HUMAN RIGHTS IN THE COUNCIL OF EUROPE AND THE EUROPEAN UNION

Confusion about the differences between the Council of Europe (the parent body of the European Court of Human Rights) and the European Union is commonplace amongst the general public. It even affects some lawyers, jurists, social scientists and students. This book will enable the reader to distinguish clearly between those human rights norms which originate in the Council of Europe and those which derive from the EU, vital for anyone interested in human rights in Europe and in the UK as it prepares to leave the EU. The main achievements of relevant institutions include securing minimum standards across the continent as they deal with increasing expansion, complexity, multidimensionality and inter-penetration of their human rights activities. The authors also identify the central challenges, particularly for the UK in the post-Brexit era where the components of each system need to be carefully distinguished and disentangled.

STEVEN GREER is Professor of Human Rights at the University of Bristol Law School.

JANNEKE GERARDS is Professor of Fundamental Rights Law at Utrecht University, the Netherlands.

ROSE SLOWE is a barrister of The Honourable Society of the Middle Temple and an Honorary Research Fellow at the University of Bristol Law School.

HUMAN RIGHTS IN THE COUNCIL OF EUROPE AND THE EUROPEAN UNION

Achievements, Trends and Challenges

STEVEN GREER

University of Bristol

JANNEKE GERARDS

Utrecht University

ROSE SLOWE

Middle Temple and University of Bristol

CAMBRIDGE
UNIVERSITY PRESS

University Printing House, Cambridge CB2 8BS, United Kingdom

One Liberty Plaza, 20th Floor, New York, NY 10006, USA

477 Williamstown Road, Port Melbourne, VIC 3207, Australia

314–321, 3rd Floor, Plot 3, Splendor Forum, Jasola District Centre, New Delhi – 110025, India

79 Anson Road, #06–04/06, Singapore 079906

Cambridge University Press is part of the University of Cambridge.

It furthers the University's mission by disseminating knowledge in the pursuit of education, learning, and research at the highest international levels of excellence.

www.cambridge.org
Information on this title: www.cambridge.org/9781107025509
DOI: 10.1017/9781139179041

© Steven Greer, Janneke Gerards and Rose Slowe 2018

First published 2018

Printed in the United Kingdom by Clays, St Ives plc

A catalogue record for this publication is available from the British Library.

Library of Congress Cataloging-in-Publication Data
Names: Greer, Steven, 1956–, author. | Gerards, J. H. (Janneke H.), author. |
Slowe, Rosie, 1991–, author.
Title: Human rights in the Council of Europe and the European Union : achievements, trends and challenges / Steven Greer, University of Bristol, Janneke Gerards, Universiteit Utrecht, The Netherlands, Rosie Slowe, Middle Temple and University of Bristol.
Description: New York : University of Cambridge Press, 2017. | Series: Cambridge studies in European law and policy | Includes bibliographical references and index.
Identifiers: LCCN 2017042296 | ISBN 9781107025509 (hardback : alk. paper)
Subjects: LCSH: Human rights–European Union countries. |
European Union. | Council of Europe.
Classification: LCC KJE5132 .G73 2017 | DDC 342.2408/5–dc23 LC record available at https://lccn.loc.gov/2017042296

ISBN 978-1-107-02550-9 Hardback

To our families and significant others

CONTENTS

SERIES EDITORS' PREFACE

The protection of human rights in Europe is the concern of many bodies, but first and foremost of the Council of Europe and the European Union. This important work by Steven Greer, Janneke Gerards and Rose Slowe discusses the achievements of these two bodies; identifies the central trends of expansion, increasing complexity, multidimensionality and interpenetration; and sets out the challenges facing these organisations with regard to matters such as their separate identity and autonomy' or coordination and harmonisation and divergence or convergence.

After an historical and conceptual discussion, the institutional structure, policy, and key treaties of the Council of Europe are examined, and then the case law of the European Court of Human Rights. Attention then turns to the European Union's institutional framework and to its internal and external policy areas focussing on fundamental rights, before moving on to the fundamental rights case law of the European Court of Justice. The summary and conclusion present the central insights of the book, noting in particular the successful institutionalisation of the respective missions of the Council of Europe and of the European Union in both the political and legal spheres. Constitutional pluralism is particularly relevant for the judicial realm in which problems and dilemmas typically arise in an extremely focused manner.

This book is most stimulating in its approach and in its analysis, offering valuable insights into the relationship between the Council of Europe and the European Union, which separately but also in various ways together set the standard for the protection of human rights and fundamental freedoms in Europe and act as guardians of the rule of law. This work will be invaluable for all who are interested in the interaction between these two bodies and in the interaction between the centralised judiciaries that they have established.

We very much welcome this book, the 29th volume in the Cambridge Studies in European Law and Policy series, which makes a major, timely and welcome contribution to the literature on European human and fundamental rights law. Policymakers, lawyers, judges, academics and graduate students will in particular profit from its analysis of bodies and case law, which are alas all too often confused and misunderstood, even in media which should know better.

Laurence Gormley
Jo Shaw

PREFACE

In our experience, the general public, some of our students and even some of our colleagues are confused about the differences between the Council of Europe (CE), the parent organisation of the European Court of Human Rights (ECtHR) and the European Union (EU), in human rights and other fields. This has been compounded as interaction between the two organisations has increased, particularly over the past decade or so. The literature is also dominated by separate studies, largely concerning their respective legal systems. As a result, more integrated accounts of the full range of relevant activities are increasingly required. This is the primary objective of this book. In what follows we seek to describe, explain, compare and contrast the human rights institutions, procedures, norms and policies of both organisations and to identify and discuss core achievements, trends and challenges.

Various key concepts, rarely sharply distinguished, litter the discourse, including 'human rights', 'fundamental rights', 'basic rights' and 'fundamental freedoms'. But, for reasons given later, the term 'human rights' provides, on balance, the best point of reference, hence the title of this study. We begin in Chapter 1 by reviewing the largely separate post–Second World War histories of the forty-seven member CE and the series of organisations which eventually became the twenty-eight, and in the wake of Brexit soon-to-become twenty-seven, member EU. Chapter 2 then considers the institutional framework and human rights policy of the CE, especially its premier treaty, the European Convention on Human Rights (ECHR) and the ECHR's core institution, the ECtHR. Chapter 3 summarises the case law of the ECtHR, Chapter 4 reviews the relevant institutional framework and the human and fundamental rights activities of the EU, while Chapter 5 considers the rights jurisprudence of the European Court of Justice (ECJ), the EU's principal judicial tribunal. Synthesising these observations and conclusions, Chapter 6 summarises how human rights in the CE and EU might be better understood and their prospects enhanced. Chapters 2 and 3 were written by Steven Greer,

Chapter 4 by Rose Slowe and Chapter 5 by Janneke Gerards. Responsibility for the others was shared.

In a nutshell, the core thesis of this book is as follows. The central achievements of the CE and the EU in the human rights field are the successful institutionalisation of their respective missions in both political and legal spheres. This, in turn, has contributed significantly to the effective securing, although not evenly or unproblematically, of at least minimum human rights standards across the continent. The central trends are their expansion and their increasing complexity, multidimensionality and interpenetration. The central challenges concern how this could, and should, be properly understood and coherently, legitimately and effectively managed, particularly with respect to two clusters of issues, both descriptive and normative, which represent the flip sides of the same coin. First, to what extent, if at all, are the autonomy, separate identity and divergence of the CE and EU in these arenas likely to be preserved as the twenty-first century progresses, and to what extent should they be? Second, to what extent, if at all, are more integration, interdependence, convergence and harmonisation likely and desirable? Our main conclusion is that, while none of the four models which, in principle, map the landscape – 'unification', 'separate development', 'organic convergence', and 'constitutional pluralism' – applies uniformly in all spheres, the most pressing challenges lie in the judicial realm, where, broadly speaking, constitutional pluralism provides the best paradigm for analytical, normative and policy-making purposes.

This book appears at a time of significant developments. The transnational protection of human rights in Europe, particularly on the legal front, is said to be at a cross roads with the centre of gravity in flux. For more than a decade, the CE failed to solve the ECtHR's burgeoning case overload. Significant improvements only started to appear in 2014. But it is not yet clear whether the crisis has been resolved or merely alleviated. In any case, important questions concerning the Court's effectiveness, authority and legitimacy and its relationship with the deepening and widening rights mission of the EU, remain. By contrast, the organisations which evolved into the EU took little formal interest in human rights for their first forty or so years. Then, at the beginning of the twenty-first century, these issues rose to the top of the agenda raising thorny questions about how this new priority might, and should, be reconciled with existing goals and the relationship it should have with the long-standing human rights activities of the CE to which all member states of the EU also belong. A much-lauded attempt by the EU to accede to the ECHR

stalled, perhaps permanently, when, in 2014, the ECJ ruled it incompatible with the EU's foundational treaties. The continent has also been
rocked by turbulence on other fronts in recent years, including, of
potentially most relevance for this study, the impact of the global economic crisis of 2008, mass migration, an increase in the frequency of
(mostly jihadi) terrorist incidents, the United Kingdom's decision to
leave the EU and legitimacy problems stemming from these and other
sources including Euro- and rights-scepticism.

Before proceeding, we would like to thank the following organisations
and individuals without whose assistance and support this project would
have been much more difficult to accomplish. Panos Koutrakos and Pat
Capps commented on earlier drafts. Lewis Graham, Dom Morton and
Eliza Jones assisted with the citations in Chapter 3. Dom also compiled
the Bibliography and Table of Abbreviations while Eliza assembled the
Table of Cases. Adriana Suarez helped edit some of the footnotes to
Chapter 5. Hana Nasif, Raeesa Rajmohamed and Georgia Tetlow assisted
with proofreading. The Strasbourg respondents cited in Chapter 2 shed
valuable light on the CE's activities not available in published sources.
The usual disclaimers apply. The University of Bristol Law School
enabled Steven to take study leave, the Nuffield Foundation provided a
small grant for the Strasbourg interviews and the staff at Cambridge
University Press offered expert assistance and advice. Finally we owe
much gratitude to our families and significant others for their patience
and forbearance.

ABBREVIATIONS

ACP	Afro-Caribbean Pacific
AFET	Foreign Affairs Committee of the European Parliament
AGs	EU Advocates General
ALDE	Alliance of Liberals and Democrats for Europe
Brexit	UK withdrawal from EU
CDDH	Council of Europe Steering Committee for Human Rights
CE	Council of Europe
CEAS	Common European Asylum System
CEE	Central and Eastern Europe
CEEC	Committee of European Economic Co-operation
CFR	EU Charter of Fundamental Rights
CFR-CDF	Network of Independent Experts on Fundamental Rights
CFSP	Common Foreign and Security Policy
CM	Council of Europe Committee of Ministers
CODEXTER	Council of Europe Committee of Experts on Terrorism
CPT	European Committee for the Prevention of Torture and Inhuman or Degrading Treatment or Punishment
CSCE	Conference on Security and Cooperation in Europe
DPC	Data Protection Convention
DPD	Data Protection Directive
EC	European Communities European Conservatives Group
ECHR	European Convention on Human Rights
ECxit	UK withdrawal from the ECHR
ECJ	European Court of Justice (refers both to the tripartite Court of Justice of the EU as an institution, and to the Court of Justice as part of this institution)
ECPT	European Convention for the Prevention of Torture and Inhuman or Degrading Treatment or Punishment
ECSC	European Coal and Steel Community
ECSR	European Committee on Social Rights
ECtHR	European Court of Human Rights
EEA	European Economic Area

EEC	European Economic Community
EFTA	European Free Trade Association
EIDHR	European Initiative for Democracy and Human Rights
EIGE	European Institute for Gender Equality
ENI	European Neighbourhood Instrument
ENO	European Network of Ombudsmen
ENP	European Neighbourhood Policy
EP	European Parliament
EPP	European People's Party
ESC	European Social Charter
ESM	European Stability Mechanism
ETUC	European Trade Union Confederation
EU	European Union
EUMC	European Monitoring Centre for Racism and Xenophobia
EURATOM	European Atomic Energy Community
EUROFOUND	European Foundation for the Improvement of Living and Working Conditions
EUSRHR	EU Special Representative for Human Rights
FC	Framework Convention for the Protection of National Minorities
FRA	EU Fundamental Rights Agency
FRONTEX	European Agency for the Management of Operational Cooperation at the External Borders
FRP	Fundamental Rights Platform
Grexit	Greek withdrawal from EU
HRC	UN Human Rights Council
IGC	Intergovernmental Conference
ILO	International Labour Organisation
IOE	International Organisation of Employers
IPA	Instrument for Pre-Accession
ISP	Internet Service Provider
LIBE	Committee on Civil Liberties, Justice and Home Affairs
MEP	Member of the European Parliament
NATO	North Atlantic Treaty Organisation
NGO	Non-Governmental Organisation
NLO	National Liaison Officer
ODIHR	OSCE Office for Democratic Institutions and Human rights
OEEC	Organisation for European Economic Co-operation
OSCE	Organisation for Security and Cooperation in Europe
PACE	Parliamentary Assembly of the Council of Europe
QMV	Qualified Majority Voting
SEA	Single European Act
SOC	Socialist Group

TEEC/TEC	Treaty establishing the European Economic Community
TEU	Treaty on European Union
TFEU	Treaty on the Functioning of the European Union
TRNC	Turkish Republic of Northern Cyprus
UEL	Group of the Unified European Left
UN	United Nations
UNHCR	UN High Commissioner for Refugees
UNSC	UN Security Council

TABLE OF CASES

European Court of Human Rights

Gäfgen v. Germany (GC), HUDOC, 1 June 2010
Gaglioni v. Italy, HUDOC, 21 December 2010
Gahramanli and Others v. Azerbaijan, HUDOC, 8 October 2015
Garaudy v. France (dec.), HUDOC, 24 June 2006
Garcia Alva v. Germany, HUDOC, 13 February 2001
Gaskin v. United Kingdom, HUDOC, 7 July 1989
Gatt v. Malta, HUDOC, 27 July 2010
Gawęda v. Poland, HUDOC, 14 March 2002
Gaygusuz v. Austria, HUDOC, 16 September 1996
Gillan and Quinton v. United Kingdom, HUDOC, 12 January 2010
Giuliani and Gaggio v. Italy (GC), HUDOC, 24 March 2011
Georgia v Russia (No 1) (2011) 52 EHRR SE 14
Georgia v Russia (No 2) (2012) 54 EHRR SE 10
Georgia v. Russia (GC), HUDOC, 3 July 2014
Georgian Labour Party v. Georgia, HUDOC, 8 July 2008
Gerasimenko and Others v Russia, HUDOC, 1 December 2016
Giniewski v. France, HUDOC, 31 January 2006
Gitonas v. Greece, HUDOC, 1 July 1997
Glimmerveen and Hagenbeek v. the Netherlands (dec.), HUDOC, 11 October 1979
Gökbulut v. Turkey, HUDOC, 29 March 2016
Golder v. United Kingdom, HUDOC, 21 February 1975
Gómez Olmeda v. Spain, HUDOC, 29 March 2016
Gongadze v. Ukraine, HUDOC, 8 November 2005
Goodwin v. United Kingdom (GC), HUDOC, 27 March 1996
Goodwin v. United Kingdom (GC), HUDOC, 11 July 2002
Gorbulya v. Russia, HUDOC, 6 March 2014
Gorzelik and Others v. Poland (GC), HUDOC, 17 February 2004
Gough v. United Kingdom, HUDOC, 24 October 2014
Gouri v. France (dec.), HUDOC, 23 March 2017
Graeme v. United Kingdom (dec.), HUDOC, 5 February 1990
Granger v. United Kingdom, HUDOC, 28 March 1990
Gratzinger and Gratzingerova v. Czech Republic (dec., GC), HUDOC, 10 July 2002
Gregory v. United Kingdom, HUDOC, 25 February 1997
Greece v. United Kingdom (1956–7) 2 Y.B. 174
Grosaru v. Romania, HUDOC, 2 March 2010
Gross v. Switzerland (GC, dec.), HUDOC, 30 September 2014
Gross v. Switzerland, HUDOC, 14 May 2013
Guerra and Others v. Italy (GC), HUDOC, 19 February 1998

European Court of Justice

Opinions

Judgments

1

Historical and Conceptual Background

1.1 Introduction

As indicated in the Preface, this book seeks to describe, explain, compare and contrast institutions, procedures, norms and policies for the protection of human rights in the CE and the EU, and to discuss core achievements, trends and challenges. The primary purpose of this chapter is to provide a brief historical overview of origins and principal milestones and to identify key conceptual frameworks to be explored in greater depth later.

But first we briefly need to consider what 'human rights' are, how, if at all, they might be distinguished from 'fundamental rights' and from other kinds of right, and what all this might imply for our purposes. Arguably the most basic distinction is between 'fundamental' rights, on the one hand, and all other 'less-fundamental' rights or 'non-fundamental' rights, on the other. But how the two categories can be demarcated, except by resorting to the circular criterion that the former is 'more fundamental' than the other, is not clear. One possibility would be to regard the category of 'fundamental rights' as an umbrella term embracing both individual human rights and some other kinds of fundamental right. However, finding a definition for these other fundamental rights which adequately identifies their key characteristics, source and rationale is not easy. By contrast, the concept of 'human rights' can be framed with greater precision. It expresses the notion that everyone possesses a set of individual entitlements, linked to the most fundamental aspects of our well-being, which recognise and give substance to our equal intrinsic worth, and which we possess independently of any other badge of difference, be it gender, race, nationality, religious or other belief, sexual orientation, ability/disability, etc.

These reflections have several implications for this study. First, if human rights are to be taken seriously, it follows that all legitimate legal and political systems, institutions and activities in the contemporary world should embody a commitment to them in some shape or form. However, because human rights are universal does not mean they apply in all contexts in precisely the same ways or without restriction or exception. Being sentenced to imprisonment for an imprisonable offence on the basis of factual and legal guilt following conviction in a fair trial is, for example, a legitimate exception to the right to liberty, not a violation. And deriving every institutionally protected right or entitlement in a contemporary liberal democracy from a human right does not make it a human right itself. So, for example, rights arising from detailed rules of civil and criminal procedure are not strictly human rights themselves but, where properly conceived, can be traced to the human right to a fair trial.

It also follows that any right which derives from a specific feature of our identity in addition to our common humanity – for example, from gender, race, ethnicity, nationality etc – cannot, by definition, itself be a 'human' right. Strictly speaking there is, therefore, no such thing as 'women's human rights' or 'gay people's human rights', or 'disabled people's human rights' in the sense of special categories of human rights only applicable to people with these characteristics. However, while women, gay people, disabled people and minorities of various kinds have the same human rights as everyone else, disadvantaged groups may require additional rights to enable them to exercise their human rights as effectively as others. But these rights are 'facilitative rights', 'rights about', or 'rights deriving from' human rights and not, strictly speaking, human rights themselves.

Since human rights are, by definition, individual rights possessed by real flesh-and-blood human beings, the collective entitlements not equally and simultaneously capable of being held by individuals cannot be genuine *human* rights either. So, for example, a faith group may appropriately be regarded as a repository of the individual human right to freedom of thought, conscience and religion also simultaneously held by each of its members. However, interests such as national self-determination or national economic development, which can only be held collectively, may more accurately be regarded as fundamental group rights, but not human rights as such. Alternatively, they can be seen as preconditions for a flourishing system of individual civil, political, social, economic and cultural human rights.

As we shall see throughout this study, the analytical distinctions between 'human rights', 'fundamental rights' and 'rights about human rights' are not clearly drawn in the law and politics of the CE or EU. Indeed, the issue is further complicated by the fact that a third term, 'fundamental freedoms', is also employed in both contexts but means something different in each. For example, debates about the ECHR have been conducted almost entirely in the language of human rights, in spite of the fact that 'fundamental freedoms' feature in its full formal title – the Convention for the Protection of Human Rights and Fundamental Freedoms – suggesting that the distinction between the two terms might be more rhetorical than substantive. By contrast, until comparatively recently, the normative language of the EU was dominated by the four 'fundamental freedoms' integral to the effective functioning of the common market – free movement of capital, goods, services and people. The increasing interest the EU has shown in human rights in the past decade or so has, therefore, raised significant questions about how these concepts can be distinguished, not only for analytical, but also for dispute resolution and policy purposes.

1.2   Chronology

For three conflicting reasons Europe occupies a central and unique place in the history of the international protection of human rights. First, it was, together with the United States, the birthplace of the now-global processes of political, social, legal and economic modernisation which embody, amongst other things, liberalisation, democratisation, marketisation and internationalisation. Second, and paradoxically, it was also the site of the Holocaust and a crucial theatre for the twentieth century's two world wars, which together constituted, or precipitated, the most systematic and serious violations of human rights the world has ever seen. Third, it was also the crucible of the Cold War at the heart of which lay a bitter ideological conflict over the profile of individual rights in social, political and economic systems. In the second half of the twentieth century, this heritage not only inspired and laid the foundations for international human rights law itself, it also led to increasing convergence in European political, constitutional, legal and economic systems around a 'common institutional model' formally defined by the values of democracy, human rights, the rule of law and the democratically regulated market. These processes now operate on three principal and overlapping dimensions: individual European states, the CE and the EU.

However, several other international institutions with a human rights brief, including the United Nations (UN), are also active across the continent. One of the most prominent is the fifty-seven-member

Organisation for Security and Cooperation in Europe (OSCE),[1] the largest regional security organisation in the world, with participating states from Europe, Central Asia and North America, which takes politically, but not legally, binding decisions on a consensual basis. The OSCE was established in December 1994 as a more permanent post–Cold War version of the Conference on Security and Cooperation in Europe (CSCE), created in the early 1970s as an ad hoc multilateral forum for dialogue and negotiation between East and West during the thaw in the Cold War known as détente. Its main achievements were the Helsinki Final Act, signed on 1 August 1975 – which contained several key commitments on political, military, economic, environmental and human rights issues, central to the so-called Helsinki process – and the Decalogue, ten fundamental rights principles governing the behaviour of states towards each other and their own citizens.

At its inception the OSCE was intended to assist in the management of the post–Cold War transition in Europe. But today its main functions cover the three core 'dimensions' of security: the politico-military; the economic and environmental; and the human. Within these fields the OSCE's activities range across traditional security issues such as conflict prevention and arms control, to fostering economic development, ensuring the sustainable use of natural resources and promoting full respect for human rights and fundamental freedoms, particularly in the fields of freedom of assembly and association, the right to liberty and fair trial and the death penalty. Its four specialist human rights–related agencies are the Office for Democratic Institutions and Human rights (ODIHR), active in election observation, democratic development and the promotion of human rights, tolerance, non-discrimination and the rule of law; the Office of the Special Representative and Coordinator for Combating Trafficking in Human Beings, which supports the development and implementation of anti-trafficking policies; the OSCE Representative on Freedom of the Media, who provides early warning on violations of freedom of expression and promotes full compliance with OSCE press freedom commitments; and the High Commissioner on National Minorities, who seeks to identify and to resolve ethnic tensions which might endanger peace, stability, or friendly relations between participating states.

---

[1] D. Galbreath, *The Organization for Security and Co-Operation in Europe* (London: Routledge, 2007).

However, only the CE and EU have trans-national legislative and/or judicial functions, without which the dynamic development of a distinctive European human rights law is not possible. Three broad, and to a certain extent overlapping phases can be distinguished in their partly separate, partly shared, histories: origins, institutionalisation and consolidation, 1945–mid-1970s; development and enlargement, mid-1970s–late 1990s; and crisis management, 2000–16. These are considered in turn.

Origins and Institutionalisation: 1945–Mid-1970s

When the Second World War ended in 1945, one question reverberated around the globe: how could such a catastrophe be prevented from recurring? It was clear that the constitutional, political and legal systems of some European countries had not effectively curbed the ambitions of political movements offering authoritarian answers to economic and political questions and military solutions to territorial disputes. The way forward for many western democrats, therefore, seemed to lie in the firmer national entrenchment of constitutional democracy, human rights and the rule of law, including their protection in much more effective international institutions than had yet been seen. There was, however, little enthusiasm for a return to the system for the protection of national minorities in Europe in the inter-war years which had involved collective complaints to the League of Nations. It had, after all, been a double failure. Not only had it proved ineffective for minorities, it had exacerbated the drift to war by intensifying the territorial squabbles between 'kin-states' and the host-states in which national minorities found themselves.[2] And the displacement of millions during the Second World War complicated these issues even further. The protection of individual rights, therefore, appeared to offer a more attractive solution.

However, the attempt to institutionalise human rights at the global level proved frustratingly slow. Indeed, it was only as a result of successful lobbying by NGOs attending the San Francisco conference which established the UN in the summer of 1945, that the UN Charter contained so many references to human rights. Three years later the UN approved the Universal Declaration of Human Rights, the significance of which has divided commentators. Some regard it as a watershed because, for the first time, representatives of western and some

[2] J. Jackson Preece, *National Minorities and the European Nation-States System* (Oxford: Clarendon Press, 1998), ch. 5.

non-western civilizations together produced a list of fundamental civil, political, social, economic and cultural rights going far beyond those the social contract and Enlightenment thinkers had regarded as natural.[3] However, for others, the Declaration's aspirational character, and its lack of enforcement machinery, made it virtually worthless.[4] Debate about two further UN human rights treaties – one on civil and political rights and the other on economic, social and cultural rights – was to last for another two decades and a further ten years would elapse before either came into force. This slow rate of progress added momentum to the campaign for a pan-European human rights regime.[5] European states were not, however, to be the sole masters of their own destiny. The defeated powers were obviously in no position to argue. But even the victors were constrained by the conflicting interests of the USA and the USSR. By 1948 it had become clear that Germany would be partitioned, that the USSR would dominate eastern and central Europe, and that the USA regarded an integrated western Europe as a constraint upon the spread of communism, the territorial expansion of the Soviet Union, and resurgent German nationalism.[6]

However, there were differing views about what kind of new arrangements western Europe should have. In a celebrated speech at the University of Zurich in September 1946 former British Prime Minister Winston Churchill advocated a 'United States of Europe', a view greatly welcomed by 'federalists' who wanted full economic integration, regulated by supranational institutions, resulting in the pooling of state sovereignty. Others, the 'intergovernmentalists', favoured a looser set of intergovernmental institutions devoted to cooperation over issues arising in the spheres of politics, defence, the rule of law, human rights and democracy, which

---

[3] M. A. Glendon, 'Knowing the Universal Declaration of Human Rights', *Notre Dame Law Review*, 73 (1998), 1153–90, 1176.

[4] A. W. B. Simpson, 'Hersch Lauterpacht and the Genesis of the Age of Human Rights', *Law Quarterly Review*, 120 (2004), 49–80, 74, 56, 62, 68, 72, 79.

[5] According to Simpson the idea of a regional human rights treaty first appeared in a British Foreign Office minute of June 1948, A. W. B. Simpson, 'Britain and the European Convention', *Cornell International Law Journal*, 34 (2001), 523–54, 540.

[6] See K. Sikkink, 'The Power of Principled Ideas: Human Rights Policies in the United States and Western Europe' in J. Goldstein and R. O. Keohane (eds.), *Ideas and Foreign Policy: Beliefs, Institutions and Political Change* (New York: Cornell University Press, 1993), pp. 139–70; A. H. Robertson, *The Council of Europe: Its Structure, Functions and Achievements* (London: Stevens & Sons, 2nd edn., 1961), p. 6; G. Lundestad, *'Empire' by Integration: The United States and European Integration, 1945–1997* (Oxford University Press, 1998), p. 13.

would preserve the traditional conception of independent nation states. The government of the United Kingdom, the only state capable of exercising significant leadership in Europe in the immediate post-war years, preferred the latter: intergovernmental arrangements based on an anti-Soviet western military alliance plus a western European organisation with largely ideological and symbolic functions. In a key speech to the House of Commons, on 22 January 1948, the British Foreign Secretary, Ernest Bevin, stated that a western European 'spiritual union', founded on respect for human rights, had become the prime aim of British foreign policy.[7] This vision, though vague on details, was to be implemented in three stages. First, in March 1948, the United Kingdom, France and the Benelux countries signed the Brussels Treaty for Economic, Social and Cultural Collaboration and Collective Self-Defence, laying the foundations for what later became the Western European Union. A Consultative Council was included and, although primarily a pact for economic, social, cultural and defence cooperation, respect for human rights became a condition of membership. Second, a wider military alliance including the United States and Canada – the North Atlantic Treaty Organisation 1949 ('NATO') – provided firmer military guarantees. Third, it was envisaged that other European countries, including West Germany, would eventually sign the Brussels Treaty when they were in a position to comply with the membership requirements, particularly respect for human rights.

However other ideas were in the air.[8] In May 1948 a Congress of Europe, sponsored by the right-of-centre international Committee of the Movements for European Unity, and attended by some 660 delegates including twenty prime ministers and former prime ministers, met in the Hague. In a keynote speech elaborating on what he had said in Zurich two years earlier, the Honorary President Winston Churchill, argued that a European Charter of Human Rights should be at the

---

[7] A. W. B. Simpson, *Human Rights and the End of Empire – Britain and the Genesis of the European Convention* (Oxford University Press, 2001), pp. 574–9. These ideas had already been discussed with the US Secretary of State, George Marshall, and the French Foreign Minister, George Bidault, at secret meetings in the Foreign Office on 17–18 December, K. Morgan, *Labour in Power* (Oxford: Clarendon Press, 1984), pp. 273, 274.

[8] For a fuller account of the debate in the 1940s see E. Bates, *The Evolution of the European Convention on Human Rights: From Its Inception to the Creation of a Permanent Court of Human Rights* (Oxford University Press, 2010), ch. 3; J. Petaux, *Democracy and Human Rights for Europe: The Council of Europe's Contribution* (Strasbourg; Council of Europe Publications, 2009), pp. 31–63.

centre of a new programme of European unification.[9] Delegates also
proposed a European Parliamentary Assembly and an individual petition process for the judicial enforcement of the Charter. The British
Labour government, which had not sent a delegation, opposed both
ideas on the grounds that such an assembly would provide an unwelcome platform for communists, while a court of human rights would
create an equally unwelcome judicial authority superior to any British
tribunal.[10] In October 1948, the various strands of European integra-
tionism were woven into the European Movement, which continued to
develop proposals including for a European Assembly selected by
national parliaments which could discuss a wide range of issues, including human rights.[11]

The Council of Europe

As 1948 drew to a close, the governments of the United Kingdom, France
and Belgium agreed to create a Council of Europe on an intergovernmental rather than integrationist model and invited Ireland, Italy, Denmark, Norway and Sweden to participate in the negotiations.
Luxembourg and the Netherlands also became founding members. In
1949 Greece joined, followed, in the 1950s, by four other states – Turkey
(1950), Germany (1950), Iceland (1950) and Austria (1956) – and a
further three in the 1960s – Cyprus (1961), Switzerland (1963) and Malta
(1965). Established by the Treaty of London on 5 May 1949, the CE had
four principal objectives: to contribute to the prevention of another war
between western European states, to provide a statement of common
values contrasting sharply with Soviet-style communism (as expressed by
the mostly civil and political rights subsequently contained in the
ECHR), to re-enforce a sense of common identity and purpose should
the Cold War degenerate into active armed conflict and to establish an
early warning device by which a drift towards authoritarianism, including communism, in any member state could be detected and addressed
by complaints from states against each other to an independent trans-
national judicial tribunal in Strasbourg. And even this 'early warning'
function was also inextricably linked to the prevention of war because the
slide towards the Second World War indicated that the rise of

---

[9] Simpson, 'Britain and European Convention', 543, claims that it is unlikely that Churchill
ever envisaged a federation which would have included the United Kingdom.
[10] Simpson, *Human Rights and the End of Empire*, pp. 619, 612.
[11] *Ibid.*, p. 629.

authoritarian regimes in Europe made the peace and security of the continent more precarious.[12]

Drafted largely by the British Foreign Office, six core principles are found in the CE's Statute. Certain unspecified 'spiritual and moral values' – 'the cumulative influence of Greek philosophy, Roman law, the Western Christian Church, the humanism of the Renaissance and the French Revolution'[13] – are said to constitute the 'common heritage' of the signatory states (the 'common heritage' principle) and to be the true source of 'individual freedom, political liberty and the rule of law' (the 'human rights' and 'rule of law' principles). These form the 'basis of all genuine democracy' (the 'democracy' principle). The promotion of these principles, and the interests of 'economic and social progress' (the principle of 'economic and social progress'), is said to require closer unity between like-minded European countries (the 'closer unity' principle). Similar ideas can be found in the Brussels and NATO Treaties.[14] And while the CE was not the only western European organisation to make adherence to the principles of human rights and the rule of law conditions of membership,[15] at the time it was unique in seeking to identify the human rights in question in a further treaty (the ECHR), in providing means for their enforcement and in promoting 'closer unity' amongst its members.

The exclusion of defence issues from the CE's remit is deliberate and understandable since these objectives were already well covered by the Brussels and NATO treaties.[16] However, curiously, Article 1 of the Statute of the CE says nothing specific about 'political' questions, possibly on the assumption that these are already entailed by the reference to social and economic issues.[17] Other provisions of the Statute deal with the establishment of the Council's principal organs – the Committee of Ministers (CM, the foreign ministers of member states), the Secretariat (the administration) and the Consultative, later Parliamentary, Assembly (a non-legislative body appointed by the legislatures of member states) – the official languages (French and English), membership (by invitation of the CM), the location (Strasbourg), financial matters, privileges and immunities (including those of representatives of member states) and arrangements for amendment, ratification and other formalities.

---

[12] S. Greer, *The European Convention on Human Rights: Achievements, Problems and Prospects* (Cambridge University Press, 2006), ch. 1.

[13] Robertson, *Council of Europe*, p. 2.

[14] *Ibid.*, p. 13.

[15] Art. 3, Statute of the Council of Europe.

[16] Art. 1 (d).

[17] Robertson, *Council of Europe*, p. 16.

By the end of the 1950s the CE had also entered into mostly informal relations with the UN and other international organisations, including the European Communities, which largely sought to affirm shared goals and values and to exchange information and expertise.[18] In addition to an expanded membership, by the end of the 1960s, seventy-five treaties and protocols, on topics as diverse as social security schemes and the payment of scholarships to students studying abroad, had been concluded. Apart from the ECHR, the most significant in the human rights field was the European Social Charter 1961 (considered more fully in Chapter 2), which provides a range of social and economic rights to such things as housing, health, education and work, but, unlike the ECHR, has no judicial or individual applications processes.

The European Convention on Human Rights

Simpson maintains that the ECHR was the product of 'conflicts, compromise and happenstance' and there are no simple explanations, either for what it is or why it came into being.[19] The discussions out of which it emerged were inevitably influenced by the intellectual and political debates in the West about rights which had been in progress since the early modern period. But they were also overwhelmingly driven by the need to find workable institutions and procedures which all parties could accept. By October 1949 the British government had concluded that a European human rights convention was urgently required – partly to remedy the lack of progress at the UN – and also because the United Kingdom was now convinced that the CE had become 'one of the major weapons of the cold war'.[20] Having embarked on this course of action, the political pressure to avoid failure was enormous since it was unlikely the CE would survive the acrimonious collapse of its first substantial project.[21]

---

[18] S. Schmahl, 'The Council of Europe within the System of International Organizations' in S. Schmahl and M. Breuer (eds.), *The Council of Europe: Its Law and Policies* (Oxford University Press, 2017), pp. 874–945.

[19] Simpson, *Human Rights*, p. ix. Other literature on the background to the Convention includes, G. Marston, 'The United Kingdom's Part in the Preparation of the European Convention on Human Rights 1950', *International and Comparative Law Quarterly*, 42 (1993), 796–826; Simpson, 'Britain and European Convention'; E. Wicks, 'The United Kingdom Government's Perceptions of the European Convention on Human Rights at the Time of Entry', *Public Law*, [2000], 438–55; D. Nicol, 'Original Intent and the European Convention on Human Rights', *Public Law*, [2005], 152–72.

[20] Simpson, *Human Rights*, p. 684.

[21] Marston, 'UK's Part in ECHR'; Simpson, *Human Rights*, 686; Wicks, 'UK's Perceptions of ECHR'.

As with many treaties, and indeed with many written agreements of any kind, Convention negotiations were marked by sharply competing visions.[22] These were also reflected in disagreement on several substantive issues – which rights should be included (those to property, education and free elections proved particularly controversial), how detailed their specification should be and whether there should be a Court and a right of individual petition. Not only did the CM take a different view from the Consultative Assembly on these matters, but the position of some states differed from that of others, and some issues even divided delegates from the same state. Some of these disputes stemmed from divergent assumptions about the appropriateness of judicial review of legislation, while others mirrored differences between the civilian and common law traditions. Those from civil law backgrounds preferred general statements of rights and limitations, a model which assumes that member states would be responsible for the provision of detailed legal mechanisms, and that effective protection would be provided by case law anchored both in the Convention's own broad principles and in the 'general principles of law recognised by civilised nations' as gradually elaborated by a trans-national court. By contrast, those who favoured the common law approach were distrustful both of catalogues of broadly defined rights and of a jurisprudence partly derived from the vague notion of 'the general principles of law'. Instead they preferred the precise specification of rights and limitations together with the provision of effective remedies.[23] However, virtually no attention was paid on any side of the debate to the question of how the Convention text would be interpreted.[24] Some also considered the ECHR merely as a first step, providing a collective guarantee of rights already well protected in contracting states, to be followed by the elaboration of a much fuller code.[25]

Sir David Maxwell Fyfe, British lawyer, Conservative MP, later Lord Chancellor and rapporteur on the CE committee charged with drafting the ECHR, and Pierre-Henri Teitgen, French lawyer, professor, government minister and later judge on the European Court of Human Rights (ECtHR), are widely regarded as the ECHR's 'founding fathers'. Nevertheless, as with the Statute of the CE, the task of producing the first drafts of the text fell to the British Foreign Office.[26] This was ironic because the

---

[22] Nicol, 'Original Intent'.
[23] Simpson, *Human Rights*, p. 713.
[24] *Ibid.*, p. 737.
[25] Simpson, 'Britain and European Convention', 547; Nicol, 'Original Intent', 158–9.
[26] Simpson, *Human Rights*, p. 642; Simpson, 'Britain and European Convention', 548–9.

Foreign Office had little legal expertise, the British rights tradition emphasised the importance of effective concrete remedies for specific wrongs rather than lofty statements of general principle, and if the British governing class had a coherent shared political morality at all, it derived from utilitarianism rather than a commitment to fundamental rights. However, the ECHR was eventually drafted and signed by the CM at the Barberini Palace in Rome on 4 November 1950.[27]

Not surprisingly it shares the general goals of the CE. But, in addition to containing a short catalogue of mostly civil and political rights, its distinctive contribution is to provide an independent judicial process at Strasbourg capable of authoritatively determining whether these have been violated by a given member state. Enforcement, considered more fully in Chapter 2, followed the judicial model favoured by the Assembly and the European Movement. Although a Court and a right of individual petition (the latter opposed only by the United Kingdom and Greece)[28] were provided, initially member states were not required to accept either. At its inception it was agreed that the Convention's main modus operandi should be complaints by states against each other (the 'inter-state process'). But, since the founding members regarded the Convention merely as a reflection of their own values and laws, none expected it ever to be used against them.[29]

Based largely on the United kingdom's proposals, the rights, considered further in Chapters 2 and 3, were broadly defined subject to various express limitations but with no obvious rationale for differences from one provision to another.[30] While acceding to the ECHR has been a condition of membership of the CE since its inception, Article 57 ECHR, in common with other international treaties, nevertheless permits states to exempt themselves from specific provisions by entering 'reservations' to this effect at the point of accession.[31] The Convention was at first, therefore, much more about protecting the democratic identity of member states through the authoritative judgment of an independent international court that human rights had been violated and about promoting international cooperation between them, than it was about

---

[27] Bates, *Evolution of the ECHR*, ch. 4.
[28] Simpson, *Human Rights*, p. 721.
[29] Simpson, 'Britain and ECHR', 553.
[30] Simpson, *Human Rights*, p. 715.
[31] For the full list see coe.int/en/web/conventions/full-list/-/conventions/treaty/005/declar ations?p_auth=E2b6tYZF.

providing individuals with individual redress for violations of their basic entitlements by a member state.

However, until the mid-1970s, the Convention had very little impact and its profile was very low.[32] In the mid-1960s its very existence was even threatened by a lack of support and interest from states. From then until the early 1970s the policies and approach of the European Commission of Human Rights caused a rift with the Court, whose supply of cases almost dried up.[33] In this period the Commission – which was able to receive individual applications from 5 July 1955 when the requisite number of states (at least six) had acceded to it – was the first port of call for both state and individual applicants. It ascertained the facts, determined whether the admissibility criteria were satisfied and explored the possibility of friendly settlement. If none could be found, a non-binding opinion about whether or not the Convention had been violated was expressed. Then, providing the jurisdiction of the ECtHR had been accepted by the state or states concerned, the case could be referred by the Commission, the respondent state, or the state of which the applicant was a national, but not by individual applicants themselves, to the Court for a legally binding decision. The CM also decided cases over which the ECtHR did not have jurisdiction and those that the Commission did not refer to the Court. Both the Commission and the Court were then staffed by part-time judges. From its inception until it was abolished in the late 1990s, the Commission declared inadmissible all applications directed against acts of the European Communities because they were not party to the ECHR.[34]

By the beginning of the 1970s there had been less than a handful of inter-state complaints. Greece brought the United Kingdom before the Commission in 1956 and 1957 over alleged mistreatment by British forces of those suspected of involvement with the armed nationalist movement, AOKA, in Cyprus. However, Cyprus gained its independence in 1960 before the issue could be considered by the CM.[35] Also in 1960, Austria complained against Italy about a breach of the right to fair trial allegedly suffered by a group of German-speaking youths accused of killing a customs officer in the border region. But in 1963 the

---

[32] Bates, *Evolution of the ECHR*, p. 12.
[33] *Ibid.*, p. 260.
[34] N. Krish, 'The Open Architecture of European Human Rights Law' *Modern Law Review*, 71 (2008), 183–216, 199.
[35] *Greece v United Kingdom* (1956–7) 2 Y.B. 174.

Commission found no violation, a decision endorsed by the CM.[36] While these cases were motivated largely by political animosity, *Denmark, Norway, Sweden and the Netherlands* v *Greece*[37] was brought largely for humanitarian reasons. The applicants complained about human rights abuses in the aftermath of the Greek military coup in 1967, and, in November 1969, the Commission found Greece to be in violation of the Convention. However, the following month Greece withdrew from the CE, denouncing the Convention before the CM could vote on a draft resolution calling for its suspension.

As for individual applications, about half of those registered in the 1960s were from detainees,[38] and by 1966, the year in which the United kingdom accepted the right of individual petition, for example, only a handful had been declared admissible and only one had been judged on the merits.[39] Although the Court had been open for business since 1959, by the beginning of the 1970s it had judged only six individual cases.[40] By the end of the 1960s, the ECHR had also been augmented by five Additional Protocols. Nos. 1 (1952) and 4 (1963) added extra rights, considered in Chapters 2 and 3, while Nos. 2 (1963), 3 (1963) and 5 (1966) made modest procedural changes.

The Three European Communities

For European integrationists the CE was a missed opportunity and a bitter disappointment. Jean Monnet, the French Planning Commissioner, regarded it as 'entirely valueless' and de Gaulle found it 'simply ridiculous.'[41] In their view, the most pressing needs were economic regeneration and the construction of international institutions which would much more effectively prevent another Franco-German war. At the end of the 1940s the effects of the Second World War remained severe. Many states faced widespread deprivation and there was an urgent need to rebuild nations, industries and prosperity. The risk of internal chaos and revolution was also thought by some to be acute. Many also believed that, if the western economic system were to be preserved and further conflict internally and internationally were to be prevented, some kind of economic transformation had to occur. Two inter-related means of achieving this were

[36] *Austria* v *Italy* (1961) 4 Y.B. 116, (1963) 6 Y.B. 740.
[37] (1968) 11 Y.B.-II 691.
[38] Bates, *Evolution of the ECHR*, p. 258.
[39] *Ibid.* p. 12.
[40] *Ibid.*
[41] Simpson, *Human Rights*, p. 646.

discussed. The first was oriented towards the external infusion of enormous material and financial aid provided by a generous benefactor. A Committee of European Economic Co-operation (CEEC) – which developed into the Organisation for European Economic Co-operation (OEEC) – was established on 16 April 1948 to coordinate and distribute aid across Europe from the United States, the only state capable of providing it. The second was through greater economic cooperation between western European states at the heart of which would be the integration of the French and West German coal and steel industries. This would not only encourage joint economic development and bind the two countries together, but would also prevent them from waging war against each other without first disaggregating such vital military assets. It was also thought that such economic integration would provide a collective western European bulwark against the Soviet threat, additional to, or greater than, that offered by the CE. A more developed western European economy along these lines had another potential benefit: by providing growing markets for American goods it would encourage greater economic support from the United States.

A scheme reflecting these goals, devised by the French bureaucrat Jean Monnet and the politician Robert Schuman, rapidly attracted the support of West Germany, Italy and the Benelux states. The Schuman Plan, made public in 1950, sought to integrate and regenerate the economies of France and Germany by establishing inter-state institutions, to which member states would cede some of their national sovereignty, and which would act to a degree independently of any particular government. In 1951 the establishment of the European Coal and Steel Community (ECSC) created, as the name suggests, a coal and steel 'community' with six founding members – France, West Germany, Italy, Belgium, the Netherlands and Luxembourg. Administered by an independent High Authority staffed by civil servants and supervised by an Assembly, the precursor of the European Parliament, the ECSC was overseen, and its policy determined, by a Special Council of Ministers or representatives from member states. A Court of Justice (also known as the European Court of Justice or ECJ) ensured the terms of the founding treaty were observed. Credited with the initial post-war reconstruction of western Europe,[42] the United States supported this venture through the Marshall Plan.[43]

---

[42] See J. L. Harper 'In Their Own Image – the Americans and the Question of European Unity, 1943–1954' in M. Bond, J. Smith and W. Wallace (eds.), *Eminent Europeans* (London: Greycoat Press, 1996), pp. 62–84.
[43] T. Judt, *Postwar: A History of Europe since 1945* (London: Pimlico, 2005). p. 90, *et seq.*

The success of the ECSC, reflected in a general economic improvement in the states concerned, enhanced the prospects for further economic integration. The six members, therefore, began to devise a more ambitious version to encompass a more comprehensive 'common market'. There were also plans to include military and political dimensions, the latter including adherence to human rights requirements. However, since the French legislature was reluctant to sanction the loss of sovereignty which the military and political dimensions suggested, these proposals were replaced by a more limited economic alternative. In 1957, following the ECSC formula, the European Economic Community (EEC) and the European Atomic Energy Community (EURATOM) were established to coexist with the ECSC. The purpose of the latter was to coordinate nuclear energy research in member states, while the EEC was designed as an intergovernmental organisation, without human rights or wider political dimensions but with some independent elements for developing and supporting an internal market based on free-trade between its members and as an external customs union controlling tariffs for goods imported from non-members. The EEC's Commission and Council paralleled the roles of the ECSC's High Authority and Council, respectively, while the ECSC's Assembly and ECJ became institutions common to all three European Communities (ECSC, EEC and EURATOM). In 1967, the Merger Treaty combined the executives of the ECSC (which continued to exist until 2002), the EEC and EURATOM to create a single Council and Commission.

However, one difficulty that quickly materialised was whether the EEC would survive without UK membership. In 1963 De Gaulle's government had shown that France could obstruct the working and threaten the very essence of the entire project by preventing the United Kingdom from joining. The problem was, however, finally resolved by the Luxembourg Accords of 1966, which provided that, in return for the Commission declining to develop a union by stealth and a recognition that any member state should be allowed to veto any decision conflicting with its key national interests, all members would refrain from boycotting EEC decisions. Although a victory for cooperation, the British membership crisis nevertheless revealed the new institution's relative instability and its lack of real power when a major player chose to act unilaterally.

Post De Gaulle, the chances of the EEC's survival improved and, at the end of the 1960s, accession negotiations began with the United Kingdom, Ireland and Denmark. UK membership was particularly prized not only because of the ballast it would add to the enterprise, but because it would also facilitate access to the trans-Atlantic alliance and the Common-wealth. To alleviate British pre-accession concerns about membership, the EEC embarked on a frenzy of institutional reforms, including the completion of the customs union.

Consolidation, Development and Enlargement: Mid-1970s–Late 1990s

For both the CE and the EEC, the 1970s–1990s were characterised by the incorporation of other western and later post-Communist European states and by the consolidation and development of their respective trans-national institutions, norms, processes and policies.

The Council of Europe and the European Convention on Human Rights

In 1974 the CE welcomed the re-democratised Greece back into membership. Portugal (1976), Spain (1977), Liechtenstein (1978), San Marino (1988) and Finland (1989) were also admitted to the fold. By the end of the 1990s, the incorporation of central and eastern European countries from the former Soviet bloc had increased mem-bership to forty-seven – every fully fledged state in Europe except Belarus – with a combined population of more than 800 million. A total of 174 treaties and protocols had also been agreed, the most significant in the human rights field being the European Convention for the Prevention of Torture and Inhuman or Degrading Treatment or Punishment 1987 (more commonly known as the Convention for the Prevention of Torture) and the European Framework Convention for the Protection of National Minorities 1995, considered further in Chapter 2. According to Polakiewicz, a 'shift from treaty-making to monitoring of compliance and assistance' also occurred with soft law instruments, such as recommendations and guidelines, gaining in importance.[44]

But, by far the most important developments for the CE in this period were the end of the Cold War in 1989, the wars in the former Yugoslavia in the early 1990s – which amongst other things together created nearly two dozen new states in Europe – and the two Chechen wars in Russia in,

---

[44] J. Polakiewicz, 'The European Union and the Council of Europe – Competition or Coher-ence in Fundamental Rights Protection in Europe?', *Jean Monnet Conference*, 27–8 May 2008, p. 2.

respectively, 1994–6 and 1999–2000. While the Chechen crisis under-scored the CE's powerlessness to intervene effectively in large-scale armed conflict involving its members and also spawned thousands of individual applications alleging serious human rights violations,[45] the end of the Cold War also deprived the CE and the Convention system of one of their core founding functions and raised deep questions about their post–Cold War roles.

As with Spain and Portugal a decade and a half earlier, the democratic transitions in the eastern bloc were precipitated largely by internal factors. The governments of the new democracies were eager to join the CE mainly to symbolise their break from Russian domination, to silence domestic and foreign critics of the transitions, to consolidate democracy and human rights, to boost their international legitimacy and to fulfil some of the minimum requirements for EU membership.[46] However, the CE nevertheless played several important secondary roles. First, it offered the 'first point of institutionalised contact' with demo-cratic Europe and a 'privileged structure for dialogue'.[47] Second, it provided moral and diplomatic support. Third, in addition to its largely rhetorical debates and declarations, the Parliamentary Assembly (PACE) organised fact-finding missions, monitored elections and instituted round table discussions for the various parties involved.[48] Fourth, expert-ise and advice about the creation and management of democratic polit-ical and legal institutions were made available through a number of specialised programmes, including those provided by CE treaties. In addition to seminars, conferences, ad hoc training programmes, transla-tion services and the provision of information, this was delivered mainly through the European Commission for Democracy through Law (the 'Venice Commission') and the Demosthenes, Lode, Demo-droit, and Themis programmes, which together provided assistance with democra-tisation, local government, legal and judicial systems and training for law

[45] R. Provost, 'Teetering on the Edge of Legal Nihilism: Russia and the Evolving European Human Rights Regime', *Human Rights Quarterly*, 37 (2015), 289–40, 317.

[46] J. E. Manas, 'The Council of Europe's Democracy Ideal and the Challenge of Ethno-National Strife' in A. Chayes and A. H. Chayes (eds.), *Preventing Conflict in the Post-Communist World – Mobilizing International and Regional Organizations* (Washington, DC: Brookings Occasional Papers, Brookings Institution, 1996), pp. 99–144, 111.

[47] D. Huber, *A Decade Which Made History: The Council of Europe 1989–1999* (Strasbourg: Council of Europe Publishing, 1999), pp. 26, 46–7.

[48] *Ibid.*, pp. 31, 152.

enforcement and related officials.[49] While the advice offered by the Venice Commission has undoubtedly been influential and enduring,[50] the Demosthenes, Lode, Demo-droit and Themis programmes have been criticised for being under-funded and 'extremely limited in scope'.[51] Fifth, and most importantly, the CE provided each of the new democracies with tailor-made accession requirements.[52] However, the processes by which former communist states sought to make their domestic laws and practices Convention-compliant, and how this was monitored by the CE, were uneven at best.[53] According to Manas, PACE – the institution with the most extensive role in the admissions process – adopted a flexible approach, loosening the membership criteria while tightening post-admission monitoring. This prompted complaints that standards had been diluted and that the Convention's legitimacy had been compromised. The accession of the Russian Federation was particularly sharply debated and Belarus's application was suspended following a constitutional coup in 1996.[54] 'Special guest status', with alternative human rights monitoring arrangements, was also established for non-member states.[55] All six states which emerged from the bloody civil wars which erupted in Yugoslavia in the 1990s also eventually joined the CE. Sweeney argues that the ECtHR's principal contribution to the post-Communist transition lay in adjudicating complaints according to 'transitional relativism', which permits certain 'rights restrictive' measures

---

[49] A. Drzemczewski, 'The Council of Europe's Co-operation and Assistance Programmes with Central and Eastern Europe in the Human Rights Field: 1990 to September 1993', *Human Rights Law Journal*, 14 (1993), 229–48; Manas, 'CE's Democracy Ideal', 114–18; Huber, *Decade Which Made History*, pp. 22 & 27.

[50] C. Grabenwarter, Constitutional Standard-Setting and Strengthening of New Democracies' in Schmahl and M. Breuer (eds.), *Council of Europe*; J. Jowell QC, 'The Venice Commission: Disseminating Democracy through Law', *Public Law*, [2001], 675–83.

[51] Manas, 'CE's Democracy Ideal', 114–15.

[52] *Ibid.*, 106–14; See T. Meron and J. S. Sloan, 'Democracy, Rule of Law and Admission to the Council of Europe', *Israel Yearbook on Human Rights*, 26 (1997), 21, 137–56 for accounts of the admissions process.

[53] Meron and Sloan, 'Democracy, Rule of Law', 155–6; A. Drzemczewski, 'Ensuring Compatibility of Domestic Law with the European Convention on Human Rights Prior to Ratification: The Hungarian Model', *Human Rights Law Journal*, 16 (1995), 241–60, 246.

[54] Meron and Sloan, 'Democracy, Rule of Law'; R. Harmsen, 'The European Convention on Human Rights after Enlargement', *International Journal of Human Rights*, 5 (2001), 18–43; Drzemczewski, 'Ensuring Compatibility', 246; Harmsen, 'ECHR After Enlargement'; P. Leach, 'The Parliamentary Assembly of the Council of Europe' in Schmahl and Breuer (eds.), *Council of Europe*, pp. 166–211, 181–91.

[55] Manas, 'CE's Democracy Ideal', 113.

and practices, conducive in the short term to democratic consolidation, particularly those regarding the electoral process in the widest sense.[56]

In the 1970s and 1980s some significant inter-state cases were brought before the Strasbourg institutions. In 1971 Ireland complained about the 'five techniques' of interrogation used against selected internees as a counter-insurgency experiment in the Northern Irish 'Troubles'. The European Commission of Human Rights found these amounted to torture, while, in a judgment delivered on 18 January 1978, the Court disagreed, declaring instead that they amounted to inhuman and degrading treatment.[57] However, in March 1972, long before this verdict was reached, the British government had already accepted the conclusions of the minority report of an official domestic inquiry that the practice could not be justified and would be discontinued.[58] The Turkish invasion of Cyprus in 1974 spawned three applications to the Commission by Cyprus, the first two of which, in 1974 and 1975, were combined in a single report delivered on 10 July 1976 and the third, submitted in 1977, in a report of 4 October 1983.[59] Each found Turkey to be in serious breach of a string of Convention provisions. Responding to the first report in 1979, the CM called on the parties to resolve their differences through further dialogue under the auspices of the Secretary General of the UN. The case of *France, Norway, Denmark, Sweden and the Netherlands* v *Turkey*,[60] which concerned widespread alleged Convention violations by the Turkish military government in the early 1980s, was resolved by friendly settlement. However, more than a decade later, Kamminga reported that there had been 'no perceptible change in the widespread and systematic torture of detainees in Turkey and scores of people . . . continued to die as a result'.[61]

In 1983 and 1984, respectively, Protocol Nos. 6 and 7 added further rights to the ECHR, while in 1985 Protocol No. 8 made some minor procedural and administrative changes. But the three main developments in the Convention system from the mid-1970s to late 1990s were, first, that the ECtHR came into its own as a 'quasi-constitutional court' in two

---

[56] J. A. Sweeney, *The European Court of Human Rights in the Post-Cold War Era: Universality in Transition* (London: Routledge, 2013), pp. 239–53.

[57] *Ireland* v *United Kingdom*, HUDOC, 18 July 1978.

[58] *Hansard*, HC, vol. 832, col.743, 2 March 1972.

[59] *Cyprus* v *Turkey*, HUDOC, 10 May 2001 (GC).

[60] (1983) 35 D.R. 143.

[61] M. T. Kamminga, 'Is the European Convention on Human Rights Sufficiently Equipped to Cope with Gross and Systematic Violations?', *Netherlands Quarterly of Human Rights*, 12 (1994), 153–64, 159.

key senses: the character of the core principles of interpretation it identified and applied, particularly that the ECHR should be treated as a 'living instrument' to be interpreted according to how European society had evolved; and the impact of its judgments on member states.[62] By the late 1970s the ECtHR had delivered some landmark judgments in individual applications, the 1980s 'saw an impressive growth in the breadth and depth of Convention jurisprudence,'[63] and by 1983 the Court had delivered fifty judgments. The next fifty were adjudicated in the following four years to 1987, and between then and 1991 more than a hundred more cases were adjudicated.[64]

The second development concerned the rapidly rising rate of individual complaints, promoting the third, a debate about reforms to the judicial system. In this period two main phases relating to the individual application rate can be distinguished: 'dormancy', from the mid-1950s to the mid-1980s, followed by the beginning of a more 'active' phase, which continued until it was superseded in the late 1990s by 'case overload'. In spite of the fact that only six cases were declared admissible in 1974 and four in 1975, by the beginning of the 1970s 'there were signs that the Convention was coming out of a long and difficult infancy.'[65] Between 1955 and 1982, 22,158 'provisional applications' (those not formally registered) were received by the Registry at Strasbourg, an average of 791 per year.[66] Of these 46 per cent (10,210) were officially registered and, of these, 3 per cent (297) were declared admissible for a decision on the merits. Things began to change significantly in the mid-1980s, however, when the annual rate of provisional applications rose to nearly quadruple the average for 1955–82, around 3,000, dropping slightly from 3,150 in 1983 to 2,831 in 1985. From then onwards it increased in three, four-to-five-year, bursts.

Between 1987 and 1998 the number of provisional applications to the ECtHR rose even more dramatically from 3,675 to 16,353.[67] This can be attributed to several factors. First, when the Convention came into force in 1953, of the then-ten signatory states, only Denmark, Ireland and Sweden opted for the right of individual petition. But, by 1960, only three

[62] Bates, *Evolution of the ECHR*, pp. 356–8.
[63] *Ibid.*, p. 18.
[64] *Ibid.*, p. 19.
[65] *Ibid.*, p. 14.
[66] European Court of Human Rights, *Survey of Activities 1999 – Development in the Number of Individual Applications Lodged with the Court (Formerly the Commission)* (Strasbourg: Council of Europe, 2000), p. 50.
[67] *Ibid.*

out of the thirteen member states withheld it, and by 1990 all of the then-twenty-two had acceded to it. Second, while the number of member states and the population over which the Court exercised jurisdiction had been increasing since the Convention came into force, it was not until the late 1990s that the impact of the post-Communist enlargement was fully felt. Third, together with a global trend towards judicially protected human rights, media interest in the Court's judgments, and in human rights generally, greatly increased in the 1980s and 1990s, raising their public profile and making litigants more likely to consider pursuing their complaints at Strasbourg.

Responding to the rising application rate, the increasing complexity of cases and enlargement, and in order to simplify the system, reduce the length of proceedings and reinforce their judicial character, the CE approved Protocol No. 11, effective from 1 November 1998.[68] The restructured Court, now a full-time institution, retained its original functions of delivering legally binding judgments on whether or not the Convention had been violated and of providing advisory opinions upon request to the CM.[69] But the European Commission of Human Rights was abolished and all its previous tasks – including registering applications, ascertaining the facts, deciding whether the admissibility criteria were satisfied and seeking friendly resolution of complaints – were transferred to the Court. The CM was stripped of its power to settle cases and was confined to supervising the execution of judgments. The right of individual petition and the Court's jurisdiction also became compulsory, although by this time, each had already been voluntarily accepted by all member states.

By the mid-1990s, according to Rolv Ryssdal, a former President of the Court, people began to turn 'to the Strasbourg institutions to seek redress for their grievances in sometimes very ordinary situations, far removed from the concern to defeat totalitarian dictatorship and genocide that motivated the Convention system's founders.' The individual

---

[68] A. Drzemczewski, 'The European Human Rights Convention: A New Court of Human Rights in Strasbourg as of November 1, 1998', *Washington and Lee Law Review*, 55 (1998), 697–736, 716; M. Madsen, 'From Cold War Instrument to Supreme European Court: The European Court of Human Rights at the Crossroads of International and National Law and Politics', *Law & Social Inquiry*, 32 (2007), 137–59.

[69] To date, the Committee of Ministers has made three requests for advisory opinions and the Court has delivered two – European Court of Human Rights, *Annual Report 2011*, 11, fn 1, echr.coe.int/Documents/Annual_report_2011_ENG.pdf – figures confirmed by Court officials to the authors as accurate up to the end of 2016.

applications process, therefore, came to be applied to 'relatively minor, sometimes highly technical issues'.[70] The ECtHR was also, by this stage, increasingly prepared to consider, albeit indirectly, some aspects of the EU's activities. For example, in *Cantoni v France*,[71] a French provision identical to an EU directive, was subjected to full scrutiny and, in 1999, the United Kingdom was found in violation of the Convention right to free and fair elections in respect of the exclusion of Gibraltar from elections to the European Parliament, the EU's assembly.[72]

By the late 1990s, the Convention, therefore, offered two different levels of protection: first, against 'bad-faith abuse of governmental power' and, secondly, against 'good-faith limitations on liberty' which nevertheless went beyond what is necessary in a democratic society.[73] As Mahoney claims, in its first forty years or so, the Convention predominantly fulfilled the second function of protecting individuals and groups from the excesses of discretion exercised by national legislative, executive and judicial authorities in healthy democracies. With respect to the first he notes, using Turkey as an illustration, that the nature of individual complaints also changed in five ways.[74] There were more allegations of serious and systematic human rights abuses, for example, destruction of villages, routine torture of detainees and the banning of political parties. But he argues that the problem with individual applications in such contexts is that they tend to focus only on the complaints of specific victims rather than upon underlying patterns of official conduct violating the Convention rights of many.[75] Second, the primary facts were increasingly contested, necessitating difficult and costly fact-finding missions by the Strasbourg institutions.[76] Third, in several cases, the Court held that

---

[70] R. Ryssdall, 'The Coming of Age of the European Convention on Human Rights', *European Human Rights Law Review*, [1996], 18–29, 22.

[71] HUDOC, 22 October 1996.

[72] *Matthews v United Kingdom*, HUDOC, 18 February 1999 (GC).

[73] P. Mahoney, 'Speculating on the Future of the Reformed European Court of Human Rights', *Human Rights Law Journal*, 20 (1999), 1–4, 2.

[74] *Ibid.*, 3.

[75] See also P. Sardaro, '*Jus Non Dicere* for Allegations of Serious Violations of Human Rights: Questionable Trends in the Recent Case Law of the Strasbourg Court', *European Human Rights Law Review*, [2003], 601–30; A. Reidy, F. Hampson and K. Boyle, 'Gross Violations of Human Rights: Invoking the European Convention on Human Rights in the Case of Turkey', *Netherlands Quarterly of Human Rights*, 15 (1997), 161–73; Kamminga, 'Is ECHR Sufficiently Equipped?'.

[76] See also P. Leach, C. Paraskeva, and G. Uzelac, 'Human Rights Fact-Finding: The European Court of Human Rights at a Crossroads', *Netherlands Quarterly of Human*

the existence of special circumstances – for example, the failure of national authorities to investigate allegations of Convention violation, and strife between local populations and the state – absolved the applicant from having to exhaust domestic remedies. The result, in such cases, was that the Court effectively turned itself into a tribunal of first instance. Fourth, in circumstances such as these, respondent states were tempted to hinder, or even obstruct, applications to Strasbourg. Finally, the cases in question were politically controversial in their country of origin. As Mahoney adds: 'this phenomenon may well be reproduced, to a greater or lesser degree, in relation to some of the new and expected participating States from the former Soviet bloc', which may require the Court to engage in more protection of the kind envisaged by the first of the two levels he distinguishes.[77] Subsequent developments, particularly with respect to the Chechen wars and the crisis in Ukraine, have partially substantiated this view.

From European Communities to European Union

For three main reasons the European Communities showed little overt interest in human rights for the first forty years of their history. First, although the ideals of democracy, human rights and the rule of law were always regarded as important and desirable, human rights were not initially seen as a priority for a project focused on economic cooperation and the creation of a common market.[78] Second, it was, in any case, assumed that fundamental human rights were adequately addressed by the CE and the ECHR, to which all members of the Communities, but not the Communities themselves, also belonged. Third, the principal judicial organ of the Communities, the ECJ in Luxembourg, generally interpreted Community law as it applied to member states – although

Rights, 28 (2010), 41–77; Harmsen, 'ECHR after Enlargement', 29; Drezemczewski, 'Prevention of Human Rights Violations', 157.

[77] Mahoney, 'Speculating on Future', 4.

[78] G. Quinn, 'The European Union and the Council of Europe on the Issue of Human Rights: Twins Separated at Birth?' *McGill Law Journal*, 46 (2001), 849–74, 856; A. von Bogdandy, 'The European Union as a Human Rights Organization? Human Rights and the Core of the European Union', *Common Market Law Review*, 37 (2000), 1307–38, 1308; M. A. Dauses, 'The Protection of Fundamental Rights in the Community Legal Order', *European Law Review*, 10 (1985), 398–419; P. Pescatore, 'Fundamental Rights in the System of the European Communities', *American Journal of Comparative Law*, 18 (1970), 343–51, 344; U. Scheuner, 'Fundamental Rights in European Community Law and in National Constitutional Law', *Common Market Law Review*, 12 (1975), 171–91, 171.

not as it applied to the institutions of the Communities themselves – in accordance with the ECHR and the jurisprudence of the Strasbourg institutions.

However, for several reasons, towards the end of the twentieth century the profile of human rights increased in the Communities, albeit in an ad hoc rather than systematic manner. First, it became clear that the success of European integration hinged upon the supremacy of Community law. A rebellion threatened since the late 1960s by national constitutional courts, fearing the risks this posed to national constitutional rights, increasingly compelled the ECJ to rule that fundamental rights, considered more fully in Chapters 4 and 5, are enshrined in general principles of Community law. Second, the Communities began to require respect for human rights as a condition of entering into formal trading and other relationships with non-members, as considered more fully in Chapter 4. It, therefore, became increasingly difficult for them not to have a human rights policy for their own internal affairs.

In 1973 the United Kingdom, Ireland and Denmark joined the EEC, transforming what had largely been a Franco-German entity, into something much more multi-national, multi-dimensional and dynamic. But the direction of travel remained controversial. Some continued to advocate closer cooperation leading to a single federal state while others, particularly in the United Kingdom, were strongly opposed. Although the Communities were gaining a sense of their own global significance, they still lacked clear objectives beyond that of a single market. And even this was beginning to stall since many national barriers to free movement of goods and people remained.

As a result, the grander ambition of European unification was downplayed (though not abandoned) in favour of further and closer economic cooperation. By seeking, in the 1980s and 1990s, to harmonise national laws, releasing the single market from domestic constraints imposed to protect national markets and by properly enforcing free competition centrally, the Communities developed into the European Union as a result of treaty reform. This process was set in motion by the more administrative than visionary Single European Act 1986, which sought to add new momentum to European integration by committing the EEC to establish a single market by 31 December 1992 and also to coordinating what would eventually become the EU's Common Foreign and Security Policy. It was an extraordinary coincidence that the completion of this project corresponded with the end of the Cold War and the dramatic political changes in Central and Eastern Europe which ensued.

Fifteen new member states eventually joined the EC/EU, attracted by the economic success and stability they offered, contrasting sharply with the plight of the former Soviet controlled states. The process also suggested that together the Communities were, or had the potential to become, a strong, independent entity capable of exercising economic leadership for the collective European good, with political authority equal to that of the United States.

Influential Community figures, particularly Jacques Delors (President of the Commission) and Presidents Mitterand and Kohl of France and Germany, respectively, began to argue that the EC should not only increase its membership but also expand its activities beyond the economic realm; in the dynamic phrase of the time, that it should 'widen and deepen'. But, to do so required a distinctive normative commitment that would provide a clearer identity both internally and externally. With the key emphasis on the institutionalisation of a single market, and given the EC's greatly increased size, the Luxembourg Accords were now also no longer appropriate and the admission of Greece, and then Spain and Portugal in the 1980s, made the prospect of the organisation being held to ransom by a recalcitrant member even more intolerable than before. Member states, therefore, also came under increasing pressure to relinquish their right of veto in defence of national interests. Although basic rules rapidly harmonised the internal market, fundamental rights were still virtually invisible, remaining the preserve of member states, complemented, as already indicated, by the CE and ECHR, each of which the EC regarded as the proper domain for any pan-European human rights regime. While the ECJ continued to regard respect for fundamental rights as a general principle of Community law, it was, however, unable to apply this, except on very few occasions, much less to develop a distinctive jurisprudence for human rights.[79]

Further reforms and transfers of sovereignty from state to Community, therefore, became inevitable. A new treaty, embodying a strange institutional compromise, was proposed to meet the aspirations of those states wanting deeper and wider union and those, such as the United Kingdom, which did not; the EC would survive but in parallel with a European Union. The new arrangements were introduced by the Treaty of Maastricht 1992 – also known as the Treaty on European Union (TEU) – which, in addition to renaming the EEC the 'European

---

[79] See Chapter 5 of this study; P. Alston with M. Bustelo and J. Heenan (eds.), *The EU and Human Rights* (Oxford University Press, 1999).

Community' (EC) and amending its founding treaty, created the 'three pillars' of the European Union: the three European Communities, police and judicial cooperation in criminal matters and a Common Foreign and Security Policy. The First Pillar, the central plank of the Community, was the internal market. This lay within the competence and control of Community institutions, which also gained control over other areas such as consumer protection, public health, transport, economic and monetary union and social policy. However, member states, such as the United Kingdom, could and did negotiate opt outs from the last two. The Second Pillar included Justice and Home Affairs, some aspects of which were to create legal obligations, including free movement of people within the EC, already accepted by some countries through the 'open border' Schengen Agreements of 1985 and 1990. However, member states could also opt not to be bound by these obligations, a choice also made by the United Kingdom and some others. The Third Pillar, which dealt with foreign and security policy, encouraged, but did not require member states to act collectively in these spheres.

Though an imaginative compromise, the Three Pillar system caused political and legal confusion. Determining where EC law applied, and where not, became, for example, a particular concern of ECJ jurisprudence at the time. The TEU did, however, recognise the importance of establishing a principled discourse for the entire EU/EC. While a rather tepid language of fundamental rights and democracy was espoused, there was now also a constitutional commitment to define the project of deeper and wider European integration more consistently in normative terms. The process of ratifying the Maastricht Treaty also proved difficult. Not only did considerable internal opposition, expressed through referenda and legal challenge, have to be overcome in various member states, but the geo-political environment in Europe was also rapidly changing. As already indicated in the previous section (The Council of Europe and the European Convention on Human Rights), in the early 1990s, the war in the former Yugoslavia and instability accompanying the transition of some central and eastern European states from authoritarianism to democracy posed difficult challenges for western Europe. While the CE provided the benefits already considered, the EU offered the prospect of political, economic and social transformation, which, by enhancing international peace across the continent and extending the reach of the internal market, necessitated a massive transfer of resources eastwards.

The success of this policy hinged particularly on two things: a clear set of core, common, yet customised, requirements that all new member

states would have to meet and a re-examination of the Community's
entire institutional framework. The first, considered more fully in Chapter 4, was both normative – what key principles defined a member of the
Community? – and administrative – what political and legal changes
were necessary for accession and how would their implementation be
monitored? Identifying the general institutional framework was more
difficult as it meant yet another re-visioning of the EU/EC and how it
could function with a vastly expanded membership.

A process of 'constitutionalisation' in all but name was, therefore,
inaugurated. In 1993 the European Council, the ultimate political authority of the EC/EU considered more fully in Chapter 4, provided fresh
membership criteria for any state wishing to join. These included economic and political requirements involving both possible changes to
national constitutional arrangements and practical mechanisms for compliance with human rights standards, the ECHR being the chief, but not
the only, guiding text. Amendments to the internal arrangements of the
EU/EC followed. Meanwhile, in 1996 the ECJ declared that, without a
formal amendment of its founding treaties, the EC lacked the powers to
accede to the ECHR, an issue explored in greater depth in Chapter 4.[80] In
1997 the Treaty of Amsterdam, more managerial than visionary in
content, established that the EU was characterised by the principles of
'liberty, democracy, respect for human rights, and the rule of law' and
stipulated that any state wishing to become a member had to abide by
them. It also created a mechanism for sanctioning existing members
which failed to do so. As a result of the perceived need to develop the
normative dimension, the European Council also decided to establish a
Bill of Rights for the EU. In 1999, a year after having been called for, a
Charter of Fundamental Rights (CFR), considered more fully in Chapters 4 and 5, was drafted and adopted. Although not then legally binding,
the CFR demonstrated a willingness to flesh out the EU's conception of
fundamental rights.

Crisis Management: Early 2000s–2017

In the first decade and a half or so of the twenty-first century the CE and
the EU have struggled with problems produced both by their own
significant successes in the previous two phases and also by several

---

[80] Opinion 2/94 of 28 March 1996, ECR 1996, I-1759, paras. 34–6.

commoncommon challenges, each with implications for their human rights activities and their legitimacy.

The Council of Europe and the European Convention on Human Rights

The new millennium began with the CE further expanding its suite of human rights institutions by creating, in 2000, the post of Commissioner for Human Rights. Considered more fully in Chapter 2, the purpose of this office is to foster the effective observance of human rights and to assist member states in the implementation of relevant standards; promote education in, and awareness of, human rights in member states; identify possible human rights–related shortcomings in domestic law and practice; facilitate the activities of national ombudsmen and other human rights institutions; and provide advice and information regarding the protection of human rights across the continent.[81] By the end of 2016 the total number of CE treaties and protocols had risen to 219, with several, particularly in the fields of data protection, child protection and human trafficking, closely mirroring EU legislation.[82]

The main challenges faced by the Convention system in this phase involved increasing engagement with the EU and the UN, and especially the ECtHR's mushrooming case overload including thousands of individual applications stemming from conflicts in Chechnya, Ukraine and the Caucasus. Of the few inter-state cases, *Denmark* v *Turkey*,[83] which concerned the alleged mis-treatment of a Danish national during pre-trial detention, was resolved by friendly settlement. In a fourth application by Cyprus relating to the Turkish invasion of 1974, the Court held, on 10 May 2001, that Turkey remained in violation of the Convention on account of discrimination by the Turkish Republic of Northern Cyprus (TRNC) against the small Greek-Cypriot minority in the Karpas region, the refusal to allow some 211,000 displaced Greek-Cypriots access to their homes or to offer compensation and the failure to conduct effective investigations into the disappearance of Greek-Cypriots.[84] In 2005,

---

[81] CM/Res (99)(50).
[82] J. Polakiewicz, 'Competition or Coherence', 8.
[83] HUDOC, 5 April 2000.
[84] HUDOC, 10 May 2001; L. G. Loucaides, 'The Judgment of the ECtHR in the *Case of Cyprus* v *Turkey*', *Leiden Journal of International Law*, 15 (2002), 225–36; F. Hoffmeister, 'Cyprus v Turkey. App.No. 25781/94. At www.echr.coe.int/Eng/Judgments.htm. ECtHR, Grand Chamber, May 10, 2001', *American Journal of International Law*, 96 (2002), 445–52.

responding to this and other judgments, the TRNC established an Immovable Property Commission to examine and to provide remedies in respect of claims relating to abandoned properties in northern Cyprus, which, in 2010, the ECtHR held had achieved these objectives.[85] Two applications made by Georgia in 2009 and 2011 concerning, respectively, multiple alleged violations of the Convention rights of Georgians living in the Russian Federation and alleged violations connected with the war between these two states in August 2008, were ruled admissible by the ECtHR.[86] Ukraine also lodged four applications against Russia concerning events in Crimea and eastern Ukraine, one of which was struck off the Court's list on 1 September 2015 when the Ukrainian government decided no longer to pursue it.[87] On 15 September 2016 Slovenia petitioned the Court alleging violations of the rights to fair trial, to peaceful enjoyment of possessions and to an effective remedy on the part of the Croatian courts and executive with respect to the attempted recovery of debts from Croatian companies by a Slovenian bank following the disintegration of Yugoslavia in the 1990s.[88]

The main doctrinal challenge from the wider international environment for the Court concerned how alleged Convention violations stemming from compliance by member states with obligations arising from their membership of other international organisations might be addressed. In 2001 the Grand Chamber ruled inadmissible an application alleging multiple Convention violations arising out of the bombing of the Serb TV station in Belgrade as part of NATO's military intervention in the Kosovan campaign, on the grounds that the aerial bombardment in question was an act of war rather than an exercise of jurisdiction as required by Article 1 ECHR.[89] The conditions under which extra-territorial jurisdiction arises and its scope arose in a series of further cases considered in Chapter 3.[90]

---

[85] *Demopoulos and Others v Turkey*, HUDOC, 1 March 2010 (dec., GC).

[86] *Georgia v Russia (No 2)*, HUDOC, 13 December 2011; *Georgia v Russia (No 1)*, HUDOC, 30 June 2009.

[87] Registrar of the European Court of Human Rights, *Press Release*, ECHR 296 (2015), 01.10.2015, hudoc.echr.coe.int/eng-press?i=003–5187816-6420666.

[88] Registrar of the ECtHR, *Press Release*, ECHR 340 (2016), 20.10.2016, hudoc.echr.coe.int/eng-press?i=003–5526060-6953663.

[89] *Banković v Belgium and Others*, HUDOC, 12 December 2001 (dec., GC).

[90] *Al-Skeini v United Kingdom* (GC), HUDOC, 7 July 2011; *Al-Jedda v United Kingdom* (GC), HUDOC, 7 July 2011; *Öcalan v Turkey* (GC), HUDOC, 12 May 2005*Ilaşcu and Others v Moldova and Russia* (GC), HUDOC, 8 July 2004; *Issa v Turkey*, HUDOC, 16 November 2004.

In a milestone ruling in 2005, the ECtHR held, in the *Bosphorus* case, that although the seizure of property by a CE state acting under an international obligation – in this instance one stemming from EU law – is justiciable under Article 1 of Protocol No. 1 of the ECHR, the state would be presumed to have complied with its ECHR obligations if the protection of human rights available in the international organisation in question was 'at least equivalent' to that provided by the ECHR, unless there was evidence that, in the specific circumstances, it was 'manifestly deficient'.[91] In 2007 the Court also ruled inadmissible two applications alleging Convention violations by several CE states acting as part of a UN military operation in Kosovo, on the grounds that the activities in question were attributable, not to the states in question, but to the UN, which is not party to the ECHR.[92]

The main procedural and administrative developments in the Convention system in this period were the case overload crisis, which had been building throughout the late 1990s, followed by its alleviation, but not at yet its definitive resolution, from 2014. Concerns that Protocol No. 11 would not be adequate were raised even before it came into effect in 1998,[93] and within eight months of its instigation, the President of the Court, Professor Luzius Wildhaber, admitted that the system was 'under pressure'. A year later he urged states to appoint a committee to consider further major reforms in order to avert 'asphyxiation' by the ever-increasing backlog of applications.[94] In 1998, 18,164 applications had been lodged with the Court. But, by 2001, this figure had nearly doubled to 31,228.[95] In November 2000 the CE officially inaugurated a fresh debate about reform. Over the next three and a half years a number of Strasbourg committees considered nearly a dozen central issues, including financial and other resources, improving Convention compliance at national level, streamlining the filtering of applications and the criteria

---

[91] *Bosphorus Hava Yollari Turizm ve Ticaret Şiket* v *Ireland*, HUDOC, 30 June 2005 (GC), at paras. 153–6.

[92] *Behrami* v *France and Saramati* v *France, Germany and Norway* HUDOC, 2 May 2007 (dec. GC).

[93] Bates, *Evolution of the ECHR*, p. 469.

[94] Council of Europe press releases of 21 June 1999 and 8 June 2000, respectively, quoted in A. Mowbray, 'Proposals for Reform of the ECtHR', *Public Law*, [2002], 252–64, 252. See also [2000] 21 *Human Rights Law Journal*, 90.

[95] European Court of Human Rights, *Annual Report – 2003* (Strasbourg: Registry of the European Court of Human Rights, 2004), p. 105, echr.coe.int/Documents/Annual_report_2003_ENG.pdf.

for admissibility, providing different procedures for different kinds of case (for example, 'clone' or 'repeat' applications involving violations the Court had already condemned in the respondent state concerned and 'straightforward' cases meriting 'fast track' management), encouraging friendly settlement, providing another instrument to deal with administrative and procedural matters capable of being amended more easily than the Convention itself, improving the enforcement and supervision of judgments, the possible accession of the EU to the Convention and the number and terms of office of judges on the ECtHR.[96] Contributions were also made by NGOs, governments, experts and other interested parties. From 1 January 2002 the formal distinction between 'provisional' and 'registered' applications was also abandoned with all written contact between an applicant and the Registry formally recorded as an 'application lodged with the Registry'. These are destroyed a year later if applicants have not submitted a written application on the correct form. Duly completed application forms were 'allocated to a decision body' to determine admissibility. Spending on the Court also increased, accounting for over a third of the CE's budget by the end of the 2000s as compared with 20 per cent a decade earlier.[97] Joining those from Turkey and Italy, which had long held this dubious honour, the Court's docket also became increasingly dominated by complaints from the post-Communist zone.

In May 2004 a modest reform package, Protocol No. 14, was unanimously endorsed by all states parties with implementation expected for late 2006 or early 2007. Amongst other things this permitted admissibility decisions to be taken by 'judicial formations' of a single judge and registry lawyer. Those disclosing patent Convention violations were also to be judged on the merits by three-judge committees in a new summary procedure intended to address the fact that some 70 per cent of the Court's judgments were then 'repeat applications' raising complaints already condemned in the specific respondent state.[98] Article 59(2) ECHR as amended by Protocol No. 14 also enables the EU to accede to the ECHR, a development endorsed in 2006 by the Juncker report, which, amongst other things, also recommended greater cooperation between the EU and CE premised on the latter being 'the Europe-wide reference

---

[96] See Greer, *European Convention*, pp. 42–3.
[97] A. Royer, *The Council of Europe* (Strasbourg: Council of Europe Publishing, 2010), p. 9.
[98] Protocol No 14bis to the Convention for the Protection of Human Rights, Explanatory Report (27 May 2009), para 16.

source for human rights'.[99] In May 2007 the CE and EU signed a
Memorandum of Understanding intended to improve coordination and
cooperation in areas of mutual interest including human rights.[100]

Meanwhile, by early 2005 concerns were expressed that the most
significant changes in Protocol No. 14 – to the applications and enforcement of judgments processes considered further in Chapter 2 – would
not make much difference to the rising tide of applications and that
something more radical was required. So, in May 2005 a Group of Wise
Persons was appointed to make further proposals. But their report, made
public in November 2006, contained nothing new of substance, largely
recycled ideas already rejected in the course of the Protocol No. 14 debate
and assumed that Protocol No. 14 would soon come into effect.[101]
However, in December 2006, to everyone's great surprise and in spite
of the fact that the Russian government had already approved it, the
Russian parliament refused to ratify Protocol No. 14, ostensibly because
of objections to the replacement of three-judge committees by single-
judge formations for admissibility decisions. This caused great conster-
nation in Strasbourg and, notwithstanding intense diplomatic pressure,
by May 2009 the Russian parliament had still not been persuaded to
change its mind. As a result, the CE provided an interim set of optional
measures in Protocol No. 14bis, intended to apply to the other forty-six
member states. However, again to everyone's surprise, in January
2010 both chambers of the Russian parliament voted in favour of ratifying Protocol No. 14, enabling it to come into effect for all forty-seven
member states on 1 June 2010. At a conference in Interlaken in February
2010 the CE also decided to conduct an official review of the impact of
Protocol No. 14 between 2012 and 2015 and to decide, by the end of
2019, whether further significant changes were still required.[102]

Various proposals – including a statute more easily modified than the
Convention itself, mandatory application fees, compulsory legal

[99] J.-C. Juncker, *Council of Europe – European Union: "A Sole Ambition for the European Continent,"* report by Jean-Claude Juncker, Prime Minister of the Grand Duchy of Luxembourg, to the attention of the Heads of State or Government of the Member states of the CE, 11 April 2006, p. 30, para. 2.
[100] *Memorandum of Understanding between the Council of Europe and the European Union,* CM(2007)74, 10 May 2007.
[101] Report of the Group of Wise Persons to the Committee of Ministers, Cm(2006)203 (15 November 2006).
[102] See A. Mowbray, 'The Interlaken Declaration – the Beginning of a New Era for the European Court of Human Rights', *Human Rights Law Review,* 10 (2010), 519–28.

representation, advisory opinions, further alterations to filtering mechanisms and admissibility criteria, increased emphasis on subsidiarity and improvements to the consistency of the case law[103] – were considered at a series of High Level Conferences on the Future of the ECtHR held in Interlaken in 2010, Izmir in 2011 and Brighton in 2012, the latter coinciding with increasingly virulent nationalism, populism, Euroscepticism and human rights–scepticism across the continent.[104] As a result, a fifteenth and sixteenth Protocol, with universal effect, were opened for signature on 24 June and 2 October 2013, but neither has yet come into effect. The details are considered in Chapter 2. In March 2015 another high-level conference, this time in Brussels, focused on Convention implementation and, amongst other things, welcomed the Court's commitment to provide brief reasons for inadmissibility decisions of single judges, invited it to do so from January 2016, and to consider providing brief reasons both for interim measures and for refusals by five-judge panels to accept requests for referral to the Grand Chamber.[105]

In a report on the long term future of the ECHR submitted to the Committee of Ministers on 11 December 2015, the CE's Steering Committee for Human Rights (CDDH), a prominent player in earlier reform debates, concluded that improvements to the selection of judges would require further modification of the ECHR but that two of the other three central challenges distinguished – national implementation and the authority of the Court including effective case management – should be addressed within existing structures. However, nothing of substance is said about the third – the place of the ECHR in European and international legal orders – except that because the 'risk of fragmentation of the European legal space in the field of human rights protection may become a major challenge to the Convention system in the longer term' and delay in EU accession to the ECHR could result in the two systems

---

[103] See, e.g., I. Cameron, 'The Court and the Member States: Procedural Aspects' in A. Føllesdal, B. Peters and G. Ulfstein (eds.), *Constituting Europe: The European Court of Human Rights in a National, European and Global Context* (Cambridge University Press, 2013), pp. 43–54.

[104] See, e.g., B. Oomen, 'A Serious Case of Strasbourg-Bashing? An Evaluation of the Debates on the Legitimacy of the European Court of Human Rights in the Netherlands', *International Journal of Human Rights*, 20 (2016), 407–25.

[105] Council of Europe, *High Level Conference on the Implementation of the European Convention on Human Rights, Our Shared Responsibility, Brussels Declaration*, 27 March 2015, p. 4, http://echr.coe.int/Documents/Brussels_Declaration_ENG.pdf.

'drifting apart', it should be the subject of further inquiry.[106] The CDDH regards inadequate national implementation of the Convention as 'among the principal challenges' or 'even the biggest challenge'[107] confronting the system, yet suggests little about how it might be addressed beyond reciting familiar mantras regarding such things as adequate training programmes, improved domestic remedies, Convention-proofing of draft legislation and the importance of national human rights structures. As far as case overload is concerned, the CDDH notes that the backlog of clearly inadmissible cases has been cleared and the expectation is that the backlog of repetitive cases will be dealt with in two or three years. It also encourages the Court to streamline its working methods in order to deal with the accumulation of non-repetitive priority and non-priority cases. While, 'strongly reiterating its attachment to the Court's mission in ensuring individual justice' and affirming that 'the quality of reasoning is essential for the authority of the case law and for the Committee of Ministers when supervising the execution of Court judgments',[108] nothing is proposed about how this might be delivered except an endorsement of Brussels Declaration proposals concerning the need for reasons to be given for single-judge decisions, for decisions regarding interim measures and for refusals by five-judge panels to accede to requests to refer cases to the Grand Chamber.

By the end of 2015, the combined effect of Protocol No. 14, the Court's prioritisation of applications according to urgency and seriousness and the Registry's stricter approach to the receipt of complaints, at last seemed to be reducing the scale of the case overload crisis. In 2014 the number of applications allocated to a judicial formation fell from an all-time high of 65,800 the previous year, to 56,200, dropping further in 2015 to 40,600, while the backlog of those awaiting a decision also declined, from an historic peak of 151,600 in 2011, to 69,900 in 2014 and to 64,850 in 2015.[109] However, by the end of 2016 the number of applications allocated to a judicial formation had risen to 53,500 with

---

[106] Council of Europe Steering Committee for Human Rights (CDDH), *CDDH report on the longer-term future of the system of the European Convention on Human Rights*, CDDH(2015)R84 Addendum I, Strasbourg, 11 December 2015, paras. 179, 181, 195(iv) and 202(ii).

[107] *Ibid.*, paras. 34, 195.

[108] *Ibid.*, para. 199(ii) and (iii).

[109] European Court of Human Rights, *Analysis of Statistics 2016* (Strasbourg: Council of Europe-European Court of Human Rights, 2017), p. 7, echr.coe.int/Documents/Stats_analysis_2016_ENG.pdf.

79,750 pending before a judicial formation.[110] By the end of January 2017, of the total cases pending, 30,500 were repetitive, 11,500 were 'priority'[111] and some 21,000 – which according to the *Annual Report 2016* constitute 'the greatest weight' on the Court's docket[112] – were neither clearly inadmissible nor repetitive. The Court itself has, therefore, acknowledged that, although more priority applications are being processed and adjudicated than before, 'this will not be sufficient' for 'substantial inroads' to be made 'into the backlog of Chamber cases' and that further reflection on 'new working methods and approaches to further streamline the proceedings for different categories of applications' including 'new forms of cooperation with national authorities' will be required.[113]

The European Union

The EU continued to develop institutionally throughout this period. While the Treaty of Nice in 2001 changed some voting arrangements to make decision making more manageable, it nevertheless complicated an already-unwieldy and confusing structure. Within a year another Treaty was already being considered, this time couched in the language of 'constitutionalisation'. At the European Council's Laeken summit in 2001, member states agreed that fundamental change was needed to address the Union's perceived 'democratic deficit', impending post-Communist enlargement, the EU's role in the world and the continuing challenges of managing the single market. Although nothing less than a re-imagining of the very nature and character of the EU was required, most attention focused on the process and what it should be called. A 'convention on the future of Europe' – convened with a mandate to draft a Constitution for the EU and to consider what the EU was and what it should become – produced a Draft Constitutional Treaty, which, amongst other things, sought to eradicate the EU/EC distinction. The EU would incorporate the new CFR, increase its control over European foreign policy, enhance its own democratic accountability and re-distribute power between itself and member states. While areas where individual states retained control would remain, the intent was clear; a

---

[110] *Ibid.* pp. 7, 8.
[111] European Court of Human Rights, *Annual Report 2016* (Strasbourg: Council of Europe-European Court of Human Rights, 2017), p. 18, echr.coe.int/Documents/Annual_report_2016_ENG.pdf.
[112] *Ibid.*, pp. 13–14.
[113] *Analysis of Statistics 2016*, p. 5; *Annual Report 2016*, p. 19.

Union more integrated on economic, legal and political dimensions was the preferred means by which the project, begun in the late 1940s, would now progress. However, although vaingloriously signed by member states, the French and Dutch derailed the process in 2005 by voting against it in referendums. The issues of enlargement and incoherence nevertheless remained acute. Within two years yet another new Treaty was, therefore, drafted, which, although dispensing with the 'constitution' tag, reintroduced many of the original features of the Draft Constitutional Treaty.

Meanwhile, developing an idea first approved in 2003, the EU formally proposed, in June 2005, to expand the remit of the European Centre on Racism and Xenophobia to create a Fundamental Rights Agency (FRA), which became operational from 1 January 2007.[114] Using the CFR as its main point of reference, attempting to avoid overlap with the CE, and networking with national institutions, the FRA is intended to be 'an independent centre of expertise on fundamental rights issues through data collection, analysis and networking', to provide 'relevant institutions and authorities of the Community and its Member states when implementing the Community law with assistance and expertise relating to fundamental rights' and to 'advise the Union institutions and the Member states on how best to prepare or implement fundamental rights related Union legislation'.[115] It does not, however, have any powers to examine individual complaints, to issue regulations or to carry out 'normative monitoring' for the purposes of Article 7 TEU, which authorises the Council of Ministers, on a reasoned proposal by one third of member states, by the European Parliament or by the Commission, to address appropriate recommendations to a member state suspected of a serious breach of the principles of liberty, democracy, respect for human rights, including those found in the ECHR and principles of legality common to member states.

The Treaty of Lisbon 2009 was also a significant milestone. While the European Community disappeared as a formal entity, its competences and responsibilities were retained under the Treaty on the Functioning of the European Union (TFEU), a revised version of the original 1957 treaty which established the EEC. Although a commitment was made to promote the now-explicit values of the EU, including respect for human rights, the CFR still lacked legal force. While the Treaty of Nice 2001 had

---

[114] P. Alston and O. De Schutter (eds.), *Monitoring Fundamental Rights in the EU: The Contribution of the Fundamental Rights Agency* (Oxford: Hart, 2005).
[115] europa.eu.int/comm/justice_home/fsj/rights/fsj_rights_agency_en.htm.

inaugurated the process of providing the EU with more formal constitutional foundations, it was not until the Treaty of Lisbon that the EU
acquired a consolidated legal personality, the 'three pillars' were abandoned and the CFR became legally binding on member states, subject to
various seemingly symbolic exemptions granted to the United Kingdom,
Poland and the Czech Republic.

The accession of the EU to the ECHR also encountered an unexpected
and not easily surmountable obstacle in December 2014. Since the 1970s
accession has been advocated as a possible solution to the lack of effective
legal redress available to victims of human rights violations arising from
the EEC/EU, a problem which has increased as the EU's powers and the
range of its interests have grown. By the beginning of the twenty-first
century, not only were the EU and the Convention system ripe for
reform, each was also more open to such developments than ever before.
Discussions between CE and EU officials culminated in the Lisbon
Treaty, which introduced Article 6(2) TEU, requiring, rather than merely
permitting or encouraging, the EU to accede to the ECHR. And, as
already indicated, Protocol No. 14 enabled the Convention system to
accommodate this. In the summer of 2010, the CDDH and the European
Commission were each mandated by their respective organisations to
negotiate a treaty enabling the EU to become a member of the ECHR
system but not to join the CE itself. A host of institutional, procedural,
normative, administrative and logistical problems bedevilled the project
from the outset, reaching agreement proved difficult and draft instruments of accession were not finalised until 5 April 2013.[116] Yet, despite
having been closely involved in the discussions, on 18 December 2014,
the ECJ ruled that accession, in the terms proposed, was beyond the
powers currently granted the EU by its foundational treaties.[117] The

---

[116] Secretariat of the Council of Europe, *Accession by the European Union to the European
Convention on Human Rights: Answers to frequently asked questions*, 30 April 2013, para
3coe.int/t/DGHL/STANDARDSETTING/hrpolicy/Accession/Meeting_reports/47_1
(2013)008_final_report_EN.pdf. The formal Accession Agreement is one of five documents facilitating accession including the Draft Explanatory Report, see Draft Explanatory
Report, appendices I–V. See V. Kosta, N. Skoutaris and V. Tzevelekos (eds.), *The EU
Accession to the ECHR* (Oxford: Hart, 2014); P. Gragl, *The Accession of the European
Union to the European Convention on Human Rights* (Oxford: Hart, 2013); Draft Accession Agreement, Art. 10(3); S. Douglas-Scott, 'The European Union and Human Rights
after the Treaty of Lisbon', *Human Rights Law Review*, 11 (2011), 645, 658–69.

[117] Opinion 2/13 of 18 December 2014, ECLI:EU:C:2014:2454; J. Odermatt, 'A Giant Step
Backwards? Opinion 2/13 on the EU's Accession to the European Convention on
Human Rights' *New York University Journal of Law and Politics*, 47 (2015), 783–98.

Court was particularly concerned that, with respect to Convention rights, accession would effectively subordinate the ECJ to the ECtHR, would compromise the transfer of sovereignty by member states to the EU and would undermine the effectiveness, autonomy and unity of EU law.[118] Therefore, unless its foundational treaties are amended – a prospect remote in the extreme – accession to the ECHR will, paradoxically, remain a formal treaty obligation which the EU is legally incapable of discharging.[119]

Recent Common Challenges

As already indicated, among several apparent and genuine human rights challenges to have confronted the CE and the EU in recent years, the most visible and pressing include the post-2008 global economic crisis, an increase in (mostly jihadi) terrorist incidents, mass migration particularly as a consequence of the Syrian civil war, Brexit and legitimacy problems stemming from these and other sources including Euro- and rights-scepticism.[120]

Although the post-2008 economic crisis has caused considerable suffering, especially in southern Europe, framing it as a human rights problem is, however, not particularly appropriate for several reasons. First, it is not clear how doing so would contribute to its resolution. Second, as an economic union with a single currency, the EU, which has been much more directly involved than the CE, has had little choice but to respond in the realm of political economy, rather than in the fundamental rights field, by embarking on a fraught and costly financial bailout to prevent Greece leaving the Union ('Grexit'). But this has not yet been required for other southern European economies, including those of

---

[118] Opinion 2/13 of 18 December 2014, ECLI:EU:C:2014:2454, paras. 165–76.

[119] X. Groussot, N.-L. Arold Lorenz and G. Þor Petursson, 'The Paradox of Human Rights Protection in Europe: Two Courts, One Goal?', pp. 19–25, and D. Björgvinsson, 'The Role of the European Court of Human Rights in the Changing European Human Rights Architecture', pp. 31–5, in O. Mjöll Arnardóttir and A. Buyse (eds.), *Shifting Centres of Gravity in Human Rights Protection: Rethinking Relations between the ECHR, EU and National Legal Orders* (London: Routledge, 2016).

[120] See, e.g., Council of Europe, *Highlights 2015: Guardian of Human Rights, Democracy and the Rule of Law – Activity Report* (Strasbourg: CE, 2016), pp. 7, 9, 13, 18, 19, 25–7, 31, slideshare.net/ssuser47a019/council-of-europe-highlights-2015; O. Dörr, 'Commissioner for Human Rights' in Schmahl and Breuer (eds.), *Council of Europe*, p. 303; M. Lezertua and A. Forde, updated by N. Sidaropoulos, 'The Commissioner for Human Rights' in T. Kleinsorge (ed.), *Council of Europe (COE)*, 2nd edn. (Alphen aan den Rijn: Wolters Kluwer, 2015), p. 118.

Spain and Portugal, which have also been under strain. Third, the EU cannot be directly blamed for causing the problem in the first place and while the austere terms of the bail-out have impacted harshly upon people's lives, they have nevertheless been accepted, albeit under protest, by a democratically elected Greek government. Finally, the suffering of people in Greece would, almost certainly, have been much worse without them.

As far as terrorism is concerned, the nationalist variety and also that of the far right and left afflicted Europe in the 1970s–90s. Jihadis also killed 192 in Madrid in March 2004 and 52 in London in July 2005 ('7/7'). After a lull of several years, since 2011 the rate of Islamist attacks has increased with fatal high profile incidents in a steadily lengthening list of European cities including Moscow, Paris, Brussels, Nice, Berlin, London, Manchester and Barcelona. There has also been a smaller number of equally savage right-wing attacks including by Anders Breivik in Norway in 2011. For the CE, the EU and European states the core challenge is effectively to counter the threat terrorism currently poses, whilst avoiding violating fundamental rights. This has been four-square within the CE's brief since its inception. But the EU only acquired it from the mid-1980s as the range of its activities and interests expanded beyond the economic sphere to include, amongst other things, common security concerns.

Unlike the EU, the CE itself has no capacity to take action directly against terrorism. Instead it is limited to providing a forum for member states in which core principles can be enunciated and/or restated. This has taken three main forms.[121] One concerns the ECHR, which, as Chapter 3 explains more fully, permits states to restrict all but a handful of rights (the 'non-derogables') in pursuit of a range of public interests including national security and the prevention of disorder or crime, providing, in particular, the principles of legality, democratic necessity and proportionality are satisfied. This has enabled most CE states to address the current terrorist challenge within the normal parameters of Convention rights. The ECtHR has also delivered a number of landmark judgments over the years, principally concerning the difference between a legitimate restriction and a violation.[122] A range of CE institutions,

---

[121] See C. Walter, 'Combating Terrorism and Organized Crime' in Schmahl and Breuer (eds.), *Council of Europe*, pp. 671–95.
[122] European Court of Human Rights Press Unit, *Factsheet – Terrorism and the European Convention on Human Rights*, September 2016, echr.coe.int/Documents/FS_Terrorism_ENG.pdf.

including particularly PACE and the ECtHR, have also condemned the involvement of member states in 'extraordinary rendition' – the 'extrajudicial transfer of persons from one jurisdiction or state to another, for the purposes of detention and interrogation outside the normal legal system, where there was a real risk of torture, or cruel, inhuman or degrading treatment'.[123] Article 15 ECHR also permits states to derogate from, ie to suspend, all but the non-derogable Convention rights in time of war or public emergency threatening the life of the nation to an extent no more than strictly required by the exigencies of the situation and in a manner consistent with other international obligations. Both the existence of such an emergency and whether the response satisfies this high-threshold proportionality requirement are justiciable at Strasbourg. The United Kingdom's highest court and later the ECtHR ruled that Britain's post-7/7 indefinite detention of a dozen or so foreign nationals violated the ECHR on the grounds that it was disproportionate and discriminatory, notwithstanding a derogation.[124] On 5 June 2015 Ukraine notified the Secretary General of the CE of its intention to derogate from certain Convention rights on account of the security crisis in the Donetsk and Lukansk regions and on 24 November 2015 France also derogated in respect of the state of emergency imposed in the wake of the terrorist attacks in Paris. A derogation was also entered by Turkey on 21 July 2016 in the aftermath of a failed military coup less than a week before.[125]

A second CE contribution has involved sponsorship of three counter-terrorism treaties. The European Convention on the Suppression of Terrorism 1977, as further extended by a Protocol in 2003, is designed primarily to facilitate the extradition of terrorist suspects by listing offences not deemed 'political' for this purpose, including hijacking aircraft, kidnapping and taking hostages, and any act of violence threatening life, physical integrity or liberty. In addition to providing for the protection and compensation of victims, the Council of Europe Convention on the Prevention of Terrorism 2005 encourages states to criminalise preparatory terrorist offences, including public provocation, recruitment and training, by reinforcing national prevention policies and

---

[123] *El Masri* v *The Former Yugoslav Republic of Macedonia*, HUDOC, 13 December 2012 (GC), at para. 221.

[124] *A and Others* v *Secretary of State for the Home Department* [2004] UKHL 56; *A and Others* v *United Kingdom*, HUDOC, 19 February 2009 (GC).

[125] European Court of Human Rights, *Factsheet – Derogation in Time of Emergency*, February 2017, echr.coe.int/Documents/FS_Derogation_ENG.pdf.

by improving extradition, mutual assistance and other relevant arrangements. A Protocol in 2015 extended these offences to include participating in an association for the purpose of terrorism, receiving terrorist training, travelling abroad for the purposes of terrorism and financing or organising travel for this purpose. The aims of the Council of Europe Convention on Laundering, Search, Seizure and Confiscation of the Proceeds from Crime and on the Financing of Terrorism 2005 are clear from the title.

A third contribution is the Committee of Experts on Terrorism (CODEXTER), the CE's principal but not its only forum responsible to the CM for the development and coordination of pan-European counter-terrorist policy in the aftermath of 9/11. Following the attacks in Europe in 2015 the CM issued a declaration on 'violent extremism and radicalisation leading to terrorism', which, amongst other things, seeks to improve the coordination of national efforts to tackle the problem of foreign terrorist fighters and lone terrorists, to prevent radicalisation through public sector measures particularly in schools and prisons and to combat hate speech.[126]

As far as the EU is concerned, three weeks after the Charlie Hebdo attack in Paris in January 2015, the European Council issued the Riga Statement, affirming that terrorism and radicalisation are amongst the principal threats to the EU's internal security and that counter-terrorism efforts need to be reinforced at both national and Union level.[127] As a result, and not without controversy, legislation has been adopted or amended in several member states. The EU has also taken numerous, mostly preventive measures, at various levels and in different forms, to tackle the common threat, including, for example, enhanced operational and investigative cooperation such as the establishment of Europol's European Counter Terrorist Centre in January 2016, and countering radicalisation by promoting the EU's founding values through such channels as employment, education and social inclusion.[128] EU institutions have also, however, unambiguously emphasised that all such measures must also respect fundamental rights and the principles

---

[126] CM Doc CM(2015)74 final of 19 May 2015.
[127] 'Council of the European Union Document 5855/15 concerning an informal meeting of Justice and Home Affairs Ministers', Riga, 29 and 30 January 2015.
[128] European Union Education Ministers, 'Declaration on Promoting Citizenship and the Common Values of Freedom, Tolerance and Non-Discrimination through Education', Paris, 17 March 2015; Europol, *European Union Terrorism Situation and Trend Report 2016 (TE-SAT 2016)*, (The Hague: European Police Office, 2016).

governing their legitimate restriction.[129] Some Union measures which strengthen the EU's external borders may, however, have an adverse impact upon core EU freedoms.[130] While Jean-Claude Junker, President of the European Commission, has, for example, underlined the need to avoid conflating refugees with terrorists,[131] far right political parties in several states, much less convinced about the distinction, have advocated stronger borders in response to both challenges.

This brings us to the third challenge – mass migration from the Middle East and Africa into Europe via Turkey, Greece and Italy, with significant loss of life in the precarious sea crossings, which greatly increased from 2011 onwards particularly as a result of militant Islamism in west and sub-Saharan Africa, instability and sectarian conflict in Afghanistan, Pakistan and Iraq, chaos following the overthrow of the Gaddafi regime in Libya and the wars in Syria and Iraq.[132] In 2015, for example, EU member states received 1,255,640 first-time asylum applications, more than double the figure for the previous year, with the following countries of origin accounting for more than half the total: Syria (362,800 applicants, 29 per cent), Afghanistan (178,200, 14 per cent) and Iraq (121,500, 10 per cent).[133] Migration clearly raises human rights issues, not least concerning how asylum applications are processed and how migrants are treated as they travel and when they arrive at their eventual destinations. However, the recent crisis is arguably more 'humanitarian' than a matter of 'human rights', the differences being largely matters of scale, intensity, causality and the kind of systemic political, economic and legal responses required. While the ECHR can be invoked by anyone, including migrants

---

[129] European Commission, *2015 Report on the Application of the EU Charter of Fundamental Rights (COM (2016) 265 final* (Brussels: European Commission, 2016), p. 5.

[130] See, e.g., European Commission, 'Recommendation of 15 June 2015 Amending the Recommendation Establishing a Common "Practical Handbook for Border Guards (Schengen Handbook)" to Be Used by Member States' Competent Authorities When Carrying Out the Border Control of Persons', C (2006) 5186 final, Brussels, 15 June 2015.

[131] See European Commission, 'Transcript of Press Conference – G20 Summit in Antalya', Speech 15/6091, Brussels, 15 November 2015.

[132] According to data provided to Eurostat pursuant to Article 4 of Regulation (EC) 862/2007, roughly 1,735,000 first-time asylum applications were lodged between January 2015 and June 2016, ec.europa.eu/eurostat/web/asylum-and-managed-migration/data/database.

[133] 'Record Number of Over 1.2 Million First Time Asylum Seekers Registered in 2015' EUROSTAT, ec.europa.eu/eurostat/documents/2995521/7203832/3-04032016-AP-EN.pdf/790eba01-381c–4163-bcd2-a54959b99ed6.

and asylum seekers within the jurisdiction of any member state,[134] the CE does not yet have any designated treaties on asylum, immigration or freedom of movement as such apart from the 1977 European Convention on the Legal Status of Migrant Workers, which is concerned with such issues as recruitment, medical examinations, occupational tests, travel, residence and work permits, the reuniting of families, working conditions, the transfer of savings and social security, social and medical assistance, the expiry of work contracts, dismissal and re-employment. By contrast, and not surprisingly since freedom of movement is one of its core internal freedoms and the right to asylum is expressly recognised in Article 18 CFR, the EU has well-developed processes. At the centre of its asylum policy is the 'Dublin System',[135] under which any given member state, usually that of first entry, is responsible for processing any given application, at least in the first instance. Since the fairness of these arrangements depends upon coordination between national systems, the EU has identified minimum standards, both for the process and for the treatment asylum seekers receive. However, harmonisation has not yet been achieved, and divergent practices, amplified by the post-2008 economic crisis, dominate the landscape.

In an attempt to promote solidarity and shared responsibility amongst member states and to maintain the credibility and sustainability of the Dublin System the EU has also recently provided additional financial and operational support to member states receiving large numbers of migrants, and/or in financial difficulty, albeit with debatable effect.[136] In an attempt to improve efficiency and effectiveness, a controversial temporary quota-based relocation mechanism for asylum seekers arriving in 'high influx' member states, has also been introduced under the Article 78(3) TFEU emergency response provision. While this was

---

[134] J. Viljanen and H.-E. Heiskanen, 'The European Court of Human Rights: A Guardian of Minimum Standards in the Context of Migration', *Netherlands Quarterly of Human Rights*, 34 (2016), 174–93; E. Psychogiopoulou, 'Does Compliance with the Jurisprudence of the European Court of Human Rights Improve State Treatment of Migrants and Asylum Seekers? A Critical Appraisal of Aliens' Rights in Greece', *Journal of International Migration and Integration*, 16 (2015), 819–40; I. Kfir, 'Refugeeship and Natural Law: The European Court of Human Rights', *Netherlands Quarterly of Human Rights*, 33 (2015), 483–511.

[135] The Dublin Convention 1990, initially signed as an intergovernmental treaty outside the EU's legal framework, was incorporated into EU law by 2003/343/EC, the 'Dublin II Regulation'.

[136] F. Trauner, 'Asylum Policy: The EU "Crises" and the Looming Policy Regime Failure', *Journal of European Integration*, 38 (2016), 311–25.

initially approved by the European Council in the form of a non-binding Resolution,[137] qualified majority voting (QMV) was subsequently used for the adoption of a legally-binding Decision,[138] enabling the EU to respond effectively to the crisis. And, in spite of having been offered financial incentives, progress in resettling asylum seekers, particularly from Greece and Italy, has been painfully slow. As of February 2017, twenty-one member states had taken in refugees under the scheme, with only 10,850 refugees relocated out of the 160,000 EU-wide quota.[139]

Domestic compliance with EU asylum policy has also generally proven to be largely inadequate. The use of QMV may even have been counter-productive, since it may reduce the initiative's legitimacy and enable overruled minority states to exploit national anti-EU sentiments to weaken, and even in some cases to evade, implementation.[140] Attempting to improve delivery, the Commission has requested regular reports from the FRA on the member states most affected and has launched numerous infringement proceedings, many resulting in the issuing of Reasoned Opinions.[141] Significant national non-compliance with the EU's response to the refugee crisis has not only posed a considerable challenge to its ability to act effectively as a regional policy coordinator. It has also fuelled right-wing extremism and Euro-scepticism across member states and undermined the Union's overall legitimacy and efficacy. Increased unemployment and diminishing living standards also appear to have triggered a rise in xenophobia and violence against third-country nationals.[142]

On 20 March 2016, an agreement between the EU and Turkey came into effect, according to which migrants entering the EU from Turkey will be sent back there if they fail to apply for asylum or their application

[137] 'Council Resolution 11131/15 of the Representatives of the Governments of the Member States Meeting within the Council on Relocating from Greece and Italy 40,000 Persons in Clear Need of International Protection', Brussels, 22 July 2015.

[138] 'Council Decision 12098/15 Establishing Provisional Measures in the Area of International Protection for the Benefit of Italy and Greece', Brussels, 22 September 2015.

[139] ec.europa.eu/home-affairs/sites/homeaffairs/files/what-we-do/policies/european-agenda-migration/press-material/docs/state_of_play_-_relocation_en.pdf.

[140] C. Roos and G. Orsini, 'How to Reconcile the EU Border Paradox? The Concurrence of Refugee Reception and Deterrence', *Institute for European Studies Policy Brief 4/2015* (Brussels: Vrije Universitei, 2015).

[141] See fra.europa.eu/sites/default/files/fra_uploads/fra-2016-annual-activity-report-2015_en.pdf at 17; europa.eu/rapid/press-release_IP-16–270_en.htm.

[142] United Nations High Commissioner for Refugees, *UNHCR Country Operations Profile – Europe* (Geneva: UNHCR, 2016).

is rejected. After this date, and following case-by-case evaluation, any further irregular migrants will also be returned. In exchange for every Syrian sent back to Turkey, up to a total of 72,000 will be resettled from Turkey to the EU with a preference for those who have not tried to enter the EU illegally. Some 2,300 experts, including security and migration officials and translators, have been sent by the EU to Greece to help implement the deal. Turkey has also been provided with $3.3 billion of aid, and in return, talks about its accession to the EU were re-opened in June 2016.[143] But a pledge to allow Turkish nationals access to the Schengen passport-free zone was not honoured by the Commission on account of concerns about the deterioration in Turkey's respect for human rights following the failed military coup on 15 July 2016. The UNHCR and four aid agencies – Médecins Sans Frontières, the International Rescue Committee, the Norwegian Refugee Council and Save the Children – have declared that, not being parties to the deal and because such blanket expulsions of refugees contravene international law, they will not participate in returns or detentions.

The fourth challenge concerns Brexit. In a referendum held on 23 June 2016, the electorate of the United Kingdom voted by 52 to 48 per cent to leave the EU, the culmination of decades of simmering discontent with this version of the European project among certain sections of the population and political classes. At this stage, the only firm conclusion which can be drawn about the human rights implications – for Britain, for the soon-to-be twenty-seven-member EU and for the forty-seven-member CE – is that they are likely to be uncertain for many years to come. Taking each of these in turn, it is clear that the human rights implications are unlikely to be immediate or direct for the United Kingdom, and their significance is also difficult to predict. Those British human rights laws which do not derive from the EU will not be affected. But this is not a straightforward distinction. The United Kingdom will also remain formally subject to EU law, including in the human rights field, as long as it remains a member of the EU, ie for the two years or more it is expected to take for the divorce, formally commenced in March 2017, to be finalised. However, it is unlikely that, in this period, any new legislation or fresh rulings of the ECJ would or could be

---

[143] Council of the European Union Press Release, 'Accession conference with Turkey: Talks opened on Chapter 33 – Financial and Budgetary Provisions', Press Release 403/16, 30 June 2016, consilium.europa.eu/en/press/press-releases/2016/06/30-turkey-acces sion-conference/.

enforced against the United Kingdom's will. But, thereafter, the status of EU law in domestic law will be difficult to ascertain. For one thing, it may depend upon whether or not, post Brexit, Britain remains a member of the single market in common with non-EU states, Iceland, Liechtenstein, Norway and Switzerland. If it does, it will continue to be subject to some EU rules which have a human rights dimension, in all probability including those concerning free movement of people. The government's stated preference is that the country should leave both the single market and the looser customs union. But Parliamentary approval may be required. However, whatever happens, once its membership of the EU finally terminates, the United Kingdom will no longer have to comply with human rights obligations enshrined in EU treaties. In the short term the European Union (Withdrawal) Bill, also known as the Repeal Bill or Great Repeal Bill which received its second reading in the House of Commons on 11 September 2017, will retain existing EU law including in the human rights field. But it is not clear which, if any, EU human rights norms – including those relating to employment, migration, equality, children, data protection and the environment considered in Chapters 4 and 5 – will ultimately survive.

One, so far largely unnoticed, possible fundamental rights consequence of Brexit is that, even if Britain leaves the single market and customs union, the EU may, nevertheless, insist upon compliance with certain fundamental rights standards in any trade deal it subsequently makes with the United Kingdom, as it routinely does with other 'third states', considered more fully in Chapter 4. It is unclear whether the ECHR would be deemed sufficient. Another, more anxiously debated implication for the United Kingdom concerns the residency status of EU nationals here and of British nationals in the remaining twenty-seven member states. While a right to asylum is provided by international human rights law to those with a well-founded fear of persecution, there is no human or fundamental right to unrestricted migration from one's own state(s) to those where citizenship is not held. And, as already indicated in this chapter and as Chapter 5 will also confirm, free movement of people within the EU is more a core characteristic of the kind of single market the Union is intended to provide – and to which some in the post Brexit United Kingdom remain eager to access – than a fundamental right as such. However, while neither British nationals living in a EU state nor EU nationals living in the United Kingdom would have a fundamental right, post Brexit, to continue so to reside, Article 19(1) of the CFR and Article 4 of Protocol No. 4 ECHR (which Britain signed in

1963 but has yet to ratify) prohibit the collective expulsion of aliens. Since deciding each individual case on its merits would present an enormous bureaucratic challenge, a deal granting permanent residence to those already living at a given date in the country of which they are not nationals seems more likely and desirable. Indeed, the possibility of British nationals being offered an individual 'opt-in' to remain EU citizens through 'associate citizenship' has already been raised at EU level.[144]

As far as the implications of Brexit for the EU itself, and for its fundamental rights activities in particular, are concerned, considerable uncertainty is also likely to prevail for years. Three clear challenges can nevertheless be discerned: Brexit underscores and compounds the EU's legitimacy problems, it strengthens Euro-scepticism in other member states and it compels the EU to respond to both. While the referendum result has already bolstered demands for similar 'in/out' referendums in other countries – such as France, the Netherlands, Sweden, Italy, Austria and Denmark – which potentially threaten all the EU's activities including human rights, it has also simultaneously reduced, though not excluded, the possibility that any government will be eager to follow the British precedent. Fundamental rights are also deeply embroiled in the legitimacy issue, not least because one of the reasons the EU embarked upon its fundamental rights mission in the early 2000s was to address the threat to its legitimacy caused by the widening gap between the elite-led project of deeper and wider integration, on the one hand, and the more limited needs and aspirations of Europe's citizens on the other. Arguably, in order to avoid stoking Euro-scepticism, the Commission and the European Council might now think twice before embarking upon any controversial legislation in the human rights arena. But the ECJ is not constrained by such factors and is likely to continue to adjudicate as it sees fit.

The implications of Brexit for the United Kingdom's membership of the CE and the ECHR are also unclear. Formally, the decision will have no impact whatever, not least because, by leaving the EU, Britain would merely join the existing nineteen non-EU CE states. However, many who campaigned and voted for Brexit are also hostile to the ECtHR, others fail to realise that departing from the EU will leave the United Kingdom's Convention commitments intact and scepticism about the ECtHR is not

---

[144] J. Stone, 'EU Negotiators Will Offer Brits an Individual Opt-in to Remain EU Citizens, Chief Negotiator Confirms', *The Independent*, 9 December 2016.

limited to Brexiteers. For example, before the referendum vote, in her then-capacity as Home Secretary, the Prime Minister Teresa May, argued that Britain should withdraw from the ECHR (call it 'ECxit') but that it should remain in the EU, in spite of the fact that membership of the Strasbourg system is effectively a condition of membership of the EU. Although, since the vote, in her bid to become Prime Minister, Teresa May ruled out ECxit post Brexit, there is no guarantee this will still be government policy when the United Kingdom final leaves the EU.[145] However, even if Britain were to renounce its membership of the Strasbourg system, Convention rights are likely to remain a feature of British law because the governing Conservative party envisages their reproduction, subject to reduced judicial enforcement, in a British Bill of Rights intended to replace the Human Rights Act, which domesticated the European Convention at the beginning of the twenty-first century.[146] Nevertheless, since Britain is one of the oldest democracies in the world, together with France and the United States is the birthplace of the human rights ideal and is a founding member of the CE, the legitimacy and authority of the Strasbourg institutions, also under strain as discussed further in Chapter 2, would be significantly damaged both internally and wider afield should the vote to leave the EU sweep the United Kingdom out of them too.

Finally, the legitimacy of both the EU and the ECtHR have been adversely affected by Euro-scepticism and (arguably less widespread) rights-scepticism, which have ebbed and flowed across the continent since the end of the Second World War. As previous parts of this chapter have demonstrated, whatever legitimacy concerns each organisation had to address at its inception tended to subside as time progressed. However, as the ECtHR's popularity with applicants rose exponentially in the 1990s, some insiders and commentators expressed concern about the damage allegedly done to its reputation by the dilution of admission criteria to enable some former Soviet bloc states to join as part of the post-Communist enlargement. The case overload crisis has also prompted a debate about the Court's efficacy, its *raison d'être* and its legitimacy, considered more fully in Chapter 2. The

---

[145] 'May Launches Tory Leadership Bid with Promise to Unite Party', *The Guardian*, 1 July 2016.

[146] See S. Greer and R. Slowe, 'The Conservatives' Proposals for a British Bill of Rights: Mired in Muddle, Misconception and Misrepresentation?' *European Human Rights Law Review*, [2015], 372–83.

development of an internal EU fundamental rights policy, conceived to boost the Union's legitimacy, credibility and popularity, ironically triggered a perception that the EU unduly interferes with domestic human rights priorities.[147] National governments and political elites across member states have historically resisted the development of an EU fundamental rights mission, not necessarily on account of any deeply held ideological objection to fundamental rights as such, but rather because deeper integration entails the expansion of supranational competences at the expense of national sovereignty, particularly in the anti-discrimination and criminal justice fields.[148] Wariness of the EU's developing interest in rights has also grown in response to a series of policy initiatives including the mainstreaming of fundamental rights across a range of internal EU policies and the consequential proliferation of fundamental rights legislation, the expansion in the types of rights receiving such protection, the inclusion of third-country nationals as rights bearers,[149] the mistaken conflation of the EU with the CE (also perceived as suffering from mission creep)[150] and, finally, the 'constitutionalisation' of EU fundamental rights protection, particularly as a result of the CFR.

1.3   Conceptual Frameworks

The principal analytical and normative questions about the relationship between the CE and the EU in the human rights field arising from this account, therefore, concern whether, on the one hand, their autonomy, separate identity and divergence are likely to and should be preserved and if so to what extent and, on the other, whether more integration, interdependence, convergence and the harmonisation of standards are likely and desirable and if so to what extent. According to the choice, two further questions arise: what kinds of arrangement to facilitate these

---

[147] P. Kopecky and P. Ucen, 'Return to Europe? Patterns of Euroscepticism among the Czech and Slovak Political Parties' in J. Rupnik and J. Zielonka (eds.), *The Road to the European Union: The Czech and Slovak Republics*, (Manchester University Press, 2003), Vol. I, pp. 164–79, 175. See C. Leconte, 'The EU Fundamental Rights Policy as a Source of Euroscepticism', *Human Rights Review*, 15 (2014), 83–96.

[148] C. Leconte, 'The EU Fundamental Rights Policy as a Source of Europscepticism', *Human Rights Review* 15 (2014), 83–96, 87–9.

[149] C. Leconte and E. Muir, 'Introduction to Special Issue 'Understanding Resistance to the EU Fundamental Rights Policy', *Human Rights Review*, 15 (2014), 7

[150] *Ibid.*, 8.

goals ought to be encouraged, and by reference to what other criteria, objectives and standards?

Any attempt to find answers needs to begin by considering the wider debate, dominated by 'pluralist' and 'constitutionalist' perspectives, over how contemporary trans-national legal processes can and should be understood and characterised. Broadly speaking, 'pluralism' maintains that, in such contexts, a plurality of institutions, processes and norms compete for recognition and authority, producing relationships governed, not by crisp prescriptive legal rules and clear vertical institutional, procedural and normative hierarchies, but by political negotiation and compromise in horizontal-heterarchical structures.[151] The 'constitutionalist' analysis, on the other hand, argues that international legal regimes, particularly those in Europe, are, and should be, firmly grounded in common constitutional fundamentals, principally those which embody democracy, the rule of law and human rights.[152]

For the purpose of this study a further distinction can be drawn between strong and weak versions of each of these alternatives. For our purposes, the strongest form of 'pluralism', 'separate development', envisages the EU and CE each retaining the maximum degree of independence and separate identity. In principle, four, not entirely discrete or mutually exclusive points may also be distinguished along a 'separate development continuum': competition, indifference, mutual respect and

---

[151] Recent contributions in both the general field of international law and the more specific field of European human rights law include N. Krisch, 'The Case for Pluralism in Postnational Law', in G. de Búrca and J. Weiler (eds.), *The Worlds of European Constitutionalism* (Cambridge University Press, 2011), pp. 203–61, *Beyond Constitutionalism: The Pluralist Structure of Postnational Law* (Oxford University Press, 2010), 'The Case for Pluralism in Postnational Law', LSE Law, Society and Economy Working Papers 12/2009, and 'The Open Architecture of European Human Rights Law' *Modern Law Review*, 71 (2008), 183–216; S. Hennette-Vauchez, 'Constitutional v International: When Unified Reformatory Rationales Mismatch the Plural Paths of Legitimacy of ECHR Law', pp. 144–63, and J. Christoffersen, 'Individual and Constitutional Justice: Can the Power Balance of Adjudication be Reversed?', pp. 181–203, in J. Christoffersen and M. Madsen (eds.), *The European Court of Human Rights between Law and Politics* (Oxford University Press, 2011).

[152] Recent contributions include P. Dobner and M. Loughlin (eds.), *The Twilight of Constitutionalism* (Oxford University Press, 2010); J. Klabbers, A. Peters and G. Ulfstein, *The Constitutionalization of International Law* (Oxford University Press, 2009); N. Tsagourias (ed.), *Transnational Constitutionalism: International and European Models* (Cambridge University Press, 2007); O. Diggelmann and T. Altwicker, 'Is There Something Like a Constitution of International Law?' *Zeitschrift für Ausländisches Öffentliches Recht und Völkerrecht*, (2008) 68, 623–50; E. de Wet, *The International Constitutional Order* (Amsterdam: Vossiuspers UvA, 2005).

voluntary cooperation. In the most extreme version, which nobody seriously advocates, EU member states would leave the CE altogether. While the separate development model has some analytical merit, particularly as far as the early history of each organisation is concerned, as the remainder of this study will seek to demonstrate, it applies today only to the activities of the CE and EU beyond Europe and to the legislative activity of the EU within Europe. A slightly less strong version of pluralism, 'organic convergence', envisages a process of convergence occurring incrementally between both systems without any overall plan or guiding goals, or any institutional, procedural or normative coordination, objectives or standards. The problem with this model, however, is that it ignores the deepening and widening cooperation between both organisations and the integrative contribution already provided by common constitutional principles. At the other end of the spectrum, the strongest version of constitutionalism, the 'unification model', advocates top-down structural integration of both the CE and the EU according to a detailed preconceived plan with, ultimately, the two organisations merging into one. This is, however, simply a non-starter, certainly for the foreseeable and probably for any conceivable future, not least because just less than half the member states of the CE do not belong to the EU.

However, a more plausible and more viable hybrid than organic convergence can be found between the stronger versions of pluralism and constitutionalism. 'Constitutional pluralism'[153] – of which there are also various conceptions, some more 'constitutional' than 'pluralist', and vice versa,[154] including 'soft' or 'interordinal' constitutionalism',[155]

---

[153] While rejecting the term 'constitutional pluralism', in the EU context, in favour of 'constitutional tolerance', Weiler nevertheless understands why others have regarded his work as 'part of the constitutional pluralist discourse', J. Weiler, 'Prologue: Global and Pluralist Constitutionalism: Some Doubts', in G. de Búrca and J. Weiler (eds.), *Worlds of European Constitutionalism*, p. 12, and, 'In Defence of the Status Quo: Europe's Constitutional *Sonderweg*' in J. Weiler and M. Wind (eds.), *European Constitutionalism beyond the State* (Cambridge University Press, 2003), pp. 7–23.

[154] For a useful typology see M. Avbelj and J. Komárek, 'Introduction' in M. Avbelj and J. Komárek (eds.), *Constitutional Pluralism in the European Union and Beyond* (Oxford: Hart, 2012), pp. 4–7.

[155] G. de Búrca, 'The ECJ and the International Legal Order: A Re-Evaluation', in de Búrca and Weiler (eds.), *Worlds of European Constitutionalism*, pp. 137–49; L. Gordillo, *Interlocking Constitutions: Towards and Interordinal Theory of National, European and UN Law* (Oxford: Hart, 2012), pp. 8, 297–307, 327.

confederalism, federalism and neo-federalism[156] – has particular relevance for the debate about the relationship between the EU and CE, especially regarding their respective courts. It is said that, in Europe, 'constitutional pluralism has now become the dominant branch of constitutional thought'[157] with the 'capacity to unleash a unique new democratic potential implicit in Europe's new post-sovereign context'.[158] According to this view, the legal systems of the CE, the EU and their member states are best understood in similar, though not identical, constitutional terms. This paradigm, therefore, provides the best empirical and normative account of their emerging relationship in the human rights field, where legitimate and defensible outcomes are negotiated through mutually respectful, though not always friction-free, dialogue, 'mutual understanding and respect', 'jurisdictional interchange', 'active engagement' or 'constructive cooperation'.[159] The human rights activities of each organisation are 'pluralistic' in their own right because interactions between the multiplicity of institutionally and normatively variable national and trans-national legal systems tend to be pragmatic, negotiated and dynamic rather than driven by formal and decisive legal

---

[156] F. Fabbrini, *Fundamental Rights in Europe: Challenges and Transformations in Comparative Perspective* (Oxford University Press, 2014), ch. 6; Avbelj and J. Komárek, 'Introduction', p. 3.
[157] K. Jaklic, *Constitutional Pluralism in the EU* (Oxford University Press, 2014), pp. 6, 8.
[158] *Ibid.*, pp. 6, 8.
[159] See, e.g., L. Glas, *The Theory, Potential and Practice of Procedural Dialogue in the European Convention on Human Rights System* (Cambridge: Intersentia, 2016); E. Bjorge, *Domestic Application of the ECHR: Courts as Faithful Trustees* (Oxford University Press, 2015), ch. 8; P. Mahoney, 'The Relationship between the Strasbourg Court and the National Courts', *Law Quarterly Review*, (2014) 130, 568–86; A. Seibert-Fohr and M. Villiger, 'Current Challenges in European Multilevel Human Rights Protection', pp. 13–24, and A. Paulus, 'From Implementation to Translation: Applying the ECtHR Judgments in the Domestic Legal Orders', pp. 267–83, in A. Seibert-Fohr and M. Villiger (eds.), *Judgments of the European Court of Human Rights – Effects and Implementation* (Baden-Baden: Nomos, 2013); Lord Kerr, 'The Need for Dialogue between National Courts and the European Court of Human Rights' in S. Flogaitis, T. Zwart and J. Fraser (eds.), *The European Court of Human Rights and Its Discontents: Turning Criticism into Strength* (Cheltenham, UK: Edward Elgar, 2013), pp. 104–15; G. Martinico and O. Pollicino, *The Interaction between Europe's Legal Systems: Judicial Dialogue and the Creation of Supranational Laws* (Cheltenham, UK: Edward Elgar, 2012); X. Groussot, 'Constitutional Dialogues, Pluralism and Conflicting Identities' in Avbelj and Komárek (eds.), *Constitutional Pluralism in the European Union and Beyond*, pp. 319–41; A. Torres Pérez, *Conflicts of Rights in the European Union: A Theory of Supranational Adjudication* (Oxford University Press, 2009), pp. 319–41.

prescription.[160] As Fabbrini points out, arrangements of this kind give rise to two distinct legitimacy challenges for which there is no definitive solution. When the trans-national level provides a floor of minimum standards, inconsistencies arise between those states which are keen to provide higher standards and those content to accept lower ones. However, when (arguably less commonly) the trans-national level imposes a ceiling of maximum standards, the challenge lies in justifying the reduced effectiveness of standards in those states willing and able to provide higher ones. The problem is further compounded by the fact that, what from one perspective presents as a challenge of inconsistency (for example, in the abortion debate, 'a woman's right to choose') from the perspective of a competing right (in this example, the 'foetus's right to life') presents as a challenge of ineffectiveness, and vice versa.[161]

But national and trans-national legal systems in Europe are also 'constitutional' because they operate, at all levels and in all directions, within the context of a formal and universal, if unevenly implemented, commitment to the following core or foundational values: democracy, the rule of law, the publicly-regulated market, the limitation of the exercise of public power by a set of justiciable 'constitutional' rights, national and trans-national courts to settle complaints about their alleged violation and other national and trans-national institutions effectively supervising the execution of these and other judicial decisions. If this is true at the level of each organisation, and both share common value commitments, it is difficult to see how it would not and should not apply to the emerging relationship between them. It is not the purpose of this study to contribute to the rapidly developing and highly sophisticated theoretical debate about the precise characteristics, or the empirical and normative pros and cons, of constitutional pluralist models for either the CE or the EU in its own right, or together.[162] Our objective is the more

---

[160] Seibert-Fohr and Villiger, 'Current Challenges', p. 27; C. Lebeck, 'The European Court of Human Rights on the Relation between ECHR and EC-law: The Limits of Constitutionalization of Public International Law', *Zeitschrift für Öffentliches Rectht,* 62 (2007), 195–236.

[161] Fabbrini, *Fundamental Rights in Europe,* pp. 37–41, 45–8, 262–5.

[162] Contributions to the debate about constitutional pluralism in Europe and more widely include Fabbrini, *Fundamental Rights in Europe,* p. 267; Jaklic, *Constitutional Pluralism in the EU;* Avbelj and Komárek (eds.), *Constitutional Pluralism in the European Union and Beyond;* Gordillo, *Interlocking Constitutions;* M. Goldoni, 'Constitutional Pluralism and the Question of the European Common Good', *European Law Journal,* 18 (2012), 385–406; Weiler, 'Prologue'; G. de Búrca, 'The ECJ and the International Legal Order',

modest one of recognising that, since the CE and EU each have constitutional and pluralistic features, this paradigm best accounts for at least one of the key dimensions of their relationship with each other, the judicial realm.

1.4 Conclusion

Although largely beyond the purview of this study, there can be little doubt that the nation-state remains a pivotal arena for the protection of human rights.[163] Where there are democratically regulated markets, and where there is civil peace and a distribution of resources which is at least not gravely inequitable, human rights are most effectively protected by genuinely democratic and rights-sensitive national legislative and executive institutions, independent, professional and rights-aware national judiciaries and the provision of national justiciable constitutional rights. Therefore, the main human rights–related functions of both the CE and the EU are to encourage the development of these elements where they have not yet firmly taken root and to contribute to their preservation and protection where they have. There is, however, no principled reason why there should be more than one such pan-European regime. The fact that there are two with legal functions – and others with political ones besides – is simply a matter of historical contingency stemming from the lack of agreement, particularly between the United Kingdom and France, over the purpose and shape of trans-national European institutions in the aftermath of the Second World War.

---

and D. Halberstam, 'Local, Global and Plural Constitutionalism: Europe Meets the World', in de Búrca and Weiler (eds.), *Worlds of European Constitutionalism*, pp. 150–202; N. Walker, 'Reconciling MacCormick: Constitutional Pluralism and the Unity of Practical Reason', *Ratio Juris*, 24 (2011), 369–85; Krisch, *Beyond Constitutionalism*, and, 'The Case for Pluralism in Postnational Law'; M. Avbelj and J. Komárek, 'Four Visions of Constitutional Pluralism', *European Journal of Legal Studies*, 2 (2008) 325–70; A. Hurrell, *On Global Order: Power, Values and the Constitution of International Society* (Oxford University Press, 2007); M. Kumm, 'The Jurisprudence of Constitutional Conflict: Constitutional Supremacy in Europe before and after the Constitutional Treaty', *European Law Journal*, 11 (2005), 262–307; M. Maduro, 'Contrapuntal Law: Europe's Constitutional Pluralism in Action', in N. Walker (ed.), *Sovereignty in Transition* (Oxford: Hart, 2003), 502–37; N. Walker, 'The Idea of Constitutional Pluralism', *Modern Law Review*, 65 (2002), 317–59; Krisch, 'The Case for Pluralism in Postnational Law'.

[163] 'Editors' Introduction' in P. Popelier, C. Van de Heyning and P. Van Nuffel (eds.), *Human Rights Protection in the European Legal Order: The Interaction between the European and the National Courts* (Cambridge: Intersentia, 2011), p. 13.

Since the end of the Cold War these arrangements have become even more complex in two main ways. First, the number of member states in the CE increased to forty-seven, twenty-seven of which, post Brexit, also belong to the EU. While most central and eastern European countries have successfully made the transition to the 'common European institutional model', as expressed by the ECHR, the process has stalled for others, particularly for Russia and some other former Soviet republics. Second, both the CE and the EU have expanded the range of their human rights–related interests and activities, raising questions about the relationship between their distinct, but increasingly overlapping, regimes. The ending of the Cold War undermined the CE's war-related founding objectives. But others, nevertheless, remain, particularly the provision of an abstract European constitutional identity and 'sounding the alarm' where member states appear to be straying significantly from it. But, in this developing environment another key objective has emerged: promoting convergence, though not harmonisation as such, in national public institutions, processes and norms around Convention principles particularly in those states where they are not yet deeply institutionalised.

In spite of having greatly expanded, intensified and specialised its formal, bureaucratic interest in the promotion and protection of an increasingly wide range of human rights, the CE's flagship treaty remains the ECHR, still the only one with an individual applications process to a trans-national court. Although the overload problem in the individual applications process has diminished over the past few years, the process continues to be criticised for the excessive involvement of judges in case management and in the adjudication of repeat violations (each at the expense of fully-reasoned judgments), and for having too many young and inexperienced judges on the bench. The Court has also been accused of lacking legitimacy and of undermining national sovereignty by failing to calibrate its role with that of national authorities.[164] The most effective contribution the CE can make to addressing these difficulties lies in enhancing the ECtHR's capacity to deliver more thoroughly-reasoned and principled judgments, which require time and reflection, coupled with better dialogue with national courts about how these should be received by national institutions and processes.

However, for the EU the challenges are different. The Lisbon Treaty has introduced a greater expectation that human rights will be promoted

---

[164] Björgvinsson, 'Role of the ECtHR', pp. 38–45.

and respected in the Union, not only as a formal value but also as viable policy. The establishment of the FRA to scrutinise the application of the CFR, combined with institutional commitments to 'mainstream' human rights across all policy areas, and to promote them externally, means the EU now has the mandate and the means to develop its role in these fields. But with EU accession to the ECHR now effectively dead in the water, how the EU can and should work with the CE and the ECHR regime, a core issue with which the remainder of this book will be concerned, remains unclear.

2

The Council of Europe

2.1   Introduction

As indicated in Chapter 1, the Council of Europe (CE) was founded in Strasbourg in 1949 by ten western European liberal democracies – Belgium, Denmark, France, Ireland, Italy, Luxembourg, the Netherlands, Norway, Sweden, and the United Kingdom – as one of several initiatives to promote their interdependence, common identity and collective security in the context of the Cold War. It now includes all but one (Belarus) of Europe's forty-eight fully fledged states with a combined population of over 800 million.[1] Five other states – Canada, the Holy See, Japan, Mexico and the United States of America – also have observer status. While the CE's main achievement is the European Convention on Human Rights (ECHR), it has also been responsible for over 200 other treaties on a wide spectrum of issues including, for example, social security, nurses' training, prevention of terrorism, human trafficking, cybercrime, drugs, data protection, and farming, amongst others.[2]

The CE's core values are human rights, democracy and the rule of law, which it pursues on three operational dimensions – standard-setting, monitoring and cooperation.[3] The vast bulk of the literature relating to it has been written by lawyers and jurists, and mostly about the ECHR and the European Court of Human Rights (ECtHR). Commentators and scholars in other disciplines, including international relations, have shown

---

[1] Europe also has several 'breakaway republics', the most fully fledged of which, but not yet recognised by every Council of Europe state, is Kosovo.

[2] C. Olsen, updated by T. Kleinsorge, 'Treaty-Making in the CoE' in T. Kleinsorge (ed.), *Council of Europe (COE)*, 2nd edn. (Alphen aan den Rijn: Wolters Kluwer, 2015), pp. 143–55.

[3] M. Bruer, 'Establishing Common Standards and Securing the Rule of Law' in S. Schmahl and M. Breuer (eds.), *The Council of Europe: Its Law and Policies* (Oxford University Press, 2017), pp. 639–70, 640.

[4] Some recent exceptions include Schmahl and Breuer (eds.), *The Council of Europe*; Kleinsorge, *Council of Europe*; K. Brummer, 'Enhancing Intergovernmentalism: The

little interest,[4] particularly compared with the mountain of material on the EU. Two main issues – one concerning why the CE was established, and the other how it can be characterised – have dominated the limited debate in this field. Moravcsik, for example, claims that human rights regimes – and the ECHR in particular – pose a considerable challenge to traditional 'realist' accounts of international relations which seek to explain the activity of states in terms of the pursuit of national self-interest.[5] This is because, prima facie, they restrict the sovereignty of liberal democracies, which already have good human rights records, without apparently giving them anything tangible in return. According to realists the explanation is that becoming parties to an international human rights treaty enables democratic states to further their interests by pressing other states to conform to their own standards and values and thus to promote easier diplomatic and other relationships with them. 'Normative' or 'ideational' models, on the other hand, maintain that democratic states sign international human rights treaties for the largely altruistic motive of persuading other less democratic, or non-democratic, states to adhere to what they take to be appropriate, or universal, values. Moravcsik claims, however, that neither of these two views is convincing and offers a third instead. 'Republican liberalism' accepts the realist premise that states pursue self-interest in international relations, but maintains that, with respect to international human rights regimes, the self-interest in question is internal rather than external. In the context of post–Second World War Europe this means that the new (or re-established) democracies advocated a strong trans-national human rights regime, not to facilitate interference in their own internal affairs by other states, but in the hope that a strong international reaction to anti-democratic developments at their own national level would trigger the appropriate response from their own domestic legislative and judicial institutions and national public opinion.

Council of Europe and Human Rights' *International Journal of Human Rights* (2010) 14(2), 280–99; G. Winkler, *The Council of Europe: Monitoring Procedures and the Constitutional Autonomy of Member States* (Vienna: Springer, 2006); A. MacMullen, 'Intergovernmental Functionalism? The Council of Europe in European Integration', *Journal of European Integration* (2004) 26, 405–29; J. Lovecy, 'Framing Decisions in the Council of Europe: An Institutional Analysis', in B. Reinalda and B. Verbeek (eds.), *Decision Making within International Organizations* (London: Routledge, 2004), 59–73; S. Trommer and R. Chari, 'The Council of Europe: Interest Groups and Ideological Mission?', *West European Politics* (2006) 29, 665–86.
[5] A. Moravcsik, 'The Origins of Human Rights Regimes: Democratic Delegation in Postwar Europe' *International Organization*, 54 (2000), 217–52.

The other debate has been between 'constructivists' such as Checkel[6] – who argue that the CE socialises members into closer adherence to its values by framing their identities and preferences, which, in turn, promotes changes in national institutions and processes – and 'rational institutionalists', such as Schimmelfennig et al.,[7] who focus instead upon the extent to which the CE's socialising is constrained by the fact that it is also an arena in which states pursue national self-interest. However, as Checkel himself points out, 'it is "both/and" and not "either/or"'.[8]

This chapter – which discusses the CE's key institutions, how its policy is formed and implemented, and which considers four of its most important human rights–related treaties – also confirms both that the CE has a socialising role, and that this is most powerfully discharged by the ECHR. However, as a result of a complex combination of national factors such as history, political culture and institutional landscape, the Convention's impact on member states is far from uniform.

2.2 Key Institutions

The CE's key institutions are the Committee of Ministers (CM), the Parliamentary Assembly (PACE), the Secretariat, the European Commissioner for Human Rights and the ECtHR. But since the Court was created by, and has an intimate relationship with, the ECHR, it is discussed in the relevant section below. A Congress of Local and Regional Authorities – with 324 members plus 324 substitutes drawn from local and regional representatives – organises conferences and training sessions, monitors local and regional democracy (including elections and fact-find missions) and also advises the CM, PACE, and member states on a wide range of local and regional issues.[9] Some 400 or so NGOs with participatory status at the CE meet three or four times a year at the

---

[6] See, e.g., J. T. Checkel, 'International Institutions and Socialization in Europe: Introduction and Framework' in J. T. Checkel (ed.), *International Institutions and Socialization in Europe* (Cambridge University Press, 2007), pp. 3–30.

[7] F. Schimmelfennig, S. Engbert and H. Knobel, *International Socialization in Europe: European Organizations, Political Conditionality, and Democratic Change* (Basingstoke, UK: Palgrave Macmillan, 2006).

[8] Checkel, *International Institutions*, vii. See also Brummer, 'Enhancing Intergovernmentalism', 294.

[9] coe.int/t/congress/Default_en.asp; B. Schaffarzik, 'Congress of Local and Regional Authorities' in Schmal and Breuer (eds.), *Council of Europe*, pp. 269–95; Affholder, updated by M. Lambrecht-Feigl, 'The Congress of Local and Regional Authorities: European Cooperation Close to the Citizen', in Kleinsorge (ed.), *Council of Europe*, pp. 170–82.

Conference of International Non-governmental Organisations constituting civil society's contribution to the CE's 'quadrilogue' with the CM, PACE and the Congress of Local and Regional Authorities.[10] There are also numerous expert advisory bodies and targeted assistance activities. The most prominent of the former include the European Commission for Democracy through Law (the 'Venice commission'), which acts as the Secretariat for the World Conference on Constitutional Justice, provides a repository of democratic constitutional standards (the Common Constitutional Heritage), mediates political conflict particularly at the request of the EU, organises seminars, and provides non-binding advice to the CE, member and other states (particularly in central and eastern Europe), on constitutional and electoral issues.[11] The European Commission against Racism and Intolerance monitors and combats racism, xenophobia, anti-Semitism, Islamophobia and other forms of intolerance in member states through advisory work with civil society, plus thematic and five-yearly country reports.[12] Targeted assistance activities, involving dozens of programmes, scores of projects and over 2,000 individual activities per annum, operate in five main areas: human rights, the rule of law, democracy/good governance, social cohesion and cultural matters/intercultural dialogue.[13]

The Committee of Ministers

The CM, the CE's main policy-making and executive body, consists of the foreign ministers of each member state, or their Deputies – the permanent diplomatic representation in Strasbourg.[14] The five states with observer status can also attend but have no right to vote. Routine

---

[10] H. Krieger, 'The Conference of International Non-Governmental Organizations of the Council of Europe' in Schmahl and Breuer (eds.), *Council of Europe*, 314–44.

[11] venice.coe.int/webforms/events/; R. Dürr, 'The Venice Commission' in Kleinsorge (ed.), *Council of Europe*, pp. 156–69.

[12] coe.int/t/dghl/monitoring/ecri/default_en.asp; T. Kleinsorge, 'General Overview' in Kleinsorge (ed.), *COE*, pp. 111–15.

[13] R. Dossow, 'Cultural Co-operation' in Kleinsorge (ed.), *Council of Europe*, pp. 194–201; A. Siegel, 'Beyond Measuring – the Council of Europe's Instruments Contributing to the Progress of Societies', OECD World Forum on *Measuring and Fostering Progress of Societies*, Istanbul, 23–30 June 2007. See also T. Kleinsorge, 'General Overview', pp. 105–15.

[14] coe.int/t/cm/home_EN.asp; S. Palmer, 'The Committee of Ministers' in Schmal and Breuer (eds.), *Council of Europe*, pp. 137–65; S. Palmer, 'Committee of Ministers' in Kleinsorge (ed.), *Council of Europe*, pp. 96–104.

bureaucratic support is provided by the CE's Secretariat. The CM's main responsibilities are implementing decisions of Summits of Heads of State and Government;[15] admitting, and if necessary suspending or expelling, member states; discussing, in collaboration with other CE institutions, pan-European problems and challenges except defence; drafting treaties to address them; monitoring state compliance with membership and treaty obligations; issuing non-binding recommendations and declarations to member states; deciding the Council's annual programme of activities; implementing cooperation and assistance programmes; adopting the annual budget drafted by the Secretary General; electing members of the European Committee for the Prevention of Torture and Inhuman or Degrading Treatment or Punishment from a list of three names submitted by the Bureau of PACE (see below) and supervising the execution of the judgments of the ECtHR, also considered further later.

Since 2006, the CM – chaired by member states from November to May on a six-month rotation basis – meets at ministerial level in Strasbourg, for a 'session' lasting a day, or two half-days in May. While these are private affairs, and the proceedings confidential, a final communiqué is issued. Ministers' Deputies meet once a week in plenary session plus several times a week (excluding August) in subsidiary groups supported by the CE's Secretariat, the Bureau of the Ministers' Deputies, a Budget Committee, several steering and expert committees (currently on such topics as human rights, terrorism, youth and culture), seven Rapporteur Groups (including ones relating to education, democracy, human rights and health), an ad hoc Working Party (on Reform of the Human Rights Convention System) and a Thematic Coordinator (on information policy). Ministers' Deputies devote four three-day meetings a year to supervising the execution of judgments of the ECtHR. The Committee's non-binding recommendations require unanimity on the part of the national representatives casting a vote, plus a majority of CM members. Resolutions adopted on the admission of new member states require a two-thirds majority of members, while a bare majority is required on

[15] So far there have only been three: Vienna (1993), which prompted Protocol No. 11 to the ECHR, the Framework Convention for the Protection of National Minorities, and the European Commission against Racism and Intolerance; Strasbourg (1997), which led to the death penalty being outlawed in all circumstances and which also affirmed the importance of social cohesion; and Warsaw (2005), which was primarily concerned with the effectiveness of the ECHR and the workload of the ECtHR.

matters relating to rules of procedure and financial or administrative regulations. The adoption of a new treaty, and the publication of the explanatory note, require a two-thirds majority of those voting and a majority of Committee members. The CM's most important institutional relationship within the CE, with PACE, is said to be 'structurally adversarial' but 'if properly managed' can produce 'creative tension' and 'constructive dialogue'.[16]

The Parliamentary Assembly

The Parliamentary Assembly of the Council of Europe (PACE) – which promotes debates on emerging European issues, identifies trends and best practices and sets benchmarks and standards – has 324 members (plus a further 324 substitutes), appointed or elected by national parliaments from their own members.[17] The parliaments of Israel, Canada and Mexico have observer status, while the parliaments of Morocco and Kyrgyzstan, the Jordanian Parliament, and the Palestinian National Council have Partners for Democracy Status. Although not entitled to vote, their representatives may speak with the President's permission. Special guest status has also been accorded other European states seeking to join the CE. But the last country in this category, Belarus, was suspended from the accession process in January 1997 following a coup. The number of PACE representatives is roughly proportionate to budgetary contributions and size, with the largest national contingent, eighteen, allocated to France, Germany, Italy, the United Kingdom and Russia. The smallest states – Andorra, Liechtenstein, Monaco, and San Marino – each have two.[18] National delegations must include at least one member of each sex, while the balance of political parties is required to reflect that of each national parliament.

PACE meets four times a year – in January, April, June and October – for a week on each occasion, in the Palais de l'Europe in Strasbourg, which it shares with the European Parliament, the EU's parliamentary

---

[16] Palmer, 'CM, 2017', pp. 138, 160–1; Palmer, 'CM, 2015', p. 104.
[17] assembly.coe.int/nw/Home-EN.asp; http://website-pace.net/documents/10643/110596/D%C3%A9pliantAPCEA5-EN.pdf/39bbf51f-aade-4438-b7ff-1dc4b02a309e. See P. Leach, 'The Parliamentary Assembly of the Council of Europe' in Schmahl and Breuer (eds.), *Council of Europe*, pp. 181–91; T. Kleinsorge, 'The Parliamentary Assembly: Europe's Motor and Conscience' in Kleinsorge (ed.), *Council of Europe*, pp. 75–95.
[18] Statute of CE, Art. 26, as amended.

body, considered further in Chapter 4. Political groups – currently the Group of the European People's Party (EPP), the Socialist Group (SOC), the European Conservatives Group (EC), the Alliance of Liberals and Democrats for Europe (ALDE) and the Group of the Unified European Left (UEL) – are required to undertake to respect the values of the CE, particularly political pluralism, human rights and the rule of law, and may be formed when at least twenty members of at least six national delegations decide to do so. Assembly members are not bound by their national party affiliation and are initially entirely free to attend meetings of any group before making up their minds about which to join. In addition to its own Secretariat, Bureau, Standing and Presidential Committees, PACE also has nine permanent committees, which, assisted by subcommittees and rapporteurs, prepare reports for debate in plenary sessions: Political Affairs and Democracy; Legal Affairs and Human Rights; Social Affairs, Health and Sustainable Development; Migration, Refugees and Displaced Persons; Culture, Science, Education and Media; Equality and Non-discrimination; the Monitoring Committee; Rules of Procedure, Immunities and Institutional Affairs; and Election of Judges to the European Court of Human Rights. Those with the highest profile are the Committees on Political Affairs and Democracy (with eighty-seven members) – which considers general CE policy and all political matters within its competence particularly urgent political crises – and on Legal Affairs and Human Rights (with eighty-six members), whose remit also includes crime, terrorism and the implementation of the judgments of the ECtHR.

PACE's other main functions are to elect its own President, Vice-President and Secretary General, and also the Secretary General and Deputy Secretary General of the CE, the European Commissioner for Human Rights, and – assisted since 2010 by the Advisory Panel of Experts on Candidates for Election as Judge to the European Court of Human Rights – judges to the ECtHR from the lists of three candidates submitted by the government of each member state; to be consulted about international treaties proposed by the CM; to liaise with the CM, other CE institutions, the EU's European Parliament, the Parliamentary Assembly of the Organization for Security and Cooperation in Europe, the Organization for Economic Cooperation and Development, and the UN's specialised agencies; to conduct periodic field visits to member states, particularly to monitor elections; and to monitor fulfilment of membership and treaty obligations by CE states and, where necessary, to withdraw the accreditation of national delegations and, as a last resort, to recommend the suspension of a given state to the CM. In 1996 PACE delayed the accession of Russia to the CE on account of the first Chechen war, and, in 2014 and 2015, some rights of the Russian delegation were suspended as a result of events in Ukraine.

While PACE can debate any issue within the CE's remit, and can propose policy, it has no legislative capacity and its decisions are not binding on other CE institutions or on member states. A two-thirds majority is required for Opinions – which express PACE's view on questions put to it by the CM, such as the accession of new member states or the drafting of a new treaty – and self-initiated policy Recommendations put to the CM and national governments. Resolutions, which relate to matters within PACE's exclusive purview, are passed by simple majority. A motion for a Resolution or Recommendation requires the support of twenty or more members from at least five national delegations and must be examined by the Bureau of the Assembly and referred to the appropriate committee(s). The reporting committee then appoints a rapporteur, who drafts a report. This is followed by consultation, which might involve hearings and the contribution of experts. Short written Declarations, which require the signature of at least twenty representatives of no fewer than four nationalities and two political groups, are published as PACE documents and distributed.

Many of the CE's 200-plus treaties – including the ECHR and its protocols, the European Social Charter, the European Convention for the Prevention of Torture, the European Charter for Regional and Minority Languages and the Convention for the Protection of Human Rights and the Dignity of the Human Being with Regard to the Application of Biology and Medicine – were drafted either by PACE or at its initiative. PACE has also campaigned against racism, xenophobia, intolerance, and violence towards women and children, and has played leading roles in promoting the rights of minorities and the abolition of the death penalty in Europe, and in exposing and condemning the involvement of European states in extraordinary rendition, the transfer of terrorist suspects by the United States to states prepared to turn a blind eye to ill-treatment of detainees. As the previous section intimated, the relationship between PACE and the CM is the most fraught of any within the CE. But, given their respective roles, such friction is both unavoidable and also dynamic and generally functional for the CE's overall goals and objectives.

The Secretariat

The Secretariat of the CE, which has a staff of over 2,000, provides bureaucratic support for all Council activities.[19] The Secretary General (currently Thorbjørn Jagland)[20] and Deputy Secretary General (currently Gabriella Battaini-Dragoni)[21] are appointed for five years by PACE on the recommendation of the CM following submission of nominations from member states. The Secretary General is accountable to the CM for the strategic management of the organisation, its budget and its day-to-day administration, and also receives notices of derogation under Article 15(3) ECHR. He or she can also request, under Article 52 ECHR, an explanation from any given member state 'of the manner in which its external law ensures the effective implementation' of the Convention. The responsibilities of the Deputy Secretary General are defined in the Secretariat's administrative regulations. Amongst other things, separate bureaucracies each service PACE, the CM, the Congress of Local and Regional Authorities, the Commissioner for Human Rights and the Court. The Secretariat's current administrative structure can be found in a chart in the *Highlights 2015* activity report published in 2016.[22]

The European Commissioner for Human Rights

The establishment of a European Ombudsman or Commissioner for Human Rights had been considered by the CE since the 1970s. But it was not until 1999, following the post-Communist enlargement and Protocol No. 11 to the ECHR, that the office was created.[23] The European Commissioner for Human Rights is elected for a non-renewable term of six years, by majority vote in PACE from a list of three candidates selected by the CM from those it has nominated or who have been nominated by member states.[24]

---

[19] M. Ruffert, 'Secretariat' in Schmahl and Breuer (eds.), *Council of Europe*, pp. 212–23; T. Kleinsorge, 'The CoE's Institutional Structure', in Kleinsorge (ed.) *Council of Europe*, pp. 71–4, para. 131; Kleinsorge, 'The CoE's Activities', pp. 105–15; Palmer, 'CM 2015', pp. 106–7.

[20] coe.int/en/web/secretary-general/home.

[21] coe.int/en/web/deputy-secretary-general/home.

[22] Council of Europe, *Highlights 2015* (Strasbourg: Council of Europe, 2016), p. 66. edoc.coe.int/en/an-overview/6912-council-of-europe-highlights-2015.html; See also Ruffert, 'Secretariat', p. 220.

[23] O. Dörr, 'Commissioner for Human Rights' in Schmahl and Breuer (eds.), *Council of Europe*, pp. 296–313.

[24] www.coe.int/en/web/commissioner.

Candidates must be nationals of a CE member state, eminent persons of high moral character with recognised expertise in human rights, a public record of attachment to CE values, and the personal authority to carry out their mission effectively. The three principal elements of the mandate – education and information, monitoring and institutional cooperation, and assistance – defined by resolution of the CM include fostering the effective observance of human rights and assisting member states in the implementation of human rights standards; promoting education in, and awareness of, human rights in member states; identifying possible human rights–related shortcomings in domestic law and practice; facilitating the activities of national ombudsmen, and other human rights institutions; and providing advice and information regarding the protection of human rights across the continent.[25] The human rights in question are not limited to those found in CE documents, which some think overstretches the scope of the Commissioner's mandate.[26]

The activities of the Commissioner fall broadly into three categories. First, he or she liaises with a broad range of international and national institutions and with human rights monitoring processes, including the UN, the OSCE, leading human rights NGOs, universities and think-tanks. Relations with the EU involve the European Parliament, the European Ombudsman, the EU Special Representative for Human Rights, the EU Fundamental Rights Agency and the EU Commissioners for Justice, Home Affairs, Employment, Social Affairs and Inclusion, and for enlargement and European neighbourhood policy. The Commissioner also works closely with national Ombudsmen, National Human Rights Structures, the European Union's Ombudsman and other human rights institutions, and organises biennial roundtables with Ombudsmen, human rights defenders, and European National Human Rights Institutions. In countries where these institutions do not exist, or are not yet fully developed, the Commissioner supports their establishment and seeks to promote their effective operation.

Second, in order to evaluate the condition of human rights in specific member states, and to engage in permanent dialogue with governments, the Commissioner conducts official country missions, extending beyond capital cities, which last between a week and ten days. These typically include meetings with the highest representatives of government, parliament, the judiciary, plus leading members of human rights institutions and civil society, and visits to institutions, such as prisons, police stations, orphanages

---

[25] CM Resolution (99)(50).
[26] Dörr, 'Commissioner for Human Rights', p. 306.

and asylum detention centres where human rights violations are most likely to occur. The Commissioner's reports, which document human rights practices and make detailed recommendations about possible improvements, are presented to the CM and PACE before being published and circulated in policy-making and NGO circles and in the media. Follow-up visits, a few years later, generally lead to widely publicised reports. The Commissioner also visits countries or regions in order to strengthen relations and to examine problems without making a formal report. States are under no formal obligation to submit reports to the Commissioner.

Third, the Commissioner's Office publishes a blog and 'Issue Papers' on topical human rights concerns. He or she may also offer opinions on draft laws and specific practices, either at the request of national bodies or on his/her own initiative. Whenever deemed appropriate, recommendations may be made regarding a specific human rights issue in a member state or states. In order to improve public awareness of human rights standards, the Commissioner's office organises, and co-organises, seminars and events on various human rights themes, and seeks to engage in permanent dialogue with governments, civil society organisations and educational institutions. Several times a year, the Commissioner also meets other key CE officials, including the Presidents of PACE and the ECtHR, and less frequently with representatives of the EU, the OSCE, NATO and the UN. As a non-judicial institution, the Commissioner can neither adjudicate, nor otherwise act directly upon, individual complaints. But he or she can draw conclusions, and take wider initiatives, on the basis of reliable information from individuals concerning alleged violations. Protocol No. 14 to the ECHR, which came into effect on 1 June 2010, enables the Commissioner on his own initiative to submit written comments to the ECtHR and to take part in Chamber and Grand Chamber hearings but not to initiate litigation. However, the Commissioner limits him/herself to providing the kind of background information contained in his/her reports and refrains from commenting on the merits of the case.[27] By the end of 2016 there had been eleven interventions of this kind.[28]

So far there have been three Commissioners.[29] Álvaro Gil-Robles (1999–2006), the former Ombudsman for Spain, shaped, and raised

[27] European Commissioner for Human Rights, *Third Party Interventions by the Commissioner for Human Rights*, coe.int/en/web/commissioner/third-party-interventions.
[28] *Ibid.*
[29] M. Lezertua and A. Forde, updated by N. Sidaropoulos, 'The Commissioner for Human Rights' in Kleinsorge (ed.), *Council of Europe*, pp. 116–26.

the international profile, of the office. He also supported national human rights actors, such as Ombudsmen and NGOs, and contributed to determining pan-European human rights priorities, including those relating to the expulsion of illegal immigrants, inter-faith dialogue, and human rights in the armed forces, the protection of human rights following the second Chechen war, the improvement of prison conditions and the promotion of minority rights. Thomas Hammarberg (2006–12), a former journalist and human rights activist from Sweden, further developed the system of country visits and dialogue with national authorities, focusing on constructive dialogue rather than 'naming and shaming' or ranking states according to their human rights records, emphasised the importance of the effective implementation of human rights standards and further raised the profile, visibility and impact of the office. Specific activities related to humanitarian work in the aftermath of the Russo-Georgian war of 2008, the defence of the human rights of Roma and migrants and raising awareness of the rights of LGBTI people. Nils Muižnieks, a former Latvian government minister appointed in 2012, has so far given priority to the human rights challenges arising from the impact of the post-2008 economic crisis and 'age of austerity', the rapidly evolving information society and the rise of racism and other forms of intolerance in Europe.

Interviews with some of the Commissioner's officials (the 'Strasbourg interviews') revealed the following.[30] Respondents thought the fact that the Commissioner is a single individual supported by a skeleton staff – now twenty-three permanent and three fixed-term positions with, in 2015, a budget of €3,345,300[31] – has its pros and cons. On the plus side it means that policy can be formulated much more rapidly compared with often more cumbersome processes in other CE institutions, which may require extensive consultation with member states. On the negative side, it was said that, while many human rights issues can be rapidly identified, limited resources militate against their being tackled effectively. Respondents also thought that the main strengths of the Commissioner's role were independence, both from government and from other

---

[30] Data were collected by Steven Greer in Strasbourg in July 2007 from formal interviews and informal discussions with Council of Europe officials, generously funded by a Nuffield Foundation Social Sciences Small Grant.

[31] N. Muižnieks, Council of Europe Commissioner for Human Rights, *Annual Activity Report 2016, Presented to the Committee of Ministers and Parliamentary Assembly*, CommDH(2017)3, 6 April 2017, p. 50, wcd.coe.int/com.instranet.InstraServlet?com mand=com.instranet.CmdBlobGet&InstranetImage=2967100&SecMode=1&DocId=2400 520&Usage=2.

CE institutions; close contact with potential sites of violation at national level, as a result of both country visits and liaison with NGOs; ready access to the highest levels of government and other national public institutions; and his/her contribution to building bridges between these institutions, NGOs and other CE bodies. In relation to specific national human rights issues, respondents distinguished three possible outcomes: the Commissioner's intervention had a decisive impact, it contributed to making a positive difference (the establishment of an Ombudsman in Chechnya was cited as an example) or it had no impact at all. Respondents thought the Commissioner's activities were well coordinated with other CE institutions, particularly with the Committee for the Prevention of Torture and other specialist agencies, and may have prompted other CE institutions to take action. They also claimed that the Commissioner accepted that there was plenty of room for multiple pan-European human rights agencies, and that there was no friction with the EU in general, or with its Fundamental Rights Agency (FRA) in particular. It was pointed out that while the FRA is better resourced, the Commissioner's office has more experience.

2.3   Policy

It is unclear whether the CE could be said to have an overall human rights policy beyond the very general one of attempting to protect, and to promote respect for, human rights by drafting treaties and other documents, by monitoring state compliance with them and by initiating and conducting various other relevant activities. As one key respondent in the Strasbourg interviews pointed out, the CE does not have a single policy-making institution as such, and most policy emanates from states – particularly from the Nordic countries, the Netherlands, Austria, Ireland, and the United Kingdom – supplemented by advice from the various committees which report to the CM, its principal decision-making body. This respondent also claimed that ambassadors from member states typically discuss policy informally amongst themselves before any formal proposal is made, and that the state which chairs the CM at any given time is in a particularly powerful position to advance its own agenda. Another maintained that policy originates in the various committees of the Secretariat, while yet another believed that particularly influential individuals play a key role.

Dörr claims that 'beside the ECtHR', the Commissioner is 'the single most influential voice on human rights issues in Europe', a view shared by some CE insiders.[32] One respondent in the Strasbourg interviews claimed that states were not sure whether to boost the functions of the office or not, and that there are problems about how the results of country visits feed back to other CE institutions. Others believe PACE has the greatest legitimacy, particularly since it consists of members of national legislatures and has good contacts with national civil society, NGOs, the ECtHR and the CM. Some claimed that PACE's main contribution lies in pressurising states to improve compliance. One respondent cited the issuing of Presidential pardons to prisoners in Azerbaijan as an example. It was also claimed that PACE's Legal Committee (now Legal Affairs and Human Rights) often 'got the ball rolling' over issues such as human rights violations in Chechnya, but that realpolitik tended to result in this being watered down by PACE itself. Kleinsorge claims that, despite its lack of formal powers, PACE has become a 'stronger' organ than the CM and is 'widely recognised as the motor and conscience' of the CE.[33] However, what 'stronger' means in this context is not clear.

Respondents in the Strasbourg interviews generally acknowledged that CE policy can be prompted or inspired by a wide range of external sources, including NGOs, national civil society, expert bodies, other international human rights treaty organisations, etc., although constitutionally, whatever its origins, the CM is the only institution which can implement it.[34] One respondent thought the CE should seek to provide more formal avenues through which NGOs and civil society organisations could make contributions and cited, as an example, the CM's rules on the supervision of the execution of the Court's judgments, which allow information to be provided by NGOs and National Human Rights Institutions. Research tends to show, however, that NGOs have limited impact both upon CE policy and upon Convention compliance in member states.[35] One respondent claimed that the CM's Steering Committee on Human Rights (the CDDH) has been so preoccupied with reforming the ECHR in recent years that it has not had time to consider broader strategy.

[32] Dörr, 'Commissioner for Human Rights', p. 312.
[33] Kleinsorge, 'Parliamentary Assembly', pp. 93, 95.
[34] For an analysis of the contributions of various CE, and other agencies, to the Protocol No. 14 debate see C. Hioureas, 'Behind the Scenes of Protocol No. 14: Politics in Reforming the European Court of Human Rights', *Berkeley Journal of International Law* (2006) 24, 718–57.
[35] H. Keller and A. Stone Sweet (eds.), *A Europe of Rights: The Impact of the ECHR on National Legal Systems* (Oxford University Press, 2008), p. 689; Hioureas, 'Behind the Scenes', p. 757.

It was also widely acknowledged in the interviews that integration and coordination between the activities of the CE's many different agencies and institutions could be improved.[36] But there was little optimism that this would happen, in spite of the fact that the CE's medium term strategy review to 2015 also accepted the need for bureaucratic rationalisation.[37] One insider claimed that liaison committees within the Secretariat ensure a higher level of coordination there than is the case within the CE as a whole. Respondents also generally thought it would be a mistake for the CE to nominate any one of its various institutions as its principal policy-making body. One claimed that, although overlap and duplication were sometimes desirable, often they were not. The condemnation, by a succession of CE representatives, of the US practice of 'extraordinary rendition' (taking terrorist suspects for interrogation to places where torture is tolerated), was cited as an illustration which had given the impression that the CE could not express its opinion in a single voice. However, another respondent thought that duplication was often desirable because positive results were more likely the more a given issue was endorsed by different agencies and by different states. This respondent also thought greater coordination between the CE's various agencies was limited by the distinct cultures and objectives of its constituent parts. Another believed that, in the longer term, the CE's human rights activities were likely to be eclipsed by the EU, and that the CE's best future lay in it restricting the scope of its activities or, as the medium term strategy paper puts it, 'doing less better'.[38]

While there is evidence that the CE has contributed to legal and/or institutional change in member states,[39] it is not always clear how critical this has been, nor how it has impacted at the grass roots. A difficulty identified by one respondent in the Strasbourg interviews is that often the most successful initiatives are those which the CE has encouraged, yet for which a given state is itself plausibly able to take the credit. One respondent noted that the CE's self-monitoring had mushroomed in recent years.

[36] See also A. Drzemczewski, 'Core Monitoring Mechanisms and Related Activities' in Schmahl and Breuer (eds.), *Council of Europe*, pp. 617–35, 633.
[37] Secretary General of the Council of Europe, *Building on Our Strengths: Eight Initiatives to Shape the CE for the Future – Towards a Medium-Term Strategy*, Information Documents SG/Inf(2007)4, 11 June 2007.
[38] *Ibid.*
[39] For examples listed by state in relation to specific treaties see Directorate General of Human Rights, *Practical Impact of the CE Human Rights Mechanisms in Improving Respect for Human Rights in Member States*, H/Inf(2007)2, April 2007.

For example, attempts have been made through 'Project Management Methodology'/'Equivalent Result-based Budgeting' to assess the performance of activities defined as 'projects', by identifying objectives and performance indicators, and by conducting performance reviews.

Respondents in the Strasbourg interviews were also asked about the CE's relationship with other intergovernmental human rights agencies in Europe particularly the EU, OSCE, NATO and the UN. In May 2007 a Memorandum of Understanding was signed with the EU according to which each organisation committed itself to 'develop their relationship in all areas of common interest ... avoiding duplication and fostering synergy ... (and) extending their cooperation to all areas where it is likely to bring added value to their action'. It was envisaged that this would be achieved by exchanging views and by preparing and implementing common strategies and programmes for human rights and fundamental freedoms; rule of law and legal cooperation; democracy and good governance; democratic stability; intercultural dialogue and cultural diversity; education, youth and promotion of human contacts; and social cohesion.[40] The Memorandum expressly identifies the CE as 'the benchmark for human rights, the rule of law and democracy in Europe'.[41] One respondent said that often different intergovernmental organisations took the lead, in relation to either particular states or particular issues. Relations between the CE and NATO were said to have been strained by the extraordinary rendition controversy, but relations with the EU were generally said to be cordial and unproblematic. However, one respondent thought there was some competition and duplication, while another stressed the need for the EU to accede to the ECHR as soon as possible. The key issue for another was that the EU should operate with the same standards as the CE and that it should avoid creating its own 'circle of legality' which might diminish rather than enhance the protection of human rights at the pan-European level. While recognising that institutions tend to value their own autonomy, another respondent acknowledged the need for greater institutional coherence. According to yet another, areas where each organisation works best needed to be more carefully identified in order to avoid

---

[40] *Memorandum of Understanding between the Council of Europe and the European Union* CM(2007)74 10 May 2007, paras. 9–14, cvce.eu/en/obj/memorandum_of_understa nding_between_the_council_of_europe_and_the_european_union_10_may_2007-en-a 30c3a25-e9f5-4bd8-878c-4445d58e015e.html.

[41] *Ibid.*, para. 10.

overlap. But another respondent said that it was important not to jeopardise the EU's relations with non-European states in the process. It was widely acknowledged in the Strasbourg interviews that the CE had initially been concerned by the creation of the EU's Fundamental Rights Agency (FRA) – on which it has a representative – especially since the latter has much greater resources than the European Commissioner for Human Rights, for example, its staff of fifty to sixty compared with the Commissioner's of less than thirty.[42] However, another respondent saw no reason for concern about any significant friction because the remit of the FRA, as a largely data-collecting organisation with some educational functions, is narrower than that of the Commissioner.

2.4 Key Treaties

The ECHR is by far the most well known, and most debated of the CE's 200-plus treaties, and, together with the ECtHR, the most significant of the CE's activities for the purposes of this study. But before turning to them, three of the most high profile of the others – the European Social Charter 1961 and 1996 (ESC), the European Convention for the Prevention of Torture and Inhuman or Degrading Treatment or Punishment 1989 (ECPT) and the Framework Convention for the Protection of National Minorities 1995 (FC) – will be considered.

The European Social Charter

As indicated in Chapter 1, since the CE was initially an affirmation of the common liberal democratic identity of western European states, expressed primarily through the medium of civil and political rights, it was not intended to enable individuals to take their own governments to an international court for allegedly violating the full panoply of their basic universal individual entitlements. But this does not mean that it was hostile to other kinds of right, or regarded them as inferior to, or less worthy of protection than, those found in the ECHR. On the contrary, since 'economic and social progress' is one of the core principles enshrined in its statute, the CE has always recognised such rights while also acknowledging – particularly because their realisation is much more a matter of political choice making them inherently less justiciable than their civil and political counterparts – that they require a distinctive

---

[42] See Chapter 4.

institutional, procedural and normative regime. Indeed, as early as 1953, the (then-Consultative) Assembly unanimously approved a memorandum from the Secretariat proposing a European Social Charter (ESC), which was available for signature in 1961 and came into force in 1965. A complex web of processes and norms was created by the addition of further Protocols in 1988, 1991 and 1995, the latter of which provided a system of collective complaints, and by the revision of the ESC itself in 1996.[43]

As the title suggests, the ESC contains a range of social and economic rights. These fall into four broad categories – individual access to and conditions of employment, collective regulation of employment, social protection outside employment and social protection of migrant workers[44] – and include such rights as those relating to health, working hours, holiday pay, collective bargaining, education, the elderly and social security. According to Harris and Darcy the ESC was created in order to fulfil three main objectives: to provide a statement of the principles of European social policy, to guide social progress in Europe and to offer a social and economic counterpart to the ECHR.[45] Like the ECHR, the ESC prohibits discrimination; restrictions upon its provisions must be both prescribed by law and necessary in a democratic society 'for the protection of the rights and freedoms of others or for the protection of public interest, national security, public health or morals';[46] derogations can be made from its provisions in time of war or public emergency threatening the life of the nation to the extent strictly required by the exigencies of the

---

[43] See coe.int/en/web/turin-european-social-charter; O. Dörr, 'European Social Charter' in S. Schmahl and M. Breuer (eds.), *The Council of Europe: Its Law and Policies* (Oxford University Press, 2017), pp. 507–41; C. Benelhocine, *The European Social Charter* (Strasbourg: Council of Europe Publishing, 2012); H. Cullen, 'The Collective Complaints System of the European Social Charter: Interpretative Methods of the European Committee of Social Rights' *Human Rights Law Review*, 9 (2009), 61–93; R. R. Churchill and U. Khaliq, 'The Collective Complaints System of the European Social Charter: An Effective Mechanism for Ensuring Compliance with Economic and Social Rights?' *European Journal of International Law* (2004) 15, 417–56; T. Novitz, 'Are Social Rights Necessarily Collective Rights? A Critical Analysis of the Collective Complaints Protocol to the European Social Charter', *European Human Rights Law Review* [2002], 50–66; T. Novitz, 'Remedies for Violation of Social Rights within the Council of Europe: The Significant Absence of a Court' in C. Kilpatrick, T. Novitz and P. Skidmore (eds.), *The Future of Remedies in Europe* (Oxford: Hart, 2000), pp. 231–51; D. Harris and J. Darcy, *The European Social Charter* (Ardsley: Transnational, 2nd edn., 2000).

[44] Dörr, 'European Social Charter', p. 524.

[45] Harris and Darcy, *European Social Charter*, p. 397. The ECSR also regards the Charter as complementary to the ECHR, Cullen, 'Collective Complaints System of the European Social Charter', p. 72.

[46] ESC, Art. 31.

situation and consistent with other international legal obligations;[47] and when a state decides to accede to the ESC, it can, within certain limits, cherry pick the provisions it wishes to adhere to and those it does not.[48]

There are, however, several significant differences between the Charter and Convention. To begin with, accession to the ESC, unlike the ECHR, is not a condition of CE membership. However, as of March 2017, all forty-seven of the CE's member states had signed the ESC (two the original, and forty-five the revised version), forty-three had also ratified it (ten the original, and thirty-three the revised version) and fifteen had acceded to the collective complaints procedure.[49] Second, although formally framed as individual rights, by contrast with the ECHR, Charter provisions tend to operate as state undertakings to secure minimum standards, subject to progressive realisation.[50] There are several other differences. Unlike the ECHR, the ESC is not intended to take effect in national law,[51] there is no right of individual complaint in the monitoring machinery discussed later, no victim requirement, and while collective complaints are required to fulfil certain specified broad admissibility criteria, domestic remedies do not have to be exhausted, and no time limits have to be observed.[52] Although described as 'decisions on the merits', the reports of the European Committee on Social Rights (ECSR), which monitors Charter compliance, not only reflect this as a bald issue, but also take account of the political, social and economic conditions in given states,[53] 'filtered by a political evaluation of the consequences of the findings of non-compliance"[54] But they do not provide remedies including compensation,[55] do not bind states[56] and are not as detailed as judgments of the ECtHR.[57] Finally, while the ECHR formally protects all those within a member state's jurisdiction, the ESC only applies to nationals of contracting states lawfully residing and working regularly within the territory of the state concerned.[58]

---

[47] ESC, Art. 30; Dörr, 'European Social Charter', pp. 512, 518, 525.
[48] Dörr, 'European Social Charter', pp. 509, 512, 514, 517, 524.
[49] coe.int/en/web/turin-european-social-charter/signature-ratifications.
[50] Dörr, 'European Social Charter', pp. 514, 525, 539; Benelhocine, *European Social Charter*, pp. 16, 23–5, 47; Novitz, 'Remedies for Violation of Social Rights', p. 241.
[51] Dörr, 'European Social Charter', pp. 509, 515, 516, 525.
[52] *Ibid.*, p. 536.
[53] Cullen, 'Collective Complaints', pp. 63, 67, 70.
[54] Dörr, 'European Social Charter', p. 533.
[55] *Ibid.*, pp. 537.
[56] *Ibid.*, pp. 533, 534, 539.
[57] Cullen, 'Collective Complaints', p. 75.
[58] Dörr, 'European Social Charter', pp. 509, 515.

The ECSR consists of fifteen independent and impartial members, currently with backgrounds as judges and jurists,[59] elected by the CM for six years renewable once. It promotes understanding of the ESC through information seminars, colloquies and training sessions, hosts seven one-week sessions a year and publishes an annual activity report.[60] ESC compliance is monitored in two ways. First, the ECSR publishes annual 'conclusions' based on self-assessment reports from signatory states, required every two years for core provisions and every four for the remainder.[61] Specific recommendations about the particular action the state needs to take in order to improve implementation may also be included. Where, in a subsequent year, the ECSR decides that a state has not responded to its conclusions appropriately, the matter is referred to the CM, which entrusts a Governmental Committee – comprising representatives of states parties to the ESC and observers from European employers' organisations and trade unions – to make a recommendation. The Governmental Committee votes by two-thirds majority and, in recent years, increasing caution on the part of state representatives has resulted in frequent abstention, hampering progress at national level.[62] Within four months of reporting to the parties, to the CM and to PACE, the ECSR's non-binding report is made public. Under Article 9 of the Protocol the CM is obliged to adopt a resolution on the basis of this report and, by a two-thirds majority, a recommendation regarding specific action.[63] However, according to Benelhocine, 'Ten years can pass before a situation is rectified and satisfies the requirements of the Charter despite repeated requests of the European Committee of Social Rights and Committee of Ministers' recommendations'.[64]

The second monitoring process is contained in an optional protocol open for signature in 1995 and in force in 1998.[65] This enables complaints about Charter non-compliance by any state which has acceded to the protocol to be lodged with the ECSR by four classes of organisation but not by individuals: (a) international organisations of employers and trade unions invited by the Governmental Committee, currently the

---

[59] Benelhocine, *European Social Charter*, p. 40.
[60] *Ibid.*, pp. 41–3.
[61] Cullen, 'Collective Complaints', p. 63.
[62] Benelhocine, *European Social Charter*, p. 47.
[63] Dörr, 'European Social Charter', pp. 537–8.
[64] Benelhocine, p. 48.
[65] See Cullen, 'Collective Complaints'; Churchill and Khaliq, 'Collective Complaints System of the European Social Charter', pp. 417–56; Novitz, 'Are Social Rights Necessarily Collective Rights?' pp. 50–66.

European Trade Union Confederation (ETUC), the International Organisation of Employers (IOE) and BUSINESSEUROPE (formerly the Union of the Confederations of Industry and Employers of Europe); (b) other international NGOs with consultative status at the CE and listed as such by the Governmental Committee; (c) representative national employers' organisations and trade unions within the jurisdiction of the contracting state against which the complaint has been lodged and; (d) any NGO with relevant competence recognised as such by, and within the jurisdiction of, any contracting state, limited so far to Finland.[66]

Where the ESCR finds a complaint admissible it communicates with the parties in writing and a public hearing may also be held before the merits are decided. The subject matter of complaints has been quite wide-ranging, with a slightly higher proportion relating to workers' than to social rights. The same broad issue has also given rise to 'repeat' complaints against the same state, for example, the impact of French working time legislation on managers.[67] The character of the decisions of the ECSR is a matter of debate. Formally they are 'administrative-bureaucratic' rather than 'judicial' and concern whether or not the Charter has been applied in an 'unsatisfactory' manner rather than whether or not it has been violated.[68] However some commentators argue that the ECSC, 'the sole entity with authority to make legal interpretations' of the Charter, has 'established itself as a clearly quasi-judicial body in the performance of its tasks under the Protocol' similar to UN human rights bodies receiving individual petitions.[69] But as Dörr observes, the ESCR's procedure is 'the only international human rights mechanism where a governmental body (the CM) has the final say in the outcome of the proceedings'.[70] Although the procedure under the Protocol is adversarial, oral hearings are, in fact, rarely held. The ECSC also regards its own former decisions as precedents, and has articulated and elaborated the underlying values of the ESC – autonomy, dignity, equality and solidarity.[71] It has been claimed that this

---

[66] Dörr, 'European Social Charter', pp. 535–6.
[67] A. Nolan, '"Aggravated Violations", Roma Housing Rights and Forced Expulsions in Italy: Recent Developments under the European Social Charter Collective Complaints System', *European Human Rights Law Review* 11 (2011), 343–6, 359; Cullen, 'Collective Complaints', pp. 68–9.
[68] Art. 1, Additional Protocol to the European Social Charter Providing for a System of Collective Complaints.
[69] Cullen, 'Collective Complaints', pp. 69, 62, 75; Churchill and Khaliq, 'Collective Complaints', p. 437.
[70] Dörr, 'European Social Charter', p. 539.
[71] Cullen, 'Collective Complaints', pp. 75, 61, 62, 71, 76–81.

approach has enabled a 'considerable economic and social rights jurisprudence' to be developed, permitting the balancing of the protection of human rights with the need for state discretion and with the resource implications of European social policy making.[72] It is said that the ECSR has also employed the methods, 'techniques of reasoning' and some core principles and concepts from the jurisprudence of the ECtHR, including positive obligations, reasonableness, minimum interference with rights, legitimate aim, legality, proportionality and margin of appreciation.[73] The fact that the ECSR has also referred to the precedents of the Strasbourg court, which has reciprocated, has also enhanced convergence between the two systems.[74] Making reference where appropriate to statistical evidence, the ECSR also considers how the law has been applied in a given state, including in ongoing situations and those not covered by country reports.[75]

Since the 1995 Protocol came into effect, the majority of complaints have been lodged by International NGOs.[76] In 2009 Cullen reported that the ETUC had been a co-complainant in only one complaint and that there had been none from any national NGO.[77] According to Benelhocine, lack of awareness of the ESC and the collective complaints mechanism appears to be the main reason why there have been so few applications from national trade unions and employers' organisations.[78] Over the period 1998–2015, the ECSR received 119 collective complaints, with France (34) and Greece (17), attracting the most.[79] Of admissible cases raised by complaints, 46–50 per cent were found to comply with the ESC while 25–35 per cent did not. The remainder were deferred.[80]

Harris and Darcy conclude that the Charter has played 'only a modest role' in providing a statement of social policy principles and in guiding harmonisation of social progress in Europe, and that it 'pales in comparison' with EU law and practice in comparable fields.[81] Nevertheless, they also maintain that its 'present significance' lies in 'its role as a

---

[72] *Ibid.*, pp. 61–2, 73, 90–92.

[73] *Ibid.*, pp. 81–90; Dörr, 'European Social Charter', pp. 518–22.

[74] Cullen, 'Collective Complaints', pp. 72, 75. Dörr, 'European Social Charter', pp. 518–22.

[75] Cullen, 'Collective Complaints', pp. 62, 71, 72, 75.

[76] Benelhocine, *European Social Charter*, p. 98

[77] Cullen, 'Collective Complaints', 67.

[78] Benelhocine, *European Social Charter*, p. 57.

[79] European Committee of Social Rights, *Activity Report 2015* (Strasbourg: Council of Europe, 2016), pp. 13, 89
https://rm.coe.int/CoERMPublicCommonSearchServices/DisplayDCTMContent?documentId=09000016805ab9c7,

[80] Dörr, 'European Social Charter', p. 535.

[81] Harris and Darcy, *European Social Charter*, pp. 397, 404.

counterpart' to the ECHR.[82] This relationship is, however, very asymmetrical, particularly given the ESC's lack of a binding judicial individual applications process, and the political role of the CM in the collective complaints machinery.[83] Dörr states that, in spite of the fact that, 'as a system for the protection of human rights, the Charter is a failure' and has been largely eclipsed by the much more effective human rights systems provided by the ECHR and the EU, it nevertheless provides an indirect but 'essential impulse' for constructing the European social model.[84] Taking 'a detour via EU law and the ECHR', it represents a necessary counterpart to their 'liberalization schemes ... adding a missing component to the European legal order and making the latter an appropriate candidate for a constitutional perspective'.[85] Moreover there can be little doubt that the ESC has had some positive impact on states and that it is regularly referred to for the purpose of interpreting national law and developing national social policy.[86] The ECSR's annual Activity Reports provide numerous examples, and the CE regularly publishes brief illustrations of changes in domestic law in response to standards specified in ECSR reports.[87] While this information is not sufficiently detailed to establish a clear and direct causal connection between ECSR conclusions and specific legislative changes, nor to determine whether the latter fully comply with the former, it would be equally difficult to claim that there has been no link whatever. Although there may be merit, as some have suggested, in extending the reach of the Charter's provisions beyond nationals of member states lawfully resident and working within the territory of a state against which a complaint is lodged, there are, however, fatal problems with proposals to make the ESC a condition of membership of the CE, to provide an individual complaints mechanism and a court capable of awarding compensation and imposing financial penalties, to integrate ESC rights more fully into the ECHR and to establish a CE body to assist complainants.[88] Not only do these aspirations lack political realism, but they also

[82] *Ibid.*, p. 397.
[83] *Ibid.*, pp. 371–4, 376, 400. See also Novitz, 'Remedies', 249–51; Cullen, 'Collective Complaints', p. 62; Churchill and Khaliq, 'Collective Complaints', 446–7, 455.
[84] Dörr, 'European Social Charter', pp. 539–40.
[85] *Ibid.*, p. 541.
[86] Dörr, 'European Social Charter', p. 540.
[87] See, e.g., Directorate General Human Rights and Rule of Law, *Practical Impact of the CE Human Rights Mechanisms in Improving Respect for Human Rights and the Rule of Law in Member States* (CE, 2014), pp. 28–34.
[88] Benelhocine, *European Social Charter*, pp. 101–10.

misunderstand the principled reasons, considered more fully elsewhere in this study, concerning why such arrangements were never included in the ECHR in the first place.

The European Convention for the Prevention of Torture

The European Convention for the Prevention of Torture and Inhuman or Degrading Treatment or Punishment 1987 (ECPT) – drafted in 1986, in force by 1989 and amended as from March 2002 – aims to strengthen 'by non-judicial means of a preventive nature'[89] the right of everyone detained by a public authority in a member state not to be subjected to torture or to inhuman or degrading treatment or punishment, in their widest senses.[90] Unlike other human rights instruments, the ECPT – now an accession requirement signed and ratified by every CE state – does not establish any new norms, but instead provides a unique enforcement regime based on visits to places of detention by the European Committee for the Prevention of Torture and Inhuman or Degrading Treatment or Punishment (CPT).[91] The CPT's findings and recommendations then form the basis of a constructive dialogue with the state concerned.[92]

Members of the CPT are persons of high moral character known for their competence in human rights or their professional experience in the areas covered by the ECPT. Elected by the CM from lists of names drawn up by the bureau of PACE, they meet in plenary session three times a year and serve part-time for periods of four years up to a maximum of twelve. The number on the CPT is equal to the number of state parties to the ECPT.[93] Members serve in their individual capacities, and not as state representatives, and are not appointed to serve on CPT visits to their own countries. While lawyers dominate the Committee, other members bring

---

[89] Preamble to the ECPT.
[90] cpt.coe.int/en/about.htm.
[91] See J. Murdoch, 'The Impact of Europe's "Torture Committee" and the Evolution of Standard-Setting in Relation to Places of Detention', *European Human Rights Law Review* [2006], 158–79 and 'Tackling Ill-Treatment in Places of Detention: The Work of the Council of Europe's "Torture Committee"', *European Journal of Criminal Policy and Research*, 12 (2006), 121–42; R. Morgan and M. Evans, *Combating Torture in Europe: The Work and Standards of the European Committee for the Prevention of Torture* (Strasbourg: Council of Europe, 2001); M. D. Evans and R. Morgan, *Preventing Torture: A Study of the European Convention for the Prevention of Torture and Inhuman and Degrading Treatment or Punishment* (Oxford: Clarendon Press, 1998).
[92] Morgan and Evans, *Combating Torture*, pp. 22, 31.
[93] *Ibid.*, p. 25.

expertise from the fields of medicine, prisons and policing. Independent experts and interpreters may also be appointed. The CPT maintains close relations with its global counterpart operating under the Optional Protocol to the UN Convention against Torture, and with the Commissioner for Human Rights, PACE, the CM, NGOs, national human rights institutions, the UN High Commissioner for Refugees, the Organization for Security and Cooperation in Europe, the EU and the International Committee of the Red Cross.[94]

The work of the CPT is directed by a bureau consisting of the President and two Vice Presidents, supported by a twenty-three member Secretariat which arranges and prepares visits, accompanies and provides administrative support to members when these take place, clerks meetings and implements the Committee's decisions regarding dialogue with member states. The CPT is obliged to inform states of its intention to conduct a visit, but no minimum notice period is required, nor the disclosure of precise inspection locations. States are obliged to provide full documentation about places where anyone is deprived of liberty, to grant the CPT unrestricted access to these sites and also to furnish any other relevant information. Government objections to the time or place of a visit can only be justified where it might harm the health of anyone concerned, compromise an urgent ongoing interrogation relating to serious crime, jeopardise national defence or public safety, or risk serious disorder. In such circumstances the state must take immediate steps to facilitate a CPT visit as soon as possible. Although all states are subject to periodic visits, usually by a team of nine CPT members – including administrative staff and experts and in principle once every four years – in practice the frequency varies according to demands on the CPT's time, resources and priorities. Ad hoc visits, typically by five-person teams – prompted by concerns from a range of possible sources that ill-treatment is occurring in a particular jurisdiction or at a particular place – are at the Committee's discretion and can occur immediately the state in question has been notified, and usually within a week or less.[95] The CPT makes follow-up visits to assess progress in implementing recommendations. Between January 2011 and December 2013 there were thirty periodic visits totalling 301 days compared with twenty-five ad hoc visits totalling 151 days,[96] and as of 3 March 2017 there

[94] H. Chetwynd, 'The European Committee for the Prevention of Torture (CPT)' in Kleinsorge (ed.), *Council of Europe*, pp. 140–1.
[95] *Ibid.*, pp. 130,135; Evans and Morgan, *Preventing Torture*, p. 168.
[96] Chetwynd, 'CPT', p. 130.

had been 406 visits (239 periodic and 167 ad hoc) with the publication of 354 reports, an average of thirteen a year.[97]

The principles of cooperation and confidentiality lie at the heart of the CPT's work and, as already indicated, the purpose of visits is to open up dialogue with the state concerned.[98] Missions, which include private interviews with detainees and various other parties, end with a meeting at which the delegation conveys its initial impressions to officials in the expectation of an official response to the subsequent report. Although formally confidential, publication of reports has become the rule rather than the exception.

The CPT itself is empowered to 'make a public statement' if a state fails to cooperate with this process, or to improve defects in its compliance with the ECPT to which the Committee has drawn its attention. But this has only happened on eight occasions, twice with respect to Turkey, three times regarding Russia, and once each concerning Greece, Belgium and Bulgaria.[99] Confidential reports are also submitted to the CM. Amongst the pan-European issues about which the CPT has expressed concern are the duty of states to combat official impunity for unlawful detention; the need for effective independent national monitoring of places of detention; the principle of equivalence of health care (that those deprived of their liberty should have the same standard of treatment as everyone else); poor sanitation; overcrowded, dilapidated and unhygienic conditions; solitary confinement; inadequate relief from cell lock-up; and the detention of foreign nationals, juveniles, women, and those held against their will in psychiatric establishments.[100]

National civil society organisations, particularly NGOs, play a critical role in the CPT's work by pursuing domestically the agenda set by its visits.[101] The Directorate General of Human Rights' *Practical Impact* document includes brief illustrations of how each of fifteen states had introduced changes conforming more closely to ECPT standards.[102] Some of these are directly linked to a CPT recommendation but others not. For example, the Austrian Ministry of the Interior set up the Human Rights Advisory Board following a CPT recommendation that an independent

---

[97] http://cpt.coe.int/en/about.htm.
[98] Chetwynd, 'CPT', p. 131. Morgan and Evans, *Combating Torture*, p. 27.
[99] http://hudoc.cpt.coe.int/eng#{"CPTDocumentType":["ps"]}.
[100] Chetwynd, 'CPT', pp. 138–40.
[101] Evans and Morgan, *Preventing Torture*, p. 168.
[102] DGHR, *Practical Impact*, pp. 13–17.

body be established to investigate complaints of police misconduct. However, there is no reference to CPT intervention regarding the establishment in Luxembourg of a detention unit outside the regular prison system. It is not, however, clear whether the ECPT has made any significant systematic difference to preventing the torture or ill-treatment of those detained by public authorities in member states because 'there are too many imponderables to be able to make a definitive assessment'.[103]

The Framework Convention for the Protection of National Minorities

As indicated in Chapter 1, in the aftermath of the Second World War, the prevailing view in western Europe was that strong, formal, collective minority rights are counterproductive, both for minorities and for the maintenance of international security, because they tend to promote division within states along ethnic, linguistic or religious lines, and, in a worst case, demands for secession. The CE was originally founded, therefore, on the alternative, individual rights, approach which accepts the existing borders of states and attempts to protect minorities within a national framework of equal, non-discriminatory individual rights, neutral on ethnic, religious, linguistic, cultural and other identity criteria. Yet, according to Manas, the trouble with this, the 'republican' perspective, is that 'equality' can often be implicitly referenced to the cultural identity of the dominant majority in any given state.[104] Since the ending of the Cold War, this has been increasingly contested in Europe and elsewhere as the profile of the 'politics of ideology' has diminished and the profile of the 'politics of identity' has increased. In other words, with both communism and fascism discredited, the sharpest conflicts in contemporary Europe are now over competing conceptions of the cultural, ethnic, linguistic and religious identity of the state and society, rather than between competing visions of the relationship between the individual, society, the state, and the market. Few western European countries have no ethnic tensions and some of the most violent of these – particularly in Northern Ireland and in the Basque region of Spain – were

---

[103] Evans and Morgan, *Preventing Torture*, p. 159; Murdoch, 'Impact of Europe's Torture Committee', 159 and 'Tackling Ill-Treatment', 141.

[104] J. E. Manas, 'The Council of Europe's Democracy Ideal and the Challenge of Ethno-National Strife' in A. Chayes and A. H. Chayes (eds.), *Preventing Conflict in the Post-Communist World – Mobilizing International and Regional Organizations* (Washington, DC: Brookings Institute, 1996) pp. 99–144, 121.

unaffected by the post–Second World War settlement. In many of the former Communist states the relaxation of authoritarian control has also reopened, or threatened to reopen, historic disputes about the relationship between ethnicity and territory. However, with the exceptions of the Balkans, Chechnya, the Caucasus and most recently Ukraine, the post–Cold War reconfiguration of Europe has involved comparatively little violence within or between states so far.

Weller claims that the 'shock of interethnic violence that afflicted Eastern Europe with the unfreezing of the Cold War' sparked a renewed interest in minority rights in Europe in the 1990s.[105] Emerging from the regionalist movement of the 1970s, and sponsored by the Conference of Local and Regional Authorities (the precursor of the later Congress with the same remit), in 1989 the CE drafted a European Charter for Regional or Minority Languages, which came into force in 1998. Favouring the terminology of 'objective standards' over both express individual and collective rights, the Charter aims to protect and encourage the use of regional or minority languages in education, judicial proceedings, administrative authorities, public services, the media and cultural, economic and social life. However, as Oeter points out, it is impossible to avoid deriving implied rights from these sources.[106] On a three-yearly cycle, member states are required to report to the Secretary General of the CE and to an expert monitoring committee, with one member per state party, which in turn reports to the CM, and can also conduct country visits. By March 2017 only twenty-five of the CE's forty-seven states had both signed and ratified/acceded to the Charter with a further five having signed but not ratified.

Notwithstanding the terrible ethnic conflict in the Balkans in the 1990s, which some attributed to Yugoslavia's multicultural foundations, the European Charter for Regional or Minority Languages was followed

---

[105] M. Weller (ed.), *The Rights of Minorities: A Commentary on the European Framework Convention for the Protection of National Minorities* (Oxford University Press, 2005), p. vii; J. Jackson Preece, *Minority Rights* (Cambridge: Polity Press, 2005), ch. 7. Martínez-Torrón argues that it was not until 1993, and partly as a result of the incorporation of central and eastern European states into the Convention system, that the Strasbourg institutions began to take an interest in questions of religious freedom, J. Martínez-Torrón, 'The European Court of Human Rights and Religion', *Current Legal Issues* [2001], 185–204, 188.

[106] S. Oeter, 'Conventions on the Protection of National Minorities', S. Schmahl and M. Breuer (eds.), *The Council of Europe: Its Law and Policies* (Oxford University Press, 2017), pp. 542–71, 560.

by a proposed minority rights protocol to the ECHR, which was later superseded by the Framework Convention for the Protection of National Minorities 1995 (the FC).[107] Since then minority-rights issues have been monitored by various CE institutions, including a Special Representative of the Secretary General on Roma Issues, a Committee of Experts on Roma and Travellers and the European Roma and Travellers Forum.[108] In 1993 the CM began the process of drafting the FC – which, unlike the European Charter for Regional or Minority Languages, was expressly intended to be a human rights instrument – by delegating responsibility to an Ad Hoc Committee for the Protection of National Minorities, which paid particular attention to the national minority commitments contained in documents of the CSCE, the forerunner of the OSCE. The FC was opened for signature on 1 February 1995 and came into force on 1 February 1998.[109] Although it is primarily a CE document, other states are entitled, at the invitation of the CM, to accede to it. The word 'Framework' indicates that the principles the FC contains are not directly applicable in the domestic legal systems of member states but require

---

[107] coe.int/en/web/minorities/home; coe.int/t/dg4/education/minlang/; see Oeter, 'Protection of national Minorities'; A. Korkeakivi, updated by C. Altenhöner-Dion, 'The CoE and the Protection of National Minorities' in Kleinsorge (ed.), *Council of Europe*, pp. 183–90; S. Berry, 'The Siren's Call? Exploring the Implications of an Additional Protocol to the European Convention on Human Rights on National Minorities', *International Journal on Minority and Group Rights* 23 (2016), 1–38; J. Ringelheim, 'Minority Rights in a Time of Multiculturalism – the Evolving Scope of the Framework Convention on the Protection of National Minorities', *Human Rights Law Review* (2010) 10, 99–128; R. Parry 'History, Human Rights and Multilingual Citizenship: Conceptualising the European Charter for Regional or Minority Languages', *Northern Ireland Legal Quarterly* (2010) 61, 329–48.

[108] A. Korkeakivi, updated by C. Altenhöner-Dion, 'The Protection of National Minorities', pp. 191–2.

[109] See A. Vertichel, A. Alen, B. De Witte and P. Lemmens (eds.), *The Framework Convention for the Protection of National Minorities: A Useful Pan-European Instrument?* (Antwerp: Intersentia, 2008); G. Pentassuglia, 'Monitoring Minority Rights in Europe: The Implementation Machinery of the Framework Convention for the Protection of National Minorities – with Special Reference to the Role of the Advisory Committee', *International Journal on Minority and Group Rights* 6 (1999), 417–61; G. Alfredsson, 'A Frame an Incomplete Painting: Comparison of the Framework Convention for the Protection of National Minorities with International Standards and Monitoring Procedures', *International Journal on Minority and Group Rights* (2000) 7, 291–304; A. Phillips, 'The 10th Anniversary of the Framework Convention for the Protection of National Minorities', *Euopäiasches Journal für Minderheitenfragen* 3 (2008), 181–9; C. F. Furtado, 'Guess Who's Coming to Dinner? Protection for National Minorities in the Eastern and Central Europe under the Council of Europe', *Columbia Human Rights Law Review* 34 (2002–3), 333–411.

implementation through positive action delivered through national legislation and public policy, subject to significant national margins of appreciation. In addition to the Preamble, the FC has thirty-two articles and is divided into five sections. Due to a lack of consensus on what constitutes a 'national minority' no definition is provided.

Section I sets out some general principles, including that the international protection of human rights extends both to national minorities and to persons belonging to them, and that everyone belonging to a national minority is free to choose to be treated, or not to be treated, as such without suffering disadvantage or discrimination either way. Section II, the main operative part of the FC, contains more detailed provisions regarding a number of minority rights to such things as the manifestation of religion, access to the media, freedom to use minority languages and education in and the promotion without discrimination of minority culture, language, religion and history. While some of these duplicate those already found in the ECHR, Oeter claims that the limited case law of the ECtHR in the field is of 'marginal importance' providing only minimum, fall-back standards in a relatively haphazard, piecemeal manner.[110] Section II prohibits policies and practices aimed at assimilation, spells out some obligations for national minorities and their members and also defines certain programmatic objectives which state parties undertake to pursue at the national level through legislation and governmental policies and also, where appropriate, by bilateral and multilateral treaties. Section III contains interpretation provisions including the principle that the FC may not be construed to derive a right to engage in activities contrary to the territorial integrity and political independence of states, and that nothing in it justifies limiting higher standards of human rights protection as found in other international instruments or in national legislation.

The CM monitors national FC compliance with the assistance of an Advisory Committee of a minimum of twelve, and a maximum of eighteen, independent and impartial members, nominated by state parties and appointed by the CM because of their recognised expertise in the protection of national minority rights. The Advisory Committee examines the reports states are required to submit at five-yearly intervals, or when the CM so requests. The expectation is that these, which are made public by the CE, will provide full information about legislative and

---

[110] Oeter, 'Protection of National Minorities', p. 549.

other measures intended to implement FC principles. In preparing an opinion about FC compliance, the Advisory Committee may request additional information from a state party and, after having notified the CM of its intention to do so, may also request information from other sources. Meetings may be held with representatives of state parties and are obligatory where the latter so requests. The Advisory Committee may also conduct country visits during the course of which it may meet people in addition to government officials. Although the Advisory Committee does not deal with individual complaints, it may, nevertheless, receive information from individuals and other sources such as NGOs.

Having received the opinion of the Advisory Committee, the CM makes its final decision ('conclusion') concerning the adequacy of the measures taken by a state party and may also, where appropriate, make recommendations. The Committee's conclusions and recommendations, the Advisory Committee's opinion and any comments by the state concerned are made public. The CM may also involve the Advisory Committee in a follow-up inquiry concerning the action taken as a result of the Advisory Committee's opinion. The first reports from state parties were due on 1 February 1999 (one year after the entry into force) and, by 2008, the Advisory Committee had delivered sixty-four opinions.[111] By March 2017 thirty-nine states had signed and ratified the Convention and a further four had signed but not ratified.[112]

The CE's *Practical Impact* documents, to which reference has already been made, contain illustrations of how compliance with the FC has been improved by changes in the law and policy in each of thirty-five states. But, as in other contexts, it is not easy to detect the extent to which, if at all, the FC prompted the particular effect and a great deal depends upon the receptiveness of civil society and public institutions in given states.[113] Many commentators welcome the FC for introducing national minority rights protection into the CE's human rights machinery and for providing the means by which compliance failure can be identified. However, they also, typically, criticise its vague, programmatic and highly qualified obligations; the lack of group rights; the scope for the arbitrary identification of national minorities by states; weaknesses in monitoring arrangements (particularly the political role of the CM); the application

---

[111] Philips, '10th Anniversary', p. 183.

[112] coe.int/en/web/conventions/full-list/-/conventions/treaty/157/signatures?p_auth=dLQ 9twHs.

[113] DGHR, *Practical Impact*, pp. 38–42; Oeter, 'Protection of National Minorities', p. 571.

of inconsistent standards by parallel organisations such as the OSCE; and the lack of remedies or any other substantial means of enforcement for non-compliance.[114]

Philips, however, argues that, as events have unfolded, some of these alleged weaknesses have, in fact, come to be seen as strengths. The FC's vague language has, for example, enabled it to be endorsed by more states than might otherwise have been the case, and the Advisory Committee has proved much more robust in its approach than some expected.[115] Other commentators are concerned about other difficulties. Manas, for example, argues that the CE currently embraces the mutually incompatible 'republican' (or individual) rights approach, which underpins the ECHR, and the 'multicultural' approach, which underpins the FC. He also maintains that any one of the three main solutions to the problem of conflict within European states ('republicanism', 'multiculturalism', or 'secessionism') tends to produce the problems associated with not choosing any of the others. While, as he argues, more flexible arrangements may be required, it is not clear what this would entail. Preferring the concept of 'co-nation' to 'national minority', Malloy argues for 'a model of accommodation based on discursive justice', and concludes that the EU's politics of integration are more likely to provide the space for this than the 'legal approach of the politics of democratization of the CE'.[116] But Oeter maintains that 'contrary to a number of fields of operation traditionally dealt with by the CoE where the EU has developed a strong competential portfolio and has taken over the initiative in standard-setting, minority protection is still a unique endeavour of the CoE'.[117] Although included in the Copenhagen accession criteria, consensus among member states about minority rights is precluded by their political sensitivity, motivating the EU and the CE to cooperate on joint programmes in which the former provides the funding and the latter the expertise. Trechsel, who also recognises the differences between arrangements for the protection of individual and minority rights, advocates the creation of a European ombudsman for minority rights,[118]

---

[114] Furtado, 'Guess Who's Coming to Dinner?' pp. 365, 367, 369, 404–11; Alfredsson, 'Incomplete Painting'; Pentassuglia, 'Monitoring Minority Rights', pp. 417–20, 458–62.

[115] Philips, '10th Anniversary' pp. 183–5, 189. See also Kleinsorge, 'Parliamentary Assembly', pp. 81–2.

[116] T. E. Malloy, *National Minority Rights in Europe* (Oxford University Press, 2005), p. 289.

[117] Oeter, 'Protection of National Minorities', pp. 547–8.

[118] S. Trechsel, 'Human Rights and Minority Rights – Two Sides of the Same Coin? A Sketch' in P. Mahoney, F. Matscher, H. Petzold and L. Wildhaber (eds.), *Protecting*

while Swimelar, who advocates a combination of legal and political approaches, praises the work of the High Commissioner on National Minorities of the OSCE as an exemplar of 'preventive diplomacy'.[119]

The Human Rights Convention and the Court

As already indicated, the Convention for the Protection of Human Rights and Fundamental Freedoms (more commonly known as the European Convention on Human Rights, or ECHR), drafted by the CE in 1950 and in force from 1953, has been a condition of membership of the CE since its foundation.[120] As also observed in Chapter 1, the distinction drawn in the formal title between 'human rights' and 'fundamental freedoms' has attracted very little scholarly attention. Nor is it clear whether it is intended to be merely rhetorical or substantive or, if the latter, how precisely it is to be understood. One possibility is that the ECHR contains human rights, in the strict sense of entitlements deriving from basic elements of individual human wellbeing, as briefly discussed in the previous chapter, plus fundamental freedoms more widely conceived, including those also, or only, held by collective rights bearers in certain contexts. As also indicated in Chapter 1, the Convention's central objective is to provide an independent judicial process at Strasbourg which can authoritatively determine whether or not an ECHR right has been violated by a given member state. In addition to issuing rare advisory opinions by invitation of the CM,[121] the ECtHR considers whether the ECHR has been violated in one of two main ways: either through the inter-state or the individual applications processes.

The remainder of this chapter considers the substantive rights found in the ECHR, the inter-state and individual applications processes, the resolution of complaints by friendly settlement and adjudication of the merits, how the CM supervises execution of judgments and finally

---

Human Rights: The European Perspective – Studies in Memory of Rolv Ryssdal (Cologne: Carl Heymans, 2000) 1443–53 at 1452–3.

[119] S. Swimelar, 'Approaches to Ethnic Conflict and the Protection of Human Rights in Post-Communist Europe: The Need for Preventive Diplomacy' *Nationalism and Ethnic Politics* 7 (2001), 120–1.

[120] echr.coe.int/Documents/Convention_ENG.pdf.

[121] To date, the Committee of Ministers has made three requests for advisory opinions and the Court has delivered two – European Court of Human Rights, *Annual Report 2011*, 11, footnote 1, echr.coe.int/Documents/Annual_report_2011_ENG.pdf – figures confirmed by Court officials to the author as accurate up to the end of 2015.

the debates about pluralism, individual and constitutional justice and the Court's legitimacy and authority. An account of how Convention rights have been interpreted by the ECtHR can be found in Chapter 3.

Content of the ECHR

The Convention is similar in content to other international and national instruments which deal with civil and political rights. It contains fifty-nine Articles in two sections – 'Rights and Freedoms' and 'European Court of Human Rights' – plus six protocols providing additional rights. Article 1 requires member states 'to secure to everyone within their jurisdiction' the rights and freedoms the Convention contains while Articles 2–13 provide the rights to life; not to be subjected to torture or to inhuman or degrading treatment or punishment; not to be held in slavery or servitude or to be required to perform forced or compulsory labour; to freedom from arbitrary arrest and detention; to fair trial; not to be punished without law; to respect for private and family life, home and correspondence; to freedom of thought, conscience and religion; to freedom of expression; to freedom of assembly and association; to marry and to found a family; and to an effective remedy before a national authority. Article 14 states that the enjoyment of any Convention right shall be secured without discrimination on any ground such as sex, race, colour, language, religion, political or other opinion, national or social origin, association with a national minority, property, birth or other status. Article 15 provides for the suspension of all but a handful of rights 'in time of war or other public emergency threatening the life of the nation', provided such departures are 'strictly required by the exigencies of the situation' and are not incompatible with other international legal obligations. Article 16 states that nothing in Articles 10, 11 and 14 shall be regarded as preventing restrictions on the political activities of aliens. Article 17 prohibits anything in the Convention from being interpreted as implying the right to engage in any activity, or to perform any act, aimed at the destruction of any Convention right or freedom, or its limitation to a greater extent than the ECHR itself permits. Article 18 limits restrictions upon rights to those purposes expressly provided in the Convention itself.

The protocols adding further optional rights include Protocol No. 1, which contains rights to education, to the peaceful enjoyment of possessions and to free elections, and Protocol No. 4 which provides the rights not to be imprisoned for debt and to freedom of movement, the right of nationals not to be expelled from the state to which they belong and the right of aliens not to be collectively expelled. Protocol No. 6 abolishes the death penalty except in time of war, and Protocol No. 7 contains procedural safeguards regarding the expulsion of aliens, the right of appeal in criminal proceedings, the right to compensation for wrongful conviction, the right not to be tried or punished twice in the same state for the same offence and the equal right of spouses under the law. Protocol No. 12 outlaws discrimination in relation to any right 'set forth by law', in contrast with Article 14 ECHR, which prohibits discrimination only with respect to Convention rights. Protocol No. 13 outlaws the death penalty even in time of war.

Some maintain the largely civil and political rights provided by the Convention reflect an outdated and limited vision, and that social, economic, cultural and other ones should be added, by either judicial interpretation or express amendment.[122] But there are at least four compelling counter-arguments. First, as already indicated in Chapter 1, the Convention was never intended to promote human flourishing in the broadest sense, as a more comprehensive rights catalogue envisages, but rather to defend the character of democratic institutions in Europe through the medium of universal civil and political human rights. In spite of the momentous developments over the past half-century this remains its most important function. Second, including even a minimum corpus of social, economic and other rights would jeopardise the fragile resolution of the case overload crisis which has only recently begun. Third, it is not clear that judicialising social and economic rights is the best way of protecting or advancing the interests they represent,[123] not least because there is no direct correlation between the justiciability of such rights and high levels of social welfare in given states. The average citizen is much worse off, for example, in some countries, such as India, which have constitutionalised social and economic rights, than in others,

---

[122] For example, M. Dahlberg, 'Should Social Rights Be Included in Interpretations of the Convention by the European Court of Human Rights?' *European Journal of Social Security* 16 (2014), 252–76; E. Møse, 'New Rights for the New Court?' in P. Mahoney, F. Matscher, H. Petzold, H. and L. Wildhaber (eds.), *Protecting Human Rights: The European Perspective – Studies in Memory of Rolv Ryssdal* (Cologne: Carl Heymans, 2000), pp. 943–56; Lord Steyn, 'Laying the Foundations of Human Rights Law in the United Kingdom', *European Human Rights Law Review* [2005], 349–62, 352.

[123] For a review of the debate in central and eastern Europe see W. Sadurski, *Rights before Courts: A Study of Constitutional Courts in Postcommunist States of Central and Eastern Europe* (Dordrecht: Springer, 2005), ch. 7.

such as the Scandinavian countries, Australia and New Zealand, which have not. Clearly many other social, political and economic factors, including national prosperity and wealth distribution, are more important than constitutionalisation. Finally, the CE has established, for good reason, the separate European Social Charter already considered.

The Inter-State Applications Process

Although not frequently used, and less than a resounding success in correcting alleged violations, the inter-state applications process has, nevertheless, had considerable symbolic significance.[124] And, as Chapter 1 demonstrates, there is life in it yet. Applicant states lodge complaints against respondent states with the Court's Registry, which then manages applications, including corresponding with the parties, preparing cases for admissibility decisions, exploring the possibility of friendly settlement and scheduling admissible applications for adjudication. As a result of Protocol No. 14, the friendly settlement procedure (see below) can be initiated at any stage of the proceedings and not just post admissibility as hitherto. Upon receipt of an application the Registry informs the President of the Court, who then notifies the respondent state and allocates the complaint to one of the Court's five Sections. A seven-judge Chamber, including the judges elected in respect of applicant and respondent states, is then constituted to consider admissibility, the requirements for which are much less exacting than those for individual applications. The ECHR must have been binding on applicant and respondent states, and applicable to the persons concerned within the jurisdiction of the respondent state at the material time and place. Except where the allegation concerns legislation or an ongoing administrative practice, all domestic remedies must have been exhausted. The application must also have been lodged with the Registry within a period of six months from the date on which the final decision on the relevant subject matter was taken in the respondent state's legal system. A prima facie case in the formal sense is not required. But inter-state applications will be rejected as inadmissible if the allegations concerned are wholly unsubstantiated. Protocol No. 14 permits the CM to refer cases decided against respondent states back to the Court for clarification about the

---

[124] S. Greer, *The European Convention on Human Rights: Achievements, Problems and Prospects* (Cambridge University Press, 2006), pp. 24–8.

original judgment or for a ruling about compliance. The processes of friendly settlement, judgment of the merits and the roles of the Court's Grand Chamber and the CM are substantially the same as under the individual applications process as amended by Protocol No. 14 considered in the following section.

The Individual Applications Process

Broadly speaking there are three stages to the individual applications process: the formal lodging of complaints with the Registry, admission for or disposal of without adjudication, and formal adjudication of the merits. In order to make a formal complaint, applicants either need to write an introductory letter to the Registry or to apply online. The Registry's key functions are to manage petitions, including corresponding with applicants and states, preparing cases for decisions about admissibility, exploring the possibility of friendly settlement, and scheduling admissible applications for judgment on the merits. All written contact between an applicant and the Registry generates a file which is destroyed a year later if an application form has not been properly submitted. The form requires such things as personal particulars, identification of the respondent state, an outline of the grievance including an indication of which Convention rights have allegedly been violated, the object of the application (including any claim for compensation), confirmation that domestic remedies have been exhausted (including details of domestic court decisions where relevant) and that no more than six months have elapsed since the last decision on the matter by the domestic legal system. A special 'filtering' section has recently been set up in the Registry which, among other things, attempts to identify patterns or problematic issues for each state.[125] Legal aid is available for individual applicants who lack sufficient means.

In addition to full adjudication of the merits, considered later, complaints may be disposed of in one of five ways: they may be struck off the list because the applicant decides not to pursue them, the respondent state may satisfy the complainant by 'unilateral declaration', they may be resolved by friendly settlement, for any other reason further examination

---

[125] I. Cameron, 'The Court and the Member States: Procedural Aspects' in A. Føllesdal, B. Peters and G. Ulfstein (eds.), *Constituting Europe: The European Court of Human Rights in a National, European and Global Context* (Cambridge University Press, 2013), pp. 25–61, 33.

is no longer considered necessary or they are ruled inadmissible. Under Protocol No. 11 the management of formal applications was the responsibility of a Judge Rapporteur assisted by a case-processing lawyer from the Registry. The Judge Rapporteur examined and prepared the file, including requiring documents and further particulars from the parties, and channelled the complaint for an admissibility decision – together with proposals about its disposal – either to a three-judge committee, if it appeared to be clearly inadmissible, or to a Chamber of seven judges if its inadmissibility was not so clear. Under Article 28 ECHR a committee could, and still can, by unanimous and final decision, declare an application inadmissible, or strike it off the list, 'where such a decision can be taken without further examination'.[126] Cases which could not be settled unanimously were referred to a Chamber for a decision on admissibility and merits, together with a report from the Judge Rapporteur summarising the facts, indicating the issues raised, and making a proposal as to what should happen next, for example, a decision against admissibility or further correspondence with the parties.

As indicated in Chapter 1, Protocol No. 14 was opened for signature on 13 May 2004, yet was not implemented until 1 June 2010. In the intervening six years both the Registry and the Court redoubled their efforts to reduce the caseload. The Registry took a more robust approach to the receipt of complaints, including by providing an online admissibility checklist and by adhering more strictly to time limits.[127] For its part, in 2009, the Court amended Rule 41 of the Rules of Court requiring it to 'have regard to the importance and urgency of the issues' raised by applications. Seven categories of application were published in November 2010: urgent (Category I); capable of impacting upon the effectiveness of the Convention system or raising important questions of general interest (Category II); prima facie concern the 'core rights' found in Articles 2–4 or 5(1) ECHR as their main complaint (Category III); potentially well founded on other provisions (Category IV); repetitive and have already been dealt with in a pilot or leading judgment (Category V); raise a problem of admissibility (Category VI); or manifestly inadmissible (Category VII).[128]

When it came into effect, Protocol No. 14 altered the applications process in several ways. First, the Registry can now explore the possibility of friendly settlement on the basis of respect for human rights, and offer

[126] ECHR, Art 28(a).
[127] Cameron, 'The Court and the Member States', pp. 28–9.
[128] ECtHR, *The Court's Priority Policy*, echr.coe.int/Documents/Priority_policy_ENG.pdf.

advice about the terms, at any stage of the proceedings and not just post admissibility as before. In individual cases such settlements typically involve offers of money by the respondent state, some other benefit – for example, a residence permit the applicant claims to have been deprived of by the alleged violation – and sometimes an undertaking to make legislative or policy changes. But these are very marginal to the Court's activities. Between 1959 and 2016 friendly settlement/striking out of judgments accounted for only 5.6 per cent of the total number of judgments (1,094 out of 19,570).[129] Second, all formal applications are now channelled to 'judicial formations' consisting of a single judge and registry rapporteur rather than to three-judge committees. The judge elected with respect to a particular state is not, however, permitted to sit on a formation hearing applications against that state. While the rapporteur continues to manage the file containing all relevant documents, the judge can reject as inadmissible, or strike off the Court's list, the vast majority of applications where such a decision can be taken without further examination. The remainder are directed to a committee or Chamber. However, according to Cameron, while the single-judge procedure 'preserves the form of a judicial determination of each application, ... in practice, in almost all cases, it is the non-judicial rapporteur who decides'.[130] Unanimous committees of three judges are now also able to decide simultaneously on admissibility and to judge the merits of those applications which, according to well-established Convention case law, disclose clear-cut violations. While states may contest recourse to this procedure, they cannot veto it. The judge elected with respect to the respondent state may be invited to participate as a member of a three-judge committee, particularly when the exhaustion of domestic remedies is at issue.

Protocol No. 14 also adds a new admissibility test to those already provided. As before, individual applications can be ruled inadmissible if the applicant (including legal persons and non-governmental organisations) was not a victim of a Convention violation, redress has not been sought through the national legal system as far as it could have been taken ('exhaustion of domestic remedies'), more than six months have elapsed between the last national decision on the matter and formal application to Strasbourg, the complaint is substantially the same as

---

[129] ECtHR, *Violation by Article and by States (1959–2016)*, echr.coe.int/Documents/Stats_ violation_1959_2016_ENG.pdf.

[130] Cameron, 'The Court and the Member States', p. 33.

one already examined, it is incompatible with the Convention, it is an abuse of process and/or it is 'manifestly ill-founded' (it obviously has no hope of being settled in the applicant's favour). The Court can also now reject as inadmissible complaints by applicants where no significant disadvantage has been suffered, providing the issue has been 'duly considered' by a domestic tribunal.[131] Until 2012 this test could only be applied by Chambers and the Grand Chamber and in 2015 only 0.1 per cent of cases declared inadmissible were disposed of in this manner.[132]

By the end of 2015, the combined effect of Protocol No. 14, the priority policy, the Registry's stricter approach to the receipt of complaints and the possibility that some applicants may have been deterred by the length of time it takes the Court to hear complaints[133] at last seemed to be reducing the scale of the case overload crisis. Between 2000 and 2016 inclusive, a total of 741,100 individual complaints were formally received ('allocated to a judicial formation'), an annual average of 43,594.[134] In 2014 the number of applications allocated to a judicial formation fell from an all-time high of 65,800 the previous year to 56,200, dropping further in 2015 to 40,600, while the backlog of those awaiting a decision also declined, from a historic peak of 151,600 in 2011 to 69,900 in 2014 and to 64,850 in 2015.[135] Between November 1998 and December 2010 only 3.8 per cent of applications allocated to a judicial formation were declared admissible.[136] But between 2000 and 2016 inclusive this figure had risen to just below 14 per cent.[137] However, although it is too early to say whether they constitute merely a temporary blip or the beginning of a new phase, the figures for 2016 also show significant reversals in some of these trends. For example, by the end of 2016 the

[131] Art 35(3)(b). See N. Vogiatzis, 'The Admissibility Criterion under Article 35(3)(b) ECHR: A "Significant Disadvantage" to Human Rights Protection', *International and Comparative Law Quarterly* 65 (2016), 185–211; D. Shelton, 'Significantly Disadvantaged? Shrinking Access to the European Court of Human Rights', *Human Rights Law Review* 16 (2016), 303–32.

[132] Information supplied by an official at the ECtHR on 2 March 2016.

[133] ECtHR, *Annual Report 2013* (Strasbourg: Council of Europe, 2014), p. 25, echr.coe.int/Documents/Annual_report_2013_ENG.pdf; ECtHR, *Annual Report 2012* (Strasbourg: Council of Europe, 2013), p. 48, hechr.coe.int/Documents/Annual_report_2012_ENG.pdf.

[134] ECtHR, *Analysis of Statistics 2016* (Strasbourg: Council of Europe – European Court of Human Rights, 2017), p. 7, echr.coe.int/Documents/Stats_analysis_2016_ENG.pdf.

[135] *Ibid.*, p. 7.

[136] ECtHR, *Annual Report 2010*, p. 155, www.echr.coe.int/NR/rdonlyres/F2735259-F638-4E83-82DF-AAC7E934A1D6/0/2010_Rapport_Annuel_EN.pdf.

[137] ECtHR, *Analysis of Statistics 2016*, pp. 7 and 9.

number of applications allocated to a judicial formation rose to 53,500[138] and, of a total case load of 79,750 applications, 1.1 per cent fell into Category I, 0.4 per cent were Category II, 23.6 per cent were Category III, 26.5 per cent were Category IV, 43.6 per cent were Category V and 4.8 were Category VI or VII.[139] By the end of January 2017, of the total cases pending, 30,500 were repetitive, 11,500 were 'priority',[140] and some 21,000 – which according to the *Annual Report 2016* constitute 'the greatest weight' on the Court's docket – were neither clearly inadmissible nor repetitive.[141] The Court has itself declared that, although more priority applications are being processed and adjudicated than before, 'this will not be sufficient' for 'substantial inroads' to be made 'into the backlog of Chamber cases', and that further reflection on 'new working methods and approaches to further streamline the proceedings for different categories of applications' will be required.[142] By the end of 2016, 85.7 per cent of pending applications were against ten countries (percentage in brackets) – Ukraine (22.8), Turkey (15.8), Hungary (11.2), Russia (9.8), Romania (9.3), Italy (7.8), Georgia (2.6), Poland (2.3), Azerbaijan (2.1) and Armenia (2.0).[143]

In particularly urgent cases, where serious consequences such as death or torture could ensue before the matter is finally resolved, a Chamber may 'indicate to the parties any interim measure which it considers should be adopted'.[144] Since the Grand Chamber's judgment in *Mamatkulov and Askarov v Turkey*,[145] the Court regards these as binding on respondent states with, in most cases, failure to comply constituting a violation of the obligation under Article 34 ECHR not to hinder the right of individual application. Breaches are, however, uncommon. Until 2006 there was an annual average of about 100 such 'Rule 39 requests'.[146] But, between 2008 and 2012 the annual average reached 2,822, mostly in cases involving imminent expulsion or extradition. Of these 23.3 per cent

[138] *Ibid.*, p. 7.
[139] *Ibid.*, p. 9; ECtHR, *The Court's Priority Policy*.
[140] ECtHR, *Annual Report 2016* (Strasbourg: Council of Europe – European Court of Human Rights, 2017), p. 18, echr.coe.int/Documents/Annual_report_2016_ENG.pdf.
[141] *Ibid.*, pp. 13–14.
[142] ECtHR, *Analysis of Statistics 2016*, p. 5; ECtHR, *Annual Report 2016*, p. 19.
[143] ECtHR, *Analysis of Statistics 2016*, p. 8.
[144] Rules of Court, rule 39.
[145] (GC), HUDOC 4 February 2005.
[146] C. Harby, 'The Changing Nature of Interim Measures before the European Court of Human Rights' (2010), *European Human Rights Law*, pp. 73–84.

were granted, 53 per cent refused and 23.7 per cent were deemed to fall outside the scope of the provision.[147] Between 2014 and 2016 inclusive there were 5,677 Rule 39 requests, an annual average of 1,892, of which 506 (8.9 per cent) were granted.[148]

The increased application rate over the past two decades has also been reflected in the delivery of more judgments. Between 1959 and 1999 fewer than 1,000 were rendered.[149] Yet, by the end of 2016, the figure had risen to a grand total of 19,570.[150] Between 2000 and 2016 the Court delivered an annual average of 1,092 judgments, including 695 in 2000, the year with the fewest within this timeframe, and 1,625 in 2009, the year with the most.[151] Eighty-four per cent of judgments,[152] and 92 per cent of judgments on the merits, result in a finding of at least one violation.[153] From 1959 to 2016 the provisions most frequently found to have been breached were the right to fair trial under Article 6 (40.32 per cent, 21.34 per cent of which concerned length of proceedings), the right to liberty and security under Article 5 (12.86 per cent), the right to peaceful enjoyment of possessions under Article 1 of Protocol No. 1 (11.93 per cent), the right not to be tortured, etc. under Article 3 (10.71 per cent), the right to an effective remedy under Article 13 (8.39 per cent), the right to respect for private and family life under Article 8 (4.69 per cent) and the right to life under Article 2 (4.58 per cent).[154] Only a

---

[147] ECtHR, *Rule 39 requests granted and refused in 2008, 2009, and 2010, 2011 and 2012 by responding state*, echr.coe.int/Documents/Stats_art_39_2008_2012_ENG.pdf; T. Zwart, 'More Human Rights than Court: Why the Legitimacy of the ECtHR Is in Need of Repair and How It Can Be Done', in S. Flogaitis et al. (eds.), *The European Court of Human Rights and Its Discontents*, pp. 71–95, 94–5.

[148] ECtHR, *Rule 39 Requests Granted and Refused in 2014, 2015 and 2016 by Respondent State*, (Strasbourg: Council of Europe, 2016), echr.coe.int/Documents/Stats_understand ing_ENG.pdf.

[149] ECtHR, *Annual Report 2011*, (Council of Europe: Strasbourg, 2012), p. 12, echr.coe.int/ Documents/Annual_report_2011_ENG.pdf.

[150] ECtHR, *Violations by Article and by State 1959–2016*, www.echr.coe.int/Documents/ Stats_violation_1959_2016_ENG.pdf.

[151] ECtHR, *Analysis of Statistics 2016*, p. 10.

[152] European Court of Human Rights, *Overview 1959–2016 ECHR*, p. 3, echr.coe.int/Docu ments/Overview_19592016_ENG.pdf.

[153] Judgments on the merits refers to 'Judgments finding at least one violation' plus 'Judgments finding no violation', ECtHR, *Violation by Article and by States (1959–2016)*.

[154] ECtHR, *Overview 1959–2016 ECHR*, p. 6. Regrettably, due to an error, p. 154, line 13 of S. Greer and F. Wylde, 'Has the European Court of Human Rights Become a "Small Claims Tribunal" and Why, If at All, Does It Matter?' *European Human Rights Law Review* [2017], 146–55 should read 'only a handful of provisions regularly feature in judgments', not 'are regularly been found to have been breached'.

small minority of states dominate the Court's docket and are repeatedly in receipt of adverse judgments. Between 1959 and 2016, more than 50 per cent of the total number of judgments (9,978 out of 19,570) and 8,767 of the 16,399 findings of at least one violation (53 per cent) involved only five states (figure in brackets – findings of at least one violation): Turkey (2,889), Italy (1,791), Russia (1,834), Romania (1,147) and Ukraine (1,106).[155]

Admissible applications not otherwise disposed of are usually judged by Chambers of seven judges – with sometimes scores or even hundreds of applications and applicants involved in a single judgment.[156] While Protocol No. 14 permits the establishment of five-judge chambers, these have not yet been established on account of difficulties in empanelling and the challenge posed to the maintenance of internal consistency in the case law.[157] Judgments, which rely mostly on written submissions from the parties (with oral public hearings in certain cases), are drafted by a Judge Rapporteur assisted by the judge elected in respect of the respondent state (or sometimes by a drafting committee), and put to a vote of all judges sitting on the particular panel. In exceptional circumstances the Court may, at its discretion, embark on fact-finding missions in respondent states.[158] Typically judgments contain summaries of the facts, the history of the dispute including a review of relevant domestic law, the arguments presented by both parties, relevant provisions of the ECHR, a concise statement of the substantive result plus concurring and dissenting opinions if any.

Subject to the consent of the parties, a Chamber may relinquish jurisdiction to a Grand Chamber of seventeen judges where the application raises a serious question affecting the interpretation of the ECHR or where there is a possibility of a departure from previous case law. Although this is not expressly limited to applications formally declared admissible, by definition, no inadmissible application could fulfil this test. Relinquishment to the Grand Chamber occurs typically in less than 1 per cent of cases.[159] A Chamber's verdict, whether unanimous or by majority, usually

---

[155] ECtHR, *Violations by Article and by States (1959–2016)*.

[156] There were 475 applications, for example, in *Gaglioni v Italy*, judgment of 21 December 2010.

[157] Cameron, 'The Court and the Member States', p. 35.

[158] P. Leach, C. Paraskeva and G. Uzelac, 'Human Rights Fact-Finding: The European Court of Human Rights at a Crossroads', *Netherlands Quarterly of Human Rights* 28 (2010), 41–77.

[159] A. Mowbray, 'An Examination of the Work of the Grand Chamber of the European Court of Human Rights', *Public Law* [2007] 507, 509.

disposes of the matter. However, rarely, exceptional cases may also be referred by one or more of the parties to the Grand Chamber within three months of the original judgment.[160] Technically, such referrals are not 'appeals', but 're-hearings', and are conditional upon the approval of the Grand Chamber's five-judge 'admissibility' panel, which is obliged to accede to them where the case in question raises, according to Article 43 (2) ECHR, 'a serious question affecting the interpretation or application of the Convention or the protocols thereto, or a serious issue of general importance'. Judgments of Chambers become final under three circumstances: when the parties declare that they will not request a reference to the Grand Chamber, three months after the date of judgment if a reference to the Grand Chamber has not been made, or where such a reference has been made but the five-judge panel has rejected it.

Historically the Court has contented itself with merely declaring whether or not any given application discloses a Convention violation. However, it has recently shown greater willingness to indicate the general type of remedial action required,[161] such as a criminal investigation, the release of an applicant from detention or reinstatement to a previously held post.[162] This is also true of the small number of so-called pilot judgments where the primary aim is to stem floods of similar complaints to Strasbourg. For example, in *Broniowski v Poland* it was held that the applicant's right to the peaceful enjoyment of possessions under Article 1 Protocol No. 1 had been violated by state expropriation of his property coupled with the payment of inadequate compensation. While in itself not an unprecedented outcome, the judgment added that, since this violation 'originated in a widespread problem which resulted from a malfunctioning of Polish legislation and administrative practice ... which has affected and remains capable of affecting a large number of persons',[163] appropriate measures were required to secure an adequate

[160] *Ibid.*, pp. 512, 513 and 518.
[161] T. Zwart, 'More Human Rights than Court', pp. 86–7; see also P. Leach, 'No Longer Offering Fine Mantras to a Parched Child? The European Court's Developing Approach to Remedies' in Føllesdal et al. (eds.), *Constituting Europe*; L.-I. Sicilianos, 'The Involvement of the European Court of Human Rights in the Implementation of its Judgments: Recent Developments under Article 46 ECHR', *Netherlands Quarterly of Human Rights* 32 (2014), 235–62.
[162] *Al Nashiri v Poland*, HUDOC, 24 July 2014, paras. 587–9; *Ataykaya v Turkey*, HUDOC, 24 July 2014, para. 75; *Oleksandr Volkov v Ukraine*, HUDOC, 9 January 2013, para. 208; *Aleksanyan v Russia*, HUDOC, 22 December 2008, para. 240.
[163] *Broniowski v Poland* (GC), HUDOC, 22 June 2004, para 189.

right to compensation or redress, not simply for the particular applicant, but for all similar potential claimants.[164] Subsequent applications complaining of violations stemming from the same state of affairs have, therefore, been directed back to the Polish authorities to settle according to the terms of this judgment without the Court having to reconsider the merits afresh in each instance. According to Leach et al., pilot judgments have been 'relatively successful' in some contexts but less so in others.[165] Perhaps not surprisingly, the key factor is the cooperation of respondent states, particularly recognition of the specific systemic problem by national constitutional or other higher courts before a pilot judgment has been delivered. A lack of cooperation at the national level may also be due to 'the extent of the political will ... the domestic political agenda, the status of the Convention in national law,... technical capacity and financial burdens'.[166] The authors also cite 'reputational pressures' but do not fully explain what these are.

Even if a judgment declares that there has been a Convention violation, an award of compensation is not automatic and, although some general principles have been identified, the relevant case law is not consistent.[167] Excluding claims under Article 1 of Protocol No. 1 (which reflect the value of the property involved) and other outliers, the average compensation per applicant is in the region of €8,300, tending to confirm that the Court has become a 'human rights small claims tribunal' rather than a 'tribunal of principle', to which many including the authors of this

---

[164] *Ibid.*, para 200.

[165] P. Leach, H. Hardman, S. Stephenson and B. K. Blitz, *Responding to Systematic Human Rights Violations – An Analysis of 'Pilot Judgments' of the European Court of Human Rights and Their Impact at National Level* (Antwerp: Intersentia, 2010), p. 178. See also T. Sainati, 'Human Rights Class Actions: Rethinking the Pilot-Judgment Procedure at the European Court of Human Rights', *Harvard International Law Journal* 56 (2015), 147–206; S. Wallace, 'Much Ado about Nothing? The Pilot Judgment Procedure at the European Court of Human Rights', *European Human Rights Law Review* [2011], 71–81; P. Leach, H. Hardman and S. Stephenson, 'Can the European Court's Pilot Judgment Procedure Help Resolve Systemic Human Rights Violations? *Burdov* and the Failure to Implement Domestic Court Decisions in Russia', *Human Rights Law Review* 10 (2010), 346–59; W. Sadurski, 'Partnering with Strasbourg: Constitutionalisation of the European Court of Human Rights, the Accession of Central and East European States to the Council of Europe, and the Idea of Pilot Judgments', *Human Rights Law Review* 9 (2009), 397–453 .

[166] Leach et al., *Responding to Systematic Human Rights Violations*, p. 179; Cameron, 'The Court and Member States', p. 38.

[167] O. Ichim, *Just Satisfaction under the European Convention on Human Rights* (Cambridge University Press, 2015), pp. 1–6, 271–6.

book argue it should instead aspire.[168] While the Court generally seeks to remain faithful to its own previous decisions, these do not constitute formally binding precedents, nor is there much doctrinal exposition as in the common law tradition. Most judgments on the merits, therefore, amount to little more than decisions on the facts where the precise circumstances of the dispute are held to constitute or not to constitute a violation of the Convention, but which establish little of general application beyond.

Before it became apparent that the case load had begun to decrease, various proposals for further micro-bureaucratic refinements to the Convention system were considered by the CE at a series of high-level conferences on the future of the Court held in Interlaken in 2010, Izmir in 2011, Brighton in 2012 and Brussels in 2015. By 2013 two further procedural protocols had emerged. Protocol No. 15, which was opened for signature on 24 June 2013, has not yet come into effect. When it does, it will have universal effect and will require candidates for appointment to the ECtHR to be less than sixty-five years of age when the three-person lists are requested by PACE, abolish the right of parties to veto relinquishment to the Grand Chamber, shorten from six to four months the time limit within which applications to the Court must be made from the last decision by the national legal system on the matter, include a reference to subsidiarity and the margin of appreciation in the Preamble to the Convention and remove the requirement from Article 35(3)(b) that an application should have been 'duly considered by a domestic tribunal' before it can be rejected as inadmissible on the grounds that the applicant has suffered 'no significant disadvantage'.[169] A further optional protocol, No. 16 – which permits national courts to request, in ongoing litigation, discretionary, non-binding advisory opinions from the Grand Chamber regarding matters of principle relating to the interpretation and application of Convention rights – was opened for signature on 2 October 2013 but has also not yet entered into force.[170] However, whether it will ever meet its core objectives – contributing to docket control and enhancing judicial dialogue between Strasbourg and national courts – is open

---

[168] Greer and Wylde, 'Has the European Court of Human Rights Become a "Small Claims Tribunal"'.

[169] *Protocol No. 15 Amending the Convention for the Protection of Human Rights and Fundamental Freedoms*, CETS No. 213, conventions.coe.int/Treaty/en/Treaties/html/213.htm.

[170] *Protocol No. 16 to the Convention for the Protection of Human Rights and Fundamental Freedoms*, CETS, No. 214, coe.int/en/web/conventions/full-list/-/conventions/treaty/214.

to question not least because of doubts about how often it will be used, and how effective it will be if and when it is.[171]

Supervision of the Execution of Judgments

Once a judgment finding a violation has been delivered, supervision of its execution passes to the CM, which considers whether the obligation under Article 46(1) ECHR, to 'abide by the final judgment of the Court', has been discharged.[172] Since this is a matter for negotiation, the respondent state effectively participates in supervising enforcement against itself. Judgments, including those involving friendly settlement, are referred to the Committee (i.e. the Deputies) by the Directorate of Human Rights and Rule of Law as soon as they are received, and are entered on the agendas of the Committee's special human rights meetings, which the Directorate also drafts and makes public. In order to manage its own workload, mushrooming in tandem with that of the Court, since 2010 the Committee has distinguished between those judgments which require 'standard' and those requiring 'enhanced' supervision. The former are largely managed by self-reporting on a publicly accessible web-based database, while the latter require more thorough consideration.

At its human rights meetings the CM first invites the respondent state to provide it with information about the remedial measures taken in response to the judgment. Applicants are not represented at these meetings, but are entitled to communicate with the CM about the implementation of individual measures including the payment of compensation.

---

[171] B. Thorarensen, 'The Advisory Jurisdiction of the ECtHR under Protocol No. 16: Enhancing Domestic Implementation or Human Rights or a Symbolic Step' in O. Mjöll Arnardóttir and A. Buyse (eds.), *Shifting Centres of Gravity in Human Rights Protection: Rethinking Relations between the ECHR, EU and National Legal Orders* (London: Routledge, 2016), pp. 79–100, 99; Cameron, 'The Court and the Member States', p. 50; K. Dzehtsiarou and N. O'Meara, 'Advisory Jurisdiction and the European Court of Human Rights: A Magic Bullet for Dialogue and Docket Control?', *Legal Studies* 34 (2014), 444–68. For a critique of the post-Brighton developments see S. Greer and L. Wildhaber, 'Revisiting the Debate about "Consitutionalising" the European Court of Human Rights', *Human Rights Law Review* 12 (2012), 655, 660–1.

[172] See E. Lambert-Abdelgawad, 'The Court as a Part of the Council of Europe: The Parliamentary Assembly and the CM' in Føllesdal et al. (eds.), *Constituting Europe*; M. Suchkova, 'An Analysis of the Institutional Arrangements within the Council of Europe and within Certain Member States for Securing the Enforcement of Judgments', *European Human Rights Law Review* [2011], 448–63.

Cases are listed for consideration at six-monthly intervals until the CM is satisfied that the violation has been properly addressed. While awaiting final execution, interim resolutions may be passed simply noting that this has not yet occurred, reporting progress and encouraging completion or threatening the respondent state with more serious measures if full compliance is further delayed. When it is satisfied that any compensation has been paid, and that any other necessary measures have been introduced, the CM publicly certifies that its responsibilities under Article 46 (2) ECHR have been discharged. This can take years, for example, more than eight and a half in the notoriously protracted case of *Marcks* v *Belgium*,which involved discrimination between legitimate and illegitimate children in the law of affiliation.[173] Not surprisingly, the Court's workload problems have also been mirrored in the enforcement process, with 9,941 cases pending by the end of 2016. Of these 8,448 (85 per cent) were repetitive – applications raising complaints already condemned in the specific respondent state stemming mostly from the absence of effective local remedies including difficulties with the enforcement of domestic court judgments.[174]

In the past the Committee's supervision of the execution of judgments was generally regarded as 'lax and deferential to national authorities'.[175] In particular, what was deemed to constitute sufficient evidence of execution varied from case to case with little apparent rationale.[176] While commentators claim this has since improved, particularly with the issuing of 'consequential orders' requiring certain kinds of remedial action,[177] the supervision process does not, of itself, ensure that the

---

[173] A. Tomkins, 'The Committee of Ministers: Its Roles under the European Convention on Human Rights', *European Human Rights Law Review*, [1995], 49–62, 61.

[174] Committee of Ministers, *Supervision of the Execution of Judgments and Decisions of the European Court of Human Rights: 10th Annual Report of the Committee of Ministers 2016*, p. 52, rm.coe.int/CoERMPublicCommonSearchServices/DisplayDCTMContent? documentId=0900001680706a3d; Cameron, 'The Court and the Member States', pp. 39–42.

[175] D. Anagnostou, 'Introduction – Untangling the Domestic Implementation of the European Court of Human Rights' Judgments' in D. Anagnostou (ed.), *The European Court of Human Rights: Implementing Strasbourg's Judgments on Domestic Policy* (Edinburgh: Edinburgh University Press, 2013), p. 7.

[176] Tomkins, 'The Committee of Ministers', 59–60; Y. S. Klerk, 'Supervision of the Execution of the Judgments of the European Court of Human Rights – the Committee of Ministers' Role under Article 54 of the European Convention on Human Rights', *Netherlands International Law Review* 45 (1998) 65–86, 77–8.

[177] A. Seibert-Fohr and M. Villiger, 'Current Challenges in European Multilevel Human Rights Protection' in A. Seibert-Foh and M. Villiger (eds.), *Judgments of the European*

source of violations is effectively addressed.[178] According to Suckova 'very few states have in place effective mechanisms and procedures (either in the executive or in the legislature) to ensure that the Court's judgments are complied with rapidly and fully so that new violations of similar kinds do not arise'.[179] A great deal will depend upon national circumstances, particularly the willingness and capacity of states to do what is required. Systemic sources of violation may be difficult to correct for various reasons including a lack of clarity in the relevant judgment, political problems, the daunting scale of the reforms required, managing complex legislative procedures, budgetary issues, adverse public opinion, the possible impact of compliance on obligations deriving from other institutions and bureaucratic inertia.[180]

Protocol No. 14 facilitates the involvement of the Court in the supervision of the execution of its own judgments in two ways, each activated by a two-thirds majority vote of the CM, but with no prospect of financial penalties or of re-opening the original verdict. First, where execution is hindered by problems in determining what the judgment means, the ECtHR may be called upon to provide further clarification. Second, the CM will be able to refer to the Grand Chamber the question of whether the respondent state has complied with the original judgment. Neither procedure has yet been used.[181] And if it ever is, it is likely to be rare. At the end of the supervision of the execution of judgments process, there is

Court of Human Rights – Effects and Implementation (Baden-Baden: Nomos/Ashgate, 2013), p. 18.

[178] C. Hillebrecht, 'The Power of Human Rights Tribunals: Compliance with the European Court of Human Rights and Domestic Policy Change', *European Journal of International Relations*, 20 (2014), 1100–23; E. Voeten, 'Domestic Implementation of European Court of Human Rights Judgments: Legal Infrastructure and Government Effectiveness Matter: A Reply to Dia Anagnostou and Alina Mungiu-Pippidi', *European Journal of International Law*, 25 (2014), 229–38; Anagnostou, 'Introduction' and 'Politics, Courts and Society in the National Implementation and Practice of European Court of Human Rights Case Law' in Anagnostou (ed.), *European Court of Human Rights*; L. Miara and V. Prais, 'The Role of Civil Society in the Execution of Judgments of the European Court of Human Rights', *European Human Rights Law Review* [2012], 528–53; E. Lambert-Abdelgawad, *The Execution of Judgments of the European Court of Human Rights* (Strasbourg: Council of Europe Publishing, Human Rights Files no. 19, 2002).

[179] Suchkova, 'Analysis', p. 462.

[180] Steering Committee for Human Rights (CDDH), *Guaranteeing the Long-Term Effectiveness of the Control System of the European Convention on Human Rights – Addendum to the Final Report Containing CDDH Proposals (long version) (9 April 2003)*, 34. See also Palmer, 'CM 2015', p. 103.

[181] Information provided to the author by officials at the European Court of Human Rights.

very little the CE can do with a state persistently in violation, short of suspending its voting rights on the CM or expelling it altogether, each of which is likely to prove counterproductive in all but the most extreme circumstances.

Pluralism, Individual and Constitutional Justice

The recent case-overload crisis fuelled debates about the Court's efficacy (its substantive impact upon the protection of Convention rights at the grass roots),[182] its efficiency (resource-effectiveness)[183] and its legitimacy and authority (shared understandings within given constituencies about, respectively, its raison d'être, and how it should discharge its responsibilities).[184] Assuming, as most informed commentators do, that the ECtHR should exist as a fully operational institution with appropriate

---

[182] See the literature on national compliance with the judgments of the European Court of Human Rights, e.g., C. Hillebrecht, *Domestic Politics and International Human Rights Tribunals* (Cambridge University Press, 2014); D. Anagnostou (ed.), *The European Court of Human Rights*; C. Hillebrecht, 'The Power of Human Rights Tribunals'; Voeten, 'Domestic Implementation of European Court of Human Rights Judgments', 229–38; A. Seibert-Fohr and M. Villiger (eds.), *Judgments of the European Court of Human Rights*; Anagnostou, 'Introduction' and 'Politics, Courts and Society'; L. Miara and V. Prais, 'The Role of Civil Society'; E. Lambert-Abdelgawad, *The Execution of Judgments of the European Court of Human Rights*; H. Keller and A. Stone Sweet (eds.), *A Europe of Rights*; Greer, *European Convention on Human Rights*, ch. 2.

[183] Y. Shany, 'Assessing the Effectiveness of International Courts – A Goal-Based Approach', *American Journal of International Law* 106 (2012), 225–70.

[184] See, e.g., B. Oomen, 'A Serious Case of Strasbourg-Bashing? An Evaluation of the Debates on the Legitimacy of Human Rights in the Netherlands', *International Journal of Human Rights* 20 (2016), 407–25; A. Føllesdal, J. Schaffer and G. Ulfstein (eds.), *The Legitimacy of International Human Rights Regimes: Legal, Political and Philosophical Perspectives* (Cambridge University Press, 2014); B. Çali, A. Koch and N. Bruch, 'The Legitimacy of Human Rights Courts: A Grounded Interpretivist Analysis of the European Court of Human Rights', *Human Rights Quarterly* 35 (2013), 955–84; T. Zwart, 'More Human Rights than Court: Why the Legitimacy of the European Court of Human Rights Is in Need of Repair and How It Can Be Done', pp. 71–95, and E. Myjer, 'Why Much of the Criticism of the European Court of Human Rights Is Unfounded', pp. 37–53, in S. Flogaitis et al. (eds.), *The European Court of Human Rights and Its Discontents*; S. Hennette-Vauchez, 'Constitutional v International: When Unified Reformatory Rationales Mismatch the Plural Paths of Legitimacy of ECHR Law' in J. Christoffersen and M. Madsen (eds.), *The European Court of Human Rights between Law and Politics* (Oxford University Press, 2011), pp. 144–63; A. Føllesdal, 'The Legitimacy of International Human Rights Review: The Case of the European Court of Human Rights', *Journal of Social Philosophy* 40 (2009), 595–607.

procedure and norms,[185] we first need to recognise that there are degrees of efficacy, efficiency and legitimacy/authority. While efficiency is largely a cost–benefit issue, what counts as efficacy will depend critically upon whether the contribution the ECtHR makes is conceived primarily in terms of the provision of individual remedies (especially compensation) for all applicants with a credible claim that their Convention rights have been violated ('individual justice'), whether it is conceived in terms of addressing systemic problems ('constitutional justice') with, up to a point, states deemed capable of discharging it themselves ('constitutional plural-ism') and whether either function is, or both are, regarded simply as one of several the Court does and should fulfil ('functional pluralism').[186]

The diminishing scale of the case overload problem has not, however, brought the curtain down on these debates.[187] Indeed, the question of the Court's legitimacy and authority, considered later in the Legitimacy and Authority section, has become sharper and much more visible since.[188] The many proposals, some mutually conflicting, currently touted as offering improvements to efficacy and efficiency, some rehearsed since the beginning of the case overload crisis and even before, include increasing/reducing the number of judges; better administrative support from the Registry; excluding as inadmissible applications which are not particularly serious; clustering repetitive complaints; referring manifestly well-founded applications back to national authorities or for pilot judg-ment; penalising states slow to pay compensation by doubling the amount after six months and then again after a year and so on; a requirement on states to provide ECHR-impact assessments for all draft legislation; and replacing the CM with a Committee of Supervision for the execution of judgments.[189]

---

[185] For a rare dissenting voice see A. Williams, 'The European Convention on Human Rights, the EU and the UK: Confronting a Heresy', *European Journal of International Law* 24 (2013), 1157–85.

[186] Shany, 'Assessing the Effectiveness of International Courts', 263–5; L. Helfer and A-M. Slaughter, 'Toward a Theory of Effective Supranational Adjudication', *Yale Law Journal* 107 (1997), 273–392.

[187] A. Føllesdal, B. Peters and G. Ulfstein, 'Conclusions' in Føllesdal et al. (eds.), *Constituting Europe*, p. 389, 392–4.

[188] See A. Føllesdal, 'Much Ado about Nothing? International Judicial Review of Human Rights in Well-Functioning Democracies' in Føllesdal et al. (eds.), *The Legitimacy of International Human Rights Regimes*.

[189] For useful summaries see J. Gerards and A. Terlouw, 'Solutions for the European Court of Human Rights: The *Amicus Curiae* Project', pp. 158–82, and J. Fraser, 'Conclusion: The European Court of Human Rights as a Common European Endeavour',

The 'official' CE contribution to the reform debate – dominated by
bureaucrats, diplomats and NGOs – was characterised by huge mountains of paperwork, containing repetitive detailed 'shopping lists' and
marked by a reluctance critically to examine core assumptions, systematically to identify a coherent governing framework or to consider the
questions of efficacy and legitimacy in any depth, if at all.[190] By contrast,
the 'academic' debate, dominated by some judges and by jurists and
scholars, involved much more serious and systematic attempts to discern
trends in the development of the Court and Convention system – and in
their interactions with national institutions, norms and processes – to
identify core contemporary functions given the seismic changes in the
wider European context since the 1950s, to diagnose the central problems
and to suggest coherent, integrated frameworks within which detailed
modifications could be identified and introduced. The two key questions
facing the Convention system were, and largely remain, first, how the CE
can best encourage the institutionalisation of those national processes
which both reduce the risk of violation of Convention rights by public
authorities in the first place and, where breaches have occurred, enable
them to be effectively addressed at national level.[191]

The available evidence indicates that the impact of the ECHR and
ECtHR 'varies widely across States and across time', and that this is

pp. 192–210, in Flogaitis et al. (eds.), *The European Court of Human Rights and Its
Discontents.*
[190] See, e.g., documents relating to the Interlaken conference (hereafter *Interlaken Docu-
ments*), coe.int/t/dc/files/events/2010_interlaken_conf/default_EN.asp?; A. Mowbray,
'The Interlaken Declaration – the Beginning of a New Era for the European Court of
Human Rights?' *Human Rights Law Review* (2010) 10, 519–28; R. Wolfrum and
U. Deutsch (eds.), *The European Court of Human Rights: Overwhelmed by Applications –
International Workshop, Heidelberg, 17–18 December 2007* (Berlin: Springer, 2007).
Preceding official CE conferences and colloquy on the future of the Court and Conven-
tion system since the finalisation of Protocol No. 14 include *Applying and Supervising the
ECHR: Towards Stronger Implementation of the European Convention on Human Rights
at the National Level*, Colloquy Organised under the Swedish Chairmanship of the
Committee of Ministers of the Council of Europe, Stockholm, 9–10 June 2008, Proceed-
ings (Strasbourg: Council of Europe, 2008); *Future Developments of the European Court
of Human Rights in the Light of the Wise Persons' Report*, Colloquy Organised by the San
Marino Chairmanship of the Committee of Ministers of the Council of Europe, San
Marino, 22–3 March 2007, Proceedings, *Human Rights Law Journal* (2007) 28, 1–40;
Report of the Group of Wise Persons to the CM, Cm(2006)203, 15 November 2006;
Applying and Supervising the ECHR: Reform of the European Human Rights System,
Proceedings of the High-Level Seminar, Oslo, 18 October 2004 (Strasbourg: Council of
Europe, 2004).
[191] Cameron, 'The Court and Member States', p. 58.

'broad and pervasive' in some but 'weak in others'.[192] While few European countries present serious persistent problems with fundamental rights, those with the longest-standing low annual average official violations, apart from the micro- and mini-states of a million or fewer inhabitants, include Ireland, Denmark, Norway and Sweden,[193] while, as already indicated, Turkey, Russia, Italy, Romania and Ukraine now have the most. However, according to calculations carried out a few years ago, when population sizes are included, Spain and Germany emerged with the fewest, and Slovakia, Italy and Greece with the most.[194] A more sophisticated ranking, which also controls for application rates, does not yet appear to have been compiled. The key to improvement in national Convention compliance appears to lie less in its formal incorporation in national legal systems, and more in its effective 'reception', i.e. its capacity to be invoked by individuals in litigation and regarded, in practice, by domestic courts as binding upon national public authorities and taking precedence over competing legal norms.[195] While the Strasbourg institutions can, and do, attempt to persuade states more effectively to 'embed'[196] Convention rights in their national processes, ultimately they lack any real coercive power to compel them do so.

The second question is how the scarce judicial resource represented by the Court could be deployed with maximum efficiency and efficacy. The models of individual and constitutional justice dominated the reform debate to which a third, pluralism, has been added relatively recently.[197] As already indicated, the former maintains that the Court exists primarily to provide redress for Convention violations for the benefit of the particular individual making the complaint, with whatever constitutional or systemic improvements at the national level might thereby result.[198]

---

[192] Heller and Stone Sweet, *Europe of Rights*, p. 4; F. Fabbrini, *Fundamental Rights in Europe: Challenges and Transformations in Comparative Perspective* (Oxford University Press, 2014), pp. 257–9.

[193] ECtHR, *Violation by Article and by States (1959–2016)*.

[194] Heller and Stone Sweet, *Europe of Rights*, p. 693.

[195] Anagnostou, 'Politics, Courts and Society'; Heller and Stone Sweet, *Europe of Rights*, pp. 14, 17, 683.

[196] L. Helfer, 'Redesigning the ECtHR: Embeddedness as a Deep Structural Principle of the European Human Rights Regime', *European Journal of International Law* 19 (2008), 125–59.

[197] See S. Greer, and L. Wildhaber, 'Revisiting the Debate about "Consitutionalising" the European Court of Human Rights', *Human Rights Law Review* 12 (2012), 655–87.

[198] See P. Egli, 'Protocol No. 14 to the European Convention for the Protection of Human Rights and Fundamental Freedoms: Towards a More Effective Control Mechanism?',

Perhaps not surprisingly, since three significant obstacles stand in the way, no coherent argument has yet been presented that this could and should be the Court's core function. First, as indicated in Chapter 1, the delivery of individual justice was not what the Convention system was originally set up for. At its inception it was intended to contribute to the peace of Western Europe in the context of the Cold War, by providing an independent, trans-national judicial forum capable of declaring authoritatively whether or not a member state was abusing the rights of its citizens. While the promotion of international peace in Europe at the trans-national level is now shared with other international institutions, not least the EU, the best and most credible conception of the Convention's fundamental role and rationale continue to be the defence of the character and integrity of European political, constitutional and legal systems through the language and medium of human rights, rather than benefiting individual applicants per se.

Second, as a result of the changes over the past half-century or so, there is no realistic prospect of justice being systematically delivered to every applicant with a legitimate complaint about a Convention violation. And, unless it is systematic, individual 'justice' becomes arbitrary and is, therefore, not justice at all. As already indicated, in any conceivable set of circumstances, the ECtHR, like national constitutional courts, is capable of judging about 10 per cent of the applications it receives, although more than 90 per cent of those judged on the merits result in a finding of at least one violation. Officially, 90 per cent or so of applications are rejected without adjudication because they fail the formal admissibility tests, for example, not being submitted in time, or being 'manifestly ill-founded', i.e. lacking an arguable case. But the 'manifestly ill-founded' criterion is not an objective test because determining whether an application has or has not satisfied it requires the exercise of judgment and the interpretation of conduct, facts and norms and is, therefore, inescapably discretionary.[199] If it were otherwise, the Court would not need to explain why an application is manifestly ill founded, as it sometimes does, and which other CE institutions increasingly require it to do. Indeed, some commentators

Journal of Transnational Law and Policy 17 (2007), 1–32; P. Leach, 'Access to the European Court of Human Rights – From a Legal Entitlement to a Lottery?' *Human Rights Law Journal* 27 (2006), 11–25.

[199] J. Gerards, 'Inadmissibility Decisions of the European Court of Human Rights: A Critique of the Lack of Reasoning', *Human Rights Law Review* 14 (2014), 148–58; Cameron, 'The Court and the Member States', p. 57.

maintain that many complaints are rejected on this basis simply because the Court does not have the resources to consider them properly.[200] Moreover, as already noted, although the right of individual petition has survived the reform process, this is largely a matter of hollow form rather than real substance. The priority policy has inescapably left many potentially well-founded applications withering on the vine, while the recent decline in the application rate may have been produced by changes in the process which have deterred some applicants with manifestly well-founded claims from lodging a complaint.[201]

Finally, for some applicants a judgment that their Convention rights have been violated may be a shallow victory because, as also already indicated, levels of compensation are generally not high and other rewards few. Although states never refuse to pay compensation where the ECtHR has ordered it, the 'justice' delivered to the lucky few otherwise tends to be more symbolic than material. For example, applicants who have managed to persuade the Court that their conviction for a criminal offence occurred in circumstances where their right to a fair trial was breached, will not automatically have their convictions quashed as a result, although criminal proceedings are now more likely to be reopened in such circumstances than was once the case.[202]

When we turn to the arguments for 'constitutionalisation' a curious paradox can be observed. 'Official' proposals about ECtHR's future have consistently dismissed suggestions that any kind of constitutionalisation might even be worth considering. The lack of a coherent defence of the case for 'individual justice' is mirrored on this side of the debate by the absence of a coherent critique of the arguments for constitutionalisation, 'constitutional justice' or 'constitutional pluralism'. Instead, all that has been offered are sweeping rejections of the very notion that the ECHR or ECtHR have any constitutional characteristics or functions, typically confined to a few sentences, and implicitly referenced to the narrow nation-state model.[203] By contrast, academic debates about the

---

[200] J. Simor and B. Emmerson (eds.), *Human Rights Practice* (London: Sweet and Maxwell, 2000), para 20.039.

[201] Cameron, 'The Court and Member States', pp. 28–9.

[202] L. Helfer, 'The Burdens and Benefits of Brighton', *European Society of International Law Reflections*, 1 (2012), esil-sedi.eu/node/138; Lambert-Abdelgawad, *The Execution of Judgments of the ECtHR* (Strasbourg: Council of Europe, Human Rights Files no. 19, 2002), pp. 15–17; Keller and Stone Sweet, *Europe of Rights*, p. 704.

[203] See Council of Europe Steering Committee for Human Rights (CDDH), *CDDH Report on the Longer-Term Future of the System of the European Convention on Human Rights,*

constitutionalisation of the Court and Convention,[204] and of international law and pan-national legal regimes more generally,[205] have spawned a sophisticated literature which has grown rapidly over the past few years, particularly since the reform debate started. While not all who have contributed to it endorse the case for constitutionalisation, or share the same conception of what it might mean, there can be no doubt that a sizable body of weighty academic opinion recognises and appreciates the implications of the ECtHR's constitutional characteristics and functions.

The central idea of 'constitutionalisation' in this context is that the Court's primary responsibility is, and should be, to select, and to adjudicate with maximum authority and impact, both in the given respondent state and in Europe generally, the most serious alleged ECHR violations brought to its attention by aggrieved applicants. This is 'constitutional'

CDDH(2015)R84 Addendum I, Strasbourg, 11 December 2015, paras. 90–5; *Contribution of the Secretary General of the CE to the Preparation of the Interlaken Ministerial Conference*, 18 December 2009, SG/Inf(2009), para. 28.

[204] See, e.g., F. De Londras, 'Dual Functionality and the Persistent Frailty of the European Court of Human Rights', *European Human Rights Law Review* [2013], 38–46; K. Dzehtsiarou and A. Greene, 'Restructuring the European Court of Human Rights: Preserving the Right of Individual Petition and Promoting Constitutionalism', *Public Law*, [2013], 710–19; G. Ulfstein, 'The European Court of Human Rights and National Courts: a Constitutional Relationship?' and B. Thorarensen, 'Advisory Jurisdiction of ECtHR under Protocol No. 16'; L. Wildhaber and S. Greer, ' Reflections of a Former President of the European Court of Human Rights', *European Human Rights Law Review* [2010], 165–75, 166–8; Sadurski, 'Partnering with Strasbourg'; R. White and I. Boussiakou, 'Voices from the European Court of Human Rights' *Netherlands Quarterly of Human Rights*, 27(2) (2009), 167–89; Helfer, 'Redesigning the ECtHR'; Greer, *European Convention*, pp. 165–9; L. Wildhaber, 'The Role of the European Court of Human Rights: An Evaluation', *Mediterranean Journal of Human Rights* 8 (2004), 9–32, and 'A Constitutional Future for the European Court of Human Rights?' *Human Rights Law Journal* 23 (2002), 161–5; P. Mahoney, 'New Challenges for the European Court of Human Rights Resulting from Expanding Case Load and Membership', *Conference on Human Rights – Dynamic Dimension*, London, 27 April 2002 and 'An Insider's View of the Reform Debate', paper presented at the *Symposium on the Reform of the European Court of Human Rights*, Strasbourg, 17 November 2003; R. Ryssdal, 'On the Road to a European Constitutional Court', Winston Churchill Lecture on the Council of Europe, Florence, 21 June 1991, quoted in E. A. Alkema, 'The European Convention as a Constitution and Its Court as a Constitutional Court' in P. Mahoney, F. Matscher, H. Petzold and L. Wildhaber (eds.), *Protecting Human Rights: The European Perspective – Studies in Memory of Rolv Ryssdall* (Cologne: Carl Heymans, 2000) 41–63.

[205] Contributions to this now-extensive literature include P. Dobner and M. Loughlin (eds.), *The Twilight of Constitutionalism* (Oxford University Press, 2010); J. Klabbers, A. Peters and G. Ulfstein, *The Constitutionalization of International Law* (Oxford University Press, 2009); N. Tsagourias (ed.), *Transnational Constitutionalism: International and European Models* (Cambridge University Press, 2007).

for several reasons.[206] For one, the Court has itself referred to the Convention as 'a constitutional instrument of the European public order'.[207] Human rights litigation in national legal systems is also, by definition, 'constitutional' because, by nature, it raises fundamental questions about the distribution of the key benefits and burdens of social life, and about the structure of social and institutional relationships, and because it impacts significantly only on the docket of national appellate courts.[208] Lower courts in all national legal systems are almost entirely concerned with fact finding, the application of positive law – which although derived from human rights is rarely directly about human rights itself – and the management of various kinds of official discretion. It is difficult to understand, therefore, how 'constitutional litigation' of this type could lose its 'constitutional' character when it moves from the national level to Strasbourg.

The reverse is also the case. As research shows, the fact that the ECHR is increasingly acquiring 'constitutional status' in member states, albeit in different ways in different places,[209] poses an intriguing question to those who reject the constitutionalisation thesis: how could this be happening at the national level without the ECHR having it in some sense already at the trans-national? The principles of interpretation used by the Court, considered in Chapter 3, are effectively constitutional because they address two distinct and quintessentially constitutional questions: the 'normative question' of what a given ECHR right means, including its relationship with other rights and collective interests, and the 'institutional question' of which institutions – judicial/non-judicial, national/European – should be responsible for providing the answer. The central constitutional issue raised by the Convention, and considered more fully in the following chapter, is, therefore, how its basic purpose can be realised institutionally, which means how responsibility for rights protection and the democratic pursuit of the public interest can be distributed between judicial and non-judicial institutions each acting according to the rule of law.

---

[206] See, e.g., Greer and Wildhaber, 'Revisiting the Debate'.

[207] *Al-Skeini and Others* v *United Kingdom*, HUDOC, 7 July 2011 (GC) at para. 141; *Loizidou v Turkey (Preliminary Objections)*, HUDOC, 23 March 1995 (GC) at para. 75.

[208] See, E. Blankenburg, 'Mobilization of the German Federal Constitutional Court' in Rogowski and Gawron (eds.), *Constitutional Courts*, pp. 157–72, 158; J. Bell, 'Reflections on Continental European Supreme Courts', *Legal Studies* 24 (2004), 156–68, 163.

[209] Keller and Stone Sweet, *Europe of Rights*, 682–9.

Several common misconceptions about the argument that the ECtHR and ECHR have constitutional characteristics can also easily be rebutted. First, limiting adjudication on the merits only to serious alleged violations does not threaten the right of individual petition as some, particularly NGOs, fear. The right of individual petition to Strasbourg is a right to *make a complaint* not a right to *have it judged on the merits*. Nobody who can currently lodge an application would be unable to do so if admissibility were to depend more critically upon the seriousness of the complaint. Second, there is no substance either in the fear that acknowledging the Court's constitutional character threatens the independence of national constitutional courts because, properly understood and applied, the constitutional functions of all relevant courts are complementary not antagonistic.[210] As Fassbender puts it: 'It is a profound misunderstanding to equate the advancement of the constitutional idea in international law with a weakening of the institution of the independent state.'[211] Third, the case for constitutional justice does not advocate that the Court should *become* a 'constitutional court'. It maintains, rather, that it *is* effectively one already and that this is a role it should perform more consistently. According to Professor Wildhaber, a former President of the ECtHR, the case for constitutional justice is much more about consolidation than it is about transformation.[212]

A fourth common misconception is that the case for constitutional justice should be rejected because it requires the Court to become like a national constitutional or supreme court *in all significant particulars*. Yet no advocate of constitutionalisation has ever made such a claim. One of the hallmarks of national constitutional courts is their conclusive judicial authority over subordinate national courts and, in some cases, their power to annul legislation or refer it back to the legislature where it has resulted in a violation of constitutional rights. But for several reasons the ECtHR does not have, nor does any credible conception of constitutionalisation require it to have, this kind of authority. To begin with, its

[210] Sadurski, 'Partnering with Strasbourg'.
[211] B. Fassbender, 'The Meaning of International Constitutional Law' in N. Tsagourias, (ed.), *Transnational Constitutionalism: International and European Models* (Cambridge University Press, 2007), pp. 307–28, 334.
[212] L. Wildhaber, Foreword to Greer, *European Convention*, p. xiii. See also Føllesdal, Peters and Ulfstein, 'Conclusions', pp. 390, 402; E. Bates, *The Evolution of the European Convention on Human Rights: From Its Inception to the Creation of a Permanent Court of Human Rights* (Oxford University Press, 2010), pp. 4, 5, 8, 17, 20, 105, 153–8; Heller and Stone Sweet, *Europe of Rights*, p. 13.

jurisdiction is largely limited to declaring whether or not the ECHR has been breached although, as already indicated, it has cautiously begun to suggest how violations might be corrected. It does not, nor should it have, the power to annul legislation nor, including under the pilot judgment process, to prescribe to states precisely what needs to be done in order to address a violation. Furthermore, the role of the ECtHR is also subsidiary to that of national authorities, which have the primary responsibility to ensure ECHR rights are not violated. Moreover, the margin of appreciation doctrine legitimately leaves considerable scope for a range of equally Convention-compliant national norms, institutions and processes. Finally, whether or not a judgment of the ECtHR is effectively implemented at national level will depend upon both the willingness and capacity of national institutions, on the one hand, and negotiation with the CM in the supervision of the execution of judgments process, on the other. Indeed, far from regarding the principles of subsidiarity, margin of appreciation and proportionality, considered more fully in Chapter 3, as characterising non-constitutionalised pluralist legal orders, many commentators regard them as integral to international constitutionalism.[213] The case against constitutional justice can in fact be turned on its head. Is it possible that any court in a contemporary liberal democratic context capable of authoritatively condemning legislative and executive action from the standpoint of an independent judicial interpretation of fundamental rights could legitimately exist and function in the absence of any constitutional framework whatever? The ECtHR would suffer serious damage to its legitimacy and authority, considered more fully later, if it were to attempt to operate in such an environment.

When we turn to pluralism we find two main forms. First, some commentators argue that, far from having a single core function, as suggested by the models of both individual and constitutional justice, the ECtHR and ECHR system have a plurality. But the most convincing accounts of pluralism in this sense are also firmly constitutionalist. While Wildhaber, for example, distinguishes six functions, each is only capable of being properly harmonised and prioritised by full recognition of, and commitment by, the Court to its core constitutional mission. First, the ECtHR filters applications, rejecting as inadmissible the vast majority on formal grounds (for example, non-exhaustion of domestic remedies), mixed grounds (for example, incompatibility with the ECHR) or

---

[213] See, e.g., Klabbers et al., *Constitutionalization of International Law*, pp. 31–6.

substantive grounds (for example, being 'manifestly ill-founded'). Nevertheless, those applicants whose petitions are rejected will, at least, have had the opportunity to raise a complaint, the second, 'wailing wall', function. Four further functions in cases judged on the merits are: borderline fine-tuning, responding to grave breaches of human rights, addressing structural or systemic problems and preventing arbitrariness by delivering administrative justice. As far as borderline fine-tuning is concerned, the ECtHR takes pride in its evolutive interpretation of the ECHR in the light of progressively developing social values and changing individual needs, with some judges apparently believing they have a duty to extend the reach of Convention rights as far as possible ('judicial activism'). The ECtHR has also had to deal with clear cases of grave, massive and systematic human rights breaches, including, for example, killings, torture, disappearances, rapes, prolonged illegal detention, thoroughly unfair or arbitrary proceedings and attempts to eliminate political opposition. According to Wildhaber there is little doubt that a human rights court should condemn such grave breaches as a matter of the utmost priority even though the governments concerned will often resent its intervention and may denounce its judgments as political rather than legal.

Heller and Stone Sweet also maintain that, depending upon which Convention rights and which states are involved, the ECtHR has several functions. For example, it behaves like a 'kind of High Cassation Court' when it comes to procedure, an 'international watchdog' regarding egregious human rights violations and massive breakdowns in the rule of law and an 'oracle of constitutional rights interpretation' in relation to Articles 8–11 and 14 of the ECHR'.[214] However, they also concede that 'the Court is increasingly engaged in delivering ... "constitutional justice"',[215] particularly, as Sadurski points out, as a result of the accession of the former communist states of central and eastern Europe.[216]

However, by contrast with the case for 'constitutional justice', which is largely normative and stems directly from the recent reform debate,[217] the term 'pluralism' is also used more widely in a second sense, as a macrolevel descriptive-analytical framework with normative implications.[218]

---

[214] Keller and Stone Sweet, *Europe of Rights*, p. 695.
[215] *Ibid.*, p. 703.
[216] Sadurski, 'Partnering with Strasbourg'.
[217] See, e.g., Greer, *European Convention*, pp. 165–89.
[218] See N. Krisch, 'The Case for Pluralism in Postnational Law', LSE Law, Society and Economy Working Papers 12/2009, 2, 19.

As a type of post-national legal regime, and unlike constitutional systems with clear and settled judicial and non-judicial hierarchies, the ECHR system is heterarchical in structure and characterised by convergence in norms and institutions, and generally by an absence of friction and conflict secured by dialogue and pragmatic political, rather than formal legal, compromise between its constituent institutions, including courts at both national and trans-national levels.[219] Europe, therefore, has a common, though an uneven, constitutional landscape since all but one (Belarus) of its forty-eight fully fledged states and all its trans-national institutions are expressly committed to the same institutional and normative model, which embodies democracy, the rule of law and human rights, as exemplified by the ECHR.[220]

But for several reasons, this landscape is also undeniably pluralistic, polyvalent and heterarchical, rather than unitary, monistic and rigidly hierarchical. First, a significant degree of harmony and convergence, based as much on political compromise as upon legal prescription, can be observed within which the question of ultimate authority is left open and contested.[221] But not only are these inevitable features of any international constitutional order, they are not unknown in national constitutional systems and processes either.[222] Second, the ECHR provides the functional equivalent of a 'constitution' for only a 'partial polity', that is to say, one with executive and judicial but no legislative functions. Third, not every European state is equally effectively integrated into it. While some adhere faithfully to the judgments of the EctHR, others do not. Some national constitutional courts, for example, in Germany, Spain and France, have even signalled their determination not to follow Strasbourg when they deem its interpretation of ECHR rights inconsistent with their interpretation of their own national constitutional documents.[223] But the fact that national courts may interpret

---

[219] N. Krisch, 'The Open Architecture of European Human Rights Law', *Modern Law Review*, 71 (2008), 183–216, *Beyond Constitutionalism: The Pluralist Structure of Post-national Law* (Oxford University Press, 2010).

[220] As more than one commentator has pointed out, the unevenness of a constitutional process is not enough in itself to deprive it of its constitutional character: Kabblers et al., *Constitutionalization of International Law*, pp. 343, 346.

[221] Krisch, 'Open Architecture'. Contributions to the debate about pluralistic constitutional orders include A. Hurrell, *On Global Order: Power, Value and the Constitution of International Society* (Oxford University Press, 2007); N. Walker, 'The Idea of Constitutional Pluralism', *Modern Law Review* 65 (2002), 317–59, 343–4.

[222] Klabbers, *Constitutionalization of International Law*, pp. 43–4, 348–51.

[223] Krisch, 'Open Architecture', 183–96; Walker, 'Constitutional Pluralism', 350.

essentially the same fundamental rights found in separate documents differently from the ECtHR is not a sufficient reason to deny that each court, and each document, is a component in a unified pluralistic 'multi-verse' of constitutional systems. Indeed, this kind of complex and contingent commitment is regarded by commentators as one of the hallmarks of constitutionalised international law.[224]

Nor, for two other main reasons, and contrary to what some have claimed, has the diminishing scale of the ECtHR's case load crisis discredited the case for constitutionalisation. First, over the past few decades the Convention system has, in fact, been substantially constitutionalised, not least by the pilot judgment procedure and the priority policy.[225] Yet, strangely, these developments have been welcomed by critics of constitutionalisation without this apparent inconsistency being recognised or explained.[226] As Sadurski argues the ECtHR could, therefore, be said to be 'largely though not fully constitutional' with the Court having become much more constitutional than before.[227]

Second, the recent 'triumph' of the individual justice model has not yet been firmly institutionalised, is more apparent than real and a coherent case that it is the best conception of the role of the ECtHR has still not been made. On the contrary, recent developments have confirmed the Court's character as a human rights small claims tribunal, hardly its most noble or most effective function. This is, regrettably, the result of an 'unholy alliance' between states, Strasbourg bureaucrats and NGOs, who for very different reasons jointly mobilised in the reform debate against any threat they perceived to the right of individual petition.[228] Yet, the unfortunate irony is that, while the right of individual complaint has been formally preserved, it has simultaneously been undermined because sending less serious prima facie ECHR violations indefinitely to 'the back of the queue' will result in 'large numbers of applications' not being

[224] Klabbers, *Constitutionalization of International Law*, p. 29.
[225] Føllesdal et al., 'Conclusions', p. 390; Cameron, 'The Court and the Member States', p. 57; L. Glas, 'Changes in the Procedural Practice of the European Court of Human Rights: Consequences for the Convention System and Lessons to be Drawn', *Human Rights Law Review* 14 (2014), 671–99; A. Stone Sweet, 'The European Convention on Human Rights and National Constitutional Reordering', *Cardozo Law Review* 33 (2012), 1859–1868.
[226] See, e.g., Leach et al., *Responding to Systematic Human Rights Violations*; P. Leach, 'On the Reform of the European Court of Human Rights', *European Human Rights Law Review* [2009], 725–35, 728, 730, 733 and 'Access to the ECtHR', 17.
[227] Sadurski, 'Partnering with Strasbourg', 447–50, italics in original.
[228] See Greer and Wildhaber, 'Revisiting the Debate'.

examined.[229] As Mahoney argues, this creates 'a structural denial of justice for certain categories of meritorious applicants whose cases cannot be handled'.[230] And even for those complaints which are eventually heard, justice is not only delayed; it is a violation of the right to be tried in a reasonable time. The state interest is clear – doing as little as possible to convince the CM that judgment has been executed. For their part, Strasbourg officials, in common with bureaucrats everywhere, tend to assume that the resolution of administrative challenges lies in micromanaging the existing system rather than in its imaginative reconceptualisation. And, by prioritising the Convention rights of actual over those of potential victims, the NGOs have endorsed, not only a highly ineffective way of promoting the structural changes which would prevent violations from occurring in the first place, but one which paradoxically institutionalises them by permitting states repeatedly to pay compensation as a modest cost of failing to deal with the source.

Legitimacy and Authority

For most of its life the ECtHR has had a low public profile and, until recently, neither its legitimacy nor its authority were discussed even by those who took an interest in it. But this has changed significantly, particularly over the past half-decade or so. In order to understand why, we first need to consider the deeper question of what the legitimacy and authority of courts and adjudication mean, and what factors determine whether they have or lack them. Of the many differences between the various approaches taken by scholars on these issues, one of the most fundamental is between, on the one hand, those which treat 'legitimacy' (an institution's 'right to exist') and 'authority' (the justifications for how it exercises its power)[231] as observable social phenomena involving

---

[229] Cameron, 'The Court and the Member States', p. 43.

[230] P. Mahoney, 'The European Court of Human Rights and Its Ever-Growing Caseload: Preserving the Mission of the Court While Ensuring the Viability of the Individual Petition' in S. Flogaitis, T. Zwart and J. Fraser (eds.), *The European Court of Human Rights and Its Discontents: Turning Criticism into Strength* (Edward Elgar, Cheltenham: 2013), p. 25.

[231] Lemmens uses the terms 'onto-legitimacy' to refer to the European Court of Human Rights' 'right to exist', and 'praxis legitimacy' to refer to the legitimacy of its verdicts, K. Lemmens, 'Chapter 2: Criticising the European Court of Human Rights or Misunderstanding the Dynamics of Human Rights Protection?' in P. Popelier, S. Lambrecht and K. Lemmens (eds.), *Criticism of the European Court of Human Rights – Shifting the Convention System: Counter-Dynamics at the National and EU Level* (Cambridge: Intersentia, 2016), pp. 23–40, 27–8.

shared understandings between those with power and those over whom it is exercised, and, on the other hand, perspectives which attempt to identify the 'true', 'objective', most persuasive or most rational normative basis for both concepts.[232]

The implications of these insights have also been explored for courts and other adjudicative and dispute resolution institutions and processes including the ECtHR.[233] The formal legitimacy of any given court, or other adjudicative/dispute resolution machinery as institutions will depend upon which kind of legitimacy – for example, according to Weber, 'traditional', 'charismatic' or 'legal-rational' – characterises the wider constitutional-political-social regime within which it operates.[234] However, this does not settle all issues regarding its authority because how its decisions are received by relevant publics is also relevant. Unpopular or heavily criticised judgments may, therefore, result in a decline in the authority of a court without significant loss of its formal institutional legitimacy, although clearly a critical mass of the former is likely to erode the latter. In other words, although controversial decisions may prompt debate about the need for changes within a given system, they need not necessarily suggest that the system itself requires radical alteration, although they may signal that both are necessary.[235] Accountability is an important element in the legitimacy and authority of democratic non-judicial institutions and generally refers to systems of checks and balances which monitor and review how they exercise power. However, since, in the judicial context, accountability tends to refer to adherence to mandate, and to how professionally, independently and

---

[232] See, e.g., Føllesdal et al. (eds.), *The Legitimacy of International Human Rights Regimes*; Çali et al., 'The Legitimacy of Human Rights Courts', pp. 958–61; J. Brunnee and S. Troope, *Legitimacy and Legality in International Law* (Cambridge University Press, 2010), ch. 2; T. Franck, 'Why a Quest for Legitimacy', *UC Davis Law Review* 21 (1987), 535–47, 542–4.

[233] See, e.g., K. Dzehtsiarou, *European Consensus and the Legitimacy of the European Court of Human Rights* (Cambridge University Press, 2015); A. Føllesdal et al. (eds.), *The Legitimacy of International Human Rights Regimes*; E. Voeten, 'Public Opinion and the Legitimacy of International Courts', *Theoretical Inquiries in Law* 14 (2013), 411–36; C. Carruba and M. Gabel, 'Courts, Compliance and the Quest for Legitimacy in International Law', *Theoretical Inquiries in International Law*, 14 (2013), 505–42; Çali et al., 'The Legitimacy of Human Rights Courts'; J. Gribnau, 'Legitimacy of the Judiciary', *Electronic Journal of Comparative Law* 6 (2002), ejcl.org/64/art64-3.html.

[234] A. Føllesdal, 'The Legitimacy of International Human Rights Review: The Case of the European Court of Human Rights', *Journal of Social Philosophy* 40 (2009), 595–607.

[235] Çali et al., 'The Legitimacy of Human Rights Courts', 983.

impartially disputes are adjudicated, it is therefore largely, if not entirely, encompassed by the concepts of legitimacy and authority themselves.

So, how does all this apply to the ECtHR? In the first place it would be difficult to deny that the Court has a high level of 'legal-rational' institutional legitimacy deriving primarily from its origins as a product of liberal democratic Europe in the Cold War aftermath of the Second World War, the character of the CE and the ECHR and the independence and professionalism of its judges.[236] But its authority arguably depends upon the perceptions of three relevant publics – the 'cognoscenti' (judges, lawyers, jurists and others who study or are otherwise professionally involved with it),[237] the politicians and political parties with partisan axes to grind and the general public in member states, most of whom have not experienced the ECHR or ECtHR directly, and who are likely to know little or nothing about it or to have heard of it only indirectly from the media and other potentially biased sources.[238] Since its first judgments, the Court has been exposed to informed and measured criticism from the cognoscenti. But it would be difficult to find any informed observers, no matter what their view of the individual/constitutional justice debate, who think it has no authority at all. In a recent study, Lambrecht found that express and implicit criticism of the ECtHR by national courts is 'very rare', except in the United Kingdom and to a lesser extent in Austria, Switzerland and Germany.[239] But, depending upon the national judicial culture, although the importance of cooperation and dialogue tends to be emphasised, judicial criticism is more common ex curia.[240] Apart from a brief but 'fierce' upsurge in the Netherlands, political and public criticism have also been significant and sustained only in France, Norway, Switzerland and the United Kingdom and, with the exception of the latter, have concerned issues of output and managerial performance rather than the ECtHR's existence as such.[241] Not surprisingly, as already intimated in Chapter 1, the greatest

---

[236] Dzehtsiarou, European Consensus, p. 144; J.-P. Costa, 'On the Legitimacy of the European Court of Human Rights' Judgments', European Constitutional Law Review 7 (2011), 173–82, 174.

[237] Çali et al., 'The Legitimacy of Human Rights Courts', 957.

[238] Voeten, 'Public Opinion and Legitimacy', 411–19.

[239] S. Lambrecht, 'Chapter 19: Assessing the Existence of Criticism of the European Court of Human Rights' in Popelier, Lambrecht and Lemmens (eds.), Criticism of the European Court of Human Rights, pp. 544–6.

[240] Lambrecht, 'Assessing the Existence of Criticism of the ECtHR', 546–50.

[241] Ibid., 509–18, 551.

political and public hostility is found on the far right of the political spectrum, where they combine with a more extensive rights- and Euro-scepticism (often compounded by the mistaken assumption that the ECtHR is an EU institution), coupled with militant forms of populist exclusionary nationalism, driven particularly by post-2008 economic austerity, jihadi terrorism, mass migration and disillusionment with multiculturalism. This has rendered some of the ECtHR's decisions unpopular, particularly in the United Kingdom, where those concerning prisoners' voting rights and the expulsion of foreigners convicted of crime or suspected of terrorism have prompted even government ministers to call for the ECHR to be repudiated.[242]

Current complaints about the legitimacy and authority of the ECtHR, some of which conflict with each other, concern such things as the professional quality of some judges, excessive/insufficient judicial activism/restraint, casuistic and inadequately reasoned judgments, insufficient adherence by the Court to its own case law, its remoteness from national public life, its lack of accountability, mission creep including the inadequately controlled minting of new rights not clearly provided by the text of the ECHR, highly variable rates of national compliance and the relationship between national democratic sovereignty and the Court's mandate to set detailed pan-European standards, allegedly skewed one way or the other depending upon a given critic's point of view.[243]

---

[242] Secretary General of the Council of Europe, *State of Democracy, Human Rights and the Rule of Law: A Security Imperative for Europe – Report by the Secretary General of the Council of Europe, 2016* (Strasbourg: Council of Europe, 2016), p. 4, edoc.coe.int/en/ fundamental-freedoms/5949-state-of-democracy-human-rights-and-the-rule-of-law-in-europe.html; Sir N. Bratza, 'Living Instrument or Dead Letter – the Future of the European Convention on Human Rights', *European Human Rights Law Review* [2014], 116–28; R. Spano, 'Universality or Diversity of Human Rights? Strasbourg in the Age of Subsidiarity', *Human Rights Law Review* 14 (2014), 487–502; Dzehtsiarou, *European Consensus*, pp. 147–8; Oomen, 'A Serious Case of Strasbourg-Bashing?' 413–9; Voeten, 'Public Opinion and Legitimacy', 418–19, 422, 435; L. Scott-Moncrieff, 'Editorial: Language and the Law: Reclaiming the Human Rights Debate', *European Human Rights Law Review* [2013] , 115–21; J. Gerards, 'The Prism of Fundamental Rights', *European Constitutional Law Review* 8 (2012), 173–202, 173–6.

[243] See the many illuminating contributions to Flogaitis et al. (eds.), *The European Court of Human Rights and Its Discontents*; Lambrecht, 'Assessing the Existence of Criticism of the ECtHR', 511–12; F. de Londras and K. Dzehtsiarou, 'Managing Judicial Innovation in the European Court of Human Rights', *Human Rights Law Review* 15 (2015), 523–47; Cameron, 'The Court and the Member States, p. 26; Føllesdal, 'Much Ado about Nothing'; R. Bellamy, 'The Democratic Legitimacy of International Human Rights Conventions: Political Constitutionalism and the European Convention on Human Rights', *European Journal of International Law* 25 (2014), 1019–42; Bratza, 'Living

Proposals under active official consideration to address these difficulties include more/less deference by the ECtHR to national authorities, prohibiting the delivery of separate opinions in judgments, more fully reasoned verdicts, a firmer commitment by the Court to its own previous judgements, increased awareness of the role of the ECtHR in member states, an enhanced role for national human rights institutions, better communication between the Court and national institutions and closer collaboration between the ECtHR and the EU's European Court of Justice (ECJ).[244]

However, as with the efficacy- and efficiency-related proposals, what becomes of these remains to be seen. But, in our view, even if 'seriousness' does not become the main substantive ground for the admissibility of complaints,[245] the efficacy, efficiency, legitimacy and authority of the Court and Convention system are unlikely to be significantly improved unless the constitutional-pluralist paradigm assumes greater prominence for both. This should include a greater sensitivity to national context in the interpretation of the more ambiguous implications of ECHR rights. A classic example is the prisoner's right to vote.[246] Since the Convention is entirely silent about whether prisoners should or should not have the vote, the matter hinges upon whether disenfranchisement should be an inevitable consequence of imprisonment, a matter upon which reasonable people equally committed to Convention rights could reasonably disagree. The ECtHR has, however, denounced the United Kingdom's

---

Instrument or Dead Letter; A. Føllesdal, B. Peters and G. Ulfstein, 'Introduction' in A. Føllesdal, B. Peters and G. Ulfstein (eds.), *Constituting Europe: The European Court of Human Rights in a National, European and Global Context* (Cambridge University Press, 2013), pp. 12–20; P. Thielborger, 'Judicial Passivism at the European Court of Human Rights', *Maastricht Journal of European and Comparative Law* 19 (2012), 341–47; D. Popovic, 'Prevailing of Judicial Activism over Self-Restraint in the Jurisprudence of the European Court of Human Rights', *Creighton Law Review* 42 (2009), 361–96; S. Andreadakis, 'The European Convention on Human Rights, the EU and the UK: Confronting a Heresy: A Reply to Andrew Williams', *European Journal of International Law* 24 (2013), 1187–93.

[244] Lambrecht, 'Assessing the Existence of Criticism of the ECtHR', 518–22, 526–34.

[245] While the CDDH still does not think this necessary, Mowbray, 'Interlaken Declaration', 521, other commentators do. See, e.g., White and Boussiakou, 'Voices', 186–8; J. Goldston, 'Achievements and Challenges: Insights from the Strasbourg Experience for Other International Courts' *European Human Rights Law Review* [2009], 603–10, 606; R. Bernhardt, 'The Admissibility Stage: The Pros and Cons of a *Certiorari* Procedure for Individual Applications' in Wolfrum and Deutch, 'ECtHR Overwhelmed by Applications'.

[246] See R. Bellamy, 'The Democratic Legitimacy of International Human Rights Conventions: Political Constitutionalism and the Hirst Case' in Føllesdal, Schaffer and Ulfstein (eds.), *The Legitimacy of International Human Rights Regimes*.

blanket ban in the face of overwhelming Parliamentary and public opposition in a contest where neither side can be said to be objectively right or wrong.

2.5 Conclusion

The CE's most obvious and visible successes are its survival, institutionalisation and expansion of membership and range of activities when it might just as easily have been marginalised by another European war, abolished as a result of the successful annexation of all, or part, of western Europe by the Soviet Union, rendered redundant by a resurgence of indigenous illiberal regimes in core states or simply wound up by common consent of its members. Its effectiveness, efficiency, authority and legitimacy are, however, much more difficult to determine.

As an intergovernmental organisation everything the CE does is based on negotiation and consent. Member states are now required only to accede to its Statute, to the ECHR and to the ECPT. Everything else is voluntary. And there is also considerable room for manoeuvre, negotiation and compromise with respect to what does, and does not, constitute compliance with any of these requirements. Although some tensions between the CM and PACE have been reported, institutionally the CE functions reasonably well with no serious or enduring friction between any of its constituent elements. Policy making is, however, diffuse. While the CM, PACE and the European Commissioner for Human Rights are each capable of developing and pursuing their own particular agendas, there is no evidence of serious disagreement on what the human rights priorities in Europe should be as the twenty-first century unfolds. But, as the CE itself recognises, growing incoherence and duplication are evident across its now-vast bureaucracies, which produce mountains of paper work and online information on a daily basis.

Apart from the ECHR, the CE's main achievement on the human rights front has been the formal enunciation of an increasingly detailed list of voluntary human rights standards and state obligations, accompanied by monitoring mechanisms. The ECPT's inspection system is a unique achievement, assisting willing states to reduce the incidence of ill treatment in places of detention and confinement, but unlikely to have much impact in states less concerned about it, nor to be replicated in any other human rights field. The CE's other principal human rights–related treaties, the European Social Charter, the European Charter for Regional or Minority Languages and the Framework Convention for the

Protection of National Minorities, share the same broad characteristics, including the specification of norms and the provision of monitoring rather than enforcement processes, which hinge upon persuasion and negotiation rather than upon proactive external investigation and/or judicial condemnation. While each allows some scope for information to be received from non-state bodies – including a limited role for individuals – the main monitoring instrument is periodic reporting by states to expert committees which, in their turn, report to the CM, which then embarks on negotiations with states about compliance leading to often-ambiguous end results. Clearly, states with poor records on the rights in question can either choose not to sign the relevant treaty in the first place or, having signed and ratified, can fail to comply with whatever recommendations are made on the basis of their reports and nevertheless avoid any significant adverse consequences. Nevertheless, there is evidence that concrete changes have occurred in many states, either directly or indirectly, as a result of the pressure brought to bear by treaty monitoring bodies. The main achievement of the CE's human rights activities apart from the ECHR is, therefore, to assist states to introduce changes to which they were not strongly opposed in the first place, but which may not have happened, either at all or as soon, without its intervention.

By contrast, the ECHR system has been widely celebrated as the world's most successful trans-national judicial process for the protection of human rights. However, while it has undoubtedly contributed to the improvement of compliance with the rights in question across the continent, the impact of the Court's judgments has been very uneven. A small minority of states which clutter its docket and persistently receive adverse judgments have been particularly impervious to its intervention. And, given that the system is inherently consensual, there is no easy solution to the problem of poor judgment compliance other than the use of diplomatic carrots and sticks. As for case load, the unfortunate irony is that, although the recent crisis has been reduced to more manageable dimensions, this has been achieved by undermining the right of individual petition in the name of preserving it since sending less serious prima facie Convention violations indefinitely to 'the back of the queue' will not only result in a large number of prima facie well-founded applications not being examined; even for those complaints which are eventually heard, justice will not only have been delayed, it will have resulted in the violation of the right to be tried in a reasonable time.

The stark and inescapable fact, persistently ignored by states, Strasbourg officials and NGOs and confirmed by these developments, is that not every meritorious complaint can possibly receive full judicial consideration in Strasbourg. Given this fact, a much wiser strategy, especially since most violations are self-evident, relatively minor, repetitive, and largely limited to certain provisions in a handful of states, would be to concentrate the ECtHR's scarce resources upon judging those which are most serious for the applicant, the respondent state, and Europe as a whole, and/or which present significant fresh challenges. This is, after all, essentially the criterion of selection at the national level. How or why they lose this characteristic when they transit from the national to the international dimension is a mystery which has yet to be explained. Indeed, their constitutional features become even more vital at this level because it is only here that the European landscape as a whole can be authoritatively judicially surveyed. The ECtHR has in fact moved and been moved significantly in this direction in recent years. But it continues to be prevented from fully capitalising on this function because of the demands made by case management and the adjudication of relatively minor repetitive applications which ultimately fail to stem the flow of similar complaints at source.

Though unwelcome, the case overload crisis nevertheless presented an opportunity for the ECHR system to be re-calibrated in order to make a more worthwhile, more legitimate and more cost-effective contribution to the protection of human rights in Europe. Regrettably, this has not happened. Nevertheless, the case for permitting it to devote itself to setting clearer and more cogently reasoned standards, better to facilitate dialogue with national authorities in more challenging cases, rather than merely requiring it continually to condemn the same relatively minor violations over and over again, remains as compelling as ever. However, needless to say, this will not provide any instant, off-the-peg solutions. But this is not the point. What it offers instead is a framework for the more thoughtful and systematic elaboration of standards, and for a more sustained attempt to cultivate rights-respecting national judicial cultures – particularly in those states which currently lack them – offering better prospects for the long-term promotion of human rights in Europe than the limited vision of the current short-sighted 'small claims' model.

Moreover, in spite of having been dismissed by official contributions to the reform debate, it is difficult to see what framework for analysis and policy offers better prospects than constitutional pluralism, since this provides a much more comprehensive framework than any conceivable alternative for recognising the ECHR's central achievements – including the transformation of laws and practices in member states as a result of successful litigation by individuals before the ECtHR – and for finding appropriate and legitimate ways of securing and developing them in the wider context of the trans-national legal protection of human rights and fundamental freedoms in Europe. Although not commanding complete consensus, a significant body of authoritative academic and judicial opinion now accepts that the ECtHR has effectively become a kind of constitutional court for greater Europe, linking former Communist states with the West and its EU with its non-EU members where the exercise of public power at every level is now formally constrained by a set of internationally justiciable, constitutional rights. It has also become increasingly clear, as the twenty-first century has progressed, that the Court's main task is to administer this system by delivering 'constitutional justice' and, in the process, gently to promote convergence around the 'common European institutional model', itself an abstract or symbolic constitution defined by the core CE and EU principles of democracy, human rights and the rule of law.

Although Europe has a plurality of both national and trans-national constitutional systems, there can be no doubt that these are now all variations on a common underlying theme, the most uniform, pervasive and internationally developed expression of which is provided by the ECHR and ECtHR. On account of their pluralistic characteristics, the constitutional justice provided by the Court is much more subtle and indirect than either the systematic delivery of individual justice (structurally incapable of being realised under any conceivable circumstances) or the more substantial constitutional justice administered by those national constitutional courts which have the power to annul legislation or refer it back to the legislature. As this study argues, it is, therefore, difficult to imagine a coherent and legitimate future for the transnational legal protection of human rights in Europe which lacks strong constitutional foundations at every level. The authority and legitimacy of the ECtHR, therefore, hinge critically on the restless and endless quest to find an appropriate balance between uniform and diverse standards across states articulated in thoroughly reasoned judgments. The most pressing challenge it faces is, therefore, for further progress to be made in this direction.

3

The Case Law of the European Court
of Human Rights

3.1 Introduction

It was not until Protocol No. 11 came into effect in November 1998 – abolishing the European Commission of Human Rights and stripping the Committee of Ministers (CM) of its quasi-judicial power to decide whether the Convention had been violated – that the European Court of Human Rights (ECtHR) became the Council of Europe's sole institution for the judicial interpretation and application of the ECHR. Strictly speaking, therefore, the jurisprudence of the Convention system prior to this point includes opinions of the European Commission of Human Rights and, to a lesser extent, decisions by the CM resolving complaints. However, over the past two decades the most important elements of these now-defunct sources of Convention case law have been incorporated by citation into the Court's own jurisprudence – hence the title of this chapter.

As already indicated in Chapter 2, between 1959 and 1999 the Court rendered fewer than 1,000 judgments. Yet, by the end of 2016, the figure had risen to a total of 19,570. Between 2000 and 2016 an annual average of 1,092 were delivered, including 695 in 2000, the year with the fewest within this timeframe, and 1,625 in 2009, the year with the most. Eighty-four per cent of judgments, and 92 per cent of cases judged on the merits result in a finding of at least one violation. From 1959 to 2016 the provisions most frequently found to have been breached were the right to fair trial under Article 6 (40.32 per cent, 21.34 per cent of which concerned length of proceedings), the right to liberty and security under Article 5 (12.86 per cent), the right to peaceful enjoyment of possessions under Article 1 of Protocol No. 1 (11.93 per cent), the right not to be tortured etc under Article 3 (10.71 per cent), the right to an effective remedy under Article 13 (8.39 per cent), the right to respect for private and family life under Article 8 (4.69 per cent) and the right to life under Article 2 (4.58 per cent).

It would be impossible in the space available here to attempt to consider this vast case law in comprehensive detail. There are, moreover, already several excellent textbooks that come much closer to doing so.[1] Nor will there be much opportunity in what follows to engage critically with controversial substantive issues. Instead, an attempt will be made simply to grasp the core elements of the Strasbourg case law, particularly in order to facilitate comparison with the human rights case law of the EU's judicial institutions, and to identify appropriate analytical paradigms. But before doing so, a few remarks are required about the process and method of adjudication.

3.2   Process and Method of Adjudication

As already indicated in Chapter 2, in judging the merits of any application, the primary issue the Court has to consider is whether, on the evidence presented, the respondent state has violated the Convention. The outcome rests mostly on written submissions from the parties. But in certain cases oral public hearings may also be held. Judgments on the merits are drafted by a Judge Rapporteur, assisted by the judge elected in respect of the respondent state, or in some cases by a drafting committee, and put to a vote of all judges sitting on the particular panel. Typically they contain summaries of the facts; the history of the dispute, including a review of relevant domestic law; the arguments presented by both parties; relevant provisions of the ECHR; a concise statement of the substantive result; plus concurring and dissenting opinions if any. They also tend to be characterised by the Court applying the Convention's sparse rights provisions to the facts by 'cutting and pasting' its earlier interpretations verbatim in judgment after judgment. Verdicts may be unanimous in all particulars, unanimous in result but divergent in reasons, or there may be a lack of consensus on both. Dissenting judgments are reported following those of the majority. Although the Court strives to be consistent with its earlier judgments, there is no formal doctrine of precedent. Therefore, judgments rarely, if ever, establish a precise legal rule; nor can they be described collectively as a closely

---

[1] See, e.g., W. Schabas, *The European Convention on Human Rights* (Oxford University Press, 2015); D. Harris, M. O'Boyle, E. Bates and C. Buckley, *Harris, O'Boyle & Warbrick: Law of the European Convention on Human Rights* (Oxford University Press, 3rd edn., 2014); B. Rainey, E. Wicks and C. Ovey, *Jacobs, White and Ovey: The European Convention on Human Rights* (Oxford University Press, 6th edn., 2014).

integrated system of legal norms, an inevitable consequence, not only of the highly abstract character of ECHR rights and principles, but also of the fact that the core elements in any judgment will probably only apply to the specific respondent state because the material legal and factual issues are unlikely to be reproduced in all relevant particulars elsewhere. The Strasbourg case law does not, therefore, establish 'authorities' for 'propositions of law' as do court decisions in common law systems. Cases tend rather to illustrate how Convention provisions and principles apply to certain facts.

In considering how the ECtHR interprets and applies the ECHR it is useful to distinguish two dimensions – 'formal' and 'stylistic'. The former concerns both how rights are expressed in the Convention text and the formal principles the Court uses to interpret and apply them, while the latter refers to how the formal issues are themselves interpreted and delivered by distinctive 'styles of adjudication' or 'judicial philosophies'. Formally, interpreting and applying the Convention involve considering the alleged misconduct in context, and determining what, according to a dozen or so 'principles of interpretation', the sparse and abstract statements of Convention rights mean, particularly where they interface with each other or with public interests such as 'national security' or the 'prevention of disorder or crime'. Principles of interpretation are not found in the text of the Convention itself but have been identified and developed from the 'teleological principle' in the process of litigation.[2] Derived from Articles 31–33 of the Vienna Convention on the Law of Treaties 1969, the teleological principle requires the text of international treaties to be interpreted in good faith according to the ordinary meaning of their terms in context – unless any special meaning was intended by the parties – and in the light of the overall object and purpose of the treaty in question.[3] But, unlike most international treaties, which are merely reciprocal agreements between states, the Convention is a 'constitutional instrument of European public order in the field of human rights,' which creates a 'network of mutual bilateral undertakings ... [and] objective obligations.'[4] The principle of effective protection of

---

[2] See S. Greer, *The European Convention on Human Rights: Achievements, Problems and Prospects* (Cambridge University Press, 2006), ch. 4.

[3] *Lithgow v United Kingdom*, HUDOC, 8 July 1986, at paras. 114–19; *Golder v United Kingdom*, HUDOC, 21 February 1975, at paras. 29–30.

[4] *Ireland v United Kingdom*, HUDOC, 18 July 1978, at para. 239; *Austria v Italy*, HUDOC, 11 January 1961 (Commission Decision) 4 YB 116, 138.

individual rights holds that the Convention 'is intended to guarantee not rights that are theoretical and illusory but rights that are practical and effective,'[5] and that what matters most is the reality of the applicant's position rather than its formal status.[6] The Court has also expressed this idea in other terms; for example, the Convention should not be interpreted in a manner that leads to unreasonable or absurd consequences.[7] The principle of implied rights and implied limitations holds that, given the Convention's primary function, rights should be interpreted broadly and exceptions narrowly.[8] This is linked to the principle of non-abuse of rights and limitations, which prohibits states, and others, from undermining the protection of rights by abusing either the rights themselves or their limitations, and to the principles of implied rights and implied limitations, which allow some scope for inherent but not extensive limitations and extensions of rights to be read into the text.[9] The principle of positive obligations also allows the Court to interpret the Convention in a manner that imposes obligations upon states actively to protect Convention rights and not merely the negative obligation to avoid violating them.[10]

Armed with the principle of autonomous interpretation the Court can define for itself some of the Convention's key terms in order to prevent states' conveniently re-defining their way around their obligations, for example, by preventing certain crimes' being re-designated as merely 'administrative infractions.'[11] Similarly, the principle of evolutive, or dynamic, interpretation enables out-moded conceptions of how terms

---

[5] *Peltier* v *France*, HUDOC, 21 May 2002, at para. 36; *Soering* v *United Kingdom*, HUDOC, 7 July 1989, at para. 87.

[6] *Welch* v *United Kingdom*, HUDOC, 9 February 1995, paras. 27 & 34; *Deweer* v *Belgium*, HUDOC, 27 February 1980, at para. 44.

[7] Ost, F., 'The Original canons of interpretation of the European Court of Human Rights' in M. Delmas-Marty and C. Chodkiewicz (eds.), *The European Convention for the Protection of Human Rights: International Protection Versus National Restrictions* (Dordrecht: Martinus Nijhoff, 1992), pp. 238–318, 304.

[8] *Ernst* v *Belgium*, HUDOC, 15 July 2003, at para. 56; *Barthold* v *Germany*, HUDOC, 25 March 1985, at para. 43; *Guzzardi* v *Italy*, HUDOC, 6 November 1980, at para. 98; *Winterwerp* v *the Netherlands*, HUDOC, 24 October 1979, at para. 37; *Sunday Times* v *United Kingdom (No. 1)*, HUDOC, 26 April 1979, at para. 65; *Klass and Others* v *Germany*, HUDOC, 6 September 1978, at para. 42.

[9] *Glimmerveen and Hagenbeek* v *the Netherlands*, HUDOC, 11 October 1979 (dec.).

[10] See A. Mowbray, *The Development of Positive Obligations under the European Convention on Human Rights by the European Court of Human Rights* (Oxford: Hart, 2004).

[11] *Ezeh and Connors* v *United Kingdom*, HUDOC, 9 October 2003 (GC), at paras. 82–9; *Engel and Others* v *the Netherlands*, HUDOC, 8 June 1976, at paras. 80–3.

in the ECHR were originally understood to be abandoned when significant, durable – and, according to the principle of commonality, pan-
European – changes in the climate of European public opinion have
occurred, for example, that homosexuality and trans-sexualism are
aspects of private life requiring respect from public authorities.[12] The
twin principles of subsidiarity and review indicate that the role of the
Court is subsidiary to that of member states and is limited to considering
Convention-compliance rather than acting as final court of appeal or
fourth instance.[13]

The principle of proportionality,[14] closely allied with the margin of
appreciation, limits interference with Convention rights to that which is
least intrusive in pursuit of a legitimate objective. The principle of, and
right to, non-discrimination found in Article 14 requires other Convention
rights and freedoms to be applied in a non-discriminatory way. The
margin of appreciation, typically described as a 'doctrine' rather than a
principle, refers to the room for manoeuvre the Strasbourg institutions are
prepared to accord national authorities in fulfilling their Convention
obligations.[15] Pervasive in the Convention are the closely related principles

[12] *I v United Kingdom*, HUDOC, 11 July 2002 (GC), paras. 53–5, 64–5 & 73.; *Dudgeon v United Kingdom*, HUDOC, 22 October 1981; S. C. Prebensen, 'Evolutive interpretation of the European Convention on Human Rights' in P. Mahoney, F. Matscher, H. Petzold and L. Wildhaber (eds.), *Protecting Human Rights: The European Perspective – Studies in Memory of Rolv Ryssdal* (Cologne: Carl Heymans, 2000), pp. 1123–37.

[13] H. Petzold, 'The convention and the principle of subsidiarity', in R. St. J. Macdonald, F. Matscher and H. Petzold (eds.), *The European System for the Protection of Human Rights* (Dordrecht: Martinus Nijhoff, 1993), pp. 41–62. According to a former President of the Court, Rolv Ryssdal, the principle of subsidiarity is 'probably the most important of the principles underlying the Convention', Ryssdall, R., 'Opinion: The coming of age of the European Convention on Human Rights', *European Human Rights Law Review*, [1996], 18–29, 24.

[14] See, e.g., J. McBride, 'Proportionality and the European Convention on Human Rights' in E. Ellis (ed.), *The Principle of Proportionality in the Laws of Europe* (Oxford: Hart, 1999), pp. 23–35; M.-A. Eissen, 'The principle of proportionality in the case-law of the European Court of Human Rights' in R. St. J. Macdonald et al. (eds.), *European System*, pp. 125–46.

[15] See, e.g., S. Greer, 'Universalism and relativism in the protection of human rights in Europe' in P. Agha (ed.) *Human Rights between Law and Politics* (Oxford: Hart, 2017), pp. 17–36; C. M. Zoethout, 'Margin of appreciation, violation and (in)compatibility: Why the European Court of Human Rights might consider using an alternative mode of adjudication', *European Public Law*, 20 (2014) 309–30; A Legg, *The Margin of Appreciation in International Human Rights Law: Deference and Proportionality* (Oxford University Press, 2012); Y. Arai-Takahashi, 'The margin of appreciation doctrine: A theoretical analysis of Strasbourg's variable geometry' in A. Føllesdal, B. Peters and G. Ulfstein (eds.), *Constituting Europe: The European Court of Human Rights in a*

of legality, the rule of law and procedural fairness – which seek to subject the exercise of public power to effective, formal legal constraints in order to avoid arbitrariness[16] – and the principle of democracy, which assumes that human rights flourish best in the context of democratic political institutions and a tolerant social climate.[17]

While the Court, and most commentators, tend to regard the principles of interpretation as a primordial soup with no particular structure or hierarchy, it has been argued that the teleological principle suggests they can, and should, be conceived in terms of three primary constitutional principles – the 'rights principle', the 'democracy principle' and the 'principle of priority to rights' each exercised according to the 'principle of legality/procedural fairness/rule of law' – to which the remaining principles of interpretation are subordinate, a distinction that would assist the Court in more consistently adhering to constitutional pluralism.[18] The 'rights' principle holds that, in a democratic society, Convention rights should be protected by national courts, and by the ECtHR, through the medium of law. The 'democracy' principle maintains that, in a democratic society, collective goods/public interests should be pursued by democratically accountable national non-judicial public bodies within a framework of law. The principle of 'priority-to-rights' mediates the relationship between the rights and democracy principles by emphasising that Convention rights take procedural and evidential, but not conclusive substantive priority over the democratic pursuit of the public interest, according to the terms of given Convention

National, European and Global Context (Cambridge University Press, 2013), pp. 62–105; J. Gerards, 'Pluralism, deference and the margin of appreciation doctrine', European Law Journal, 17 (2011), 80–120; J. Kratochvíl, 'The inflation of the margin of appreciation by the European Court of Human Rights', Netherlands Quarterly of Human Rights, 29 (2011), 324–57; G. Letsas, 'Two concepts of the margin of appreciation', Oxford Journal of Legal Studies, 26 (2006), 705–32; J. A. Sweeney, 'Margins of appreciation: Cultural relativity and the European Court of Human Rights in the post–Cold War era', International and Comparative Law Quarterly, 54 (2005) 459–74; Y. Arai-Takahashi, The Margin of Appreciation Doctrine and the Principle of Proportionality in the Jurisprudence of the ECHR (Antwerp: Intersentia, 2002).

[16] See, G. Lautenbach, The Concept of the Rule of Law and the European Court of Human Rights (Oxford University Press, 2013).

[17] See C. Gearty, 'Democracy and human rights in the European Court of Human Rights: A critical appraisal', Northern Ireland Legal Quarterly, 51 (2000), 381–96; A. Mowbray, 'The role of the European Court of Human Rights in the promotion of democracy', Public Law [1999], 703–25; S. Marks, 'The European Convention on Human Rights and its "democratic society"', British Yearbook of International Law, 66 (1995), 209–38.

[18] Greer, European Convention, ch. 4.

provisions. It should be observed that each of these three primary constitutional principles incorporates what might otherwise be regarded as a fourth, the principle of legality/rule of law. However, providing it is recognised as integral to the other three, little of consequence results from counting them one way or the other.

As far as matters of 'judicial style' are concerned, a distinction can be drawn between 'activism' and 'restraint', or between 'perfectionism' and 'realism'.[19] 'Judicial activists'/'perfectionists' tend to regard the Court's mission as the steady expansion of human rights on a widening front, side-lining both limiting principles such as subsidiarity and margin of appreciation in favour of ambitious standard-setting, and largely ignoring the distinction between grave violations and the 'fine-tuning' of relatively minor breaches of the ECHR in largely Convention-compliant states. The implication is that the simple concept of 'ECHR violation' is all that matters, however serious or systematic. On the other hand, advocates of 'judicial self-restraint'/'realism' would not go so far. For them the ECtHR's dependence upon, and interconnectedness with, national courts, parliaments and governments necessarily require a sense of proportion, prioritisation and restraint. Judges adhering to this perspective see the Court as providing, above all, inspiration, guidelines, minimal standards and an acknowledgement that, while 'human rights' are undeniably an ideal, their fulfilment must be tempered by a realistic appreciation of what can and cannot be achieved in the ECHR context.[20] However, activism/restraint and perfectionism/realism merely identify points on a continuum rather than a comprehensive and mutually exclusive classification of judicial styles. While some Strasbourg judges

---

[19] For discussions of 'activism' and 'restraint' as styles of adjudication in the Convention context see: P. Thielborger, 'Judicial passivism at the European Court of Human Rights', *Maastricht Journal of European and Comparative Law*, 19 (2012), 341–47; E. Voeten, 'Politics, judicial behaviour and institutional design' in J. Christoffersen and M. Madsen (eds.), *The European Court of Human Rights between Law and Politics* (Oxford University Press, 2011), pp. 61–76; D. Popovic, 'Prevailing of judicial activism over self-restraint in the jurisprudence of the European Court of Human Rights', *Creighton Law Review*, 42 (2009), 361–96; P. Mahoney, 'Judicial activism and judicial self-restraint in the European Court of Human Rights: Two sides of the same coin', *Human Rights Law Journal*, 11 (1990), 57–88. For a discussion of the distinction between 'scepticism', 'realism' and 'perfectionism' in relation to human rights see S. Greer, 'Being 'realistic' about human rights?' (2009) 60 *Northern Ireland Legal Quarterly*, 145–61.

[20] L. Wildhaber, 'Rethinking the European Court of Human Rights', in Christoffersen and Madsen (eds.), *The European Court of Human Rights between Law and Politics*, pp. 2014–29.

may be wholeheartedly committed to one of these options, others might not adhere firmly or consistently to either, content instead to oscillate somewhere in between according to the case under consideration.

3.3 Substantive Provisions

There are many ways of approaching the Convention's substantive provisions. But the one followed here, though not necessarily the most imaginative, is the most obvious: simply to discuss them as they appear in the text which can be found in Appendix A.

Article 1 – Obligation to Respect Human Rights

The obligation on member states under Article 1 ECHR to 'secure to everyone within their jurisdiction the rights and freedoms' found in the Convention, applies, not only to any given national territory, but also to break-away or autonomous regions, and may also extend beyond ('extra-territorial effect'), particularly regarding military operations abroad. States generally exercise jurisdiction without difficulty throughout their territory. But this may be partially or totally ousted in exceptional circumstances such as military occupation by the forces of another state, acts of war or rebellion or the acts of a foreign state supporting a separatist regime.[21]

The key to understanding extra-territoriality lies in determining what 'jurisdiction' means and, in particular, whether, and if so to what extent, it can be distinguished from other exercises of state power. In ruling the case of *Chagos Islanders* v *United Kingdom* inadmissible, the Court summarised six relevant principles articulated by the Grand Chamber in the leading case of *Al-Skeini and others* v *UK:*[22]

> i. A State's jurisdictional competence under Article 1 is primarily territorial; ii. Only exceptional circumstances give rise to exercise of jurisdiction by a State outside its own territorial boundaries; iii. Whether there is an exercise of jurisdiction is a question of fact; iv. There are two principal exceptions to territoriality: circumstances of "State agent authority and control" and "effective control over an area"; v. The "State agent authority

---

[21] *Ilaşcu and Others* v *Moldova and Russia*, HUDOC, 8 July 2004 (GC), at para. 312. See also *Catan and Others* v *Moldova and Russia*, HUDOC, 19 October 2012 (GC), at paras. 105–7; *Ivanţoc* v *Moldova and Russia*, HUDOC, 15 November 2011, at paras. 105–6 & 120; *Assanidze* v *Georgia*, HUDOC, 8 April 2004 (GC), at paras. 137–43.

[22] *Al-Skeini and Others* v *United Kingdom*, HUDOC, 7 July 2011 (GC).

and control" exception applies to the acts of diplomatic and consular agents present on foreign territory; to circumstances where a Contracting State, through custom, treaty or agreement, exercises executive public powers or carries out judicial or executive functions on the territory of another State; and circumstances where the State through its agents exercises control and authority over an individual outside its territory, such as using force to take a person into custody or exerting full physical control over a person through apprehension or detention. vi. The "effective control over an area" exception applies where through military action, lawful or unlawful, the State exerts effective control of an area outside its national territory.[23]

While this clarifies the position, it does not fully settle whether, and if so under what conditions, acts of war such as aerial bombing by a Convention state (particularly those that are lawful under the international law of armed conflict) would bring casualties in the enemy state under the 'jurisdiction' of a member state for the purposes of this provision.

Article 2 – Right to Life

Article 2 does not provide a right to life as such. Assuming such a right exists, this provision seeks instead to protect it by way of two distinct obligations. The first sentence of Article 2(1) creates a positive obligation on the part of the state to protect everyone's right to life through law, while the second sentence of Article 2(1) and Article 2(2) together create a negative state obligation not to deprive anyone of life except through lawful execution,[24] or by the use of no more force than is absolutely necessary to defend someone from unlawful violence, in order to effect a lawful arrest or to prevent the escape of a person lawfully detained or lawfully to quell a riot or insurrection. It was not until 1995 that the ECtHR had the opportunity to deliver its first judgment on the merits of an Article 2 complaint. Since then the positive obligations in the first paragraph, including and especially the duty to investigate, have significantly expanded, while the content of the negative obligation not to take

---

[23] *Chagos Islanders* v *United Kingdom*, HUDOC, 11 December 2012 (dec.), at para. 70.

[24] Protocol No. 6 abolishes the death penalty except in wartime while Protocol No. 13 abolishes it in all circumstances. Execution no longer occurs in any Council of Europe state and, according to *Al Nashiri* v *Poland*, HUDOC, 24 July 2014, at para. 577, Art. 2 prohibits deportation or extradition where there are 'substantial grounds ... for believing' there is a 'real risk of being subjected to the death penalty'.

life arbitrarily has also been clarified, particularly as a result of conflicts in Northern Ireland, Turkey and Chechnya.

The positive obligation under Article 2(1) is to protect everyone's *right to life* through law, but not to provide legal protection for everyone's *life* through law. This is because, and unlike any other interest protected by the Convention, life necessarily embraces its own negation, death. It follows, therefore, that death as such does not necessarily constitute an interference with the right to life. States do not, therefore, have to justify every death of their citizens as they are required, for example, to justify restrictions upon their liberty. Instead, the obligation to 'protect the right to life by law' implies, at a minimum: the provision of appropriate health care;[25] independent and effective legal and administrative processes capable of establishing the cause of unexplained deaths that also criminalise, deter and provide appropriate remedies for culpable killing;[26] effective responses by national authorities to serious threats to life;[27] rapid responses to disappearances plus effective and independent investigations thereafter;[28] effective and independent investigations into deaths in custody,[29] deaths at the hands of security forces,[30] deaths as a result of

---

[25] *Aydoğdu* v *Turkey*, HUDOC, 30 November 2016, at para. 56; *Cyprus* v *Turkey*, HUDOC, 10 May 2001 (GC), at para. 219 (GC); *Calvelli and Ciglio* v *Italy*, HUDOC, 17 January 2002 (GC), at paras. 49 & 51.

[26] *Kitanovska Stanojkovic and Others* v *the Former Yugoslav Republic of Macedonia*, HUDOC, 13 October 2016, at paras. 26 & 33; *Halime Kılıç* v *Turkey*, HUDOC, 28 June 2016, at paras. 101–2; *Kasap and Others* v *Turkey*, HUDOC, 14 January 2014, at paras. 57 & 60–1; *Öneryildiz* v *Turkey*, HUDOC, 30 November 2004 (GC), at paras. 92 & 96; *Menson and Others* v *United Kingdom*, HUDOC, 7 May 2003 (dec.), at para. 1; *Sabuktekin* v *Turkey*, HUDOC, 19 March 2002, at paras. 97–8; *Osman* v *United Kingdom*, HUDOC, 28 October 1998 (GC), at para. 115; *McCann and Others* v *United Kingdom*, HUDOC, 27 September 1995 (GC), at para. 161.

[27] *Civek* v *Turkey*, HUDOC, 23 February 2016, at paras. 65 & 66.

[28] *Ortsuyeva and Others* v *Russia*, HUDOC, 22 November 2016, at paras. 93–4; *Makayeva* v *Russia*, HUDOC, 18 September 2014, at paras. 104–6; *Turluyeva* v *Russia*, HUDOC, 20 June 2013, at paras. 83 & 99; *Aslakhanova and Others* v *Russia*, HUDOC, 18 December 2012 at paras. 121–3; *ER and Others* v *Turkey*, HUDOC, 31 July 2012 at paras. 80–2; *Varnava and Others* v *Turkey*, HUDOC, 18 September 2009 (GC), at para. 184; *Imakayeva* v *Russia*, HUDOC, 9 November 2006, at paras. 139–43 *Gongadze* v *Ukraine*, HUDOC, 8 November 2005, at paras. 164 & 170; *Timurtaş* v *Turkey*, HUDOC, 13 June 2000, at paras. 82–6.

[29] *Keller* v *Russia*, HUDOC 17 October 2013, at paras. 81–3; *Mižárová* v *Slovakia*, HUDOC, 14 December 2010, at para. 89; *Anguelova* v *Bulgaria*, HUDOC, 13 June 2002, at para. 110; *Paul and Audrey Edwards* v *United Kingdom*, HUDOC, 14 March 2002, at para. 56; *Salman* v *Turkey*, HUDOC, 27 June 2000 (GC), at paras. 99 & 102–3.

[30] *Armani Da Silva* v *the United Kingdom*, HUDOC, 20 March 2016 (GC), at paras. 283–8; *Ramsahai and Others* v *the Netherlands*, HUDOC, 15 May 2007 (GC), at paras. 323–5;

possibly negligent official conduct[31] and other suspicious deaths;[32] and Article 2 – compliant legal regulation and training of security forces with respect to use of lethal force.[33] The positive obligation also implies a right to be adequately protected from foreseeable and reasonably avoidable life-threatening self-harm or harm from third parties,[34] and from potentially life-threatening risks arising from man-made[35] and natural hazards.[36] However states have wide margins of appreciation with the result that arrangements may vary from one country to another.[37] While the right to have one's life protected by law cannot be balanced against competing public interests, such as the costs and administrative convenience of official investigations, there is, however, scope for discretion on the part of national non-judicial institutions, for example, concerning whether or not any particular death is 'suspicious'. The obligation to protect everyone's right to life through law does not, however, entail an obligation to make lethal medication available in order to facilitate suicide,[38] or to permit assisted suicide by mentally competent persons

---

Hugh Jordan v United Kingdom, HUDOC, 4 May 2001, at paras. 105–9; *McCann and Others v United Kingdom*, HUDOC, 27 September 1995 (GC), at para. 161.

[31] *Ioniţă v Romania*, HUDOC, 10 January 2017, at para. 72; *Isenc v France*, HUDOC, 4 February 2016, at paras. 46 & 47; *Šilih v Slovenia*, HUDOC, 9 April 2009 (GC), at para. 195; *Dodov v Bulgaria*, HUDOC, 17 January 2008, at paras. 80–3; *Calvelli and Ciglio v Italy*, HUDOC, 17 January 2002 (GC), at para. 49.

[32] *Muradyan v Armenia*, HUDOC, 24 November 2016, at para. 133; *Ramsahai and Others v the Netherlands*, HUDOC, 15 May 2007 (GC), at paras. 323–5; *McCann and Others v United Kingdom*, HUDOC, 27 September 1995 (GC), at para. 161.

[33] *Gerasimenko and Others v Russia*, HUDOC, 1 December 2016, at para. 103; *Nachova and Others v Bulgaria*, HUDOC, 6 July 2005 (GC), at para. 99; *Makaratzis v Greece*, HUDOC, 20 December 2004 (GC), at para. 59; *McCann and Others v United Kingdom*, HUDOC, 27 September 1995 (GC), at para. 150;

[34] *Tagayeva and Others v Russia*, HUDOC, 13 April 2017, at para. 438; *Talpis v Italy*, HUDOC, 2 March 2017, at para. 101; *Hiller v Austria*, HUDOC, 22 November 2016, at para. 48; *F. G. v Sweden*, HUDOC, 23 March 2016 (GC), at paras. 155–8; *Opuz v Turkey*, HUDOC, 9 June 2009, at paras. 128–30; *Branko Tomašić and Others v Croatia*, HUDOC, 15 January 2009, at paras. 50–1; *Gongadze v Ukraine*, HUDOC, 8 November 2005, at para. 164; *Keenan v United Kingdom*, HUDOC, 3 April 2001, at para. 90; *Osman v United Kingdom*, HUDOC, 28 October 1998 (GC), at para. 115.

[35] *Öneryildiz v Turkey*, HUDOC, 30 November 2004 (GC), at para. 71; *Guerra and Others v Italy*, HUDOC, 19 February 1998 (GC).

[36] *Budayeva and Others v Russia*, HUDOC, 20 March 2008, at paras. 129–31 & 141–3.

[37] *Öneryildiz v Turkey*, HUDOC, 30 November 2004 (GC), at para. 107; *Paul and Audrey Edwards v United Kingdom*, HUDOC, 14 March 2002, at para. 55

[38] *Gross v Switzerland*, HUDOC, 14 May 2013, at para. 69. See also: *Gross v Switzerland*, HUDOC, 30 September 2014 (GC, dec.); *Koch v Germany*, HUDOC, 19 July 2012; *Haas v Switzerland*, HUDOC, 20 January 2011.

enduring great suffering who, because of their condition, cannot end their lives themselves.[39]

Potentially one of the most contentious issues under Article 2(1) concerns abortion. Although the Commission heard several cases in the 1980s and 1990s[40] it was not until 2004 that the Court considered the matter. In *Vo v France* a majority of the Grand Chamber ruled that there had been no violation of Article 2 as the result of an involuntary termination caused by medical negligence because, although no offence had been committed, the domestic law provided adequate civil remedies and the requisite procedural requirements had been fulfilled. It was observed that the Convention is silent about when human life attracting the protection of Article 2 begins and that there is, at best, a consensus in Europe that embryos and foetuses are part of the human race with the potential to develop into persons with full legal rights. But, because there is no consensus on when, legally, morally and scientifically, human life begins, member states must be permitted a margin of appreciation in responding to these challenges. The majority, therefore, declined to judge whether the foetus in this case was a person or not. Nor, given that the interests of the foetus and the mother coincided, was there any need to speculate on possible conflicts between their respective rights.[41] Subject to certain gestational limits, abortion is available on request in thirty Council of Europe states, on health grounds in forty and in the interests of the mother's well-being in thirty-five. Only three states – Malta, San Marino and Andorra – prohibit it in all circumstances, while Ireland permits it only to save the life or health of the mother.[42]

Article 2(2) states that killing shall not be regarded as a violation of the right to life 'when it results from the use of force which is no more than absolutely necessary: (a) in defence of any person from unlawful violence;

---

[39] *Pretty v United Kingdom*, HUDOC, 29 April 2002, at paras. 39–41. See A. Pedain, 'The Human rights dimension of the *Diane Pretty* case', *Cambridge Law Journal*, 62 (2003), 181–206.

[40] *H v Norway*, HUDOC, 19 May 1992 (dec.); *Paton v United Kingdom* (1980) 19 D.R. 244; *Brüggemann and Scheuten v Germany*, HUDOC, 19 May 1976. G. Hogan, 'The right to life and the abortion question under the European Convention on Human Rights' in L. Heffernan with J. Kingston (eds.), *Human Rights: A European Perspective* (Blackrock: Round Hall Press, 1994), pp. 104–16.

[41] HUDOC, 8 July 2004 (GC). A further five judges agreed with the majority's decision but disputed the application of Art. 2, two others agreed with the majority verdict in spite of concluding that Art. 2 did apply while three judges dissented from the majority (two of whom delivered a joint opinion) on the grounds that Art. 2 had been violated.

[42] *A, B and C v Ireland*, HUDOC, 16 December 2010 (GC), at para. 112.

(b) in order to effect a lawful arrest or to prevent the escape of a person lawfully detained; (c) in action lawfully taken for the purpose of quelling a riot or insurrection'. As the Court held in *McCann v United Kingdom*: 'the use of the term "absolutely necessary" ... indicates that a stricter and more compelling test of necessity must be employed from that normally applicable when determining whether State action is "necessary in a democratic society" under paragraph 2 of Articles 8–11 ECHR. In particular, the force used must be strictly proportionate to achieving the aims set out in subparagraphs 2(a), (b) and (c) of Article 2.'[43] The provisions of Article 2(2) must, therefore, be 'strictly construed'[44] and are limited only by the 'exhaustive and ... narrowly interpreted'[45] objectives listed. The lethal force must be no more than the minimum necessary depending upon 'the nature of the aim pursued, the dangers to life and limb inherent in the situation and the degree of the risk that the force employed might result in loss of life ... (with) due regard to all the relevant circumstances',[46] a test that also applies in armed conflict, subject to international humanitarian law and with different implications for proportionality.[47] The Court also expects that such cases will be effectively investigated by the defendant state itself,[48] and it may conclude that the manner in which an operation resulting in the use of potentially lethal force was conceived, planned and executed made the force itself excessive,[49] even where those who used it, honestly though

---

[43] *McCann and Others v United Kingdom*, HUDOC, 27 September 1995 (GC), at para. 149. See also *Giuliani and Gaggio v Italy*, HUDOC, 24 March 2011 (GC), at paras. 175–6; *Isayeva, Yusupova and Bazayeva v Russia*, HUDOC, 24 February 2005, at paras. 169, 172 & 191; *McShane v United Kingdom*, HUDOC, 28 May 2002, at para. 93; *Oğur v Turkey*, HUDOC, 20 May 1999 (GC), at para. 78.

[44] *Isayeva, Yusupova and Bazayeva v Russia*, HUDOC, 24 February 2005, at para. 168; *Andronicou & Constantinou v Cyprus*, HUDOC, 9 October 1997, at para. 171; *McCann and Others v United Kingdom*, HUDOC, 27 September 1995 (GC), at para. 147.

[45] *Stewart v United Kingdom* (1984) 39 D.R. 162, at para. 13.

[46] See also *Isayeva, Yusupova and Bazayeva v Russia*, HUDOC, 24 February 2005, at para. 171.

[47] *Hassan v United Kingdom*, HUDOC, 16 September 2014 (GC), at paras. 77 & 102–3.

[48] *Finogenov and Others v Russia*, HUDOC, 20 December 2011, at paras. 268–72; *Isayeva, Yusupova and Bazayeva v Russia*, HUDOC, 24 February 2005, at paras. 209–24; *Tepe v Turkey*, HUDOC, 9 May 2003, at paras. 177–82.

[49] *Tagayeva and Others v Russia*, HUDOC, 13 April 2017, at para. 574; *Finogenov and Others v Russia*, HUDOC, 20 December 2011 at para. 266; *Nachova and Others v Bulgaria*, HUDOC, 6 July 2005 (GC), at para. 95; *Isayeva, Yusupova and Bazayeva v Russia*, HUDOC, 24 February 2005, at paras. 174–6; *McCann and Others v United Kingdom*, HUDOC, 27 September 1995 (GC), at paras. 150 & 200–1.

mistakenly, believed that it was no more than absolutely necessary in pursuit of the legitimate objectives specified in Article 2(2).[50] In *McCann*, for example, the Court concluded that it was not absolutely necessary in all the circumstances to kill three IRA suspects in order to prevent the detonation of a bomb in Gibraltar, which British security forces mistakenly believed they were carrying and which, had this been true, would have killed many when it exploded. Although on a bombing mission, the three suspects were not, in fact, about to detonate a bomb at the time they were shot, and the Court held they could have been arrested as they crossed the frontier into the British territory having parked their car with the explosives on the Spanish side.[51]

Here, as with respect to most other Convention rights, the principle of proportionality plays a pivotal role, appearing in Article 2(1) as a necessarily implicit component of the obligation to protect the right to life rather than life itself, and in the high threshold 'no more force than absolutely necessary' test in Article 2(2). By and large, the ECtHR has understood and applied this well, treading the sometimes-thin line between being too demanding of or too generous to the state in resolving the dilemmas sometimes created by these onerous obligations. The margin of appreciation doctrine quite properly plays a particularly significant role concerning the vexed issue of when a life attracting Article 2 protection begins.

Article 3 – Prohibition of Torture

Although the substance of Articles 3, 4(1) and 7(1) is different, they share the same form,[52] containing not rights as such but unqualified and non-derogable negative or prohibitive principles or imperatives, from which rights may be derived. In order to fall within the scope of Article 3, the

---

[50] *Giuliani and Gaggio* v *Italy*, HUDOC, 24 March 2011 (GC), at paras. 178 & 191; *McCann and Others* v *United Kingdom*, HUDOC, 27 September 1995 (GC), at para. 200.

[51] *McCann and Others* v *United Kingdom*, HUDOC, 27 September 1995 (GC), at paras. 195–214.

[52] Some of the provisions found in the Protocols also take the form of unqualified prohibitions, for example, deprivation of liberty merely because of inability to fulfil a contractual obligation (Art. 1 of Protocol No. 4); the expulsion of nationals from, or refusal of entry to, their national state (Art. 3 of Protocol No. 4); the collective expulsion of aliens (Art. 4 of Protocol No. 4); and the death penalty (Arts. 1 of Protocol No. 13). But not all Council of Europe states have agreed to be bound by these Protocols and there is very little case law on any.

prohibited conduct, torture, inhuman or degrading treatment or punishment, must cross a seriousness threshold, which may depend on subjective and/or context-specific factors. For example, while beating a detainee to obtain information or a confession will invariably be a violation of Article 3, the same force may be justified when making an arrest.[53] And not every affront to dignity will amount to degrading treatment for the purpose of this provision.[54] As with Article 2, Article 3 also generates positive state obligations, which include criminalising the proscribed ill-treatment in domestic law, adequately preventing it, including by third parties[55] and by other states, including by refusing to facilitate extraordinary rendition,[56] extradition and deportation where there are 'substantial grounds' for believing there is a 'real risk' of an Article 3 violation in the receiving state.[57] There is also a duty to conduct independent and effective investigations[58] and to enforce the prohibition appropriately, including through prosecution and punishment and by providing other remedies.[59]

Much of the case law on Article 3 is concerned with how torture, inhuman or degrading treatment or punishment should be understood and distinguished.[60] Degrading treatment or punishment is that which,

---

[53] *Ali Güneş v Turkey*, HUDOC, 10 April 2012, at paras. 34–43.

[54] See *Wainwright v United Kingdom*, HUDOC, 26 September 2006, at para. 46.

[55] *Irina Smirnova v Ukraine*, HUDOC, 13 October 2016, at para. 70; *Abdu v Bulgaria*, HUDOC, 11 March 2014, at para. 40; *Opuz v Turkey*, HUDOC, 9 June 2009, at paras. 159 & 176; *Z and Others v United Kingdom*, HUDOC, 10 May 2001 (GC), at para. 73; *Mahmut Kaya v Turkey*, HUDOC, 28 March 2000, at para. 115.

[56] The 'extra-judicial transfer of persons from one jurisdiction or state to another for the purpose of detention and interrogation outside the normal legal system where there is a real risk of torture, inhuman or degrading treatment', *Nasr and Ghali v Italy*, HUDOC, 23 February 2016, at paras. 288–91.

[57] *Paposhvili v Belgium*, HUDOC, 13 December 2016 (GC), at paras. 174 & 181; *J. K. and Others v Sweden*, HUDOC, 23 August 2016 (GC), at para. 79; *MYH and Others v Sweden*, HUDOC, 27 June 2013, at para. 52; *Al-Saadoon and Mufdhi v United Kingdom*, HUDOC, 2 March 2010, at para. 123; *Soering v United Kingdom*, HUDOC, 7 July 1989, paras. 88 & 91. The Court has been prepared to accept assurances by the receiving state that this will not happen. See, e.g., decision on inadmissibility in *Aswat v United Kingdom*, HUDOC, 6 January 2015 (dec.), at paras. 29–31.

[58] *Beortegui Martinez v Spain*, HUDOC, 31 May 2016, at para. 47; *Alpar v Turkey*, HUDOC, 26 January 2016, at para. 50.

[59] *Jeronovičs v Latvia*, HUDOC, 5 July 2016 (GC), at paras. 103–6; *Abdu v Bulgaria*, HUDOC, 11 March 2014, at paras. 41–3; *Gäfgen v Germany*, HUDOC, 1 June 2010 (GC), at paras. 116–19; *Opuz v Turkey*, HUDOC, 9 June 2009, at 168; *Assenov and Others v Bulgaria*, HUDOC, 28 October 1998, at para. 102.

[60] See J. Vorhaus, 'On degradation. Part one. Article 3 of the European Convention on Human Rights', *Common Law World Review*, 31 (2002), 374–99 and 'On degradation. Part two. Degrading treatment and punishment', *Common Law World Review* 32 (2003),

intentionally or otherwise, humiliates and/or severely debases, and/or shows a lack of respect for dignity, and/or which arouses feelings of fear, anguish and/or inferiority capable of breaking moral and/or physical resistance.[61] Examples in the context of detention include the absence of any possibility of review regarding release;[62] overcrowded, unsanitary and otherwise unacceptable conditions;[63] strip searches without sufficient reason and/or in breach of appropriate procedures;[64] being forced to undress for no reason;[65] solitary confinement or segregation, particularly for long periods without periodic review and/or lacking adequate justification in terms of security, discipline, the administration of justice, the prevention or crime or the safety of the detainee or others;[66] inadequate provision for specific needs including routine medical care;[67] medical intervention against a detainee's will in breach of appropriate procedures and in the absence of a therapeutic necessity in terms of physical or mental health, including forced feeding;[68] and physical

---

65–92; M. D. Evans and R. Morgan, *Preventing Torture: A Study of the European Convention for the Prevention of Torture and Inhuman and Degrading Treatment or Punishment* (Oxford: Clarendon Press, 1998), pp. 79–105. As Evans argues, for the Court, this is less about finding 'definitions' than developing an 'approach', M. D. Evans, 'Getting to grips with torture', *International and Comparative Law Quarterly*, 51 (2002), 365–83 at 368–9.

[61] *Pretty v United Kingdom*, HUDOC, 29 April 2002, at para. 52; *Kudła v Poland*, HUDOC, 26 October 2000 (GC), at para. 92.

[62] *Hutchinson v United Kingdom*, HUDOC, 17 January 2017 (GC), at para. 44; *Hutchinson v United Kingdom*, HUDOC, 3 February 2015, at paras. 19–20; *Vinter and Others v United Kingdom*, HUDOC, 9 July 2013 (GC), at paras. 110–15 & 119.

[63] *Muršić v Croatia*, HUDOC, 20 October 2016 (GC), at paras. 104 & 137; *Korneykova and Korneykov v Ukraine*, HUDOC, 24 March 2016, at para. 147; *Modarca v Moldova*, HUDOC, 10 May 2007, paras. 63–9; *Kalashnikov v Russia*, HUDOC, 15 July 2002, at paras. 96–103.

[64] *Wiktorko v Poland*, HUDOC, 31 March 2009, at paras. 53–7; *Wainwright v United Kingdom*, HUDOC, 26 September 2006, at para. 45.

[65] *Enver Aydemir v Turkey*, HUDOC, 7 June 2016, at para. 63.

[66] *Ramirez Sanchez v France*, HUDOC, 4 July 2006 (GC), at paras. 120–50; *Ilaşcu and Others v Moldova and Russia*, HUDOC, 8 July 2004 (GC), at paras. 428–33, 438–9 & 451–2.

[67] *Wenner v Germany*, 1 September 2016, at paras. 55–7; *Yunusova and Yunusov v Azerbaijan*, HUDOC, 2 June 2016, at para. 150; *Murray v the Netherlands*, HUDOC, 26 April 2016 (GC), at paras. 125–7; *Gorbulya v Russia*, HUDOC, 6 March 2014, at para. 75; *Dybeku v Albania*, HUDOC, 18 December 2007, at paras. 41–52; *Khudobin v Russia*, HUDOC, 26 October 2006, at paras. 92–7; *Kudła v Poland*, HUDOC, 26 October 2000 (GC), at para. 94.

[68] *Jalloh v Germany*, HUDOC, 11 July 2006 (GC), at para. 69; *Herczegfalvy v Austria*, HUDOC, 24 September 1992, at para. 82.

restraint that is not reasonable in the circumstances.[69] Examples from other contexts include certain kinds of discrimination;[70] failure to meet the basic needs of asylum seekers and those subject to collective expulsion;[71] pressuring a young woman into having an abortion;[72] requiring a seventy-year-old man to do military service including training designed for much younger people;[73] corporal punishment in some forms and contexts but not others;[74] and the removal of tissue from a dead man's body for pharmaceutical purposes without the knowledge or consent of his wife.[75]

Inhuman treatment or punishment is the infliction of degrading treatment or punishment, not necessarily intentional, which causes either actual bodily injury or intense physical and/or mental suffering above a certain threshold and sustained for considerable periods.[76] It is distinguished from torture primarily by the lesser degree of suffering involved. Examples include assaults,[77] oppressive psychological interrogation techniques beyond merely robust questioning,[78] ill-treatment of detainees[79] and anticipation of capital punishment.[80]

Torture is deliberate, purposive and prolonged inhuman treatment that causes very serious and cruel physical and/or mental suffering.[81]

---

[69] *Korneykova and Korneykov v Ukraine*, HUDOC, 24 March 2016, at paras. 165 & 166; *Svinarenko and Slyadnev v Russia*, HUDOC, 17 July 2014 (GC), at para. 117; *Erdoğan Yağiz v Turkey*, HUDOC, 6 March 2007, at paras. 45–8.

[70] *Cyprus v Turkey*, HUDOC, 10 May 2001 (GC), at para. 305.

[71] *Z. A. and Others v Russia*, HUDOC, 28 March 2017, at paras. 102–11; *Shioshvili and Others v Russia*, HUDOC, 20 December 2016, at paras. 81–6; *VM and Others v Belgium*, HUDOC, 7 July 2015, at paras. 156–63; *MSS v Belgium and Greece*, HUDOC, 21 January 2011 (GC), at para. 263.

[72] *P and S v Poland*, HUDOC, 30 January 2013, at paras. 163–4 & 168–9.

[73] *Taştan v Turkey*, HUDOC, 4 March 2008, at paras. 27–33.

[74] *Costello-Roberts v United Kingdom*, HUDOC, 25 March 1993, at paras. 31–2; *Tyrer v United Kingdom*, HUDOC, 25 April 1978, at paras. 32–5.

[75] *Elberte v Latvia*, HUDOC, 13 January 2015, at paras. 137 & 140–3.

[76] *Kudła v Poland*, HUDOC, 26 October 2000 (GC), at para. 92; *Tekin v Turkey*, HUDOC, 9 June 1998, at para. 52; *Ireland v United Kingdom*, HUDOC, 18 July 1978, at para. 167.

[77] *Najafli v Azerbaijan*, HUDOC, 2 October 2012, at paras. 39–41; *Denizci and Others v Cyprus*, HUDOC, 21 May 2001, at paras. 329–42 & 384–7; *Ribitsch v Austria*, HUDOC, 4 December 1995, at para. 38; *Tomasi v France*, HUDOC, 27 August 1992, at para. 115.

[78] *Ireland v United Kingdom*, HUDOC, 18 July 1978, at paras. 96 & 167–8.

[79] *Mader v Croatia*, HUDOC, 21 June 2011, at paras. 108 & 110.

[80] *Al Nashiri v Poland*, HUDOC, 24 July 2014, at para. 577.

[81] *Virabyan v Armenia*, HUDOC, 2 October 2012, at para. 156; *Ireland v United Kingdom*, HUDOC, 18 July 1978, at para. 167.

Examples include beatings,[82] suspension by the arms tied behind the back ('Palestinian hanging'),[83] rape and the threat of rape,[84] electric shock treatment,[85] extreme solitary confinement,[86] threats to the victim's family[87] and mock executions.[88] Inhuman treatment may constitute torture when it is particularly intense or prolonged, or when several types, for example, being blindfolded and paraded naked, are combined with each other and/or with physical abuse.[89]

Although the Court has repeatedly emphasised that the rights derived from Article 3 are 'absolute' and, therefore, subject to no exceptions whatsoever, this cannot be strictly true for two main reasons. First, what constitutes the prohibited conduct is relative both to circumstance and to the subjective characteristics of the victim with the language of proportionality sometimes used to determine whether or not this threshold has been crossed.[90] Second, where two instances of the same Article 3 right are in conflict, one must necessarily be an exception to ('less absolute') than the other.[91] On the rare occasions when this might occur, the empty repetition of the absoluteness mantra is no substitute for a choice based upon a comprehensive evaluation of all the issues at stake. Nevertheless, Article 3, together with the other formally unqualified non-derogable rights, are 'virtually absolute' and deserve a 'specially protected status' not conferred on other Convention rights.[92]

---

[82] *Dikme v Turkey*, HUDOC, 11 July 2000, at paras. 91 & 96; *Selmouni v France*, HUDOC, 28 July 1999 (GC), at paras. 102 & 105; *Greek Case*, HUDOC, 5 November 1969 (Commission Decision) 12 YB 1, 504.

[83] *Aksoy v Turkey*, HUDOC, 18 December 1996, at para. 64.

[84] *Zontul v Greece*, HUDOC, 12 January 2012, at para. 91; *Aydin v Turkey*, HUDOC, 25 September 1997 (GC), at paras. 83 & 86.

[85] *Mikheyev v Russia*, HUDOC, 26 January 2006, at para. 129; *Akkoçv Turkey*, HUDOC, 10 October 2000, at para. 116.

[86] *Ilaşcu and Others v Moldova and Russia*, HUDOC, 8 July 2004 (GC), at para. 438.

[87] *Akkoçv Turkey*, HUDOC, 10 October 2000, at para. 116.

[88] *Ilaşcu and Others v Moldova and Russia*, HUDOC, 8 July 2004 (GC), at para. 435.

[89] *Aydin v Turkey*, HUDOC, 25 September 1997 (GC), at paras. 80–7.

[90] J. Simor and B. Emmerson, Q.C. (eds.), *Human Rights Practice* (London: Sweet & Maxwell, 2000), para. 1.079.

[91] *Gäfgen v Germany*, HUDOC, 1 June 2011 (GC). See S. Greer, 'Should police threats to torture suspects always be severely punished? Reflections on the Gäfgen case', *Human Rights Law Review*, 11 (2011), 67–89.

[92] S. Greer, 'Is the prohibition against torture, cruel, inhuman or degrading treatment really "absolute" in international human rights law?' *Human Rights Law Review*, 15 (2015), 101–37.

Article 4 – Prohibition of Slavery and Forced Labour

Although Article 4, expressed as a non-derogable and formally unquali-fied prohibition, has generated very little case law, it has become more relevant recently as a result of increased awareness about the problem of human trafficking.[93] The Court has endorsed the classic meaning of slavery found in Article 1 of the UN Slavery Convention 1926 as 'the status or condition of a person over whom any or all of the powers attaching to the right of ownership are exercised' and has defined servi-tude as 'an obligation to provide one's services that is imposed by the use of coercion' coupled with being required 'to live on another's property and the impossibility of changing one's situation'.[94]

As far as 'forced or compulsory labour' is concerned the definition found in the International Labour Organisation's Forced Labour Convention 1930 – 'all work or service which is exacted from any person under the menace of any penalty and for which the said person has not offered himself voluntarily' – has been taken as 'a starting point'.[95] However, while Article 4(2) provides that '(n)o one shall be required to perform forced or compulsory labour', Article 4(3) provides a series of definitional exclusions, for example, military service and prison or com-munity work. Unlike those derived from Article 4(1), these rights are derogable. The little other litigation there has been on these provisions has been dominated by mostly unsuccessful attempts by dentists, phys-icians, and lawyers to evade discharging limited public service obligations as part of their professional responsibilities.[96] Nor does forced or compulsory labour include the deduction of social security payments or income tax from an employee's salary at source,[97] a prisoner working without remuneration[98] or beyond retirement age[99] or an unemployed person accepting suitable employment as a condition for receiving unemployment benefit.[100] Relying on the principles of proportionality,

---

[93] *Rantsev v Cyprus and Russia*, HUDOC, 7 January 2010, at paras. 278–81. See also *Siliadin v France*, HUDOC, 26 July 2005, at paras. 48–51.

[94] *Siliadin v France*, HUDOC, 26 July 2005, at para. 122–4.

[95] *Stummer v Austria*, HUDOC, 7 July 2011 (GC), at para. 118.

[96] *Reitmayr v Austria*, HUDOC, 28 June 1995 (dec.); *Van der Mussele v Belgium*, HUDOC, 23 November 1983, at paras. 37–40; *Van Droogenbroeck v Belgium*, HUDOC, 24 June 1982, at paras. 57–60

[97] *Four Companies v Austria*, HUDOC, 27 September 1976 (dec.).

[98] *Floroiu v Romania*, HUDOC, 12 March 2013 (dec.) at paras. 17–21 & 35–7.

[99] *Meier v Switzerland*, HUDOC, 9 February 2016, at para. 80.

[100] *Schuitemaker v the Netherlands*, HUDOC, 4 May 2010 (dec.).

commonality, legality and non-discrimination, the Strasbourg institutions have, therefore, defined 'normal civic responsibilities' in Article 4 (3)(d) to mean those permitted by domestic law or professional codes, encompassing a foreseeable possibility when joining the profession in the country concerned, common amongst member states, applied without discrimination or arbitrariness, and not excessively burdensome considering time spent, connection with normal professional duties, remuneration received and service rendered. Therefore, in spite of its different format, the right not to be subjected to forced or compulsory labour is a strongly protected one with a universal European character, similar to those in Articles 3, 4(1) and 7(1).

As with Articles 2 and 3, states also have positive obligations under Article 4 to prohibit the behaviour and conditions in question, to act appropriately without assuming an 'impossible or disproportionate burden' where they are 'or ought to have been aware of circumstances giving rise to credible suspicions' that a specific person was being or was at real risk of being subjected to the prohibited conduct, to conduct effective investigations and adequately to punish offenders.[101]

Article 5 – Right to Liberty and Security

The purpose of Article 5 is to prohibit arbitrary/unlawful deprivations of liberty without consent,[102] though not all restrictions upon movement, the distinction being largely a matter of degree, type, context, duration, effects, manner of implementation and the presence or absence of coercion.[103] Apart from unacknowledged disappearances, it is, however, difficult to find a credible example of a violation of the 'right to security of the person' that, in this context, would not also constitute a violation

---

[101] *JA v France*, HUDOC, 27 May 2014 (dec.), at para. 37; *Rantsev v Cyprus and Russia*, HUDOC, 7 January 2010, at para. 286; *Siliadin v France*, HUDOC, 26 July 2005, at paras. 84 & 89.

[102] *El Masri v The Former Yugoslav Republic of Macedonia*, HUDOC, 13 December 2012 (GC), at paras. 230–3; *Austin v United Kingdom*, HUDOC, 15 March 2012 (GC), at para. 58; *İ Bilgin v Turkey*, HUDOC, 17 July 2001, at para. 149; *Engel and Others v the Netherlands*, HUDOC, 8 June 1976, at para. 58. See R. Kolb, 'The jurisprudence of the European Court of Human Rights on detention and fair trial in criminal matters from 1992 to the end of 1998', *Human Rights Law Journal*, 21 (2000), 348–73.

[103] *Austin v United Kingdom*, HUDOC, 15 March 2012 (GC), at paras. 53–60; *Gillan and Quinton v United Kingdom*, HUDOC, 12 January 2010, at para. 57; *Guzzardi v Italy*, HUDOC, 6 November 1980, paras. 92–5.

of the 'right to liberty'.[104] The core assumption underpinning Article 5 is that liberty should be presumed unless one or more of a number of express exceptions falling broadly into two categories apply: those concerning the law enforcement process and specific types of detainee.

Providing they are lawful (a concept explored later), the following law enforcement deprivations of liberty are permissible, do not constitute arbitrary deprivations and therefore do not amount to violations of Article 5: following conviction by a competent court;[105] for non-compliance with a lawful court order[106] or to secure fulfilment of a legal obligation;[107] applied to those reasonably, and not just honestly, suspected of having committed an offence whether or not charge or trial follow; [108] and to prevent the commission of an offence, or to prevent escape thereafter where, in each case, it is reasonably necessary to do so.[109] Provided it complies with 'a procedure prescribed by law,'[110] and any other detainee-specific requirements derived from this principle, the arrest/detention of various nominated types of detainee also does not violate Article 5. Minors may be detained by lawful order for the purpose of educational supervision or lawful detention for the purpose of being brought before a competent legal authority.[111] Those suffering from infectious diseases may be lawfully detained where, striking a fair balance with the right to liberty, less severe measures would not adequately safeguard public health.[112] Persons of 'unsound mind' may be lawfully detained where there is medical evidence that this is the case and that,

---

[104] See, for example, *ER and Others* v *Turkey*, HUDOC, 31 July 2012; *Kurt* v *Turkey*, HUDOC, 25 May 1998.

[105] Art. 5(1)(a). *James, Wells and Lee* v *United Kingdom*, HUDOC, 18 September 2012, at paras. 188 & 197; *Weeks* v *United Kingdom*, HUDOC, 2 March 1987, at para. 61; *Van Droogenbroeck* v *Belgium*, HUDOC, 24 June 1982, at para. 39.

[106] Art. 5(1) (b). *X* v *Germany* (1975) 3 D.R. 92.

[107] Art. 5(1)(b). *Ostendorf* v *Germany*, HUDOC, 7 March 2013, at paras. 69 & 90–103; *Ciulla* v *Italy*, HUDOC, 22 February 1989, at paras. 41–2.

[108] *Gusinskiy* v *Russia*, HUDOC, 19 May 2004, at para. 53; *O'Hara* v *United Kingdom*, HUDOC, 16 October 2001, at para. 38; *Fox, Campbell and Hartley* v *United Kingdom*, HUDOC, 30 August 1990, at para. 32; *Brogan* v *United Kingdom*, HUDOC, 29 November 1988, at para. 53.

[109] Art. 5(1)(c). *Kasparov* v *Russia*, HUDOC, 11 October 2016, at paras. 51–4; ; *Ostendorf* v *Germany*, HUDOC, 7 March 2013, at para. 66; *Schwabe and MG* v *Germany*, HUDOC, 1 December 2011, paras. 70, 72 & 77–80.

[110] Art. 5(1).

[111] Art. 5(1)(d). *Blokhin* v *Russia*, HUDOC, 23 March 2016 (GC), at paras. 171 & 172; *Bouamar* v *Belgium*, HUDOC, 29 February 1988, at paras. 48 & 52–3.

[112] Art. 5 (1)(e). *Enhorn* v *Sweden*, HUDOC, 25 January 2005, at paras. 43–6 & 55–6.

subject to adequate safeguards against arbitrariness, compulsory confinement is necessary in the circumstances either to protect them from themselves or to protect others, and/or for appropriate and proportionate therapeutic reasons.[113] Where no other equally effective alternatives are available, alcoholics or drug addicts whose behaviour poses a threat to themselves or the public may also be lawfully detained.[114] While Article 5(1)(e) envisages the lawful detention of 'vagrants,'[115] this 'rather archaic provision' is 'almost certainly obsolete today.'[116] Those seeking unauthorised entry into a country or subject to extradition or deportation proceedings could be considered as falling into either the 'law enforcement' or 'specific type of detainee' categories.[117] Although the detention of those seeking entry is subject to a legality/non-arbitrary (but not a reasonable necessity) test, the place and conditions of detention should be appropriate and the duration of detention should not exceed that reasonably required for the purpose of settling the authorisation issue.[118] Similarly, providing duly diligent action in the circumstances is being taken genuinely with a view to extradition or deportation, and there are appropriate safeguards against arbitrariness, detention for these purposes must be 'lawful' rather than 'necessary' and for no longer than the proceedings themselves last.[119]

The 'principle of legality' provides the bedrock for Article 5, with the term 'law' or 'lawful' appearing twelve times, and 'court', 'judge', 'competent legal authority' or 'officer authorised by law' six times.[120] In the ECHR generally, and in Article 5 in particular, this means both

---

[113] Art. 5 (1)(e). *Ruslan Makarov v Russia*, HUDOC, 11 October 2016, at paras. 20–5; *Bergmann v Germany*, HUDOC, 7 January 2016, at paras. 133 & 134; *Radu v Germany*, HUDOC, 16 May 2013, at paras. 105–8; *Varbanov v Bulgaria*, HUDOC, 5 October 2000, at para. 46; *Winterwerp v the Netherlands*, HUDOC, 24 October 1979, paras. 39 & 41.

[114] Art. 5 (1)(e). *Gukovych v Ukraine*, HUDOC, 20 October 2016, at para. 51; *Witold Litwa v Poland*, HUDOC, 4 April 2000, at paras. 61–2.

[115] Art. 5 (1)(e). *De Wilde, Ooms and Versyp ("Vagrancy") v Belgium*, HUDOC, 18 June 1971, at paras. 69–70.

[116] Schabas, *European Convention*, p. 243.

[117] Art. (5(1)(f).

[118] *Saadi v United Kingdom*, HUDOC, 29 January 2008 (GC), at paras. 66 & 78–80.

[119] *Khlaifia and Others v Italy*, HUDOC, 15 December 2016 (GC), at paras. 90 – 92; *A and Others v United Kingdom*, HUDOC, 19 February 2009 (GC), at para. 171; *Chahal v United Kingdom*, HUDOC, 15 November 1996 (GC), at paras. 112–19; *Bozano v France*, HUDOC, 18 December 1986, at paras. 59–60.

[120] *Assanidze v Georgia*, HUDOC, 8 April 2004 (GC), at para. 170; *Čonka v Belgium*, HUDOC, 5 February 2002, at para. 42; *Dougoz v Greece*, HUDOC, 6 March 2001, at para. 61; *Chahal v United Kingdom*, HUDOC, 15 November 1996 (GC), at para. 127; *Ireland v United Kingdom*, HUDOC, 18 July 1978, at para. 194.

compliance with domestic law,[121] and with a more abstract principle of legality, which includes the requirements of precision, accessibility, foreseeability, judicial accountability, the provision of adequate remedies and the exclusion of arbitrariness by, for example, giving reasons, keeping adequate records[122] and adhering to the principles of proportionality, last resort, limited duration and due diligence.[123] While 'arrest' and 'detention' are not formally defined by Article 5, detention involving particularly severe restrictions on freedom of movement, does not require arrest, and arrest need not coincide with, or depend upon, being charged with an offence. Two rights apply both to arrest and to detention. Article 5(4) provides a right to have the legality of arrest and/or detention decided speedily by an independent and impartial 'court'[124] empowered, in adversarial proceedings where the principle of equality of arms is observed,[125] to order release if confinement is found to be unlawful.[126] Article 5(5) provides an enforceable right to compensation for breaches of any part of the entire provision.

A number of other rights apply only to those under arrest. Article 5(2) requires arrestees to be informed 'promptly' (taken to mean within a matter of hours), in a language they understand, of at least the bare legal reasons for arrest and of any charge against them, subject to whatever information they themselves may also glean from the circumstances.[127] Those arrested under Article 5(1)(c) must also be brought 'promptly' (taken to mean within a maximum of four days), and, where relevant, at

---

[121] *Ruslan Makarov v Russia*, HUDOC, 11 October 2016, at para. 28; *Creangă v Romania*, 23 January 2012 (GC), at para. 101.

[122] *Oleynik v Russia*, HUDOC, 21 June 2016, at paras. 38–9.

[123] *Lelyuk v Ukraine*, HUDOC, 17 November 2016, at paras. 43–6; *El Masri v The Former Yugoslav Republic of Macedonia*, HUDOC, 13 December 2012 (GC), at para. 230; *James, Wells and Lee v United Kingdom*, HUDOC, 18 September 2012, at para. 195; *Creangă v Romania*, 23 January 2012 (GC), at para. 120; *Medvedyev v France*, HUDOC, 29 March 2010 (GC), at para. 80; *Saadi v United Kingdom*, HUDOC, 29 January 2008 (GC), at para. 70; *Denizci and Others v Cyprus*, HUDOC, 21 May 2001, at paras. 392–3; *Kurt v Turkey*, HUDOC, 25 May 1998, at para. 124.

[124] *Khlaifia and Others v Italy*, HUDOC, 15 December 2016 (GC), at para. 131; *Derungs v Switzerland*, HUDOC, 10 May 2016, at paras. 53–6; *Hutchinson and Reid v United Kingdom*, HUDOC, 20 February 2003, at para. 64.

[125] *A and Others v United Kingdom*, HUDOC, 19 February 2009 (GC), at paras. 204 & 219–20; *Garcia Alva v Germany*, HUDOC, 13 February 2001, at paras. 39 & 42–3.

[126] *Van Droogenbroeck v Belgium*, HUDOC, 24 June 1982, at para. 48.

[127] Art. 5(2). *Fox, Campbell and Hartley v United Kingdom*, HUDOC, 30 August 1990, at para. 41.

reasonable intervals,[128] before an independent and impartial 'judge or other officer authorised by law to exercise judicial power'.[129] They must also be tried within a reasonable time,[130] or released pending trial (upon surety if appropriate), unless the state can provide 'relevant and sufficient' reasons to justify continued detention.[131] The Strasbourg institutions have recognised four risks with respect to which bail may legitimately be refused: absconding, interfering with the course of justice, committing crime and disturbing public order.[132] While certain circumstances, including, for example, the struggle against terrorism, may legitimately prolong the period of pre-trial detention, or the period of detention before suspects are brought before a judge, the 'promptness' criterion should not be so flexible as to impair the 'very essence' of the right to liberty. It has been held that even a delay of four days, six hours is too long.[133]

While the express justifications for arrest and detention provided by Article 5 are exhaustive and open only to narrow interpretation,[134] there is, nevertheless, room for some national discretion in determining, for example, whether an individual is of 'unsound mind' for the purpose of Article 5(1)(e), and in applying the adjectives and adverbs 'promptly', 'speedily', 'reasonable' and 'reasonably' in Article 5(1)(c), 5(2) and 5 (3).[135] Since these terms cannot be conclusively defined, national non-judicial authorities may be capable of choosing among a range of

---

[128] *Bezicheri* v *Italy*, HUDOC, 25 October 1989, at paras. 20–3; *Winterwerp* v *the Netherlands*, HUDOC, 24 October 1979, at para. 55.

[129] *Hood* v *United Kingdom*, HUDOC, 18 February 1999 (GC), at paras. 50 & 57–8; *Schiesser* v *Switzerland*, HUDOC, 4 December 1979, at paras. 29–31.

[130] Art. 5(3). *McKay* v *United Kingdom*, HUDOC, 3 October 2006 (GC), at para. 47; *Brogan* v *United Kingdom*, HUDOC, 29 November 1988, at paras. 59 & 62; *De Jong, Baljet and Van Den Brink* v *the Netherlands*, HUDOC, 22 May 1984, at para. 51; *Winterwerp* v *the Netherlands*, HUDOC, 24 October 1979, at paras. 42 & 49; *Stogmüller* v *Austria*, HUDOC, 10 November 1969, at paras. 2 & 13–16 of the section 'As to the law'.

[131] *Buzadji* v *the Republic of Moldova*, HUDOC, 5 July 2016 (GC), at paras. 87–8 & 92–102; *Idalov* v *Russia*, HUDOC, 22 May 2012 (GC), at para. 140; *Wemhoff* v *Germany*, HUDOC, 27 June 1968, at para. 12.

[132] *Letellier* v *France*, HUDOC, 26 June 1991, at paras. 37–53; *Matznetter* v *Austria*, HUDOC, 10 November 1969, at paras. 8–9; *Stogmüller* v *Austria*, HUDOC, 10 November 1969, at para. 15 of the section 'As to the law'; *Wemhoff* v *Germany*, HUDOC, 27 June 1968, at paras. 13–14.

[133] *Chraidi* v *Germany*, HUDOC, 26 October 2006, at para. 37; *Brogan* v *United Kingdom*, HUDOC, 29 November 1988, at para. 62.

[134] *Al-Jedda* v *United Kingdom*, HUDOC, 7 July 2011, at para. 99; *Winterwerp* v *the Netherlands*, HUDOC, 24 October 1979, at para. 37.

[135] *Winterwerp* v *the Netherlands*, HUDOC, 24 October 1979, at para. 40.

alternatives at least as effectively and appropriately as the ECtHR. But this must be within strict limits. The 'reasonable suspicion' requirement in Article 5(1)(c), for example, requires some objective grounds in addition to an 'honest belief'. A high-threshold proportionality/'strictly necessary' test must also be observed when balancing the right to liberty against any risk posed by the 'socially problematic' individuals listed in Article 5(1)(e), either to themselves or to the public if they were left at large. However, proportionality is not relevant, and legality is the only criterion applicable to the detention of minors under Article 5(1)(d), those seeking unauthorised entry into a country and candidates for extradition or deportation under Article 5(1)(f). Article 5 also permits little scope for a national margin of appreciation in the strict sense of a discretion available to national non-judicial bodies in determining how conflicts should be settled between the right to liberty and other human rights or implicit public interests such as protection from harm or crime.

Article 6 – Right to a Fair Trial

Article 6 ECHR provides a right to fair trial. Paradoxically this right could be said to be both 'absolute', in the sense that an unfair trial can never be justified by reference to any other competing right or public interest, and 'relative' because what constitutes 'fairness' can legitimately vary according to context and may depend upon technical procedural issues and wider circumstances including public interests. A 'fair trial' is also both a right available to the accused and a general public interest.[136] Strangely, although its provisions apply where they are available, Article 6 does not expressly require rights of appeal.

In the non-criminal context, the key goal of a fair trial is to enable, as far as possible, each side in a legal dispute adequately to present its case, while in the criminal context it is to manage two sharply competing risks: wrongfully acquitting the guilty if the standard is set too high, and wrongfully convicting those who cannot be proven to be guilty (including the innocent) if the standard is set too low. However, because every viable democratic criminal justice system must compromise between the competing aims of effective crime control and the highest conceivable standards of due process, 'fairness' in criminal trials is essentially a matter of judgement rather than exactitude and cannot realistically mean procedures

---

[136] Kolb, 'Jurisprudence', 361.

guaranteeing absolute certainty of guilt as a condition for conviction. However, Article 6, together with the Convention's primary constitutional principles, require that whatever balancing occurs, greater though not conclusive weight should be placed upon rights than upon competing public interests.

Article 6(1) ECHR provides that, in the determination of civil rights and obligations or of any criminal charge, everyone is entitled to a fair and public (and by implication an oral) hearing,[137] within a reasonable time, by an independent and impartial tribunal established by law.[138] While the Strasbourg institutions initially excluded administrative law proceedings from the term 'the determination of civil rights and obliga- tions',[139] the ECtHR has since included at least those that are pecuniary in nature, except where, as with taxation but not with social security, they 'form part of the hard core of public authority prerogatives'.[140] However, the rationale for drawing a distinction between those administrative proceedings that attract Article 6 guarantees and those that do not is unclear. Similarly, the expression 'the proper administration of justice' may refer both to normative standards and to administrative necessity. The Court takes the term 'criminal charge' to have 'autonomous mean- ing'. That is to say, in order to prevent states' neutralising Article 6 safeguards by re-designating criminal offences as mere administrative infractions, it decides for itself whether or not any given domestic proceeding involves a criminal charge.[141] While it will always accept a 'charge' as 'criminal' if this is how it is defined domestically, it may, nevertheless, regard as criminal those 'charges' that are not so defined, where they are enforceable by a public body with punitive or deterrent rather than compensatory statutory powers hinging upon a finding of culpability, or are regarded by other member states generally as criminal. Nevertheless, the most influential factor tends to be the severity of the applicable sanction.[142] However, the distinction between, on the one hand, criminal offences and, on the other, disciplinary, regulatory or

---

[137] *Jussila v Finland*, HUDOC, 23 November 2006 (GC), at para. 40; *Campbell and Fell v United Kingdom*, HUDOC, 28 June 1984, at para. 87.

[138] *Whitfield and Others v United Kingdom*, HUDOC, 12 April 2005, at para. 43.

[139] *König v Germany*, HUDOC, 28 June 1978, at para. 95; *Ringeisen v Austria*, HUDOC, 16 July 1971, at para. 94.

[140] *Ferrazzini v Italy*, HUDOC, 12 July 2001 (GC), at para. 29.

[141] *Engel and Others v the Netherlands*, HUDOC, 8 June 1976, at paras. 80–3.

[142] *Öztürk v Germany*, HUDOC, 21 February 1984, at para. 52; *Engel and Others v the Netherlands*, HUDOC, 8 June 1976, at paras. 80 & 82.

administrative infractions – the sanctions for which might include professional disqualification – is not always clear cut, and the Court has not
always applied the 'severity' criterion consistently.[143]

What constitutes a 'reasonable time' will depend on all the circumstances
of any given case including the complexity of facts, law and domestic judicial
procedure, the conduct of both parties, what is at stake for the applicant and
ensuring that justice is neither unreasonably delayed[144] nor excessively
swift.[145] While this test is not technically subject to a margin of appreciation,[146] determining what is 'reasonable' clearly involves judgement and
discretion rather than the application of an objective standard. However,
although judgement shall also be 'pronounced publicly', though not necessarily in open court,[147] according to Article 6(1), the 'press and public may
be excluded from all or part of the trial in the interests of morals, public
order or national security in a democratic society, where the interests of
juveniles or the protection of the private life of the parties so require, or to
the extent strictly necessary in the opinion of the court in special circumstances where publicity would prejudice the interests of justice'. While this is
an exhaustive list, the application of any one or more of these exceptions to
single cases, or to whole classes of case, is subject to the test of proportionality to a pressing social need,[148] such as protecting the safety or ensuring the
privacy of witnesses, or promoting the free exchange of information and
opinion in pursuit of justice.[149] Some national discretion is, therefore,
implied even though no margin of appreciation as such has been recognised
at Strasbourg.[150]

---

[143] *Wilson v United Kingdom*, HUDOC, 21 May 1998 (dec.).
[144] *Sismanidis and Sitaridis v Greece*, HUDOC, 9 June 2016, at para. 67; *L. E. v Greece*, HUDOC, 21 January 2016, at para. 97.
[145] *Lupeni Greek Catholic Parish and Others v Romania*, HUDOC, 29 November 2016 (GC), at paras. 142–3; *Moiseyev v Russia*, HUDOC, 9 October 2008, at para. 189; *Scordino v Italy (No. 1)*, HUDOC, 29 March 2006 (GC), at paras. 222–7; *Frydlender v France*, HUDOC, 27 June 2000, at para. 43; *König v Germany*, HUDOC, 28 June 1978, at para. 99; *Neumeister v Austria*, HUDOC, 27 June 1968, at paras. 20–1 of the section 'As to the law'.
[146] Harris et al., *Law of the European Convention on Human Rights*, p. 440.
[147] *Chaushev and Others v Russia*, HUDOC, 25 October 2016, at para. 23; *B and P v United Kingdom*, HUDOC, 24 April 2001, at paras. 45–8; *Werner v Austria*, HUDOC, 24 November 1997, at para. 55; *Campbell and Fell v United Kingdom*, HUDOC, 28 June 1984, at paras. 87–8; *Pretto and Others v Italy*, HUDOC, 8 December 1982, at paras. 26–7.
[148] *Jones and Others v United Kingdom*, HUDOC, 14 January 2014, at paras. 186 & 189.
[149] *B and P v United Kingdom*, HUDOC, 24 April 2001, at para. 37.
[150] Harris et al., *Law of the European Convention on Human Rights*, p. 434.

In considering compliance with Article 6, the Strasbourg institutions have principally been concerned, therefore, with procedural fairness rather than with either the merits of judicial decisions or the details of trial machinery over which states have wide 'implementation discretion'. It has also been held that 'the right to a fair administration of justice holds so prominent a place in a democratic society that it cannot be sacrificed to expediency'[151] and that in camera proceedings 'must be strictly required by the circumstances'[152] and are 'exceptional'.[153]

A 'tribunal established by law' is one rooted in legislation and governed by law, though not necessarily staffed by professional judges, which has the jurisdiction to examine all relevant questions of fact and law, and the decisions of which are legally binding and incapable of being overturned by the executive.[154] While 'independence' and 'impartiality' are interwoven concepts, the former refers particularly to the character of courts and tribunals as institutions, and denotes their structural separation and the appearance of separation from other public institutions, particularly the executive and the parties to litigation. But since it would be neither possible nor desirable for judicial institutions to be entirely insulated from other public bodies, including the government, independence is, therefore, a relative rather than an absolute characteristic. The ECtHR has held that, in determining whether a court is independent both of the executive and of the parties, consideration must be given to the manner by which its members are appointed, the duration of their term of office, the provision of guarantees against outside pressures and whether there is also an appearance of independence.[155] While renewable terms of judicial office are not generally approved – since they may create opportunities subtly to influence career-conscious judges – appointment by the executive is permitted provided judges are free from interference when carrying out their duties.[156] Judicial independence also includes immunity from dismissal at executive discretion, protection from being subject to

---

[151] *Kostovski v the Netherlands*, HUDOC, 20 November 1989, at para. 44.
[152] *Diennet v France*, HUDOC, 26 September 1995, at para. 34.
[153] *Stallinger and Kuso v Austria*, HUDOC, 23 April 1997, at para. 51.
[154] *Van de Hurk v the Netherlands*, HUDOC, 19 April 1994, at para. 45; *Belilos v Switzerland*, HUDOC, 29 April 1988, at para. 64.
[155] *Incal v Turkey*, HUDOC, 9 June 1998 (GC), at para. 65; *Langborger v Sweden*, HUDOC, 22 June 1989, at paras. 32 & 35; *Campbell and Fell v United Kingdom*, HUDOC, 28 June 1984, at para. 78.
[156] *Incal v Turkey*, HUDOC, 9 June 1998 (GC), at paras. 67–73.

governmental instruction about how cases should be decided and the capacity to make decisions binding even on government.[157]

'Impartiality', on the other hand, refers to the integrity of the process of adjudication and to the need to avoid the risk of actual, and/or apparent, judicial bias towards either party. Unlike independence, it is, therefore, an absolute standard since not even the slightest whiff of partisanship is tolerable. Although impartiality is, therefore, compromised by a lack of judicial independence, a structurally independent tribunal may nevertheless fail to be impartial for other contingent reasons, including, for example, where a judge fails to disclose a personal or financial interest in a case he or she adjudicates,[158] there is, or was, a close professional association between the judge in a particular case and the advocate for either party,[159] a decision to reject an application made under a statutory scheme is upheld by a court presided over by a judge who had also previously presided over the drafting of the scheme in question,[160] or where a jury shows evidence of racial bias.[161]

Other rights not expressly provided by Article 6(1) have also been derived from it. These include a general residual right to fairness not exhausted by full compliance with the express terms of Article 6,[162] and the rights of effective access to a court, capable of delivering a properly considered[163] and definitive[164] judgment, the grounds for which are indicated with sufficient clarity to enable any available right of appeal to be exercised,[165] possibly involving the provision of free legal

---

[157] *Sramek v Austria*, HUDOC, 22 October 1984, at paras. 38 & 41–2.

[158] *Micallef v Malta*, HUDOC, 15 October 2009 (GC) at para. 93; *Sigurðsson v Iceland*, HUDOC, 10 April 2003, at paras. 39–46; *Demicoli v Malta*, HUDOC, 27 August 1991, at paras. 41–2.

[159] *Micallef v Malta*, HUDOC, 15 October 2009 (GC) at para. 102; *Piersack v Belgium*, HUDOC, 1 October 1982, at para. 31.

[160] *McGonnell v United Kingdom*, HUDOC, 8 February 2000, at para. 57.

[161] *Zubac v Croatia*, HUDOC, 11 October 2016, at para. 40; *Sander v United Kingdom*, HUDOC, 9 May 2000, at paras. 23 & 32–3; *Gregory v United Kingdom*, HUDOC, 25 February 1997, at paras. 45 & 49; *Remli v France*, HUDOC, 23 April 1996, at paras. 46–8.

[162] *Perez v France*, HUDOC, 12 February 2004 (GC), at para. 64; See, e.g., *Barberà, Messegué and Jabardo v Spain*, HUDOC, 6 December 1988, at para. 89, where the cumulative effect of a number of procedural irregularities was deemed to have rendered a criminal trial unfair.

[163] *Dulaurans v France*, HUDOC, 21 March 2000, at para. 33.

[164] *Brumărescu v Romania*, HUDOC, 28 October 1999 (GC), at para. 61.

[165] *Lhermitte v Belgium*, HUDOC, 29 November 2016 (GC), at paras. 67 & 80–4; *Hadjianastassiou v Greece*, HUDOC, 16 December 1992, at para. 33.

aid.[166] Others implied rights include the following: to adversarial proceedings where each party is informed of, and can comment upon, all evidence and make submissions capable of influencing the court's decision,[167] including reasonable opportunity to present their case while avoiding being placed at a substantial disadvantage in relation to each other (the principle of equality of arms);[168] those of defendants, and litigants in some non-criminal cases (subject to waiver),[169] to a hearing in their presence in which they can effectively participate;[170] to be tried upon evidence obtained in a manner that does not compromise the fairness of the proceedings as a whole;[171] to a result not grossly at variance with any objective assessment of the evidence;[172] to freedom from improperly compelled self-incrimination that would otherwise destroy the very essence of this right;[173] and those of litigants not to have pending court claims undermined by retrospective legislation lacking a compelling public interest justification.[174]

The rights expressly or implicitly found in Article 6(2) and (3) apply only to those charged with a criminal offence. Article 6(2) provides a right to be

---

[166] *Urbšienė and Urbšys v Lithuania*, HUDOC, 8 November 2016, at paras. 43–6; *Ibrahim and Others v United Kingdom*, HUDOC, 13 September 2016 (GC), at paras. 266–9; *Steel and Morris v United Kingdom*, HUDOC, 15 February 2005, at paras. 61–2; *Aćimović v Croatia*, HUDOC, 9 October 2003, at para. 29.

[167] *Gökbulut v Turkey*, HUDOC, 29 March 2016, at paras. 69–72; *Vermeulen v Belgium*, HUDOC, 20 February 1996 (GC), at para. 33; *Feldbrugge v the Netherlands*, HUDOC, 29 May 1986, at paras. 42–4.

[168] *Al-Dulimi and Montana Management Inc. v Switzerland*, HUDOC, 21 June 2016 (GC), at paras. 151 & 155; *Ternovskis v Latvia*, HUDOC, 29 April 2014, at paras. 65 & 72; *Steel and Morris v United Kingdom*, HUDOC, 15 February 2005, at paras. 62 & 72; *Kress v France*, HUDOC, 7 June 2001 (GC), at para. 72; *Dombo Beheer BV v the Netherlands*, HUDOC, 27 October 1993, at paras. 33 & 35; *Feldbrugge v the Netherlands*, HUDOC, 29 May 1986, at para. 44.

[169] *Sejdovic v Italy*, HUDOC, 1 March 2006 (GC), at para. 86; *Colozza v Italy*, HUDOC, 12 February 1985, at para. 28.

[170] *Gómez Olmeda v Spain*, HUDOC, 29 March 2016, at paras. 36–40; *T v United Kingdom*, HUDOC, 16 December 1999 (GC), at paras. 83–4; *Feldbrugge v the Netherlands*, HUDOC, 29 May 1986, at para. 44.

[171] *Gäfgen v Germany*, HUDOC, 1 June 2010 (GC), at para. 178; *Ramanauskas v Lithuania*, HUDOC, 5 February 2008 (GC), at para. 51; *Jalloh v Germany*, HUDOC, 11 July 2006 (GC), at para. 94; *Khan v United Kingdom*, HUDOC, 12 May 2000, at para. 34.

[172] *Khamidov v Russia*, HUDOC, 15 November 2007, at para.174.

[173] *Jalloh v Germany*, HUDOC, 11 July 2006 (GC), at para. 101; *Weh v Austria*, HUDOC, 8 April 2004, at paras. 39–43; *Heaney and McGuiness v Ireland*, HUDOC, 21 December 2000, at para. 48; *John Murray v United Kingdom*, 8 February 1996 (GC), at paras. 45–6.

[174] See, e.g., *National and Provincial Building Society, Leeds Permanent Building Society and Yorkshire Building Society v United Kingdom*, HUDOC, 23 October 1997, at paras. 75–6 & 112–13.

presumed innocent until proven guilty according to law, which is also intimately linked to the privilege against self-incrimination, and is, more widely, an element of the general notion of fairness under Article 6(1). In common law terms this means that the burden of proof lies with the prosecution, while in civil law systems it means that, in its inquiry into the facts, a court should find in favour of the accused where doubts about guilt have not been dispelled. It has also been held that Article 6(2) is violated by prejudicial remarks, before verdicts in criminal trials and also following acquittal, on the part of those with authority and influence.[175] But this is not true of, amongst other things, strict liability offences or presumptions of fact or law,[176] inferences from silence under fair and appropriate conditions,[177] disclosure of an accused's criminal record prior to verdict[178] or sentencing-only proceedings on guilty pleas.[179] The ECtHR has not insisted either on any particular formula for the standard of proof.[180]

Article 6(3) provides the following minimum set of rights, essential for the effective preparation and conduct of the defence on equal terms to that of the prosecution (the principle of equality of arms). Under Article 6(3) (a) there is a right to be informed promptly, and in detail, in a language that either the accused or his/her lawyer understands, of the nature and grounds for the accusation, i.e. the specific criminal charge, plus relevant facts and inferences indicated by questions asked in the course of the criminal investigation, provided these are sufficient to facilitate the preparation of the defence case.[181] Article 6(3)(b) provides a right to adequate time and facilities to prepare a defence, including access to relevant documents, the precise requirements of which will vary according to the particular facts, circumstances and complexity of the case.[182] Overlapping

---

[175] *Turyev v Russia*, HUDOC, 11 October 2016, at para. 21; *Stoyanov and Others v Bulgaria*, HUDOC, 31 March 2016, paras. 106–8; *Allen v United Kingdom*, HUDOC, 12 July 2013 (GC), at paras. 125–6 & 134–5; *Sekanina v Austria*, HUDOC, 25 August 1993, at paras. 29–30; *Minelli v Switzerland*, HUDOC, 25 March 1983 at para. 37.

[176] *Salabiaku v France*, HUDOC, 7 October 1988, at paras. 28–30.

[177] *John Murray v United Kingdom*, 8 February 1996 (GC), at para. 54.

[178] *Iasir v Belgium*, HUDOC, 26 January 2016, at paras. 32 & 33; *X v Austria*, HUDOC, 30 May 1967 (dec.).

[179] *X v United Kingdom*, HUDOC, 23 March 1972 (dec.).

[180] Harris et al., *Law of European Convention*, at 461.

[181] *Mattoccia v Italy*, HUDOC, 25 July 2000, at paras. 59–60; *Péllister and Sassi v France*, HUDOC, 25 March 1999 (GC), at paras. 51 & 62; *Kamasinski v Austria*, HUDOC, 19 December 1989, at paras. 78–86.

[182] *Moiseyev v Russia*, HUDOC, 9 October 2008, at paras. 224–5; *Albert and Le Compte v Belgium*, HUDOC, 10 February 1983, at para. 41

with this provision, Article 6(3)(c) provides the accused with the right to defend themselves in person, or with effective legal assistance[183] of their own choosing, freely provided where they lack sufficient means and where the interests of justice, including what is at stake for the applicant, the complexity of the case and doubts about the capacity of any accused to defend themselves adequately, so require.[184] Restrictions may, however, be justified in pursuit of the interests of justice, security and the safety of others.[185] The accused also have the right under Article 6(3)(d) to obtain the attendance of, examine and cross-examine witnesses under the same conditions as the prosecution, except for those who – for legitimate reasons, including death or intimidation, and subject to sufficient counterbalancing factors – provide evidence but do not testify.[186] Finally, a right to a competent interpreter, which is not means tested and also applies to the translation of documents, is provided by Article 6(3)(e).[187]

Article 7 – No Punishment without Law

Article 7(1), which prohibits both retrospective criminalisation and the imposition of heavier penalties than those applicable at the time the offence was committed, derives from the rule of law principle. Amongst other things, this requires that crimes and penalties are defined only by law and that 'the criminal law must not be extensively construed to an accused's detriment'.[188] The prohibition against the retrospective criminalisation of conduct only applies to punishment following conviction resulting from changes to substantive law (consistent with the principle of legality),[189] but not to non-punitive penalties (such as the preventive

---

[183] *Öcalan v Turkey*, HUDOC, 12 May 2005 (GC), at para. 135; *Artico v Italy*, HUDOC, 13 May 1980, at paras. 34–7.

[184] *Twalib v Greece*, HUDOC, 9 June 1998, at paras. 46 & 52–4; *Granger v United Kingdom*, HUDOC, 28 March 1990, at para. 44.

[185] *Ibrahim and Others v the United Kingdom*, HUDOC, 13 September 2016 (GC), at paras. 258–9; *Ibrahim and Others v the United Kingdom*, HUDOC, 16 December 2014, at para. 193; *Salduz v Turkey*, HUDOC, 27 November 2008 (GC), at para. 55.

[186] *Manucharyan v Armenia*, HUDOC, 24 November 2016, at paras. 45–8; *Schatschaschwili v Germany*, HUDOC, 15 December 2015 (GC) at paras. 107 & 119; *Al-Khawaja and Tahery v United Kingdom*, HUDOC, 15 December 2011 (GC), at paras. 120–5, 146–7 & 152.

[187] *Cuscani v United Kingdom* HUDOC, 24 September 2002, at paras. 37–40; *Kamasinski v Austria*, HUDOC, 19 December 1989, at para. 74.

[188] *Veeber v Estonia (No. 2)*, HUDOC, 21 January 2003, at paras. 30–1; *Kokkinakis v Greece*, HUDOC, 25 May 1993, at para. 52.

[189] *Scoppola v Italy (No 2)*, HUDOC, 17 September 2009 (GC), at paras. 106 & 109.

detention of terrorist suspects compliant with Article 15) or to other elements of the criminal justice process, such as procedural or evidential changes.[190] The ECtHR has also held that the Article 7(1) prohibition includes, on the one hand, the retrospective extension of the scope of existing offences to acts and omissions not previously covered,[191] but not, on the other, to repetitive criminal conduct the mere formal definition of which was changed as the offender repeatedly committed it[192] or to the judicial interpretation of an offence which, by resolving doubts about its scope, retrospectively extends its reach, especially where this, accessibly and foreseeably,[193] eliminates an unjust and anomalous exception, such as the marital rape defence.[194] Article 7(2) provides that 'this article shall not prejudice the trial and punishment of any person for any act or omission which, at the time it was committed, was criminal according to the general principles of law recognised by civilised nations.'[195] There can be no derogation from the rights in Article 7 under Article 15 ECHR considered further below.

Article 8 – Right to Respect for Private and Family Life

Articles 8–11 have a common structure. The first paragraphs state a specific right while, subject to the 'rule of law' and 'democratic necessity' tests, the second provide a range of express exceptions including national security, public safety, the economic well-being of the country, the

---

[190] *K-H W* v *Germany*, HUDOC, 22 March 2001 (GC), at paras. 44–6 & 114; *Streletz, Kessler and Krenz* v *Germany*, HUDOC, 21 February 2001 (GC), at paras. 8, see also concurring opinion of Judge Zupancic; *Welch* v *United Kingdom*, HUDOC, 9 February 1995, at paras. 27–35.

[191] *Contrada* v *Italy (No. 3)*, HUDOC, 14 April 2015.

[192] *Rohlena* v *Czech Republic*, HUDOC, 27 January 2015 (GC), at paras. 63–4 & 69.

[193] *Dallas* v *the United Kingdom*, HUDOC, 11 February 2016, at paras. 77 & 78; *Rohlena* v *Czech Republic*, HUDOC, 27 January 2015 (GC), at paras. 57–64; *Del Rio Prada* v *Spain*, HUDOC, 21 October 2013 (GC), at para. 93; *Camilleri* v *Malta*, HUDOC, 22 January 2013, at para. 43; *Kononov* v *Latvia*, HUDOC, 17 May 2010 (GC), at para. 185; *Korbely* v *Hungary*, HUDOC, 19 September 2008 (GC), at para. 71; *Kafkaris* v *Cyprus*, HUDOC, 12 February 2008, at para. 140; *Streletz, Kessler and Krenz* v *Germany*, HUDOC, 21 February 2001 (GC), at para. 85; *SW* v *United Kingdom*, HUDOC, 22 November 1995, at para. 36. For the principle of foreseeability in relation to heavier penalties see *Achour* v *France*, HUDOC, 29 March 2006 (GC), at paras. 35–7.

[194] *Del Rio Prada* v *Spain*, HUDOC, 21 October 2013 (GC), paras. 115–17; *SW* v *United Kingdom*, HUDOC 22 November 1995, at para. 44.

[195] *Kononov* v *Latvia*, HUDOC, 17 May 2010 (GC) at para. 213 & 238–44; *Korbely* v *Hungary*, HUDOC, 19 September 2008 (GC), at paras. 78–85.

prevention of disorder or crime, the protection of health or morals and the protection of the rights and freedom of others. In litigation under these provisions the respondent state will typically admit interfering with the right in question but will seek to justify it under one of more of these limitations. Therefore, in these circumstances, an interference only becomes a violation of one of these rights when none of the second paragraph defences is successfully invoked. The legality test requires the interference to be prescribed by, or to be in accordance with, domestic law, which in its turn should be clear, accessible, precise, enable consequences of non-compliance to be foreseen and should exclude arbitrariness by providing adequate safeguards against abuse. The Strasbourg institutions have not yet produced a clear conception of 'democratic necessity' apart from affirming that democracy includes pluralism, tolerance and broadmindedness, and the protection of minorities.[196] Although various patterns have been identified in the Articles 8–11 case law, most commentators agree that the 'legitimate purposes' are fluid and are not underpinned by any clear or coherent rationale.[197] This is largely attributable to a lack of clarity concerning the Convention's constitutional principles, and, in particular, the loose and unprincipled use of the margin of appreciation doctrine, coupled with confusion about which party has the burden of proving that a specific interference was proportionate.

Article 8, which provides a right *to respect* for private and family life, home and correspondence rather than rights to these interests themselves,

---

[196] Art. 2 of Protocol No. 4 provides rights to freedom of movement, choice of residence and departure from any country, subject to a general 'public interest' exception, plus specific public interest restrictions similar to those found in Art. 8–11, and the rights and freedoms of others. However, it has been the subject of very few judgments.

[197] See W. B. Simpson, *Human Rights and the End of Empire – Britain and the Genesis of the European Convention* (Oxford University Press, 2001), p. 715; A. McHarg, 'Reconciling human rights and the public interest: Conceptual problems and doctrinal uncertainty in the jurisprudence of the European Court of Human Rights', *Modern Law Review*, 62 (1999), 671–96 at 685–95; S. Greer, *The Exceptions to Articles 8 to 11 of the European Convention on Human Rights* (Strasbourg: Council of Europe, Human Rights Files No. 15, 1997), pp. 42–4; F. G. Jacobs, 'The "limitation clauses" of the European Convention on Human Rights' in A. de Mestral, S. Birks, M. Bothe, I. Cotler, D. Klinck and A. Morel (eds.), *The Limitation of Human Rights in Comparative Constitutional Law* (Cowansville, Canada: Les Éditions Yvon Blais, 1986), pp. 21–40; B. Hovius, 'The limitation clauses of the European Convention on Human Rights: A guide for the application of Section 1 of the Charter?', *Ottawa Law Review*, 17 (1985), 213–61. For a discussion of limitation clauses in rights documents generally see M. E. Badar, 'Basic principles governing limitations on individual rights and freedoms in human rights instruments', *International Journal of Human Rights*, 7 (2003), 63–92.

has generated an ever-expanding bundle of intertwined express and implied entitlements, and both positive and negative obligations, which interface with other Convention provisions in a variety of congruent and conflicting ways. There is, for example, a connected right under Article 12 to marry and found a family, many of the rights deriving from Article 8 are also 'civil rights' for the purpose of Article 6 and the right to respect for private life could, in principle, embrace various forms of religious practice and expression also protected by Articles 9 and 10, respectively. Article 8 rights can also conflict with the right to freedom of expression, particularly regarding the unwelcome publication of allegations about private conduct. There is, however, no obvious rationale for the express specification of 'family life', 'private life', 'home' and 'correspondence', rather than any of the other rights capable of being derived from the underlying range of relevant interests, and some interferences also span several of these. Article 8 has also increasingly become a residual category, potentially accommodating claims failing on other grounds.

A useful preliminary, though not a wholly watertight distinction, is between, on the one hand, the right to respect for family life and, on the other, the right to respect for private life, home and correspondence. As far as the scope of the right to respect for family life is concerned, the Strasbourg institutions have recognised, for example, that Convention jurisprudence should reflect the fact that contemporary families in Europe are complex and fluid, and that the de facto reality may matter more than the formal legal status of family relationships.[198] For different and same-sex couples without children, cohabitation, length of relationship, commitment to each other and an intention to raise children tend to indicate 'family life.'[199] However, 'family life' may also include, not just children born to married or cohabiting parents but also single mothers and their children.[200] But, for non-cohabiting fathers, a relationship beyond mere biological paternity is required.[201] Divorced parents may

---

[198] *Şerife Yiğit v Turkey*, HUDOC, 2 November 2010 (GC), at paras. 97–8. *X, Y and Z v United Kingdom*, HUDOC, 22 April 1997 (GC), at para. 36.

[199] *Van der Heijden v the Netherlands*, HUDOC, 3 April 2012 (GC), at para. 50; *Şerife Yiğit v Turkey*, HUDOC, 2 November 2010 (GC), at paras. 95–6; *Schalk and Kopf v Austria*, HUDOC, 24 June 2010, at paras. 93–4; *X, Y and Z v United Kingdom*, HUDOC, 22 April 1997 (GC), at para. 36.

[200] *Marckx v Belgium*, HUDOC, 13 June 1979, at para. 31.

[201] *Schneider v Germany*, HUDOC, 15 September 2011, at para. 83; *Boughanemi v France*, HUDOC, 24 April 1996, at paras. 32–5.

have a family life with their children, though not with each other.[202] Depending upon the circumstances, children taken into care may become part of the family life of foster parents[203] or remain part of the family life of their natural parents.[204] Family life also includes same-sex couples who adopt or live with the child, or children, of one partner,[205] and may also include the relationship between siblings and between children and other relatives.[206] While the Strasbourg authorities regard the formal official recognition of parentage as part of the 'family life' element of Article 8,[207] procedures for establishing paternity have been considered under 'private life'.[208]

'Respect' for family life also involves positive obligations to provide appropriate legal recognition and procedures, for example, regarding adoption,[209] rights of succession,[210] plus custody and rights of access to children following divorce.[211] The 'rights and freedoms of others' and the 'prevention of disorder and crime' are often pleaded by states to defend claims that, although the right to respect for family life may have been infringed, it has not been violated. For example, in cases where parents complain about the authorities taking their children into care, or about limitations upon rights of access thereafter, the Strasbourg institutions have required – subject to the paramountcy of the best interests of the child, the principle of proportionality, proper consideration of parental rights and the margin of appreciation – that fair bureaucratic procedures are followed and that convincing reasons have been provided.[212] The

---

[202] *Berrehab v the Netherlands*, HUDOC, 21 June 1988, at para. 21.
[203] *Paradiso and Campanelli v Italy*, HUDOC, 24 January 2017 (GC), at paras. 148–9; *Gaskin v United Kingdom*, HUDOC, 7 July 1989, at paras. 36–7
[204] *Kearns v France*, HUDOC, 10 January 2008, at paras. 72 & 74.
[205] *Schalk and Kopf v Austria*, HUDOC, 24 June 2010, at para. 91; *Elzholz v Germany*, HUDOC, 13 July 2000 (GC), at para. 43.
[206] *Moustaquim v Belgium*, HUDOC, 18 February 1991, at para. 36; *Marckx v Belgium*, HUDOC, 13 June 1979, at para. 45.
[207] *X, Y and Z v United Kingdom*, HUDOC, 22 April 1997 (GC), at paras. 42–4 & 52; *Marckx v Belgium*, HUDOC, 13 June 1979, at para. 31.
[208] *Paulík v Slovakia*, HUDOC, 10 October 2006, at paras. 41–2; *Rasmussen v Denmark*, HUDOC, 28 November 1984, at para. 33.
[209] *Wagner and JMWL v Luxembourg*, HUDOC, 28 June 2007, at paras. 121, 123–4 & 133–5.
[210] *Marckx v Belgium*, HUDOC, 13 June 1979, at paras. 49–59.
[211] *Hokkanen v Finland*, HUDOC, 23 September 1994, at paras. 56 & 60–2.
[212] *Soares de Melo v Portugal*, HUDOC, 16 February 2016, at paras. 118–23; *X v Croatia*, HUDOC, 17 July 2008, at paras. 48–55; *K and T v Finland*, HUDOC, 12 July 2001 (GC), at paras. 166–70; *Olsson v Sweden (No. 1)*, HUDOC, 24 March 1998, at paras. 80–3.

'prevention of disorder and crime' exception has caused particular controversy in cases where an alien, whose family lawfully resides in a given CE state, contests exclusion, expulsion or deportation on the grounds that this would breach his/her right to respect for family life.[213] The principle of proportionality and the margin of appreciation play pivotal roles, and while the exception tends to prevail, the right has, nevertheless, been upheld in the case of a known recidivist who had lived in the member state since early childhood and had no personal connection with his family's country of origin.[214]

The wide range of privacy-related interests derived by the Strasbourg institutions from Article 8 has, so far, defied every attempt at comprehensive, rational, consistent and discrete classification. However, one of the most useful is that which distinguishes between, on the one hand, the 'negative freedom' from unwelcome active interference with well-being or integrity and, on the other, the 'positive freedom' to develop personality, identity, life-style, and to exercise autonomy, avoiding unjustified hindrance and requiring appropriate official recognition.[215] Within the first category, a further distinction can be drawn between unwelcome interferences with bodily and non-bodily integrity. The Strasbourg institutions have, for example, held that, among other things, compulsory medical and psychological examinations without consent,[216] corporal punishment,[217] body searches,[218] preventing a prisoner from growing body hair[219] and health risks arising from environmental pollution and other sources[220] may constitute an interference with the right to avoid unwelcome interferences with bodily and psychological integrity, but may, nevertheless, be justified in certain circumstances under the Article

---

[213] Üner v Netherlands, HUDOC, 18 October 2006 (GC), at paras. 44–5 & 62; Beldjoudi v France, HUDOC, 26 March 1992, at paras. 64 & 74–80.

[214] Moustaquim v Belgium, HUDOC, 18 February 1991, at paras. 41–7.

[215] This is a re-working of a distinction drawn by N. Moreham, 'The right to respect for private life in the European Convention on Human Rights: A re-examination', European Human Rights Law Review, [2008], 44–79.

[216] MAK and RK v United Kingdom, HUODC, 23 March 2010, at paras. 75 & 78–9; Bogumil v Portugal, HUDOC, 7 October 2008, at paras. 83–91.

[217] Costello-Roberts v United Kingdom, HUDOC, 25 March 1993, at paras. 35–6.

[218] Colon v the Netherlands, HUDOC, 15 May 2012 (dec.), at para. 65; Gillan and Quinton v United Kingdom, HUDOC, 12 January 2010, at paras. 64–5; Wainwright v United Kingdom, HUDOC, 26 September 2006, at para. 46.

[219] Biržietis v Lithuania, HUDOC, 14 June 2016, at para. 58.

[220] Otgon v the Republic of Moldova, HUDOC, 25 October 2016, at para. 15; Hatton and Others v United Kingdom, HUDOC, 8 July 2003 (GC), at paras. 98 & 119; López Ostra v Spain, HUDOC, 9 December 1994, paras. 16–22.

8(2) limitations. National law and procedures may also be deemed to have fallen short of the positive obligation to provide adequate protection from physical and other kinds of abuse by third parties.[221]

Within the non-bodily category a further distinction can be drawn between, on the one hand, protection from unwelcome intrusions into personal physical space, including those occasioned by the exercise of powers of search and seizure,[222] and, on the other, from eaves-dropping upon, and the collection, storage, and disclosure of personal information/images,[223] including by the media,[224] and as a result of state surveil-lance.[225] But, in common with other aspects of this provision, while any of these is likely to constitute an interference with the right to respect for private life, home and correspondence, it may, nevertheless, be capable of being justified if it accords with law, is necessary in a democratic society in pursuit of one of more of the Article 8(2) exceptions, is within the margin of appreciation and complies with the principle of proportionality.

The same is true of the freedom to develop personality, identity, autonomy, sexual relationships, reputation and life-style, and for this to receive appropriate official recognition. The relevant case law is domin-ated by the quest for a 'fair balance' between the applicant's Article 8(1) rights and the competing legitimate interests found in Article 8(2). Departing from earlier decisions, the Court has now accepted, for example, that states have positive obligations under Article 8 to provide appropriate arrangements both for gender reassignment, and for its

---

[221] *Hajduova v Slovakia*, HUDOC, 30 November 2010, at para. 46; *X and Y v Netherlands*, 28 March 1985, at paras. 23–7.

[222] *Knecht v Romania*, HUDOC, 2 October 2012, at paras. 55–8; *Funke v France*, HUDOC, 25 February 1993, at para. 48; *Niemietz v Germany*, HUDOC, 16 December 1992, at paras. 29–33.

[223] *Surikov v Ukraine*, HUDOC, 26 January 2017, at para. 75; *Vukota-Bojić v Switzerland*, HUDOC, 18 October 2016, at paras. 58–9; *Bremner v Turkey*, HUDOC, 13 October 2015, at paras. 62–70; *S and Marper v United Kingdom*, HUDOC, 4 December 2008 (GC), at para. 67; *Sciacca v Italy*, HUDOC, 11 January 2005, at para. 25; *Leander v Sweden*, HUDOC, 26 March 1987, at para. 48; *Silver and Others v United Kingdom*, HUDOC, 25 March 1983, at para. 84.

[224] *Von Hannover v Germany (No. 2)*, HUDOC, 7 February 2012 (GC), at paras. 95–8; *Mosley v United Kingdom*, HUDOC, 10 May 2011, at para. 131; *Sciacca v Italy*, HUDOC, 11 January 2005, at para. 27; *Von Hannover v Germany*, HUDOC, 24 June 2004, at paras. 50–3 & 59.

[225] *Bašić v Croatia*, HUDOC, 25 October 2016, at paras. 32–6; *Karabeyoğlu v Turkey*, HUDOC, 7 June 2016, at para. 96; *Uzun v Germany*, HUDOC, 2 September 2010, at para. 46; *Peck v United Kingdom*, HUDOC, 28 January 2003, at para. 59–63; *Kopp v Switzerland*, HUDOC, 22 March 1998, at para. 53; *Klass and Others v Germany*, HUDOC, 6 September 1978, at para. 41.

official recognition including in birth certificates, passports and other identity documents.[226] The ECtHR has also decided that, although abortion is not mandated by the Convention, where it is legally available in any state, the criteria should be clear, and adequate procedures should be available to challenge decisions relating to how they have been applied.[227] Similarly, it has also been held that voluntary assisted dying, including withdrawal of artificial nutrition and hydration,[228] may be permissible in certain circumstances where appropriate legal safeguards have been provided.[229] On account of its inherent importance for autonomy, identity, and personal well-being, the Strasbourg institutions have, however, insisted upon the universal pan-European decriminalisation of private, consensual, adult homosexual relationships and activities, no matter how strong national or regional objections.[230] However, because gay marriage remains a controversial matter of official status rather than a vital aspect of private life, it has not yet been regarded as mandated by Article 8.[231] Notwithstanding national margins of appreciation, prosecution and conviction for consensual incest between adult siblings, and for group sadomasochistic activities deemed to have caused more than trivial harm, have been held not to violate Article 8.[232] Arrangements for nomadic lifestyles,[233] and for access to official information concerning, for example, exposure to health risks,[234] and to information about childhood,[235] have also raised issues under both paragraphs of this provision.

---

[226] *YY v Turkey*, HUDOC, 10 March 2015, at paras. 57 & 65; *L v Lithuania*, HUDOC, 11 September 2007, at para. 56; *Christine Goodwin v United Kingdom*, HUDOC, 11 July 2002 (GC), at paras. 71 & 91–3.

[227] *A, B and C v Ireland*, HUDOC, 16 December 2010 (GC), at paras. 248–9 & 253–68; *Tysiąc v Poland*, HUDOC, 20 March 2007, at paras. 110 & 116–30.

[228] *Lambert and Others v France*, HUDOC, 5 June 2015 (GC), at paras. 12, 181 & 183–84.

[229] *Gross v Switzerland*, HUDOC, 14 May 2013, at para. 60 & 67; *Haas v Switzerland*, HUDOC, 20 January 2011, at paras. 51 & 56; *Pretty v United Kingdom*, HUDOC, 29 April 2002, at para. 67.

[230] *ADT v United Kingdom*, HUDOC, 31 July 2000, at paras. 32–3; *Modinos v Cyprus*, HUDOC, 22 April 1993, at paras. 17–24; *Norris v Ireland*, HUDOC, 26 October 1988, at paras. 38 & 46; *Dudgeon v United Kingdom*, HUDOC, 22 October 1981, at paras. 41 & 60.

[231] *Schalk and Kopf v Austria*, HUDOC, 24 June 2010, at paras. 105 & 110.

[232] *Stübing v Germany*, HUDOC, 12 April 2012, at paras. 61–7; *Laskey, Jaggard and Brown v United Kingdom*, HUDOC, 19 February 1997, at para. 50.

[233] *Connors v United Kingdom*, HUDOC, 27 May 2004, at paras. 86–95; *Chapman v United Kingdom*, HUDOC, 18 January 2001, at paras. 92–6 & 105–16.

[234] *McGinley and Egan v United Kingdom*, HUDOC, 9 June 1998, at paras. 96–103; *Guerra and Others v Italy*, HUDOC, 19 February 1998 (GC), at paras. 56–60.

[235] *Odièvre v France*, HUDOC, 13 February 2003 (GC), at paras. 44–9; *Gaskin v United Kingdom*, HUDOC, 7 July 1989, at para. 49.

Article 9 – Freedom of Thought, Conscience and Religion

It was not until 1993 that the Court examined the right to freedom of thought, conscience and religion provided by Article 9 in any detail.[236] Since then three key questions, with particular significance given the increasing public profile of religion in 'post-secular' European states and societies, have emerged: what kind of beliefs are covered; to what extent do they give rise to negative and/or positive obligations on the part of states and to corresponding rights on the part of believers; and to what extent may the exercise of these rights be legitimately restricted? Article 9 protects not only freedom *of* but freedom *from* religion,[237] and not only individual religion and belief but also that of faith communities.[238] But to enjoy the protection of Article 9, a belief system must have a 'certain level of cogency, seriousness, cohesion and importance,'[239] and it must also respect the ideals and values of the ECHR and a democratic society.[240] Therefore, 'not all opinions or convictions constitute beliefs' in the sense envisaged by Article 9(1).[241] The manifestation of thought, opinion and conscience may also be considered an exercise of the right to freedom of expression under Article 10.[242]

The right to believe in the 'pure', 'internal' sense precludes forced conversion, and modification, renunciation or (usually) compelled disclosure of belief.[243] Once the 'seriousness' threshold has been crossed, the state's principal negative obligation is to remain neutral and tolerant, and to refrain from privileging any faith or belief system over any other, or expressing views about how it should be practiced, about who should

---

[236] *Kokkinakis v Greece*, HUDOC, 25 May 1993, at para. 31.

[237] *Sinan Işik v Turkey*, HUDOC, 2 February 2010, at para. 38; *Buscarini v San Marino*, HUDOC, 18 February 1999 (GC), at para. 34.

[238] *Jehovah's Witnesses of Moscow and Others v Russia*, HUDOC, 10 June 2010, at para. 99; *Moscow Branch of the Salvation Army v Russia*, HUDOC, 5 October 2006, at para. 72; *Metropolitan Church of Bessarabia and Others v Moldova*, HUDOC, 13 December 2001, at paras. 101 & 105; *Hasan and Chaush v Bulgaria*, HUDOC, 26 October 2000 (GC), at para. 62; *Kokkinakis v Greece*, HUDOC, 25 May 1993, at paras. 38 & 45.

[239] *Campbell and Cosans v United Kingdom*, HUDOC, 25 February 1982, at para. 36.

[240] *Refah Partisi (The Welfare Party) and Others v Turkey*, HUDOC, 13 February 2003 (GC), at paras. 98–9.

[241] *Pretty v United Kingdom*, HUDOC, 29 April 2002, at para. 82.

[242] M. Evans, *Religious Liberty and International Law in Europe* (Cambridge University Press, 1997), p. 285.

[243] *Sinan Işik v Turkey*, HUDOC, 2 February 2010, at para. 52; *Nolan and K v Russia*, HUDOC, 12 February 2009, at para. 73; *Folgerø and Others v Norway*, HUDOC, 27 June 2007 (GC), at paras. 96–102 & 105; *Kokkinakis v Greece*, HUDOC, 25 May 1993, at paras. 31 & 51.

lead it[244] or about its truth or falsity, including in the educational context where Article 2 of Protocol No. 1 – the right of parents to ensure their children are taught in conformity with their own religious and philosophical convictions – may also arise.[245] In some circumstances – for example, requesting time off work to attend a religious festival –some proof that the claimant genuinely subscribes to the faith in question may be required.[246] Positive obligations, exercisable on a non-discriminatory basis,[247] include granting religious and other views official recognition and/or official registration where appropriate,[248] decriminalising refusals to undertake compulsory military service on well-founded conscientious grounds and offering non-military alternatives instead,[249] making adequate provision for prisoners and others to practice their faith[250] and protecting faith groups from harassment and physical attack.[251] Providing these responsibilities are satisfactorily discharged, it is unlikely that established religions, such as Anglicanism in England, and state religions such as the Orthodox faith in Greece, will be condemned as incompatible with Article 9.

---

[244] *Hasan and Eylem Zengin v Turkey*, HUDOC, 9 October 2007, at para. 70; *Metropolitan Church of Bessarabia and Others v Moldova*, HUDOC, 13 December 2001, at para. 117; *Hasan and Chaush v Bulgaria*, HUDOC, 26 October 2000 (GC), at paras. 78 & 82; *Serif v Greece*, HUDOC, 14 December 1999, at para. 52.

[245] *Lautsi v Italy*, HUDOC, 18 March 2011 (GC), at paras. 59–60; *Folgerø and Others v Norway*, HUDOC, 27 June 2007 (GC), at para. 84.

[246] *Kosteski v Former Yugoslav Republic of Macedonia*, HUDOC, 13 April 2006, at para. 39. See also *Wasmuth v Germany*, HUDOC, 17 February 2011, at para. 61.

[247] *Cumhuriyetç Eğitim Ve Kültür Merkezi Vakfi v Turkey*, HUDOC, 2 December 2014, at para. 48.

[248] *İzzettin Doğan and Others v Turkey*, HUDOC, 26 April 2016 (GC), at para. 135; *Jehovah's Witnesses of Moscow and Others v Russia*, HUDOC, 10 June 2010, at para. 101; *Church of Scientology Moscow v Russia*, HUDOC, 5 April 2007, at para. 83; *Moscow Branch of the Salvation of Army v Russia*, HUDOC, 5 October 2006, at para. 74; *Metropolitan Church of Bessarabia and Others v Moldova*, HUDOC, 13 December 2001, at para. 105. This may have both symbolic and instrumental value since official recognition is generally required for conducting legally valid marriages, often leads to tax concessions and may also strengthen the case for state funding of schools in the faith concerned. See *The Church of Jesus Christ of Latter Day Saints v United Kingdom*, HUDOC, 4 March 2014, at para. 30.

[249] *Savda v Turkey*, HUDOC, 12 June 2012, at paras. 91–101; *Bayatyan v Armenia*, HUDOC, 7 July 2011 (GC), at paras. 112 & 124–8.

[250] *Association for Solidarity with Jehovah Witnesses and Others v Turkey*, HUDOC, 24 May 2016, at paras. 103–8; *Jakóbski v Poland*, HUDOC, 7 December 2010, at paras. 52–5.

[251] *Karaahmed v Bulgaria*, HUDOC, 24 February 2015, at para. 111; *Members of the Gldani Congregation of Jehovah's Witnesses and Others v Georgia*, HUDOC, 3 May 2007, at paras. 133–5.

Two key questions arise with respect to the public manifestation of religion and belief: what conduct is covered by 'worship, practice, teaching and observance' and under what circumstances can it legitimately be restricted in the interests of public safety, the protection of public order, health, morals or the rights and freedoms of others? 'Practices' and 'manifestations' held not to be protected by Article 9(1) have included distributing leaflets to British soldiers urging them not to serve in Northern Ireland,[252] religiously motivated objections by pharmacists to selling contraceptive pills[253] and the exemption of a Jehovah's Witness pupil from a school parade commemorating the Second World War.[254] But when determining what constitutes a manifestation of religion or belief, the Court no longer requires that the applicant acted upon a religious obligation, as opposed to a religious choice. It will instead consider whether, on the facts, there was 'a sufficiently close and direct nexus between the act and the underlying belief'.[255] The ECtHR has also distinguished between permissible and impermissible forms of proselytising. While the former involves merely the attempt to persuade or to convert, the latter is characterised by threats, violence, brainwashing or improper pressure such as the offer of material or social inducements or the attempted conversion of subordinates by higher-ranking military officers.[256] The Court has also departed from its earlier view that the Article 9 rights of those seeking leave from work on the grounds of religious obligation – for example, Christians unwilling to work on Sundays[257] or Muslims seeking extended Friday lunch breaks to pray at mosques[258] – had not been violated because those concerned were 'free to resign'.[259] Instead, a reasonable accommodation between the competing interests of employer and employee is now required.[260]

---

[252] *Arrowsmith v United Kingdom*, HUDOC, 16 May 1977 (dec.).

[253] *Pichon and Sajous v France*, HUDOC, 2 October 2001 (dec.).

[254] *Valsamis v Greece*, HUDOC, 18 December 1996, at paras. 37–8.

[255] *Eweida and Others v United Kingdom*, HUDOC, 15 January 2013, at para. 82; *Jakóbski v Poland*, HUDOC, 7 December 2010, at para. 45; *Leyla Şahin v Turkey*, HUDOC, 10 November 2005 (GC), at para. 78.

[256] *Jehovah's Witnesses of Moscow and Others v Russia*, HUDOC, 10 June 2010, at paras. 128–30; *Barankevich v Russia*, HUDOC, 26 July 2007, at para. 34; *Larissis v Greece*, HUDOC, 24 February 1998, at para. 45; *Kokkinakis v Greece*, HUDOC, 25 May 1993, at para. 48.

[257] *Stedman v United Kingdom*, HUDOC, 9 April 1997 (dec.).

[258] *Ahmad v United Kingdom* (1982) 4 EHRR 126, at para. 11.

[259] *Eweida and Others v United Kingdom*, HUDOC, 15 January 2013, at para. 83.

[260] *Eweida and Others v United Kingdom*, HUDOC, 15 January 2013, at paras. 91–5.

Legitimate restrictions upon the manifestation of religion or belief that pass the prescribed by law test[261] are then subject to the democratic necessity test where the principle of proportionality[262] and the margin of appreciation doctrine[263] are of particular importance. Those accepted by the Court as justified in order to maintain public order have included restrictions on access to a Druid summer festival at Stonehenge[264] and the confiscation of a prisoner's religious book containing information about martial arts.[265] It has also been held that the protection of public health and safety justified requiring a Christian hospital nurse to remove a necklace bearing a cross.[266] The 'rights and freedoms of others' has proven particularly elastic in the Article 9 context. In *Eweida and others* v *United Kingdom*[267] the Court held that this justified the dismissal of a Christian Council Registrar who objected to conducting same-sex marriages and a Christian relationship counsellor who refused to counsel gay couples, especially since the employers in both cases explicitly promoted equal opportunities.

The Court has relied heavily on the margin of appreciation in adjudicating complaints concerning the particularly contentious issue of religious dress and symbols in contexts other than that already discussed. For example, in *Leyla Şahin* v *Turkey* it declined to condemn, as a violation of Articles 8–10, Article 14 or Article 2 of Protocol No. 1, the banning of headscarves in institutions of higher education on the grounds that, in the specific context, the headscarf was difficult to reconcile with gender equality and because of the threat, given its connection with political Islam, the Turkish authorities considered it posed to the stability of the secular state upon which the 'rights and freedoms of others' depend.[268] It has also been decided that, because of the need to

---

[261] Those failing this test have included *Kuznetsov* v *Russia*, HUDOC, 11 January 2007, at para. 74; *Poltoratskiy* v *Ukraine*, HUDOC, 29 April 2003, at para. 170.

[262] *Manoussakis* v *Greece*, HUDOC, 26 September 1996, at para. 44.

[263] *Eweida and Others* v *United Kingdom*, HUDOC, 15 January 2013, at para. 84; *Cha'are Shalom Ve Tsedek* v *France*, HUDOC, 27 June 2000 (GC), at para. 84; *Manoussakis* v *Greece*, HUDOC, 26 September 1996, at para. 44.

[264] *Chappell* v *United Kingdom*, HUDOC, 14 July 1987 (dec.).

[265] *X* v *United Kingdom*, HUDOC, 18 May 1976 (dec.).

[266] *Eweida and Others* v *United Kingdom*, HUDOC, 15 January 2013, at para. 100.

[267] *Eweida and Others* v *United Kingdom*, HUDOC, 15 January 2013.

[268] *Leyla Şahin* v *Turkey*, HUDOC, 10 November 2005 (GC), at paras. 112–16. See also *Ahmet Arslan and Others* v *Turkey*, HUDOC, 23 February 2010, at para. 43; *Köse and Others* v *Turkey*, HUDOC, 24 January 2006 (dec.); *Kurtulmuş* v *Turkey*, HUDOC, 24 January 2006 (dec.).

protect the right of state school pupils to be taught in a denominationally neutral context – in order to preclude the risk of subtle proselytisation, especially where the children in question were between four and eight years old, and to affirm the principle of gender equality – a Muslim primary school teacher in Switzerland was not improperly dismissed for refusing to remove her headscarf in class.[269] While requiring veils and turbans to be removed for identification purposes has been upheld on the grounds of public safety and public order,[270] a legal ban on wearing the face veil in public was also upheld in *SAS* v *France*, on the grounds that, taking Articles 8–10 separately and together with Article 14, it lay within the state's margin of appreciation and could be justified by the principle of 'living together' and communicating effectively, derived from the 'rights and freedoms of others'.[271] The pursuit of a certain corporate image, arguably a borderline 'rights and freedoms of others' issue at best, was held not to justify prohibiting a Christian British Airways employee from wearing a small cross at work.[272] The Court has also decided – on account of Italy's historic Catholic culture, and because in the case in question there was evidence of religious pluralism and no evidence of indoctrination – that non-Catholics do not have the right under Articles 9 or 14, or under Article 2 of Protocol No. 1, to have crucifixes removed from the walls of Italian state schools.[273]

Article 10 – Freedom of Expression

Article 10(1) provides a right to freedom of expression, including 'to hold opinions and to receive and impart information and ideas without interference by public authority and regardless of frontiers'. The ECtHR has affirmed that this right is vital for the kind of ideas, views, opinions and outlooks – including those that 'offend, shock and disturb' – upon which a pluralistic, tolerant, broadminded, progressive and democratic society depends.[274] States have both the negative obligation not to violate Article 10 and the positive obligation to ensure that the right to

---

[269] *Dahlab* v *Switzerland*, HUDOC, 15 February 2001 (dec.).

[270] *El Morsli* v *France*, HUDOC, 4 March 2008 (dec.); *Phull* v *France*, HUDOC, 11 January 2005 (dec.); *X* v *United Kingdom*, HUDOC, 12 July 1978 (dec.).

[271] *SAS* v *France*, HUDOC, 1 July 2014 (GC), at paras. 121–2, 141–2 & 157. See also *Ebrahimian* v *France*, HUDOC 26 November 2015, at paras. 54–72.

[272] *Eweida and Others* v *United Kingdom*, HUDOC, 15 January 2013, at paras. 93–5.

[273] *Lautsi* v *Italy*, HUDOC, 18 March 2011 (GC), at paras. 63–78.

[274] *Handyside* v *United Kingdom*, HUDOC, 7 December 1976, at para. 49

freedom of expression is adequately protected between private parties.[275] In certain circumstances, this may include access to information.[276]

The majority of complaints about breaches of Article 10 concern liability for alleged defamation,[277] where fine balances typically have to be struck between freedom of expression and the protection of reputations.[278] Three core questions, similar to those in the Article 9 context, arise more generally: what counts as 'expression', what kinds of expression are protected and what kinds of restriction may legitimately be imposed under what circumstances? The distinction between the second and third issues is not, however, clear-cut. As for the first issue, 'expression', for the purpose of Article 10, includes the spoken and written word, drama, art, graphics, dress, nudity, symbolic acts and symbols that convey opinions and ideas of a political, social, cultural/artistic or commercial kind, through publications, meetings, broadcasting, theatre, cinema, the Internet and advertising.[279] In addition to some areas of friction considered later, Article 10 also has positive relationships with other Convention provisions, particularly with Article 8 (a form of expression, for example, dress, music or dance, may also be part of private life), Article 9 (a type of expression, for example, a sacred ritual, may also be a manifestation of religion) and Article 11 (the right to freedom of assembly and association would be largely redundant without the right to free expression in such circumstances).

---

[275] *Appleby and Others v United Kingdom*, HUDOC, 6 May 2003, at para. 39; *Özgür Gündem v Turkey*, HUDOC, 16 March 2000, at paras. 42–6.

[276] *Magyar Helsinki Bizottság v Hungary*, HUDOC, 8 November 2016 (GC), at para 156; *Kalda v Estonia*, HUDOC, 19 January 2016, at paras. 48–54.

[277] Rainey et al., *The European Convention on Human Rights*, p. 436.

[278] *Cumpǎnǎ and Mazǎre v Romania*, HUDOC, 17 December 2004 (GC), at para. 91; *Pedersen and Baadsgaard v Denmark*, HUDOC, 17 December 2004 (GC), at para. 91; *Prager and Oberschlick v Austria*, HUDOC, 26 April 1995, at para. 31; *Oberschlick v Austria*, HUDOC, 23 May 1991, at para. 58; *Lingens v Austria*, HUDOC, 8 July 1986, at para. 42.

[279] *Semir Güzel v Turkey*, HUDOC, 13 September 2016, at para. 29; *M'Bala M'Bala v France*, HUDOC, 10 November 2015 (dec.), at para. 31; *Gough v United Kingdom*, HUDOC, 24 October 2014, at para. 147; *Murat Vural v Turkey*, HUDOC, 21 October 2014, at paras. 47–52; *Tatár and Fáber v Hungary*, HUDOC, 12 June 2012, at para. 29; *Perrin v United Kingdom*, HUDOC, 18 October 2005 (dec.); *Hashman and Harrup v United Kingdom*, HUDOC, 25 November 1999 (GC), at para. 28; *Otto-Preminger-Institut v Austria*, HUDOC, 20 September 1994, at para. 43; *Barthold v Germany*, HUDOC, 25 March 1985, para. 42; *Handyside v United Kingdom*, HUDOC, 7 December 1976, at para. 43.

Certain forms of expression are, however excluded from the scope of Article 10 in principle such as: those inherently hostile towards core Convention values[280] (an invocation of Article 17, which denies the protection of the Convention to those engaged in the destruction of any of its rights or their more extensive limitation than the Convention itself permits), those seeking to deny, belittle or defend the Holocaust (and possibly, in certain circumstances, other clearly established crimes against humanity)[281] or those that incite violence or hatred, providing any formalities, conditions, restrictions or penalties imposed are proportionate.[282] Content, form, tone, context and consequences – including the applicant's status, the addressees, any relevant legitimate public interest and the likely public impact – will often be critical in determining whether any particular expression is deemed permissible or impermissible.[283]

According to Article 10(2), the exercise of this right also 'carries with it duties and responsibilities' and may be

> 'subject to such formalities, conditions, restrictions or penalties as are prescribed by law and are necessary in a democratic society in the interests of national security, territorial integrity or public safety, for the prevention of disorder or crime, for the protection of health or morals, for the protection of the reputation or rights of others, for preventing the disclosure of information received in confidence, or for maintaining the authority and impartiality of the judiciary'.

These are to be construed narrowly and are subject to the principle of proportionality and to the margin of appreciation.[284] In cases where any interference with the right to freedom of expression is admitted but

---

[280] *Vejdeland and Others v Sweden*, HUDOC, 9 February 2012, at para. 55; *Refah Partisi (The Welfare Party) and Others v Turkey*, HUDOC, 13 February 2003 (GC), at para. 123.

[281] *M'Bala M'Bala v France*, HUDOC, 10 November 2015 (dec.), at paras. 33 & 42-3; *Perinçek v Switzerland*, HUDOC, 15 October 2015 (GC), at paras. 209-12; *Garaudy v France*, HUDOC, 24 June 2006 (dec.); *Lehideux and Isorni v France* HUDOC, 23 September 1998 (GC), at paras. 47-53; *Marais v France*, HUDOC, 24 June 1996 (dec.).

[282] *Gündüz v Turkey* HUDOC, 4 December 2003, at para. 51; *Sürek v Turkey (No. 1)*, HUDOC, 8 July 1999 (GC), at paras. 63-5; *Karataş v Turkey*, HUDOC, 8 July 1999 (GC), at paras. 51-4.

[283] *Perinçek v Switzerland*, HUDOC, 15 October 2015 (GC), at para. 207; *Leroy v France*, HUDOC, 2 October 2008, at paras. 38-9; *Sürek v Turkey (No. 1)*, HUDOC, 8 July 1999 (GC), at para. 62; *Ceylan v Turkey*, HUDOC, 8 July 1999 (GC), at paras. 35-6; *Jersild v Denmark*, HUDOC, 23 September 1994 (GC), at para. 34.

[284] *Karataş v Turkey*, HUDOC, 8 July 1999 (GC), at para. 48; *Vereinigung Demokratischer Soldaten Österreichs and Gubi v Austria*, HUDOC, 19 December 1994, at para. 37; *Informationsverein Lentia v Austria*, HUDOC, 24 November 1993, at para. 35.

justification pleaded, the severity of the penalty will often be the deciding factor in determining whether there has been a violation or not.[285] It should also be noted that, in addition to withholding licenses for broadcasting, TV and cinema (expressly recognised by Article 10(1)), freedom of expression can be restricted in much more varied ways than can the interests protected by most other Convention rights, including by pre-publication notification requirements,[286] refusal of permission to publish,[287] prior restraint,[288] confiscation,[289] criminal and civil sanctions,[290] reprimands in disciplinary proceedings,[291] orders to account for profits and costs,[292] compulsory withdrawal from sale,[293] and attempts to compel disclosure of journalists' sources.[294]

The Strasbourg institutions have generally sought to identify and specify relevant 'duties and responsibilities' according to the characteristics of the applicant. So, for example, journalists, NGOs and campaigning organisations have an obligation to act with due diligence in seeking to provide verifiably accurate and reliable information, and grounded opinion, in good faith according to their professional ethics.[295] Judges and lawyers should maintain the authority and impartiality of the legal process by

---

[285] *Steel and Morris v United Kingdom*, HUDOC, 15 February 2005, at paras. 94–6; *Cumpănă and Mazăre v Romania*, 17 December 2004 (GC), at para. 116; *Tolstoy Miloslavsky v United Kingdom*, HUDOC, 13 July 1995, at para. 51.
[286] *Mosley v The United Kingdom*, HUDOC, 15 September 2011, at para. 117; *Observer and Guardian v The United Kingdom*, HUDOC, 26 November 1991, at para. 60.
[287] *Ulusoy and Others v Turkey*, HUDOC, 3 May 2007, at paras. 45–55; *Vereniging Weekblad Bluf! v the Netherlands*, HUDOC, 9 February 1995, at paras. 8–9 & 45–6.
[288] *Mosley v United Kingdom*, 10 May 2011, HUDOC, at para. 117; *Gawęda v Poland*, HUDOC, 14 March 2002, at para. 35.
[289] *Kaos GL v Turkey*, HUDOC, 22 November 2016, at para. 51; *Otto-Preminger-Institut v Austria*, HUDOC, 20 September 1994, at para. 43.
[290] *Zana v Turkey*, HUDOC, 25 November 1997 (GC), at paras. 52–3 & 61–2; *Tolstoy Miloslavsky v United Kingdom*, 13 July 1995, at paras. 49–51.
[291] *Szanyi v Hungary*, HUDOC, 8 November 2016, at para. 26; *Steur v the Netherlands*, HUDOC, 28 October 2003, at paras. 44–6.
[292] *Times Newspapers and Neil v United Kingdom*, HUDOC, 11 April 1991 (dec.).
[293] *Leempoel & S. A. Ed. Cine Revue v Belgium*, HUDOC, 9 November 2006, at para. 84.
[294] *Financial Times Ltd and Others v United Kingdom*, HUDOC, 15 December 2009, at paras. 46 & 56; *Goodwin v United Kingdom*, HUDOC, 27 March 1996 (GC), at para. 28.
[295] *Kunitsyna v Russia*, HUDOC, 13 December 2016, at para. 45; *Dorota Kania v Poland (No. 2)*, HUDOC, 4 October 2016, at paras. 63–6; *Braun v Poland*, HUDOC, 4 November 2014, at paras. 50–1; *Times Newspapers Ltd (Nos. 1 and 2) v United Kingdom*, HUDOC, 10 March 2009, at para. 42; *Steel and Morris v United Kingdom*, HUDOC, 15 February 2005, at para. 90; *Bladet Tromsø and Stensaas v Norway*, HUDOC, 20 May 1999 (GC), at para. 65; *Goodwin v United Kingdom*, HUDOC, 27 March 1996 (GC), at para. 39; *Prager and Oberschlick v Austria*, HUDOC, 26 April 1995, at para. 37.

expressing their opinions with discretion.[296] Civil servants should refrain from joining extreme political parties and from expressing views that might compromise their neutrality.[297] On the other hand, while politicians have considerable latitude with respect to the opinions they express,[298] in doing so they should, nevertheless, show appropriate respect for the democratic process.[299] Employees should also avoid personal attacks when publicly criticising colleagues or their employers.[300]

The first issue to note with respect to restrictions stemming from the pursuit of the 'legitimate purposes' in Article 10(2) is that the elements of the 'prescribed by law' test most strongly emphasised by the Strasbourg institutions in this context are foreseeability/clarity[301] and safeguards against arbitrary abuse.[302] Second, the form, purpose and nature of the expression, together with who is expressing it and in what context, should be taken into account along with the extent of the restriction and the possibility of alternative outlets for the views in question. For example, on account of its importance for the proper functioning of democracy, greater scope for social and political expression, particularly by politicians and journalists,[303] than for their artistic and commercial counterparts is permiited by the Court[304] which also recognises that

---

[296] *Nikula* v *Finland*, HUDOC, 21 March 2002, at paras. 45–6; *Wille* v *Lichtenstein*, HUDOC, 28 October 1999 (GC), at paras. 59–60 & 70.

[297] *Karapetyan and Others* v *Armenia*, HUDOC, 17 November 2016, at paras. 49 & 59; *Ahmed* v *United Kingdom*, HUDOC, 2 September 1998, at para. 56; *Vogt* v *Germany*, HUDOC, 26 September 1995 (GC), at para. 53.

[298] *Karácsony and Others* v *Hungary*, HUDOC, 17 May 2016 (GC), at paras. 159–62.

[299] *Szanyi* v *Hungary*, HUDOC, 8 November 2016, at para. 33; *Willem* v *France*, HUDOC, 10 December 2009, at para. 37.

[300] *De Diego Nafria* v *Spain*, HUDOC, 14 March 2002, at para. 40

[301] *Semir Güzel* v *Turkey*, HUDOC, 13 September 2016, at paras. 33–40; *Telegraaf Media Nederland Landelijke Media BV and Others* v *the Netherlands*, HUDOC, 22 November 2012, at para. 90; *Sanoma Uitgevers BV* v *the Netherlands*, HUDOC, 14 September 2010 (GC), at para. 81; *Markt Intern Verlag GmbH* v *Germany*, HUDOC, 20 November 1989, at paras. 29–30; *Barthold* v *Germany*, HUDOC, 25 March 1985, at para. 45; *Sunday Times* v *United Kingdom (No. 1)*, HUDOC, 26 April 1979, at para. 49.

[302] *Telegraaf Media Nederland Landelijke Media BV and Others* v *the Netherlands*, HUDOC, 22 November 2012, at paras. 90 & 97–102; *Sanoma Uitgevers BV* v *the Netherlands*, HUDOC, 14 September 2010 (GC), at paras. 82 & 100.

[303] *Bilen and Çoruk* v *Turkey*, HUDOC, 8 March 2016, at paras. 57–61.

[304] *Szél and Others* v *Hungary*, HUDOC, 16 September 2014, at paras. 63 & 85; *Mouvement Raëlien Suisse* v *Switzerland*, HUDOC, 13 July 2012 (GC), at para. 61; *Ceylan* v *Turkey*, HUDOC, 8 July 1999 (GC), at para. 34; *Piermont* v *France*, HUDOC, 27 April 1995, at para. 76; *Castells* v *Spain*, HUDOC, 23 April 1992, at paras. 42–3; *Markt Intern Verlag GmbH* v *Germany*, HUDOC, 20 November 1989, at para. 33.

audio-visual media have greater immediacy and impact than print.[305] Third, in considering, in any given circumstances, whether the right to freedom of expression should prevail over any legitimate limitation, or vice versa, the Court is not only concerned with the particular dispute before it, but also with the possible 'chilling effect' upon freedom of expression generally if the restriction were to be upheld.[306]

The legitimate purposes are not always easy to distinguish from each other and the Strasbourg institutions do not always indicate clearly the ground upon which a limitation upon freedom of expression has been accepted. For example, in cases involving terrorism, the criminalisation of the expression of certain views may be permitted in the interests of national security, public safety and/or the prevention of disorder or crime. But the Strasbourg institutions are generally unsympathetic to blanket bans and are typically mostly concerned about the proportionality of restrictions and sanctions, and with the provision of adequate procedural safeguards against arbitrariness.[307]

The 'protection of morals' is arguably the most controversial of the Article 10(2) limitations largely because morality is so nebulous, it varies over time and space and there may be little or no European consensus on detailed content or upon what is necessary and legitimate to protect it. Although the Strasbourg institutions have repeatedly affirmed that the right to freedom of expression encompasses views and representations that 'offend, shock and disturb', they have, nevertheless, invoked both the protection of morals and the rights of others to endorse limitations upon forms of expression precisely on this basis.[308] The legitimate limits of the right to express critical, satirical or 'obscene' views about a given religion have also proven difficult to specify with precision. While, as already noted, incitement to religious hatred is not protected by Article 10, and notwithstanding generous margins of appreciation, a shift can be detected in the

---

[305] *Times Newspapers Ltd (Nos. 1 and 2)* v *United Kingdom*, HUDOC, 10 March 2009, at para. 45; *Pedersen and Baadsgaard* v *Denmark*, HUDOC, 17 December 2004 (GC), at para. 79; *Jersild* v *Denmark*, HUDOC, 23 September 1994 (GC), at para. 31

[306] *Dammann* v *Switzerland*, HUDOC, 25 April 2006, at para. 57; *Giniewski* v *France*, HUDOC, 31 January 2006, at para. 55; *IA* v *Turkey*, HUDOC, 13 September 2005, dissenting opinion of Judges Costa, Cabral Barreto and Jungwiert, at para. 6.

[307] *Leroy* v *France*, HUDOC, 2 October 2008, at paras. 44–5; *Vereniging Weekblad Bluf!* v *the Netherlands*, HUDOC, 9 February 1995, at paras. 39–46; *Brind and Others* v *United Kingdom*, HUDOC, 9 May 1994 (dec.).

[308] *Wingrove* v *United Kingdom*, HUDOC, 25 November 1996, at paras. 48–9 & 64; *Otto-Preminger-Institut* v *Austria*, HUDOC, 20 September 1994, at para. 48; *Müller* v *Switzerland*, HUDOC, 24 May 1988, at paras. 39–43; *Handyside* v *United Kingdom*, HUDOC, 7 December 1976, at para. 52.

development of the 'gratuitous insult/abusive attack' test in the case law, from concern for the sensitivities of religious believers to more scope for the right to criticise and satirise religious faith.[309] However, determining whether or not the test has been satisfied can be highly controversial and, in some of its key judgments, the Court has been split over it.[310]

The 'rights of others' is also the axis around which conflicts between the media's freedom of expression and the right to respect for the private and family life of celebrities, public figures and others in the public eye revolve. Here, as in other areas, proportionality and context, including the extent to which the information is already in the public domain, are of particular importance.[311] The scope of the right to respect for private life tends to be limited by the right to freedom of expression according to how convincingly the alleged intrusion can be justified, for example, in terms of the disclosure of discreditable private conduct inconsistent with a positive public image or by reference to a genuine public interest in, for instance, the honourable discharge of an important public responsibility.[312] In the advertising context, in order to prevent unfair competition and to secure a level playing field, wide margins of appreciation have also been applied to the 'protection of the reputation or rights of others' limitation, especially with respect to broadcast media and to the circulation of ideological viewpoints, particularly during election campaigns.[313]

The relationship between freedom of expression and the protection from disclosure of information received in confidence is subject to the

---

[309] Harris et al., *Law of the European Convention on Human Rights*, pp. 669–70; Rainey et al., *The European Convention on Human Rights*, p. 457.

[310] *Leroy v France*, HUDOC, 2 October 2008, at paras. 40–8; *Klein v Slovakia*, HUDOC, 31 October 2006, at paras. 52–4; *Giniewski v France*, HUDOC, 31 January 2006, at paras. 52–5; *IA v Turkey*, HUDOC, 13 September 2005, at paras. 25–32; *Wingrove v United Kingdom*, HUDOC, 25 November 1996, at paras. 59–64; *Otto-Preminger-Institut v Austria*, HUDOC, 20 September 1994, at paras. 49 & 56; *Müller v Switzerland*, HUDOC, 24 May 1988, at paras. 42–4.

[311] *Axel Springer AG v Germany*, HUDOC, 7 February 2012 (GC), at paras. 89–95; *MGN Ltd v United Kingdom*, HUDOC, 18 January 2011, at para. 151; *Egeland and Hanseid v Norway*, HUDOC, 16 April 2009, at para. 60.

[312] *Do Carmo de Portugal e Castro Câmara v Portugal*, HUDOC, 4 October 2016, at paras. 37 & 40; *Von Hannover v Germany (No. 2)*, HUDOC, 7 February 2012 (GC), at paras. 102, 109 & 111; *Axel Springer AG v Germany*, HUDOC, 7 February 2012 (GC), at paras. 91–2, 100–1 & 108; *Von Hannover v Germany*, HUDOC, 24 June 2004, at paras. 60 & 63–5.

[313] *Oran v Turkey*, HUDOC, 15 April 2014, at para. 51; *Jacubowski v Germany*, HUDOC, 23 June 1994, at para. 26; *Markt Intern Verlag GmbH v Germany*, HUDOC, 20 November 1989, at para. 33; *Barthold v Germany*, HUDOC, 25 March 1985, at paras. 28 & 55.

proportionality principle and to a wide margin of appreciation. Which of these rights should prevail over the other will typically hinge upon the precise facts, including the severity of the penalty, and how national (particularly judicial) authorities seek to balance the competing public interests in, on the one hand, maintaining confidentiality and, on the other, the disclosure of wrongdoing or discreditable conduct, especially by public-spirited whistle-blowers acting in good faith on reliable information where other means of addressing the problem have been tried and failed or are not realistically available.[314]

Finally, although measured, responsible and well-grounded criticism of judges and the legal process about matters of public interest is permitted by Article 10, particularly where it contributes to informed public debate, the 'maintenance of the authority and impartiality of the judiciary' exception can justify the prohibition of the release of information about ongoing trials in order to prevent prejudicing outcomes or compounding the personal distress of those involved,[315] and, where much depends on context, substance, tone, proportionality and penalty, the sanctioning of insult or intemperate allegations, and the unsubstantiated impugning of judicial integrity.[316]

Article 11 – Freedom of Assembly and Association

Article 11 provides rights to freedom of peaceful assembly and to freedom of association, the latter of which expressly includes the rights to form and join trade unions. Similar in format to Articles 8–10, no restriction is permissible, except as prescribed by law and necessary in a democratic society for a range of legitimate purposes, including lawful limits upon the exercise of these rights by members of the armed forces, police or state administration. Associations and assemblies also have the right to express themselves subject to the Article 10 limitations. The past decade has seen an increase in adverse judgments in cases on freedom of

---

[314] *Matúz v Hungary*, HUDOC, 21 October 2014, at paras. 39–51; *Guja v Moldova*, HUDOC, 23 February 2008 (GC), at paras. 72–8; *Stoll v Switzerland*, HUDOC, 10 December 2007 (GC), at paras. 112–62.

[315] *Egeland and Hanseid v Norway*, HUDOC, 16 April 2009, at paras. 60 & 63; *Worm v Austria*, HUDOC, 29 August 1997, at paras. 40, 50 & 54; *Sunday Times v United Kingdom (No. 1)*, HUDOC, 26 April 1979, at paras. 63–4 & 66.

[316] *Guja v Moldova*, HUDOC, 23 February 2008 (GC), at paras. 74 & 91; *De Haes and Gijsels v Belgium*, HUDOC, 24 February 1997, dissenting opinion of Judge Morenilla, at para. 11.

assembly and association, particularly regarding the dissolution of political parties and the refusal to register associations in the new democracies of central and eastern Europe.[317]

Peaceful assemblies include private and public meetings, marches, demonstrations, sit-ins and pickets, for political, religious, cultural, social, or other purposes.[318] The positive duty on states to protect the right to peaceful assembly may require finely tuned public order measures to enable both demonstrators and counter-demonstrators to exercise it.[319] Where appropriate and proportionate, these can include requirements for prior notification or authorisation, with or without express conditions, and sensitive policing including re-routing, dispersal or complete bans, with proportionate penalties for non-compliance,[320] including for failing to dissociate from a lawful demonstration when it turns violent.[321] There is no right to peaceful assembly on private property, unless the proprietor's refusal to give permission neutralises the very essence of the right, as, for example, where a corporate body controls an entire town.[322] It is also clear that the unpopular, and even provocative, content of any message conveyed, or sought to be conveyed, by peaceful assembly is not a legitimate reason for restricting the exercise of Article 11 rights on any of the second paragraph grounds.[323] The precipitate and forceful dispersal of peaceful, though unlawful, assemblies has also been held to constitute a disproportionate interference and, therefore, a violation.[324]

---

[317] Harris et al., *Law of the European Convention on Human Rights*, p. 752.

[318] *Barankevich v Russia*, HUDOC, 26 July 2007, at para. 32; *The Gypsy Council and Others v United Kingdom*, HUDOC, 14 May 2002 (dec.); *G v Germany*, HUDOC, 6 March 1989 (dec.); *Rassemblement Jurassien Unité Jurassienne v Switzerland*, HUDOC, 10 October 1979 (dec.).

[319] *Identoba and Others v Georgia*, HUDOC, 12 May 2015, at para. 94; *United Macedonian Organization Ilinden and Ivanov v Bulgaria*, HUDOC, 20 October 2005, at paras. 114–15.

[320] *Gafgaz Mammadov v Azerbaijan*, HUDOC, 15 October 2015, at para. 59; *Kudrevičius and Others v Lithuania*, HUDOC, 15 October 2015 (GC), at para. 147; *Çelik v Turkey (No. 3)*, HUDOC, 15 November 2012, at para. 90; *Berladir and Others v Russia*, HUDOC, 10 July 2012, at paras. 40–2

[321] *Oya Ataman v Turkey*, HUDOC, 5 December 2006, at paras. 40–4; *Ezelin v France*, HUDOC, 20 April 1991, at paras. 41 & 51–3.

[322] *Appleby and Others v United Kingdom*, HUDOC, 6 May 2003, at para. 41; *Anderson v United Kingdom*, HUDOC, 27 October 1997 (dec.).

[323] *Alekseyev v Russia*, HUDOC, 21 October 2010, at para. 73; *Stankov and United Macedonian Organization Ilinden v Bulgaria*, HUDOC, 2 October 2001, at para. 86.

[324] *Kasparov and Others v Russia*, HUDOC, 3 October 2013, at paras. 91 & 95; *Cisse v France*, HUDOC, 9 April 2002, at para. 50.

While the right to freedom of association is one of the critical features of a democratic society, it does not entail an individual right to be admitted to any particular association; nor does any association have an obligation to admit any particular individual as a member.[325] Equally, Article 11 also implies the so-called negative freedom not to be compelled to join an association against one's will, a right that has given rise to particular controversy in the context of compulsory trading associations[326] and 'closed shop' trade unions considered later.[327] For the purposes of this provision, an 'association' is something more than an informal network or gathering of friends or acquaintances,[328] but may not necessarily be a formal entity under national law.[329] The judicial institutions at Strasbourg have also ruled that professional associations, with compulsory membership established by law, are not 'associations' for the purpose of Article 11.[330] States also have positive obligations to ensure that legitimate associations receive some form of official recognition (though not necessarily registration)[331] and that the right to freedom of association is observed between private parties, including by providing adequate and effective laws to protect employees from dismissal on political grounds.[332] It has also been held that, where states maintain official registers of associations – which in certain circumstances may also lead to various material benefits such as tax concessions – decisions not to register must be prescribed by law, proportionate, taken in good faith according to the duty of neutrality and impartiality, non-arbitrary and supported by convincing and compelling reasons based on solid evidence.[333]

The Article 11(2) limitations 'have given rise to no serious difficulties for states'.[334] Few complaints about the violation of the right to peaceful

---

[325] *Cheall* v *United Kingdom*, HUDOC, 13 May 1985 (dec.).

[326] *Mytilinaios and Kostakis* v *Greece*, HUDOC, 3 December 2015, at para. 53 & 65–7.

[327] *Young, James and Webster* v *United Kingdom*, HUDOC, 13 August 1981, at paras. 13 & 55–7.

[328] *McFeeley* v *United Kingdom*, HUDOC, 15 May 1980 (dec.).

[329] *Sigurjónsson* v *Iceland*, HUDOC, 30 June 1993, at para. 31.

[330] *Le Compte, Van Leuven and De Meyere* v *Belgium*, HUDOC, 23 June 1981, at paras. 64–5.

[331] *House of Macedonian Civilisation* v *Greece*, HUDOC, 9 July 2015, at paras. 20 & 44.

[332] *Redfearn* v *United Kingdom*, HUDOC, 6 November 2012, at paras. 42 & 57.

[333] *Moscow Branch of the Salvation of Army* v *Russia*, HUDOC, 5 October 2006, at paras. 86–7; *Gorzelik and Others* v *Poland*, HUDOC, 17 February 2004 (GC), at paras. 97–105; *Sidiropoulos and Others* v *Greece*, HUDOC, 10 July 1998, at paras. 31–2 & 47.

[334] Harris et al., *Law of the European Convention on Human Rights*, p. 716.

assembly have, for example, succeeded in Strasbourg with most either falling at the admissibility hurdle or being successfully defended on the grounds that the restriction in question was prescribed by law and, taking the margin of appreciation and proportionality into account, was necessary in a democratic society, typically in the interests of public safety and/ or to protect the rights and freedoms of others.[335] The bulk of the limited litigation has concerned the scope of the legitimate limitations. A key distinction concerns political parties and other types of association. Because of their importance for democracy, states have only a narrow margin of appreciation to restrict, and particularly to ban or dissolve, political associations in pursuit of any of the Article 11(2) exceptions. This has been a particular issue in Turkey, where the ECtHR has condemned the legal dissolution of several secular political parties because of their peaceful support for Kurdish autonomy, anathema to the rigorously unitary Kemalist republic.[336] By contrast, the banning of the moderately Islamist Refah Partisi (Welfare party) was upheld because, in the view of the majority of the Grand Chamber, this was within the national margin of appreciation, was not disproportionate, was prescribed by law and was necessary in a democratic society to prevent disorder and crime and in pursuit of the protection of national security, public safety and the rights and freedoms of others. In the Court's opinion, there were evidence-based doubts about Refah's commitment to non-violence, and its advocacy of a plurality of legal systems and Sharia law was deemed incompatible with ECHR values.[337] The ECtHR has also held that, in addition to political parties, other kinds of association, formed for political or other objectives, are also protected by Article 11.[338] Rights to form and to join religious associations are, for example, implied by the combined effect of Articles 9 and 11. Where proportionate, the interests of public safety, the prevention of disorder or crime and the protection of the rights and freedoms of others also provide legitimate grounds for banning associations that seek to incite

---

[335] Rainey et al., *The European Convention on Human Rights*, p. 454.
[336] *Freedom and Democracy Party (ÖZDEP) v Turkey*, HUDOC, 8 December 1999 (GC), at paras. 44–8; *United Communist Party of Turkey and Others v Turkey*, HUDOC, 30 January 1998 (GC), at paras. 43 & 57–61; *Socialist Party and Others v Turkey*, HUDOC, 25 May 1998 (GC), at paras. 41 & 50–4.
[337] *Refah Partisi (The Welfare Party) and Others v Turkey*, HUDOC, 13 February 2003 (GC), at paras. 104–36. See also *Herri Batasuna and Batasuna v Spain*, HUDOC, 30 June 2009, at paras. 83 & 88–91.
[338] *Gorzelik and Others v Poland*, HUDOC, 17 February 2004 (GC), at para. 92.

racial or other forms of social hatred, particularly those organised along paramilitary lines and holding intimidating rallies.[339]

Although there is a clear trend in the Strasbourg case law towards greater recognition of trade union rights in accordance with international labour law standards, their scope and content have been amongst the most contentious issues raised by Article 11. States have both the negative obligation not to interfere with the right to form or join a trade union of one's choice and positive obligations to uphold the rights of unions and their members against employers and the rights of members and non-members against unions themselves. Employers may also have rights under the rights and freedoms of others exception in Article 11(2). It has been held, for example, that although there is a right to strike, it is not unlimited,[340] and that there is a limited right to collective bargaining.[341] The expulsion or exclusion of members by, or from, a trade union is not a violation of Article 11, providing it does not constitute an abuse of a dominant position, it is not against union rules, it is not wholly arbitrary and it does not result in exceptional hardship such as job loss.[342] The ECtHR has also held that 'closed shops'– where, in the interests of effective collective bargaining, an employer requires every employee to join a specific trade union – are generally, though not invariably, incompatible with Article 11. The compulsion in question is regarded as tending to undermine the very essence of the rights protected by Article 11, the national margin of appreciation is narrow, closed shops have declined in acceptability internationally and the principle of proportionality requires a fair balance to be struck between all relevant interests.[343] While members of the armed forces, police and civil servants have the right to form and join associations including trade unions – and to participate in their activities including by going on strike – the ECtHR accepts that the scope of these rights is much narrower in this context

---

[339] *Vona v Hungary*, HUDOC, 9 July 2013, at paras. 55, 66–7 & 71.

[340] *Sindicatul "Păstorul cel Bun" v Romania*, HUDOC, 9 July 2013 (GC), at paras. 172–3; *Federation of Offshore Workers' Trade Unions v Norway*, HUDOC, 27 June 2002 (dec.).

[341] *Demir and Baykara v Turkey*, HUDOC, 12 November 2008 (GC), at paras. 147–54.

[342] *Associated Society of Locomotive Engineers and Firemen (ASLEF) v United Kingdom*, HUDOC, 27 February 2007, at para. 39; *Sibson v United Kingdom*, HUDOC, 20 April 1993, at paras. 29–30; *Cheall v United Kingdom*, HUDOC, 13 May 1985 (dec.).

[343] *Sørensen and Rasmussen v Denmark*, HUDOC, 11 January 2006 (GC), at para. 54, 58 & 76; *Sigurjónsson v Iceland*, HUDOC, 30 June 1993, at para. 41; *Young, James and Webster v United Kingdom*, HUDOC, 13 August 1981, at paras. 55 & 65.

than in others.[344] The relevant margin of appreciation is limited, the proportionality test more easily accommodates restriction and bans on strikes by certain public servants can be more easily justified.[345]

Article 12 – Right to Marry

Article 12, which had generated comparatively little litigation at Strasbourg,[346] provides rights to marry and to found a family according to 'national laws'. While states have a positive obligation to facilitate marriage, this does not include providing the material conditions to make it effective by, for example, granting benefits to married couples not available to co-habitees.[347] Nor is there a positive obligation to promote the 'legitimate' family, although a legitimate family may be treated more favourably than an illegitimate one, provided there is no violation of the Article 8 rights of the latter.[348] Although the right to marry includes couples who do not intend to have children, Article 12 does not provide a right to found a family in the absence of marriage, a matter covered, however, by Article 8.[349] Providing the Strasbourg legality test has been met, the principles of proportionality, reasonableness and non-arbitrariness are satisfied and any restriction does not impair their very essence, states have a wide margin of appreciation concerning how to regulate the rights to marry and to found a family, regarding, for example, form, capacity, conditions and exclusions.[350] Since the beginning of the twenty-first century the Court has also acknowledged that transsexuals have the right to marry those of the post-operative opposite sex.[351] But, given the lack of European consensus, states are currently permitted a margin of appreciation about whether or not to recognise

---

[344] *Junta Rectora Del Ertzainen Nazional Elkartasuna (ERNE.) v Spain*, HUDOC, 21 April 2015, at paras. 29 & 39.
[345] *Tüm Haber Sen and Çinar v Turkey*, HUDOC, 21 February 2006, at para. 35; *S v Germany*, HUDOC, 5 July 1984 (dec.).
[346] Harris et al., *Law of the European Convention on Human Rights*, 762.
[347] *Marckx v Belgium*, HUDOC, 13 June 1979, at para. 67.
[348] *Andersson v. Sweden*, HUDOC, 4 March 1986 (dec.); *B, R and J v Germany*, HUDOC, 15 March 1984 (dec.).
[349] *Hamer v United Kingdom*, HUDOC,13 December 1979, at para. 58.
[350] *O'Donoghue and Others v United Kingdom*, HUDOC, 14 December 2010, at paras. 83–4; *Şerife Yiğit v Turkey*, HUDOC, 2 November 2010 (GC), at para. 44; *Rees v United Kingdom*, HUDOC, 17 October 1986, at para. 50.
[351] *Christine Goodwin v United Kingdom*, HUDOC, 11 July 2002 (GC), at paras. 100–1.

same-sex marriage.[352] The rights to marry and to found a family do not entail a right to divorce,[353] or a right to procreate by natural or artificial means.[354] Nor does Article 12, or any other Convention provision, provide a right to adopt.[355]

Article 13 – Right to an Effective Remedy

Article 13, largely dormant in the Strasbourg case law until the past decade or so, provides an autonomous, though subsidiary, right to 'an effective remedy before a national authority' where an 'arguable case' can be made that another Convention provision has been violated, whether or not this is eventually confirmed.[356] Provided the authority in question is sufficiently independent, its decisions have some degree of enforceability and minimum procedural guarantees are observed, national remedies – which may also be cumulative, variable according to the right and other relevant interests and open to a degree of national discretion concerning form and details – need not be judicial.[357] They must, however, operate effectively in practice as well as in law, and where violations of Articles 2, 3 and 5 have been alleged, thorough and effective investigations capable of establishing culpability and dispensing punishment, to which victims have effective access, should also be conducted.[358] Appropriate relief should be provided and, where necessary, compensation, particularly for delays in the administration of justice in breach of Article 6(1).[359] Generally, though not invariably, if the ECtHR is satisfied that the procedural aspects of other provisions have been adequately

---

[352] *Schalk and Kopf v Austria*, HUDOC, 24 June 2010, at para. 105.

[353] *Babiarz v Poland*, HUDOC, 10 January 2017, at paras. 49 & 54; *Johnston and Others v Ireland*, HUDOC, 18 December 1986, at paras. 51–4.

[354] *SH and Others v Austria*, HUDOC, 3 November 2011 (GC), at paras. 115–18.

[355] *EB v France*, HUDOC, 22 January 2008 (GC), at para. 41.

[356] *Bubbins v United Kingdom*, HUDOC, 17 March 2005 at para. 170; *Kaya v Turkey*, HUDOC, 19 February 1998, at para. 107; *Silver and Others v United Kingdom*, HUDOC, 25 March 1983, at para. 113.

[357] *De Souza Ribeiro v France*, HUDOC, 13 December 2012 (GC), at para. 79; *Hasan and Chaush v Bulgaria*, HUDOC, 26 October 2000 (GC), at para. 98; *Kudła v Poland*, HUDOC, 26 October 2000 (GC), at para. 151; *Klass and Others v Germany*, HUDOC, 6 September 1978, para. 57.

[358] *Kudła v Poland*, HUDOC, 26 October 2000 (GC), at para. 157; *Kaya v Turkey*, HUDOC, 19 February 1998, at paras. 106 & 108; *Kurt v Turkey*, HUDOC, 25 May 1998, at paras. 138–42; *Aksoy v Turkey*, HUDOC, 18 December 1996, at paras. 98–100.

[359] *L. E. v Greece*, HUDOC, 21 January 2016, at paras. 99 & 100; *Krasuski v Poland*, HUDOC, 14 June 2005, at para. 68; *Kudła v Poland*, HUDOC, 26 October 2000 (GC), at paras. 159–60.

fulfilled, it will not consider whether Article 13 itself has been violated.[360] Article 13 does not create an obligation for the Convention to be incorporated into domestic legal systems – although this is now universal in some form or other throughout member states. Nor does it require the Convention compliance of legislation to be open to challenge at national level.[361] Effective implementation of Article 13 could contribute to alleviating the ECtHR's case management problems by enabling more complaints to be settled domestically.[362]

Article 14 – Prohibition of Discrimination

Article 14 prohibits discrimination in the 'enjoyment of the rights and freedoms set forth in this Convention ... on any ground such as sex, race, colour, language, religion, political or other opinion, national or social origin, association with a national minority, property, birth or other status'.[363] It is, arguably, both a 'principle', governing how other Convention rights and freedoms are applied (in a non-discriminatory manner), and a 'right' capable of being breached whether or not any other Convention right has been violated. Protocol 12, which has not as yet received much support from member states, provides much wider protection by prohibiting discrimination in relation to the 'enjoyment of any right set forth by law'.[364] In recent years the profile of Article 14 has

---

[360] *Ramsahai v Netherlands*, HUDOC, 15 May 2007 (GC), at paras. 362–3; but see, e.g., *Nuri Kurt v Turkey*, HUDOC, 25 November 2005 at paras. 115–22.

[361] *James and Others v United Kingdom*, HUDOC, 21 February 1986, at para. 85.

[362] See Chapter 2.

[363] See e.g., O. Mjöll Arnardóttir, 'Discrimination as a magnifying lens: Scope and ambit under Article 14 and Protocol No. 12' in E. Brems and J. Gerards (eds.), *Shaping Rights in the ECHR: The Role of the European Court of Human Rights in Determining the Scope of Human Rights* (Cambridge Universtiy Press, 2013); R. Wintemute, '"Within the ambit": How big is the "gap" in Article 14 European Convention on Human Rights? Part 1', *European Human Rights Law Review* (2004), 366–82 and 'Filling the Article 14 "gap": Government ratification and judicial control of Protocol No. 12 ECHR: Part 2', *European Human Rights Law Review* (2004), 484–99; O. M. Arnardóttir, *Equality and Non-Discrimination under the European Convention on Human Rights* (The Hague: Martinus Nijhoff, 2003); J. Schokkenbroek, 'The prohibition of discrimination in Article 14 of the convention and the margin of appreciation', *Human Rights Law Journal*, 19 (1998), 20–3; S. Livingstone, 'Article 14 and the prevention of discrimination in the European Convention on Human Rights', *European Human Rights Law Review* (1997), 25–34.

[364] N. Grief, 'Non discrimination under the European Convention on Human Rights: A critique of the United Kingdom government's refusal to sign and ratify Protocol 12', *European Law Review*, 27 (2002), 3–18.

increased in the Strasbourg jurisprudence as various kinds of discrimination, for example, that faced by the Roma in eastern Europe or stemming from sexual orientation, have been litigated.

In the Article 14 context, 'discrimination' means the direct or indirect[365] allocation of goods or benefits on an unequal basis without adequate justification by reference to the rights and freedoms of others and/or to legitimate public interests. Not every difference in treatment will, therefore, be discriminatory, and, while not every private or social disadvantage is discriminatory either, the state has a positive obligation[366] to address those that are, including, if it wishes, through appropriate and necessary programmes of affirmative action.[367] Providing a difference in treatment has been established, three principal questions arise:[368] is the alleged discrimination covered by one or more of the stipulated grounds; does the complaint fall within the scope or 'ambit' of another Convention right; and was the differential treatment the applicant claims to have suffered reasonably and objectively justified when compared with the more favourable experience of an analogous or comparable group or class? On account of the 'any grounds such as' clause, and because the boundaries of 'other status' are indeterminate, the possible sources of discrimination under Article 14 are non-exhaustive and may extend beyond innate personal characteristics to include contingent ones such as residence[369] or former employment.[370]

In the case law, the 'ambit test', and the fact that Article 14 is 'parasitic' upon other ECHR rights, can lead, in principle, to five different outcomes. At one end of the continuum, the Court may decide that both Article 14 and another Convention right (call it 'x') have been violated,[371]

---

[365] *DH and Others v Czech Republic*, HUDOC, 13 November 2007 (GC), at paras. 175–6, 189 & 195.

[366] *Members of the Gldani Congregation of Jehovah's Witnesses and Others v Georgia*, HUDOC, 3 May 2007, at paras. 140–2; *DH and Others v Czech Republic*, HUDOC, 13 November 2007 (GC), at para. 176.

[367] Case *"relating to certain aspects of the laws on the use of languages in education in Belgium" v Belgium, the 'Belgian Linguistics Case'*, HUDOC, 23 July 1968, 'The six questions referred to the court', at para. 32.

[368] *Rasmussen v Denmark*, HUDOC, 28 November 1984, at paras. 29–42.

[369] *Gouri v France*, HUDOC, 23 March 2017 (dec.), at para. 23; *Carson and Others v United Kingdom*, HUDOC, 16 March 2010 (GC), at para. 70.

[370] *Sidabras and Džiautas v Lithuania*, HUDOC, 27 July 2004, at paras. 40–1.

[371] *Biao v Denmark*, HUDOC, 24 May 2016 (GC), at paras. 138 & 139; *Taddeucci and McCall v Italy*, HUDOC, 30 June 2016; *Nachova and Others v Bulgaria*, HUDOC, 6 July 2005 (GC) (concerning the culture of impunity surrounding investigations into assaults

while, at the other end, it may conclude that neither has.[372] However, since more than 90 per cent of admissible applications to the ECtHR result in a finding of at least one violation, the latter is statistically unlikely. In between are three other possibilities. First, and until recently the most likely outcome, the Court may decide that Article x has been violated but will expressly decline to consider whether or not this is also true of Article 14.[373] Second, Article x may be found to have been violated but not Article 14.[374] Third, the ECtHR may find the converse – a violation of Article 14 but not Article x – which means that a right connected, but not integral, to Article x has been applied in a discriminatory manner. For example, although the right to respect for family life provided by Article 8 does not expressly grant single people a right to adopt – and is not, therefore, required by this or any other Convention provision – where adoption on this basis is available, it must be applied without discrimination on the basis of sexual orientation.[375] The same is true of social security provisions that, although linked to the right to the peaceful enjoyment of possessions under Article 1 of Protocol No. 1, are not expressly provided as of right by the Convention.[376]

The identity of the 'comparable group' is sometimes easily determined by the complaint itself. For example, if the alleged discrimination is based on gender, the comparator will be members of the opposite sex not suffering the same alleged disadvantage.[377] But in some circumstances this can be a circular test. For example, whether a 'comparable' group is in an 'analogous' situation may depend upon whether or not the difference in treatment can be justified.[378] A failure to treat differently persons whose circumstances are significantly different will also constitute

by the police with an allegedly racist dimension). *Rasmussen* v *Denmark*, HUDOC, 28 November 1984

[372] *Carson and Others* v *The United Kingdom*, HUDOC, 16 March 2010 (GC), at paras. 59 & 90.

[373] See, for example, *Dudgeon* v *United Kingdom*, HUDOC, 22 October 1981, at paras. 67–70.

[374] See, for example, *Soare and Others* v *Romania*, HUDOC, 22 February 2011, at paras. 200–209; *Dimitrova and Others* v *Bulgaria*, HUDOC, 27 January 2011, at paras. 92–9; *Bouamar* v *Belgium*, HUDOC, 29 February 1988, at para. 67; *Sunday Times* v *United Kingdom (No. 1)*, HUDOC, 26 April 1979, at paras. 69–73.

[375] *EB* v *France*, HUDOC, 22 January 2008 (GC), at paras. 89–90 & 93–8.

[376] *Stec and Others* v *United Kingdom*, HUDOC, 12 April 2006 (GC), at para. 53.

[377] *Schmidt* v *Germany*, HUDOC, 18 July 1994, at paras. 25–9.

[378] *Gouri* v *France*, HUDOC, 23 March 2017 (dec.), at para. 27; *British Gurkha Welfare Society and Others* v *United Kingdom*, HUDOC, 15 September 2016, at para. 79; *Burden* v *United Kingdom*, HUDOC, 29 April 2008 (GC), at para. 65.

discrimination,[379] as will, in certain circumstances, a failure to tackle inequality through differential treatment.[380] If the applicant can show adverse differential treatment by comparison with an analogous or comparable group or class, it then falls to the state to demonstrate that the difference was reasonably and objectively justified and, therefore, did not constitute discrimination.[381] Reference to the policy goals that the different treatment is said to facilitate,[382] supported by evidence including statistics where appropriate,[383] will be required. The pursuit of even legitimate aims must not, however, be disproportionate in their overall effects, even if they have a disparate impact upon some individuals.[384] Alternative means for achieving the same end might also have to be considered, and 'a fair balance between the protection of the interests of the community and respect for the rights and freedoms safeguarded by the Convention' must be struck.[385] National margins of appreciation may, therefore, vary 'according to the circumstances, the subject-matter and its background.'[386] Whether the practice in question is regarded as non-discriminatory in other democratic states has also been significant in determining their scope.[387] Particularly wide margins are permitted with respect to social and economic policy.[388] By contrast, on the express or implicit grounds that they run counter to major priorities of European social policy, the margin is narrow, and the justifications for differential treatment must be particularly compelling, with respect to characteristics

---

[379] *Thlimmenos v Greece*, HUDOC, 6 April 2000 (GC), at para. 44.

[380] *Stummer v Austria*, HUDOC, 7 July 2011 (GC), at para. 88.

[381] *Belgian Linguistics Case*, HUDOC, 23 July 1968, 'Interpretation adopted by the court', at para. 10; See, e.g., *Swedish Engine Drivers Union v Sweden*, HUDOC, 6 February 1976, at paras. 44–8.

[382] *Abdulaziz, Cabales, Balkandali v United Kingdom*, HUDOC, 28 May 1985, at paras. 74–83.

[383] *EB v France*, HUDOC, 22 January 2008 (GC), at para. 74; *DH and Others v Czech Republic*, HUDOC, 13 November 2007 (GC), at para. 80; *Abdulaziz, Cabales, Balkandali v United Kingdom*, HUDOC, 28 May 1985, at para. 38.

[384] *Petrovic v Austria*, HUDOC, 27 March 1998, at para. 30; *James and Others v United Kingdom*, HUDOC, 21 February 1986, at paras. 75–7.

[385] *Zarb Adami v Malta*, HUDOC, 20 June 2006, at para. 73.

[386] *Petrovic v Austria*, HUDOC, 27 March 1998, at para. 38; *Rasmussen v Denmark*, HUDOC, 28 November 1984, at para. 40.

[387] *Petrovic v Austria*, HUDOC, 27 March 1998, at paras. 38–9; *Rasmussen v Denmark*, HUDOC, 28 November 1984, at paras. 40–1.

[388] *British Gurkha Welfare Society and Others v United Kingdom*, HUDOC, 15 September 2016, at para. 81; *Burden v United Kingdom*, HUDOC, 29 April 2008 (GC), at para. 60.

such as race,[389] sex/gender,[390] sexual orientation,[391] religion,[392] birth,[393] nationality[394] and (but only comparatively recently) health and disability.[395] Marital status arguably lies somewhere in between.[396]

Article 15 – Derogation in Time of Emergency

Article 15, the 'derogation provision', permits the suspension of most Convention rights in war and public emergencies. However, notwithstanding security concerns in various parts of the continent both pre- and post-9/11, only a small minority of states have ever resorted to it. This is at least partly because Convention rights may legitimately be restricted to address the challenges posed by terrorism without derogation being required.[397]

Compliance with Article 15 requires the fulfilment of several conditions. First, there must be a 'time of war or public emergency threatening the life of the nation'. According to the Strasbourg institutions this must be actual or imminent, threatens the continuance of the organised life of the community and presents an exceptional and possibly prolonged crisis or danger, notwithstanding phases when the risk decreases. Normal Convention-compliant measures must be plainly inadequate, and the effects must involve the whole nation, although not all parts need be equally exposed to the risk of violent attack.[398] While these are ultimately

---

[389] *DH and Others v Czech Republic*, HUDOC, 13 November 2007 (GC), at paras. 176 & 196.

[390] *Van Raalte v the Netherlands*, HUDOC, 21 February 1997, at para. 42.

[391] *Eweida and Others v United Kingdom*, HUDOC, 15 January 2013, at para. 105; *Schalk and Kopf v Austria*, HUDOC, 24 June 2010, at para. 97; *EB v France*, HUDOC, 22 January 2008 (GC), at para. 91; *Smith and Grady v United Kingdom*, HUDOC, 27 September 1999, at paras. 89–90.

[392] *Eweida and Others v United Kingdom*, HUDOC, 15 January 2013, at paras. 94 & 99.

[393] *Fabris v France*, HUDOC, 7 February 2013 (GC), at para. 59 ; *Marckx v Belgium*, HUDOC, 13 June 1979, at para. 58.

[394] *A. H. and Others v Russia*, HUDOC, 17 January 2017, at para. 407; *Gaygusuz v Austria*, HUDOC, 16 September 1996, at para. 42.

[395] *Kiyutin v Russia*, HUDOC, 10 March 2011, at para. 63.

[396] *Sahin v Germany*, HUDOC, 8 July 2003 (GC), at para. 94; *McMichael v United Kingdom*, HUDOC, 24 February 1995, at paras. 97–8.

[397] See, for example, *Aksoy v Turkey*, HUDOC, 18 December 1996; *Murray v United Kingdom*, HUDOC, 28 October 1994; *Brogan v United Kingdom*, HUDOC, 29 November 1988.

[398] *A and Others v United Kingdom*, HUDOC, 19 February 2009 (GC), at para. 177; *Marshall v United Kingdom*; HUDOC, 10 July 2001 (dec.); *Lawless v Ireland (No. 3)*, HUDOC, 1 July 1961, at paras. 28–30.

matters for the Court, they are also subject to a wide margin of appreciation, justified by the 'better position rationale' – national authorities acting in good faith are likely to be better able to make the appropriate risk assessment than any Strasbourg institution – and by an acknowledgement that the choice is also political by nature and may be controversial in the state in question.[399] Different responses may also be justified to similar emergencies in different states.

Second, any derogating measure must be limited to 'the extent strictly required by the exigencies of the situation', a high threshold proportionality test. The issues here, and the division of responsibility between the Court and domestic authorities, are similar to those applicable to the existence of an emergency itself. The Court will consider the adequacy of existing non-emergency measures, 'precise reasons relating to the actual facts' rather than generalisations will be required[400] and appropriate weight will also be given to such relevant factors as the provision of adequate safeguards against abuse (including effective judicial remedies and regular legislative review), the nature of the rights affected, the circumstances, the duration of the emergency[401] and its geographical reach.[402] But it is not for the Court to determine how prudent or expedient any given emergency measure might be. It must confine itself merely to considering its compatibility, given the national margin of appreciation, with the Article 15 'strict necessity' test.[403]

Third, there can be no derogation from the 'non-derogable rights' to life (except for lawful acts of war), not to be tortured or inhumanly or degradingly treated or punished, not to be held in slavery or servitude and not to be punished retrospectively or more severely for conduct than was the case at the time it occurred. Protocol 6 also outlaws the death penalty except in time of war, while Protocol 13 outlaws it in all circumstances including time of war. Differences in the impact of counter-terrorist

---

[399] *Aksoy* v *Turkey*, HUDOC, 18 December 1996, at para. 53; *Brannigan and McBride* v *United Kingdom*, HUDOC, 26 May 1993, at paras. 41 & 43; *Ireland* v *United Kingdom*, HUDOC, 18 July 1978, at para. 207.

[400] *Demir and Others* v *Turkey*, HUDOC, 23 September 1998, at para. 52.

[401] *Aksoy* v *Turkey*, HUDOC, 18 December 1996, at paras. 79–82; *Brannigan and McBride* v *United Kingdom*, HUDOC, 26 May 1993, at paras. 63–6; *Ireland* v *United Kingdom*, HUDOC, 18 July 1978, at para. 217; *Lawless* v *Ireland (No. 3)*, HUDOC, 1 July 1961, at paras. 36–8.

[402] *Sakik and Others* v *Turkey*, HUDOC, 26 November 1997, at paras. 38–9.

[403] *A and Others* v *United Kingdom*, HUDOC, 19 February 2009 (GC) at para. 174; *Ireland* v *United Kingdom*, HUDOC, 18 July 1978, at para. 214.

measures upon different social groups will amount to discrimination if no objective or reasonable justification can be found.[404] Fourth, any derogation must not be inconsistent with the other international obligations of the state concerned. While this is 'of little significance' in practice,[405] the most substantial other international obligation is the derogation provision in Article 4(1) of the International Covenant on Civil and Political Rights, which contains a longer list of non-derogable rights than that found in Article 15 ECHR. Finally, the Secretary General of the Council of Europe must be informed of the derogating measures without delay, but not necessarily in advance of their introduction, the reasons for them and when they no longer apply.[406]

Articles 16–18 – Additional Restrictions upon Convention Rights

While, as already observed, most of the rights in the Convention are expressly restricted, Articles 16–18 provide additional generic limitations. Article 16 states that nothing in Articles 10, 11 and 14 shall be regarded as preventing restrictions on the political activities of aliens.[407] Article 17 (the 'abuse clause') prohibits anything in the Convention from being interpreted as implying, for any state, group or person, the right to engage in any activity, or to perform any act, aimed at the destruction of any Convention right or freedom, or its limitation to a greater extent than the Convention itself permits.[408] Article 18, frequently invoked by litigants but much less frequently formally addressed by the ECtHR,[409] prohibits the use of restrictions upon rights for purposes other than those prescribed (call this the 'bad faith' clause), for example, detentions for political reasons disguised as legitimate exceptions to Article 5, the bad faith motives for which will, typically, be difficult to prove.[410]

---

[404] *A and Others* v *United Kingdom*, HUDOC, 19 February 2009 (GC), at para. 190; *Ireland* v *United Kingdom*, HUDOC, 18 July 1978, paras. 225–30.

[405] Harris et al., *Law of the European Convention*, p. 844.

[406] *Ireland* v *United Kingdom*, HUDOC, 18 July 1978, at para. 39; *Lawless* v *Ireland (No. 3)*, HUDOC, 1 July 1961, at paras. 41–5.

[407] *Piermont* v *France*, HUDOC, 27 April 1995, at paras. 60–4.

[408] *Ždanoka* v *Latvia*, HUDOC, 16 March 2006 (GC), at paras. 99–101; *Norwood* v *United Kingdom*, HUDOC, 16 November 2004 (dec.); *Lehideux and Isorni* v *France* HUDOC, 23 September 1998 (GC), at paras. 57–8.

[409] *Navalnyy and Yashin* v *Russia*, HUDOC, 4 December 2014, at para. 117.

[410] *Ilgar Mammadov* v *Azerbaijan*, HUDOC, 22 May 2014, at para. 137; *Gusinskiy* v *Russia*, HUDOC, 19 May 2004, at para. 77.

The Protocols

Six subsequent substantive protocols to the Convention have added further rights, which, unlike the procedural protocols, are optional for states. Protocol No. 1 provides rights to the peaceful enjoyment of possessions, to education and to free elections. Protocol No. 4 provides the right not to be imprisoned for debt, the right to freedom of movement, the right of nationals not to be expelled from the state to which they belong and the right of aliens not to be collectively expelled. As already indicated, Protocol No. 6 abolishes the death penalty except in time of war. Protocol No. 7 contains procedural safeguards regarding the expulsion of aliens, the right of appeal in criminal proceedings, the right to compensation for wrongful conviction, the right not to be tried or punished twice in the same state for the same offence plus the equal right of spouses under the law. Protocol No. 12 outlaws discrimination in relation to any right 'set forth by law', in contrast with Article 14 of the Convention, which prohibits discrimination only with respect to Convention rights.[411] And, as also already indicated, Protocol No. 13 outlaws the death penalty even in time of war. The remaining Protocols concern procedural matters discussed in the preceding two chapters.

Article 1, Protocol No. 1 - Protection of Property

The right to property proved to be one of the most controversial human rights when the ECHR was being drafted. As a result it was omitted from the main text and included in a highly qualified form in what eventually became the first Protocol, Article 1 of which recognises the right of 'every natural or legal person' to the peaceful enjoyment of his or her possessions. Being deprived of possessions is prohibited, 'except in the public interest and subject to the conditions provided for by law and by the general principles of international law'.[412] Article 1 also preserves the right of a state to 'enforce such laws as it deems necessary to control the use of property in accordance with the general interest or to secure the payment of taxes or other contributions or penalties.' Given the substantial values of property that may be at stake, a successful claim

---

[411] *Sejdić and Finci v Bosnia and Herzegovina*, HUDOC, 22 December 2009 (GC), at paras. 39 & 54.

[412] International law prohibits the arbitrary expropriation of foreign property without compensation.

can result in substantial compensation, for example, €24 million as in *Stran Greek Refineries*.[413]

For the purpose of this provision, a 'possession' means something of economic value that the applicant already has – including a legitimate expectation, adequately supported by domestic law[414] – but not property rights no longer capable of being exercised effectively, as in claims for the restitution of property expropriated by the communist states of central and eastern Europe.[415] In common with most other rights in the ECHR, and taking appropriate account of market-related loss of value,[416] states have both preventive and remedial positive obligations to ensure that the right to peaceful enjoyment of possessions is adequately protected.[417]

Three core issues arise under Article 1 of the first Protocol – the scope of the right to 'peaceful enjoyment' of possessions, legitimate grounds for being deprived of them and the limited right of states to control the use of property.[418] The distinctions between 'interference', 'deprivation' and 'control' are not always easy to draw and, even when finding a violation, the Court does not always clearly identify which has occurred.[419] Providing no one ends up bearing an 'individual and excessive burden' (although this does not mean avoiding all individual disadvantage),[420] states are entitled to balance fairly the right in question against the public or community interest. Subject to the legality test,[421] and the principles of proportionality[422] and

---

[413] *Stran Greek Refineries and Stratis Andreadis v Greece*, HUDOC, 9 December 1994.

[414] *Béláné Nagy v Hungary*, HUDOC, 13 December 2016 (GC), at paras 74–9 & 106–7; *Gratzinger and Gratzingerova v Czech Republic*, HUDOC, 10 July 2002 (dec., GC), at para. 69; *Pressos Compania Naviera SA and Others v Belgium*, HUDOC, 20 November 1995, at para. 31.

[415] *Von Maltzan and Others v Germany*, HUDOC, 2 March 2005 (dec. GC), at paras. 85–102

[416] *Akkuş v Turkey*, HUDOC, 9 July 1997, at paras. 30–1.

[417] *Öneryildiz v Turkey*, HUDOC, 30 November 2004 (GC), at para. 134.

[418] *James and Others v United Kingdom*, HUDOC, 21 February 1986, at para. 37; *Sporrong and Lönnroth v Sweden*, HUDOC, 23 September 1982, at para. 61.

[419] *Papamichalopoulos and Others v Greece*, HUDOC, 24 June 1993, at paras. 45–6.

[420] *Baczúr v Hungary*, HUDOC, 7 February 2017, at para. 32; *Alentseva v Russia*, HUDOC, 17 November 2016, at para. 77; *JA Pye (Oxford) Ltd and JA Pye (Oxford) Land Ltd v United Kingdom*, HUDOC, 30 August 2007 (GC), at paras. 75 & 84.

[421] *Broniowski v Poland*, HUDOC, 22 June 2004 (GC), at paras. 147 & 154; *Carbonara and Ventura v Italy*, HUDOC, 30 May 2000, at para. 63; *Beyeler v Italy*, HUDOC, 5 January 2000 (GC), at paras. 118–19;

[422] *Tomina and Others v Russia*, HUDOC, 1 December 2016, at paras. 37–43; *Kjartan Ásmundsson v Iceland*, HUDOC, 12 October 2004, at paras. 40 & 42–5.

non-discrimination[423] – which imply, amongst other things, the avoidance of arbitrariness,[424] consideration of alternative means to achieve the same result,[425] the availability of procedures for challenging and remedying decisions[426] and, in all but the most exceptional cases, the provision of adequate compensation[427] – the Court recognises generous margins of appreciation in deciding how this should be achieved.[428]

'Interferences' not amounting to 'deprivations' or 'controls' have spanned a wide spectrum, including denial of access to property;[429] an inflexible and unpredictable system of land expropriation for urban redevelopment resulting in owners being unable, and without remedy, to build upon their own land in some cases for decades;[430] the reduction or discontinuation of pensions or social security benefits;[431] and the exercise of a right of pre-emption over an art work purchased under contract.[432] To qualify as a 'deprivation' all the property owners' legal rights have to be extinguished by law rather than merely in fact.[433] The latter will, nevertheless, constitute an 'interference'.[434] 'Control' of property can take a variety of forms, including restrictions on use reducing its value and limiting its disposability[435] and regulations governing rent, planning, the environment,[436] import and export[437] and the conduct of

---

[423] *Pine Valley Developments and Others v Ireland*, HUDOC, 29 November 1991, at paras. 61–4.

[424] *Carbonara and Ventura v Italy*, HUDOC, 30 May 2000, at paras. 65 & 72–3.

[425] *Kjartan Ásmundsson v Iceland*, HUDOC, 12 October 2004, at para. 45.

[426] *Öneryildiz v Turkey*, HUDOC, 30 November 2004 (GC), at paras. 145–9.

[427] *Broniowski v Poland*, HUDOC, 22 June 2004 (GC), at para. 186; *Hentrich v France*, HUDOC, 22 September 1994, at paras. 43 & 48–9; *Lithgow v United Kingdom*, HUDOC, 8 July 1986, at para. 121.

[428] *Lithgow v United Kingdom*, HUDOC, 8 July 1986, at paras. 122 & 147; *James and Others v United Kingdom*, HUDOC, 21 February 1986, at para. 50; *Sporrong and Lönnroth v Sweden*, HUDOC, 23 September 1982, at paras. 69 & 73.

[429] *Loizidou v Turkey*, HUDOC, 18 December 1996 (GC), at paras. 60–1.

[430] *Barcza and Others v Hungary*, HUDOC, 11 October 2016, at para. 47; *Sporrong and Lönnroth v Sweden*, HUDOC, 23 September 1982, at paras. 58–60.

[431] *Béláné Nagy v Hungary*, HUDOC, 13 December 2016 (GC), at paras. 11–22; *Klein v Austria*, HUDOC, 3 March 2011, at para. 48.

[432] *Beyeler v Italy*, HUDOC, 5 January 2000 (GC), at para. 107.

[433] *Lithgow v United Kingdom*, HUDOC, 8 July 1986, at paras. 105–7.

[434] *Hentrich v France*, HUDOC, 22 September 1994, at paras. 40–9.

[435] *Anthony Aquilina v Malta*, HUDOC, 11 December 2014, at para. 54.

[436] *Statileo v Croatia*, HUDOC, 10 July 2014, at para. 140; *Fredin v Sweden (No. 1)*, HUDOC, 18 February 1991, at paras. 41–7; *Mellacher and Others v Austria*, HUDOC, 19 December 1989, at paras. 42–4.

[437] *AGOSI v United Kingdom*, HUDOC, 24 October 1986, at para. 51.

business.[438] Since forfeiture and confiscation orders typically penalise breaches of norms regulating the use of property, the Court regards them as means of control rather than as deprivations of possessions.[439]

Article 2, Protocol No. 1 – Right to Education

As with the right to property, the debate over the right to education proved so controversial that it was diverted into an optional protocol, and in acceding to it, 'an unusually large number of states' entered reservations.[440] Article 2 of Protocol No. 1 provides that 'no one shall be denied the right to education', and that in discharging educational responsibilities, the state shall respect the right of parents to ensure education and teaching conform to 'their religious and philosophical beliefs'. It has two principal dimensions: the negative obligation on states not to deny the right to education, and the positive obligation to respect the right of parents to ensure education and teaching conform with their religious and philosophical convictions, each of which must be discharged in a non-discriminatory manner.[441]

Although they must refrain from prohibiting private education,[442] states, therefore, have no positive obligation either to provide a publicly provisioned education system or to subsidise private education at any level.[443] And, since the right to education is not absolute, providing the effects are foreseeable and reasonably proportionate to a legitimate aim, it may be subject to regulation in both public and private sectors according to a national margin of appreciation.[444] A key issue concerns access to, and exclusion from, educational institutions. States may, for example, insist on education being provided at school rather than at home,[445] authorise the suspension or exclusion of disruptive children[446] and

---

[438] *Denimark Ltd and Others v United Kingdom*, HUDOC, 26 September 2000 (dec.).

[439] *Raimondo v Italy*, HUDOC, 22 February 1994, at para. 25; *AGOSI v United Kingdom*, HUDOC, 24 October 1986, at para. 51; *Handyside v United Kingdom*, HUDOC, 7 December 1976, at para. 62.

[440] Harris et al., *Law of the European Convention on Human Rights*, p. 906.

[441] *DH and Others v Czech Republic*, HUDOC, 13 November 2007 (GC), at paras. 196–210; *Belgian Linguistics Case*, HUDOC, 23 July 1968, 'Interpretation adopted by the court', at para. 8.

[442] *Kjeldsen, Busk Madsen and Pedersen v Denmark*, HUDOC, 7 December 1976, at para. 54.

[443] *Velyo Velev v Bulgaria*, HUDOC, 27 May 2014, at para. 34; *Belgian Linguistics Case*, HUDOC, 23 July 1968, 'The meaning and scope of the Protocol', at para. 1.

[444] *Leyla Şahin v Turkey*, HUDOC, 10 November 2005 (GC), at para. 154.

[445] *Konrad v Germany*, HUDOC, 11 September 2006 (dec.).

[446] *Ali v United Kingdom*, HUDOC, 11 January 2011, at paras. 54 & 62.

choose the state school any child, particularly those with special needs, should attend.[447] The language of instruction must not be discriminatory,[448] and while the right in question is to an effective education,[449] claims based on such issues as resources, management, curriculum and the role of parents 'are unlikely to succeed in the absence of clearly arbitrary action or the lack of a legal base'.[450]

The positive obligation to respect parents' religious and philosophical convictions, primarily intended to protect against indoctrination, is subject to four main limitations. First, the beliefs at issue must be 'religious' or 'philosophical' and not merely 'ideas' or 'opinions'.[451] Second, mere incidental treatment of matters pertaining to them will not raise an arguable issue under this branch of Article 2 if the lessons and other relevant activities are conducted in 'an objective, critical and pluralistic manner'.[452] Third, the state's obligations can be discharged by exempting pupils from the offending class(es).[453] Finally, whether dress codes or the display of religious symbols on the premises of educational establishments violates Article 2 will depend upon proportionality, likely impact and the national margin of appreciation.[454]

Article 3, Protocol No. 1 – Right to Free Elections

Article 3 of Protocol No. 1 – which provides that the 'High Contracting Parties undertake to hold free elections at regular intervals by secret ballot, under conditions which will ensure the free expression of the opinion of the people in the choice of legislature' – imposes a positive obligation on states from which two core electoral rights derive: the right to vote and the right to stand for election. In recent years, the number of complaints about violation of this provision has increased,

---

[447] *Graeme* v *United Kingdom*, HUDOC, 5 February 1990 (dec.).

[448] *Catan and Others* v *Moldova and Russia*, HUDOC, 19 October 2012 (GC), at paras. 137–43; *Belgian Linguistics Case*, HUDOC, 23 July 1968, 'The six questions referred to the court', at para. 7.

[449] See *Belgian Linguistics Case*, HUDOC, 23 July 1968.

[450] Harris et al., *Law of the European Convention on Human Rights*, pp. 912, 918.

[451] *Campbell and Cosans* v *United Kingdom*, HUDOC, 25 February 1982, at para. 36.

[452] *Folgerø and Others* v *Norway*, HUDOC, 27 June 2007 (GC), at para. 85; *Kjeldsen, Busk Madsen and Pedersen* v *Denmark*, HUDOC, 7 December 1976, at para. 53.

[453] *Mansur Yalçin* v *Turkey*, HUDOC, 16 September 2014 at para. 77; *Folgerø and Others* v *Norway*, HUDOC, 27 June 2007 (GC), at paras. 96–100.

[454] *Lautsi* v *Italy*, HUDOC, 18 March 2011 (GC), at paras. 68–72; *Leyla Şahin* v *Turkey*, HUDOC, 10 November 2005 (GC), at paras. 117–23.

many from the relatively new democracies of central and eastern Europe.[455] Although the text makes no express reference to 'democracy', the ECtHR has, nevertheless, strongly affirmed that 'democracy constitutes a fundamental element of the "European public order" ... (and) ... is the only political model contemplated by the Convention and, accordingly, the only one compatible with it.'[456] Since the text of Article 3 is expressly confined to 'the choice of legislature', the obligation does not include presidential elections or referendums.[457] In spite of the absence of an express 'legality' requirement, it has, nevertheless, also been held that, taking national margins of appreciation and any relevant European consensus into account, limitations upon electoral rights must comply with the legality principle, and, in particular, must preserve the essence and effectiveness of these rights, pursue a legitimate aim in a proportionate manner, protect legitimate expectations and not be arbitrary or thwart the free expression of the people in the choice of legislators.[458] Subject to these principles, no particular type of legislature or electoral system is required.[459] Laws requiring political parties to gain a certain proportion of the total vote before being able to take their seats, typically 5 per cent, are also compatible with Article 3.[460] While Article 6 ECHR (the right to a fair trial) does not apply to Article 3, Article 13 ECHR (the right to an effective remedy) does.[461] Article 3 also implies fair and impartial practices and institutions, such as properly constituted and effective election commissions for managing the conduct of elections including counting ballots, announcing results and

---

[455] Rainey et al., *The European Convention on Human Rights*, pp. 538–9.

[456] *Ždanoka v Latvia*, HUDOC, 16 March 2006 (GC), at para. 98.

[457] *Baškauskaitė v Lithuania*, HUDOC, 21 October 1998 (dec.); *Castelli and Others v Italy*, HUDOC, 14 September 1998 (dec.).

[458] *Yabloko Russian United Democratic Party and Others v Russia*, HUDOC, 8 November 2016, at para. 66; *Communist Party of Russia and Others v Russia*, HUDOC, 19 June 2012, at paras. 102 & 110; *Sitaropoulos and Giakoumopoulos v Greece*, HUDOC, 15 March 2012 (GC), at para. 64; *Tănase v Moldova*, HUDOC, 27 April 2010 (GC), at para. 161; *Yumak and Sadak v Turkey*, HUDOC, 8 July 2008 (GC), at para. 109; *Hirst v United Kingdom (No. 2)*, HUDOC, 6 October 2005 (GC), at para. 62; *Mathieu-Mohin and Clerfayt v Belgium*, HUDOC, 2 March 1987, at para. 52.

[459] *Sitaropoulos and Giakoumopoulos v Greece*, HUDOC, 15 March 2012 (GC), at para. 65; *Liberal Party, R and P v United Kingdom*, HUDOC, 18 December 1980 (dec.).

[460] *Yumak and Sadak v Turkey*, HUDOC, 8 July 2008 (GC), at paras. 113–15.

[461] *Grosaru v Romania*, HUDOC, 2 March 2010, at paras. 158–62; *Petkov v Bulgaria*, HUDOC, 11 June 2009, at paras. 74–83; *Pierre-Bloch v France*, HUDOC, 21 October 1997, at para. 64.

registering voters;[462] state funding for political parties;[463] and regulating the media.[464] Impartial, independent and effective judicial procedures should also be provided for resolving disputes about electoral process and outcomes.[465]

The principle of universal suffrage lies at the heart of the right to vote. But, because it is not absolute, disqualifications and exclusions may, therefore, be implied and justified. In addition to condemning the disenfranchisement of those declared bankrupt, the Court's other relevant decisions have turned on arguments about disproportionality.[466] Subject to this, and the other principles outlined in the previous paragraph, the ECtHR has accepted, for example, that suffrage may be limited according to age, residence, citizenship and mental incapacity.[467] Two particularly controversial exclusions concern the voting rights of expatriates and prisoners. With regard to the former, the ECtHR has applied the proportionality test generously.[468] As far as the latter is concerned, wide margins of appreciation reflecting divergent practice across Europe have also been acknowledged. While condemning blanket prisoner voting bans, the Court has also declined to condemn potentially permanent bans on some prisoners even after their sentences have been served.[469]

The rights to stand for election, and if successful to sit in the legislature, are subject to potentially greater restriction, and wider margins of appreciation, than voting rights.[470] Subject to the principles discussed in the first paragraph of this section, and in addition to familiar limitations

---

[462] *Gahramanli and Others v Azerbaijan*, HUDOC, 8 October 2015, at paras. 70, 78 & 87; *Georgian Labour Party v Georgia*, HUDOC, 8 July 2008, at paras. 101 & 104–11.

[463] *Özgürlük ve Dayanişma Partisi (ÖDP) v Turkey*, HUDOC, 10 May 2012, at paras. 34–5.

[464] *Communist Party of Russia and Others v Russia*, HUDOC, 19 June 2012, at paras. 126–8.

[465] *Grosaru v Romania*, HUDOC, 2 March 2010, at paras. 53–7 & 62; *Petkov v Bulgaria*, HUDOC, 11 June 2009, at paras. 82–3.

[466] Harris et al., *Law of the European Convention on Human Rights*, p. 929.

[467] *Sitaropoulos and Giakoumopoulos v Greece*, HUDOC, 15 March 2012 (GC), at para. 68; *Alajos Kiss v Hungary*, HUDOC, 20 May 2010, at paras. 36 & 42–4; *Hirst v United Kingdom (No. 2)*, HUDOC, 6 October 2005 (GC), at paras. 60–2; *Mathieu-Mohin and Clerfayt v Belgium*, HUDOC, 2 March 1987, at para. 52.

[468] *Oran v Turkey*, HUDOC, 15 April 2014, at para. 66; *Shindler v United Kingdom* HUDOC, 7 May 2013, at paras. 116 & 118; *Sitaropoulos and Giakoumopoulos v Greece*, HUDOC, 15 March 2012 (GC), at paras. 75 & 81.

[469] *Kulinski and Sabev v Bulgaria*, HUDOC, 21 July 2016, at para. 32; *Scoppola v Italy (No. 3)*, HUDOC, 22 May 2012 (GC), at paras. 103–10; *Hirst v United Kingdom (No. 2)*, HUDOC, 6 October 2005 (GC), at paras. 82–5.

[470] *Russian Conservative Party of Entrepreneurs and Others v Russia*, HUDOC, 11 January 2007, at para. 48; *Melnychenko v Ukraine*, HUDOC, 19 October 2004, at para. 57.

relating to age, residency and citizenship applicable to the franchise, certain restrictions on the right to stand, for example, the exclusion of prisoners and certain public servants, may be legitimate.[471] Various other rules may also be appropriate, relating, for example, to language proficiency,[472] to the conduct of elections (for example, candidate deposits)[473] and to various types of electoral malpractice such as fraud or bribery and to previous criminal or unlawful conduct.[474] Subject to legitimate expectations and other principles cited above, particularly wide margins of appreciation are also available to states regarding the disqualification of legislators for misconduct.[475]

Miscellaneous

In addition to Protocol No. 1, substantive rights are found in the fourth, sixth, seventh, twelfth and thirteenth protocols. Protocol Nos. 6, 12 and 13 have already been discussed. What follows, therefore, is a brief overview of the other relatively infrequently litigated rights in the other provisions. Article 1 of Protocol No. 4 provides the right to be free from imprisonment merely for non-fulfillment of a contractual obligation,[476] while Article 2 provides, subject to legality and democratic necessity tests similar to those found in Articles 8–11 ECHR (with the 'public interest' providing an extra legitimate purpose), the right of everyone lawfully within a territory to liberty of movement including freedom to choose residence there, and the right of everyone to leave any country including his or her own. As already indicated, the right not to be deprived of liberty, which Article 5 strictly circumscribes, should not be confused with the right to freedom of movement. Subject to the express legitimate

---

[471] *Zornić* v *Bosnia and Herzegovina*, HUDOC, 15 July 2014, at para. 30; *Scoppola* v *Italy (No. 3)*, HUDOC, 22 May 2012 (GC), at paras. 81–3 & 103–10; *Tănase* v *Moldova*, HUDOC, 27 April 2010 (GC), at para. 180; *Melnychenko* v *Ukraine*, HUDOC, 19 October 2004, at para. 56; *Gitonas* v *Greece*, HUDOC, 1 July 1997, at para. 44.

[472] *Podkolzina* v *Latvia*, HUDOC, 9 April 2002, at paras. 34–5.

[473] *Sukhovetskyy* v *Ukraine*, HUDOC, 28 March 2006, at paras. 62 & 73–4.

[474] *Uspaskich* v *Lithuania*, HUDOC, 20 December 2016, at para. 89; *Paksas* v *Lithuania*, HUDOC, 6 January 2014 (GC), at para. 100; *Abil* v *Azerbaijan*, HUDOC, 21 February 2012, at para. 32; *Russian Conservative Party of Entrepreneurs and Others* v *Russia*, HUDOC, 11 January 2007, at paras. 64–7; *Ždanoka* v *Latvia*, HUDOC, 16 March 2006 (GC), at para. 110.

[475] *Gitonas* v *Greece*, HUDOC, 1 July 1997, at para. 39, cf. *Sadak and Others* v *Turkey (No. 2)*, HUDOC, 11 June 2002, at paras. 35–40.

[476] *Gatt* v *Malta*, HUDOC, 27 July 2010, at paras. 53–6.

purposes in Article 2 of Protocol No. 4, plus proportionality, reliable evidence and the national margin of appreciation, restrictions on movement imposed by bail conditions,[477] preventive house arrest,[478] travel bans[479] and confinement within, or exclusion from, a particular area[480] can, therefore, be justified. Article 3 of Protocol No. 4 provides a formally unqualified prohibition against expulsion from, or denial of entry to, the state of which one is a national. But this does not include extradition.[481] Article 4 of Protocol No. 4 provides a formally unqualified prohibition against the collective expulsion of aliens, including stateless persons, while Article 1 of Protocol No. 7 prohibits the individual expulsion of lawfully resident aliens, except in accordance with law and certain specified due process rights, the latter of which can be suspended until after expulsion where necessary and proportionate to the pursuit of public order or national security.[482] Mass individual expulsions, where the individual merits of each case have been considered, do not amount to 'collective expulsion' for the purpose of this provision.[483]

Except for minor offences, Article 2 of Protocol No. 7 recognises the right of everyone convicted of a crime to have his or her conviction or sentence reviewed by a higher tribunal according to law, where the original trial was conducted by the highest court, or where conviction followed an appeal against acquittal. Providing a legitimate aim is pursued and the very essence of the right is not infringed, the right to 'review' – which does not mean a right to appeal the merits – is subject to a wide national margin of appreciation.[484] Article 3 of Protocol No. 7 provides a right to compensation for conviction and punishment as a result of new, or newly discovered, facts indicating a miscarriage of

---

[477] *Schmid v Austria*, HUDOC, 9 July 1985 (dec.).

[478] *Labita v Italy*, HUDOC, 6 April 2000 (GC), at paras. 189–97.

[479] *Riener v Bulgaria*, HUDOC, 23 May 2006, at paras. 110–11 & 130.

[480] *Rosengren v Romania*, HUDOC, 24 April 2008, at paras. 32–40; *Olivieira v the Netherlands*, HUDOC, 4 June 2002, at paras. 39–66.

[481] *IB v Germany*, HUDOC, 24 May 1974 (dec.), at para. 13 of the section 'The Law'.

[482] *Khlaifia and Others v Italy*, HUDOC, 1 September 2015, at paras. 169 & 171–2; *Nolan and K v Russia*, HUDOC, 12 February 2009, at paras. 114–16; *Bolat v Russia*, HUDOC, 5 October 2006, at paras. 81–3; *Lupsa v Romania*, HUDOC, 8 June 2006, at paras. 54–61.

[483] *Georgia v Russia*, HUDOC, 3 July 2014 (GC), at paras. 167 & 175–6; *Hirsi Jamaa and Others v Italy*, HUDOC, 23 February 2012 (GC), at para. 184; *Sultani v France*, HUDOC, 20 September 2007, at para. 81; *Čonka v Belgium*, HUDOC, 5 February 2002, at paras. 61–3.

[484] *Krombach v France*, HUDOC, 13 February 2001, at para. 96.

criminal justice has occurred, unless non-disclosure can wholly or partly be attributed to the defendant.[485]

Article 4 of Protocol No. 7 prohibits the trial or punishment of anyone under the jurisdiction of a given state for an offence arising from identical or substantially similar facts in relation to which he or she has already been prosecuted in accordance with law in that state (the principle of *ne bis in idem* or 'double jeopardy').[486] But it does not preclude the reopening of cases, in accordance with law and national penal procedure, where there is evidence of new or newly discovered facts or where some fundamental defect in the original proceedings, which could have affected the outcome, occurred.[487] Subject to necessary measures taken by states within their margin of appreciation in the interests of children, Article 5 of Protocol No. 7 provides for the equal rights and responsibilities of spouses in private law, regarding and during marriage, in the event of dissolution and in relations with their children.[488]

3.4 Impact of International and EU Law

As Chapter 5 describes in more detail, when it comes to the adjudication of fundamental rights, until recently the ECJ has tended to follow in the footsteps of its older sister, the ECtHR. And, by the same token, this has not been true the other way around. Nevertheless, although fairly marginal so far, international, including EU, law can impact upon the ECtHR in several ways.[489]

---

[485] *Poghosyan and Baghdasaryan v Armenia*, HUDOC, 12 June 2012, at paras. 49–52.

[486] *Kiiveri v Finland*, HUDOC, 10 February 2015, at paras. 37 & 45–9; *Österlund v Finland*, HUDOC, 10 February 2015, at paras. 41 & 49–52; *Lucky Dev v Sweden*, HUDOC, 27 November 2014, at para. 58.

[487] *Marguš v Croatia*, HUDOC, 27 May 2014 (GC), at paras. 140–1.

[488] *Konstantin Markin v Russia*, HUDOC, 7 October 2010, at para. 61.

[489] C. Ryngaert, 'Oscillating between embracing and avoiding Bosphorus: The European Court of Human Rights on member state responsibility for acts of international organisations and the case of the EU', *European Law Review*, 39 (2014), 176–92; V. Tzevelekos, 'When Elephants Fight It Is the Grass That suffers: "Hegemonic struggle" in Europe and the side-effects for international law' in K. Dzehtsiarou, T. Konstadinides, T. Lock and N. O'Meara (eds.), *Human Rights in Europe: The Influence, Overlaps and Contradictions of the EU and the ECHR* (London: Routledge, 2014); L. Gordillo, *Interlocking Constitutions: Towards and Interordinal Theory of National, European and UN Law* (Oxford: Hart, 2012), pp. 122–81; C. Van de Heyning and R. Lawson, 'The EU as a party to the European Convention of (sic) Human Rights: EU law and the European Court of Justice case law as inspiration and challenge to the ECtHR jurisprudence', in P. Popelier, C. Van de Heyning and P. Van Nuffel (eds.), *Human Rights Protection in the*

First, it has long been accepted that the ECHR should be interpreted in accordance with international law.[490] International and/or EU law, including the jurisprudence of the ECJ, may also shed light upon the interpretation of ECHR provisions, such as the right not to be subject to gender, and other forms of discrimination (Article 14 ECHR),[491] the right to peaceful enjoyment of possessions (Article 1 of Protocol No. 1 ECHR),[492] issues arising under child abduction (Article 8 ECHR)[493] and generic legal concepts such as the *non bis in idem* principle (Article 7 ECHR).[494] It has also long been accepted, since the EU is not a party to the Convention, that any complaint that it, or any of its constitutive organs, has violated the ECHR will be ruled inadmissible at Strasbourg. Nor is it possible for the ECtHR to hold member states of the CE responsible for Convention violation by the EU.

Elements of EU law may, however, be integral to the domestic law of a respondent state and may, therefore, be relevant for a given Strasbourg complaint. For example, in *Aristimuño Mendizabal* v *France*, the French authorities, concerned about the applicant's links with the Basque terrorist organisation ETA, gave her only short-term permission to reside in France on sixty-nine occasions over fourteen years, instead of the full residence permit to which, as a Spanish citizen, she was entitled under EU law. The ECtHR found that, as the interference was not 'in accordance with the law' as required by Article 8 ECHR, which for this purpose included relevant EU provisions, her right to respect for her family life under this provision had been violated.[495] The ECtHR has also taken EU directives into account to determine the legality of the detention of

European Legal Order: The Between the European and the National Courts (Cambridge: Intersentia, 2011), pp. 35–64; J. Callewaert, 'The European Convention on Human Rights and European Union law: A long way to harmony', *European Human Rights Law Review*, [2009], 768–83.

[490] *Schalk and Kopf* v *Austria*, HUDOC, 24 June 2010, para. 52; *Marckx* v *Belgium*, HUDOC, 13 June 1979, para. 41; *Golder* v *United Kingdom*, HUDOC, 21 February 1975, para. 29. See also L. Wildhaber, 'The European Convention on Human Rights and international law', *International and Comparative Law Quarterly*, 56 (2007), 217–32.

[491] *Goodwin* v *United Kingdom*, HUDOC, 11 July 2002 (GC), para. 100; *DH* v *Czech Republic*, HUDOC, 13 November 2007 (GC), para. 187.

[492] *Dangeville* v *France*, HUDOC, 16 April 2002, para. 57.

[493] *Neulinger and Schuruk* v *Switzerland*, HUDOC, 6 July 2002 (GC), para. 132.

[494] *Scoppola* v *Italy (no. 2)*, HUDOC, 17 September 2009 (GC), para. 105; *Sergey Zolotukhin* v *Russia*, HUDOC, 10 February 2009 (GC), para. 79.

[495] *Aristimuño Mendizabal* v *France*, HUDOC, 17 January 2006, para. 79; See also *Cantoni* v *France*, HUDOC, 15 November 1996 (GC), para. 26.

asylum seekers[496] and of expulsions in the immigration context.[497] Applying the right to fair trial (Article 6 ECHR) the ECtHR can also sometimes provide individual applicants, who cannot themselves appeal directly to the ECJ, with a remedy for a failure by a respondent state to honour its commitments under EU law. For example, in *Hornsby* v *Greece*, it was held that the right of a British couple to fair trial had been violated by the failure of the respondent state to grant them a work permit to which the domestic courts had confirmed they were entitled under EU law.[498] The ECtHR has also held that an arbitrary refusal by a domestic court to initiate the preliminary ruling procedure – according to which an issue of EU law that has arisen in domestic proceedings may be referred to Luxembourg for an authoritative opinion – may constitute a breach of Article 6 ECHR.[499]

Finally, an alleged Convention violation may arise from the respondent state acting in pursuit of an obligation deriving from another international organisation, including the EU, to which it also belongs. However, as Chapter 1 indicated, if the international organisation in question provides at least 'equivalent', though not necessarily identical, substantive and procedural protection for ECHR rights, Convention-compliance will be presumed unless the facts indicate that the arrangements were 'manifestly deficient', the respondent state exercised a discretion conferred by the specific international legal obligation (a feature of EU directives but not regulations) in a Convention-violating manner and/or the international obligation was freely undertaken by the respondent state and is not subject to judicial review within the legal order of the other international association.[500] For example, in *Matthews*, it was held that the United Kingdom had violated the right to free elections provided by Article 3 of Protocol No. 1 ECHR. Britain had been involved in drafting all relevant EU legal instruments, which were not open to judicial review by the ECJ, and which excluded Gibraltarians, to whom EU law applied and for whom the United Kingdom is

---

[496] *Saadi* v *United Kingdom*, HUDOC, 29 January 2008 (GC).

[497] *Maslov* v *Austria*, HUDOC, 23 June 2008 (GC), paras. 82 & 93.

[498] *Hornsby* v *Greece*, HUDOC, 19 March 1997, para. 44.

[499] *Coéme* v *Belgium*, HUDOC, 22 June 2000, para. 114.

[500] *Michaud* v *France*, HUDOC, 6 December 2012, para. 103; See also *Cooperatieve Producentenorganisatie can de Nederlandse Kokkelvisserij U. A.* v *the Netherlands*, HUDOC, 20 January 2009 (dec.); *Bosphorus Hava Yollari Turizm ve Ticaret Anonim Şirketi* v *Ireland*, HUDOC, 30 June 2005 (GC), at paras. 154–6.

responsible under the ECHR, from elections to the European Parliament.[501] It was also held in *Bosphorus* that Article 1 of Protocol No. 1 ECHR (the right to peaceful enjoyment of possessions) had not been violated when – acting proportionately to comply with an EU obligation stemming from economic sanctions imposed upon Yugoslavia by the UN Security Council (UNSC) – Ireland impounded a civil aircraft leased by the Turkish applicant from the Yugoslav national airline.[502] However in *MSS v Belgium and Greece* it was held that the presumption does not apply universally to EU law but only to those fields of policy hitherto regarded as 'Third Pillar' issues discussed in Chapters 1 and 4.[503] Similarly, when the armed forces of a CE state engage in military operations under NATO command, itself acting on the authority of the UNSC, their conduct is attributable to the UNSC rather than to the member state concerned.[504] It is also presumed that 'clear and explicit language would be used' to indicate whether action should be taken that conflicts with international human rights law.[505] According to some commentators, the most convincing underlying rationale for all these decisions is to preserve the integrity and coherence of international law of which both EU and Convention law are constituent parts.[506]

3.5 Conclusion

The meaning, scope and limits of substantive Convention rights hinge critically upon the design and structure of the ECHR and how the Court interprets and applies its provisions. For present purposes several observations can be made about the former. First, for reasons more fully explained in Chapter 1, the ECHR contains mostly civil and political

---

[501] *Matthews v United Kingdom*, HUDOC, 18 February 1999 (GC), para. 34.

[502] *Bosphorus Hava Yolları Turizm ve Ticaret Anonim Şirketi v Ireland*, HUDOC, 30 June 2005 (GC), at paras. 154–6; Ryngaert, 'Oscillating between embracing and avoiding Bosphorus'; Lock, 'Beyond Bosphorus'; C. Eckes, 'Does the European Court of Human Rights provide protection from the European Community? – The case of Bosphorus Airways', *European Public Law*, 13 (2007), 47–67; C. Costello, 'The Bosphorus ruling of the European Court of Human Rights: Fundamental rights and blurred boundaries in Europe', *Human Rights Law Review*, 6 (2006), 87–130.

[503] *MSS v Belgium and Greece*, HUDOC, 21 January 2011 (GC), para. 338.

[504] *Behrami and Saramati v France, Germany and Norway* (dec. GC), HUDOC, 2 May 2007, para. 143.

[505] *Al-Jedda v United Kingdom*, HUDOC, 7 July 2011 (GC), at para. 102; *Nada v Switzerland*, HUDOC, 12 September 2012 (GC), para. 172.

[506] See, for example, Tzevelekos, 'When Elephants Fight It Is the Grass That suffers'.

rights, distilled from at least three centuries of reflection and debate about what these are and how they should be expressed. This does not, however, deny or detract from the importance of socio-economic and other kinds of human right and other kinds of right. It stems, rather, as already observed, from the fact that civil and political rights lend themselves better to judicial protection, and are more integral to the democratic character of post–Second World War western Europe than any other kind of right. It is also well recognised that the various categories of human right are not mutually exclusive. The Court has, indeed, derived some significant socio-economic rights from the ECHR's civil and political rights catalogue, particularly as a result of the prohibition against discrimination in Article 14.

Second, several formal distinctions can be made between Convention rights. The 'irreducible core' is found in the main body of the ECHR, to which all member states are required to accede, while extra, optional ones are provided by the Protocols. Only a handful of rights – those found in Articles 3, 4(1), and 7(1), and in Articles 3 and 4 of Protocol No. 4 – are subject to no express exceptions at all ('formally unrestricted/unlimited' rights), the first three of which also cannot be suspended under Article 15. The remainder ('formally restricted/limited' rights) are limited by various express restrictions and can also be suspended according to the terms of Article 15. It is, however, not clear whether any of the formally unrestricted rights are genuinely 'absolute', not least because any attempt to resolve a conflict between two competing instances of the same 'absolute' right must necessarily result in one becoming an exception to, and therefore 'less absolute' than, the other. Within the formally limited category, Articles 8–11 have a common structure, with the first paragraphs stating a specific right and the second a range of express exceptions subject to the rule of law and democratic necessity tests. While Article 2 of Protocol No. 4 is also in a roughly similar form, the other formally limited rights do not share any common format, although 'definitional exclusions' – statements about what the right does not include – are common to Articles 2, 4, 5 and Articles 1 and 4 of Protocol No. 7.

As far as the interpretation of the Convention is concerned, the principles of democracy (which, amongst other things, gives rise to the margin of appreciation doctrine), effective protection (from which negative and positive obligations also derive), legality and proportionality are the most pervasive of the dozen or so express and implicit principles of interpretation found in the case law. While the principle of legality, and the procedural implications of positive obligations, have a relatively objective character, the application of the others is, primarily, a matter of judgement. The process of interpretation would also, arguably, be improved if the principles of interpretation – which as Chapter 2 argued are fundamentally constitutional in character – were reconfigured, with 'democracy', 'rights' and 'priority to rights' assuming a primary, and the remainder a secondary supportive, role. Because the boundaries between rights are not always clear-cut, and also because a great deal depends upon how much the scope of a particular right depends upon variable contexts, it is impossible to determine how many express and implied Convention rights there are, much less to provide an authoritative canonical list. Arguably, the more any given right derives from a Convention right, and the more it depends upon variable circumstances, the less it is a human right and the more it is some other kind of right generated by, but not itself, a human right.

Finally, commentators and others have, needless to say, criticised the way in which the Court has interpreted and applied the Convention both generically and in relation to specific complaints about violation. These have included its alleged failure to affirm certain rights as universal rather than state-specific (to gay marriage, for instance), its purported readiness to recognise other putatively unwarranted rights (for example, the right to sleep) and criticism of the scope and other characteristics attributed to both express and implied rights the existence of which may not be in serious dispute. But probably the most pervasive generic criticism concerns the allegedly over-generous application of the principle of proportionality and the margin of appreciation doctrine, and the resulting failure to condemn interferences as violations. The credibility of such critiques depends, however, upon what the core purpose, objective or 'mission' of the ECtHR is taken to be and what constitutional theory this implies, something that critics are much less willing to consider. If, according to the 'activist' model, the Court's goal is deemed, for example, to provide a uniquely authoritative 'judicial truth' about the character, scope and limits of Convention rights, it should judge all disputes, both when condemning egregious systematic violations and when fine-tuning adherence in highly compliant states, according to its own notions of proportionality and the other principles of interpretation, permitting only the narrowest national margins of appreciation, if any. However, if on the other hand, according to the model of 'constitutional pluralism', its core mission is to condemn serious systemic violations according to a thoroughly reasoned 'jurisprudence of principle', but to be more flexible and pluralistic about the rest, it should be more circumspect about insisting upon its own conception of proportionality and upon how the other principles of interpretation should be applied, and should permit variable national margins of appreciation instead. A central element in the core thesis of this study is that this model already largely is, but should more fully become, the governing paradigm for the judicial protection of human rights in both the EU and the Council of Europe.

4

The European Union

4.1 Introduction

The European Union – the product of an incremental expansion from what was initially a purely economic six-member state coal and steel trade community, to what is now a twenty-eight-member political entity – is a uniquely complex regional organisation that exists concurrently with the Council of Europe (CE) and its European Court of Human Rights (ECtHR). Successive enlargements, in membership and competence, have left it with a haphazard treaty basis. Its complex institutional architecture is indicative of evolving compromise between national sovereignty and supranational supremacy. In addition to the European Central Bank and Court of Auditors, which are not of relevance to this study, there are five official EU institutions, each representing distinct manifestations of different sectoral interests. Compensating member states for transferring considerable authority to the supranational level, the policy and law-making ministerial Council of the EU (Council) represents the competing interests of national governments, not to be confused with the European Council, which incorporates each member state's head of state or government and sits at the pinnacle of all EU decision-making. As guardian of the Treaties, the European Commission (Commission) is the EU's executive branch, legislative initiator, internal mediator and external representative, independently performing its duties ostensibly in the general interest of the Community. The only directly elected international legislature in the world, the European Parliament (EP) is the voice of all EU citizens, exercising supervisory, legislative, budgetary and external mandates. Finally, the Court of Justice of the EU (ECJ) constitutes the judicial branch in this composite institutional landscape.

Today, fundamental rights occupy a central position in the EU's constitutional discourse and institutional practice. However, as Chapter 1 indicated, unlike the four single market freedoms – free movement of goods, services, capital and persons – fundamental rights did not overtly feature in the establishment of the three European Communities during the 1950s. It has been the progressive deepening of European integration that has seen respect for fundamental rights gain increasing centrality within the EU legal order and become a key aspect of the Union's internal and external activities. It should be observed that, despite some contradictory terminology in official EU discourse most notably in the external sphere, the EU has a *fundamental* rights policy, broader than a *human* rights policy in the strict sense of the term (a distinction considered in Chapter 1).

Section 4.2 (Institutional Framework) discusses more fully the origins, composition, fundamental rights-related functions and intra-institutional relationships of the EU's core institutions, together with those of other relevant bodies, offices and agencies of the EU, collectively referred to as 'bodies'. Section 4.3 (Internal Policy) endeavours to shed light on the EU's multifaceted internal fundamental rights policy. It starts by addressing the gradual incorporation of this normative dimension into EU primary law, namely, general principles, the Treaties, and, as of 2009, the Charter of Fundamental Rights (CFR). The most recent reform Treaty, signed in Lisbon in 2007, heralded major constitutional change in the field of fundamental rights. Not only did it bestow upon the CFR the same legal status as the EU Treaties, but it also obligated the EU to accede to the CE's European Convention on Human Rights (ECHR), a development since indefinitely stalled. In what follows, the CFR's key characteristics will be discussed, along with the provision of fundamental rights in EU secondary law and the proliferation of coincident soft law instruments. The fundamental rights enforcement mechanisms available to the EU also receive critical examination. Section 4.4 (External Policy) addresses the EU's external fundamental rights policy, which was incentivised by, but evolved separately from, the EU's internal normative activity. In addition to examining how the Union ensures respect for fundamental rights in third states, applicant states, and non-EU states that belong to the European Economic Area (EEA), this section highlights the inconsistencies and double standards in the EU's external promotion of fundamental rights, and addresses the damage this causes to its credibility as a normative actor on the world stage.

4.2   Institutional Framework

The following EU institutions and bodies, of relevance to this study, are considered in this chapter: the European Council, the European

Commission, the European Parliament, the Council of the EU, the Court of Justice of the EU, the European Ombudsman, the EU Agency for Fundamental Rights, the European Institute for Gender Equality, and Expert Networks in the field of fundamental rights.

The European Council

At least four times a year, member states' heads of state or government, along with the President of the Commission and the High Representative of the Union for Foreign Affairs and Security Policy (High Representative), gather as the European Council, the highest-level intergovernmental institution in the EU, which must be distinguished from the Council, a less elevated intergovernmental body, made up of ministers from each member state. As the ultimate decision-making authority, the European Council is responsible for setting the EU's broad policy agenda. Enjoying a monopoly over launching new fields of EU activity, it has been the principal source of historic decisions and systemic change.[1] While member states have transferred considerable competence to the EU at the expense of domestic policy independence, institutionalised summitry in the European Council has, to some extent, provided a substitute. Further, since its members are democratically accountable to their national parliaments and/or citizens, the European Council's indirect democratic legitimacy ought not be overlooked.

The European Council was born out of ad hoc informal practice; state leaders took it upon themselves to meet sporadically to address important matters of European integration requiring resolution at the highest political level. In 1974, the heads of state or government of the then-nine-member states, along with the Ministers of Foreign Affairs and President of the Commission, met in Paris and decided that such meetings should be institutionalised and, as of 1975, held on a regular basis in order to ensure 'progress and overall consistency' in the Union's activities.[2] The European Council attained legal recognition for the first time in 1986 under the Single European Act (SEA).[3] However, it was not until

---

[1] P. de Schoutheete, 'The European Council' in J. Peterson and M. Shackleton (eds.), *The Institutions of the European Union*, 3rd edn., (Oxford University Press, 2012), p. 46.

[2] Final communiqué of the meeting of heads of Government of the Community (Paris, 9 and 10 December 1974), paragraph 2.

[3] Single European Act 1986 (*Official Journal of the European Communities* ('OJ'), 1987), vol. 30, L 169.

the Treaty of Lisbon,[4] which came into effect in 2009, that it was accorded formal institutional status.[5] While the Commission President and High Representative remain *de jure* members of the European Council, the Lisbon Treaty stripped foreign ministers of their entitlement to participate. Despite the inefficiency of the procedure, almost all decisions must be taken unanimously, de facto practice prior to Lisbon, now a Treaty obligation.[6] The European Council's decision-making capacity is further hindered by the infrequency of its quarterly meetings, although the President may assemble a special meeting 'when the situation so requires'.[7]

Despite these limitations, the European Council has, nevertheless, successfully utilised its ultimate political authority, and limited treaty base, to self-determine its originally ill-defined function. Initially establishing the remit of its roles and responsibilities through Declarations,[8] it continued this process of self-empowerment through treaty reform, placing itself at the pinnacle of decision-making, exercising a near-monopoly over launching innovative fields of Union activity and providing the momentum behind major political and institutional developments. Despite a tendency to involve itself in micro policy-making, the European Council's primary purpose is to 'provide the Union with the necessary impetus for its development and' to 'define the general political directions and priorities thereof',[9] establishing the overall outline within which other institutions develop specific policy initiatives. It identifies and defines strategic guidelines in the EU's internal and external policy spheres,[10] performing the latter function on the basis of the objectives and principles espoused in Article 21 Treaty on European Union (TEU), which include consolidating democracy and universal human rights. Having momentously established respect for fundamental rights as one of several core eligibility conditions for membership (see later discussion),

---

[4] *Treaty of Lisbon Amending the Treaty on European Union and the Treaty Establishing the European Community*, (OJ, 2007), 2007/C 306/01 ('Lisbon Treaty').

[5] Article 13 *Consolidated Version of the Treaty on European Union* (OJ C 326/13, 26.10.2012) ('TEU').

[6] Article 15(4) TEU.

[7] Article 15(3) TEU.

[8] See for example European Council, *Solemn Declaration on European Union* (Stuttgart, 19 June 1983) Bulletin of the European Communities, No. 6/1983.

[9] Article 15(1) TEU.

[10] Article 68 *Treaty on the Functioning of the European Union* (OJ, 2012/C 326/01) ('TFEU') and Article 26(1) TEU.

the European Council takes most important decisions concerning accession applications. Internally, under the Article 7 TEU sanctioning procedure (discussed later), it is the European Council that is empowered to 'determine the existence of a serious and persistent breach by a member state of the values referred to in Article 2 [TEU]', including democracy, equality and respect for human and minority rights.

As the European Council evolved, the decision-making authority of the ministerial Council (discussed later) decreased, with most major initiatives now subjected to the political approval of the former. The subservience of the Council is also illustrated by the appeal element in its relationship with the European Council, with important issues in deadlock at ministerial level being referred up to the heads of state or government for settlement. The Commission's unique position as policy initiator has also been somewhat thwarted, only marginally compensated by the Commission President's participation at European Council summits. While the EP has a notable lack of input into the European Council's 'agendas or deliberations',[11] the ECJ's position in relation to the European Council has been strengthened by the Lisbon Treaty. Having been granted institutional status, the European Council is now able to adopt acts with legal effect, judiciable by the ECJ. Further, the ECJ has been granted jurisdiction to review acts adopted under Article 7 TEU.[12] The European Council is also no longer immune from infringement proceedings (discussed later) brought against it before the ECJ.[13]

The European Commission

Performing its duties independently of member states, the Commission represents the EU's general interest. Existing at the heart of the institutional framework, this distinctive supranational institution performs hybrid tasks, acting as the EU's external representative, executive branch and initiator of legislation.

The origins of the Commission can be traced back to the creation of the European Coal and Steel Community (ECSC) in 1952. The ECSC equivalent of the Commission was its High Authority, an independent supranational collegiate executive, responsible for achieving the Treaty's

---

[11] N. Nugent, *The Government and Politics of the European Union*, 7th edn. (Basingstoke: Palgrave Macmillan, 2010), pp. 177–8.
[12] Article 269 TFEU.
[13] Article 265 TFEU.

objectives and acting in the general interest of that particular Community. It comprised at least one appointee from every member state, each obligated to act entirely independently and not as a national delegate. This principle persists in the Commission today. Formally appointed every five years by the European Council following the EP's approval,[14] the Commission consists of individual Commissioners, each nominated to the post by a member state. Despite the contradictory wording of Article 17(5) of the Lisbon Treaty, each member state appoints one Commissioner.[15] Accordingly, there are, at present, twenty-eight Commissioners. Although nominated by their member state's government, Commissioners are not supposed to act as national representatives. Upon taking office, each must swear an oath renouncing any advocacy of national interest, and undertaking instead to perform the duties independently and in the EU's general interest.[16] Each Commissioner is allocated at least one 'portfolio', a particular area of responsibility, and is assisted by a personal office known as a 'cabinet'. Commissioners meet as the College of Commissioners and, according to the principle of collective responsibility, they must all publicly support the Commission's actions and decisions. As the College makes decisions by majority voting, the majority's view is, therefore, imposed upon dissenting Commissioners, who then have to support it.

As time has progressed, the Commission has become increasingly 'presidential', with treaty reforms giving its President 'a progressively stronger grip over the College.'[17] The President not only is the Commission's external representative, both in the EU institutional landscape and on the international stage, but also has considerable internal competences, including the power to request a Commissioner's resignation, to allocate portfolios and to determine the policy agenda. Pursuant to the Treaties, it is for the European Council, taking account of EP elections, to propose a presidential candidate, who is then elected by the EP.[18] In 2014, however, a new Spitzenkandidaten system was introduced, whereby the EP's political

---

[14] Article 17(7) TEU.

[15] European Council Decision 2013/272/EU of 22 May 2013 concerning the number of members of the European Commission (*Official Journal of the European Union*, L 165/98, 18.6.2013) and European Council Decision 2014/749/EU of 23 October 2014 appointing the European Commission (*Official Journal of the European Union*, L 331/36, 31.10.2014).

[16] Article 17 TEU.

[17] Peterson in Peterson and Shackleton, *The Institutions of the European Union*, p. 107.

[18] Article 17(7) TEU.

groups nominated a candidate for Commission President, whom the European Council was then under pressure to endorse or risk accusations of acting undemocratically. The 2014 Commission also saw a special post of First Vice President created in addition to the existing vice-president positions, one of which is held by the High Representative. The First Vice President is responsible for steering and coordinating the Commission's work in the areas of better regulation, inter-institutional relations, the rule of law and the CFR. This includes, *inter alia*, ensuring that every Commission proposal complies with the CFR.

The Commission's formal independence and associated duty to act solely in the EU's interest are fundamental to its raison d'etre, reflected in its overarching obligation to ensure the advancement of EU policies in light of the Treaties, which it is equipped to accomplish through its four primary functions: representation, initiation, implementation and enforcement.

The Commission's representative task is twofold. Externally, it represents the EU in the international arena in all areas except for Common Foreign and Security Policy (CFSP),[19] acting as its key point of contact with third states and international bodies, including the UN and CE.[20] It has negotiating and managerial responsibilities in relation to the EU's various external agreements – including trade, partnership, cooperation and association agreements, as well as political dialogues and the provision of financial aid – and plays an important role vis-à-vis membership applications, undertaking detailed examinations of applicant states and monitoring their progress throughout the negotiation process. Internally, the Commission represents the Union's general interests and plays an important negotiating role within its institutional framework.

The Commission ensures that 'the principles of the treaties are turned into laws and policies',[21] thereby acting as an engine of integration. It has an almost exclusive right to propose legislation (initiation). Only under the Special Legislative Procedure can legislative initiatives arise from a request or recommendation by a group of member states or an EU institution other than the Commission.[22] Since the Treaty of Lisbon, under certain conditions, EU citizens are also able to invite the Commission to submit a

---

[19] Article 17(1) TEU.
[20] Article 220 TFEU.
[21] J. McCormick, *Understanding the European Union: A Concise Introduction*, 6th edn. (Basingstoke: Palgrave Macmillan, 2014), p. 76.
[22] Articles 228, 308 and 349 TFEU.

specific proposal.[23] In addition to its power of legislative initiative, the Commission is the EU's primary executive body (implementation). The Treaties confer on it key administrative responsibilities concerning the management, supervision and implementation of the EU's policies, laws and budget, the latter of which the Commission drafts, proposes and guides through to adoption, as it does with legislation.

Together with the ECJ, it is the Commission's role to ensure member states properly apply EU law (enforcement). It has powers of investigation, which it can utilise on its own initiative, or in response to an Article 259 Treaty on the Functioning of the European Union (TFEU) member state communication alleging another member state has infringed EU law (in such circumstances it falls on the Commission as guardian of the Treaties to proceed against the alleged defaulter) or an individual complaint by an EU citizen about any domestic practice, measure or absence of such, by a public authority, that is believed to be in breach of EU law. Further, the Commission can instigate infringement proceedings under Article 258 TFEU (see later discussion). However, doing so is constrained by resource limitations, inadequate information and political considerations.[24]

The increasing institutional prowess of the EP (discussed next) has come at the Commission's expense. Alongside the Council, the EP exercises an important role in Commissioners' appointment,[25] its power to approve nominees having gradually increased. When consenting to the College's appointment, the EP examines each Commissioner and may express objections to his or her suitability for assigned responsibilities. As the Commission is formally accountable to the EP, which may vote on a motion of censure compelling its resignation,[26] failure by the Commission President to take account of the EP's objections to particular Commissioners risks rejection of the entire body. In addition to powers of appointment and dismissal, the EP has an informal right of scrutiny.

The European Parliament

Ostensibly espousing the democratic will of its 500-million-person electorate, the EP represents EU citizens' interests at EU level. It has evolved

---

[23] Article 11(4) TEU.
[24] Nugent, *The Government and Politics of the European Union*, p. 131.
[25] Articles 17 and 18 TEU.
[26] Article 234 TFEU.

from a powerless and ineffectual appointed assembly vested with weak supervisory powers[27] into a directly elected institution exerting considerable influence within the EU, including the exercise of legislative and supervisory powers far in excess of those it had at its inception.

First constituted in 1952 as the ECSC's General Assembly, the EP provided accountability in an international organisation where supranational power was predominantly vested in the High Authority, as the Commission was then known. However, although created to lend democratic legitimacy to the Community, for the first twenty-eight years of its existence, membership of the EP was confined to national parliamentarians appointed by their national legislatures. Although the option for directly elected European parliamentarians existed from the outset,[28] this did not come into effect until 1979, when it considerably enhanced the EU's democratic legitimacy and the EP's clout in the institutional firmament.

The number of parliamentarians increased coincident with the Union's enlargement, until the Lisbon Treaty set the cap at 751 Members of the European Parliament (MEPs), including the EP President.[29] MEPs are assigned to permanent policy-specialised committees, and may also be allotted to specially created temporary committees as and when required. Committees carry out most of the EP's detailed work, including the examination of legislative proposals. Some committees have a specific fundamental rights mandate in the internal policy sphere, notably the Committee on Civil Liberties, Justice and Home Affairs (LIBE). The EP's Foreign Affairs Committee (AFET) and its Subcommittee on Human Rights (DROI) seek to promote and protect fundamental rights beyond the EU's borders. Parliamentary delegations, which maintain and develop the EP's international relations by facilitating dialogue with parliaments of third states in order to promote the EU's founding values, are also of importance to the EU's external fundamental rights policies.

Although its formal powers remain less extensive than those of national legislatures, a slow process of 'parliamentarisation' within the EU's institutional framework has enlarged the EP's functions far beyond its early role as a modest advisory and supervisory body. It has assumed

---

[27] Articles 20 and 24 *Treaty Constituting the European Coal and Steel Community*, Paris, 18 April 1951, unpublished ('TECSC').

[28] Article 21 TECSC.

[29] Under Article 14(4) TEU, the EP elects its own President from amongst its elected members.

an augmented influence within the EU system by, on the one hand, interpreting and utilising its existing powers to the maximum and, on the other, by pushing for fundamental institutional reform to its advantage.[30] Treaty reforms have extended not only the EP's initial prerogative of executive supervision, but also its role in the EU's legislative process, budgetary procedure and external relations.

The EP exerts democratic supervision over the EU executive. As already indicated, it elects the Commission President, and has power of approval over the Commission as a whole.[31] It can dismiss the entire College by a motion of censure, which obliges all Commissioners, President and High Representative included, to resign.[32] Political accountability to the EP also manifests in the ability of MEPs to ask the Commission and Council written or oral questions, to which they are obliged to respond.[33] The EP is responsible for appointing the Ombudsman (discussed later), and monitoring the performance of the office.[34] Further, the EP is empowered to establish a temporary Committee of Inquiry to investigate alleged maladministration, including violation of fundamental rights, by an EU institution or body in the implementation of Community law.[35] EU citizens or residents are also able to submit to the EP a petition, in the form of a request or complaint, concerning any EU activity that directly affects them.[36]

Within the legislative process, the EP has also incrementally evolved to become a co–decision maker on an equal footing with the Council in most policy areas. The SEA strengthened the EP's position by introducing the 'cooperation procedure', under which it was entitled to two readings of proposed legislation, as opposed to just one, thereby increasing its ability to amend. In 1992 the Maastricht Treaty[37] introduced what was later dubbed the 'co-decision procedure', granting the EP a third

---

[30] For detailed discussion, see Nugent, *The Government and Politics of the European Union*, p. 205.

[31] Article 17(7) TEU.

[32] Article 17(8) TEU.

[33] Article 230 TFEU.

[34] *Decision of the European Parliament on the regulations and general conditions governing the performance of the Ombudsman's duties*, adopted on 9 March 1994 (OJ L 113, 4.5.1994), p. 15 and amended by its decisions of 14 March 2002 (OJ L 92, 9.4.2002) p. 13 and 18 June 2008 (OJ L 189, 17.7.2008) p. 25.

[35] Article 226 TFEU.

[36] Article 227 TFEU.

[37] *Treaty on European Union*, signed at Maastricht on 7 February 1992 (OJ 1992, 92/C 191/01) ('Maastricht Treaty').

reading and accordingly establishing it as a legally equal co-legislature with the Council in some policy areas. Co-decision was extended through subsequent treaty reforms, culminating in the Treaty of Lisbon, which established it as the new 'ordinary legislative procedure', applicable in all fields with a few limited exceptions. Further, under this procedure the EP and Council are obliged to negotiate in order to reach agreement on draft legislation. While the EP seldom blocks proposals, many are significantly altered by it during the course of the legislative process, enhancing the democratic legitimacy of EU law as a whole. The EP can also invite the Commission to submit appropriate proposals,[38] to which the Commission generally responds promptly and positively.[39]

Exercising democratic oversight of the EU purse since the 1970s, the EP has been able to influence supranational spending through treaty-based budgetary powers. Although, it constitutes the EU's fiscal authority in conjunction with the Council – with both institutions having equal powers of amendment when reviewing the Commission's proposed annual budget under the 'budgetary co-decision procedure' – the EP has a stronger position. Able either to approve or to reject the budget in its entirety at the end of the process, it is the EP that effectively has the final say.

In addition to its control of the annual budget, which includes external expenditure, and supervisory powers over the High Representative as Vice-President of the Commission, the EP can influence the EU's external policy through various other means. It must be consulted over the main aspects of the CFSP, and may ask questions of the Council or make recommendations.[40] While neither its consultation nor its consent is required with regard to external agreements relating exclusively to this field,[41] it must be kept 'immediately and fully informed' throughout the decision-making process.[42] The EP's assent is required for all accession treaties and trade agreements, and it has relied on this to advance the EU's external fundamental rights policy, which it also endeavours to influence through Resolutions and reports. Notably, since 1983, the EP

---

[38] Article 225 TFEU.
[39] S. Hagemann, 'Strength in Numbers? An Evaluation of the 2004–2009 European Parliament', *European Policy Centre Issue Paper*, 58 (2009), 15.
[40] Article 36 TEU.
[41] Article 218(6) TFEU.
[42] Article 218(10) TFEU; Case C-658/11, *European Parliament v Council of the European Union*, paragraph 72.

has adopted an annual report and Resolution on the human rights situation in the world. While the content of these reports varies according to current affairs, certain topics, such as eradication of the death penalty, are repeatedly addressed. EP delegations maintain relations with parliaments in third states, a particular focus being upon the promotion of human rights, and the EP also addresses certain prioritised human rights concerns by tabling questions to the Commission or Council, with concrete action often taken by them as a result.

Recognising that if the EU is credibly to promote fundamental rights beyond its borders it must also take this issue seriously internally,[43] the EP has taken action to monitor fundamental rights compliance at the EU and member state levels. It regularly issues Resolutions addressing particular fundamental rights concerns in specific member states, as well as on the fundamental rights situation in the Union as a whole. Its LIBE committee also issues reports highlighting areas of concern, and has produced a report on the fundamental rights situation within the EU almost every year since 1993. Although the latter was envisaged to mirror the EP's annual reports on respect for fundamental rights outside the EU, the provision of a comparable internal monitoring mechanism was fundamentally undermined by lack of resources.[44] Almost entirely dependent upon external sources of information, the reports are written in such vague terms that, unlike their external counterpart, 'the notion of scrutiny is difficult to discern from the process'.[45]

The EP's increased power has come at the expense of the Commission and Council. In order to facilitate inter-institutional cooperation in decision-making, both institutions participate in the EP's plenary meetings, where debates are held and decisions made. The EP utilises its supervisory powers to exercise institutional oversight, and has been active in holding the Council and Commission to account for inconsistent application of human rights clauses in external agreements, as discussed more fully later.

---

[43] Committee on Citizens' Freedoms and Rights, Justice and Home Affairs, 'Annual Report on Respect for Human Rights in the European Union (1998–1999)' (Document A5-0050/2000), p. 20.

[44] Committee on Citizens' Freedoms and Rights, Justice and Home Affairs, 'Report on the Situation as Regards Fundamental Rights in the EU' (Document A5-0223/2001, 2000), p. 24.

[45] A. J. Williams, *EU Human Rights Policies: A Study in Irony* (Oxford University Press, 2004), pp. 97–8.

The Council of the European Union

The Council of the EU, still often referred to by its historic title 'the Council of Ministers', is commonly called 'the Council' in contradistinction to the European Council. Acting as the EU's main decision-making authority, it represents the governments of member states at EU level, providing a unique international forum in which national interests are articulated, defended and aggregated by ministerial representatives. In conjunction with the European Council as the EU's ultimate decision maker, the Council compensates member states for pooling their sovereignty and delegating considerable decision-making control to the supranational level.

Originally the ECSC's Special Council of Ministers, comprising a ministerial representative from each of the national governments of the then-six member states, the Council's creation followed traditional intergovernmental interaction between states and was accordingly less innovative than that of the supranational Commission and EP. It held weak supervisory powers that, it was assumed, would decline as the trust of member states in joint policies increased. While the Council has witnessed some transfer of authority to the Commission and EP since inception, it has also seen a massive increase in its mandate. As it exists and operates today, the Council is symbolic of the member states' enduring influence within the EU institutional system.

While legally there is one Council, in practice it meets in different configurations depending on the policy area under discussion, with every specialised Council composed of those ministers with the relevant portfolio. As state representatives, all ministers are authorised to commit their government, and are accordingly bound by national interest and their government's instructions. While this does hinder decision-making to some extent, ministerial accountability at national level, along with the EP's involvement, give the Council's decisions indirect democratic authority. Nevertheless, as ministers take their seats ex officio, the Council's democratic deficit remains an issue of concern for both proponents and opponents of European integration.

The Council endeavours to reach decisions through negotiation, with both the Commission and Council President playing an important mediating role. Ministerial meetings are just the apex of the Council hierarchy. Most compromises are reached at lower levels in specialised Working Parties and Committees, thus easing the ministerial Council's workload. Decision-making procedure depends on the subject matter, with the Treaties specifying when simple majority (with each state casting a single vote), qualified majority or unanimity is required. Under qualified majority voting (QMV) votes were initially weighted so that the assent of some smaller member states was required. However, the system now ensures a majority of the EU's population is also represented through demographic weighting. Refined and extended by treaty reform, QMV has become the normal mode of decision-making. This, in turn, has reduced the role of unanimity and individual member states' corresponding veto, thereby facilitating decision-making and enabling the Council to cope effectively with the EU's enlarged policy portfolio and membership. Today, unanimous decisions are only required for particularly sensitive policy areas, including those relating to the CFSP, membership applications and EU citizens' rights. As indicated in Chapter 1, in the face of opposition from some eastern European member states, the Council relied on QMV to enact a legally binding system of refugee resettlement quotas.[46] Although breaking from the informal norm of consensus-seeking in a sovereignty-sensitive issue in this manner enabled the EU to respond efficiently and effectively to the refugee crisis, using QMV arguably decreases the initiative's legitimacy, enabling the overruled minority to exploit anti-EU sentiments and possibly evade implementation.[47]

Acting as policy and law maker, executive and mediator,[48] the Council exercises an array of responsibilities. In addition to coordinating member states' economic and political policies in areas where the Community does not possess ultimate supranational competence, the Council is formally responsible for decision-making across almost all areas of EU activity, sharing this authority with other institutions to varying degrees. Authorised to approve the annual budget in conjunction with the EP, the two institutions also act jointly in amending, debating and reaching decisions on legislative proposals in most policy areas, although historically the Council has had the final say. In addition to its loss in legislative authority, the Council's law-making prowess is hampered by the fact that it is not the EU's executive body and, as

---

[46] Council Decision 12098/15 establishing provisional measures in the area of international protection for the benefit of Italy and Greece (Brussels, 22.9.2015).

[47] C. Roos and G. Orsini, 'How to Reconcile the EU Border Paradox? The Concurrence of Refugee Reception and Deterrence', *Institute for European Studies Policy Brief 4/2015* (Brussels: Vrije Universitei, 2015).

[48] Nugent, *The Government and Politics of the European Union*, p. 139–41.

such, is not responsible for initiating legislation, although it can request the Commission to submit proposals.[49]

The Council possesses some executive powers, predominantly in the field of the CFSP, where it takes executive decisions and is responsible for ensuring implementation. It is also empowered to ensure implementation of the EU's founding values. Under Article 7 TEU, it is for the Council to determine whether there is a clear risk of serious and persistent breach by a member state of the values espoused in Article 2 of the same treaty. Further, following a determination by the European Council that such a breach has occurred, it is for the Council alone to sanction the offending state by suspending some of its membership rights, including the voting rights of its Council representative.[50] However, due to its high procedural thresholds and member states' political unwillingness to use it, the Article 7 sanctioning procedure is commonly regarded as merely symbolic (see later discussion).

It is for the Council, upon a recommendation from the Commission, to authorise negotiation of external agreements between the EU and third states or international organisations (discussed later). Further, it is responsible for signing such agreements upon completion of the negotiation process, and has the authority to order their suspension if a human rights clause is breached. The Council's annual reports on human rights, issued since 1999, provide a general overview of EU action in this field. While these initially included some comment on the state of fundamental rights within the Union, the reports now have an almost exclusively external focus, with country-specific accounts regarding third states, applicant states and non-EU EEA states, distinctions considered further later. As far as accession to the EU is concerned, it is for the Council, having invited the Commission to submit its opinion on the applicant, to decide whether or not to initiate the process. If this occurs, the Commission provides the Council with regular reports on the applicant's progress towards eligibility. These serve as a basis for the Council's decisions concerning conduct of the accession negotiations on which it keeps the EP informed. Upon conclusion, the Council approves a draft Accession Treaty, which is then submitted to the EP for its assent before being sent for ratification by member states and the applicant state in question.

Since its inception, the Council has seen both an expansion of its responsibilities and a reduction in its authority as other EU institutional

[49] Article 241 TFEU.
[50] Article 7(3) TEU.

actors have been empowered at its expense. The greater mandate the European Council has assumed for itself has tended to overshadow the Council's policy impact, with the former responsible for the EU's most historic political decisions. The EP's increased role in the legislative process has reduced the Council to co-legislature in most fields. Both institutions nevertheless engage with each other under formal cooperation procedures, with much informal dialogue also occurring between them and the Commission. The Council and Commission's institutional roles make them highly interdependent. Commission representatives attend Council meetings, where they act as protagonists and mediators in order to ensure adoption of proposed legislation. The Commission also acts as broker between the Council and EP, although opinion in the Council appears to be that the Commission tends to side against member states in negotiations.[51]

The European Court of Justice

The Court of Justice of the European Union is the EU's composite judicial tribunal consisting of three distinct courts – the Court of Justice, General Court and Civil Service Tribunal. The Court of Justice, commonly referred to as the 'European Court of Justice' or 'ECJ',[52] is the EU's original, and most renowned, judicial authority. Established in 1952 as the ECSC's supranational court, it was envisaged as a legal guarantee against arbitrary decision-making by the Community's executive body, the High Authority.[53] In 1989 the Court of First Instance, now named the General Court, was created to reduce the workload of the Court of Justice by determining more routine cases at first instance. The Civil Service Tribunal was established in 2005 to adjudicate employment disputes between the EU and its staff.

While the Civil Service Tribunal consists of seven judges, the Court of Justice and General Court are each composed of one judge from every

---

[51] Hayes-Renshaw, 'The Council of Ministers' in Peterson and Shackleton, *The Institutions of the European Union*, p. 90.

[52] This book uses 'ECJ' to refer to both the Court of Justice of the EU as an institution and the Court of Justice as a part of this institution.

[53] See D. Tamm, 'The History of the Court of Justice of the European Union since Its Origin' in The Court of Justice of the European Union (eds.), *The Court of Justice and the Construction of Europe: Analyses and Perspectives on Sixty Years of Case-law – La Cour de Justice et la Construction de l'Europe: Analyses et Perspectives de Soixante Ans de Jurisprudence* (The Hague: TMC Asser Press, 2013), pp. 9–35.

member state. The Court of Justice also has eleven Advocates General (AGs),[54] mandated to prepare a non-binding advisory opinion to assist the Court of Justice in determining cases raising especially complex or novel questions of law. Both the Court of Justice and General Court operate through a system of chambers, with most cases heard by either a three-judge or five-judge chamber. The formation of a Grand Chamber, comprising at least thirteen judges, is reserved for legally significant cases or upon request of the member state or institution party to the proceedings. Although this raises concerns about consistency and coherence in judicial decision-making, the organisation of the Court of Justice and General Court into chambers is essential to ensure the efficient and effective management of their respective workloads.[55]

The Court of Justice and General Court have two main functions: ensuring member states and EU institutions abide by EU law, and ensuring that EU law is interpreted and applied uniformly across member states. The General Court has jurisdiction to deal with most cases against an EU institution or body, while the Court of Justice has jurisdiction to hear: appeals from the GC; infringement actions against member states; preliminary references by national courts; and actions for annulment of EU legislation. The role of both courts in relation to fundamental rights is considered in Chapter 5.

Treaty reforms have brought about gradual expansion in the ECJ's competences, enabling it to exercise increasing judicial control over other EU institutions. An example is that, prior to the Treaty of Lisbon, the European Council predominately operated outside the ECJ's remit. Further, through two landmark rulings in the 1980s,[56] the ECJ included the EP within the list of institutions able to bring, or be subject to, annulment proceedings, an alteration subsequently incorporated into the Treaties. In addition to granting the EP the power to challenge the legality of those Council and Commission acts which have legal effect, the creation of the General Court enabled the ECJ to review the Commission's decisions in more detail. The ECJ's horizontal power within the EU legal order (namely, its ability to review legislation and decisions taken by other

---

[54] The ECJ has had at least one AG since the outset.

[55] N. Nic Shuibhne in Peterson and Shackleton, *The Institutions of the European Union*, p. 159.

[56] Case 294/83, *Les Verts* v *European Parliament* [1986] ECR -01339; Case C-70/88, *European Parliament* v *Council of the European Communities (Chernobyl)* [1990] ECR I-02041.

EU institutions) has, however, received little academic attention,[57] with legal scholarship predominately focusing on the more crucial interrelationship between the ECJ and member states, as considered in Chapter 5.

Other Bodies

The European Ombudsman

The Ombudsman is responsible for monitoring EU institutions and bodies, existing alongside the ECJ and EP as one of the EU's three channels for complaint. Acting as an intermediary between them and the people of Europe, the Ombudsman is primarily a reactive investigatory office intended to encourage good administration at EU level. It was created in the 1990s to complement the introduction of EU citizenship as a component of European integration, an integral aspect of which was deemed to be the provision of an effective mechanism for safeguarding citizens' rights.[58] The Ombudsman's independence and impartiality are guaranteed by treaty,[59] reiterated in the Ombudsman Statute,[60] though weakened by the fact that (s)he[61] is appointed and financed by the EP. At any time during the five-year mandate, the EP can also request that the ECJ dismiss the Ombudsman if 'he no longer fulfils the conditions required for the performance of his duties or if he is guilty of serious misconduct.'[62]

---

[57] Research in this regard has also primarily focused on the influence of ECJ's jurisprudence in the legislative process, see G. Davies, 'Legislative Control of the European Court of Justice', *Common Market Law Review*, 51(6) (2014), 1579–1607; T. Nowak, 'Of Garbage Cans and Rulings: Judgments of the European Court of Justice in the EU Legislative Process', *West European Politics*, 33(4) (2010), 753–69; and D. Wincott, 'The Court of Justice and the European Policy Process' in J. Richardson (ed.), *European Union, Power and Policy-Making* (London: Routledge, 2001), pp. 179–97.

[58] Spanish Delegation to the Intergovernmental Conference on Political Union, 'The Road to European Citizenship' (unpublished Council Document SN 3940/90); Spanish Delegation to the Intergovernmental Conference on Political Union, 'European Citizenship', (21.2.1991).

[59] Article 228(3) TFEU.

[60] Articles 6(2) and 9(1) Ombudsman Statute, adopted by Parliament on 9 March 1994 (OJ L 113, 4.5.1994), p. 15 and amended by its decisions of 14 March 2002 (OJ L 92, 9.4.2002), p. 13 and 18 June 2008 (OJ L 189, 17.7.2008), p. 25 ('Ombudsman Statute').

[61] The pronoun 'he' is lifted directly from the text of the Treaty and used here in a gender-neutral sense. Emily O'Reilly was elected as the European Ombudsman in July 2013 and took office on 1 October 2013. She was re-elected in December 2014 for a five-year mandate.

[62] Article 195(2) *Treaty Establishing the European Community* (OJ C 325, 24.12.2002) ('TEC'); Article 8 Ombudsman Statute.

Any EU citizen, and any natural or legal person residing or having its registered office in a member state, is permitted to lodge a complaint with the Ombudsman,[63] either directly or through his or her MEP.[64] The Ombudsman can receive complaints concerning maladministration by any EU institution or body, except for the ECJ acting in its judicial capacity.[65] Maladministration is defined by the Ombudsman as non-adherence to the principles of good administration, failure to act within the law or violation of human rights.[66] Complaints of domestic mal-administration are beyond the Ombudsman's mandate.

Upon receiving an admissible complaint, the Ombudsman is empowered to conduct an inquiry, 'except where the alleged facts are or have been the subject of legal proceedings'.[67] This is instigated by the matter being referred to the institution or body concerned for an opinion, which must be returned within three months.[68] If the Ombudsman determines that there has been maladministration, he will endeavour to cooperate with the institution or body concerned to achieve a 'friendly settlement'.[69] This mediatorial, rather than adversarial, approach stems from to the Ombudsman's lack of enforce-ment powers. However, in spite of this, compliance with his findings is consistently high. If efforts to achieve amicable resolution are unsuccessful, the Ombudsman can then close the case with a 'critical remark'[70] or attempt to achieve conciliation by issuing draft recommendations.[71] If these are rejected, the Ombudsman can submit a special report to the EP,[72] which can then take whatever political action it deems necessary. Although subsidiary to complaint handing, the Ombudsman is also empowered to open inquiries into possible maladministration on his own initiative. Powers of investigation and procedure, similar to those pertaining to complaints, are available.[73]

---

[63] Article 195(1) TEC, Article 43 *Charter of Fundamental Rights of the European Union*, (*Official Journal of the European Union*), 2012/C 326/02 ('CFR').

[64] Article 2(2) Ombudsman Statute.

[65] Article 195(1) TEC.

[66] European Ombudsman, *The European Ombudsman's Guide to Complaints: A Publication for Staff of the EU Institutions, Bodies, Offices, and Agencies* (European Union, 2011), p. 7.

[67] Article 195(1) TEC.

[68] Ibid.

[69] Article 6(1) Ombudsman Statute.

[70] Article 7 Ombudsman Statute.

[71] Article 8(1) Ombudsman Statute.

[72] Article 8(4) Ombudsman Statute.

[73] Article 9(2) and (3) Ombudsman Statute.

The contribution made by the Ombudsman to the improvement of the quality of EU administration is controversial. On average, a quarter of complaints lodged annually before, and investigated by, the Ombudsman concern violations of the right to access information and documentation, of which the Commission is the predominant alleged offender. The Ombudsman's inquiries appear to yield positive results, with the Commission generally releasing the requested documents. However, the Commission has not always proved willing to cooperate, and in the past the Ombudsman has had to resort to its seldom-invoked power of lodging a special report before the EP to elicit the Commission's timely response.[74] Although the most recent statistics indicate a 90 per cent overall compliance rate with the Ombudsman's findings,[75] the long-term impact of the office on EU administrative practice is also questionable. As indicated by the Commission's persistent violation of the right to access information, the piecemeal complaint-led investigations appear to result in little overall behavioural change in EU institutions and bodies. Accordingly, the Ombudsman appears merely to be a reactive watchdog delivering individual justice without ensuring any administrative reform. This is hardly surprising since systematic review of EU administration was never within its remit; the office was created largely on the classic redress model, 'which does not lend itself to the introduction or pursuit of systemic changes across a system of governance.'[76]

The Ombudsman, however, asserts that positive development in institutional administrative practice can be assured, claiming that, in situations where complaints are a symptom of an underlying systemic issue, identification of the problem by the office reduces the likelihood of recurrence.[77] Further, a number of ad hoc investigations have been opened on his initiative, some of which have produced concrete results. The Ombudsman's claim to have initiated administrative reform appears

---

[74] European Ombudsman, Special report from the European Ombudsman to the European Parliament concerning lack of cooperation by the European Commission in complaint 676/2008/RT (24 February 2010); European Ombudsman, Decision of the European Ombudsman closing his inquiry into complaint 676/2008/RT against the European Commission (7.7.2010).

[75] The European Ombudsman, *Annual Report 2015*, p. 39.

[76] M. Smith, 'Developing Administrative Principles in the EU: A Foundational Model of Legitimacy?', *European Law Journal*, 18(2) (2012), 269–88 at 287.

[77] European Ombudsman, *The European Ombudsman's Guide to Complaints: A Publication for Staff of the EU Institutions, Bodies, Offices, and Agencies* (European Union, 2011), p. 10.

to be further substantiated by the production of the Code of Good Administrative Behaviour (Code) for EU institutions and bodies, which sets out the Ombudsman's definition of good administration. The Code was created for the purpose of establishing unequivocal standards against which the Ombudsman could base investigations, providing an administrative guide to EU institutions and bodies and informing EU citizens of their administrative entitlements.[78] However, while it has been, to varying degrees, the influence and blueprint for EU institutions and bodies adopting their own administrative Codes of Conduct,[79] analysis reveals it to be merely a partial success. Its substantive content is neither progressive nor conceptually clear. Effectively amalgamating existing principles of good administration,[80] its provisions are 'neither wide ranging nor revolutionary in character'.[81] Further, by incorporating an eclectic set of principles, the Code arguably complicates the concept of good administrative behaviour.[82] Article 1 provides that EU institutions and bodies shall respect the principles laid down therein, and in the Preamble the Ombudsman treats it as binding. However, the Code seemingly lacks enforceability. The Commission, opposed to what it perceives as excessive regulation of its discretionary powers, rejected the Ombudsman's initial call for the Code to be adopted as binding law by way of Regulation. During the drafting of the CFR, the Ombudsman focused on ensuring the Code's binding status by ensuring the inclusion of a right to good administration, specifically aimed at EU institutions and bodies.[83] Nevertheless, while the Ombudsman asserts that the Code

---

[78] The European Ombudsman, *Annual Report 1998*, pp. 18–9.

[79] European Ombudsman, 'Draft recommendation to the European institutions, bodies and agencies in the own initiative inquiry' (Case: OI/1/98/OV, 13.9.1999), paragraph 1.1–1.3. It should be noted that the internal non-binding administrative Codes of the Commission (*Code of Good Administrative Behaviour for Staff of the European Commission in Their Relations with the Public* (OJ L 267/20, 2000)) and Parliament (*Guide to the obligations of officials and other servants of the European Parliament (Code of conduct)* (OJ C 97, 2000, 1)) differ somewhat to the Ombudsman's Code; those of the EU's decentralised agencies adhere to it considerably.

[80] M. Hirsch-Ziembińska, 'In Pursuit of Good Administration' (European Conference, Strasbourg, 10 January 2008) DA/ba/Conf (2007), 9.e.

[81] M. Smith, 'Developing Administrative Principles in the EU: A Foundational Model of Legitimacy?', *European Law Journal*, 18(2) (2012), 269–88 at 285.

[82] J. Mendes, 'Good Administration in EU Law and the European Code of Good Administrative Behaviour', *EU Working Papers* 2009/09 (European University Institute, Florence, Department of Law), p.4.

[83] J. Söderman, 'Public Hearing before the Convention on the Draft Charter of Fundamental Rights of the European Union', speech delivered on 2 February 2000 in Brussels.

informs EU citizens what their right to good administration under
Article 41 CFR 'means in practice',[84] it has been convincingly argued
that the Code should not be read as explicating the content of this
provision.[85] While the CFR, Article 41 included, is legally binding, the
Code contains both legal and non-legal dimensions of good administration and thus exists, in part, beyond the legal realm.[86] Accordingly,
Article 41 CFR should not be read as affording the Code, in its entirety,
legally binding force.

As the Ombudsman's mandate is restricted to examining maladministration by EU institutions and bodies, he is unable to investigate any
alleged or apparent violation of fundamental rights arising from the
administrative actions of member states. The Ombudsman has, however,
endeavoured to mitigate this limitation. The European Network of
Ombudsmen (ENO), set up in 1996 to improve cooperation in case
handling, enables the Ombudsman to deal promptly and effectively with
domestic complaints that fall outside his mandate, by facilitating their
transfer to the competent ombudsman or alternative authority in a
member state.[87] The ENO also shares guidance about substantive CFR
rights so that national ombudsmen are better able to defend the CFR in
situations where EU law is applied. National ombudsmen may submit to
the Ombudsman additional queries about the application and interpretation of EU law, and by extension, the CFR.[88]

The European Union Agency for Fundamental Rights

The EU Agency for Fundamental Rights (FRA) is one of the EU's
independent specialised decentralised agencies. Having evolved from a
previous monitoring body with a more limited remit, it is designed to
assist EU institutions and member states in safeguarding fundamental
rights. In June 1996, the European Council affirmed the Union's determination to combat racism and xenophobia in member states, and
approved the establishment of a monitoring centre at the supranational
level. The European Monitoring Centre for Racism and Xenophobia

---

[84] European Ombudsman, *Code of Good Administrative Behaviour* (Foreword), p.2.
[85] Mendes, 'Good Administration in EU Law and the European Code of Good Administrative Behaviour'.
[86] Ibid., p.13.
[87] The European Ombudsman, *Annual Report 2009*, p. 18.
[88] The European Ombudsman, *Annual Report 2009*, p. 78.

(EUMC) was subsequently established,[89] to provide the EU and member states 'with objective, reliable and comparable data ... in order to help them when they take measures or formulate courses of action within their respective spheres of competence'.[90] Annual reports, and a series of smaller-scale thematic studies, were the EUMC's principal output. Coordination with the CE was envisaged from the outset,[91] and regular contact was subsequently facilitated by way of an agreement.[92] In 2003, the European Council, 'stressing the importance of human rights data collection and analysis with a view to defining Union policy in this field', decided to extend the EUMC's mandate,[93] and in 2007 the FRA was established as the EUMC's successor.[94] The Management Board of the FRA consists of independent members appointed by each member state and the CE, together with a Commission representative. Representatives of the CE's Secretariat are also present as observers at Management Board meetings.

Devoid of the powers associated with a positive fundamental rights enforcement body, such as an individual complaint-handing mechanism, the FRA's objective is simply to provide EU institutions and bodies, and member states when implementing EU law, with assistance, information and expertise regarding fundamental rights. This limited role enables the FRA to participate within the EU's crowded institutional framework, without encroaching on the mandate of any other institution or body. The scope of its activities, almost entirely confined to the EU and member states, is also territorially restricted.[95] While applicant states are able to participate in the FRA's work to a self-determined extent,[96] so far Croatia has been the only state to do so. Granted observer status in

---

[89] Council Regulation (EC) No. 1035/97 of 2 June 1997 establishing a European Monitoring Centre on Racism and Xenophobia, OJ C 171, 5.6.1998.

[90] Article 2(1) Council Regulation 1035/97.

[91] Article 7(3) Council Regulation 1035/97.

[92] Council Decision 1999/132/EC of 21 December 1998 relating to the conclusion of an Agreement between the European Community and the Council of Europe for the purpose of establishing, in accordance with Article 7(3) of Council Regulation (EC) No 1035/97 of 2 June 1997 establishing a European Monitoring Centre on Racism and Xenophobia, close cooperation between the Centre and the Council of Europe, OJ L 44, 18.02.1999.

[93] European Council, 'Presidency Conclusions – Brussels, 12/13 December 2003,' 5381/04 POLGEN 2, Brussels (2004), 27.

[94] Council Regulation (EC) No. 168/2007 of 15 February 2007 establishing a European Union Agency for Fundamental Rights, OJ 2007 L 53/1, 22.2.2007 ('FRA Regulation').

[95] Founding FRA Regulation Art.3(3).

[96] Article 28 FRA Regulation.

July 2010,[97] Croatia permitted the FRA to treat it on a par with member states before it joined the EU on 1 July 2013.

The FRA's principal function is to collect and analyse objective, reliable and comparable information on fundamental rights within the EU.[98] On its own initiative or in response to a request from the Council, Commission or EP, it can carry out, cooperate with and encourage such research, surveys and studies as it deems necessary.[99] As well as collecting data directly, through various, and often combined, methodologies ranging from large-scale quantitative survey research to in-depth focus groups and individual interviews, it also relies on data communicated to it by EU institutions, member states, third states, relevant national bodies, civil society and international organisations, notably the CE.[100] Unlike national research institutions, by collecting and/or analysing data gathered from across member states, the FRA is able to fill a gap in the existing knowledge base.

The FRA is responsible for disseminating its amalgamated and assessed information through various channels. It publishes annual reports on its activities[101] and the fundamental rights issues covered, highlighting examples of good practice.[102] These are presented directly to the relevant bodies in the Commission and Council, enhancing their potential to influence EU policy. Along with thematic reports,[103] the FRA is tasked with publishing, either on its own initiative or at the request of the Council, Commission or EP, 'conclusions and opinions on specific thematic topics',[104] a potentially politically powerful charge.[105] Since 2007, the FRA has experienced an upsurge in ad hoc requests from institutions for advice on a broad spectrum of thematic issues, with its response often serving as a tangible direct input into decision-making

---

[97] Decision No 1/2010 of the EU-Croatia Stabilisation and Association Council of 25 May 2010 on the participation of Croatia as an observer in the European Union Agency for Fundamental Rights' work and the respective modalities thereof ((2010/636/EU) *Official Journal of the European Union*, L 279/68).

[98] Article 4(1)(a) FRA Regulation.

[99] Article 4(1)(c) FRA Regulation.

[100] Article 4(1)(a) FRA Regulation.

[101] Article 4(1)(g) FRA Regulation.

[102] Article 4(1)(e) FRA Regulation.

[103] Article 4(1)(f) FRA Regulation.

[104] Article 4(1)(d) FRA Regulation.

[105] G. Toggenburg, 'The Role of the New EU Fundamental Rights Agency: Debating the "Sex of Angels" or Improving Europe's Human Rights Performance?', *European Law Review*, 3(385) (2008), 393.

and concrete initiatives.[106] Nevertheless, the FRA has predominantly been kept out of the EU's law-making process, permitted merely a limited role in commenting on specific legislative developments.[107] It can only issue conclusions, opinions and reports concerning Commission proposals, or positions taken by another institution in the course of legislating, if requested to do so by the institution in question.[108] In addition, despite recommendations to the contrary,[109] the FRA has no role with regard to Article 7 preventive and sanctioning procedures discussed further later. Not only is member state compliance in this context broader than implementation of EU law, and therefore outside the FRA's field of competence, but the FRA is also prohibited from systematically monitoring member states' fundamental rights adherence or producing country reports, 'in order to avoid overlap with existing reporting systems'.[110] While these restrictions to the FRA's legislative, monitoring and enforcement mandate undoubtedly hinder its potential for influence, each can be circumvented to a certain extent. In addition to institutions being able to request its input in the legislative process, the FRA could theoretically, on its own initiative, report on issues *of relevance* to proposed legislation, without actually falling foul of the prohibition against unsolicited opinions *concerning* legislative proposals or an EU institution's relevant position.[111] With regard to the FRA's inability to monitor member state compliance, some form of regular indirect monitoring is arguably required in order to highlight examples of good national practice.[112] Vis-à-vis Article 7 TEU, the Council can consult the FRA, either as a source of expertise or as an 'independent person'.[113]

The FRA works closely with relevant national, regional and international institutions and bodies. It has a network of National Liaison Officers (NLOs), government officials appointed by their member state to

---

[106] FRA 2012, *External Evaluation of the European Union Agency for Fundamental Rights: Final Report* (Copenhagen: European Union Agency For Fundamental Rights, 2012), pp. 17 and 96.

[107] Article 4(2) FRA Regulation.

[108] Ibid.

[109] Article 4(e) European Commission Proposal (COM [2005] 280 final); European Parliament Resolution of 8 September 2015 on the situation of fundamental rights in the European Union (2013–2014) (P8_TA PROV (2015) 0286), paragraph 9(b).

[110] Annex to European Commission Proposal (COM [2005] 280 final).

[111] Toggenburg, 'The Role of the New EU Fundamental Rights Agency', 394.

[112] Ibid.

[113] The respective declaration in Council Document 6166/07, p. 4.

act as the FRA's primary point of contact, and engages in structured cooperation with UN organisations and other EU institutions and bodies. Within the EU, pursuant to Cooperation Agreements,[114] the FRA collaborates with the European Foundation for the Improvement of Living and Working Conditions (Eurofound) in overlapping fields of research, and with the European Agency for the Management of Operational Cooperation at the External Borders (Frontex) to strengthen respect for fundamental rights in border management. It also has a Cooperation Agreement with the CE,[115] under which the two organisations pledge to maintain regular contact[116] and to 'provide each other with information and data collected in the course of their activities',[117] so as to avoid duplication and to ensure their work is complementary.[118] Collaboration between the FRA and CE takes various forms, including thematic operational cooperation and joint projects. The CE is also associated with the FRA's dialogue with civil society, primarily by participating in its Fundamental Rights Platform (FRP),[119] a network designed to enable organisations at all levels to participate with the FRA through information exchange. In order to raise public awareness, the FRA disseminates information about its work through its annual and thematic reports, events and digital channels. Nevertheless, hampered by resource limitations, it has been obliged to enhance its impact at the domestic level by concentrating upon tailor-made material addressing specific target groups, such as teachers and public sector broadcasters.

The European Institute for Gender Equality

The European Institute for Gender Equality (EIGE) is another autonomous specialised decentralised fundamental rights agency, which exists alongside the FRA with a more specific rights remit. Established in

---

[114] Cooperation agreement between EUROFOUND and the FRA of 8 October 2009; Cooperation arrangement between FRONTEX and the FRA of 26 May 2010.

[115] Agreement between the European Community and the Council of Europe on cooperation between the European Union Agency for Fundamental Rights and the Council of Europe (*Official Journal of the European Union*, L 186/7, 15.7.2008) ('CE Cooperation Agreement').

[116] Articles 3 and 12 CE Cooperation Agreement.

[117] Article 7 CE Cooperation Agreement.

[118] Article 2 CE Cooperation Agreement.

[119] Council of Europe – Secretariat of the Committee of Ministers, *Overview of the Cooperation between the European Union Agency for Fundamental Rights and the Council of Europe*, p. 4 paragraph 3.1.

2006,[120] following repeated calls for its creation from the EP,[121] and ultimately with the European Council's endorsement,[122] the EIGE consists of a Management Board acting as its decision-making body, a Directorate as its executive and an Experts' Forum fulfilling an advisory consultative function.

The overall objective of the EIGE is to contribute to, and to strengthen, the struggle against sex discrimination, by raising public awareness and by providing technical support to EU institutions and member states.[123] It is mandated to meet this objective through various means,[124] including collecting, analysing and disseminating objective, comparable and reliable information on gender equality; carrying out relevant surveys; and publishing positive examples on non-gender-stereotyped practices. It publishes numerous thematic reports, has created a Gender Equality Index – the first statistical measurement instrument assessing the variation in gender equality trends across member states – and, in 2011, launched an online database, *Women and Men in the EU: Facts and Figures*, which is regularly updated.

To avoid duplication and maximise effectiveness, the EIGE has a close working relationship with the FRA, formalised in a Cooperation Agreement,[125] which goes beyond merely sharing information and notifying each other of upcoming research. For example, the FRA invited an EIGE representative to attend all its expert meetings concerning development of the FRA's EU-wide survey on violence against women. Like the FRA, by permitting applicant states to participate in its activities, the EIGE potentially has impact beyond the EU's borders. Since 2013, it has cooperated with six pre-accession states from the western Balkans and Turkey,[126] engaging them in its regular activities and building relationships with relevant national authorities so as to facilitate compliance with the EU's gender equality policies. The EIGE not only offers technical

[120] European Parliament and Council Regulation (EC) No. 1922/2006 of 20 December 2006 establishing a European Institute for Gender Equality, OJ 2006 L 403/9, 30.12.2006, p. 1 ('EIGE Regulation').

[121] See for example European Parliament, *Role of a Future European Gender Institute*, IPOL/C/IV/2003/16/03 (June 2004).

[122] Presidency Conclusions, Brussels European Council Meeting, 17 and 18 June 2004, 10679/2/04 REV 2, p. 14 paragraph 43.

[123] Article 2 EIGE Regulation.

[124] Article 3(1) EIGE Regulation.

[125] Cooperation agreement between EIGE and the FRA of 22 November 2010.

[126] European Institute for Gender Equality, 2015 'European Institute for Gender Equality – EIGE in brief' at 18.

assistance and expertise to applicants, but also provides EU institutions with information on gender equality in applicant states.[127]

Expert Networks

In order to contribute advice and analysis to EU policy-making, the Commission has established numerous independent expert networks, including in the field of fundamental rights. Having been financed under a three-year non-renewable 'preparatory action', which expired in September 2006, the Network of Independent Experts on Fundamental Rights (CFR-CDF) is no longer active. It was established by the Commission in 2002 following an EP Resolution[128] that, accepting that the Commission and Council would not then approve an EU fundamental rights agency, requested a less formal monitoring body.[129] Composed of one expert per member state, headed by a coordinator, the CFR-CDF's function was systematically to monitor, and to report on, the fundamental rights situation in the EU and its member states by reference to the CFR. During its tenure, the CFR-CDF published four annual reports in this respect, identifying, *inter alia*, positive practices and reasons for concern at the member state level. In contradistinction to the FRA, the CFR-CDF was permitted to make a judgement about compliance with legal obligations, and empowered to contribute to the Article 7 preventive sanctioning procedures. Mandated as a consultation body, the Commission was also able to request non-binding opinions on issues relating to fundamental rights protection within the EU, thereby ensuring better account was taken of fundamental rights in the early stages of the legislative process.

The High Level Group on Non-Discrimination, Equality and Diversity (Expert Group) was set up by the Commission in 2015 to replace, in the field of non-discrimination, the Government Expert Group, whose mandate expired in 2013. The current Expert Group is composed of two representatives per member state, and open to participation from EEA states. Its members discuss common concerns and exchange experiences in relation to eliminating discrimination and achieving equality. In order

---

[127] Article 3(1)(l) EIGE Regulation.

[128] European Parliament Resolution of 5 July 2001 on the situation of fundamental rights in the European Union (2000/2231(INI), 5.7.2000).

[129] M. Nowak, 'The Agency and National Institutions for the Promotion and Protection of Human Rights' in P. Alston and O. de Schutter (eds.), *Monitoring Fundamental Rights in the EU: The Contribution of the Fundamental Rights Agency*, p. 97.

to solicit feedback, the Council presidency updates the Expert Group on plans, activities and results in the field of equality and anti-discrimination. The Commission provides secretarial and logistic support, and a Commission representative chairs the Group's meetings in close cooperation with the Council Presidency.

The European Network of Legal Experts in Gender Equality and Non-Discrimination (Equality Network) comprises domestic experts from thirty-five countries, all member states or members of the EEA and every current applicant state except Albania. It was established by the Commission in 2014 to merge the mandates of two previously existing Networks – the European Network of Legal Experts in the Field of Gender Equality, established in 1983, and the European Network of Legal Experts in the Non-Discrimination Field, established in 2004 – to inform the Commission 'about implementation of EU equality law and developments at the national level regarding policies, legislation, case law and activities of equality bodies in their respective fields'.[130] The Equality Network continues the functions of its predecessors, providing the Commission with independent advice, analysis and information in the fields of gender equality and non-discrimination. It addresses: national transposition of, and compliance with, EU Directives; national initiatives and political developments; domestic jurisprudence; the impact of ECJ and ECtHR judgments on national law; and EU policy developments. In addition to publishing a biannual *European Equality Law Review* setting out the key legal developments in gender equality and non-discrimination at the EU and member state levels, the Equality Network produces various thematic reports focusing on particular policy areas, and comparative analyses summarising domestic equality law to highlight key issues. The legalistic focus of its mandate enables it to coexist with, and complement, the work of the EIGE. An Academic Network of European Disability Experts was also created by the Commission in 2007 to collaborate with the Commission in support of policy development in this field.

4.3 Internal Policy

Although initially deemed irrelevant to European integration, fundamental rights have, nevertheless, become increasing central to the EU legal

---

[130] S. Burri, 'The European Network of Legal Experts in the Field of Gender Equality', *European Anti-Discrimination Law Review*, 6 (1993), 11–12.

order. Originally incorporated as negative obligations, the EU has slowly gained competences positively to develop relevant standards and has established mechanisms for their enforcement. A multifaceted and uniquely complex internal fundamental rights policy now exists, which, perhaps paradoxically, has the potential to undermine the EU's authority and legitimacy, particularly in the face of the current and recent crises discussed in Chapter 1. The following, particularly salient issues are considered later: incorporation of fundamental rights into EU primary law; EU accession to the ECHR; the EU Charter of Fundamental Rights; fundamental rights in EU secondary legislation; EU soft law instruments addressing fundamental rights; and enforcement mechanisms.

Incorporation of Fundamental Rights into EU Primary Law

As indicated in Chapter 1, although European political integration was already a long-term goal for some in the immediate aftermath of the Second World War,[131] fundamental rights provided little, if any, direct motivation for the creation of the three Economic Communities – the ECSC, the European Economic Community (EEC) and the European Atomic Energy Community (Euratom) – in the early 1950s. The founding Treaties of the three Economic Communities,[132] therefore, only addressed well-defined economic issues without any explicit reference to fundamental rights, although the 1957 Treaty Establishing the European Economic Community (TEEC) contained a few articles directly impacting on individual entitlements, such as those concerning equal pay for men and women.[133]

However, the attempt to confine European integration to the economic dimension proved unsustainable, not least because it eventually became apparent that the legitimacy of the Union's activities was dependent on its supranational institutions being constrained by respect for fundamental rights, as public authorities in member states are by their national constitutions and the ECHR. The ECJ was one of the first EU institutions

---

[131] See in particular G. Ionescu, *The New Politics of European Integration* (London: Macmillan, 1972) and U. W. Kitzinger, *The Politics and Economics of European Integration* (Westport, CT: Greenwood Press, 1963).

[132] Treaty establishing the European Coal and Steel Community, signed in Paris in 1951, expired on 23 July 2002; Treaty establishing the European Economic Community, signed in Rome in 1957; Treaty establishing the European Atomic Energy Community, signed in Rome in 1957.

[133] Article 119 TEEC.

to realise this but not because of its own untrammelled insight. In the face of concerns on the part of national constitutional courts that without a Community commitment to fundamental rights national constitutional rights were jeopardised, it held that fundamental rights common to the constitutional traditions of member states, and/or protected in international agreements to which the member states were party, are enshrined in the general principles of Community law (see Chapter 5). While praised as a great achievement 'in the process of constitutionalising the founding Treaties',[134] this was, nevertheless, an assumption about the Union's unwritten normative origins.

Other Community institutions complemented the ECJ's conclusion through various legally non-binding instruments. The first occurred in December 1973, when, before the European Council was officially formed, the Heads of State and Government identified respect for fundamental rights as a vital element of 'European identity'.[135] In 1975, the Commission asserted that it was politically important for a potentially enlarged Union to rest upon general principles held by all member states, including the protection of human rights,[136] which it later proposed the Community's political institutions should formally endorse.[137] The Commission, Council and EP subsequently published a joint Declaration stressing their commitment to fundamental rights arising from the sources identified by the ECJ, and pledged to respect them in exercising their powers.[138] At its Copenhagen summit in 1978, the Heads of State and Government, now officially the European Council, confirmed their commitment to safeguarding respect for human rights, declared such

---

[134] A. von Bogdandy, 'The European Union as a Human Rights Organization? Human Rights and the Core of the European Union', *Common Market Law Review*, 37(6) (2000), 1320.

[135] Meeting of the Heads of State or Government (Copenhagen, 14–15 December 1973), *Communique of the European Community "Summit" Meeting and Annexes*, European Community Background Information No. 29/1973, Annex II, 'Declaration on European Identity', p. 9.

[136] Report on the European Union (EC Bulletin, Supplement 5-1975, paragraph 4), p. 9.

[137] Report of the Commission of 4 Feb 1976 (EC Bulletin, Supplement 5/76) p.16; *The Protection of Fundamental Rights as Community Law Is Created and Developed, Report of the Commission Submitted to the European Parliament and the Council* (COM [76] 37 final), 4.2.1976.

[138] Joint Declaration by the European Parliament, the Council and the Commission concerning the Protection of Fundamental Rights and the European Convention for the Protection of Human Rights and Fundamental Freedoms, (Official Journal of the European Communities 1977, C 103/1, 5.4.1977).

respect to be an essential element of membership and endorsed the joint Declaration.[139] While not as important as the Declaration itself, this indicated support for fundamental rights at the highest political level and, as such, added momentum to the affirmation of other institutions.

The introduction of direct universal suffrage, in 1979, bestowed democratic legitimacy upon the EP conferring a moral authority, which, in the 1980s, enabled it to expand its fundamental rights initiatives.[140] In 1984, the EP adopted a draft Treaty establishing the European Union,[141] declaring respect for fundamental rights to be indispensable for the Community's legitimacy and providing a control mechanism to ensure member states' adherence to them.[142] Although, in the event, the 1984 draft Treaty was not adopted, many of its proposals re-appeared in the first major revision of the Treaties, the 1986 SEA, which made an explicit, albeit brief, reference to fundamental rights in the Preamble.

By this point, a written Bill of Rights for the Community was being declared to be desirable, and two options were under consideration: the creation of a Community Charter and the Union's accession to the ECHR.[143] In 1989 the EP adopted a Declaration on a List of Fundamental Rights,[144] identifying a catalogue of fundamental civil, political and socio-economic entitlements specific to the Community. Although other EU institutions did not accept it as legally binding,[145] the EP's subsequent Resolution[146] proved to be the precursor to the Community Charter of the Fundamental Social Rights of Workers ('Social Charter'),[147] adopted in December 1989 as a legally non-enforceable political Declaration by eleven of the then-twelve member states in what was the first in a series of rights-related 'opt-outs' by the United Kingdom. The

---

[139] Conclusions from the session of the European Council at Copenhagen, 7 and 8 April 1978, pp. 99–100.

[140] D. Napoli, 'The European Union's Foreign Policy and Human Rights' in N. A. Neuwahl and A. Rosas (eds.), The European Union and Human Rights (The Hague: Martinus Nijhoff, c. 1995), p. 302.

[141] Draft Treaty Establishing the European Union (OJ 1984, C 77/33, 14.2.1984).

[142] Article 4 Draft Treaty Establishing the European Union.

[143] E. C. Landau, 'New Regime of Human Rights in the EU', European Journal of Law Reform, 10 (2008), 559.

[144] European Parliament Resolution adopting the Declaration of Fundamental Rights and Freedoms of 12 April 1989 ('De Gucht Report') (OJ C 120/51, Doc. A2-3/89, 16.5.1989).

[145] Ibid.

[146] European Parliament Resolution on the Community Charter of Fundamental Social Rights of 22.11.1989 (OJ, C 323/44, 27.12.1989).

[147] Community Charter of Fundamental Social Rights – Draft (COM [89] 471 final, 2.10.1989).

Commission's action programme, published alongside the Social Charter,[148] ushered in an intensive period of legislative activity in this field.

The 1992 Maastricht Treaty on European Union created the EU and paved the way to political integration. *Inter alia*, it introduced the concept of EU citizenship,[149] and, by providing that the Union would 'respect fundamental rights, as guaranteed by the [ECHR]... and as they result from the constitutional traditions common to the member states, as general principles of Community law',[150] converted the ECJ's aforementioned fundamental rights jurisprudence into a treaty obligation. Following ratification of the Maastricht Treaty, the Community's competences expanded dramatically into such areas as immigration and asylum, security and data protection, impinging more on citizens' daily lives and increasing the possibility that fundamental individual rights might be infringed. This gave rise to a corresponding expansion in the EU's fundamental rights competence,[151] which in turn rendered the need for legal clarity through a written catalogue of community rights all the more necessary. In 1994, the EP adopted a Draft Constitution,[152] Title VII of which incorporated a revised version of its 1989 list of rights. The following year the Commission set up a Comité des Sages to consider social and civic rights. In its 1996 report, the Comité asserted that the 'inclusion of civil and social rights in the treaty would help to nurture [EU] citizenship and prevent the EU being perceived as a bureaucracy assembled by technocratic elites far removed from daily concerns.'[153]

The 1997 Treaty of Amsterdam[154] was the first of three successive Treaties amending the EU's two core functional treaties (the TEU and TEC)[155] in order to accommodate enlargement. Described as a turning

---

[148] European Commission Communication concerning its Action Programme relating to the Implementation of the Community Charter of Basic Social Rights for Workers (COM [89] 568 final, 29.11.1989).

[149] Article B Maastricht Treaty.

[150] Article F(2) Maastricht Treaty.

[151] F. Ferraro and J. Carmona, 'Fundamental Rights in the European Union: The Role of the Charter after the Lisbon Treaty' (European Union: European Parliament Research Service, 2015), p. 7.

[152] Draft Constitution for the European Union of 10 February 1994 (OJ 1994, C61/155).

[153] Report of the Comité des Sages chaired by Maria de Lourdes Pintasilgo, *From a Europe of Civic and Social Rights* (Brussels: 1996), pp. 95–6.

[154] *Treaty of Amsterdam Amending the Treaty on European Union*, the Treaties Establishing the European Communities and Certain Related Acts (OJ 97/C 340/01, 10.11.1997, p. 1), ('Treaty of Amsterdam').

[155] The TEEC became the *Treaty establishing the Economic Community* ('TEC') in 1992 when the Treaty of Maastricht retrospectively deleted the word 'economic' from the Treaty's official title.

point for the positive promotion, as opposed to negative protection, of fundamental rights at EU level,[156] it added a new provision to Article 6 (ex Article F) TEU, affirming that 'the Union is founded on the principles of liberty, democracy, respect for human rights and fundamental freedoms, and the rule of law, principles which are common to the member states',[157] thereby providing a constitutional basis for the retrospectively articulated moral dimension of what was originally an exclusively economic Community. The Treaty of Amsterdam preserved the TEU provision stipulating that the Community would respect fundamental rights arising from the sources identified by the ECJ,[158] and, by granting the ECJ appropriate jurisdiction, provided a legal guarantee that EU institutions would adhere to it.[159] The Amsterdam Treaty also enshrined a new EU objective, namely, 'to maintain and develop the Union as an area of freedom, security and justice',[160] complemented by several Treaty articles providing new legal bases from which the EU could adopt legislation giving specific expression to fundamental rights. By introducing a mechanism for sanctioning breach of fundamental rights at the national level, discussed later, the Treaty of Amsterdam rendered the EU's internal fundamental rights policy applicable to member states, as opposed merely to EU institutions, which complemented the establishment of respect for fundamental rights as a prerequisite for EU membership, also discussed further later. Moreover, while stopping short of creating directly enforceable rights, the Amsterdam Treaty referenced the 1989 Social Charter and the CE's 1961 European Social Charter (ESC) (see Chapter 2) as instruments to be taken into account by EU institutions and member states in pursuit of social policy objectives.[161]

Since the Commission initially saw accession to the ECHR, rather than a Community Bill of Rights, as an imminently preferable option, in the wake of the Amsterdam Treaty it established an Expert Group on Fundamental Rights to review and report on the status of this issue in the Union. The report concluded that visibility of fundamental rights was crucial, and stipulated that the provisions of the ECHR, and its Protocols,

---

[156] Ferraro and Carmona, 'Fundamental Rights in the European Union', p. 8.
[157] Article 6(1) *Consolidated Version of the Treaty on European Union* (OJ 1997, 97/C 340/02) ('TEU 1997').
[158] Article 6(2) TEU 1997.
[159] Article 46(d) TEU 1997.
[160] Article 2 TEU 1997.
[161] Article 136 *Consolidated Version of the Treaty Establishing the European Community* (OJ 1997, 97/C 340/03) ('TEC 1997').

ought to be incorporated into EU law, in order to prevent different sets of rights evolving in Europe.[162] Inspired by this report, in June 1999, the Cologne European Council made the landmark decision to establish a CFR, asserting that the 'protection of fundamental rights is a founding principle of the Union and an indispensable prerequisite for her legitimacy'.[163] The theory was that by collating, in a single document, the disparate sets of rights 'scattered across the landscape of the Community's laws' their nature and scope would be more coherently expressed[164] and their importance enhanced. Unlike the procedure for all previous Treaty reforms, whereby member states negotiated amendments at Intergovernmental Conferences (IGCs), the Cologne European Council entrusted the task of drafting the Charter to an ad hoc Convention. More representative than the traditional IGC, this body comprised representatives of the Commission, EP, Heads of State and Government and national parliaments. Although the draft CFR it adopted was solemnly proclaimed in December 2000 at the European Council summit in Nice,[165] the CFR's constitutional impact was initially hampered by its ambiguous legal status as a mere Proclamation, an inter-institutional agreement that did not legally bind member states. The UK government had been 'particularly keen to neutralise any legal effects . . . by opposing any incorporation into the founding treaties'.[166]

With twelve non-EU states seeking membership as early as 2004, the Treaty of Nice, signed in 2001 shortly after the CFR was proclaimed, primarily made technical amendments to the EU facilitating future enlargement. It had little impact on fundamental rights, other than to incorporate a preventive mechanism into Article 7 TEU enabling the Council to determine a 'clear risk', rather than an actual occurrence, of a serious breach of fundamental rights; to make appropriate recommendations to the member state in question; and to monitor its progress

---

[162] Report of the Expert Group on Fundamental Rights, the European Commission, *Affirming Fundamental Rights in the EU: Time to Act*, February 1999.

[163] Presidential Conclusions, Cologne European Council meeting 3–4 June 1999, Annex IV 'European Council Decision on the Drawing up of a Charter of Fundamental Rights of the European Union'.

[164] A. J. Williams, *EU Human Rights Policies: A Study in Irony*, p. 2.

[165] *Charter of Fundamental Rights of the European Union (Official Journal of the European Union*, 2000/C 364/01) ('CFR').

[166] X. Groussot and L. Pech, 'Fundamental Rights Protection in the European Union post Lisbon Treaty', *Policy Papers of the Foundation Robert Schuman (European Issue)*, 173 (2010), 3.

accordingly (see later discussion). In order to rectify the increasingly complex European legal architecture – with repeated reforms having amended the founding Treaties, while adding further protocols, annexes and Declarations – a Treaty establishing a Constitution for Europe was conceived to replace the founding Treaties, except for that which established Euratom. The CFR was incorporated into Part II of the Constitutional Treaty, which was signed by the Heads of State and Government at the Rome European Council summit in October 2004. However, before entering into force, it had to be ratified by all member states, and this process failed. Following referendum rejections in France and the Netherlands, the constitutional project was abandoned, and a new amending treaty was drawn up instead.

Incorporating the majority of the institutional and political reforms envisaged in the Constitutional Treaty, but amending, rather than replacing, the founding Treaties,[167] the Treaty of Lisbon was signed in December 2007 and entered into force two years later. Seen as marking 'a new era' for the EU's fundamental rights activities, it considerably consolidated protection through various provisions relating to written and direct sources of rights.[168] First, it unequivocally granted the now-amended and re-proclaimed[169] CFR (discussed later) the same legal value as the Treaties,[170] rendering it a legally binding core element of the EU's legal order. Second, it explicitly recognised the single legal personality of the EU,[171] thus enabling it to become a member of international organisations and to join international conventions as an independent entity. Accordingly, Article 216 TFEU empowered the EU to become party to international human rights treaties that would then become binding on EU institutions and member states. The first time this happened was in December 2010, when the EU formally ratified the UN Convention on the Rights of Persons with Disabilities. Further, Article 6(2) TEU granted the EU an explicit constitutional mandate to seek accession to the ECHR, considered next.[172]

---

[167] The TEC, what was originally the TEEC, was renamed the *Treaty on the Functioning of the European Union*.

[168] E. Muir, 'The Fundamental Rights Implications of EU Legislation: Some Constitutional Challenges', *Common Market Law Review*, 51(1) (2014), 219–45 at 219.

[169] European Commission Press Release, 'Charter of Fundamental Rights: The Presidents of the Commission, European Parliament and Council Sign and Solemnly Proclaim the Charter in Strasbourg' (IP/07/1916, Brussels, 12.12.2007).

[170] Article 6(1) TEU.

[171] Article 47 TEU.

[172] Article 6(2) TEU.

EU Accession to the ECHR

The Commission first raised the possibility of the Union's accession to the ECHR in its 1976 report.[173] But it concluded that, provided the ECJ took ECHR provisions into consideration when deliberating cases,[174] it was sufficient for the latter to be generally binding in the context of Community law.[175] Dissatisfied, the EP urged the Commission to conduct a follow-up study. In the resulting memorandum, published three years later, the Commission reversed its opinion and favoured accession.[176] It maintained that the ECJ's protection of fundamental rights was adequate, but asserted that the absence of a written catalogue of rights undermined legal certainty. While acknowledging that a comprehensive Community Bill of Rights would be more effective, the Commission proposed ECHR accession as a simpler short term solution,[177] and advocated that the legal acts of EU institutions be subject to scrutiny by the ECHR's monitoring machinery.[178] Yet its detailed pro-accession report did not persuade the Council.

In the wake of the SEA, which contained the first explicit Treaty reference to fundamental rights, the Commission revived the debate by formally asking the Council to authorise accession negotiations.[179] However, the ECJ held that there were no Treaty provisions at that time that gave the institutions 'any general power to enact rules on fundamental rights or to conclude international conventions in this field'.[180] In 1994, the EP, a consistent advocate of ECHR accession, adopted a Resolution maintaining that, in order to fill 'a conspicuous gap in the Community legal system', the Council ought to authorise the Commission to

---

[173] Report of the European Commission, *The protection of fundamental rights as Community law is created and developed. Report of the Commission submitted to the European Parliament and the Council* (COM [76] 37 final, 4.2.1976, Bulletin of the European Community ('EC Bulletin'), Supplement 5/76), pp. 5–16.

[174] Ibid., pp. 9–10.

[175] Ibid., p. 14.

[176] European Commission Memorandum on the accession of the Communities to the European Convention for the Protection of Human Rights and Fundamental Freedoms (COM [79] 210 final, 2.5.1979, EC Bulletin, Supplement 2/79), adopted by the European Commission on 4 April 1979.

[177] Ibid., p. 5.

[178] Ibid., p. 15.

[179] European Commission Communication of 19 November 1990 on Community Accession to the European Convention for the Protection of Human Rights and Fundamental Freedoms and Some of Its Protocols' (SEC (90) 2087 final, EC Bulletin 11/1990).

[180] Opinion 2/94 of the Court, [1996] ECR I-1759, paragraph 27.

negotiate with the CE about accession to the ECHR.[181] While stipulating
that this would constitute 'a step forward' in fundamental rights protection, the Resolution also endorsed the concurrent establishment of a
Community Bill of Rights as a complementary measure rather than an
alternative. In 1996, however, the ECJ issued another opinion, again
finding that accession was beyond the Community's competence under
EU law as it then stood.[182] It was held that accession would entail a
substantial systemic change in the Community's protection of fundamental rights,[183] and, since such a modification 'would be of constitutional
significance', it could only be brought about by Treaty amendment.[184]

However, by the beginning of the twenty-first century, not only were
the EU and the Convention system ripe for reform, each was also more
open to accession than ever before. The Lisbon Treaty required, rather
than merely permitted or encouraged, the EU to accede to the ECHR.[185]
And Protocol No. 14 enabled the Convention system to accommodate it.
But a host of institutional, procedural, normative, administrative and
logistical problems bedevilled the project, and reaching agreement
proved difficult. One unacknowledged difficulty concerned the credibility
of the underlying premise that accession would contribute significantly to
the protection of human rights. The success of the entire exercise would,
for example, be highly contingent upon its use by applicants. If the
experience of the inter-state procedure in the Convention system is
anything to go by, complaints to the ECtHR by states against the EU,
and by the EU against states, would not be common. The individual
application rate would be even more difficult to predict and would
depend particularly upon how visible the prospect of lodging a complaint
with the ECtHR about EU-related violations of the ECHR would be to
potential applicants. Although, thus far, complaints about the violation of
civil and political rights, including by secondary EU law, have provided a
focal point for ECJ case law, it is not clear that this would have remained
the case post accession nor that such violations would be effectively
corrected. The enduring sclerosis in the administration of justice in many
European states, particularly Italy, provides a salutary reminder that even

---

[181] European Parliament Resolution on Community Accession to the European Convention
on Human Rights (OJ C44/32, 14.2.1994).
[182] Opinion 2/94 of the Court.
[183] Ibid., paragraph 34.
[184] Ibid., paragraph 35.
[185] Article 6(2) TEU, A summary of the negotiating process can be found in the draft
explanatory report, paragraphs 8–16.

thousands of successful applications to Strasbourg can fail to remedy the source of perennial violations. It is, therefore, possible, even if accession went ahead, that the most systemic human rights violations by the EU would not be solved by litigation at the instigation of victims at Strasbourg or elsewhere.

There is also a further unacknowledged challenge at the heart of the accession project. If EU accession to the ECHR results in a substantial increase in applications to the ECtHR, it could jeopardise the resolution of the case overload crisis, which has only just begun. Yet, if there is little additional litigation, it is difficult to see how accession could make a major contribution to the protection of human rights in Europe, unless the ECtHR, and the Convention system generally, operate more consistently according to the requirements of 'constitutional' rather than 'individual' justice, a prospect deeply opposed by the CE itself.

Draft instruments of accession were, nevertheless, finalised on 5 April 2013 and sent for an opinion to the ECJ. Yet, in spite of having been closely involved in the discussions, on 18 December 2014, the ECJ ruled that accession, in the terms proposed, was beyond the powers granted to the EU by its foundational treaties.[186] The Court was particularly concerned that, with respect to Convention rights, accession would effectively subordinate the ECJ to the ECtHR, would compromise the transfer of sovereignty by member states to the EU and would undermine the effectiveness, autonomy and unity of EU law.[187] Therefore, unless its foundational treaties are amended – a prospect remote in the extreme – accession to the ECHR will, paradoxically, remain a formal treaty obligation which the EU is legally incapable of discharging.[188] The ECJ's ruling

---

[186] Opinion 2/13 of the Court, [2014] ECR I-2454; J. Odermatt, 'A Giant Step Backwards? Opinion 2/13 on the EU's Accession to the European Convention on Human Rights' (2015) 47 New York University Journal of Law and Politics, 783–98; for detailed discussion on the future of EU accession, see T. Lock, 'The Future of EU Accession to the ECHR after Opinion 2/13: Is It Still Possible and Is It Still Desirable?', European Constitutional Law Review, 11(2) (2015), 239–73.

[187] Ibid., paragraphs. 165–76. For a critique see J. Polakiweicz, 'Accession to the European Convention on Human Rights (ECHR) — an Insider's View Addressing One by One the CJEU's Objections in Opinion 2/13', Human Rights Law Journal, 36 (2016), 10–21.

[188] X. Groussot, N-L. Arold Lorenz and G. Thor Petursson, 'The Paradox of Human Rights Protection in Europe: Two Courts, One Goal?', pp. 19–25; D. Björgvinsson, 'The Role of the ECtHR in the Changing European Human Rights Architecture', pp. 26–35 in O. Mjöll Arnardóttir and A. Buyse (eds.), Shifting Centres of Gravity in Human Rights Protection: Rethinking Relations between the ECHR, EU and National Legal Orders (London: Routledge, 2016).

against EU accession has undoubtedly soured relations with the ECtHR. In his foreword to the ECtHR's Annual Report 2014, for example, the then-President Dean Speilmann stated that this opinion would deprive citizens of 'the right to have acts of the European Union subjected to the same external scrutiny as regards respect for human rights as that which applies to each member state' and would increase 'the onus on the Strasbourg Court to do what it can in cases before it to protect citizens from the negative effects of this situation.'[189] But, as the President of the Spanish Constitutional Court has also observed, 'the crisis' triggered by the ECJ's opinion 'will probably prove to be beneficial because ultimately it will make each stakeholder face up to its own responsibilities'.[190] This may be especially true as new human rights issues emerge. The ECJ may, for example, be increasingly required to interpret fundamental rights before the ECtHR has had the chance to do so, and the ECtHR may effectively have to acknowledge the leading role of the ECJ in fields such as data protection, asylum and the Internet, in which EU law provides more precise regulation than the ECHR.

The EU Charter of Fundamental Rights

As already indicated, in the pre-CFR EU legal order, there was no single text containing a comprehensive list of fundamental rights. The fact that such entitlements derived from diverse sources was both theoretically and practically problematic. Allied to the need to make citizens feel closer to the EU with their rights better protected, in 1999 the CFR was drafted and adopted to identify, codify and consolidate EU-applicable fundamental rights in a single written instrument. By providing a rights basis for the EU's governance as a European polity, the CFR has been described as one of the most explicit statements of the EU's commitment to direct legitimacy[191] and, accordingly, 'represents a very important development in the constitutionalisation of the EU'.[192]

The CFR is divided into seven Chapters, referred to as Titles, of which the first six contain its substantive provisions deriving from a number of

---

[189] ECtHR, *Annual Report 2014* (Strasbourg: Council of Europe, 2015), p. 6.
[190] ECtHR, *Annual Report 2015* (Strasbourg: Council of Europe, 2016), p. 49.
[191] E. O. Eriksen, 'Why a Charter of Fundamental Human Rights in the EU?' *Ratio Juris*, 16 (3) (2003), 352–73 at 356.
[192] E. O. Eriksen, *The Unfinished Democratization of Europe*, new edn. (New York: Oxford University Press, 2009), p. 94.

international and regional instruments, including the ECHR, EU and CE Social Charters, ILO and UN Conventions, as well as from the ECJ's case law and the common constitutional traditions of member states. The CFR differs from the ECHR in five principal ways.[193] First, it includes rights contained in the latter but not in precisely the same terms. For example, Article 6 CFR provides the right to liberty and security of the person in a single clause – 'everyone has the right to liberty and security of the person' – while Article 5 ECHR has no fewer than five clauses, one of which has six further sub-clauses (twelve elements in total) for the same right. Conversely, the CFR also expands and updates rights found in the ECHR formally to provide more extensive protection in the light of scientific and technological developments, societal changes and the emergence of new forms of potential infringement. For example, reflecting advances in bio-medicine since the ECHR was drafted, the right to the integrity of the person (Article 3(2) CFR) expressly includes respect for free and informed consent as well as the prohibition of eugenic practices and reproductive cloning. Although some of these rights have since been enshrined in the CE's 1997 Convention on Human Rights and Biomedicine, not many of the forty-seven CE member states, including several that also belong to the EU, have ratified it. While reflecting the prohibition of slavery in Article 4 ECHR, Article 5 CFR includes an additional paragraph prohibiting human trafficking, a problem that also only became visible after the ECHR was drafted. Similarly, echoing the right to property enshrined in Article 1, Protocol 1 ECHR, Article 17(2) CFR expressly adds the right to intellectual property.

Second, the CFR contains a more extensive catalogue of rights than the ECHR. While the latter is largely confined to civil and political rights, the CFR also includes a wide range of social, economic, cultural and citizenship rights, similar in kind to those found in the CE's ESC discussed in Chapter 2.[194] The CFR also introduces 'new' rights, such as the right to

---

[193] See, e.g., G. de Búrca, 'The drafting of the European Union Charter of Fundamental Rights', *European Law Review*, 26 (2001), 126–38; A. W. Heringa and L. F. M. Verhey, 'The EU Charter: Text and Structure', *MJ*, 8 (2001), 11–32; C. Ladenburger, 'European Union Institutional Report', in J. Laffranque (ed.), *The Protection of Fundamental Rights Post-Lisbon* (Tartu, Estonia: Tartu University Press, 2012) 141–215.

[194] See further, e.g., M. H. S. Gijzen, 'The Charter: A Milestone for Social Protection in Europe?', *MJ*, 8 (2001), 33ff; D. Guðmundsdóttir, 'A Renewed Emphasis on the Charter's Distinction between Rights and Principles: Is a Doctrine of Judicial Restraint More Appropriate?', *Common Market Law Review*, 52 (2015), 685–720 at 687; J. Krommendijk, 'Principled Silence or Mere Silence on Principles? The Role of the EU Charter's Principles in the Case Law of the Court of Justice', *European Constitutional*

good administration (Article 41 CFR), by elevating the status of existing entitlements, already protected to a variable degree, but not explicitly recognised as fundamental rights per se.[195] Further, the substantive scope of the CFR is also broader than that of the ECHR in that it includes a number of 'fundamental rights' that are not, strictly speaking, 'human rights' because they are incapable of being possessed by all individuals without distinction purely on account of their humanity. These include rights allocated to specific classes of people, such as the elderly (Article 25 CFR) and the disabled (Article 26 CFR); rights that can only be held collectively, such as the right to collective bargaining and other collective action in the employment context (Article 28 CFR); and rights that can be invoked by natural and legal persons, such as companies. The CFR also employs the term 'principles' to distinguish entitlements, considered further in Chapter 5, which are not judicially cognisable rights per se.

Third, the ECHR and CFR deal with restrictions upon rights in different ways. The former attaches specific limitations to certain provisions and enables all but a handful of particularly fundamental rights ('non-derogables') to be suspended in war or public emergency threatening the life of the nation. By contrast, Article 52 CFR provides a general limitation for all substantive CFR rights in the following terms. They must be provided for by law, respect the essence of the rights and freedoms in question and be subject to the principle of proportionality. They must also be necessary and genuinely meet objectives of the general interest recognised by the EU or protect the rights and freedoms of others. Rights found in the CFR, which derive from EU Treaties, must also be exercised under the conditions and within the limits defined. Unlike the ECHR, the CFR does not formally provide for derogation. Further, although some CFR provisions are framed in formally unrestricted terms, others are only afforded 'in accordance with Union law and national law and practices'.

The fourth difference between the ECHR and the CFR is that the former generally binds member states in any and all of their activities, while Article 51 CFR indicates that it is predominantly aimed at constraining the actions of EU institutions and bodies, only engaging member states when implementing EU law. Additional 'horizontal

---

Law Review, 11 (2015), 321–56. For an overview of the Charter rights and the way the ECJ has interpreted and applied them, see Chapter 5, Section 5.6.

[195] European Commission Communication on the Charter of Fundamental Rights of the European Union, (COM [2000] 559 final, Brussels, 13.9.2000), 4.

clauses' dealing with the scope, interpretation and application of the CFR also appear under Title VII. These general provisions were included because, during the drafting process, some member states expressed concern that the Charter could act as a federalising device, threatening national sovereignty and culture. To deal with particular concerns over whether the CFR would enlarge the EU's powers through the back door via 'competence creep', Article 6(1) TEU, reiterated by Article 51(2) CFR, explicitly states that the CFR's provisions 'shall not extend in any way' EU competences 'as defined in the Treaties'. As such, in conformity with the principle of competence conferral,[196] the CFR itself cannot offer a legal basis for the EU to legislate, but only applies to areas of law where the member states have bestowed such competence on the EU. Dissatisfied with the assurances offered under Title VII, and devised as a means of domestic political compromise, the United Kingdom and Poland negotiated Protocol 30 to the Lisbon Treaty, addressing certain aspects of the CFR's application. Nevertheless, Protocol 30 fails to function as an opt-out or genuine derogation regime, since none of its provisions has any tangible impact on the application of the CFR in practice.[197]

Finally, the CFR does not provide any additional right of individual petition. As such, the only recourse to the ECJ open to individual litigants for a breach of a CFR right remains the existing limited ones addressed in Chapter 5.

Since 1 December 2009, when the Lisbon Treaty entered into force, the CFR acquired the status of primary EU law, equal to the Treaties.[198] As the outcome of a pan-European political consensus, ratified by member states on behalf of their citizens, the CFR enjoys a high degree of formal legitimacy,[199] and since it became a binding document, its role and importance for the ECJ's case law, have also changed significantly. For a start, largely as a result of an increase in the exercise of EU competences – in areas such as migration and asylum law, employment, protection of personal data and sanctioning mechanisms in relation to international terrorism, where fundamental rights issues are prominent[200] – the ECJ now has to deal with,

---

[196] Article 5 TEU.
[197] For detailed analysis, see Groussot and Pech, 'Fundamental Rights Protection in the European Union post Lisbon Treaty'.
[198] For detailed analysis, see Groussot and Pech, 'Fundamental Rights Protection in the European Union post Lisbon Treaty'.
[199] Ferraro and Carmona, 'Fundamental Rights in the European Union', p. 10.
[200] G. de Búrca, 'After the EU Charter of Fundamental Rights: The Court of Justice as a Human Rights Adjudicator?', MJ, 20 (2013), 168–84.

and judge, a growing number of fundamental rights complaints considered more fully in Chapter 5.[201] The enhanced activity of the EU in these areas, combined with the CFR's wide rights catalogue, appear to have alerted individuals and others to the CFR's litigation potential.[202] Having clarified and interpreted many CFR provisions, and by building its own fundamental rights jurisprudence on a par with that of the ECtHR, the ECJ is also fast becoming a fundamental rights court itself.[203]

Binding all EU institutions and bodies, the CFR is also now a significant point of reference during the legislative process, regardless of whether the legislation in question gives specific expression to fundamental rights or concerns EU policy potentially affecting fundamental rights.[204] Even before it became legally binding, the Commission proclaimed that it would treat the CFR as such[205] and would use it to scrutinise the compatibility of all proposed legislation.[206] In order to ensure greater attention to the potential impact of any legislative proposal on CRF entitlements, in 2005 the Commission adopted a new set of guidelines on the preparation of impact assessments.[207] Since the Lisbon Treaty, such *ex ante* scrutiny has been implemented by the Commission via its 'Strategy for the Effective Implementation of the CFR' ('CFR Strategy'),[208] which aims to promote a 'fundamental rights culture' at all stages of the legislative process, from preparatory consultations and

---

[201] See European Commission, *2014 Report on the Application of the EU Charter of Fundamental Rights*, Brussels, 8 May 2015, COM(2015) 191 final, p. 1. See also C. Ladenburger, 'European Union Institutional Report', in J. Laffranque (ed.), *The Protection of Fundamental Rights Post-Lisbon* Tartu (Estonia: Tartu University Press, 2012) pp. 141–215 at pp. 149–51.

[202] Cf. Ladenburger, p. 150 and, more implicitly, S. Iglesias Sánchez, 'The Court and the Charter: The Impact of the Entry into Force of the Lisbon Treaty on the ECJ's Approach to Fundamental Rights', *Common Market Law Review*, 49 (2012), 1565–612 at 1577.

[203] Cf. J. Kühling, 'Fundamental Rights', in A. Von Bogdandy and J. Bast (eds.), *Principles of European Constitutional Law*, 2nd rev. edn. (Oxford: Hart/Beck, 2010) pp. 479–514 at p. 481.

[204] Ferraro and Carmona, 'Fundamental Rights in the European Union', p. 3.

[205] European Commission Communication on the Legal Nature of the Charter of Fundamental Rights of the Union (COM [2000] 644 final, Brussels, 11.10.2000).

[206] European Commission Memorandum from the President and Mr. Vitorino on the application of the Charter of Fundamental Rights of the European Union (SEC (2001) 380/3, Brussels, 13.3.2001).

[207] European Commission, *Impact Assessment Guidelines on Procedural Rules* (SEC (2005) 791/3, 15.6.2005).

[208] European Commission Communication on a Strategy for the Effective Implementation of the Charter of Fundamental Rights by the European Union, (COM [2010] 573 final, Brussels, 19.10.2010).

initial drafting, through amendment up to legality checks of the final text. The impact assessment, to which all draft legislation is subject, is to include, if relevant, examination of CFR compliance. This involves identifying, on the basis of a 'fundamental rights checklist' which mirrors Article 52(1) CFR, fundamental rights that are liable to be affected, the degree of interference, and its necessity and proportionality.[209] The CFR Strategy checklist, included in the fundamental rights section of the Commission's 'better regulation toolbox',[210] and introduced to accompany the Commission's 2015 Better Regulation Guidelines,[211] provides step-by-step guidance on how to assess fundamental rights when conducting impact assessments. After assessment, proposals linked with fundamental rights must include a specific non-standardised recital explaining their CFR compliance.[212] If EU legislation interfering with fundamental rights does not conform with the generic limitation provision in Article 52(1) CFR, the legislation in question is considered void. Since 2010, in accordance with its role as guardian of the Treaties, the Commission has also published annual reports on the application of the CFR. These act as frameworks for monitoring progress, indicating how the CFR has been taken into account by EU institutions and by national authorities when implementing EU law.

Similar initiatives have also been implemented by the Council through the adoption of detailed Guidelines,[213] which act as non-binding advice to 'help the Council's preparatory body take the steps necessary to identify and deal with fundamental rights issues arising in connection with the proposals under discussion'.[214] In ensuring the CFR's effective implementation, the Council has also stressed the importance of

---

[209] More detailed guidance on this is provided to Commission staff by way of the European Commission Staff Working Document, *Operational Guidance on Taking Account of Fundamental Rights in Commission Impact Assessments* (SEC (2011) 567 final, Brussels, 6.5.2011).

[210] See 'Tool #24: Fundamental Rights and Human Rights', in the European Commission *Better Regulation Toolbox*, available from: ec.europa.eu/smart-regulation/guidelines/docs/br_toolbox_en.pdf, pp. 176–9.

[211] European Commission Staff Working Document, *Better Regulation Guidelines* (SWD (2015) 110 final, Strasbourg, 19.5.2015).

[212] European Commission Communication (COM [2010] 573 final), p. 7.

[213] Council of the European Union, *Fundamental Rights Compatibility: Guidelines for Council Preparatory Bodies* (Luxembourg: Publications Office of the European Union, 2015).

[214] Ibid., p. 2.

cooperation with the FRA regarding policy and legislative development.[215] To this end it has, for example, requested the FRA to submit opinions on legislative proposals. Nevertheless, whether or not the Council's commitment to considering the CFR actually contributes to increased fundamental rights scrutiny of legislative proposals is a matter of opinion.[216] The EP also scrutinises draft legislation for its CFR compatibility, and did so even prior to the Lisbon Treaty. In addition, MEPs use written and oral questions to scrutinise the Council and Commission's legislative proposals for CFR compliance.[217] The EP also uses its Article 263 TFEU powers of annulment effectively to ensure that all adopted EU legislation respects fundamental rights.[218]

Fundamental Rights in EU Secondary Legislation

The EU's internal fundamental rights policy is not restricted to primary law, namely, the Treaties, the CFR and general principles, but is influenced by 'soft law', considered later, and finds expression in three types of secondary legislation:[219] Regulations, which are of general application and directly applicable in all member states; Directives, which must be transposed by member states into their national law; and Decisions of general application, or aimed at a specific addressee, which are legally binding.

Because the EU has competence only to develop a fundamental rights policy where the Treaties provide the requisite legal basis, secondary EU legislation giving effect to a broad spectrum of fundamental rights is fragmented and its visibility varied. Typically, it either gives specific expression to a particular fundamental right, for which there are few

---

[215] Council of the EU Conclusions on the role of the Council of the European Union in ensuring the effective implementation of the Charter of Fundamental Rights of the European Union (Doc. 6387/11, Brussels, 11.2.2011) , pp. 18–20.

[216] G. N. Toggenburg, 'The EU Charter: Moving from a Fundamental Rights Ornament to a European Fundamental Rights Order', in G. Palmisano (ed.), *Making the Charter of Fundamental Rights a Living Instrument* (Leiden: Brill Nijhoff, 2015), p. 22; J. Morijn, 'Kissing Awake a Sleeping Beauty? The Charter of Fundamental Rights in EU and Member States' Policy Practice' in V. Kosta, N. Skoutaris and V. Tzevelekos (eds.), *The EU Accession to the ECHR* (Oxford: Hart, 2014), p. 138.

[217] See, for example, European Commission Staff Working Document, *2013 Report on the Application of the EU CFR of Fundamental Rights* (SWD (2014) 141 final, Brussels, 14.4.2014), p. 8.

[218] For example, the EP sought the partial annulment of the Family Reunification Directive in Case C-540/03, *Parliament v Council*, which led to the judgment of 27 June 2006 (OJ L 251, 3.10.2003, p. 12).

[219] Article 288 TFEU defines the basic attributes of each.

legal bases, or is designed to implement another EU competence, which must be balanced with fundamental rights and, as such, incidentally sets fundamental rights standards.[220] The various categories of fundamental rights enshrined in the CFR find some expression in EU secondary law, of which the following are some of the more prominent examples.

Equality and Discrimination

Gender equality, now enshrined in Article 23 CFR, was the earliest manifestation of the EU's internal fundamental rights policy, with a legal basis dating back to the Article 119 TEEC prohibition of sex discrimination regarding remuneration, incorporated at the EEC's inception for purely economic reasons. Preventing member states from gaining a competitive advantage by offering lower rates of pay to women ensured a level playing field. It is not surprising, therefore, that the first legislative act adopted in the field of gender equality was the 1975 Equal Pay Directive,[221] shortly succeeded by the Equal Treatment Directive,[222] which broadened the scope of gender equality to other aspects of employment. Other legislative instruments were adopted in the late 1970s and 1980s to ensure equal treatment between men and women in the fields of occupational social security[223] and self-employment,[224] although the latter included only weak member state obligations and played a minor role in practice.[225] The protection of gender equality in employment

---

[220] For detailed discussion, see E. Muir, 'The Fundamental Rights Implications of EU Legislation: Some Constitutional Challenges'.

[221] Council Directive 75/11/EEC of 10 February 1975 on the approximation of the laws of the member states relating to the application of the principle of equal pay for men and women (OJ L 045, 19.02.75) (repealed by the Recast Directive 2006/54).

[222] Council Directive 76/207/EEC of 9 February 1976 on the implementation of the principle of equal treatment for men and women as regards access to employment, vocational training and promotion and working conditions (OJ L 039, 14.02.76) (amended by Directive 2002/73, repealed by the Recast Directive 2006/54).

[223] Council Directive 79/7/EEC of 19 December 1978 on the progressive implementation of the principle of equal treatment for men and women in matters of social security (OJ L 006, 10.01.79), and Council Directive 86/378/EEC of 24 July 1986 on the implementation of the principle of equal treatment for men and women in occupational social security schemes (OJ L 225, 12.08.86) (amended by Directive 96/97).

[224] Council Directive 86/613/EEC of 11 December 1986 on the application of the principle of equal treatment between men and women engaged in an activity, including agriculture, in a self-employed capacity, and on the protection of self-employed women during pregnancy and motherhood (OJ L 359, 19.12.86) (repealed by Directive 2010/41).

[225] European Network of Legal Experts in the Field of Gender Equality, S. Burri and S. Prechal, *EU Gender Equality Law: Update 2013* (European Commission, 2014), p. 13.

expanded in the 1990s through Directives on pregnancy and maternity leave,[226] parental leave,[227] part-time work[228] and the burden of proof in sex discrimination cases,[229] many of which have since been amended, repealed or replaced, in order to modernise, harmonise and strengthen the protection they provide.

Prior to the introduction of provisions in the 1997 Treaty of Amsterdam dealing expressly with gender equality, general Treaty provisions, relating to the single market or objectives of the Treaties, had to be relied on as the legal basis for secondary legislation in this field.[230] Although a vast range of legislation had been adopted, it only applied in the context of employment and social security, and only addressed discrimination on the ground of sex. Lobbying by public interest groups in the 1990s, combined with concerns of resurgent extreme nationalism in some member states, stimulated enough political will among EU leaders to grant the Community competence to combat discrimination, both inside and outside the labour market, on grounds other than sex (Article 13(1) TEC), the Treaty of Amsterdam's most significant contribution to ensuring equality at the EU level.

Article 13(1) TEC (now Article 19 TFEU) provided the legal basis for two landmark Directives, adopted in 2000, prohibiting direct and indirect discrimination in the employment field on grounds other than sex. The Employment Equality Directive[231] prohibited discrimination on the basis of sexual orientation, religion or belief, age or disability, while the Race Directive[232] prohibited discrimination on the basis of race or ethnicity in

---

[226] Council Directive 92/85/EEC of 19 October 1992 on the introduction of measures to encourage improvements in the safety and health at work of pregnant workers and workers who have recently given birth or are breastfeeding (OJ L 348, 28.11.92).

[227] Council Directive 96/34/EC of 3 June 1996 on the framework agreement on parental leave concluded by UNICE, CEEP and the ETUC (OJ L 145, 19.06.96). (repealed by Council Directive 2010/18/EU). 'A directive on parental leave had been proposed as long ago as 1984, but was consistently opposed by the UK Government on financial grounds' (E. Ellis and P. Watson, *EU Anti-Discrimination Law*, 2nd edn., (Oxford University Press, 2013), p.18).

[228] Council Directive 97/81/EC of 15 December 1997 concerning the Framework Agreement on part-time work concluded by UNICE, CEEP and the ETUC (OJ L 014, 20.01.98).

[229] Council Directive 97/80/EC of 15 December 1997 on the burden of proof in cases of discrimination based on sex (OJ L 014, 20.01.98).

[230] E. Ellis and P. Watson, *EU Anti-Discrimination Law*, p.16.

[231] Council Directive 2000/78/EC of 27 November 2000 establishing a legal framework for equal treatment in employment and occupation (OJ L 303/16, 2.12.2000).

[232] Council Directive 2000/43/EC of 29 June 2000 implementing the principle of equal treatment between persons irrespective of racial or ethnic origin (OJ L 180/22, 19.7.2000).

the context of employment, access to goods and services, welfare and social security. These significant extensions to EU anti-discrimination law 'recognised that in order to allow individuals to reach their full potential in the employment market, it was also essential to guarantee them equal access to areas such as health, education and housing.'[233] In 2004 the first Directive to address sex discrimination beyond employment was adopted,[234] broadening the scope of gender equality to include access to, and the supply of, goods and services. However, it failed to offer protection as extensive as the Race Directive, only guaranteeing equal treatment in relation to social security and not to the broader welfare system. The Horizontal Directive,[235] aimed at extending equal treatment under the Employment Equality Directive beyond the labour market, has been under debate in the EU's legislative institutions since 2008.[236] However, while some progress has been made to break deadlock over the proposal in the Council, where unanimity is required for its adoption,[237] there are indications that it might be too controversial ever to be accepted.

Data Protection

Data protection, a manifestation of the right to privacy, is another of the EU's long-standing fundamental rights concerns, with the need for a Union regime in this regard first recognised in the 1970s.[238] A right to protection of personal data, which finds expression in Article 16 TFEU (ex Article 286 TEC), was elevated to a free-standing fundamental right,

---

[233] European Union Agency for Fundamental Rights and Council of Europe, *Handbook on European Non-Discrimination Law* (Luxembourg: Publications Office of the European Union, 2010), p. 14.

[234] Council Directive 2004/113/EC of 13 December 2004 implementing the principle of equal treatment between men and women in the access to and supply of goods and services (OJ L373/37, 21.12.2004).

[235] Commission Proposal for a Council Directive on implementing the principle of equal treatment between persons irrespective of religion or belief, disability, age or sexual orientation (COM/2008/426 final, 2.7.2008).

[236] See Council of the European Union Press Release, 'Employment, Social Policy, Health and Consumer Affairs' (17943/1/11 REV 1, Brussels, 1.12.2011), p. 11.

[237] Council of the European Union Proposal for a Council Directive on implementing the principle of equal treatment between persons irrespective of religion or belief, disability, age or sexual orientation – Progress Report (9336/16, Brussels, 3.6.2016).

[238] The European Parliament passed a series of resolutions on the protection of the rights of the individual in the face of technical developments in data processing including those of 13 March 1975 [1975] OJ C60/48; of 3 May 1976 [1976] OJ C100/27; of 8 May 1979 [1979] OJ C140/34; and of 9 March 1982 [1982] OJ C87/39.

distinct from the right to respect for private life (Article 7 CFR), by Article 8 CFR. The protection of personal data under secondary EU law, however, predates these primary law provisions. Encompassing two of the core ambitions of European integration, the protection of fundamental rights and the effective functioning of the single market, the Data Protection Directive (DPD)[239] was adopted in 1995 to harmonise member states' data protection laws and to give substance to, and to expand, the CE's 1981 Data Protection Convention (DPC),[240] to which all the then-fifteen EU member states were party. However, as a result of limitations in EU competence at the time, the material scope of the DPD was restricted to only single market matters and was, therefore, narrower than that of the DPC. The scope of data protection in the EU has since been extended to cover judicial cooperation and law enforcement,[241] as well as certain types of information exchange between member states.[242] Additional, more detailed secondary legislation to achieve the necessary clarity in balancing data privacy with other legitimate interests has also been adopted regarding areas covered by the DPD.[243]

In December 2015, the EP and Council agreed on a data protection reform package.[244] Described as a key building block of the digital single market, and essential to protect the fundamental rights to privacy and protection of personal data,[245] it consists of a general Data Protection

---

[239] Council Directive 95/46/EC on the protection of individuals with regard to the processing of personal data and on the free movement of such data (OJ L281/31, 1995).

[240] Council of Europe Convention for the Protection of Individuals with regard to Automatic Processing of Personal Data (Strasbourg, CETS No. 108, 1981).

[241] Council of the European Union (2008), Council Framework Decision 2008/977/JHA of 27 November 2008 on the protection of personal data processed in the framework of police and judicial cooperation in criminal matters (OJ L 350, 2008) ('Data Protection Framework Decision').

[242] Council of the European Union (2009), Council Framework Decision 2009/315/JHA of 26 February 2009 on the organisation and content of the exchange of information extracted from the criminal record between member states (OJ L 93, 2009); Council of the European Union (2000), Council Decision 2000/642/JHA of 17 October 2000 concerning arrangements for cooperation between financial intelligence units of the member states in respect of exchanging information, (OJ L 271, 2000).

[243] See for example Council Directive 2002/58/EC of the European Parliament and of the Council of 12 July 2002 concerning the processing of personal data and the protection of privacy in the electronic communications sector (OJ L 201/37, 2000).

[244] See European Commission Press Release, 'Agreement on Commission's EU data protection reform will boost Digital Single Market' (IP/15/6321, Brussels, 15.12.2015).

[245] European Commission, '2015 Report on the Application of the EU Charter of Fundamental Rights' (COM [2016] 265 final, Brussels, 19.5.2016).

Regulation[246] and a Data Protection Directive for police and criminal justice authorities,[247] which will replace existing legislation when they come into operation in May 2018.

Social and Economic Rights

Although the EU's commitment to improving working conditions was explicit from the inception of the European integration project, its social policy has been slow to break free from the 'economic imperative' of justifying supranational interference in this field on the single market rationale.[248] Notwithstanding the fact that socio-economic entitlements were explicitly mentioned in the Preamble to the 1986 SEA – where the CE and EU's Social Charters were listed as sources of fundamental rights for the Community – member states remained reluctant to delegate social policy competences to the EU, except in the field of occupational health and safety, deemed closely associated with the single market.[249] Pursuant to Article 153 TFEU (ex Article 137 TEC), the EU has been mandated to protect workers by establishing minimum working environment requirements since the 2001 Treaty of Nice. The Commission has interpreted this provision widely so as to adopt such legislation as that on working time.[250] Health and safety at work continue to be ensured generally through the Framework Directive,[251] and a number of specific directives regarding particular risks have been adopted more recently.[252]

---

[246] European Commission Proposal for a Regulation of the European Parliament and Council on the protection of individuals with regard to the processing of personal data and on the free movement of such data (COM [2012] 11 final, Brussels, 25.1.2012).

[247] European Commission Proposal for a Directive on the protection of individuals with regard to the processing of personal data by competent authorities for the purposes of prevention, investigation, detection or prosecution of criminal offences or the execution of criminal penalties, and the free movement of such data (COM [2012] 10 final, Brussels, 25.1.2012).

[248] T. K. Hervey and J. Kenner, *Economic and Social Rights under the EU Charter of Fundamental Rights: A Legal Perspective* (Portland, OR: Hart, 2006), p. 45.

[249] G. Schwellnus, 'Social Rights: The EU and ILO', in G. Falkner and P. Müller (eds.) *EU Policies in a Global Perspective: Shaping or Taking International Regimes?* (London: Routledge, 2014).

[250] Council Directive 2003/88/EC of 4 November 2003 concerning aspects of the organisation of working time (OJ L 299, 18.11.2003), consolidating Directive 93/104/EC and its amending Directive 2000/34/EC.

[251] Council Directive 89/391/EEC of 12 June 1989 on the introduction of measures to encourage improvements in the safety and health of workers at work (OJ L 183, 29.6.1989).

[252] See for example Council Directive 2009/148/EC of 30 November 2009 on the protection of workers from the risks related to exposure to asbestos at work (OJ L 330, 16.12.2009); Council Directive 2006/95/EC (OJ L 96, 29.3.2014) ('Low Voltage Directive').

Other Fundamental Rights

EU legislation often sets standards for the protection of classical fundamental rights in relation to a specific category or class of persons, including victims of crime and children. However, because of the EU's lack of competence, there is a notable absence of Union legislation giving effect to collective rights. While some collective rights, such as information and consultation rights concerning collective redundancies[253] and transfers of undertakings,[254] have been enshrined in secondary law, others have not. In 2012 the Commission adopted a proposal on the right to take collective action, which clarified that, in the single market, economic freedoms do not prevail over the right to strike.[255] There was no explicit provision in the Treaties bestowing competence upon the EU to legislate in this respect. Indeed, Article 153(5) TFEU excluded the right to strike from the issues capable of being regulated by way of Directives setting minimum standards. Accordingly, the appropriate legal basis for the proposal, relied on by the Commission, was Article 352 TFEU, reserved for cases where the Treaties do not provide the power to implement action necessary to obtain a Treaty objective.[256] A dozen national parliaments issued reasoned opinions stipulating why they believed the proposal did not comply with the principle of subsidiarity.[257] As a result, the Commission recognised that its proposal was unlikely to gather the necessary political support in the EP and Council to secure adoption[258] and decided to withdraw it.[259]

Soft Law Instruments Addressing Fundamental Rights

In addition to hard law sources discussed earlier, the EU's fundamental rights policy includes a vast array of soft law measures intended to

---

[253] Council Directive 98/59/EC of 20 July 1998 on the approximation of laws regarding collective redundancies (OJ L 225, 12.8.1998).

[254] Council Directive 2001/23/EC (OJ L 82, 22.3.2001).

[255] European Commission Proposal for a Council Regulation on the exercise of the right to take collective action within the context of the freedom of establishment and the freedom to provide services ('Monti II') (COM [2012] 130 final, Brussels, 21.3.2012).

[256] Ibid., 3.2.

[257] See Article 6 and Article 7(2) TFEU Protocol No. 2 on the application of the principles of subsidiarity and proportionality (OJ 115, 9.05.2008).

[258] Report from the Commission, *Annual Report 2012 on Subsidiarity and Proportionality* (COM [2013] 566 final, Brussels, 30.7.2013), p. 8.

[259] European Commission Minutes of the 2017th meeting of the Commission on 26 September 2012 (PV (2012) 2017, Brussels, 10.10.2012).

influence, but not direct, institutional or member state practice. Although not without its ambiguities, the term 'soft law' generally refers to a variety of non-binding quasi-legal instruments with some normative quality,[260] several of which have been encountered already, including the EU's historic Declarations relating to respect for fundamental rights, the CFR in its original form as a proclamation and the internal strategy documents, guidelines and rules of procedure of various EU institutions aimed at ensuring CFR compliance. Numerous rights-specific soft law instruments, aimed at ensuring effective realisation of particular fundamental rights enshrined in EU hard law, have also been adopted by different institutional actors in various forms, including Communications, Opinions, Guidelines, Action Plans, Working Papers, Handbooks and Strategies. A comprehensive overview of all rights-specific soft law documents is beyond the scope of this study. The following example will, therefore, serve merely as an illustration.

The prohibition of slavery and forced labour (Article 5 CFR) is enshrined in various enforceable pieces of EU legislation, such as the Human Trafficking Directive.[261] In turn, these are complemented by a wide range of soft law measures adopted to influence the policy taken by the EU and member states. The Commission's 'EU Strategy towards the Eradication of Trafficking in Human Beings 2012–16,'[262] for example, proposes a series of concrete actions, at both the EU and member state levels. In order to deliver on these commitments, in 2014 the FRA adopted a handbook on guardianship for children deprived of parental care, recognising the risks of such minors becoming victims of human trafficking or other forms of exploitation.[263] The same year the EP passed two Resolutions, one on undocumented women migrants, noting their

---

[260] For further discussion on the concept and classification of EU soft law, see L. A. J. Senden, 'Soft Law and Its Implications for Institutional Balance in the EC', *Utrecht Law Review*, 1(2) (2005), 79–99 at 81-3.

[261] European Parliament Directive 2011/36/EU of 5 April 2011 on preventing and combating trafficking in human beings and protecting its victims, and replacing Council Framework Decision 2002/629/JHA (OJ L 101/1, 15.4.2011).

[262] Commission Communication on the EU Strategy towards the Eradication of Trafficking in Human Beings 2012–2016 (COM [2012] 286 final, Brussels, 19.6.2012).

[263] Fundamental Rights Agency, *Guardianship for Children Deprived of Parental Care – a Handbook to Reinforce Guardianship Systems to Cater for the Specific Needs of Child Victims of Trafficking* (Luxembourg: Publications Office of the European Union, 2014).

particular vulnerability to traffickers,[264] and the other on sexual exploitation, specifically addressing prostitution.[265]

Enforcement Mechanisms

Just as the Ombudsman endeavours to ensure that the EU administration complies with fundamental rights, EU institutions have various other mechanisms at their disposal to ensure compliance by member states. When political pressure, such as the Commission's public condemnation,[266] fails to yield positive results, two enforcement mechanisms – 'infringement proceedings' and 'Article 7 preventive and sanctioning procedures' – can be activated.

Infringement Proceedings

Pursuant to Article 258 TFEU, if the Commission considers that a member state has failed to fulfil a Treaty obligation, such as correctly transposing a Directive, a letter of formal notice can be sent to the member state inviting it to submit its observations. If it fails to respond, or the Commission is not persuaded by its reply, the Commission may issue a reasoned opinion on the matter. If the member state fails to comply within the time provided, the Commission may then bring the matter before the ECJ. In the event of non-compliance with the ECJ's judgment, the process is repeated, culminating in the matter being brought before the ECJ again, this time with the prospect of a financial penalty under Article 260 TFEU.

The Commission has used its Article 258 TFEU powers effectively on a number of occasions to ensure respect for fundamental rights at national level. For example, in 2012 it launched infringement proceedings against Malta for its failure to implement correctly the right of same-sex spouses to join EU citizens residing there. The offending Maltese legislation was subsequently modified to ensure compatibility with EU non-discrimination law.[267] In 2014 and 2015, proceedings were launched against the Czech Republic and Slovakia, respectively, for discrimination

---

[264] European Parliament Resolution of 4 February 2014 on undocumented women migrants in the European Union (2013/2115(INI)).

[265] European Parliament Resolution of 26 February 2014 on sexual exploitation and prostitution and its impact on gender equality (2013/2103(INI)).

[266] See for example Commission Press Release IP/03/1047 'Commission concerned at member states' failure to implement new racial equality rules.'.

[267] European Commission, '2012 Report on the Application of the EU Charter of Fundamental Rights' (COM [2013] 271 final, Brussels, 8.5.2013), p. 8.

against Roma children in education, resulting in domestic legislative amendments in both member states.[268] In May 2016, the Commission initiated infringement proceedings against Hungary on the same grounds.[269] The Hungarian Government initially responded to the letter of formal notice dismissively.[270] Defiance of Article 258 TFEU action on the part of the Hungarian government is not novel. In April 2012, the Commission initiated infringement proceedings against Hungary concerning various issues, only one of which was satisfactorily resolved. Consequently, for the first time, the Commission brought infringement proceedings before the ECJ regarding Hungary's non-compliance with certain Directives and corresponding key provisions of the CFR.[271] The ECJ's adverse ruling against Hungary, in November 2012, prompted a remedial judicial and legislative response at the domestic level.[272]

Article 7 Preventive and Sanctioning Procedures

Article 7 TEU provides that if, following a proposal by either the Commission or one-third of member states, and having obtained the EP's consent, the European Council unanimously determines there to be a 'serious and persistent breach' by a member state of the founding values enshrined in Article 2 TEU, including respect for human rights, democracy and equality, some of the offending state's Treaty rights can be suspended.

Concern for fundamental rights standards in central and eastern European (CEE) applicant states once they joined the EU provided the impetus for providing this sanctioning procedure.[273] It could accordingly be described as an internalisation of the Copenhagen accession criteria

---

[268] FRA, *Fundamental Rights Report 2016* (Luxembourg: Publications Office of the European Union, 2016), p. 85; and European Commission News Report, 'Parliament Adopting a Schools Act Amendment with Provisions Likely to Perpetuate Segregation of Roma Children' (European Network of Legal Experts in Gender Equality and Non-Discrimination, 4.8.2015).

[269] European Commission Fact Sheet, 'May Infringements' Package: Key Decisions – 'Commission requests Hungary to put an end to the discrimination of Roma children in education" (MEMO/16/1823, Brussels, 26.5.2016).

[270] János Lázár, Minister of the Prime Minister's Office of Hungary, 'No one can be sent back to Hungary' (Website of the Prime Minister's Office, 26.5.2016), available from www .kormany.hu/en/prime-minister-s-office/news/no-one-can-be-sent-back-to-hungary.

[271] The Court's ruling upheld the Commission's assessment (Case C-286/12, *European Commission v Hungary*).

[272] See European Commission Press Release, 'European Commission closes infringement procedure on forced retirement of Hungarian judges' (IP/13/1112, Brussels, 20.11.2013).

[273] S. Peers and A. Ward (eds.), *The European Union Charter of Fundamental Rights*, (Oxford: Hart, 2004), p. 59.

(discussed later), which rendered respect for fundamental rights a prerequisite of membership. Nevertheless, its inadequacies became apparent in 2000 when addressing a potential fundamental rights crisis in Austria, prompting substantial revision of the Treaty provision. The 2001 Nice Treaty accordingly added the less cumbersome Article 7(1) TEU preventive procedure. Nevertheless, neither the preventive nor sanctioning mechanisms enshrined in Article 7 TEU have ever been applied in practice, arguably because of the high procedural threshold, partisan politics and weak normative consensus.[274]

By 2012 the EP had voiced various concerns about constitutional and other developments in Hungary to which reference has already been made.[275] A 2012 LIBE report in this regard[276] suggested assessing the appropriateness of various measures, including Article 7(1) TEU, but did not recommend resorting to the sanctioning procedure at that time. In 2015, this time regarding a domestic consultation on migration and a call for public debate on the death penalty, the EP urged the Commission to activate the initial in-depth monitoring stage of the Article 7(1) preventive mechanism against Hungary.[277] In its official response, the Commission, deeming the procedure to be a political mechanism of last resort, intended only for exceptional situations,[278] stipulated that the conditions to activate Article 7 had not yet been met.[279] In December 2015 the EP repeated its call to the Commission, but to no avail.[280]

With Article 258 TFEU infringement proceedings seemingly ineffective in tackling systematic failures, and an apparent reluctance at the EU level to utilise Article 7 TEU, the EP has repeatedly called for

[274] See U. Sedelmeier, 'Anchoring Democracy from Above? The European Union and Democratic Backsliding in Hungary and Romania after Accession', *Journal of Common Market Studies*, 52(1) (2014), 105–21.

[275] J. Sargentini and A. Dimitrovs, 'The European Parliament's Role: Towards New Copenhagen Criteria for Existing Member States?' *Journal of Common Market Studies*, 54(5) (2016), 1085–92, p. 1108.

[276] European Parliament, 'Recent Political Developments in Hungary' (P7_TA (2012) 0053, Strasbourg, 2013/C 249 E/08).

[277] European Parliament, 'Situation in Hungary' (P8_TA (2015) 0227, Strasbourg, adopted 10.06.2015).

[278] European Commission Communication, *Article 7 TEU - Respect for and Promotion of the Values on Which the Union Is Based* (COM [2003] 606 final, 15.10.2003).

[279] European Commission, 'Follow up to the European Parliament Resolution on the Situation in Hungary' (SP (2015) 529, 23.9.2015).

[280] European Parliament, 'Situation in Hungary: Follow-Up to the European Parliament Resolution of 10 June 2015' (P8_TA PROV (2015) 0461, Strasbourg, adopted 16.12.2015).

improvements in the EU's enforcement mechanisms, including the creation of a 'new Copenhagen mechanism',[281] whereby member states' adherence to the EU's founding values is ensured by ongoing monitoring of their compliance with the Copenhagen criteria. The EP has not been alone in criticising the existing institutional arrangements and calling for improvements. In 2012, the Commission President demanded a more developed set of instruments as an alternative to the 'nuclear option' of Article 7,[282] and scholars have made various proposals to this effect.[283] In 2014, the Commission established a new EU framework to resolve situations of systemic threat to the rule of law that could not be effectively dealt with by infringement proceedings.[284] Entailing assessment, recommendations and follow-up, the assumption is that, by addressing an emerging problem through structured dialogue, there will be no need for recourse to Article 7 TEU. Nevertheless, the framework has been subject to criticism[285] and calls for additional mechanisms systematically to monitor compliance by member states with the EU's founding values persist.

4.4   External Policy

Today, the EU is 'one of the most important, if not the most important, normative powers in the world',[286] a value-driven standard-setting force compelling other actors to adhere to certain norms, including respect for fundamental rights. However, in keeping with the Community's original

---

[281] European Parliament, 'Situation of Fundamental Rights in the European Union (2012)' (P7_TA PROV (2014) 0173, Strasbourg, 27.2.2012).

[282] President of the European Commission, 'State of the Union 2012 Address' (SPEECH/12/596).

[283] See for example, J.-W. Müller, 'Safeguarding Democracy Inside the EU: Brussels and the Future of Liberal Order', *Transatlantic Academy 2012–2013 Paper Studies No. 3* (2013); S. Carrera and A. F. Atger, 'L'affaire des Roms: A Challenge to the EU's Area of Freedom, Security and Justice', *CEPS Paper 'Liberty and Security in Europe'* (2010).

[284] European Commission Communication on a new EU Framework to strengthen the Rule of Law (COM [2014] 158 final, Brussels, 11.3.2014).

[285] See C. Closa, 'Reinforcing EU Monitoring of the Rule of Law: Normative Arguments, Institutional Proposals and the Procedural Limitations' in C. Closa and D. Kochenov (eds.), Reinforcing Rule of Law Oversight in the European Union (Cambridge University Press, 2016), pp. 15–35; D. Kochenov and L. Pech, 'Monitoring and Enforcement of the Rule of Law in the EU: Rhetoric and Reality', *European Constitutional Law Review*, 11(3) (2015), 512–40.

[286] I. A. Manners, 'The Normative Ethics of the European Union', *International Affairs*, 84 (1) (2008), 45–60 at 59.

conception as a resolutely economic supranational organisation, ethical considerations were initially entirely absent from its external affairs. The subsequent establishment of respect for fundamental rights as a founding value of European integration, and a key element of Community identity, provided the normative basis upon which the EC/EU established its distinctive international identity as a protector and promoter of 'human rights' worldwide.[287] External events, such as the Ugandan atrocities in the 1970s and the conclusion of the Cold War in 1991, in conjunction with the evolution of the international human rights regime,[288] also influenced, and gave impetus to, the Community's gradual emergence as a normative actor on the world stage. Insisting on the universality of human rights and rejecting the objection that their promotion interferes with national sovereignty,[289] the EU now incorporates human rights considerations into all its external activities.

Political conditionality, present in all the EU's external relations, has been aptly defined as 'the linking, by a state or international organisation, of perceived benefits to another state – such as aid, trade concessions, cooperation agreements, political contacts, or international organisation membership – to the fulfilment of conditions relating to the protection of human rights and the advancement of democratic principles'.[290] In the positive sense, this involves the provision of benefits in exchange for fulfilment of certain conditions, while negative conditionality manifests in the reduction, suspension or termination of those benefits upon violation of these requirements.

While the EU uses common instruments to promote human rights in its relations with all other states, these pursue different policy objectives according to whether the state in question is incapable of joining the EU, because, for example, it is not in Europe, or although it may be European,

---

[287] The EU deploys the better-known term 'human rights' in relation to its external policy, despite technically referring to the broader category of fundamental rights, including, for example, the rights of the child.

[288] For detailed discussion on how the international human rights regime influenced the Community's evolution as a normative player, see G. Balducci, 'The Study of the EU Promotion of Human Rights: The Importance of International and Internal Factors', GARNET Working Paper No. 61/08 (2008).

[289] European Political Cooperation, 'Statement by the Twelve on Human Rights', Brussels, 21 July 1986, reprinted in Press and Information Office of the Federal Republic of German, European Political Co-Operation (EPC), 5th edn. (1988), p. 264.

[290] K. E. Smith, 'The Use of Political Conditionality in the EU's Relations with Third Countries: How Effective?', SPS Working Paper 1997/7 (1997), San Domenico di Fiesole: EUI: 1–37.

is unlikely to join in the foreseeable future (a third state); is a member of the EEA and by extension the single market (a non-EU EEA state) or is a candidate for EU membership (an applicant state).

Third States

For the first few decades of its existence, the Community promoted human rights in third states primarily through dialogue and declaratory diplomacy with more robust instruments deployed only from the late 1980s. Regarding the promotion and protection of human rights abroad as an intrinsic part of its duty in representing the European electorate,[291] the EP was instrumental in bringing about this change. Having gained direct democratic legitimacy in 1979, and in the light of public discontent, the EP took a more vocal stand in enunciating the principle of European responsibility[292] by increasing pressure on other institutional actors through the various means at its disposal, notably by issuing Resolutions and reports, and by refusing to approve external agreements lacking sufficient human rights safeguards.[293] These activities are documented extensively elsewhere.[294]

However, the arguably mixed motives behind the Community's adoption of human rights as an external policy objective have been subject to debate. While there was seemingly a genuine altruistic consensus that all people are entitled to respect for their fundamental human rights, regardless of their nation state, security interests in strengthening the international order and identity-building imperatives ought not to be overlooked. It has also been argued that the Community initially chose to

---

[291] European Parliament, *The European Parliament and Human Rights* (Luxembourg: OOPEC, 1994) p. 7.

[292] See European Parliament Resolution on Human Rights in the World (OJ C 161/58, 20/6.1983).

[293] See for example European Parliament Resolution on the financial protocols with Syria, Morocco, Algeria, Egypt, Tunisia, Jordan, Lebanon and Israel and these countries' respect for human rights and international agreements (OJ C39/50, 15.1.1992); European Parliament Resolution on the draft agreement on the conclusion of customs union between the EU and Turkey (OJ C56/99, 16.2.1995).

[294] See H. Fischer, S. Lorion and G. Ulrich, *Beyond Activism: The Impact of the Resolutions and Other Activities of the European Parliament in the Field of Human Rights outside the European Union* (Venice: Marsilio, 2007), ch. 2; E. Fierro, *The EU's Approach to Human Rights Conditionality in Practice* (The Hague: Martinus Nijhoff, 2003), ch. 1; and P. Alston (ed.), *The EU and Human Rights* (Oxford University Press, 1999), ch.25.

promote human rights through its external activities in order to enhance its legitimacy in the international arena.[295]

Whatever the reason, the Community gradually gave its external projection of human rights a legal basis. In the aftermath of the Cold War, the 1992 Maastricht Treaty declared the development and consolidation of human rights to be an objective of both the Community's CFSP and development cooperation.[296] The 2001 Treaty of Nice subsequently established the promotion of human rights as an objective of all forms of Community cooperation with third states.[297] The Lisbon Treaty later situated human rights at the epicentre of all the EU's external relations by stipulating that 'the Union's action on the international scene shall be guided by the principles which have inspired its own creation ... and which it seeks to advance in the wider world', namely, democracy, the rule of law and the universality and indivisibility of human rights.[298] Giving practical expression to the Lisbon Treaty's unequivocal commitment, in 2012 the Council agreed on an ambitious 'EU Strategic Framework on Human Rights and Democracy', which professed that 'the EU will promote human rights in all areas of its external activity without exception'.[299] With regard to policy formation and implementation, the Strategic Framework was accompanied by a 2012–14 Action Plan, which listed almost one hundred actions for the EU and member states to implement in order to achieve the overarching aim of enhancing the coherence and effectiveness of the EU as a normative power. This has since been succeeded by a new Action Plan on Human Rights and Democracy, covering the period 2015–19.[300] Like its predecessor, the current Action Plan reiterates the EU's rhetorical commitment to human rights 'mainstreaming' (integrating human rights considerations into the planning, design, implementation and monitoring of policies and

---

[295] A. Williams, *EU Human Rights Policies: A Study in Irony*, p. 171.

[296] Articles J.1(2) and 130u(2) Maastricht Treaty.

[297] Article 181a(1) *Nice Consolidated Version of the Treaty Establishing the European Community* (OJ C 325/33, 24.12.2002) ('TEC 2002').

[298] Article 21(1) TEU. A similar commitment was also included at Article 3(5) TEU, which states that 'in its relations with the wider world, the Union shall uphold and promote its values... It shall contribute to ... the protection of human rights'.

[299] Council of the EU, *EU Strategic Framework and Action Plan on Human Rights and Democracy* (Document 11855/12, Luxembourg, 25.6.2012), p. 2.

[300] Council Conclusions on the Action Plan on Human Rights and Democracy 2015–2019, adopted on 20 July 2015 (Document 10897/15, Brussels, 20.7.2015).

programmes) across all its external activities – a long-endorsed concept[301] that has yet to be fully realised in practice – and recognises the importance of producing individual country strategies tailored to target states, an initiative that was already under way. Among the EU institutions that closely scrutinise the human rights situation in third states, the EP's ad hoc state-specific Resolutions raise awareness about particular concerns, while the Council's annual human rights reports monitor third states on an individual basis. The Commission also has several processes that enable it to scrutinise external fundamental rights adherence, including its own evaluative mechanisms and a programme of EU delegations, fact-finding missions and research.[302]

Since 1998, the Council has selectively developed, and updated, a series of non–legally binding guidelines, pragmatic practical tools aimed at ensuring coherence in its external human rights policy.[303] These soft law instruments, addressed to EU institutions and member states, include thematic guidelines on priority issues of concern – such as the death penalty, torture and other ill treatment, children and armed conflict, human rights defenders, the rights of the child, discrimination and violence against women, freedom of religion or belief, LGBTI[304] rights and freedom of expression – and are designed to provide direction and concrete tools for coherent human rights–related action. Policy-instrument-specific guidelines on human rights dialogues with third states were also adopted by the Council in 2001, and updated in 2009, in order to strengthen the coherence and consistency of the EU's approach towards launching and conducting such diplomacy following the rapid expansion of this policy tool.

---

[301] The first formal EU commitment to human rights mainstreaming at a practical level across all policy areas is found in the 2001 Commission of the European Communities Communication to the Council and Parliament on the European Union's Role in Promoting Human Rights and Democratisation in Third Countries (COM[2001] 252 final, Brussels, 8.5.2001) and in the Council Conclusions on the European Union's Role in Promoting Human Rights and Democratisation in Third Countries, adopted on 25 June 2001 (Document 10228/01, Brussels, 25.6.2001) which endorsed the Commission's communication.

[302] A. Williams, *The Ethos of Europe: Values, Law and Justice in the EU* (Cambridge University Press, 2010), p. 137.

[303] For detailed assessment see J. Wouters and M. Hermez, 'EU Guidelines on Human Rights as a Foreign Policy Instrument: An Assessment', *Leuven Centre for Global Governance Studies Working Paper No. 170* (Leuven, Belgium: Leuven Centre for Global Governance Studies, 2016).

[304] Lesbian, Gay, Bisexual, Transgender and Intersex.

In order to pursue its external human rights objectives, the EU has established a range of instruments including political conditionality, diplomacy, financial assistance and military or civilian missions. While sanctions are available as a last resort, the Community's overall approach is characterised by a long-standing preference for positive incentive-providing measures.[305] Encompassing both incentives and sanctions, political conditionality has arguably proved the most effective means by which the EU ensures respect for human rights in third states. As early as the mid-1970s, the EP was advocating the drafting of development aid agreements to enable the imposition of sanctions in the event of human rights violations by third states. These calls were, however, rejected as unacceptable by the Commission on the grounds that maintaining trade ties was more important and that, at that time, the Union valued itself as an international actor with a non-political development aid programme including a 'neutral' stance regarding third states' human rights records.[306] It was the atrocities committed in Uganda in the 1970s by the brutal dictatorship of Idi Amin Dada that compelled the Community to change its mind. Bound by the Lomé I Convention – a trade and aid agreement between the EEC and Afro-Caribbean Pacific (ACP) states signed in 1975 that included payment obligations to Idi Amin's regime – the Community's apolitical approach gave the impression that it endorsed, or was at least indifferent to, the large-scale systematic human rights violations taking place. In 1977, prompted by an EP question,[307] the Council issued a Declaration,[308] known as the 'Uganda Guidelines', vaguely stipulating that indeterminate steps would be taken, within the existing Lomé I framework, to ensure Community assistance would not contribute to the reinforcement or prolongation of human rights violations in Uganda. This, the first manifestation of negative political conditionality in the Community's external relations, was a milestone.

---

[305] European Commission Report on the implementation in 1993 of the Resolution on human rights, democracy and development (COM [94] 42 final), p. 11. See also EU Council Conclusions on the EU's role in promoting human rights and democratisation in third countries (Luxembourg, 25.6.2001), paragraph 14.

[306] K. E. Smith, *European Union Foreign Policy in a Changing World*, 3rd edn. (London: Polity Press, 2014), pp. 100–1.

[307] Written Question No. 941/76 by Mr. Van der Hek of 28 February 1977 to the Council of the European Communities on the Human Rights Situation in Uganda (OJ C 214/1, 7.9.1977).

[308] Council Declaration on the Situation in Uganda, adopted 21 June 1977 (European Community Bulletin 6-1977), paragraph 2.2.59.

Despite the Council extending the Uganda Guidelines to all ACP states,[309] Lomé relations contained no such political conditionality until a non-operative provision referencing commitment to human rights, but not providing for sanctions in cases of violation, was incorporated in the 1985 Lomé III Convention. Following a European Council Declaration in 1988,[310] an operative provision permitting appropriate responses to human rights violations was eventually incorporated into the 1989 Lomé IV Convention, Article 5 of which made it the first ever multilateral development agreement to incorporate political conditionality. However, as a concession to ACP states, an automatic suspension procedure was not included. Such so-called basis clauses, which merely stipulate that cooperation is based on respect for democratic principles and human rights, were also soon incorporated into agreements with Argentina, Chile, Uruguay and Paraguay.

A number of landmark developments occurred in 1991. The Commission issued a communication affirming the need to include human rights considerations in the Community's development and cooperation policy, with the option of 'a negative response to serious systematic violations'.[311] The European Council, admittedly taking a cautious line on human rights clauses, subsequently asserted that the important bearing respect for human rights had on the Community's relations with developing countries was 'bound to develop further',[312] and adopted a Declaration in this respect.[313] Following the European Council's endorsement of political conditionality, in November 1991 the Council went further, and made this practice mandatory by adopting a historic Resolution, in which it declared that human rights clauses would be inserted into *all* future cooperation agreements with developing countries.[314] Championing political conditionality in both the positive and

---

[309] Agence Europe No. 2793, *Internal Regulations on EEC aid to the ACP* of 21 November 1979, p. 6.

[310] European Council Declaration of 3 December 1988 on the international role of the European Community (Rhodes 2–3/XII/1988, SN 4446/88).

[311] Commission of the European Communities Communication to the Council and Parliament on Human Rights, Democracy and Development Cooperation Policy (SEC (91) 61, Brussels, 25.3.1991), p. 7.

[312] European Council, Presidency Conclusions of 28–29 June 1991 (SN 151/3/91, Luxembourg), p. 17.

[313] European Council Declaration on Human Rights of 28–29 June 1991 (European Communities Bulletin 6-1991, I. Annex V), p. 17.

[314] Development Council Resolution on human rights, democracy and development (European Communities Bulletin 11–1991).

negative senses, the Resolution gave 'high priority' to positive meas-ures,[315] while also providing that, in the event of 'grave and persistent human violations', the Community would take an appropriate response corresponding to the severity of the case.[316] A range of graded negative measures – from the application of pressure through confidential *démarches* (formal statements of values or preferences issued by an EU delegation) to altering the content or channels of the agreement, but stopping short of discontinuing development cooperation entirely – was provided, indicating that conditionality was predominantly an instru-ment for dialogue.

However, the Council's rejection of suspension as a sanctioning mechan-ism did not last long.[317] The 1992 agreements, concluded with the three Baltic countries and Albania, defined respect for democracy and human rights as an essential element of cooperation, functioning as a trigger for the application of a suspension clause where these undertakings were breached. In the EU's 1992 agreements with Romania and Bulgaria the suspension clause was replaced by a non-execution clause incorporating a prior con-sultation mechanism except in cases of special urgency. In 1995 the Com-mission approved these refinements when it asserted that an 'essential element clause' of this type should be included in all EU agreements with third states.[318] Their incorporation has subsequently become standard prac-tice in all trade, cooperation, dialogue, partnership and association agree-ments, a laudable development in the EU's external human rights policy.

However, if not applied in practice, the mere existence of political conditionality is insufficient to ensure respect for human rights. The EP has long subjected human rights clauses to scrutiny, and has expressed concern about their inadequate implementation,[319] repeatedly calling on the Council and Commission to apply sanctions. However, with no clear guidelines on when or how human rights clauses should be invoked,[320]

---

[315] Ibid., 2.3.1.4.

[316] Ibid., 2.3.1.6.

[317] 1573rd Council Meeting, General Affairs (Political Co-Operation), Brussels, 11 May 1992, 6326/92, press release 71 (European Communities Bulletin 5-1992), p. 120.

[318] Communication from the Commission on the inclusion of respect for democratic principles and human rights in agreements between the Community and third countries (COM [95] 216 final, Brussels, 23.5.1995).

[319] See for example European Parliament Resolution on human rights in the world in 2000 and the European Union Human Rights Policy (2000/2105 (INI)).

[320] European Parliament, *Study: Human Rights Mainstreaming in EU's External Relations* (Brussels: European Parliament, 2009, EXPO/B/DROI/2008/66) pp. 59–60.

their inconsistent application has been one of the EP's greatest bones of contention with other EU institutions. As early as 1997, the EP condemned as discriminatory in nature the EU's exclusive reliance on human rights clauses in relation to ACP states,[321] particularly its focus on the poorest.[322] While the EP continues to highlight disparate treatment,[323] its demands for effective and non-selective application of negative political conditionality appear to have had little or no effect so far.

Despite its limitations, especially if not combined with incentives or pressure in the form of political conditionality,[324] the EU still relies heavily on diplomacy to encourage third states to improve their human rights records. In cooperation with civil society, it conducts various types of human rights dialogues with third states and regional organisations, including those of a general nature within the framework of a legally binding association or cooperation agreement; ad hoc dialogues addressing CFSP-related topics, including human rights; regular, institutionalised exchanges structured to focus exclusively on human rights, enabling more detailed discussion with specific partners; and dialogues in the context of special relations with like-minded third states. Each dialogue is established in accordance with EU guidelines on human rights dialogues. The matters to be addressed are decided on a case-by-case basis in agreement with the partner country concerned, although certain priority issues, such as abolition of the death penalty and combating torture, are always on the agenda.

While the particular objective of any given dialogue depends on its context, the common overarching aim is to improve the human rights situation in the relevant third state and to keep diplomatic channels of communication open. However, as most are held behind closed doors, external assessments are kept confidential and EU reports are often silent on resultant action taken, it is difficult to assess their effectiveness.

---

[321] Human rights clauses were invoked 15 times between 1995 and 2009, all in relation to ACP States (European Parliament, *Study: Human Rights Mainstreaming in EU's External Relations*, p. 36).

[322] European Parliament Interim Report on the proposal for a Council Decision on a framework procedure for implementing Article 366a of the Fourth Lomé Convention (COM [96] 69, A4-0175/97, 10).

[323] See for example European Union, *EU Annual Report on Human Rights and Democracy in the World in 2010* (European External Action Service, 2011), p. 14.

[324] K. E. Smith, 'The EU as a Diplomatic Actor in the Field of Human Rights' in J. Koops and G. Macaj (eds.), *The European Union as a Diplomatic Actor* (Basingstoke, Palgrave Macmillan, 2015), p. 157.

Nevertheless, it does appear that, despite their widespread proliferation, human rights dialogues have had minimal impact in improving third states' human rights records.[325]

In addition to dialogues, the EU applies diplomatic pressure on third states through public Declarations and confidential *démarches*. Declarations are relied on extensively to express particular concerns or to welcome positive developments, while *démarches* are delivered if private diplomacy is deemed more appropriate in the circumstances. These instruments are arguably more effective than dialogues, particularly when deployed on a case-by-case basis.[326] Diplomatic sanctions, such as suspension of official visits, can also be imposed on third states, but require the Council to act unanimously.

The EU also actively engages diplomatically in multilateral fora to pursue it external human rights objectives.[327] For example, it issues statements and sponsors Resolutions in the UN's Human Rights Council (HRC), an arena in which the member states aspire to act collectively. However, despite increasing internal coherence,[328] the EU struggles to influence HRC output, primarily because of the divisive external environment in which it operates,[329] with voting blocs within the HRC often outweighing the EU. As a result, the EU has been proposing, with increasing success, fewer Resolutions, particularly in relation to state-specific situations that are less likely to attract consensus. However, such an approach significantly limits the EU's external impact on the HRC's agenda, and has been criticised by the EP.[330] In 2005, the High

[325] For a detailed critique, see K. Kinzelbach, 'The EU's Human Rights Dialogues - Talking to Persuade or Silencing the Debate?' presented at the Kolleg-Forschergruppe (KFG) Conference: *The Transformative Power of Europe* at Freie Univesität Berlin, 10–11 December 2009), pp. 10–11.

[326] M. Fouwels, 'The European Union's Common Foreign and Security Policy and Human Rights', *Netherlands Quarterly of Human Rights*, 15, 3 (1997), 309.

[327] For detailed discussion of the EU's legal standing at the UN, see D. Zaru and C.-M. Guerts, 'Legal Framework for EU Participation in Global Human Rights Governance' in J. Wouters, H. Bruyninckx, S. Basu and S. Schunz (eds.), *The European Union and Multilateral Governance: Assessing EU Participation in United Nations Human Rights and Environmental Fora* (Basingstoke: Palgrave Macmillan, 2012) pp. 49–65.

[328] For detailed discussion, see K. E. Smith, 'The European Union at the Human Rights Council: Speaking with One Voice but Having Little Influence,' *Journal of European Public Policy*, 17(2) (2010), 224–41.

[329] S. Basu, 'The European Union in the Human Rights Council' in Wouters et al. (eds.), *The European Union and Multilateral Governance*, p. 91.

[330] European Parliament Resolution of 14 January 2009 on the development of the UN Human Rights Council, including the role of the EU (2008/2201 (INI), P6_TA (2009) 0021), paragraph 49.

Representative for Foreign Affairs appointed a 'personal representative for human rights'.[331] In July 2012, following the adoption of the Strategic Framework, this post was replaced by an EU Special Representative for Human Rights (EUSRHR),[332] which undertakes diplomatic activities identical to those of its predecessor. Exercising a mandate under the High Representative's supervision, the EUSRHR is to 'engage with the UN, chair high-level human rights dialogues and lead consultations with third countries on human rights issues'.[333] The new EUSRHR post is indicative of the increasing importance the EU places on the promotion of human rights in the wider world.

In conjunction with political conditionality and diplomacy, the EU relies on financial assistance to pursue its external human rights policy objectives. The Community started giving small amounts of aid to certain third states to help them improve their human rights records and democratic processes in 1986.[334] In addition to incorporating political conditionality into its development aid agreements, the EU has various financial instruments to support human rights and democracy world-wide. While this study does not permit all such instruments, or the CFSP budget, to be comprehensively reviewed, two that deserve particular attention will be discussed as illustrations instead. It ought first to be noted that, while the EU's budget is essential for financing many external human rights activities and operations, it is still relatively small and its policy impact is therefore limited.[335]

Following pressure from the EP, the European Initiative (now Instrument) for Democracy and Human Rights (EIDHR) was created as a chapter in the EU budget in 1994.[336] By amalgamating previously separate budget headings addressing democratisation and the promotion of human rights abroad, the EIDHR provides grants to groups or individuals independent from the state whose activities contribute to promoting human rights and democracy. By channelling financial

---

[331] Commission and Council of Ministers, *EU Annual Report on Human Rights 2006* (Luxembourg: Office for Official Publications of the European Communities, 2006), p. 4.

[332] Council of the European Union Decision 2012/440/CFSP of 25 July 2012 appointing the European Union Special Representative for Human Rights (OJ L 200/21, 27.12.2012).

[333] European Parliament EPP Group Press Release, 'The EU Special Representative for Human Rights Should Have Worldwide Authority' (Strasbourg, 13.6.2012).

[334] K. E. Smith, *European Union Foreign Policy in a Changing World*, p. 113.

[335] Nugent, *The Government and Politics of the European Union*, p. 415.

[336] It has a budget of €1.249 billion for the period 2014–20.

assistance independent of the consent or collaboration of the targeted third state, the EIDHR is thereby able effectively to complement other EU human rights instruments, or to compensate for their absence. Because of its decentralised nature, the EIDHR does not include political conditionality provisions, and can be used to promote human rights in third states where other EU programmes have been suspended on human rights grounds. However, its effectiveness is limited in third states with the worst human rights records where NGOs struggle to operate.[337] The European Neighbourhood (previously Partnership) Instrument (ENI) is the main financial instrument for implementing the political initiatives shaping the European Neighbourhood Policy (ENP), with a budget of €15.433 billion for the period 2014–20. Launched in 2003, the ENP governs the EU's relations with its closest eastern and southern neighbours. Encompassing a vast geographical area and a diverse range of third states, it offers 'more than partnership and less than membership, without precluding the latter'.[338] Assisting neighbours with implementing EU-compatible reforms, while neither offering nor ruling out the prospect of accession,[339] the ENP offers access to the EU single market in exchange for compliance with economic and political conditions.[340] Financial support for such reforms is provided under ENI targets, in part, the promotion of human rights.[341] Following a review of the ENP undertaken by the Commission in the wake of the 'Arab Spring',[342] additional ENI funding has been provided on the basis of a 'more-for-more' principle, an incentive-based approach that rewards, with increased financial support, those third states successfully implementing progressive change. As of 2014, the ENI, and various other financial instruments seeking to advance human rights, no longer embody negative political conditionality in the form of an explicit reference to the

---

[337] K. E. Smith, *European Union Foreign Policy in a Changing World*, p. 114.

[338] R. Prodi, 'A Wider Europe: A Proximity Policy as the Key to Stability', speech to the Sixth ECSA World Conference in Brussels, 5–6 December 2002 (SPEECH/02/619), p. 3.

[339] D. Bechev and K. Nicolaïdis, 'From Policy to Polity: Can the EU's Special Relations with Its 'Neighbourhood' Be Decentred?', *JCMS: Journal of Common Market Studies*, 48(3) (2010), 475–500.

[340] Communication from the Commission to the European Parliament and Council, 'A Strong European Neighbourhood Policy' (COM [2007] 774 final, Brussels, 5.12.2007).

[341] Article 2(2) European Parliament and Council Regulation No. 232/2014 of 11 March 2014 establishing a Neighbourhood European Instrument (OJ L 77/27, 15.3.2014).

[342] European Commission Joint Communication, 'Review of the European Neighbourhood Policy' (JOIN (2015) 50 final, Brussels, 18.11.2015, SWD (2015) 500 final).

possibility of assistance being suspended if the beneficiary third state fails to respect human rights.[343]

The EU has also deployed civilian and military operations in third states in order to ensure respect for human rights, undertaking, for example, more than one hundred election observation and assistance missions since 1993 to ensure third states' democratic processes adhere to international standards. In addition, as of 2003, it has also launched various crisis management interventions as part of its CFSP, usually upon receiving a mandate to do so by the UN Security Council, upon the conclusion of a peace agreement, or having acquired the consent of the host state in question.[344] These predominantly civilian, but also military,[345] operations range from large-scale deployments to more modest assignments.[346] While their immediate priority is not the promotion of human rights per se, the overarching aim of ensuring stability contributes to the practical realisation of human rights in the countries concerned. Many, such as those concerning police training or judicial support, are also directly linked to the protection of human rights, and the EU also mainstreams human rights in the planning and conduct of all its crisis management interventions.[347]

Principled objections have been raised against the EU incorporating human rights considerations into its external policy. Some have argued that it could undermine national sovereignty and the international norm

---

[343] See European Parliament and Council Regulation No. 233/2014 of 11 March 2014 establishing a financing instrument for development cooperation for the period 2014–20 (OJ L 77/44, 15.3.2014), European Parliament and Council Regulation No. 232/2014 of 11 March 2014 establishing a Neighbourhood European Instrument (OJ L 77/27, 15.3.2014), and European Parliament and Council Regulation No. 234/2014 of 11 March 2014 establishing a Partnership Instrument for cooperation with third countries (OJ L 77/77, 15.3.2014).

[344] F. Naert, 'Accountability for Violations of Human Rights Law by EU Forces' in S. Blockmans (ed.), *The European Union and Crisis Management: Policy and Legal Aspects* (The Hague: TMC Asser Press, 2008), p. 377.

[345] See for example Council Decision 2006/412/CFSP of 12 June 2006 on the launching of the European Union military operation in support of the United Nations Organisation Mission in the Democratic Republic of the Congo (MONUC) during the election process (OJ L 163/16, 15.6.2006).

[346] Detailed discussions of the strengths and weaknesses of such missions is beyond the scope of this chapter, see European Parliament, *Study: CSDP Missions and Operations: Lessons Learned Processes* (Brussels: European Parliament, 2012, EXPO/B/SEDE/DWC/2009-01/Lot6/16).

[347] See C. M. Carrasco, 'The Applicability of Human Rights Instruments to European Union's CSDP Operations: Framing the Challenges', *Cuadernos Europeos de Deusto*, 53 (2005), 53–80.

of non-interference in domestic affairs.[348] More abstractly, the universality of human rights has been called to question, with protestations that the manner in which the EU promotes them amounts to an imposition of Eurocentric standards.[349] The EU's external human rights policy has also come under criticism for its ineffectiveness in practice, although detractors tend to overlook the fact that a conducive external context is of primary importance for an effective normative impact. Nevertheless, the predominant complaint levied against the EU is that of inconsistency and differential treatment, both in the context of its external relations and regarding the internal/external policy disparity. As one commentator puts it, 'The legitimacy, credibility and effectiveness of EU policies to promote human rights will inevitably continue to suffer if the gaps are not closed.'[350]

The EU's strong rhetorical commitment to the promotion of human rights worldwide is not always consistently observed. Rather, a reactive and flexible approach is employed in practice. Despite the EP's repeated calls for third states with similar human rights records to be treated in the same manner,[351] indisputably differential treatment confirms that the promotion of human rights is not the EU's principal priority. Take, for example, the cases of Myanmar and China.[352] While human rights violations in Myanmar have been met with a vast array of restrictive sanctions,[353] comparable contraventions in China have resulted in few

---

[348] See K. E. Smith, *European Union Foreign Policy in a Changing World*; and D. M. Hill, 'Human Rights and Foreign Policy: Theoretical Foundations' in D. M. Hill (ed.), *Human Rights and Foreign Policy: Theoretical Foundations* (Basingstoke: Macmillan, 1989) pp. 3–20.

[349] A useful review of the literature which claims that human rights are merely an artefact of western civilization is R. Cruft, S. Matthew Liao and M. Renzo, 'The Philosophical Foundations of Human Rights: An Overview' in R. Cruft, S. Matthew Liao and M. Renzo (eds.), *Philosophical Foundations of Human Rights* (Oxford University Press, 2015), pp. 31–4.

[350] K. E. Smith, *European Union Foreign Policy in a Changing World*, p. 121.

[351] See for example European Parliament Resolution of 4 September 2008 on the evaluation of EU sanctions as part of the EU's actions and policies in the area of human rights (A6-0309/2008, P6_TA-PROV(2008)0405).

[352] For detailed discussion of the EU's differing approach towards human rights promotion in Myanmar and China, see N. Borreschmidt, 'The EU's Human Rights Promotion in China and Myanmar: Trading Rights for Might?', *EU Diplomacy Paper 5/2014* (Department of EU International Relations and Diplomacy Studies, 2014).

[353] For details, see C. Portela and J. Orbie, 'Sanctions under the EU Generalised System of Preferences and Foreign Policy: Coherence by Accident?', *Contemporary Politics*, 20(1) (2014), 68; M. Bünte and C. Portela, 'Myanmar: The Beginning of Reforms and the End of Sanctions', *GIGA Focus*, 3 (2012), 5; C. Portela and P. Vennesson, 'Sanctions and Embargos in EU-Asia Relations' in T. Christiansen, E. Kirchner and P. Murray (eds.),

negative measures by the EU.[354] Instead of pursuing political conditionality, quiet diplomacy in the form of institutionalised structured human
rights dialogue has been, and continues to be, the EU's preferred
approach in pursuit of tangible improvements to China's human rights
record, despite the negligible impact this has had to date.[355] As is further
illustrated by the EU's lenient treatment of the United States and Russia,
both of which are important trading and security partners,[356] the Union's
response to human rights infringements in third states is clearly dependent upon other variables, not least the offending state's economic, political and strategic significance, prompting accusations of selectivity
motivated by self-interest. However, the genuine dilemmas the EU
encounters ought not to be underestimated. Other external policy objectives or security imperatives may necessitate prioritisation in any given
case, not to mention practical feasibility, with economic supremacy an
apparent precondition to exerting effective influence over third states.

Further, any evaluation of inconsistencies in the EU's external human
rights policy would also be incomplete without reference to internal factors.
While there is clearly an EU consensus on the desirability of promoting
human rights externally, how to do so in a particular case is more contentious.[357] Legitimate disagreements over the effectiveness of sanctions versus
strengthening economic and political ties are, for example, exacerbated by
the fact that the question of when to resort to negative measures has not
been comprehensively addressed in the EU's official discourse. In addition,
the EU's internal architecture militates against uniformity. The differing
opinions of member states on the desirability of sanctions, particularly when
competing national interests are at play, coupled with the unanimity
requirement in the Council for most external policy matters, repeatedly
renders the EU incapable of taking the strong stance it rhetorically espouses,
particularly against powerful third states.

Whatever the reasons, the EU's failure consistently to practice what it
preaches has considerable adverse repercussions. With its authenticity,
legitimacy and credibility as a human rights actor called into question,

---

The Palgrave Handbook of EU-Asia Relations (Basingstoke: Palgrave MacMillan, 2013),
p. 203.

[354] It has only subjected it to an arms embargo and brief period of diplomatic sanctions in
the late 1980s and early 1990s.

[355] See K. Kinzelbach, The EU's Human Rights Dialogue with China: Quiet Diplomacy and
Its Limits (Abingdon: Routledge, 2015), vol. VII.

[356] For more on the cases of inconsistency, see K. Brummer, 'Imposing Sanctions: The Not So
"Normative Power Europe"', European Foreign Affairs Review, 14(2) (2009), 280–99.

[357] K. E. Smith, European Union Foreign Policy in a Changing World, p. 105.

the EU's position as a normative power on the world stage is compromised. And as if this were not enough, the impact of its external human rights policy is further diminished by the fact that disparate enforcement undermines the impact of political conditionality, with knock-on effects on the EU's persuasiveness as a diplomatic actor in multinational fora, weakened further by internal coordination problems. A given institution may, for example, condemn a third state while another fails to reflect this in its own practice. In 2004, for instance, the Council criticised Israeli raids in Gaza and the West Bank, but the Commission continued negotiating an ENP action plan with Israel notwithstanding.[358] There are also occasions when member states take negative measures against a third state but the EU does not, such as when the Netherlands and Sweden, but not the EU, froze aid to Ethiopia in 2005.[359] Failing to speak with a unified voice on the world stage weakens the EU's moral authority and standing as a global normative power.

However, it is the inconsistency between the EU's internal and external fundamental rights policies that has received most attention in the academic literature, and understandably so, as it undermines the Union's entire ethos as an organisation with fundamental rights as a founding value. While substantive disparity cannot be denied – with the EU basing its external policy on a wider range of sources, including several international human rights treaties that have not been ratified by all member states[360] – this is not the predominant cause for concern. The differential fundamental rights monitoring and enforcement between member states, on the one hand, and third states, on the other, is rather the main criticism. While the fundamental rights situation in third states is kept under close scrutiny, with large-scale monitoring by various institutions through intrusive and extensive processes,[361] the EU still fails systematically to monitor member states' fundamental rights practices. While this *was* within the historic CFR-CDF's competence, it is explicitly omitted from the FRA's mandate. The EU maintains that member states are already subject to a rigorous system of scrutiny as signatories to the

---

[358] See N. Tocci, *The EU and Conflict Resolution: Promoting Peace in the Backyard* (London: Routledge, 2007), p. 117.

[359] See R. Youngs (ed.), *Survey of European Democracy Promotion Policies 2000–2006* (Madrid: Fundacíon para las Relaciones Internacionales y el Diálogo Exterior (FRIDE), 2006), pp. 149–50, 195–6 and 220–1.

[360] For detailed discussion, see A. Williams, *The Ethos of Europe*, pp. 117–135.

[361] Ibid., pp. 136–8.

ECHR, thereby abdicating responsibility to the CE. Vis-à-vis powers of enforcement, whereas internal enforcement mechanisms are comparatively weak (as discussed previously), political conditionality is a powerful tool in ensuring respect for fundamental rights in third states. EU institutions have long acknowledged the internal/external discrepancy, and the direct impact it has on the EU's 'ability to implement an effective external human rights policy'.[362] While some steps, such as the establishment of the FRA, taken to address the disparity are commendable, others have had a marginal, if not detrimental, effect. Earlier versions of the Council's annual reports on human rights, published since 1999, focused primarily on the EU's external activities, while also addressing fundamental rights within the EU, the attention internal fundamental rights activities received diminished over the years then ceased entirely, with the 2008 report and all subsequent publications[363] focusing solely on fundamental rights abroad, thereby contributing to the entrenchment of differential treatment. The EP's annual reports on fundamental rights within the EU, issued since 1993 to complement its external counterpart, have failed to provide an effective internal monitoring mechanism because of resource limitations and the absence of an accompanying enforcement apparatus. Unless effective action is taken at the EU level, accusations of 'double standards' could fatally undermine the credibility of the EU as a normative power. As matters stand, there is an indefensible incongruity in the EU's active approach to the promotion of fundamental rights beyond its borders when juxtaposed with its near-abdication of responsibility for the internal dimension.

Non-EU European Economic Area States

The EEA was established by the 1992 EEA Agreement[364] with all contracting parties granted full participation in the EU's single market. EEA membership includes all EU states plus Iceland, Liechtenstein and Norway, which, together with Switzerland (not a member of the EEA),

---

[362] European Parliament Resolution of 7 May 2009 on the Annual Report on Human Rights in the World 2008 and the European Union's policy on the matter (2008/2336 (INI), P6_TA(2009)0385), paragraph E.

[363] Titled *EU Annual Report on Human Rights and Democracy in the World* to reflect the exclusively external focus.

[364] Agreement on the European Economic Area (OJ L 1, 3.1.1994, as amended) ('EEA Agreement').

are part of the European Free Trade Association (EFTA), a regional intergovernmental organisation established in parallel with the EU for the promotion of free trade among its members. The three non-EU EEA states are closely affiliated with the EU, yet little, if any, scholarly attention has been paid to the fundamental rights impact EEA membership has on them, perhaps because they were all widely regarded as states with good fundamental rights records in any case.

In order to ensure the creation of a homogeneous EEA, with uniform national laws relating to the single market, all relevant EU legislation is integrated into the EEA Agreement. Incorporated EU legislation, listed in the Annexes and updated continuously, is to be interpreted in conformity with EU jurisprudence prior to 1992.[365] It is binding on all contracting parties, and must be part of their internal legal order.[366] Accordingly, in the numerous policy fields encompassed by the EEA Agreement, EEA states are affiliated to the same extent as EU member states are 'as far as policy harmonization is concerned'.[367] While EEA states are not permitted access to the formal decision-making process of EU institutions, unable to either sit or vote in the EP or Council, they are able to participate in the Commission during the early preparative stages of EEA-relevant legislative proposals, and have the right to submit comments on pertinent Commission initiatives.[368]

The fundamental rights implications of this external EU governance are simple. First and foremost, while the EEA Agreement does not cover CFSP or justice and home affairs, EEA states are bound by certain rights-related EU secondary legislation, notably, although not exclusively, in the fields of social security, labour law, gender equality and data protection. Second, EEA states must continuously incorporate into their legal orders such EU legislation without having had any substantial input into the legislative process. This constitutes yet another form of political conditionality in the EU's external human rights policy since, if a non-EU EFTA state wishes to join the EEA, it must accept the EU's extensive internal fundamental rights legislation relating to the single market.

---

[365] Article 6 EEA Agreement.
[366] Article 7 EEA Agreement.
[367] M. Egeberg and J. Trondal, 'Differentiated Integration in Europe: The Case of EEA Country, Norway', *JCMS: Journal of Common Market Studies*, 37(1) (1999), 113–42 at 134.
[368] For more information, see the EFTA Bulletin, 'Decision Shaping in the European Economic Area' (March 2009).

Applicant States

Accession to the EU is arguably the Union's most effective external policy tool, with the best overall success rate in ensuring positive developments in human rights beyond its historic heartlands. 'Passive' and 'active' leverage is exercised on applicant states' domestic policies, the former resulting from the inherent attraction of European integration, with the latter a consequence of the EU's accession policy,[369] which encompasses political conditionality, monitoring and financial assistance in conjunction with accession negotiations that now include a specific chapter on the 'judiciary and fundamental rights'.[370]

Political conditionality for accession was articulated as early as 1962, when the EP adopted the Birkelbach Report, stating that only those states guaranteeing respect for human rights could join the Community.[371] Having established, in 1973, that respect for human rights was a cornerstone of European identity, and European integration was open 'to other European nations who share the same ideals and objectives',[372] in 1978 the European Council solemnly declared that respect for human rights and democracy were 'essential elements of membership'.[373] Following the collapse of its dictatorial regime in 1974, political conditionality was first applied to Greece, albeit in a weak embryonic form of procedural democratic criteria. The fall of the Iron Curtain, and aspirations of CEE states to become members, motivated the Union to strengthen its accession policy. The implicit accession *conditio sine qua non* of respect for human rights and democracy was formalised by the European Council at its Copenhagen summit in 1993, which endorsed the Commission's 1992 opinion regarding the preconditions for enlargement.[374] While the latter required applicant states to demonstrate

---

[369] M. A. Vachudová, *Europe Undivided: Democracy, Leverage and Integration after Communism* (Oxford University Press, 2005).

[370] The introduction of this chapter is discussed in C. Hillion, 'Enlarging the European Union and Deepening Its Fundamental Rights Protection', *SIEPS European Policy Analysis*, 11 (2013), at 4–7.

[371] Birkelbach Report quoted in L. Whitehead, *The International Dimensions of Democratization: Europe and the Americas*, 2nd edn. (Oxford University Press, 2001), p. 267.

[372] Declaration on European Identity, paragraph 4 (Bulletin of the European Communities 12–1973), pp. 118–22.

[373] Declaration on Democracy, issued by the European Council on 8 April 1978 in Copenhagen (Bulletin of the European Communities 3-1978), pp. 5–6.

[374] European Commission, 'Europe and the Challenge of Enlargement, 24 June 1992', prepared for the European Council, Lisbon, 26–27 June 1992 (Bulletin of the European Communities Supplement 3/92).

'stability of institutions guaranteeing democracy, the rule of law, human rights and respect for and protection of minorities',[375] the Copenhagen European Council formulated objective economic, political and *acquis*[376] criteria for accession. Although established in the specific context of post-Communist eastern enlargement, compliance with the Copenhagen criteria remains a prerequisite for the opening of accession negotiations with any state and a yardstick for progress throughout. The political conditionality encompassed was constitutionalised by the 1997 Treaty of Amsterdam, which proclaimed respect for human rights and democracy as explicit preconditions for accession, by amending Article 49 TEU (ex Article O) specifying that only a European State 'which respects the principles set out in Article 6(1) may apply to become a member of the Union'. Previously Article O TEU contained no formal requirements other than that an applicant must be European. Alluding to the Copenhagen criteria, the most recent formulation of Article 49 TEU provides that 'the conditions of eligibility agreed upon by the European Council shall be taken into account.'

It was left to the Commission to specify the content of the Copenhagen criteria. In 1997, it published 'Agenda 2000',[377] which disaggregated the general criteria into more specific practical requirements.[378] Against these, the Commission monitored the progress of applicant states via a process of benchmarking, naming and shaming, conducted through official visits, fact-finding missions and public reports.[379] The Commission's initial Opinions on CEE applicants, annexed to Agenda 2000, made it apparent from the outset that its investigations would go beyond a formal description of political institutions, and would instead entail a 'systematic examination of the main ways in which public authorities are organized and operate, and the steps that have been taken to protect fundamental rights'. With scrutiny deemed to be an ongoing process, in

---

[375] European Council, Presidency Conclusions of 21–22 June 1993, Copenhagen (Bulletin of the European Communities 6-1993), p. 13, paragraph I.13.

[376] The expression *acquis* (or *acquis communautaire*) is used to describe all EU's rules and policies. It comprises the entire body of Union legislation, founding Treaties and the judgments of the ECJ. It includes all hard law relating to the EU's internal fundamental rights policy.

[377] European Commission, 'Agenda 2000: For a stronger and wider Union. Document drawn up on the basis of COM(97) 2000 final, 15 July 1997' (EU Bulletin Supplement 5/97).

[378] Ibid., pp. 41–52.

[379] G. Balducci, 'The Study of the EU Promotion of Human Rights', 10.

December 1997 the Luxembourg European Council adopted a review procedure as part of its 'enhanced pre-accession strategy', mandating the Commission to report regularly on progress made by applicant states towards accession.[380] Since 1998, the Commission's chief instrument for monitoring and evaluating applicants' eligibility has been its annual reports on compliance with the Copenhagen criteria. 'Accession Partnerships', another key instrument introduced in the Luxembourg European Council's pre-accession strategy, identify priority areas for reform itemised as short- and medium-term objectives from each applicant's annual reports. With implementation subject to systematic monitoring by the Commission, applicant states are required to act in accordance with the EU's directions if they wish to advance their application and ultimately joint the EU. Negotiation frameworks for accession also now include a mechanism for the possible suspension of the negotiation process in cases of 'serious and persistent breach' of the EU's foundational principles, including respect for human rights, by an applicant state.

Empirical analysis demonstrates a positive correlation between the extent of annual pre-accession monitoring and an applicant state's compliance with accession criteria.[381] This combination of conditionality and constant scrutiny is effectively supplemented by pre-accession assistance programmes also conditional on progress. Technical and financial instruments aimed at supporting applicant states' advance towards eligibility include the Instrument for Pre-Accession (IPA), which supports the implementation of various reforms required to satisfy accession requirements. Despite having amongst its specific objectives the protection and promotion of human rights and the strengthening of democracy, the current IPA under the 2014–20 budget contains no explicit reference to the possibility of suspending assistance if the beneficiary state fails to observe these principles.[382]

While the EU's accession policy appears to have yielded positive results in incentivising improvements in respect for human rights in applicant states, focusing, as the Commission does, on legal reforms such as constitutional amendments, legislative developments and treaty

---

[380] European Council, Presidency Conclusions of 12 and 13 December 1997 meeting in Luxembourg (EU Bulletin 12–1997,), pp. 29–30, paragraph 29.

[381] S. Khan-Nisser, 'Conditionality, Communication and Compliance: The Effect of Monitoring on Collective Labour Rights in Candidate Countries', *JCMS: Journal of Common Market Studies*, 51(6) (2013), 1040–56.

[382] European Parliament and Council Regulation No. 231/2014 of 11 March 2014 establishing an Instrument for Pre-Accession Assistance (IPA II) (OJ L 77/11, 14.3.2014).

ratification as opposed to evidence of improvement in practice, has opened the doors of the EU to several applicant states with weak human rights records.[383] Ensuring that reforms undertaken by applicant states endure after they have been admitted as members also presents considerable challenges, with Hungary as a particularly striking example of regression.[384]

To conclude, the internal/external discrepancy over the monitoring of human rights compliance by the EU manifests in various forms in relation to applicant states.[385] First, there are discrepancies in the scope of rights to be respected, for example, the unparalleled emphasis on minority rights in applicant states.[386] Second, monitoring mechanisms pre and post accession differ considerably, with no effective counterpart to the Commission's systematic scrutiny of applicants once they become EU members. Third, there is a disparity in the enforcement machinery available. Outside the scope of Article 7 TEU, member states are only bound by the EU's CFR and general principles when implementing EU law. By contrast, any conduct by an applicant state is relevant when evaluating its Copenhagen criteria compliance. The limitations of the Article 7 TEU fundamental rights enforcement mechanism when member states are acting beyond the scope of EU law has already been discussed. Notably, the Article 7 sanctioning mechanism has a much higher procedural threshold than suspension of accession negotiations, with the latter capable of being triggered by QMV in the Council. The logical effect of all the disparities is that the EU is able to exercise less influence over the fundamental rights records of applicant states once they have attained membership. Further, they undermine the credibility of its accession policy. If not preparing applicant states for the obligations of membership, the EU's extensive intervention in their domestic affairs can hardly be justified. Enlargement represents a self-identification exercise for the EU,[387] a means by which it can project the image by which it

---

[383] See L. Conant, 'Compelling Criteria? Human Rights in the European Union', *Journal of European Public Policy*, 21(5), 713–29.

[384] See B. Wright, 'The Europeanisation of Hungary: Institutional adjustment and the effects of European Union integration', *POLIS Journal*, (2013), 271.

[385] For detailed discussion, see Hillion, 'Enlarging the European Union', 7–9.

[386] E. G. Heidbreder, *The Impact of Expansion on EU Institutions: The Eastern Touch on Brussels* (New York: Palgrave Macmillan, 2011), pp. 82–5.

[387] 'By articulating what is required to be(come) a Member State, enlargement offers glimpses of the Union's constitutional identity' (Hillion, 'Enlarging the European Union', 1).

wishes to be perceived.[388] There is, however, evident hypocrisy in vigorously enforcing normative requirements on applicants when members are not themselves held comparably to account.

4.5   Conclusion

The main observations to be drawn from the preceding analysis are as follows. Fundamental rights considerations were seemingly irrelevant at the Community's inception, and found no explicit mention in the Founding Treaties. However, in 1969, in spite of the absence of a clear constitutional justification, the ECJ retrospectively declared respect for fundamental rights to be enshrined in the general principles of Community law. Deemed necessary in order to avoid a potentially fatal clash between supranational supremacy and national constitutionalism, this also provided a legitimising function by binding Community institutions to respect rights in ways similar to public authorities in member states. A series of developments followed. In 1973 the heads of state or government established that respect for fundamental rights was a vital feature of the Community's identity, subsequently declaring it an essential element of membership in 1978. Projecting its newly established normative character externally enabled the Community to prove its fidelity to its founding values and to establish a distinctive profile for itself on the world stage. With political conditionality mandatory in all external agreements from 1991, respect for fundamental rights became a requirement for third states seeking to benefit from association with the Union. It naturally followed that those states wishing to associate with the EU to the highest degree, through membership, found themselves similarly obligated. Indeed, the EU has a far greater interest in ensuring that applicant states respect fundamental rights, as reflected in the extensive and intrusive monitoring of adherence to the Copenhagen criteria for accession. Having rendered respect for fundamental rights to be a strictly enforceable prerequisite for membership, it would be paradoxical for the EU no longer to hold applicant states to similar account upon them gaining admission. Indeed, monitoring third and applicant states' adherence to fundamental rights while abdicating such a responsibility for

---

[388] Further, see e.g., H. Sjursen, 'Enlargement in Perspective: The EU's Quest for Identity', *Recon Online Working Paper* 2007/15, and K. E. Smith, 'The Conditional Offer of Membership as an Instrument of EU Foreign Policy: Reshaping Europe in the EU's Image?' *Marmara Journal of European Studies*, 33 (2000), p. 33.

member states had already exposed the EU to accusations of double standards, which it has sought to address by introducing the Article 7 sanctioning mechanism under the 1997 Treaty of Amsterdam. As integration deepened and the EU evolved from more than an economic community to something akin to a political union, the promotion of fundamental rights gained further prominence and the need for legal certainty through a written catalogue of Community rights became all the more apparent. This was subsequently achieved by the adoption of the CFR in 2000, which clarified the EU's respect for fundamental rights in the negative sense but stopped short of bestowing upon the EU competence to protect fundamental rights proactively through legislation to this effect.

The European Council can be credited with providing the political impetus for the establishment of the EU's internal and external fundamental rights policies. In addition to adopting relevant treaty revisions, its contributions in this field include declaring respect for fundamental rights an essential element of membership; formalising this in the Copenhagen criteria for accession; providing impetus for the emergence of political conditionality in relations with third states; authorising the creation of the FRA; and deciding to establish the CFR. The European Council is also entrusted with most of the important decisions on membership applications and with determination of breach under Article 7 TEU. For its part, the EP has been, and continues to be, a leading and successful proponent of fundamental rights internally and externally, deeming this part of its democratic duty. It issues reports and Resolutions on fundamental rights both within and outside the Union, and subjects to scrutiny the fundamental rights records of other EU institutions and bodies. As for the Commission, it makes sense that, as representative of the Union's general interest and given the legitimising and identity-building function of the EU's fundamental rights policy, it has been particularly closely associated with the EP's efforts to develop and enforce it. It was the Commission, for example, that first asserted, in 1976, that the Community's political institutions should formally declare their respect for fundamental rights. Over the years it has since utilised available treaty bases to propose a battery of rights-related legislation, advocated the establishment of the CFR and established expert networks to provide EU policy-making advice and analysis in the fundamental rights field, and it continues to ensure that all legislative proposals are fully CFR compliant. It has also monitored member states' implementation of EU law in the fundamental rights field and utilises the powers at its disposal to ensure the effectiveness thereof. Externally, the Commission supported the EP in championing the inclusion of political conditionality vis-à-vis third states, called for political preconditions for accession and developed the Copenhagen criteria, and it continues to ensure regular scrutiny of applicant states' compliance. As a primary EU decision maker, the Council has also played a central and multi-faceted role with respect to fundamental rights, albeit with rhetoric often stronger than action. With national governments reluctant to transfer sovereignty to the EU in the fundamental rights field, or to put the enforcement of norms abroad above their national interests, the Council's reserved stance in practice is unsurprising given its composition.

Because of its institution-led, ad hoc and highly reactive evolution, the EU's fundamental rights policy is uniquely complex and incoherent. In the internal sphere, while the CFR enhances transparency and legal certainty, the EU's lack of competence to develop a fully-fledged policy has left its promotion of fundamental rights patchy and incomplete at best, although this could be remedied if it were provided with competence to legislate in relation to each CFR provision. Further, it is clearly inconsistent that EU legislation is subject to considerable scrutiny for its fundamental rights compliance but that no comparable mechanism exists to hold member states to similar account. With strategic interests and other policy objectives preventing the EU from taking a uniform hardline approach to all those with whom it associates, its external fundamental rights policy is plagued with inconsistent treatment of third states. While this may be the product of genuine political dilemmas to which there are no obvious principled solutions, it nevertheless exposes the EU to the differential treatment accusation, which, in turn, undermines its capacity to exert normative influence beyond its borders. Internal inter-institutional inconsistency with regard to external human rights conditionality also damages the EU's authority in the international arena, further exacerbated by it imposing its founding values more forcefully in third and applicant states than within its own borders. Although the practical and pragmatic work of the FRA in monitoring member states lessens the internal/external dichotomy, it lacks powers of positive enforcement. Its mandate should be expanded to include subjecting member states to systematic scrutiny and contributing to Article 7 TEU decisions. Further, an internal enforcement mechanism, broader than infringement proceedings but less severe than the symbolic Article 7 sanctioning procedure, is also sorely needed. However, though highly desirable, enhanced harmonisation of monitoring and enforcement machinery is unlikely to be politically palatable to member states.

Ironically, the development and successive expansion of the EU's internal fundamental rights policy, although always aimed at legitimation, has in fact contributed to a rise in Euro-scepticism across member states, as discussed in Chapter 1. Specifically, it has triggered a new form of 'value-based Euroscepticism', whereby the EU is perceived as unduly interfering with domestic preferences on ethical issues,[389] with EU initiatives that touch upon highly sensitive areas of national sovereignty, notably in the fields of anti-discrimination and criminal justice, proving particularly unfavourable in some countries, especially the United Kingdom.[390]

The following key question for this study therefore arises: Which, if any, of the conceptual models considered – 'unification', 'separate development', 'organic convergence' or 'constitutional pluralism' – might best apply to the EU's fundamental rights activities on both external and internal dimensions? As far as the external dimension is concerned, three different spheres need to be distinguished: third states entering trade agreements with the EU, EEA-EFTA states and applicant states. Taking third states first, 'unification' can promptly be excluded because there is, by definition, no shared institutional framework of sufficient substance beyond that provided by the terms of the specific agreement. 'Separate development' is not particularly applicable either because fundamental rights commitments shared by the EU itself are nevertheless included. However, neither of the remaining two models quite fits the bill. Since the EU drives the 'convergence' in question, it cannot be adequately described as 'organic.' Yet, although the relationship between the EU and third states is unquestionably 'pluralistic', it would be a stretch to describe it as genuinely 'constitutional'. This suggests a 'separate development/constitutional-pluralism' hybrid, 'guided convergence', the key feature of which is the attempt by the EU to incentivise third states, through trade agreements, to improve compliance with fundamental rights, itself a normative project with constitutional and pluralistic characteristics. It is 'constitutional' because the effective institutionalisation of fundamental rights in any legal system is inherently constitutional, yet it is 'pluralistic' because this can and should be achieved in a wide variety of

---

[389] See C. Leconte, 'The EU Fundamental Rights Policy as a Source of Euroscepticism', *Human Rights Review*, 15(1) (2014), 83–96.

[390] Leconte, 'The EU Fundamental Rights Policy as a Source of Europscepticism', 87–9.

ways, the differences being particularly marked between EU and non-EU states and especially between European and non-western ones. By allowing for cultural and other legitimate forms of relativity to be taken into account, the pluralistic component addresses accusations that the EU enforces Eurocentric standards beyond its borders. For the same reasons this paradigm would also best fit the EEA-EFTA category, while 'constitutional pluralism' is most suitable for accession states on the grounds that their relationship with the EU clearly has both constitutional and pluralistic dimensions, and because 'unification' suggests a degree of standardisation and harmonisation at variance with national sovereignty even in a supranational system.

However, constitutional pluralism provides a much more convincing paradigm for the internal dimension, with the CFR functioning as the key constitutional text providing, in principle, the basis of legality reviews for both EU institutions and member states. The EU's legitimacy to govern would also be enhanced by this model if EU institutions were bound to respect fundamental rights in the same manner as member states are by their national constitutions, if it applied to existing and proposed EU legislation and if this prompted the creation of a new enforcement apparatus aimed at ensuring adherence to fundamental rights by member states in all areas of activity and not just to the implementation of EU law as at present. It is unlikely, however, that this would resolve the crisis of legitimacy, undeniably further damaged by Brexit, which currently confronts the EU. Its failure to tackle current crises in an effective and coordinated manner (as discussed in Chapter 1) also calls into question the value of supranational governance as an effective way to address common threats, and tests the EU's resilience potentially to breaking point. With xenophobic sentiment more vocal and visible across the continent, and the possibility of secessionist referendums in other member states, the EU's survival is no longer as assured as it seemed even a couple of years ago. The Union has, of course, demonstrated its capacity for self-renewal time and time again. The establishment of the European Council, for example, brought much needed political direction to European integration, while the strengthening of the EP vis-à-vis other EU institutions has served to enhance the Union's democratic legitimacy and accordingly undermine one of the main Euro-sceptic arguments levelled against it. The complaint that it is an undemocratic organisation, run by unelected bureaucrats, overlooks the complexity of the institutional framework, the inter-institutional division of powers, developing parliamentary supervision and the new

Spitzenkandidaten system. However, the irony is that, while the establishment of respect for fundamental rights as a founding value of European integration was designed to enhance the Community's legitimacy, it has, instead, contributed to the opposite across member states. While constitutional pluralism may offer enhanced conceptual clarity and coherence, on its own it is unlikely to reverse this trend.

5

The Fundamental Rights Jurisprudence of the European Court of Justice

5.1 Introduction

As this study has already observed many times, while the CE has always concentrated on the further realisation of the rule of law, human rights and fundamental freedoms, the EU and its predecessors focused on economic cooperation and the creation of a common market.[1] For an international organisation with such goals, fundamental rights seemed to be of limited importance, which explains why the ECJ has long remained a relatively unimportant player in the European human rights field.[2] Rather than developing its own human rights doctrines, the ECJ applied existing concepts and notions derived from a variety of national and European sources.[3] Another characteristic of the ECJ's initial approach is that, in cases of conflict, it generally favoured typically EU interests such as free movement rights, over fundamental rights.[4] As discussed in Chapter 1, however, the EU fundamental rights landscape started to change once the CFR became a binding document in 2009 with the result that the ECJ is now growing into a fundamental rights court in its own right, building a fundamental rights *acquis* on a par with that of the ECtHR.[5] As explained in Chapters 1 and 4, the ECJ does not clearly

---

[1] See further Chapter 1.

[2] E.g., B. de Witte, 'The Past and Future Role of the European Court of Justice in the Protection of Human Rights', in P. Alston, M. Bustelo and J. Heenan (eds.), *The EU and Human Rights* (Oxford University Press, 1999), pp. 859–97 at 869–70; G. de Búrca, 'The Evolution of EU Human Rights Law', in P. Craig and G. de Búrca (eds.), *The Evolution of EU Law*, 2nd edn. (Oxford University Press, 2011) pp. 465–97.

[3] Cf., e.g., J. Kühling, 'Fundamental Rights', in A. Von Bogdandy and J. Bast (eds.), *Principles of European Constitutional Law*, 2nd edn. (Oxford: Hart/Beck, 2010), pp. 479–514 at 490; S. Douglas-Scott, 'The European Union and Human Rights after the Treaty of Lisbon', *Human Rights Law Review*, 11 (2011), 645–82 at 649.

[4] E.g., J. Coppel and A. O'Neill, 'The European Court of Justice: Taking Rights Seriously?' *Common Market Law Review*, 29 (1992), 669–92; De Witte, 'The Past and Future Role of the European Court of Justice', 880–1.

[5] Cf. Kühling, 'Fundamental Rights', 481.

distinguish between human and fundamental rights. Furthermore, it has put the classic EU free movement provisions on a par with fundamental rights, calling them 'fundamental freedoms'.[6] In line with the ECJ's approach, the wider term 'fundamental rights' is used throughout this chapter, instead of the notion of 'human rights'. To prevent confusion with the ECHR's terminology, however, 'free movement rights' is used rather than 'fundamental freedoms' to indicate issues of free movement of goods, persons, services and the like.

This chapter reviews the fundamental rights case law of the ECJ. After a brief description of the legal context in which the ECJ delivers its judgments in Section 5.2, it discusses the origins and development of fundamental rights in the ECJ's case law. Sections 5.3 and 5.4 are devoted to the central fundamental rights principles the ECJ has developed in its pre- and post-binding CFR case law, while Section 5.5 deals with the interaction between the CFR, national constitutional rights and the ECHR. Before some conclusions are drawn in Section 5.7, Section 5.6 offers a review of the various substantive rights protected in the CFR to further illustrate their potential and the ECJ's practice.

5.2   Structure and Nature of the EU Judicial System

Principles and Notions Guiding the ECJ[7]

The ECJ has defined its main task as guaranteeing the 'primacy, unity and effectiveness of European Union law'[8] and as 'the pursuit of the EU's objectives', concretised as 'providing for the free movement of goods, services, capital and persons, citizenship of the Union, the area of freedom, security and justice, and competition policy'.[9] Much of the ECJ's case law is based on principles directly related to these objectives

---

[6] See, e.g., *Bosman*, C-415/93, para. 78. On this, see e.g., M. Poiares Maduro, *We the Court* (Oxford: Hart 1998) pp. 166ff. One of the fundamental (market) freedoms (the free movement of persons) even has been 'upgraded' to a real fundamental right by including it in Article 45 of the EU Charter of Fundamental Rights (see Section 6.4).

[7] This section is loosely based on J. H. Gerards, 'Who Decides on Fundamental Rights Issues in Europe?' in S. Weatherill and S. de Vries (eds.), *Five Years Legally Binding EU Charter of Fundamental Rights* (Oxford: Hart 2015), pp. 47–74.

[8] *Melloni*, C-399/11, para. 60.

[9] Opinion 2/13 of 18 December 2014 on the accession of the EU to the ECHR, para. 172. See also, e.g., G. De Búrca, 'Europe's Raison d'Etre', *NYU Public Law & Legal Theory Research Paper Series*, 13-09 (2013), 13. http://ssrn.com/abstract=2224310.

and to the duties of member states in pursuing them.[10] These core principles can be seen to impact upon the ECJ's judicial strategies and the legal-political choices it makes, including in relation to fundamental rights.[11] Important principles are those of direct effect and supremacy, harmony and uniformity in the interpretation of the internal market and competition law, mutual respect and mutual recognition, effectiveness and equivalence of national procedural mechanisms to enforce EU law and, more recently, EU citizenship and the notion of EU autonomy.[12]

Whilst these principles push the ECJ towards strong protection of typical EU values, others pull in the direction of restraint.[13] Regardless of all its important competences, the EU has always remained an organisation that may act 'only' in pursuance of the aims expressly defined in the Treaties. This follows in particular from the principles of attribution and conferral, which imply that EU institutions may exercise only those powers and competences expressly accorded to them by the Treaties.[14] This clearly also limits the degree to which the ECJ may provide for extensive interpretation of fundamental rights.[15]

The principles of attibution and conferral are closely related to those of subsidiarity and proportionality, which also inform the exercise of powers by EU institutions. These imply that what can be regulated on the national level should not be taken up on the level of the EU.[16] The

---

[10] Cf. C. Van de Heyning, *Fundamental Rights Lost in Complexity* (Antwerp: Antwerp University, 2011), pp. 84ff.

[11] E.g., M. Poiares Maduro, 'Interpreting European Law: Judicial Adjudication in a Context of Constitutional Pluralism', *European Journal of Legal Studies*, 1 (2007), 137–52; A. Stone Sweet, 'The European Court of Justice' in P. Craig and G. de Búrca (eds.), *The Evolution of EU Law*, 2nd edn. (Oxford University Press, 2011) pp. 121 at 131–40.

[12] Van de Heyning (ed.), 'Fundamental Rights', p. 84; see also A. Torres Pérez, *Conflicts of Rights in the European Union* (Oxford University Press, 2009), pp. 50ff.

[13] Cf. J. Snell, 'Fundamental Rights Review of National Measures: Nothing New under the Charter?' *European Public Law*, 21 (2015), 285–308 at 300.

[14] E.g., S. Prechal, S. de Vries and H. van Eijken, 'The Principle of Attributed Powers and the "Scope of EU Law"' in L. F. M. Besselink, F. Pennings and S. Prechal (eds.), *The Eclipse of the Legality Principle in the European Union* (Alphen aan den Rijn: Kluwer Law International, 2010), pp. 213–47. This principle has been emphasised even more strongly in the Lisbon Treaty; see M. Dougan, 'The Treaty of Lisbon 2007: Winning Minds, not Hearts', *Common Market Law Review*, 45 (2008), 617 at 654.

[15] See, e.g., S. Prechal, 'Competence Creep and General Principles of Law', *Review of European Administrative Law*, 3 (2010), 5–22.

[16] See Article 5(2) TEU and the Protocol on the Application of the Principles of Subsidiarity and Proportionality; see further, e.g., Dougan, 'The Treaty of Lisbon 2007', 657. Importantly, this limitation also concerns legislation and policy-making in the area of

observance of these principles is strictly scrutinised by member states, in particular some national constitutional courts.[17] Consequently, when the EU institutions, including the ECJ, are perceived to transgress the limits of their powers or to intrude on national (constitutional) law, this may lead to member state protest and, for example, to setting aside or ignoring European law and ECJ judgments.[18]

Finally, an important principle for the ECJ's fundamental rights jurisprudence is that of respect for national constitutional identity (Article 4 (2) TEU).[19] This requires that the ECJ heed central national constitutional principles, including fundamental rights. Like the principles of subsidiarity and conferral, this principle influences the degree to which the ECJ can act in the field of fundamental rights.

Procedural Context

The ECJ's approach to fundamental rights cases is further determined by procedural specificities.[20] Most fundamental rights issues come before the ECJ in the form of a preliminary reference by one of the national courts.[21] Consequently, unlike the ECtHR, the ECJ does not deal with a case that has been fully examined on the national level and closed by a judgment with *res judicata*. Instead, the ECJ is asked for its opinion and interpretation in an ongoing case where the national courts may still have

---

fundamental rights; cf., e.g., S. Besson, 'The Human Rights Competences in the EU – the State of the Question after Lisbon' in G. Kofler, M. Poiares Maduro and P. Pistone (eds.), *Human Rights and Taxation in Europe and the World* (Amsterdam: IBFD, 2011), pp. 37–63.

[17] Cf. the *Lisbon* judgment of the German Federal Constitutional Court of 30 June 2009, 2 BvE 2/08, para. 231 and the *ESM* order of the same court of 18 March 2014, 2 BvR 1390/12, paras. 160ff. See further, e.g., P. Craig, 'The ECJ and Ultra Vires Action: A Conceptual Analysis', *Common Market Law Review*, 48 (2011), 395–437 at 403.

[18] E.g., R. Barents, 'The Precedence of EU Law from the Perspective of Constitutional Pluralism', *European Constitutional Law Review*, 5 (2009), 421–46; Torres Pérez (ed.), 'Conflicts of Rights', 50.

[19] See further, e.g., Van de Heyning (ed.), 'Fundamental Rights', 116–19; L. F. M. Besselink, 'National and Constitutional Identity before and after Lisbon', *Utrecht Law Review*, 6 (2010), 36–49 at 42ff.; A. von Bogdandy and S. Schill, 'Overcoming Absolute Primacy: Respect for National Identity under the Lisbon Treaty', *Common Market Law Review*, 48 (2011), 1417–54 at 1418–19.

[20] Cf. P. Pescatore, 'Fundamental Rights and Freedoms in the System of the European Communities', *American Journal of Comparative Law*, 18 (1970), 343–51, 347; De Witte, 'The Past and Future Role of the ECJ', p. 869; Stone Sweet, 'The European Court of Justice', p. 149.

[21] Article 267 TFEU.

important work to do in terms of establishing and qualifying the facts and assessing the reasonableness of an interference.[22] Preliminary questions thereby usually relate to the interpretation of concrete provisions of primary or secondary EU law, such as the CFR, the Data Protection Directive or the Employment Discrimination Directive, as considered in Chapter 4. The ECJ's aim then is to provide the referring court with the necessary tools and clarification to allow it to apply the provision in a concrete case. Alternatively, a national court may want to know whether a provision of EU law is compatible with EU law, including EU fundamental rights.[23]

Fundamental rights issues may arise also in connection with the infringement procedure of Article 269 TFEU and the direct appeals procedure of Article 263 TFEU discussed in Chapter 4. In infringement proceedings, a member state can be held responsible for not (fully) complying with fundamental rights provisions, such as those contained in fundamental rights directives.[24] By contrast, a member state may be held responsible for a violation of its EU obligations, such as those related to the internal market, and invoke the need to protect fundamental rights as a justification for its lack of compliance. Direct appeals, brought under Article 263 TFEU, require the ECJ to direct its attention to the compatibility of EU decisions and (sometimes) legislation with fundamental rights. The ECJ's task here consists of assessing validity as much as interpretation.[25] In doing so it has to take account of the fact that decisions have been taken by co-equal 'branches of government'.

The procedural set-up in the EU implies that the ECJ's approach is primarily reactive. The ECJ can only interpret and review existing legislation and decisions in response to direct appeals or infringement proceedings, or it can answer national questions on interpretation or validity. The partnership between national courts and the ECJ, created by the preliminary reference system, also means that the ECJ may leave

---

[22] See further, e.g., M. Broberg and N. Fenger, *Preliminary References to the European Court of Justice* (Oxford University Press, 2010); M. Bobek, 'The Court of Justice, the National Courts and the Spirit of Cooperation: Between *Dichtung und Wahrheit*', in A. Lazowski and S. Blockmans (eds.), *Research Handbook on EU Institutional Law* (London: Edward Elgar, 2014) pp. 353–78.

[23] See also, e.g., F. van den Berghe, 'The EU and Issues of Human Rights Protection: Same Solutions to More Acute Problems?', *European Law Journal*, 16 (2010), 112–57 at 114–15.

[24] E.g., *Commission v Hungary*, C-286/12.

[25] Cf. Van den Berghe, 'The EU and Issues of Human Rights Protection', 115.

certain questions to be decided by national courts.[26] The judgments of the ECJ therefore can remain rather open-ended. The principles of conferral and subsidiarity further limit the possibility for it to develop fundamental rights. For example, it cannot simply decide to read new positive obligations into the fundamental rights provisions of the CFR if there is no competence for the EU to act.[27]

5.3   Development of Fundamental Rights by the ECJ

Fundamental Rights as General Principles of EU Law

As already indicated elsewhere in this study, given the mainly economic nature of the original conception of what eventually became the EU, it is not surprising that, initially, it was hardly considered necessary to include any fundamental rights provisions in the Treaties.[28] Over time, however, it became evident that the exercise of powers by the EU institutions could have an impact on fundamental rights.[29] For example, sanctions and surcharges imposed under the common agricultural policy or the competition law regime were seen to interfere with the right to property, the right to a fair trial and the principle of equal treatment.[30]

In response to growing national concern over such interferences, in the 1970s the ECJ started to provide for protection of fundamental rights through its case law.[31] In *Stauder*, it dropped a brief line to the effect that 'the provision at issue contains nothing capable of prejudicing the fundamental human rights enshrined in the general principles of Community law and protected by the Court'.[32] It thereby recognised that

---

[26] D. Sarmiento, 'The Silent Lamb and the Deaf Wolves', in M. Avbelj and J. Komárek (eds.), *Constitutional Pluralism in the European Union and Beyond* (Oxford University Press, 2012), pp. 285–318.

[27] Cf. M. Beijer, *The Limits of Fundamental Rights Protection in the EU* (Antwerp: Intersentia, 2017).

[28] U. Scheuner, 'Fundamental Rights in European Community Law and in National Constitutional Law', *Common Market Law Review*, 12 (1975), 171–91.

[29] M. A. Dauses, 'The Protection of Fundamental Rights in the Community Legal Order', *European Law Review*, 10 (1985), 398–419 at 400.

[30] Pescatore, 'Fundamental Rights', 345; Scheuner, 'Fundamental Rights in European Community Law', 174.

[31] Cf. Dauses, 'The Protection of Fundamental Rights', 400; Coppel and O'Neill, 'Taking Rights Seriously?' 670–1; De Witte, 'The Past and Future Role of the ECJ', p. 866; De Búrca, 'The Evolution of EU Human Rights Law', p. 478; Van de Heyning (ed.), 'Fundamental Rights', 36.

[32] *Stauder*, C-29/69, para. 7.

fundamental rights could form part of the Community legal system in the shape of general principles of Community law.[33] In later judgments the ECJ gradually clarified how certain rights could be identified as forming part of the Community's general principles.[34] In *Internationale Handelsgesellschaft*[35] and *Nold*[36], it made clear that for a right to be regarded as a 'common' principle, there should be sufficient consensus on its fundamental rights character.[37] The ECJ relied on different sources to recognise such consensus, such as the constitutions of member states and human rights treaties ratified by them.[38] The ECJ thereby frequently referred to ECHR provisions as confirmation of the existence of a general principle.[39] With the growth of the body of case law on fundamental rights as principles, the ECJ could also refer to its own precedents in which it had established that a certain right formed part of the general principles of EU law.[40]

This 'fundamental rights as general principles' approach has allowed the ECJ to build its own catalogue of fundamental rights, an approach given further legitimacy by Article 6(2) of the Treaty of Maastricht in 1992.[41] It might have been expected that the ECJ would change its approach following the proclamation of the CFR in Nice in 2000.[42] After all, as discussed in Chapter 1, the drafters of the CFR made a great effort to provide for a modern codification of fundamental rights.[43] It filled some of the gaps of the ECHR, in particular the lack of social and economic rights, and added a number of rights and principles of special

---

[33] Cf. Scheuner, 'Fundamental Rights in European Community Law', 182.

[34] See also Dauses, 'The Protection of Fundamental Rights', 401; Coppel and O'Neill, 'Taking Rights Seriously?' 671; F. G. Jacobs, 'Human Rights in the European Union: The Role of the Court of Justice', *European Law Review*, 26 (2001), 331–41 at 332–3.

[35] *Internationale Handelsgesellschaft*, C-11/70.

[36] *Nold*, C 4/73; see later also, e.g., *Hauer*, C-44//9, para. 15.

[37] Scheuner, 'Fundamental Rights in European Community Law', 183; De Búrca, 'The Evolution of EU Human Rights Law', 478.

[38] E.g., *Rutili*, C-36/75, para. 32; *Hauer*, C-44/79, paras. 17, 20, 22. See in detail, H. C. K. Senden, *Interpretation of Fundamental Rights in a Multilevel Legal System* (Antwerp: Intersentia, 2011), p. 324. See also Van de Heyning, 'Fundamental Rights', p. 39.

[39] See further Senden, 'Interpretation', pp. 356–8.

[40] E.g., *Schräder*, C-265/87, para. 15. See also Senden, 'Interpretation', pp. 330–1.

[41] Cf. De Búrca, 'The Evolution of EU Human Rights Law', 480.

[42] See further B. de Witte, 'The Legal Status of the Charter: Vital Question or Non-Issue?' *Maastricht Journal of European and Comparative Law*, 8 (2001), 81–9 at 84.

[43] G. de Búrca, 'The Drafting of the European Union Charter of Fundamental Rights', *European Law Review*, 26 (2001), 126–38.

importance to the EU. Nevertheless, whilst the General Court used the CFR relatively often,[44] the ECJ continued to rely mainly on its well-established method of referring to general principles and the ECHR.[45] Only in more recent years has the ECJ started to refer to the CFR as a source of interpretation.[46]

The ECJ as a Fundamental Rights Court?

Regardless of the ECJ's efforts to develop a fundamental rights cata-logue as part of the general principles of EU law, its fundamental rights jurisprudence has often been said to be rather reactive. This may be explained by the factors discussed previously, in particular the ECJ's desire to respect and promote the economic 'raison d'être' of European cooperation. Seemingly reasoning from an economic rather than a fundamental rights perspective, for example, the ECJ held in its 1989 *Hoechst* judgment that searches of business premises did not constitute an interference with fundamental rights.[47] In the ECJ's view, enter-prises could not claim the same protection offered by the principle of respect for private life as individuals could under Article 8 ECHR.[48] Similarly, in more recent cases the ECJ has made clear that, in principle, the EU freedoms of movement should prevail over socio-economic rights, such as taking collective action.[49] The ECJ also has been criticised for restricting the *ius standi* of individuals before it in relation to regulatory measures.[50] In the eyes of critics, such judgments

---

[44] *Jégo-Quéré*, T-177/01, para. 42.

[45] *Connolly*, C-274/99 P, paras. 39ff.

[46] *Varec*, C-450/06, para. 48; *Viking Line*, paras. 43–4; *Dynamic Medien*, C-244/06, para. 39; *Promusicae*, C-275/06, paras. 61ff. Possibly this can be explained by the Court's wish to support the Lisbon Treaty – see Dougan, 'The Treaty of Lisbon 2007', 662.

[47] *Hoechst*, C-46/87.

[48] *Ibid.*, paras. 17–18; see further Van den Berghe, 'EU and Issues of Human Rights Protection', at 120.

[49] *Viking Line*, C-438/05, paras. 85–90. Similarly, in *Laval* the Court set rather high demands to be met by trade unions in order to justify a blockade, a specific form of collective action; *Laval un Parteri*, C-341/05, para. 110. See more specifically S. Douglas-Scott, 'The European Union and Human Rights after the Treaty of Lisbon', *Human Rights Law Review*, 11 (2011), 645–82, 678. For a nuanced account, see L. Azoulai, 'The Court of Justice and the Social Market Economy: The Emergence of an Ideal and the Conditions for Its Realisation', *Common Market Law Review*, 45 (2008), 1335.

[50] E.g., J. Heliskoski, 'Fundamental Rights versus Economic Freedoms in the European Union: Which Paradigm?' in J. Klabbers and J. Petman (eds.), *Nordic Cosmopolitanism: Essays in International Law for Martti Koskenniemi* (Leiden: Martinus Nijhoff, 2003)

indicate that the ECJ does not have a favourable attitude towards fundamental rights.[51]

However, this image of the ECJ as a reluctant and strongly market-oriented protector of fundamental rights does not fully do justice to its contribution to the development of human rights in Europe. In some fields the ECJ has always played the role of forerunner and its case law is even further developed than that of the ECtHR.[52] A prime example is the field of non-discrimination and equal treatment.[53] Although the relevant treaty provisions reflect clearly economic motives, they have allowed the ECJ to develop a variety of important concepts, such as those of substantive and indirect discrimination.[54] Similarly, the ECJ has seized on the notion of EU citizenship to infuse EU principles with fundamental rights.[55] This is especially true in the area of freedom, security and justice and in relation to immigration and asylum law, where the ECJ has recognised important rights related to the protection of family life, social interests and residence.[56] Hence, even if the ECJ's fundamental-rights-as-principles jurisprudence might be strongly inspired and informed by the ECJ's economic raison d'être, in many fundamental rights cases it has offered real and meaningful protection.

pp. 417–43; S. Weatherill, 'From Economic Rights to Fundamental Rights', in S. de Vries et al. (eds.), *The Protection of Fundamental Rights in the EU after Lisbon* (Oxford: Hart, 2013), pp. 11–36 at 26.

[51] See more generally, e.g., S. Garben, 'The Constitutional (Im)Balance between "the Market" and "the Social" in the European Union', *European Constitutional Law Review*, 13 (2017), 23–61.

[52] See also Douglas-Scott, 'European Union and Human Rights after Lisbon', 675, although she also mentions that the real concern of the CJEU may not have been the desire to protect fundamental rights effectively as much as to maintain and bolster the autonomy of the EU legal order.

[53] See, e.g., M. Bell, 'The Principle of Equal Treatment: Widening and Deepening', in P. Craig and G. de Búrca (eds.), *The Evolution of EU Law*, 2nd edn. (Oxford University Press, 2011) pp. 611–39 at 615; J. H. Gerards, 'The Discrimination Grounds of Article 14 ECHR', *Human Rights Law Review*, 13 (2013), 99–124.

[54] See further E. Muir, 'The Transformative Function of EU Equality Law', *European Review of Private Law* (2013), 1231–54 at 1236ff.

[55] E.g., *Orfanopoulos*, C-493/01; see further D. Sarmiento, 'Who's Afraid of the Charter? The Court of Justice, National Courts and the New Framework of Fundamental Rights Protection in Europe', *Common Market Law Review*, 50 (2013), 1267–304 at 1271; A. von Bogdandy et al., 'Reverse *Solange* – Protecting the Essence of Fundamental Rights against EU Member States', *Common Market Law Review*, 49 (2012), 489–520 at 503.

[56] E.g., *Baumbast and R*, C-413/99; *Sayn-Wittgenstein*, C-208/09.

5.4   Fundamental Rights in the ECJ's Case Law after Lisbon

Although the CFR has been in place since its proclamation in Nice in 2000, its lack of legal force originally caused the document to play a minor role in the ECJ's case law. This has changed significantly since the Lisbon Treaty entered into force on 1 December 2009 and the CFR has obtained the same status as the Treaties.[57] The number of preliminary questions on fundamental rights issues has surged since that moment, presenting the ECJ with many opportunities to develop its fundamental rights standards and doctrines and to elucidate the text of the CFR.[58] Building on notions and principles it has developed in its earlier jurisprudence on fundamental rights as general principles, the ECJ has set out a number of relatively clear jurisprudential doctrines on a variety of topics, such as the material and personal scope of application, conditions for justification and the relationship between the CFR and national constitutional rights.[59] This section discusses a selection of the most important of these.

Material Scope of Application

Acts and Omissions of EU Institutions

The text of Article 51(1) makes clear that the CFR first and foremost applies to acts, measures and decisions taken by EU institutions, bodies, offices and agencies. The ECJ has confirmed that they may not act against the CFR and it is prepared to review the compatibility of EU legislation and decisions with the CFR provisions.[60] This includes acts of EU institutions that, strictly speaking, fall outside the EU framework, such as the adoption of a memorandum of understanding by the European Commission in connection to the treaty on the European Stability Mechanism

---

[57] On the roles to be played by the binding Charter, see also K. Lenaerts, 'Exploring the Limits of the EU Charter of Fundamental Rights', *European Constitutional Law Review*, 6 (2012), 375–403 at 376–7.

[58] Opinions on the impact of the CFR's becoming binding differ; compare, e.g., S. Weatherill, 'From Economic Rights to Fundamental Rights', in S. de Vries et al. (eds.), *The Protection of Fundamental Rights in the EU after Lisbon* (Oxford: Hart, 2013), pp. 11–36 at 30 and, in the same volume, S. A. de Vries, 'The Protection of Fundamental Rights within Europe's Internal Market after Lisbon – an Endeavour for More Harmony', pp. 59–94 at 74.

[59] Cf. Sarmiento, 'Who's Afraid of the Charter?' 1270.

[60] E.g., *Schecke*, C-92/09, para. 46; *Digital Rights Ireland*, C-293/12.

(ESM).[61] Moreover, the ECJ has held that the CFR entails an obligation to interpret EU measures and decisions in such a way that fundamental rights are respected.[62]

The limit of the applicability of the CFR to EU acts is laid down in Article 51(2), which stipulates that the CFR does not extend the field of application of Union law beyond the powers of the Union. Thus, the CFR cannot be regarded as providing any new competences to EU institutions to act in active protection of fundamental rights, a limitation in line with the fundamental principles underlying EU law, explained earlier.

Importantly, the application of the CFR to acts of the EU may result in the ECJ holding that a legislative act – such as a Directive – is invalid.[63] This may raise questions about the effects of such invalidity for national laws transposing EU legislation. In *Tele2 Sverige* the ECJ provided an answer by holding that national legislation is permitted only as long as it provides solutions to the flaws and omissions the ECJ has found in relation to the original EU legislation.[64] Thus, the responsibility of EU institutions to protect and respect the CFR runs parallel to that of member states.

Acts and Omissions of Member States

Member states of the EU are bound to comply with the CFR only 'when they are implementing Union law' (Article 51(1) CFR).[65] The ECJ's leading judgment on the applicability of the CFR to such implementation is *Åkerberg Fransson*.[66] This builds on the classic *Wachauf* case, where the ECJ held that when a member state transposes a directive into national law, or implements the obligations stemming from a regulation, it must do so in conformity with fundamental rights as recognised by the ECJ.[67] This is logical from the perspective of the principles discussed

---

[61] *Ledra Advertising*, C-8/15 P to C/10–15 P, para. 67.

[62] E.g., *Gueye*, C-483/09, para. 55; *Google Spain*, C-131/12.

[63] E.g., *Digital Rights Ireland*, C-293/12.

[64] C-2013/15 and C-698/15.

[65] E.g., T. von Danwitz and K. Paraschas, 'A Fresh Start for the Charter: Fundamental Questions on the Application of the European Charter of Fundamental Rights', *Fordham International Law Journal*, 35 (2012), 1396–1424 at 1405.

[66] *Åkerberg Fransson*, C-617/10, ECLI:EU:C:2013:105. See elaborately, e.g., A. Ward, 'Article 51 – Field of Application', in S. Peers, T. Hervey, J. Kenner, A. Ward (eds.), *The EU Charter of Fundamental Rights: A Commentary* (Oxford: Hart, 2014), pp. 1413–54 at 1433ff.

[67] *Wachauf*, C-5/88, paras. 19 and 22; see also Jacobs, 'Human Rights in the European Union', 333.

previously since, if member states could decide to disrespect EU fundamental principles unilaterally, the effectiveness of EU law as a whole
would be put at risk.[68] In *Åkerberg Fransson* the ECJ confirmed that
applicability of the CFR should follow the applicability of EU law,
because it would be undesirable if situations existed that would be
covered by EU law without there being any fundamental rights protection.[69] By contrast, if a legal situation does not come within the scope of
EU law, the ECJ has no jurisdiction to rule on it and, accordingly, the
provisions of the CFR cannot be applied either.[70]

In *Siragusa*, the ECJ formulated some criteria to help it decide whether
a national act is covered by EU law and, consequently, by the CFR.[71] The
mere fact that the topic addressed by national legislation is one on which
there is a considerable amount of EU legislation is not sufficient to bring
a case related to national legislation about that topic within the scope of
the CFR.[72] As the ECJ held, 'a certain degree of connection' would be
required 'above and beyond the matters covered being closely related or
one of those matters having an indirect impact on the other'.[73] Some
points to be taken into account in this respect are 'whether the national
legislation is intended to implement a provision of EU law; the nature of
that legislation and whether it pursues objectives other than those
covered by EU law, even if it is capable of indirectly affecting EU law;
and also whether there are specific rules of EU law on the matter or
capable of affecting' it.[74] In addition, even if a national act or omission is
not expressly intended to implement EU law, it can still come within the
scope of the CFR if it aims to pursue typical EU objectives or if it relates
to fundamental rights issues that are of such a nature that the unity,
primacy or effectiveness of EU law could be at stake.[75]

It can be noted that the *Siragusa* criteria are not very precisely formulated, and their interrelationship is not particularly straightforward
either. Perhaps for that reason, they are not often expressly applied. Thus
far, the ECJ mostly rather generally assesses whether a legal situation is

---

[68] *Ibid.*, para. 19.
[69] *Åkerberg Fransson*, C-617/10, para. 21. On this, see also Sarmiento, 'Who's Afraid of the
Charter?' 1278.
[70] *Ibid.*, para. 22.
[71] *Siragusa*, C-206/13.
[72] *Ibid.*, para. 23.
[73] *Ibid.*, para. 24.
[74] *Ibid.*, para. 25.
[75] *Ibid.*, paras. 25 and 31.

governed by EU law.[76] The CFR thus will apply when a member state is acting under an express mandate contained in a rule of EU law, when they are implementing an exhaustively regulated area by EU law yet have received the explicit possibility to make a choice, and when a national court is empowered to guarantee the effectiveness of the rights and obligations derived from EU law.[77]

The scope of application of the CFR in respect of implementation might be rather broad, but the ECJ's jurisprudence reveals several legal situations that do *not* come within EU law. These are situations in which national authorities either exercise powers that are not governed by EU law or they have such a degree of discretion that the choices made must be considered fully their own.[78] In all such cases the determining factor appears to be whether or not the *specific* exercise of powers is dictated or governed by EU law.[79] However, even if a case is excluded from the protection of the CFR, this does not yet mean that individuals derive no protection from fundamental rights. The ECJ has emphasised that national authorities are still bound to respect the ECHR and that domestic courts may examine the compatibility of national measures with the Convention.[80]

In its case law applying fundamental rights as general principles, most notably in the classic *ERT* case, the ECJ has further held that acts and omissions of member states come within the scope of EU law when the member states interfere with EU fundamental freedoms or when they discriminate directly or indirectly on the basis of nationality.[81] The ECJ has also held that Article 51(1) CFR should be read as a continuation of this case law.[82] Consequently, the CFR applies to all cases where a member state fails to discharge its obligations under the Treaty and

---

[76] E.g., *Érsekcsanádi Mezőgazdasági*, C-56/13, para. 54. See further, e.g., Ward, 'Article 51', p. 1452.

[77] Sarmiento, 'Who's Afraid of the Charter?' 1280–5.

[78] E.g., *Pelckmans*, C-483/12, paras. 22–5; *Poclova*, C-117/14; *Sindicato dos Bancários do Norte*, C-128/12, para. 12; *Nagy*, C-488/12; *X and X*, C-638/16PPU. This is a difficult field, however, because in some cases of discretion the Charter still will be held to apply; see, e.g., *N. S.*, C-411/10; cf. Lenaerts, 'Exploring the Limits of the EU Charter', 380; Ward, 'Article 51', p. 1437.

[79] *Kaltoft*, C-354/13, paras. 36–40; *Érsekcsanádi Mezőgazdasági*, para. 54; *Hernández*, C-198/13, para. 39; *Dano*, C-333/13, paras. 89–91; *Eurosaneamientos*, C-532/15, para. 54.

[80] E.g., *Dereci*, C-256/11, paras. 72–3; *Jeremy F.*, C-168/13 PPU, para. 48.

[81] See also Jacobs, 'Human Rights in the European Union', 335.

[82] *Pfleger*, C-390/12, para. 36; see also Snell, 'Fundamental Rights', 298.

invokes one of the exceptions in justification,[83] such as where a member state invokes the need to protect or respect a fundamental right in justification of the infringement of EU law, or where a member state infringes a fundamental right as a consequence of its restriction of one of the EU freedoms of movement.[84] In the latter case, however, the ECJ may be inclined to apply the EU provisions on fundamental freedoms rather than the provisions of the CFR, especially if the right invoked is closely related to these freedoms (e.g. the freedom to conduct a business or the right to property).[85] The free movement right is then considered to encapsulate this particular fundamental right or freedom, rendering it unnecessary to pay separate attention to the CFR.

Application of the CFR in Relation to Private Parties

The question may arise to what extent private parties (such as companies or employers) can be held responsible for not respecting the provisions of the CFR and whether national courts could apply the CFR provisions in civil law cases. The notion of horizontal effect, i.e., the application of fundamental rights in relations between private parties, has created particular difficulties for the ECJ.[86] Four different situations can be distinguished regarding the extent to and the way in which EU fundamental rights may affect private parties.

Effect of Primary EU Law in Relations between Private Parties

First, it is well recognised that most of the fundamental freedoms laid down in primary EU law also have effect in horizontal relationships.[87]

---

[83] See critically on this Snell, 'Fundamental Rights', 302–4.

[84] For the latter situation, see, e.g., Runevič-Vardyn, C-391/09.

[85] E.g., Sokoll-Seebacher, C-367/12, paras. 22–3; Pfleger, C-390/12, paras. 57–60.

[86] There is much confusion over the use of different concepts, typologies and distinctions. For the sake of clarity, it has been attempted here to avoid controversial notions and describe the various situation types instead. On terminology, see in particular A. S. Hartkamp, 'The Concept of (Direct and Indirect) Horizontal Effect of EU Law', in U. Bernitz, X. Groussot and F. Schulyok (eds.), General Principles of EU Law and European Private Law (Alphen aan den Rijn: Wolters Kluwer, 2013), pp. 189–97. See also, e.g., M. Safjan and P. Miklasziewicz, 'Horizontal Effect of the General Principles of EU Law in the Sphere of Private Law', European Review of Private Law (2010), 475–86; and M. Fornasier, 'The Impact of EU Fundamental Rights on Private Relationships: Direct or Indirect Effect?' European Review of Private Law (2015), 29–46.

[87] There is some uncertainty as to the horizontal applicability of the free movement of goods.

The ECJ has held, for example, that free movement of workers can as easily be impeded by employers or trade unions as by member state authorities, and for that reason, they too have to respect the relevant treaty provisions.[88] In addition, a private party, such as an employer, may invoke fundamental rights in order to justify limitations upon the free movement of workers or services.[89] In this category of cases, no real difference appears to be discernible between horizontal and vertical situations as regards the way in which the ECJ applies fundamental rights.[90]

Interpretation of Secondary Legislation Applicable to Relations between Private Parties

Second, some EU legislation expressly aims to apply to relations between private parties. The EU non-discrimination directives, for example, are clearly intended to regulate employment relationships.[91] Similarly, for many private actors, the data protection directive and the directives in the field of the media and intellectual property law are of great relevance.[92] When civil law disputes arise over the implementation or application of such directives, national courts may refer preliminary questions about it to the ECJ, thereby raising the issue of CFR compliance.[93] Since

---

[88] See classically, e.g., *Walrave and Koch*, C-36/74; *Bosman*, C-415/93; *Angonese*, C-281/98.

[89] See in particular, e.g., *Omega*, C-36/02; *Viking Line*, C-438/05, paras. 33–37 and 77ff. See also, e.g., C. Sieburgh, 'General Principles and the Charter in Private Law Relationships', in U. Bernitz, X. Groussot and F. Schulyok (eds.), *General Principles of EU Law and European Private Law* (Alphen aan den Rijn: Wolters Kluwer, 2013), pp. 233–47 at 237 and 242–3.

[90] There could be good reason for making such a difference, however; see, e.g., C. Mak, 'Unchart(er)ed Territory – EU Fundamental Rights and National Private Law', in A. S. Hartkamp, J. S. Kortmann, C. Sieburgh and M. Wissink (eds.), *The Influence of EU Law on National Private Law* (Deventer: Kluwer, 2014), pp. 323–53 at 325–6.

[91] See in particular Directive 2000/43 (on race and ethnicity) and Directive 2000/78 (establishing a general framework for equal treatment in employment and occupation). On the impact of these directives for private law, see, e.g., Muir, 'The Transformative Function', p. 1241.

[92] On this form of horizontal effect, see also M. Claes, 'The EU, Its Member States and Their Citizens', in D. Leczykiewicz and S. Weatherill (eds.), *The Involvement of EU Law in Private Law Relationships* (Oxford: Hart, 2013), pp. 29–52.

[93] E.g., *Hennigs and Mai*, C-297/10, paras. 65–8. See further D. Leczykiewicz, 'Horizontal Effect of Fundamental Rights: In Search of Social Justice or Private Autonomy in EU Law?' in U. Bernitz, X. Groussot and F. Schulyok (eds.), *General Principles of EU Law and European Private Law* (Alphen aan den Rijn: Wolters Kluwer, 2013), pp. 171–86 at 172.

they determine how the EU legislation has to be understood and applied by the national courts, the ECJ's answers may have an impact on the outcome of private law disputes.[94] For example, the ECJ has held that the use of surveillance cameras by natural persons, such as home owners, can be regarded as data processing.[95] Such use of cameras, even for purely private purposes such as providing security against burglary, might infringe Article 7 CFR insofar as it constitutes video surveillance (even partially) of a public space.[96] Although exceptions to the obligation to protect personal data are allowed,[97] individuals can, thus, be held responsible for respecting and protecting the fundamental rights of others.

Claims That a Provision of National Law Is Incompatible with EU Fundamental Rights

Third, it is sometimes claimed in a horizontal conflict that a provision of national law, such as legislation on unfair dismissal, is incompatible with one of the EU fundamental rights principles.[98] In these cases, although the question of validity stems from a horizontal conflict, the ECJ may be asked to determine whether the national legislation is compatible with EU fundamental rights. From the perspective of the ECJ, these cases concern a 'vertical' issue, even though, eventually, the interpretation given in its judgment may have implications for the national private law dispute. This situation does not seem to present the ECJ with any particular difficulties, as it can apply its normal CFR review to the national legislation (or the EU legislation lying at its basis), in conformity with the standards discussed later.[99]

---

[94] See M. Wissink, 'Interpretation of Private Law in Conformity with EU Directives', in A. S. Hartkamp, J. S. Kortmann, C. Sieburgh and M. Wissink (eds.), *The Influence of EU Law on National Private Law* (Deventer: Kluwer, 2014), pp. 119–58. This impact may be far-reaching; see, e.g., *Test-Achats*, C-236/09 and *Prigge*, C-447/09; see further Mak, 'Unchart (er)ed territory'.

[95] *Ryneš*, C-212/13.

[96] *Ibid.*, para. 33.

[97] This question was left to be answered by the national courts – see *ibid.*, para. 34.

[98] E.g., *Rasmussen*, C-441/14.

[99] See section 4.4.1. On this situation, see C. Ladenburger, 'European Union Institutional Report', in J. Laffranque (ed.), *The Protection of Fundamental Rights Post-Lisbon* (Tartu: Tartu University Press, 2012), pp. 141–215 at 190.

Direct Applicability of the CFR in Relations between Private Parties

Finally, matters become rather more complex if a case between two private parties concerns fundamental rights laid down in a directive.[100] According to classic EU doctrine, a directive cannot of itself impose obligations on individuals; nor can it be relied on against a private party.[101] However, the question has been raised if this could be different where a party to a national private law dispute could support a claim by pointing to a fundamental right protected by EU law.[102] In the pre-Lisbon *Mangold* case, which concerned a horizontal conflict about an arguably discriminatory employment contract, the ECJ held that the relevant directive merely codified the fundamental principle of non-discrimination.[103] Although it would not be possible to invoke the directive as such in this private law dispute, the ECJ concluded that the national court had the responsibility to provide 'the legal protection which individuals derive from the rules of Community law and to ensure that those rules are fully effective, setting aside any provision of national law which may conflict with that law'.[104] This approach was consolidated in later ECJ case law, most notably in *Kücükdeveci*.[105] Nevertheless, it has remained unclear whether the ECJ will be inclined to apply this line of

---

[100] Cf. C. Sieburgh, 'A Method to Substantively Guide the Involvement of EU Primary Law in Private Law Matters', *European Review of Private Law* (2013), 1165–88 at 1179; X. Groussot, T. Lock and G. T. Petursson, 'The Reach of EU Fundamental Rights on Member State Action after Lisbon', in S. de Vries, U. Bernitz and S. Weatherill (eds.), *The Protection of Fundamental Rights in the EU after Lisbon* (Oxford: Hart, 2013), pp. 97–118 at 109.

[101] See classically *Faccini Dori*, C-91/92, para. 20.

[102] See more elaborately, e.g., Sieburgh, 'A Method to Guide', 1179; W. Devroe and P. Van Cleynenbreugel, 'The Impact of General Principles of EU Law on Private Law Relationships', in A. S. Hartkamp, J. S. Kortmann, C. Sieburgh and M. Wissink (eds.), *The Influence of EU Law on National Private Law* (Deventer: Kluwer, 2014), pp. 187–218 at 194.

[103] *Mangold*, C-144/04, para. 74.

[104] *Ibid.*, para. 77. It may be argued that this is an indirect horizontal effect, since it is actually the national omission to implement (which is a vertical situation) that is reviewed, rather than the act of the private party to the national case; see Ladenburger, 'European Union Institutional Report', p. 190. Nevertheless, it is evident that the horizontal relationship is impacted; see Sieburgh, 'A Method to Guide', 1179 and M. de Mol, '*Kücükdeveci*: *Mangold* Revisited – Horizontal Effect of a General Principle of EU Law', *European Constitutional Law Review*, 6 (2010), 293–308.

[105] *Kücükdeveci*, C-555/07, para. 53; see also De Mol, '*Kücükdeveci*: *Mangold* Revisited', 293–308. In turn, this will impact the way the private law dispute is decided on the national level; see further, e.g., Sieburgh, n. 98, at 241.

reasoning to other fundamental rights and whether it will be willing to do so even if there is no similarly strong history of recognition of the right as a central EU principle.[106] Moreover, it has remained an open question whether it would be possible to invoke EU fundamental rights successfully in purely horizontal cases, without there being an intermediary in the form of EU secondary legislation.[107] Thus far, the Court has shown itself reluctant to deal with these questions.[108] The following clarifications have, nevertheless, emerged.

First, the ECJ's judgment in *Kristensen* seems to make clear that it is not strictly necessary to invoke a 'vertical' element in a purely private relationship in order to trigger the application of EU fundamental rights.[109] In *Mangold*, the parties to the private law dispute had argued that a legislative provision governed their interrelationship, which was incompatible with EU non-discrimination rights. In effect, the case thus contained a 'vertical' element in the sense described earlier. By contrast, the *Kristensen* case concerned an occupational pension scheme that was not prescribed by legislation or by a collective agreement, but stemmed from the employment contract concluded between a private employer and its employees.[110] The ECJ emphasised in its judgment that the employment non-discrimination directive could not as such impose any obligations on the employer as a private party, but it also recalled its earlier holding that the principle of non-discrimination must be regarded as a general principle of EU law.[111] Moreover, since the directive expressly addressed all persons, as regards both the public and the private sectors, the principle of equal treatment could be invoked against the employer.[112] Consequently, the

---

[106] Cf., e.g., Safjan and Miklasziewicz, 'Horizontal Effect', 480; De Mol, '*Kücükdeveci*: *Mangold* Revisited', 302–3.

[107] Cf. Devroe and Van Cleynenbreugel, 'The Impact of General Principles of EU Law', 195; Claes, 'The EU, Its Member States and Their Citizens'; Groussot, Lock and Petursson, 'The Reach of EU Fundamental Rights', pp. 111; Safjan and Miklasziewicz, 'Horizontal Effect', 478. On the terminology see also Hartkamp, 'The Concept of Horizontal Effect', p. 193.

[108] See, e.g., *Dominguez*, C-282/10, where the Court construed the conflict as in fact being of a vertical nature, since the employer could be regarded as a public authority and thus as part of the state.

[109] *Kristensen*, C-476/11.

[110] *Ibid.*, para. 12.

[111] *Ibid.*, para. 18.

[112] *Ibid.*, para. 24.

ECJ could review the compatibility of the occupational pension scheme with the CFR.[113] Thus, this judgment seems to confirm that the equality principle not only applies in horizontal conflicts when there is an 'intermediary' in the shape of national legislation, but also when the interference with the equality principle is directly caused by a private party.

Second, the *AMS* case concerned a conflict between a trade union and an association organising reintegration activities for unemployed persons (AMS).[114] The national court had asked the ECJ whether the fundamental right of workers to information and consultation, as recognised by Article 27 CFR, could be invoked in a dispute between private parties in order to assess the compliance with EU law of a national measure implementing the relevant directive. This case did not concern a purely horizontal situation, since the litigation really only served to challenge a national legislative measure. Nevertheless, the ECJ felt obliged to explain whether the CFR could be directly invoked in a dispute between private parties.[115] It thereby focused on the interpretation of Article 27 CFR, holding that 'for this article to be fully effective, it must be given more specific expression in European Union or national law'.[116] By contrast with the prohibition of age discrimination, which played a central role in the *Mangold* case, this provision 'could not be seen to confer on individuals an individual right which they may invoke as such'.[117] Accordingly, the ECJ decided that Article 27 CFR could not be invoked in a horizontal dispute in order to conclude that a national provision that is not in conformity with a directive should not be applied.[118] It can be gleaned from this that the ECJ will not easily hold CFR provisions to be applicable in horizontal cases outside the particular area of non-discrimination law. Therefore, it does not seem to make much difference whether such cases on the national level concern a 'vertical' issue, i.e. the compatibility of national legislation with EU law, or whether they are fully 'horizontal', e.g. where a decision of an employer directly infringes an EU fundamental right. There is considerable room for uncertainty here, however, as in

---

[113] *Ibid.*, para. 32.
[114] *AMS*, C-176/12.
[115] *Ibid.*, para. 36. On the qualification of this case as one of horizontal effect, see also Fornasier, 'The Impact of EU Fundamental Rights', 44.
[116] *AMS*, C-176/12, para. 45.
[117] *Ibid.*, para. 47.
[118] *Ibid.*, para. 48.

the *AMS* case the ECJ carefully restricted its reasoning to one specific CFR provision only.[119]

Rights Holders: Individuals, Legal Persons and Public Authorities

The CFR makes many distinctions between the groups who may claim a fundamental right.[120] Certain rights are expressly accorded to 'citizens', such as the right to vote in Article 39, while other rights, such as to protection against unfair dismissal in Article 30, can be claimed only by 'workers'. For the principle of fair administration, now codified in Article 41 CFR, the ECJ has held that it 'does not, in itself, confer rights on individuals, except where it constitutes the expression of specific rights for the purposes of Article 41'.[121] Sometimes the rights holders are not even clear. In particular, the CFR leaves some uncertainty as to whether the rights can be claimed only by individuals, or also by legal persons. In the *DEB* case the ECJ clarified that provisions that are addressed to 'persons' generally will also cover legal persons.[122] This will not be the case for all CFR rights, however. Rights that are closely connected to human dignity, such as the right to life or the right to integrity of the person, can only be invoked by human beings.[123]

A related question is whether CFR rights can be claimed by public authorities or by legal persons closely connected to the state. The ECtHR has consistently rejected claims that such authorities can benefit from the protection of Convention rights and has held that ECHR rights are only available to private parties.[124] By contrast, the ECJ has held that at least the rights of the defence and of effective judicial protection 'may be invoked by any natural person or any entity bringing an action before the Courts of the European Union', even if such an entity is of a public law nature.[125] Generally, therefore, it may be said that when a

---

[119] See also Fornasier, 'The Impact of EU Fundamental Rights', 43–5.
[120] See also D. Curtin and R. van Ooik, 'The Sting Is Always in the Tail: The Personal Scope of Application of the EU Charter of Fundamental Rights', *Maastricht Journal of European and Comparative Law*, 8 (2001), 102–14 at 103.
[121] *Growth Energy*, T-276/13, para. 304.
[122] *DEB*, C-279/09, para. 38.
[123] *Idem*, para. 39.
[124] E.g., *Radio France and Others* v *France* (dec.), HUDOC, 23 September 2003, para. 26; *Ljubljanska Banka D. D.* v *Croatia* (dec.), HUDOC, 12 May 2015.
[125] *Bank Mellat*, C-176/13 P, para. 49.

fundamental right is capable of being invoked by a legal person, under EU law it can also be invoked by a state body or public authority.

Judicial Review of Rights and Principles

As indicated in Chapter 4, the CFR includes a much wider set of fundamental rights than does the ECHR. In particular it also covers a number of socio-economic rights, a right to good administration and several citizen's rights.[126] Since the protection of these rights might involve claims on national budgets or influence national policy priorities, the relevant provisions were extensively debated in the drafting process.[127] Initially, this was not considered particularly problematic, because the CFR would not be a binding document and its provisions would merely serve as aids to the interpretation of already existing legal obligations.[128] When it was decided that the CFR would be given the same legal value as the Treaties, however, a new section 5 was added to Article 52.[129] This stipulates that provisions of the CFR that contain principles 'may be implemented by legislative and executive acts taken by institutions, bodies, offices and agencies of the Union, and by acts of Member States when they are implementing Union law, in the exercise of their respective powers. They shall be judicially cognisable only in the interpretation of such acts and in the ruling on their legality'.

On a narrow reading, Article 52(5) could be understood as meaning that principles serve as guidance when the ECJ is interpreting secondary law that directly and specifically implements them, but they cannot serve as an independent basis for legality review.[130] On a wider reading, however, in cases involving implementation legislation, principles could be used as a judicial touchstone for reviewing the legality of such

---

[126] See further Chapter 4 and Section 5.6 of this chapter.

[127] See in more detail, e.g., D. Guðmundsdóttir, 'A Renewed Emphasis on the Charter's Distinction between Rights and Principles: Is a Doctrine of Judicial Restraint More Appropriate?', *Common Market Law Review*, 52 (2015), 685–720 at 688–9; J. Krommendijk, 'Principled Silence or Mere Silence on Principles?' *European Constitutional Law Review*, 11 (2015), 321–56.

[128] In fact, it was precisely because social rights had also been included that the Charter originally was proclaimed as a non-binding document; see Krommendijk, 'Principled Silence or Mere Silence on Principles?'

[129] On this, see, e.g., Ladenburger, 'European Union Institutional Report', p. 183; Krommendijk, 'Principled Silence or Mere Silence on Principles?'

[130] Cf. Guðmundsdóttir, 'A Renewed Emphasis', 691; Krommendijk, 'Principled Silence or Mere Silence on Principles?'

legislation.[131] Thus far the ECJ has not clarified whether and when it will adopt a narrow or a wide reading. Possibly the choice will depend on the degree to which the relevant CFR provisions can be considered justiciable, i.e. whether they are deemed sufficiently precise and unconditional to provide a sufficiently operational standard.[132]

Article 52(5) raises the further question of how it can be determined which provisions in the CFR contain principles and which 'subjective', judicially enforceable rights.[133] The Explanatory Notes to the CFR provide some guidance by stating relatively clearly that some provisions contain principles rather than rights. In relation to other provisions, however, the Explanatory Notes are ambiguous and not of much help.[134] The ECJ has not yet been in a position to provide much clarity in these matters.[135] An exception is *Glatzel*, which concerned Article 26 CFR on the rights of disabled persons.[136] Briefly referring to the Explanation Notes, and mentioning that in order for that article to be fully effective it must be given more specific expression in EU or national law, the ECJ held that this provision contains a principle rather than a right.[137]

Review of Justification

Article 52(1) CFR contains an express and generic limitation clause that makes very clear the requirements interferences should meet in order to be justified.[138] At the same time, the generic nature of Article 52(1) means that it is not linked with the content of concrete fundamental rights.[139] It does not contain any specifically formulated legitimate aims, for example, but states that limitations can be acceptable if they

---

[131] Cf., e.g., Krommendijk, 'Principled Silence or Mere Silence on Principles?'

[132] Cf. Ladenburger, 'European Union Institutional Report', p. 185.

[133] See A. W. Heringa and L. F. M. Verhey, 'The EU Charter: Text and Structure', *Maastricht Journal of European and Comparative Law*, 8 (2001), 11–32 at 14.

[134] Cf. Dougan, 'The Treaty of Lisbon 2007', 663; Von Danwitz and Paraschas 'A Fresh Start for the Charter', 1412; Lenaerts, 'Exploring the Limits of the EU Charter', 400; Ward, 'Article 51', p. 1417; S. Peers and S. Prechal, 'Article 52 – Scope and Interpretation of Rights and Principles', in Peers et al., 'The EU Charter', 1506–7.

[135] See further Guðmundsdóttir, 'A Renewed Emphasis', 694.

[136] *Glatzel*, C-356/12.

[137] *Ibid.*, paras. 74 and 78. See also Krommendijk, 'Principled Silence or Mere Silence on Principles?'

[138] In some cases the ECJ has continued to apply the standards developed in its previous case law (see, e.g., *Deutsches Weintor*, C-544/10).

[139] Cf. Peers and Prechal, 'Article 52 – Scope and Interpretation', 1476.

'genuinely meet objectives of general interests'.[140] While the fundamental-rights-as-principles approach allowed the ECJ to formulate specific standards for specific types of right and for specific types of situation, the justification clause of Article 52(1) CFR leaves less room for doing so. The ECJ has not really seemed to be bothered by this in practice, however. In cases where the CFR's justification clause seems difficult to apply, or where specific standards have been well entrenched in its case law, the ECJ either does not refer to Article 52(1) at all, or, on the basis of its pre-Lisbon case law, it redefines or adds to the criteria it mentions. Examples of this are visible in cases regarding the scope or proportionality of punitive sanctions,[141] the freezing of assets[142] and cases related to equal treatment.[143]

It is also important to note that some CFR provisions contain specific requirements for limitation, regardless of Article 52(1). An example is Article 8 on data protection, the second section of which specifies that data must be processed fairly for specified purposes and on the basis of the consent of the person(s) concerned or some other legitimate basis in law, while the third section provides that compliance with these rules shall be subject to control by an independent authority. These clauses do not bypass the applicability of Article 52(1). Instead, limitations of the right to protection of one's personal data must be compatible with both the specific requirements of Article 8(2) and (3) and the general requirements of Article 52(1).[144]

The generic nature of the justification clause of Article 52(1) CFR theoretically allows for exemptions to be made to *all* fundamental rights listed in the CFR, including otherwise ostensibly 'absolute', non-derogable rights such as the prohibition of torture, freedom of conscience and the prohibition of the retroactive application of criminal law.[145] However, it follows from Article 52(3) that insofar as the CFR contains rights that correspond to the rights guaranteed by the ECHR, the meaning and scope of those rights shall be the same as those laid down

---

[140] *Ibid.*

[141] E.g., *Chalkor*, C-386/10P, paras. 57ff; *Texdata*, C-418/11.

[142] E.g., *Al-Aqsa*, C-539/10P, paras. 121ff.

[143] E.g., *Chatzi*, C-149/10, para. 64; *Soukupóva*, C-401/11; *Glatzel*, C-356/12.

[144] E.g., *Schwartz*, C-291/12, paras. 31 and 34.

[145] Although Peers has convincingly argued that even a literal reading of the text does not expressly say so; Peers and Prechal, 'Article 52 – Scope and Interpretation', 1469.

there.[146] Consequently, regardless of the wording of Article 52(1) CFR, where the ECtHR has held that certain rights should be regarded as subject to no exceptions, the CFR follows suit.[147]

Furthermore, Article 52(1) explicitly states that any limitation should 'respect the essence' of CFR rights. It is not yet clear how the ECJ intends to apply this 'core rights notion'.[148] In some cases it has begun its review of the justification for limitations by assessing whether the individual right asserted can be considered part of the very core of a right as defined in the CFR.[149] If this is the case, the ECJ would not need to go any further in scrutinising the justification, since limitations of the essence of the right are not acceptable anyway.[150] However, in most cases the ECJ seems to adopt a less 'absolute' approach by reviewing the reasonableness of a limitation of a human right without establishing a priori whether a core right is at stake. It will then find a violation only if the assessment reveals that, in the circumstances of the case, the 'very essence' of the human right has been affected.[151] If that is so, what constitutes the core of a right is merely what is left of it after the limitation: this discloses a 'relative' rather than 'absolute' approach towards core Charter rights.[152]

When the ECJ applies the other requirements of Article 52(1) CFR, it usually does do so with great care and precision, determining the compliance with each requirement individually, including new elements such as that the interference must be 'provided for by law'.[153] In some cases, it

---

[146] See also Heringa and Verhey, 'The EU Charter', 24–5; see in more detail on Article 52(3), Peers and Prechal, 'Article 52 – Scope and Interpretation', 1491ff.

[147] See also Lenaerts, 'Exploring the Limits of the EU Charter', 388.

[148] There is much scholarly debate on this and a variety of meanings have been accorded to the notion; for a good overview, see A. E. M. Leijten, *Core Rights and the Protection of Socio-Economic Interests by the European Court of Human Rights* (Leiden: Leiden University, 2015).

[149] E.g., *Digital Rights Ireland*, C-293/12, paras. 38–40; *Schrems*, C-362/14, para. 94. See also T. Ojanen, 'Making the Essence of Fundamental Rights Real: The Court of Justice of the European Union Clarifies the Structure of Fundamental Rights under the Charter', *European Constitutional Law Review*, 12 (2016), 318–29 at 322ff.

[150] See in particular *Schrems*, C-362/14, para. 94 and Ojanen, 'Essence of Fundamental Rights'.

[151] E.g., *UPC*, C-314/12, paras. 51–3.

[152] E.g., *Romonta*, T-614/13, para. 59; *Sky Österreich*, C-283/11, para. 49. On the different possible approaches, see further Leijten, 'Core Rights'.

[153] E.g., *Schecke*, C-92/09; *Digital Rights Ireland*, C-293/12. Sometimes the reasoning is rather cursory, but even then most elements of Article 52(1) are briefly touched upon; see, e.g., *Holcim (Romania)*, T-317/12, para. 169. On the requirement of a legal basis, see

has set higher requirements for the legal basis of interferences than the ECtHR. For example, the ECJ has expressly required that conditions for the deprivation of liberty are laid down in binding rules of general application, rather than in well-established case law.[154]

The various proportionality requirements contained in the CFR help the ECJ structure its reasoning in a clear fashion.[155] It thereby tends to pay more attention to the different elements of the proportionality test than the ECtHR. Whilst the latter often resorts to a rather general balancing approach, the ECJ typically applies requirements of suitability and necessity and often relies on a 'least onerous means' test.[156] By comparison with its classic case law on the application of the rule of reason and the proportionality test in relation to cases on free movement rights,[157] the ECJ now also more readily seems to include an element of balancing.[158] In particular it has demanded that national authorities and EU institutions, when dealing with conflicting fundamental rights (either when devising new legislation or when applying or interpreting existing legislation), ensure a fair balance between the different rights and interests concerned.[159] Finally, the ECJ has noted that in addition to the requirements expressly mentioned in Article 52(1), it may be important to provide for procedural safeguards to ensure effective protection of the right concerned against the risk of abuse.[160]

Deference and the Margin of Appreciation

In its case law reviewing the justification for limitations upon fundamental rights, the ECJ has not developed a fully fledged 'margin of

---

further, e.g., Lenaerts, 'Exploring the Limits of the EU Charter', 390 and Peers and Prechal, 'Article 52 – Scope and Interpretation', 1471ff.

[154] Al Chodor, C-528/15, para. 45.

[155] There are some exceptions; see Peers and Prechal, 'Article 52 – Scope and Interpretation', 1479.

[156] E.g., Schecke, C-92/09, para. 78; Digital Rights Ireland, C-293/12.

[157] E.g., Dynamic Medien, C-244/06, paras. 46ff.

[158] E.g., Romonta, T-614/13, paras. 75ff. In some cases, the ECJ restricts itself to a test of necessity; see, e.g., Schwartz, C-291/12 and Achbita, C-157/15 – in the latter case, it thereby took a different approach and reached a different outcome than the ECtHR did in a similar case, without further explanation.

[159] See, e.g., ASNEF, C-468/10, para. 43; Deckmyn, C-201/13, para. 27.

[160] E.g., Digital Rights Ireland, C-293/12, paras. 66ff; the Court seems to derive this requirement from the text of Article 8(2) and (3).

appreciation doctrine' or a 'doctrine of deference'.[161] Especially in pre-Lisbon cases it hardly ever stated which factors determined the intensity of its review of interferences with fundamental rights, and it rarely highlighted the impact of a certain degree of deference for the standard of review and the burden of proof.[162] Since the CFR became binding, the ECJ's overall approach seems to have changed. In recent years, for example, the presence of a fundamental rights dimension to a case has become a factor the ECJ increasingly refers to in determining the strictness of review.[163] This is particularly evident from the *Digital Rights Ireland* case, where the ECJ mentioned factors such as 'the nature of the right at issue guaranteed by the CFR, the nature and seriousness of the interference and the object pursued by the interference'.[164] Similarly, in *Google Spain* the ECJ held that national courts should carefully balance the interests of protection of personal data against the (commercial) interests of the enterprise engaged in data processing, given the potential seriousness of the interference with the right to data protection.[165] In the context of cases about expulsion or extradition of aliens to states where there might be a risk of prosecution or of inhuman or degrading treatment, the ECJ also has left little discretion to member states.[166] In all such cases, the importance of a fundamental right and the seriousness of an interference clearly invite strict review, either by the ECJ or by national courts, regardless of any factors arguing for judicial restraint, such as the 'better placed' factor, the sensitivity and complexity of the aims

---

[161] In some cases the Court does not even clarify whether it will apply deferential, 'standard' or strict review – e.g., *Schecke*, C-92/09. For a further analysis, see, e.g., J. H. Gerards, 'Pluralism, Deference and the Margin of Appreciation Doctrine', *European Law Journal*, 17 (2011), 80–120. Some commentators have stated that there would be no place for such a doctrine in the EU; see Peers and Prechal, 'Article 52 – Scope and Interpretation', p. 1481.

[162] See in more detail Gerards, 'Pluralism, Deference'.

[163] Cf. also, e.g., G. Anagnostaras, 'Balancing Conflicting Fundamental Rights: The *Sky Österreich* Paradigm', *European Law Review*, 39 (2014), 111–24 at 118.

[164] *Digital Rights Ireland*, C-293/12 para. 47. See similarly, but in relation to national legislation rather than EU legislation, *Tele2 Sverige*, C-203/15.

[165] *Google Spain*, C-131/12, para. 81. For another situation type in which the Court reached a similar outcome, see, e.g., *Scarlet Extended*, C-70/10, paras. 48–9.

[166] See, e.g., *N. S. and Others*, C-411/10; in cases on medical care, however, the margin of discretion appears to be wider and member states may more easily presume that the level of health care in other member states is adequate; see *C. K.*, C-578/16PPU, para. 70, but see also paras. 81ff.

pursued, the policy area or the lack of a European common approach.[167]

By contrast, the ECJ seems willing to be more deferential if a fundamental right does not appear to be seriously affected, if the case concerns a less important aspect of a fundamental right or if it deals with socioeconomic principles rather than subjective rights.[168] An example can be found in *Sky Österreich*, which concerned the freedom to conduct a business.[169] Although the ECJ did not expressly deal with the notion of deference or the margin of appreciation in this case, it set slightly lower standards for accepting the justification for the interference, for example by merely requiring that the 'disadvantages caused must not be disproportionate to the aims pursued'. Similarly, the ECJ has allowed for a wide margin of appreciation in cases where there is little European consensus on a certain matter, such as concepts of public policy.[170] In cases where EU institutions have exercised powers in areas requiring complex economic, technical or medical assessments, the ECJ has also accorded a margin of discretion,[171] which usually results in a test of manifest arbitrariness or manifest disproportionality.[172]

Finally, it should be noted that deferential review is not the only way for the ECJ to keep its distance in controversial or sensitive cases. In many instances it responds to national differences by avoiding the really thorny issues,[173] by narrowing its interpretation to the exact circumstances of the case[174] or by leaving certain matters to be decided by national courts. The latter approach is chosen mainly in relation to the necessity and proportionality of restrictions upon fundamental rights[175] with the ECJ then often leaving to the national courts the exact balance to be struck.[176]

---

[167] For the relevance of such factors for the Court's older case law, see, e.g., Gerards, 'Pluralism, Deference'.

[168] E.g., *Specht*, C-501/12, para. 46.

[169] *Sky Österreich*, C-283/11.

[170] E.g., *Sayn-Wittgenstein*, C-208/09, para. 87; *Bogendorff von Wolffersdorff*, C-438/14, para. 79.

[171] E.g., *Chalkor*, C-386/10P, para. 54; *Glatzel*, C-356/12, paras. 52–3.

[172] E.g., *Chalkor*, C-386/10P, para. 54; *Otis*, C-199/11, para. 59.

[173] E.g., *C. D.*, C-167/12; *Z.*, C-363/12.

[174] E.g., *Brüstle*, C-34/10; *International Cell Corporation*, C-364/13.

[175] See further Sarmiento, 'The Silent Lamb'.

[176] E.g., *Kušionová*, C-34/13, para. 68; cf. also *Ryneš*, C-212/13, para. 34; *A. B. and C.*, C-148/13, para. 72. In some cases the Court is more willing to provide for the answer to be given by the national courts; see, e.g., *Deckmyn*, C-201/13.

Positive Obligations

Compared to the ECtHR, the ECJ has had little opportunity to develop a full-fledged doctrine of positive obligations.[177] This can be explained by the legal context explained previously. Procedural restraints, as well as the limitations posed by the principles of conferral and attribution, make it difficult for the ECJ to define obligations and requirements beyond those that are already contained in EU treaties and in secondary legislation.[178] Indeed, in its CFR case law the ECJ does not expressly refer to the notion of positive obligations; nor has it relied on any of the factors used by the ECtHR, such as the fair balance test or the reasonable knowledge test, to define them.[179]

Nevertheless, the ECJ has imposed some positive obligations on member states and EU institutions.[180] For example, member states have been required to ensure the rights of the defence in all cases where they could be negatively affected by application of EU law, even where the applicable legislation does not (yet) expressly provide for this.[181] Member states should further designate competent courts and tribunals and should provide for detailed procedural rules allowing individuals to enforce rights derivable from EU law.[182] For EU institutions, the obligations include providing adequate reasons for decisions, access to information, a possibility to be heard and adequate judicial review.[183] It is clear from these examples that the positive obligations defined by the ECJ have been limited to the procedural sphere.[184] Indeed, for the reasons

---

[177] See in more detail M. Beijer, 'Active Guidance of (Procedural) Fundamental Rights Protection by the European Court of Justice', *Review of European Administrative Law*, 8 (2015), 127–50; C. Stubberfield, 'Lifting the Organisational Veil: Positive Obligations of the European Union Following Accession to the European Convention on Human Rights', *Australian International Law Journal*, 19 (2012), 117–42 at 125; Beijer, 'The Limits of Fundamental Rights'.

[178] Cf. Besson, 'The Human Rights Competences'; P. van Cleynenbreugel, 'Judge-Made Standards of National Procedure in the Post-Lisbon Constitutional Framework', *European Law Review*, 37 (2012), 90–100.

[179] Beijer, 'The Limits of Fundamental Rights'.

[180] *Ibid.*; see also Van Cleynenbreugel, 'Judge-Made Standards', 92ff; Prechal, De Vries and Van Eijken, 'The Principle of Attributed Powers', 239ff.

[181] E.g., *ZZ*, C-300/11, paras. 53/55; *M. G. and N. R.*, C-383/13PPU; *Texdata*, C-418/11, paras. 79ff; *Kamino*, C-129/13, para. 31; *Mukarubega*, C-166/13, paras. 46ff.

[182] E.g., *Inuit*, C-583/11P, para. 102; *UPC/Telekabel Wien*, C-314/12, para. 57; *Liivimaa Lihaveis MTÜ*, C-562/12, para. 68.

[183] E.g., *Trabelsi*, T-187/11, para. 66; *Bamba*, C-417/11P, paras. 50ff; *Kadi (II)*, C-584/10P, paras. 97ff.

[184] Cf. Beijer, 'The Limits of Fundamental Rights'.

mentioned earlier, it is not very likely that the ECJ would be willing to impose any substantive positive obligations, such as to introduce legislation.[185] Even in rare cases where substantive obligations can be identified, such as to ensure adequate length of parental leave for parents of twins or to provide an asylum seeker with emergency health care and essential treatment of illness, they derive from the provisions and obligations laid down in EU legislation, rather than from the ECJ's judgments.[186]

Filling the Gaps – Interpretation and Further Development of Fundamental Rights

While the codification of rights in the CFR is a relatively recent manifestation of fundamental rights thinking, views on fundamental rights will continue to change. In addition, the CFR leaves certain lacunas, as the drafters cannot possibly have foreseen all potential fundamental rights cases and covered them in advance. Moreover, many terms and notions contained in the CFR are rather open and underdetermined, allowing much room for interpretation and gap filling. In some cases, the ECJ fills such gaps by referring to the case law of the ECtHR, especially if questions concern corresponding provisions in the ECHR that the ECtHR has interpreted in previous case law.[187] When such guidance is lacking, the ECJ also may rely on the Explanatory Notes.[188] Article 52(7) CFR expressly provides that these 'shall be given due regard by the courts of the Union and the Member States'.[189] Moreover, the explanations to Article 52(4) CFR indicate how the ECJ can deal with any gaps left by the CFR by stating that 'the Charter rights concerned should be interpreted in a way offering a high standard of protection which is adequate for the law of the Union and in harmony with the common constitutional

---

[185] It has been argued that there is sufficient basis for such recognition of positive obligations in the CFR (cf. O. De Schutter and I. De Jesus Butler, 'Binding the EU to International Human Rights Law', *Yearbook of European Law* 27 (2008), 277–320), but this has not yet been accepted by the Court.

[186] Cf. *Chatzi*, C-149/10, para. 75; *N. S.*, C-411/10; *Puid*, C-4/11; *Abdida*, C-562/13, para. 62. See further also Beijer, 'The Limits of Fundamental Rights'.

[187] E.g., *Achbita*, C-157/15, para. 27.

[188] See also Von Danwitz and Paraschas, 'A Fresh Start for the Charter', 1422; Lenaerts, 'Exploring the Limits of the EU Charter', 402; and, elaborately, J. P. Jacqué, 'The Explanations Relating to the Charter of Fundamental Rights of the European Union', in Peers et al., 'The EU Charter', 1714–24.

[189] *Spacic*, C-129/14PPU, para. 54; *Abdida*, C-562/13, para. 51.

traditions'.[190] Gap filling thus can be based on the classic approach of recognising fundamental rights as general principles of EU law.[191] The ECJ has held that where the CFR cannot be applied directly because the facts of the case pre-date the entry into force of the Lisbon Treaty, a right can be invoked as a general principle if it is among the fundamental rights that form an integral part of the EU legal order.[192] The methods the ECJ has used during the first decades of development of fundamental rights therefore continue to play an important role.[193]

5.5   The Relationship Between the Charter of Fundamental Rights, National Constitutional Rights and the ECHR

The CFR and National Constitutional Rights

The interrelationship between EU law and national constitutional law has always been complex, especially as far as fundamental rights are concerned. The German Federal Constitutional Court has held that member states are the masters of the Treaties and they may apply *ultra vires* review in cases where fundamental rights are affected.[194] It is thus not excluded that constitutional courts may hold that protection of national constitutional rights should prevail over application of EU law.[195]

Seemingly, this national position is in tune with Article 53 CFR, which states that

> nothing in this Charter shall be interpreted as restricting or adversely affecting human rights and fundamental freedoms as recognised, in their respective fields of application, by Union law and international law and by international agreements to which the Union or all the Member States are party, including the European Convention for the Protection of Human Rights and Fundamental Freedoms, and by the Member States' constitutions.

---

[190] See also, e.g., Peers and Prechal, 'Article 52 – Scope and Interpretation', p. 1505; Ladenburger, 'European Union Institutional Report', p. 145.

[191] See, e.g., *DEB*, C-279/09, paras. 38–53, 59; *Polkomtel*, C-397/14, paras. 59ff.

[192] *Sabou*, C-276/12, para. 28; *Kamino*, C-129/13, para. 29; *Polkomtel*, C-397/14.

[193] This is in line with Article 52(4), which stipulates that the CFR provisions must be interpreted in conformity with the constitutional traditions of the member states; see also Ward, 'Article 51', 1418.

[194] See, e.g., the *Lisbon* judgment of the German Federal Constitutional Court of 30 June 2009, 2 BvE 2/08, Judgment of paras. 231 and 241; see also Craig, 'The ECJ'.

[195] See also Snell, 'Fundamental Rights', 295.

To all appearances, this provision, which finds a parallel in Article 53 ECHR, implies that the highest level of protection of fundamental rights should be respected, even if this level is provided for in national rather than EU law, and even if this would mean that respect for national constitutional law should prevail over the application of EU law.[196] Nevertheless, legal scholars have suggested different possible readings of the clause,[197] and in 2013, in *Melloni*, the ECJ added its own, authoritative, alternative to the list.[198] The case concerned an extradition request regarding a person who had been sentenced *in absentia*, a situation with respect to which the Spanish constitution sets exceptionally high procedural standards, which were not in line with the EU legislation on the European arrest warrant. This led the Spanish constitutional court to ask the ECJ whether Article 53 CFR could be held to imply that the national constitutional protection could prevail over the obligations resulting from the European arrest warrant system. The ECJ began its answer by making clear that the relevant EU legislation did not leave any discretion to national authorities to refuse to execute a European arrest warrant. Moreover, it held that it was itself compatible with fundamental rights as protected by the CFR.[199] Subsequently, the ECJ addressed the question whether, in these circumstances, surrender of a person could still be made conditional on compliance with fundamental procedural rights as guaranteed in a national constitution.[200] The ECJ noted that such an interpretation would have the effect that national constitutional law would be given priority over the application of provisions of EU law.[201] It added that 'such an interpretation of Article 53 of the Charter cannot be accepted'[202] because it 'would undermine the principle of the primacy of EU law inasmuch as it would allow a Member State to disapply EU legal rules which are fully in compliance with the Charter where they

---

[196] See, e.g., Besselink, n. 100, p. 73.

[197] See specifically e.g., J. B. Liisberg, 'Does the EU Charter of Fundamental Rights Threaten the Supremacy of Community Law?' *Common Market Law Review*, 38 (2001), 1171; C. van de Heyning, 'No Place Like Home: Discretionary Space for the Domestic Protection of Fundamental Rights' in P. Popelier, C. van de Heyning and P. van Nuffel (eds.), *Human Rights Protection in the European Legal Order* (Antwerp: Intersentia, 2011), 65; Torres Pérez, 'Conflicts of Rights'.

[198] *Melloni*, C-399/11; see also A. Torres Pérez, '*Melloni* in Three Acts: From Dialogue to Monologue', *European Constitutional Law Review*, 10 (2014), 308–31.

[199] *Ibid.*, paras. 49, 52–3.

[200] *Ibid.*, para. 55.

[201] *Ibid.*, para. 56.

[202] *Ibid.*, para. 57.

infringe the fundamental rights guaranteed by that State's constitution',[203] and since settled case law of the ECJ holds that 'rules of national law, even of a constitutional order, cannot be allowed to undermine the effectiveness of EU law on the territory of that State'.[204] Consequently, the ECJ held that Article 53 would only allow national constitutional rights to be applied to the level specifically provided by them if 'the primacy, unity and effectiveness of EU law are not thereby compromised'.[205]

It should be noted that the judgment in *Melloni* concerned a rather special situation, as the framework decision on the European arrest warrant leaves hardly any discretion to member states to apply their own national (constitutional) law. Instead, it provides for full regulation of fundamental rights issues.[206] Indeed, on the same day the ECJ handed down the *Melloni* judgment, it held in *Åkerberg Fransson* that 'in a situation where action of the Member States is not entirely determined by European Union law (...), national authorities and courts remain free to apply national standards of protection of fundamental rights, provided that the level of protection provided for by the Charter, as interpreted by the Court, and the primacy, unity and effectiveness of European Union Law are not thereby compromised'.[207] The ECJ also made clear, however, that, in case of doubt, it is not up to national courts to decide whether or not national constitutional rights might be applied. In *Åkerberg Fransson* the ECJ held that 'where national courts find it necessary to interpret the Charter they may, and in some cases must, make a reference to the Court of Justice for a preliminary ruling'.[208]

Hence, the ECJ does not acknowledge any pretence by national constitutional courts of maintaining their 'mastership' of the Treaties, and it will not accept appeals by states to their obligations under the ECHR to provide a high level of protection that would conflict with the protection provided under EU law.[209] Instead, the ECJ strives to provide a high level

---

[203] *Ibid.*, para. 58.
[204] *Ibid.*, para. 59.
[205] *Ibid.*, para. 60.
[206] See also Sarmiento, 'Who's Afraid of the Charter?' 1289.
[207] *Åkerberg Fransson*, C-617/10, para. 29; see also B. de Witte, 'Article 53 – Level of Protection', in Peers et al., 'The EU Charter', 1530.
[208] *Ibid.*, para. 30.
[209] *Ibid.*, paras. 184, 186, 188. In some circumstances the ECJ may be open to justifications of interferences with fundamental rights that are clear expressions of national

of human rights protection of its own, especially in recent cases on the European arrest warrant.[210]

The CFR and the ECHR

According to Article 52(3) CRF and the Explanatory Notes, CFR rights that correspond to rights guaranteed by the ECHR must be given the same meaning and scope as ECHR rights, although this obligation does not stand in the way of a more extensive protection in EU law.[211] This provision serves to harmonise the fundamental rights obligations imposed on member states and ensures that the generic limitation clause of Article 52(2) CFR is not applied to allow limitations and restrictions upon non-derogable rights such as the prohibition of torture.[212] The ECJ has confirmed that CFR provisions containing rights corresponding to those guaranteed by the ECHR must be given the same scope and meaning as Convention provisions as interpreted in the ECtHR's case law.[213]

In the light of Article 52(3) CFR, it might be expected that the ECJ would frequently take the ECtHR's jurisprudence into account, and developments over the past few years show that this has indeed been the case.[214] Notably, however, the number of references to the Strasbourg case law has recently declined and been increasingly replaced by references to the ECJ's own precedents.[215] The ECJ now even takes the position that the CFR should be the primary source for fundamental rights in the EU and that it is no longer necessary to refer to the ECHR in

---

constitutional values; see, e.g., *Sayn-Wittgenstein*, C-208/09, paras. 85ff. See also Von Bogdandy and Schill, 'Overcoming Absolute Primacy', 1423.

[210] See, e.g., *Petruhhin*, C-182/15.

[211] On the background and drafting history of this provision, see P. Lemmens, 'The Relation between the Charter of Fundamental Rights of the European Union and the European Convention on Human Rights – Substantive Aspects', *Maastricht Journal of European and Comparative Law*, 8 (2001), 49–67.

[212] K. Lenaerts and E. de Smijter, 'The Charter and the Role of the European Courts', *Maastricht Journal of European and Comparative Law*, 8 (2001), 90–101 at 96ff.

[213] E.g., *McB.*, C-400/10PPU, para. 53. In some cases the General Court has continued to apply the ECHR; see *Degussa*, T-341/12, paras. 123–6.

[214] E.g., *DEB*, C-279/09; *McB.*, C-400/10PPU, para. 54; *N. S.*, C-411/10, paras. 88ff.

[215] G. de Búrca, 'After the EU Charter of Fundamental Rights: The Court of Justice as a Human Rights Adjudicator?' *Maastricht Journal of European and Comparative Law*, 20 (2013), 168–84; J. Krommendijk, 'The Use of ECtHR Case Law by the Court of Justice after Lisbon: The View of Luxembourg Insiders', *Maastricht Journal of European and Comparative Law*, 22 (2015), 812–35.

cases where a fundamental right is also to be found in the CFR.[216] Moreover, the General Court has taken a rather restrictive interpretation of Article 52(3), holding that there is a need to apply ECtHR precedents only in cases where the facts are sufficiently comparable to those of cases decided by the ECtHR.[217]

However, such 'flying solo' by the ECJ is not necessarily problematic since the ECJ still refers to the ECtHR's case law when there is a risk of divergence, when new questions arise on which there is already relevant ECtHR, or when the ECJ wants to stress the convergence between the two human rights instruments for other reasons.[218] Although some scholars have pointed out that the two Courts sometimes take a different approach towards fundamental rights, and may approach similar factual and legal situations differently,[219] the lack of citation does not appear to disclose an intentional departure from the ECtHR's approach.[220]

Nevertheless, as already indicated in Chapter 1, it seems that friendly relations between the two courts have come under strain. This is most apparent with respect to the ECJ's rejection of the intended accession of the EU to the ECHR on the grounds that the ECtHR would become the final arbiter in all fundamental rights matters, including those in which EU law plays a central role. From the outset it was clear that this prospect would be difficult to reconcile with the EU's claim to autonomy.[221] Yet, in the accession negotiations, representatives of member states, the EU and the CE tried to find ways around it and an Accession Agreement was eventually drafted that was acceptable to all and that contained a number of complex procedural elements to guarantee the EU's involvement in all stages of the procedure before the ECtHR.[222] Yet, when the ECJ was asked to give its (binding) opinion on the compatibility of the Accession Agreement with EU law and with fundamental EU principles, it

---

[216] See expressly, e.g., *Chalkor*, C-386/10 P, para. 51; *Otis*, C-199/11, para. 47; *Paoletti*, C-218/15, paras. 21–22.

[217] *Association Justice & Environment*, T-727/15, para. 73.

[218] E.g., *Jeremy F.*, C-168/13 PPU, para. 43; *M'Bodj*, C-542/13, para. 39; *Abdida*, C-562/13, para. 47; *Bogendorff von Wolffersdorff*, C-438/14, para. 55; *JZ*, C-294/16PPU, paras. 48ff.

[219] E.g., *Delvigne*, C-650/13.

[220] De Búrca, 'After the EU Charter'; Krommendijk, 'Use of ECtHR Case Law after Lisbon'.

[221] E.g., De Búrca, 'The Evolution of EU Human Rights Law' at 488.

[222] E.g., T. Lock, 'End of an Epic? The Draft Agreement on the EU's Accession to the ECHR', *Yearbook of European Law*, 31 (2012), 162–97; X. Groussot, T. Lock and L. Pech, 'EU Accession to the European Convention on Human Rights: A Legal Assessment of the Draft Accession Agreement of 14th October 2011', *European Issues No. 218*, 7 November 2011.

transpired that it had a far stronger view on the need to protect EU autonomy than the negotiating parties expected.[223] In its Opinion 2/13 of 18 December 2014 the ECJ identified various consequences of accession that would be incompatible with the autonomy, effectiveness and uniformity of EU law at risk.[224] The legal consequences of this opinion are not yet clear, but it is widely expected that accession will, at least, be put on hold, with the result that the two supranational courts will continue to coexist as before, with equal power to decide on European fundamental rights issues, until new relations are settled, if they ever are. In some cases since the ECJ delivered its opinion, it seems to have taken a rather aggressive approach to the matter. In *J. N.*, for example, the ECJ emphasised that the obligation to ensure consistency between the CFR and the ECHR may not adversely affect 'the autonomy of Union law and that of the Court of Justice of the European Union'.[225] Yet, in others, it has made a deliberate effort to align its own approach with that of the Convention. In the *Aranyosi* case, the ECJ even accepted that the core EU principles of mutual trust and mutual recognition should be set aside if this would be the only way to guarantee respect for the prohibition of inhuman or degrading treatment, in line with the ECtHR's settled case law.[226] It is, therefore, rather difficult to predict how the relations between the two European Courts will develop in future.

5.6   Rights Protected by the CFR

As discussed in Chapter 4, it was the express intention of the drafters of the CFR to provide a broad and modern fundamental rights catalogue, comprising not only classic rights and freedoms, but also socioeconomic rights and rights directly related to EU law. The result is a list of fifty substantive provisions, which typically contain more than one right. In fact, it can easily be said that the CFR encompasses at least seventy-five different (aspects of) substantive rights. A great many of these have already been invoked before the ECJ, although some provisions appear more frequently than others. This has allowed the

---

[223] Cf. also Lenaerts, 'Exploring the Limits of the EU Charter', 393, who stresses the importance of the EU's autonomy in interpreting the EU Charter in the light of the Convention.

[224] Opinion 2/13 of 18 December 2014.

[225] *J. N.*, C-601/15 PPU, para. 47.

[226] *Aranyosi*, C-404/15 and C-659/15 PPU, paras. 88ff; cf also *Meroni*, C-559/14, para. 42.

ECJ to develop and specify further the notions and doctrines discussed in previous sections.

The substantive provisions of the CFR are grouped together in six chapters or Titles. Title I contains dignity-related rights, Title II comprises freedoms (such as freedom of religion and freedom to conduct a business), Title III lists a number of equality-related rights, Title IV contains 'solidarity rights' (mostly socio-economic rights), Title V is on citizens' rights (such as the right to vote and freedom of movement), while Title VI concerns justice rights (such as the right to a fair trial).

Title I – Dignity

The CFR opens with a chapter devoted to 'Dignity'. Articles 2 to 5 relate to specific aspects, such as the rights to life and to integrity, while Article 1 protects the right to human dignity as such by stipulating that human dignity is inviolable and that it must be respected and protected.[227] Thus, human dignity constitutes a fundamental right in itself, which can be directly invoked by individuals.[228] The right to dignity has not as such surfaced in the ECJ's case law yet.[229] However, since the Explanatory Notes also mention that human dignity 'constitutes the real basis of fundamental rights', it is also a foundational principle for the CFR as a whole and a value that must inform the interpretation of all EU law.[230] In this respect the ECJ frequently uses the provision as an interpretative aid when it comes to interpretation of primary and secondary EU law, such as directives and decisions on the patentability of biotechnological inventions,[231] or the rights of asylum seekers or prisoners.[232] Furthermore, the notion of human dignity has be invoked by member states to justify limitations upon EU law, such as those concerning the freedom to provide services.[233] The Explanatory Notes stress that human dignity

---

[227] See more elaborately C. Dupré, 'Article 1. Human Dignity', in Peers et al., 'The EU Charter', 3–24.

[228] Explanatory Notes to Article 1 CFR.

[229] Cf. Dupré, 'Human Dignity', para. 01.44.

[230] Especially when read in conjunction with Article 2 TEU; see Dupré, 'Human Dignity', para. 01.03.

[231] See, e.g., *Brüstle*, C-34/10; *International Stem Cell Corporation*, C-364/13. Often the Court merely pays lip service to it; e.g., *Cimade*, C-179/11, para. 42.

[232] E.g., *Saciri*, C-79/13, para. 35; *A., B. and C.*, C-148/13, para. 65; *Aranyosi*, C-404/15 and C-659/15PPU, para. 85.

[233] *Omega*, C-36/02.

constitutes the very core of all rights contained in the Charter and emphasises that 'it must therefore be respected, even where a right is restricted'. This is particularly relevant in connection with Article 52(1) CFR, which states that restrictions upon CFR rights can only be justified if the very essence of the right remains unaffected, which may be connected with human dignity.

Article 2 CFR states that everyone has the right to life and prohibits the death penalty and execution.[234] This provision has proved relevant mainly as an interpretative aid for secondary EU legislation in the field of asylum and immigration law, as well as in relation to health and human reproduction issues.[235]

In practice, the prohibition of torture and inhuman and degrading treatment or punishment in Article 4 CFR plays a more important role.[236] For example, asylum seekers and migrants qualify for subsidiary protection under Directive 2004/38 when there is a real risk of suffering 'serious harm', which includes not only the death penalty and execution and other serious individual threats to life or to the person, but also 'torture or inhuman or degrading treatment or punishment of an applicant in the country of origin' (Article 15 (b)). The ECJ has held that this directive must be read in line with Article 4 and Article 19(2) CFR, which provides an express prohibition on non-refoulement for cases in which removal, expulsion or extradition would expose someone to a serious risk of the death penalty, torture or other inhuman or degrading treatment or punishment. The ECJ further interprets Article 4 in conformity with the identical provision of Article 3 ECHR, which means that the right guaranteed by Article 4 CFR is considered 'absolute'.[237] While the ECJ generally follows the lead of the ECtHR in setting standards,[238] it, nevertheless, sometimes provides slightly different interpretations.[239] In *Aranyosi*, for example, it set some strict and specific requirements of its

---

[234] In more detail, see E. Wicks, 'Article 2. Right to Life', in Peers et al., 'The EU Charter', 25–38.

[235] Cf. Wicks, 'Right to Life', paras. 02.02–08.

[236] Cf. M. Nowak and A. Charbord, 'Article 4. Prohibition of Torture and Inhuman or Degrading Treatment or Punishment', in Peers et al., 'The EU Charter', 61–99, para. 04.03.

[237] *Aranyosi*, C-404/15 and C-659/15 PPU, para. 86.

[238] See, e.g., *N. S.*, C-411/10, paras. 86, 88–90 and 106; *C. K.*, C-578/16 PPU, para. 68. See also Nowak and Charbord, 'Prohibition of Torture', para. 04.30.

[239] *Abdida*, C-562/13, para. 50; compare with *N. v the United Kingdom*, HUDOC, 27 May 2008 (GC), paras. 42–3.

own for domestic courts considering whether to refuse to surrender a prisoner to another member state because of problematic prison conditions there.[240] Finally, in common with the ECtHR, the ECJ has held that procedural safeguards and effective remedies are essential to protection against torture and inhuman or degrading treatment or punishment. By contrast with the ECtHR, however, the ECJ usually does not read these safeguards into the substantive provision of Article 4 CFR, but applies the procedural provisions of Article 47 CFR instead.[241]

The other two provisions of Title I relate to the integrity of the person (Article 3) and the prohibition of slavery and forced labour (Article 5); Article 5 also expressly prohibits trafficking in human beings. Both the right to integrity of the person and the prohibition of trafficking have no clearly corresponding provision in the ECHR.[242] As yet, Article 3 has not played any concrete role in the ECJ's case law, including in cases where this would have been possible.[243] Where it has been invoked, it has been referred to as forming part of the right to human dignity more generally.[244]

No cases have yet been presented to the ECJ on the prohibition of trafficking in Article 5 either.[245] Similarly, the number of cases on the prohibition of forced labour thus far has been limited, although there is some potential for the provision to play a role in cases brought by civil servants working for EU institutions or in national employment cases.[246] If the ECJ is ever confronted with any such case, it will probably apply the standards and criteria developed by the ECtHR in its case law on the corresponding provision of Article 4 ECHR.[247]

---

[240] *Aranyosi*, C-404/15 and C-659/15 PPU, paras. 88ff.

[241] E.g., *Abdida*, C-562/13.

[242] See further on this provision S. Michalowski, 'Article 3. Right to the Integrity of the Person', in Peers et al., 'The EU Charter', 39–60.

[243] The Court could have referred to it in the *Léger* case on blood donation by homosexual men (*Léger*, C-528/13) or the aforementioned cases on patentability of biotechnological inventions involving stem cells and human embryos (*Brüstle*, C-34/10; *International Stem Cell Corporation*, C-364/13). See also Michalowski, 'Right to Integrity of the Person', paras. 03.47–51.

[244] See, e.g., *Abdida*, C-562/13, para. 30; see earlier also *Netherlands v European Parliament and Council*, C-377/86, para. 70.

[245] See further on this H. Askola, 'Article 5. Prohibition of Slavery and Forced Labour', in Peers et al., 'The EU Charter', 101–19, para. 05.02.

[246] Cf. *Ruipérez Aguirre and ATC Petition v Commission*, T-487/10 and C-111/11 P.

[247] Cf. Askola, 'Prohibition of Slavery', para. 05.15ff.

Title II – Freedoms

Title II CFR encompasses a number of 'classic' fundamental rights and freedoms, most of which correspond to rights contained in the ECHR. Consequently, in line with the obligation under Article 52(3) CFR, the ECJ needs to interpret these rights in conformity with the ECtHR's case law.

The first freedom protected by Title II CFR is the right to liberty and security (Article 6).[248] Compared to Article 5 ECHR the right is stated very briefly, but according to the Explanatory Notes this is not intended to have any bearing on its interpretation: the rights are to be given the same meaning and scope. The provision is of particular importance to migration and asylum law, as some EU directives allow member states to detain third country nationals pending the decision on their admission or awaiting their expulsion or return.[249] Similarly, the right to liberty and security plays a role in the area of freedom, security and justice (Title V TFEU), which provides a legal basis for cooperation in relation to criminal justice.[250] In its interpretation of Article 6 CFR, the ECJ sometimes expressly refers to the requirements set by the ECtHR in its case law on Article 5 ECHR,[251] while in other cases it has provided interpretations of its own.[252] The case of *J. N.*, for example, is related to Directive 2013/33 (the Return Directive), which allows for detention of aliens required to leave a member state.[253] The ECJ held that, on condition that the principle of proportionality is taken into account, Article 6 CFR allows for such detention when it is intended to protect national security and public order. It also pointed out that the ECtHR has held that a deprivation of liberty will be justified only for as long as deportation or extradition proceedings are in progress. If such proceedings are not prosecuted with due diligence, the detention will cease to be permissible under Article 5(1)(f) ECHR. In *J. N.*, the ECJ concluded that this

---

[248] See further also D. Wilsher, 'Article 6. Right to Liberty and Security', in Peers et al., 'The EU Charter', 121–52.

[249] Wilsher, 'Right to Liberty and Security', paras. 06.04–06.05.

[250] E.g., in relation to the European arrest warrant (OJ 2009 L 81, p. 24); cf., e.g., *Lanigan*, C-237/15PPU; *JZ*, C-294/16PPU; *Vilkas*, C-640/15. See for other potential areas of application, Wilsher, 'Right to Liberty and Security', para. 06.03.

[251] *Lanigan*, C-237/15PPU, paras. 55–6 and 59–61.

[252] Sometimes it is necessary to do so as secondary legislation contains a different term, such as 'detention'; such terms are interpreted in the light of Article 6 CFR, as in *JZ*, C-294/16PPU, paras. 48ff and *Vilkas*, C-640/15, paras. 40ff.

[253] *J. N.*, C-601/15PPU.

judgment of the ECtHR could justify certain cases of prolonged and continued detention for security reasons.[254]

An exception to the overall correspondence between the freedoms of Title II of the CFR and the ECHR provisions is Article 8 CFR, which protects personal data.[255] Other aspects of privacy are protected by Article 7 CFR. In relation to personal data cases, the ECJ regards Articles 7 and 8 as so closely connected as to be hardly separable, and, probably for that reason, it generally applies them jointly without specifying which aspects of its judgment relate to which provision.[256] This is unfortunate given that Article 8(2) and (3) CFR contain a number of specific exemptions in addition to the possible justifications under Article 52(1) CFR.[257] Thus far, the ECJ has not really explained the relationship between the different exemption clauses.[258]

Articles 7 and 8 CFR have proved to be of great importance in relation to personal data. Indeed, this is one of the areas where the ECJ provides more detailed protection than the ECtHR and where it has taken the lead in setting standards for review.[259] The ECJ has generally held that 'the right to respect for private life with regard to the processing of personal data (...) concerns any information relating to an identified or identifiable individual',[260] a notion covering a wide number of situations, ranging from the publication of the names of beneficiaries of a funding scheme,[261] to taking and storing fingerprints for use in passports,[262] and intercepting telecommunications or emails.[263] A decisive issue is whether the data 'objectively contain unique information about individuals which

---

[254] *Ibid.* paras. 78ff.
[255] See, e.g., J. Vested-Hansen, 'Article 7. Respect for Private and Family Life (Private Life, Home and Communications)', in Peers et al., 'The EU Charter', 153–82; H. Kranenborg, 'Article 8. Protection of Personal Data', in Peers et al., 'The EU Charter', pp. 223–66.
[256] See, e.g., *Schecke*, C-92/09; *Schwarz*, C-291/12; *Digital Rights Ireland*, C-293/12; *Schrems*, C-362/14, para. 39.
[257] Cf. *Google Spain*, C-131/12, para. 69.
[258] See further in particular Kranenborg, 'Protection of Personal Data', paras. 08.152ff; G. G. Fuster, *The Emergence of Personal Data Protection as a Fundamental Right of the EU* (Cham: Springer, 2014), p. 214; for an exception, see *Google Spain*, C-131/12, para. 69.
[259] For a review and assessment, see, e.g., M. Brkan, 'The Unstoppable Expansion of the EU Fundamental Right to Data Protection: Little Shop of Horrors?' *Maastricht Journal of European and Comparative Law*, 23 (2016), 812–41.
[260] E.g., *Schecke*, C-92/09, para. 52.
[261] *Ibid.*
[262] *Schwarz*, C-291/12.
[263] *WebMindLicences*, C-419/14, paras. 70–2.

allows those individuals to be identified with precision'.[264] The ECJ also has indicated that a wide number of interferences are covered by Article 7, whether they relate to storage or retention of data, the possibility for certain authorities to have access to it,[265] or video surveillance by a private person, which also covers (even partially) a public space.[266]

The ECJ tends to review rather strictly whether EU legislation allowing processing of personal information is compatible with Articles 7 and 8 CFR.[267] It pays considerable attention to the effectiveness and appropriateness of collecting and storing certain information, as well as to the 'strict necessity' of doing so.[268] In many cases it also examines whether a 'proper balance' has been struck between the right to protection of one's private life and personal data and the particular general interest allegedly served by processing personal data in a specific way.[269] Moreover, the ECJ has consistently held that individuals should be effectively protected from misuse and abuse of their personal data by means of clear and precise rules imposing minimum safeguards.[270] Specific restrictions and guarantees must be provided concerning, for example, who is authorised to read certain information;[271] what types of information should be processed and stored;[272] how and where information should be stored;[273] how to prevent information being used for purposes other than those provided for;[274] the duration of storage;[275] and how fraudulent use can be prevented.[276] Storage for an unlimited, or a very long period of time, and highly generalised storage of information are generally considered

[264] *Schwarz*, C-291/12, para. 27.
[265] *Digital Rights Ireland*, C-293/12, paras. 34–5.
[266] *Ryneš*, C-212/13, para. 33.
[267] *Digital Rights Ireland*, C-293/12; *Schrems*, C-362/14; *Tele2 Sverige*, C-203/15.
[268] For good examples, see *Schwarz*, C-291/12, paras. 40ff; *Digital Rights Ireland*, C-293/12, paras. 49ff; *Schrems*, C-362/14, paras. 93ff; *Tele2 Sverige*, C-203/15, paras. 96, 109.
[269] E.g., *Schecke*, C-92/09 and C-93/09, para. 79. In cases where the interpretation, rather than the validity, of secondary legislation is concerned, the Court also may require national decision-making authorities to seek actively to strike a fair balance; see, e.g., *Google Spain*, C-131/12, para. 81.
[270] E.g., *Schwarz*, C-291/12, para. 55; *Digital Rights Ireland*, C-293/12, para. 54; *Schrems*, C-362/14, para. 91.
[271] *Schwarz*, C-291/12, para. 57; *Digital Rights Ireland*, C-293/12, paras. 60–1.
[272] *Digital Rights Ireland*, C-293/12, para. 56.
[273] *Schwarz*, C-291/12, para. 58.
[274] *Ibid.*, para. 58.
[275] *Digital Rights Ireland*, C-293/12, paras. 56 and 63–5.
[276] *Schwarz*, C-291/12, para. 63; see generally also *Tele2 Sverige*, C-203/15.

unacceptable.[277] Transfers of personal data to third countries not ensuring an adequate level of protection are not allowed either.[278] Finally, the ECJ has held that 'legislation permitting the public authorities to have access on a generalised basis to the content of electronic communications must be regarded as compromising the essence of the fundamental right to respect for private life, as guaranteed by Article 7 of the Charter'.[279]

Occasionally, the private life aspect of Article 7 CFR is applied in contexts other than that of data protection.[280] The ECJ has held, for example, that respect for one's name is a constituent element of the right to protection of one's identity and private life, and is therefore covered by Article 7 CFR.[281] In quite another context, the ECJ has considered that private life may be affected by the freezing of funds and economic resources resulting from a sanction regime.[282]

Article 7 CFR further protects the right to respect for one's home and communication, which is particularly relevant for searches of business premises in relation to alleged violations of the EC's competition law regime. After some initial reluctance,[283] the ECJ has accepted the ECtHR's stand that the protection of Article 8 ECHR may extend to 'certain commercial premises',[284] which is also true for Article 7 CFR. In this context, and because of the close correspondence between Article 7 CFR and Article 8 ECHR, the ECJ has generally accepted the same standards as used by the ECtHR. It has also stressed, however, that an 'interference by a public authority could go further for professional or commercial premises or activities than in other cases'.[285]

Article 7 also encompasses the right to respect for one's family life. For EU law this aspect of this provision is mainly relevant in the area of migration and free movement of persons, in particular in relation to family reunion and expulsion of family members. Before the CFR became binding, it was mainly Article 8 ECHR that prompted the development of

---

[277] *Digital Rights Ireland*, C-293/12.

[278] *Schrems*, C-362/14, para. 49.

[279] *Ibid.*, para. 94.

[280] Cf. Vested-Hansen, 'Respect for Private and Family Life', paras. 07.07Aff.

[281] E.g., *Sayn-Wittgenstein*, C-208/09, para. 52; *Runevič-Vardyn*, C-391/09, para. 66; *U. v Stadt Karlsruhe*, C-101/13, para. 48; *Bogendorff von Wolffersdorff*, C-438/14, para. 54. See further Vested-Hansen, 'Respect for Private and Family Life', paras. 07.23Aff.

[282] For an express application of Article 7 in this regard, see *Makhlouf*, T-383/11, para. 96.

[283] See originally, *Hoechst*, 46/87. See further on this, e.g., Vested-Hansen, 'Respect for Private and Family Life', paras. 07.13Aff.

[284] *Deutsche Bahn*, C-583/13P, para. 20.

[285] *Ibid.*

the right to free movement and citizenship in relation to families.[286] While it might have been expected that this would have changed when CFR entered into force as a binding instrument, initially Article 7 played a marginal role in the ECJ's case law and was mainly used to help the ECJ and national courts to interpret secondary EU legislation on family law matters in accordance with fundamental rights.[287] More recently, however, the ECJ has also started to apply the provision in relation to expulsion of EU citizens for reasons of public policy and public security. In *Rendón Marín*, for example, it held that member states retain the power to expel such citizens, but in their assessment of an individual situation they must take account of the right to respect for private and family life, as laid down in Article 7 CFR, read in conjunction with the obligation to take into consideration the child's best interests as provided by Article 24(2) CFR.[288]

Article 9 CFR protects the rights to marry and to found a family. This provision is notable mainly because it is formulated differently from the corresponding provision of Article 12 ECHR, which states that 'men and women' have this right. As the Explanatory Memorandum notes, however, this difference is not intended to have much significance, as 'this Article neither prohibits nor imposes the granting of the status of marriage to unions between people of the same sex' and the right 'is thus similar to that afforded by the ECHR, but its scope may be wider when national legislation so provides'. Although the ECtHR has attached some relevance to Article 9 CFR for its own case law on same-sex marriages,[289] it has not yet played any significant role in the ECJ's case law.[290]

Title II also contains a number of classic freedoms closely corresponding to Articles 9, 10 and 11 ECHR. Article 10 CFR protects the freedom of thought, conscience and religion. While it is not very likely that EU

[286] See classically *Baumbast*, C-413/99, para. 72 and see *European Parliament v Council*, C-540/03.
[287] *O., S. and L.*, C-356/11 and 357/11; cf. Vested-Hansen, 'Respect for Private and Family Life', para. 07.38A.
[288] *Rendón Marín*, C-165/14, para. 66; see also *CS*, C-304/14, para. 36.
[289] In fact, the ECtHR has made mention of the more 'modern' wording of Article 9 CFR in its interpretation of Article 12 ECHR; see *Schalk and Kopf v Austria*, HUDOC, 24 June 2010, para. 61.
[290] There is important potential for its application in the future, in particular also in relation to same-sex marriages; cf. S. Choudry, 'Article 9. Right to Marry and Right to Found a Family', in Peers et al., 'The EU Charter', 269–90, paras. 09-01ff and 09.31.

law would directly breach this provision,[291] it has, nevertheless, proven of relevance in interpreting secondary legislation, in particular in relation to expulsion of asylum seekers and non-discrimination in employment. In asylum cases, the ECJ has provided a wide definition of religion and has found it 'unnecessary to distinguish acts that interfere with the "core areas" ("forum internum") of the basic right to freedom of religion, which do not include religious activities in public ("forum externum"), from acts which do not affect those purported "core areas".[292] The ECJ has also been reluctant to distinguish between public and private and between collective and individual aspects of this freedom on the grounds that such distinctions are incompatible with the broad definition of 'religion' provided by relevant EU legislation, which is mainly aimed at protecting individuals from significant harm in third countries.[293] As a result it has considered it irrelevant whether someone would risk a 'severe violation' of these rights in his home country by practicing his faith in private circles or by living that faith publicly.[294] In employment cases, the Court has taken a different approach. For example, in a case about a company policy to prohibit all expressions of religious, philosophical or political beliefs, it accepted that the aim of displaying neutrality in relations with customers constituted a legitimate justification.[295] The only requirements are that the policy should be restricted only to workers who are required to come into contact with customers and that it is genuinely pursued in a consistent and systematic manner. By contrast with similar ECtHR cases,[296] the ECJ has not reviewed whether such a policy strikes a fair balance between the employer's interests and those of employees. However, in another, similar case, the ECJ held that if an employer's decision to dismiss an employee because of her headscarf amounts to direct discrimination, it cannot be justified by the employer's willingness to take account of the particular wishes of the customer.[297]

---

[291] Although the provision may play a role in justifying certain limitations of free movement; cf. R. McCrea, 'Article 10. Freedom of Thought, Conscience and Religion', in Peers et al., 'The EU Charter', 291–309, para. 10.03.

[292] Y. and Z., C-71/11, para. 62; see also McCrea, 'Freedom of Religion', para. 10.33 and cf Achbita, C-157/15 para. 28 and Bougnaoui, C-188/15, para. 30.

[293] Ibid., para. 63.

[294] Ibid.

[295] Achbita, C-157/15.

[296] In particular Eweida, HUDOC, 15 January 2013, paras. 94–5.

[297] Bougnaoui, C-188/15.

Article 11 CFR protects freedom of expression and information. Although the ECJ has closely followed the ECtHR in its interpretation of this freedom in the past,[298] it has more recently adopted its own approach. Several cases have been brought before it relating to the regulation of television broadcasting,[299] disclosure of personal data through the Internet[300] and the protection of intellectual property rights relating to films and television series.[301] While the ECJ usually decides these cases by applying secondary EU law, in interpreting the applicable provisions it has consistently held that a careful balance should be struck between the CFR rights at stake. In copyright cases, for example, it has balanced copyrights and related rights under Article 17 CFR, the freedom to conduct a business, which economic agents such as Internet service providers enjoy under Article 16 CFR, and the freedom of information of Internet users under Article 11 CFR.[302] Moreover, given the importance of Article 11, the ECJ has held that limitations should be carefully assessed to see whether they would not unnecessarily deprive Internet users of the possibility of lawfully accessing the information available.[303] The margin of appreciation allowed to national authorities seems limited in this context, and, in most cases, runs parallel to that granted by the ECtHR.[304] Both the ECtHR and the ECJ tend, for example, to grant generous margins of appreciation to national authorities in relation to restrictions of commercial expression.[305]

Like Article 11 ECHR, Article 12 CFR provides a right to form and belong to all kinds of associations, including political parties and trade unions.[306] In practice trade union freedom would seem most relevant to EU law, in particular because Article 12 can also be said to cover connected rights, such as the right to collective action. However, there

---

[298] See originally, e.g., *Connolly*, C-274/99P; in more detail, see L. Woods, 'Article 11. Freedom of Expression and Information, in Peers et al., 'The EU Charter', paras. 11.25ff.

[299] E.g., *Mesopotamia Broadcast and Roj TV*, C-244/10; *Sky Österreich*, C-283/11.

[300] E.g., *Lindqvist*, C-101/01; *Satamedia*, C-73/07.

[301] E.g., *Laserdisken*, C-479/04; *UPC Telekabel Wien*, C-314/12.

[302] *UPC Telekabel Wien*, C-314/12, para. 47. See also, e.g., *Sky Österreich*, C-283/11, para. 59.

[303] *UPC Telekabel Wien*, para. 63.

[304] Although it has been said that there is not a fully parallel application; cf. Woods, 'Freedom of Expression', para. 11.41.

[305] See, e.g., *Neptune Distribution*, C-157/14, para. 76.

[306] Article 12(2) indeed exclusively deals with political parties; on this, see J. Shaw and L. Khadar, 'Article 12(2). Freedom of Assembly and Association', in Peers et al., 'The EU Charter', 371–7.

is little need to bring such aspects within the scope of Article 12, since Article 28, contained in Title IV on solidarity rights (considered later), specifically protects the rights of collective bargaining and collective action.[307] The ECJ does not always clearly distinguish between the different provisions. In the *Viking Line* and *Laval* cases, for example, although collective action had hampered the free movement of services,[308] the ECJ did not devote much attention to the definition and delineation of trade union rights; nor did it make mention of the CFR. It merely balanced the general principle of collective action against the typically economic values protected by EU free movement clauses, giving priority to free movement.

Article 13 CFR protects the freedom of arts and sciences which finds no express parallel in the ECHR, although it is generally regarded as an aspect of freedom of expression.[309] As yet there is no ECJ case law on Article 13, and indeed it is rather difficult to see how and where it might apply, given restrictions on the scope of the CFR and the lack of relevant EU competences.[310] It may theoretically play a role, however, in relation to broadcasting freedom, free movement of students and university staff and research funding.[311]

Article 14 CFR protects the right to education and is similar to Article 2 P1 ECHR. Again, there does not seem to be much potential for its application, since there are only limited EU competences in this field.[312] Nevertheless, Article 14 may be relevant to the interpretation of secondary union law in relation to migration and citizen's rights, for example access to education by migrant workers, students and third country nationals, topics on which the ECJ had already developed an elaborate case law,[313] which contains no references to Article 14 because it predates

---

[307] There are a few relevant differences, however; see further F. Dorssemont, 'Article 12(1). Freedom of Assembly and of Association', in Peers et al., 'The EU Charter', 341–77, para. 12(1).14–17.

[308] *Laval*, C-341/05; *Viking Line*, C-438/05.

[309] E.g., *Sorguç v Turkey*, HUDOC, 23 June 2009, para. 34; *Mustafa Erdoğan and Others v Turkey*, HUDOC, 27 May 2014, para. 40.

[310] Cf. D. Sayers, 'Article 13. Freedom of the Arts and Sciences', in Peers et al., 'The EU Charter', 379–400, para. 13.39ff.

[311] *Ibid.*

[312] Although the provision might have some relevance for cases about financing of education; see, e.g., *Dirextra Alta Formazione*, C-523/12.

[313] E.g., *Gravier*, C-293/83; *Grzelczyk*, C-184/99; *Commission v Austria*, C-147/03; *Bidar*, C-209/03; *Förster*, C-158/07, ECLI:EU:C:2008:630; *Bressol*, C-73/08. See further G. Gori, 'Article 14. Right to Education', in Peers et al., 'The EU Charter', 401–22.

the entry into force of the CFR as a binding instrument. If a similar case were to come before the ECJ now, it is likely the ECJ would endeavour to interpret the applicable provisions of secondary EU law in line with Article 14 CFR.[314] Given that this provision parallels Article 2 P1 ECHR, the ECJ thereby probably would dovetail its interpretation with that of the ECtHR on freedom of education.

Articles 15–17 CFR contain a set of closely connected freedoms, relating to economic issues at the core of EU law, which play a significant role in the ECJ's jurisprudence. The first is the freedom to choose an occupation and engage in work (Article 15 CFR), which is mainly based on a mixture of TEU provisions related to the rights of workers and the concomitant case law.[315] It clearly is a freedom and therefore an enforceable right, rather than a socio-economic principle, which aims to protect individuals from unwarranted interference by governments with their choice of occupation. Thus far, the ECJ has not used Article 15 CFR as a standard of review of the legality of national acts, apparently because it does not add much to what is already contained in the TFEU.[316] In one case, after having stressed that the provision 'reiterates inter alia the free movement of workers guaranteed by Article 45 TFEU', the ECJ stated that a separate analysis of the case under Article 15 would not be warranted.[317] Nevertheless, as with other CFR provisions, Article 15 may have a role to play as an interpretive aid, guiding the ECJ in its engagement with secondary legislation.[318]

The closely related freedom to conduct a business is protected by Article 16 CFR. In common with Article 15, this provision has its basis in the general principles of EU law as recognised by the ECJ.[319] Given the strongly economic character of the EU it is not surprising that this provision ranks amongst those most often invoked before the

---

[314] Cf. Gori, 'Right to Education', para. 14.45.

[315] In particular cases like *Hauer*, C-44/79, para. 16; see Explanatory Notes to Article 15 and in more detail, D. Ashiagbor, 'Article 15. Freedom to Choose an Occupation', in Peers, et al., 'The EU Charter', 423–35. This was confirmed by the ECJ in *ONEm and M.*, C-284/15, para. 33.

[316] Although there is some potential here; see e.g., *Deutsches Weintor*, C-455/120.

[317] *Gardella*, C-233/12, paras. 39–41; cf. also *Pfleger*, C-390/12, paras. 57–60; *ONEm and M.*, C-284/15, para. 34.

[318] See, e.g., *Hörnfeldt*, C-141/11, para. 37.

[319] See originally *Nold*, C-4/73; *Eridania*, C-230/78; more recently, see *Interseroh Scrap*, C-1/11, para. 54. See also M. Everson and R. Correia Gonçalves, 'Article 16. Freedom to Conduct a Business', in Peers et al., 'The EU Charter', para. 16.01.

ECJ.[320] In *Sky Österreich* the ECJ held that the protection afforded by this provision covers 'the freedom to exercise an economic or commercial activity, the freedom of contract and free competition',[321] including 'the freedom to choose with whom to do business and the freedom to determine the price of a service'.[322] The meaning and potential of Article 16 may further be gleaned from the wide variety of cases in which the ECJ has applied it, for example those involving enterprises limited by EU law in making nutrition and health claims,[323] companies required to disclose information about their sources of supply,[324] and airlines required to provide certain care and facilities to their customers.[325] Its application can also be seen in several cases where national courts obliged Internet service providers (ISPs) to filter or block data or entire web sites,[326] and even in a case where a company, having dismissed an employee wearing a headscarf, had invoked Article 16, claiming a right to do so in order to project an image of neutrality towards customers.[327]

The ECJ has emphasised that the freedom to conduct a business 'must be considered in its social function', which means that it may be 'subjected to a broad range of interventions on the part of public authorities which may limit the exercise of economic activity in the public interest'.[328] It thereby applies the standard criteria of Article 52(1), paying particular attention to whether the 'essence' of the freedom in question has been impaired.[329] Most of the measures it has examined only affected specific aspects of conducting a business, such as labelling or advertising, or compelling a commercial broadcasting company to make available to the general public a small portion of its programmes.[330] In the ECJ's view, such limitations do not affect the actual substance of the freedom to

---

[320]   European Commission, *Staff Working Document on the Application of the EU Charter of Fundamental Rights in 2015* (SWD(2016), 158 final) p. 9. See also R. Babayev, 'Private Autonomy at Union Level: On Article 16 CFREU and Free Movement Rights', *Common Market Law Review*, 53 (2016), 979–1005.

[321]   *Sky Österreich*, C-283/11, para. 42.

[322]   Ibid., para. 43; see also *Alemo-Herron*, C-426/11, para. 32.

[323]   E.g., *Deutsches Weintor*, C-544/10; *Neptune Distributions*, C-157/14.

[324]   *Interseroh Scrap*, C-1/11.   [325]   *McDonagh*, C-12/11.

[326]   E.g., *Scarlet Extended*, C-70/10; *UPC Telekabel Wien*, C-314/12.

[327]   *Achbita*, C-157/15, para. 38.

[328]   *Sky Österreich*, C-283/11, paras. 45–6; see also *Deutsches Weintor*, C-544/10, para. 54; *McDonagh*, C-12/11, para. 60; *Neptune Distributions*, C-157/14, para. 66.

[329]   E.g., *Deutsches Weintor*, C-544/10, para. 54.

[330]   *Sky Österreich*, C-283/11, para. 49; *Neptune Distributions*, C-157/14, para. 71.

conduct a business,[331] especially if it is clear that they pursue an important general interest – such as the protection of human health, itself protected by Article 35 (2) CFR, consumer protection as protected by Article 38 CFR, or the freedom to receive information under Article 11 CFR, and where national decision-making authorities are accorded a wide margin of discretion.[332] In other cases, however, the ECJ has found the imposition of certain measures or injunctions overly broad and burdensome, for example, where an ISP was required to monitor all electronic communications made through its network in order to avoid infringements of intellectual property rights without any time limit.[333] According to the ECJ, such an injunction would result in a serious infringement of the ISP's freedom to conduct its business since it would require the installation of a complicated, costly and permanent computer system at its own expense,[334] which would fail to strike a fair balance between, on the one hand, the protection of the intellectual property rights enjoyed by copyright holders, and, on the other, the ISP's right under Article 16 CFR.[335]

Article 17 CFR protects the right to property. Like the freedom to conduct a business, this is a core right for the EU system, which has been recognised as a general principle of EU law from a very early stage.[336] Worded to correspond with Article 1 P1 ECHR, the provision has, nevertheless, been modernised to include a separate clause on intellectual property. According to the Explanatory Notes, however, the two provisions should be interpreted in parallel and these differences do not have any consequence for the level of protection provided. Indeed, the ECJ sometimes refers to the ECtHR's case law, for instance to support its view that the right to property does not cover future income.[337] In other cases it prefers to apply its own, well-established jurisprudence on the right to property as a general principle of law.[338] According to this case law, the

---

[331] *Deutsches Weintor*, C-544/10, para. 58.
[332] See expressly *Neptune Distributions*, C-157/14, para. 76.
[333] *Scarlet Extended*, C-70/10, para. 48. For an example in the different context of freedom of contract, see *Alemo-Herron*, C-426/11, para. 35.
[334] *Scarlet Extended*, C-70/10, para. 48.
[335] *UPC Telekabel Wien*, C-314/12, ECLI:EU:C:2014:192, paras. 51–3.
[336] Initially in *Hauer*, C-44/79. See further F. Wollenschläger, 'Article 17(1). Right to Property', in Peers et al., 'The EU Charter', 469–87.
[337] *Inuit Tapiriit Kanatami*, C-398/13P, para. 61.
[338] E.g., *Al-Aqsa*, C-539/10P, paras. 120ff. The Court may choose not to deal with an Article 17 complaint if it already has addressed the substance of the case in relation to a TFEU provision; e.g., *Berlington*, C-98/14, paras. 89–91.

right to property applies to pecuniary rights as well as to many immaterial rights representing economic value,[339] including quota and imposition of taxes or levies, emission allowances, rules on advertising[340] and in cases concerning sanctions (for example relating to the freezing of the assets of terrorist suspects or in relation to sanctions imposed on account of competition law violations).[341] By contrast, Article 17 is inapplicable where a subsidy or aid has to be repaid because an eligibility condition has not been satisfied.[342]

In cases where Article 17 applies, the key notion is proportionality,[343] but the notions of legitimate expectations and legal certainty are also of relevance.[344] According to the ECJ, these generally require that measures restricting property rights are clear, precise and predictable in their effect, especially where they have negative consequences for individuals and undertakings.[345] In reviewing the proportionality of interferences in this context, the ECJ usually leaves a considerable margin of discretion to EU institutions.[346]

Although Article 17(2) CFR pertains specifically to intellectual property,[347] it has been held to apply only to rights with an asset value that create a legal entitlement enabling the holder to exercise those rights autonomously and for his own benefit.[348] However, the protection does not include mere commercial interests or opportunities.[349] Furthermore, the right can only be claimed by actual proprietors of intellectual property rights, not by third parties who want to dispute those rights acquired by others.[350] The right to intellectual property is not absolute,[351] and the ECJ aims to reconcile, or if needed balance, it with other fundamental rights, such as protection of personal data,[352] the freedom to conduct a

---

[339] Wollenschläger, 'Right to Property', para. 17(1).16ff.
[340] For some examples out of many, see *Berlington*, C-98/14; *Romonta*, T-614/13.
[341] E.g., *Kadi I*, C-402/05P, para. 355; *Al-Aqsa*, C-539/10P.
[342] *ZS 'Ezernieki'*, C-273/15, paras. 47–51. In that case, the general principle of proportionality can be applied instead.
[343] E.g., *Križan*, C-416/10.
[344] In much more detail, see Wollenschläger, 'Right to Property', paras. 17(1).25ff.
[345] *Berlington*, C-98/14, para. 77.
[346] See further Wollenschläger, 'Right to Property', paras. 17(1).52–4.
[347] See above (Article 16) and see further, e.g., P. Torremans, 'Article 17(2). Right to Property', in Peers et al., 'The EU Charter', 489–517.
[348] *Sky Österreich*, C-283/11, para. 34.
[349] *Ibid.*
[350] *Bericap Záródástechnikai*, C-180/11, para. 77.
[351] E.g., *SABAM*, C-360/10, para. 41.
[352] E.g., *Coty Germany*, C-580/13, para. 30–3.

business[353] and the right to receive information.[354] The EU and national authorities are generally accorded a wide margin of discretion in this respect. For example, measures restricting other fundamental rights in order to safeguard intellectual property can be justified even if they do not fully realise this objective.[355]

The last two provisions of Title II concern asylum issues.[356] Article 18 provides a right to asylum which, according to the Explanatory Memorandum, is based on the EU's obligation under the TFEU to respect the UN Convention Relating to the Status of Refugees. However, it has only limited practical relevance, since the EU already has a well-developed system of asylum and related law, the Common European Asylum System (CEAS). There is usually little need for applying the CFR right to asylum since the more detailed rules of the CEAS are preferred.[357] If Article 18 is mentioned in the case law at all, it mainly serves to support the ECJ in interpreting the latter.[358]

Article 19(1) CFR prohibits collective expulsions and thus corresponds to Article 4 P4 ECHR. Thus far, it has not been applied by the ECJ. By contrast, the ECJ has rather often mentioned Article 19(2) CFR, which contains an independent prohibition of returning, extraditing or expelling third-country nationals ('refoulement') where there is a serious risk that they would be subjected to the death penalty, torture or other inhuman or degrading treatment or punishment. This prohibition is a codification of the ECtHR's case law on Article 3, and therefore it has to be interpreted in line with this case law.[359] As a consequence of the close correspondence between Article 19(2) and Article 3 ECHR, there is also significant overlap with the dignity rights protected by Articles 1, 2 and 4 CFR.[360] In many cases, the ECJ therefore jointly applies Article 19(2) and the dignity provisions. In particular, the ECJ has made it part of its case law that the relevant secondary legislation must be interpreted in

---

[353] *SABAM*, C-360/10, para. 47.
[354] E.g., *UPC Telekabel Wien*, C-314/12, para. 47; Cf. also Torremans, 'Right to Property', para. 17(2).41.
[355] *UPC Telekabel Wien*, C-314/12, para. 63.
[356] As such they do not really fit in well with the overall theme of 'freedoms', but probably the drafters found it difficult to place them elsewhere.
[357] Cf. M. den Heijer, 'Article 18. Right to Asylum', in Peers et al., 'The EU Charter', 519–41.
[358] E.g., *N. S.*, C-411/10, para. 75; *Cimade*, C-179/11, para. 42; *H. T.*, C-373/13, para. 65.
[359] E.g., *Tall*, C-239/14, para. 54.
[360] Cf. E. Guild, 'Article 19. Protection in the Event of Removal', in Peers et al., 'The EU Charter', para. 19.05.

harmony with the ECtHR's substantive and procedural standards.[361] For example, just like the ECtHR, the ECJ has held that appeal measures against a return decision must have suspensive effect[362] and that the existence of declarations and accession to international treaties guaranteeing respect for fundamental rights is not in itself sufficient to ensure adequate protection against the risk of ill-treatment upon expulsion.[363]

Title III – Equality

The third title of the CFR contains a variety of equality and non-discrimination provisions. Not only does it contain an article safeguarding equality before the law (Article 20) and one on non-discrimination (Article 21, corresponding to Article 14 ECHR), but there are also a number of provisions concerning specific groups and grounds of discrimination indicating that diversity is valued as much as equal treatment. Article 22 CFR expressly states that the EU shall respect cultural, religious and linguistic diversity.

Equal treatment and non-discrimination have always been core concepts of EU law, although, initially, their function was mainly that of helping to remove economic and financial obstacles to European integration.[364] It was only in Schröder, a case decided in 2000, that the ECJ recognised that the principle of equal treatment of men and women did not merely have economic value, but also, and even more so, could be regarded as a fundamental right of its own.[365] The central importance of the equality and non-discrimination principles to EU law, including the large body of primary and secondary legislation on equal treatment in employment, has made the ECJ a forerunner in the conceptual development of these principles.[366] This has not only resulted in many preliminary references being made to the ECJ on equality issues, but has also helped the ECJ develop case law related to positive action, harassment, the burden of proof and so on.[367]

---

[361] Cf., e.g., M'Bodj, C-542/13, para. 38; Tall, C-239/14, paras. 56ff.
[362] Abdida, C-562/13, para. 50; Tall, C-239/14, para. 58.
[363] Petruhhin, C-182/15, para. 57.
[364] See further, e.g., Bell, 'Principle of Equal Treatment'.
[365] Schröder, C-50/96, para. 57.
[366] Cf. Muir, 'The Transformative Function'.
[367] In more detail, see M. Bell, D. Schiek and L. Waddington (eds.), Cases, Materials and Text on National, Supranational and International Non-Discrimination Law (Oxford: Hart, 2007).

Given the elaborate body of case law and relevant secondary legislation, the added value of Title III CFR in practical terms may seem to be relatively limited. Indeed, the ECJ has sometimes held that member states must primarily respect EU legislation that specifically concerns the principle of discrimination. For that reason, it often examines national compliance with secondary legislation rather than with the CFR.[368] Nevertheless, several provisions of Title III have proven relevant for the ECJ's case law.[369]

The ECJ has, for example, clarified that the principle of equal treatment in Article 20 is a general principle of EU law, of which the principle of non-discrimination laid down in Article 21(1) CFR is a particular expression.[370] Crucially, the provisions only apply to internal EU situations – discrimination occurring in external relations with third countries is not covered.[371] There is no strict boundary between Articles 20 and 21 and often there is no real need to distinguish between them.[372] In some cases, the ECJ mainly cites these provisions to inform its own interpretation of the underlying secondary legislation, or to allow or require states to take these rights into account when implementing EU law.[373] In other judgments, the importance of the articles is shown by the fact that the ECJ uses them as a touchstone for reviewing the legality of national or EU legislation.[374] In cases on national legislation, the ECJ may leave it to national courts to decide whether there was a sufficient justification for a difference in treatment contained in national legislation implementing EU law.[375] While it sometimes mentions the general justification requirements of Article 52(1) in this regard,[376] in many cases

---

[368] E.g., *Schmitzer*, C-530/13, paras. 22–4; *Felber*, C-529/13, paras. 15–17; *Tirolean Airways*, C-132/11, paras. 21ff.

[369] Cf., e.g., *Ziegler*, C-439/11P, paras. 166ff; *Soukupová*, C-401/11, paras. 22ff.

[370] *Glatzel*, C-356/12, para. 43.

[371] *Swiss International Air Lines*, C-272/15, paras. 26–35.

[372] See further M. Bell, 'Article 20. Equality before the Law', in Peers et al., 'The EU Charter', paras. 20.06–07 and, in the same volume, C. Kilpatrick, 'Article 21. Non-Discrimination', in Peers et al., 'The EU Charter', 579–603.

[373] E.g., *Sayn-Wittgenstein*, C-208/09, para. 89; *Prigge*, C-447/09, para. 38; *HK Danmark*, C-476/11; *Szatmári Malom*, C-135/13, para. 65; *Deckmyn*, C-201/13, para. 30; *CHEZ*, C-83/14.

[374] On Article 20, see, e.g., *Baltic Agro*, C-3/13, paras. 41–6; on Article 21, e.g., *Test-Achats*, C-236/09, para. 17; *Glatzel*, C-356/12, para. 46.

[375] *Léger*, C-528/13, para. 69.

[376] See also, e.g., *Glatzel*, C-356/12, para. 42.

it applies its own, well-established criteria, developed long before the CFR became a binding document.[377]

According to the classic case law, comparable situations must not be treated differently and different situations must not be treated in the same way, unless such treatment is objectively justified.[378] A difference in treatment is justified if it is based on an objective and reasonable criterion, that is, if the difference relates to a legally permitted aim pursued by the legislation in question, and is proportionate to the aim pursued by the treatment concerned.[379] These general criteria closely resemble those contained in Article 52(1) CFR, but may be specified for certain situation types. In *Glatzel*, for example, the ECJ held that

> a difference of treatment which is based on a characteristic (...) [such as sex or age] does not constitute discrimination (...) where, by reason of the nature of the particular occupational activities concerned or of the context in which they are carried out, such a characteristic constitutes a genuine and determining occupational requirement, provided that the objective is legitimate and the requirement is proportionate.[380]

In applying this justification test, the intensity of the ECJ's review may differ according to the circumstances of the case.[381] While it may be rather strict in some cases,[382] more leeway is given in complex or sensitive policy areas such as public health.[383] The ECJ has also started to define the meaning of the different grounds of discrimination listed in Article 21 CFR, such as 'disability',[384] thereby expressly building on its existing case law regarding secondary non-discrimination legislation. In doing so it has refused to accept that cases of 'intersectional' or 'multi-ground' discrimination, such as discrimination on the combined effect of sexual orientation and age, constitute a new or special category of discrimination that should be assessed in a different way.[385]

---

[377] E.g., *Copydan Båndkopi*, C-463/12; *Glatzel*, C-356/12.
[378] *IBV & Cie*, C-195/12, para. 50; *Glatzel*, C-356/12, para. 43; *Copydan Båndkopi*, C-463/12, para. 32.
[379] *Glatzel*, C-356/12, para. 43.
[380] Para. 49.
[381] Cf. Bell, 'Equality before the Law', paras. 20.32–3.
[382] E.g., *Test-Achats*, C-236/09.
[383] E.g., *Glatzel*, C-356/12, para. 64.
[384] Para. 44ff; see also *Dadouidi*, C-395/15.
[385] *Parris*, C-443/15, paras. 79–81. See further, e.g., *Tackling Multiple Discrimination: Practices, Policies, and Laws* (Brussels: European Commission, 2007) and D. Schiek, 'Intersectionality and the Notion of Disability in EU Discrimination Law', *Common Market Law Review*, 53 (2016), 35–64.

The diversity provision of Article 22 CFR has symbolic importance as it is closely related to the values of diversity and pluralism underlying the EU Treaties.[386] Thus far it has been invoked mainly to support other arguments, such as those relating to the importance of the EU's multi-lingualism in a case about patent registration.[387] It has also been used in a case to strengthen the justification for an interference with free movement provisions, where it was held that the interference was needed to protect, promote and encourage the use of an official national language.[388]

Article 23 CFR is based on the TFEU's provisions on gender equality and codifies the ECJ's well-established case law on this topic,[389] and thus far has mainly been cited by the ECJ as underlying and inspiring its interpretation of primary and secondary EU law.[390] Article 23 may also provide a basis for review of the validity of legislation in much the same way as Articles 20 and 21.[391]

The rights of the child, as protected by Article 24, have considerable impact on the ECJ's case law,[392] mainly in relation to migration and asylum issues, where it can help establish, for example, that unaccompanied minors need additional protection.[393] It may also provide guidance for the interpretation of secondary legislation, such as provisions on family reunification,[394] as well as for the interpretation of the right to respect for one's family life under Article 7 CFR.[395] It has also been referred to in cases on cross-border family law matters, such as cooperation between member states in child abduction cases.[396] In this regard,

---

[386] See in particular Articles 2, 4 (2) and 6 TEU; see further R. Craufurd Smith, 'Article 22. Cultural, Religious and Linguistic Diversity', in Peers et al., 'The EU Charter', 605–31, para. 22.02.

[387] *Spain v Commission*, C-147/13, para. 42.

[388] *Las*, C-202/11, para. 26; *Runevič-Vardyn*, C-391/09, para. 86.

[389] See the Explanatory Notes to Article 23; in much more detail, see D. Schiek, 'Article 23. Equality between Women and Men', in Peers et al., 'The EU Charter', 633–60.

[390] E.g., *Z*, C-363/12, para. 64; *Soukupová*, C-401/11, para. 28; *Danosa*, C-232/09, para. 71.

[391] See above; an example is *Test-Achats*, C-236/09, in which the Court reviewed the compatibility of EU legislation with Articles 21 and 23 jointly.

[392] See further, e.g., R. Lamont, 'Article 24. The Rights of the Child', in Peers et al., 'The EU Charter', 661–91.

[393] E.g., *M. A.*, C-648/11.

[394] *O. and S.*, C-356/11, paras. 76–80.

[395] *Rendón Marín*, C-165/14, para. 66; see also *CS*, C-304/14, para. 36.

[396] On child abduction, see, e.g., *McB*, C-400/10PPU, paras. 60ff; *Bradbrooke*, C-498/14PPU. On other family law related matters, see, e.g., *A. v B.*, C-184/14, para. 46; *Bohez*, C-4/14, para. 58.

the ECJ has noted that the relevant EU legislation must be interpreted in such a way as to ensure 'respect for the fundamental rights of the child as set out in Article 24 CFR, which include the right to maintain on a regular basis personal relationships and direct contact with both of his or her parents'.[397] Moreover, the ECJ has held that procedural arrangements in cross-border family law cases, such as allocation of jurisdiction, must be compatible with the rights of the child.[398]

Generally, in this and in other contexts the yardstick is the notion of 'the best interests of the child' found in the UN Children's Rights Convention, which the ECJ has accepted as constituting a primary consideration in relevant decision making.[399] However, its precise meaning depends on the concrete circumstances of the case and its application may require flexible measures including considering alternatives most conducive to a child's welfare, taking decisions with particular expedition and providing for procedures that guarantee that children can freely express their views 'in accordance with their age and maturity'.[400]

Since the rights of the elderly, protected by Article 25, have not yet been invoked before the ECJ,[401] it is not clear who would qualify as belonging to this category.[402] By contrast, for the rights of disabled persons protected by Article 26, the case law provides clarification for what 'disability' means.[403] The significance of the provision for the ECJ's case law has remained limited, however, largely because the UN Disability Convention, which provides for more detailed rights and obligations than can be found in Article 26, has been ratified by the EU.[404] Many cases on the rights of disabled persons refer to this UN Convention rather than to the CFR.[405] Another reason for the UN Convention being preferred over the CFR is that the Explanatory Notes on the latter expressly indicate that Article 26 contains a 'principle' and

---

[397] *Bradbrooke*, C-498/14 PPU, para. 42.
[398] Ibid., para. 52.
[399] E.g., *M. A.*, C-648/11, para. 59; *Health Service Executive*, C-92/12PPU, para. 127.
[400] E.g., *McB*, C-400/10PPU, para. 62; *Aguire Zarraga*, C-491/10PPU, para. 63ff; *Health Service Executive*, C-92/12PPU, paras. 127ff; *M. A.*, C-648/11, paras. 61ff.
[401] Although there is some potential for relevant application; see further C. O'Cinneide, 'Article 25. The Rights of the Elderly', in Peers et al., 'The EU Charter', 693–708.
[402] *Ibid.*, para. 25.36.
[403] For a definition, see, e.g., *HK Danmark*, C-476/11.
[404] See in particular Directive 2000/78; see further, e.g., C. O'Brien, 'Article 26. Integration of Persons with Disabilities', in Peers et al., 'The EU Charter', 709–48. There are some limitations to its review, however; see *Z*, C-363/12.
[405] See, e.g., *HK Danmark*, C-476/11; *Z*, C-363/12.

the ECJ has confirmed that it does not contain an enforceable individual right.[406] For the article to become more effective it must first 'be given more specific expression in European Union or national law'.[407]

Title IV – Solidarity

Most of the socio-economic 'rights' included in the CFR have been brought together in Title IV on Solidarity, which, by contrast with most of the rights and freedoms contained in the first three Titles, is generally considered to state principles rather than enforceable individual rights. As already discussed, this means they will mainly play a role as a source of interpretation for primary or secondary EU law. It is not entirely clear, however, which of the provisions of Title IV really have the character of a principle, and which could be seen as containing subjective rights. The ECJ has provided clarification for some provisions but less for others.

The text of Article 27 CFR, regarding workers' right to information and consultation with employers,[408] states that they are to be guaranteed in cases and under the conditions provided for by EU law and national laws and practices. The ECJ held, in the *AMS* case, that 'for this article to be fully effective, it must be given more specific expression in European Union or national law'.[409] Thus, Article 27 CFR cannot, as such, support an argument that a national provision should not be applied in a horizontal situation because it is not in conformity with EU law.[410] It is not entirely clear whether this also means that Article 27 CFR cannot be directly invoked in a 'vertical' conflict between an individual and a public authority. However, it is likely that the provision will merely serve as an interpretative guide to such legislation.

The right of collective bargaining and collective action in Article 28 CFR has already been mentioned in relation to Article 12, freedom of association, including trade union freedom. Although the ECJ has not expressly discussed the nature of this right, it is likely that it will be capable of being directly claimed as an enforceable right by either trade

---

[406] *Glatzel*, C-356/12, para. 78.

[407] *Ibid.*

[408] See more specifically, e.g., F. Dorssemont, 'Article 27. Workers' Right to Information and Consultation within the Undertaking', in Peers et al., 'The EU Charter', 749–71.

[409] *Association de médiation sociale (AMS)*, C-176/12, para. 45.

[410] *Ibid.*, paras. 48–9.

unions or employers if only because of the clear parallel with the ECtHR's case law on Article 11 ECHR.[411]

Thus far, the ECJ has applied Article 28 mainly to define its limits. In particular, that it cannot be claimed unconditionally, and the right to negotiate and conclude collective agreements must be exercised in accordance with EU law.[412] Collective or individual agreements that establish direct or indirect discrimination will be null and void.[413] More generally, social partners must comply with specifications of the non-discrimination principles contained in secondary legislation.[414] Moreover, when exercising this right, they must take care to strike a balance between the various interests concerned.[415] The framework for reviewing restrictions, and their justification, is thereby clearly different from that laid down in Article 52(1) CFR.

Article 29 CFR states that everyone has the right to a free placement service. It is not yet clear whether this should be considered an enforceable right, as the wording seems to suggest, or rather a principle, and its practical meaning has not yet been illuminated in the ECJ's case law either.[416]

Drawing on Article 24 of the revised European Social Charter, Article 30 CFR stipulates that every worker has the right to protection against unfair dismissal in accordance with EU law and national laws and practices. The ECJ has not yet had an opportunity to elucidate the nature of this provision as a right or principle. However, it may be concluded from the fact that it is worded similarly to Article 27 that it cannot be directly invoked in horizontal relations to claim that a provison of national law should be disapplied because of its incompatibility with this provision.[417] It is more likely, however, that it may provide guidance in explaining relevant secondary legislation, such as on the consequences of insolvency of employers, collective redundancies or transfers of undertakings.[418]

---

[411] See also the Explanatory Notes.
[412] *Prigge*, C-447/09, para. 47; *Erny*, C-172/11, para. 50.
[413] *Erny*, C-172/11, para. 52.
[414] *Prigge*, C-447/09, para. 48; *Hennigs and Mai*, C-297/10, para. 68.
[415] *Hennigs and Mai*, C-297/10, para. 66.
[416] See further, D. Ashiagbor, 'Article 29. Right of Access to Placement Services', in Peers et al., 'The EU Charter', 795–803.
[417] Cf. *AMS*, C-176/12, paras. 48–9.
[418] Cf. Explanatory Notes to Article 30; see further J. Kenner, 'Article 30. Protection in the Event of Unjustified Dismissal', in Peers et al., 'The EU Charter', 805–32.

Articles 31, 32 and 33 concern other aspects of the rights of workers, concerning, for example, paid leave, working hours, reasonable working conditions, protection against dismissal (whether or not on account of maternity related reasons), maternity leave and parental leave,[419] all at least partly based on secondary legislation. In its case law, the ECJ has continued to apply these rights as expressed in secondary legislation, rather than as in Articles 31–33 as such, the only difference being that it now usually supports its findings by also referring to them.[420] Whether the various rights contained in these provisions are capable of becoming fully fledged and enforceable rights, or will remain as principles, is not clear.[421]

Entitlements to social security benefits and social advantages are recognised and respected by the EU on the basis of Article 34(1) CFR. Although questions about this provision have been referred to the ECJ, it has as yet refrained from clarifying its nature as an enforceable right or mere principle, as well as from seeking to define 'social security' and 'social advantages'.[422] Instead, it has decided social security cases by relying on general principles of primary or secondary EU law.[423]

Article 34(2) stipulates that everyone residing and moving legally within the EU is entitled to social security benefits and to social advantages in accordance with EU law, national laws and practices. Since this provision is also in line with existing primary and secondary legislation, it is unlikely to have much impact on the ECJ's judgments.[424] The same is true for Article 34(3), which states that the EU recognises and respects the right to social and housing assistance so as to ensure a decent existence for all those who lack sufficient resources.

---

[419] See further A. Bogg, 'Article 31. Fair and Just Working Conditions', in Peers et al., 'The EU Charter', 833–68; H. Stalford, 'Article 32. Prohibition of Child Labour and Protection of Young People at Work', in Peers et al., 'The EU Charter', 869–89; C. Costello, 'Article 33. Family and Professional Life', in Peers et al., 'The EU Charter', 891–925.

[420] See, e.g., *Sähköalojen ammattiliitto ry*, C-396/13, paras. 64, 66; *Fenoll*, C-316/13, paras. 18, 23, 26. For references to Article 33 CFR, see, e.g., *Maïstrellis*, C-222/14, para. 39. Article 32 has not yet been mentioned in the Court's case law. There is more potential for these provisions, however; see Bogg, 'Fair and Just Working Conditions', para. 31.05.

[421] More elaborately on Article 31, see Bogg, 'Fair and Just Working Conditions', paras. 31.33–5; on Article 33, see Costello, 'Family and Professional Life', para. 33.02.

[422] Cf. R. White, 'Article 34. Social Security and Social Assistance', in Peers et al., 'The EU Charter', 927–68, para. 34.45.

[423] E.g., *Wojchiechowski*, C-408/14; *Melchior*, C-647/13, para. 29.

[424] Cf. White, 'Social Security', paras. 34.46 and 34.78–9.

Thus far, the ECJ has only mentioned the latter provision in cases concerning secondary law, where it left much interpretive leeway to national courts.[425]

Article 35 CFR, on the right to health, has two different aspects. The first sentence contains the right of access to preventive health care and the right to benefit from medical treatment under the conditions established by national laws and practices. This provision has not yet figured in the Luxembourg case law, which is hardly surprising given that regulation of the organisation of, and access to, health care is not one of the EU's competences.[426]

The second sentence, which states that a high level of human health protection shall be secured in the definition and implementation of all EU policies and activities, contains a clear aspiration that has had some impact on cases involving conflicting rights.[427] As explained previously, restrictions upon, for example, the freedom to conduct a business or the right to property may be justified by an important general interest. Article 35 indicates that public health must be considered such an interest, and it therefore has been placed on a par with other CFR provisions and the TFEU's free movement clauses in balancing exercises.[428] Moreover, Article 35 may colour the interpretation of secondary EU law on health-related matters.[429]

By stating that the EU recognises and respects access to services of general economic interest (i.e., public and social services, such as telecommunication or electricity), Article 36 protects a typical EU right.[430] The Explanatory Notes explain that 'this Article is fully in line with Article 14 of the Treaty on the Functioning of the European Union and does not create any new right. It merely sets out the principle of respect by the Union for the access to services of general economic interest as provided for by national provisions, when those provisions are compatible with Union law'. In practice, the ECJ has referred to the

---

[425] *Kamberaj*, C-571/10, para. 80; *Sánchez Morcillo*, C-539/14.

[426] See Article 168 TFEU; cf. T. Hervey and J. McHale, 'Article 35. Health Care', in Peers et al., 'The EU Charter', para. 35.01.

[427] Cf. Hervey and McHale, 'Health Care', para. 35.23.

[428] E.g., *Venturini*, C-159/12, para. 41; *Deutsches Weintor*, C-544/10; *Philip Morris*, C-547/14, paras. 153ff.

[429] See, e.g., *Léger*, C-528/13, para. 57; cf. Hervey and McHale, 'Health Care', para. 35.25.

[430] See further E. Szyszczak, 'Article 36. Access to Services', in Peers et al., 'The EU Charter', 969–82, para. 36.37.

provision only to strengthen arguments made in relation to Article 14 TFEU.[431] Thus, its added value seems very limited.

Finally, Articles 37 – on environmental protection – and 38 – on consumer protection – have much the same impact on the ECJ's case law as Article 35. Both clearly express aspirations and principles and cannot be invoked as enforceable individual rights.[432] Like the right to health, however, the CFR's codification of interests relating to environmental protection and consumer protection has allowed the ECJ to give them additional weight and importance in balancing them against other CFR rights (such as the freedom to conduct a business) and EU free movement provisions.[433] Furthermore, the ECJ may interpret secondary legislation on consumer and environmental law matters in the light of Articles 38 and 37.[434] In doing so it has specified for Article 38 that, because of the nature and wording of the provision, it cannot by itself impose an interpretation upon a directive that would encompass a concrete right to consumer protection.[435] Given the similarity in formulation, the same will be true for Article 37.

Title V – Citizens' Rights

Title V contains a number of rights promoting transparency, openness and participation in the EU's decision-making processes and codifies specific rights for EU citizens. Most of these, including voting rights and freedom of movement, were already part of the TFEU provisions on citizenship, and are not really new. More innovative is the elevation of the general principle of good administration to the status of fundamental right.

While the Title itself seems to suggest that these rights can only be invoked by EU citizens, this is true only for the provisions relating to voting rights (Articles 39–40), freedom of movement and of residence (Article 45 (1)) and the right to diplomatic and consular protection (Article 46). The others can be invoked by all natural or legal persons

---

[431] *ANODE*, C-121/15, para. 51.

[432] See E. Morgera and G. Marín Durán, 'Environmental Protection', in Peers et al., 'The EU Charter', 983–1003, para. 37.01 and S. Weatherill, 'Article 38. Consumer Protection', in Peers et al., 'The EU Charter', 1005–25.

[433] For Article 37, see, e.g., *Commission v Austria*, C-28/09, para. 121; for Article 38, see, e.g., *McDonagh*, C-12/11, para. 63.

[434] See, e.g., *Kušionová*, C-34/13, para. 46.

[435] *Pohotovosť*, C-470/12, para. 52.

residing or having their registered office in a member state, and even by 'every person' (Article 41).

Articles 39 and 40 CFR, which are also included in EU treaties and secondary legislation,[436] relate to different aspects of the right to vote. Article 39 concerns elections for the European Parliament and contains the active and passive rights to participate in them. Article 40 grants EU citizens the same rights as nationals in municipal elections in any member state where they happen to reside. Consequently, the challenge for the ECJ is to align its interpretation of these provisions with its case law on the relevant TEU and TFEU provisions and with the secondary legislation defining the limits and conditions on the right to vote.[437] While these also refer to the ECtHR's interpretation of Article 3 P1 ECHR,[438] the ECJ has, more recently, been taking its own approach. For example, as discussed in Chapter 2, the ECtHR generally submits legislation excluding certain categories of detainees to a rather strict test. In *Delvigne*, by contrast, the ECJ accepted that all prisoners who had been convicted to a sentence of five years or more were deprived of their voting rights, including their rights to vote in the elections for the European Parliament.[439]

Article 41 CFR codifies a number of rights and principles of good administration, with no parallel in any other fundamental rights catalogue. They have largely been derived from the case law of the ECJ.[440] Importantly, Article 41(1) states that 'every person has the right to have his or her affairs handled impartially, fairly and within a reasonable time *by the institutions, bodies, offices and agencies of the Union*'. Initially, the ECJ did not attach any express value to the italicised part of this sentence

---

[436] Article 39(1) corresponds to Article 20(2)(b) TFEU; Article 39(2) to Article 14(3) TEU; Article 40 to Articles 20(2)(b) and 22(2) TFEU. On the TFEU right to vote, see, e.g., *Eman and Sevinger*, C-300/04. See further L. Khadar and J. Shaw, 'Article 39. Right to Vote and Stand as a Candidate at Elections to the European Parliament', in Peers et al., 'The EU Charter', 1027–56; K. Groenendijk, 'Article 40. Right to Vote and Stand as a Candidate at Municipal Elections', in Peers et al., 'The EU Charter', 1057–67.

[437] See further Khadar and Shaw, 'Right to Vote in Elections for the European Parliament', paras. 39.27ff and 39.71ff and Groenendijk, 'Right to Vote in Municipal Elections', para. 40.27.

[438] See, e.g., *Eman and Sevinger*, C-300/04, para. 54.

[439] *Delvigne*, C-650/13.

[440] See further H. C. H. Hofman and B. C. Mihaescu, 'The Relation between the Charter's Fundamental Rights and the Unwritten General Principles of EU Law: Good Administration as the Test Case', *European Constitutional Law Review*, 9 (2013), 86–101; P. Craig, 'Article 41. Right to Good Administration', in Peers et al., 'The EU Charter', 1069–98.

and it seemed to suggest that Article 41(1) could also be applied to decisions taken by national authorities in the exercise of EU competences or in implementing EU law.[441] More recently, however, the ECJ has held that the provision can only be directly invoked in cases concerning decisions taken by EU institutions.[442] Nonetheless, it has avoided creating a protection gap by accepting that the rights of the defence can still be regarded as a general principle of EU law,[443] enabling individuals and companies to claim them in their relations with national authorities.

The general right to good administration, found in Article 41(1) CFR, is specified in Article 41(2), (3) and (4), which contain a non-exhaustive list of the rights of those involved in administrative proceedings (the right to be heard, the right to have access to one's file),[444] the obligation on the authorities to give reasons, the right to compensation for damage caused by EU institutions and the right to use any of the EU's official languages. But these rights do not apply to judicial proceedings, for which special provision is made in Article 47 CFR.[445]

The rights and principles expressed in Article 41 are of particular importance, because Articles 6 and 13 ECHR only partly cover the fairness and procedural correctness of the primary decision-making process. Moreover, Article 6 ECHR applies only to civil rights and obligations and criminal charges and has not, as yet, been seen to cover asylum and migration procedures. It is therefore not surprising that the rights contained in Article 41 rank among those most frequently invoked before the ECJ.[446]

The application of Article 41 may vary for the different categories of case in which it is invoked, depending on the specific context of decision making and the interests of procedural fairness raised by the circumstances of the case.[447] Extensive lists of requirements have been established, for example, in relation to sanctions based on lists drawn up by

---

[441] E.g., *H. N.*, C-604/12, paras. 49–50; *M. G. and N. R.*, C-383/13PPU.

[442] Originally in *Y. S.*, C-141/12, para. 67.

[443] E.g., *Mukarubega*, C-166/13, para. 45; *Boudjlida*, C-249/13, para. 34.

[444] *AJD Tuna*, C-221/09, para. 49.

[445] Cf. Explanatory Notes to Article 41.

[446] It ranks second, just after Article 47; see EC Staff Working Document 2016, n. 320, at 9. Article 41 is often invoked in cases against the EU institutions; see e.g *Versorgungswerk der Zahnärztekammer Schleswig-Holstein*, T-376/13.

[447] *Kadi II*, C-584/10P, para. 102. See also already *Solvay*, C-110/10P, para. 63.

the UN sanction committee,[448] including, for example, the right to be heard, procedural guarantees offered, the reasoning provided, the need for authorities to respect confidentiality and the availability of procedures to deal with security interests with respect to the right of access to information.[449] However, the ECJ has generally permitted more discretion in relation to asylum and migration decisions taken by the authorities of member states by, for example, emphasising that the principle is not absolute, and that 'not every irregularity in the exercise of the rights of the defence in an administrative procedure (...) will constitute an infringement of those rights'.[450] Indeed, 'infringement of the principle of respect for the rights of the defence results in the annulment of the decision in question only if, had it not been for that infringement, the outcome of the procedure could have been different'.[451] The same appears to be true for the right to be heard, which may be limited as long as its core is not affected.[452] The ECJ has, nevertheless, imposed considerable procedural obligations on member states. As soon as an individual is adversely affected by any measure, he must be placed in a position in which he can effectively make his views known regarding the information on which the authorities intend to base their decision[453] and the authorities must pay due attention to the observations submitted, examining carefully and impartially all the relevant aspects of the individual case and giving a detailed statement of the reasons for their decision[454] that must be sufficiently specific to allow the person concerned to understand why his application has been rejected.[455]

Article 42 CFR provides a right of access to documents held by the institutions, bodies, offices and agencies of the Union.[456] This right was already protected by Article 255 TFEU. As with Article 41, the scope of this right is limited in that Article 42 does not provide a right of access to documents of national governmental bodies. Nevertheless, this is an

---

[448] See in particular *Kadi II*, C-584/10P; see for a more recent confirmation *Fulmen*, C-280/12P.
[449] See very elaborately *Kadi II*, C-584/10P, paras. 118ff.
[450] E.g., *M. G. and N. R.*, C-383/13PPU, para. 39.
[451] *Kamino*, C-129/13, para. 80.
[452] E.g., *Texdata*, C-418/11, para. 85.
[453] See *Sopropé*, C-349/07, para. 38; under the CFR, see, e.g., *Mukarubega*, C-166/13, para. 49; *Kamino*, C-129/13, paras. 30–1.
[454] *Boudjlida*, C-249/13, para. 38; *Sopropé*, C-349/07, para. 50.
[455] *M. M.*, C-277/11, para. 88.
[456] See more elaborately, D. Curtin and J. Mendes, 'Article 42. Right of Access to Documents', in Peers et al., 'The EU Charter', 1099–119.

important provision for EU law, as it helps to ensure the transparency of EU decision-making processes and, as a result, may promote good administrative practices.[457]

The right of access to documents is regulated by secondary legislation, which the ECJ tends to apply instead of Article 42.[458] It has, for example, observed that disclosure of documents that contain personal information may conflict with the privacy and the integrity of the individual as regulated by the data protection directive.[459] Requests for access to documents must, therefore, be examined and assessed to ensure conformity with the directive and with Article 8 CFR.[460]

There is some overlap between Article 42 and the more general right to receive information provided by Article 11 CFR. In many cases, both provisions are invoked, but sometimes only Article 11 is mentioned.[461] It is clear from the ECJ's case law, however, that the right to access to documents is not unlimited and that exception may be made where, for example, disclosure would harm the EU's international relations or endanger investigations or audits.[462]

Articles 43 and 44 CFR are closely related, in that both provisions give a voice to everyone residing in the EU who wants to express views, wishes and complaints regarding EU law and policy. Article 43 reaffirms the possibility of referring cases of maladministration – the neglect of principles of good administration, a lack of respect for fundamental rights and, more generally, unlawful behaviour by the EU institutions, bodies and agencies[463] – to the European Ombudsman, an alternative, non-judicial remedy available to EU citizens already provided by Articles 20 and 228 TFEU.[464]

Article 44 recognises the right to petition the European Parliament in conformity with Articles 20 and 227 TFEU,[465] recognised by the ECJ as an instrument of citizen participation in the democratic life of the EU[466]

---

[457] Dennekamp, T-115/13, para. 40.
[458] E.g., Spirlea, T-669/11; Schenker, T-534/11.
[459] See already Bavarian Lager, C-28/08P, para. 59.
[460] Dennekamp, T-115/13, para. 87.
[461] Ibid.; Besselink, T-331/11.
[462] See further Curtin and Mendes, 'Right of Access to Documents', paras. 42-28ff.
[463] Ibid., paras. 43.41ff.
[464] I. Harden, 'Article 43. European Ombudsman', in Peers et al., 'The EU Charter', 1121–50, para. 43.29.
[465] See further M. Lindfeldt, 'Article 44. Right to Petition', in Peers et al., 'The EU Charter', 1151–60.
[466] Schönberg, C-261/13P, para. 17.

and one of the means of ensuring direct dialogue between EU citizens and their representatives.[467] The ECJ has held that, rather than the CFR provisions, the TFEU clauses should be applied in concrete cases concerning such petitions, since they provide more details and conditions for the invocation of these rights.[468] Article 227 specifies, for example, that a petition must relate to one of the EU's 'fields of activity' and must 'directly' affect the person or persons submitting it.[469] Once a petition is taken up, the European Parliament has broad political discretion to decide on how to deal with it.[470] The decisions taken in this regard are not amenable to judicial review.[471]

Article 45 deals with freedom of movement and of residence for EU citizens (pargraph 1)—one of the classic EU citizens' rights also recognised in Article 20 TFEU—and of third country nationals (paragraph 2).[472] Although the Explanatory Notes do not make mention of it, and the ECJ has not as yet made any reference to the ECHR, the provision is paralleled by the free movement provision of Article 2 P4 ECHR. In the few cases in which reference was made to Article 45, the ECJ has also held that primary or secondary EU law was applicable,[473] indicating that the former does not have much independent value.[474] Since Article 20(2) TFEU states that freedom of movement has to be exercised 'under the conditions and within the limits defined by the Treaties and by the measures adopted pursuant thereto', the ECJ considers it appropriate to deal with Article 45 claims under the more detailed legislation alone.[475] The ECJ has cited Article 45 CFR mainly as confirmation that, as one of the fundamental freedoms of the internal market, the free movement of persons is to be regarded as a fundamental right.[476]

Title V concludes with the rather unusual Article 46 CFR, which states that every citizen of the Union who finds himself unrepresented by his member state in the territory of a third country is entitled to protection

---

[467] Ibid.
[468] Ibid., para. 14.
[469] Ibid., para. 15.
[470] Ibid., para. 24.
[471] Ibid.
[472] See further E. Spaventa, 'Article 45. Freedom of Movement and of Residence', in Peers et al., 'The EU Charter', 1161–76.
[473] Zeman, C-543/12; McCarthy, C-434/09; Lassal, C-162/09.
[474] Cf. Spaventa, 'Free Movement of Persons', para. 45.01.
[475] E.g., Zeman, C-543/12, para. 39.
[476] McCarthy, C-434/09, para. 27; Lassal, C-162/09, para. 29.

by the diplomatic or consular authorities of any member state on the same conditions as the nationals of that member state.[477] This is a right of EU citizens already contained in Article 20 TFEU. Its meaning has not yet been clarified by the ECJ's case law, and its value may be primarily symbolic.[478]

Title VI – Justice

The last substantive title of the CFR contains four provisions, each relating to different aspects of procedural and criminal justice. Article 47 in particular is very important and is the most frequently invoked provision in the entire document.[479] It guarantees the right to an effective remedy before a tribunal to everyone whose rights and freedoms guaranteed by the law of the Union are violated (paragraph 1); a fair and public hearing within a reasonable time by an independent and impartial tribunal previously established by law; and a right to be advised, defended and represented (paragraph 2). Finally, paragraph 3 states that legal aid shall be made available to those who lack sufficient resources in so far as it is necessary to ensure effective access to justice. This provision therefore reflects the rights protected by Articles 6 and 13 ECHR but seeks to protect them much more widely. For example, Article 47 does not restrict the guarantees of access to court and to fair trial to civil rights and obligations and to a criminal charge, as does Article 6(1) ECHR; nor does it limit the right to an effective remedy to 'arguable claims' about fundamental rights, as does Article 13 ECHR. In addition, the scope of Article 47 is not limited to judicial review of decisions taken by EU institutions, as is the right to good administration provided by Article 41 CFR, but it extends to all decisions and legislation made by EU institutions and bodies or national authorities.

Procedural justice and access to remedies have always been core principles of EU law. From a very early stage, the ECJ recognised that effective judicial protection has to be offered to individuals, companies and administrative bodies whose interests are affected by EU law (the

---

[477] E. Denza, 'Article 46. Diplomatic and Consular Protection', in Peers et al., 'The EU Charter', 1177–95.

[478] Denza, 'Diplomatic Protection', para. 46.18.

[479] In 2014, in 20 per cent of all cases in which the CFR was invoked, reference was made to Article 47; Commission Report 2014, n. 320, p. 27. See also A. Ward et al, 'Article 47. Right to an Effective Remedy and to a Fair Trial', in Peers et al., 'The EU Charter', 1197–1275.

principle of effectiveness) and that this protection ought to be at least equivalent to that which would normally be offered in similar cases governed by national law (the principle of equivalence).[480] In its case law on Article 47, the ECJ has striven for continuity with its well-established case law relating to these general principles and this is why only few references can be found in it to the standards for justification laid down in Article 52(1).[481] Similarly, although there are some references to the ECtHR's case law under Articles 6 and 13, the ECJ has expressly stated that, now that 'Article 47 of the Charter secures in EU law the protection afforded by Article 6(1) of the ECHR (...) it is necessary (...) to refer only to Article 47'.[482] On topics where the ECJ has established few precedents of its own, however, references to the Strasbourg case law can be found.[483] Article 47 covers a wide number of issues including, as the ECJ has summarised, 'in particular, the rights of the defence, the principle of equality of arms, the right of access to a tribunal and the right to be advised, defended and represented'.[484]

The rights to an effective remedy and of access to a court or tribunal have been applied in a variety of cases.[485] According to the case law, member states must provide remedies sufficient to ensure effective legal protection in all fields covered by EU law,[486] and the ECJ has consistently held that it is for the national legal order of each member state to institute such remedies, and provide such procedural rules, in accordance with the principles of procedural autonomy, equivalence and effectiveness.[487] As regards the right to effective access to a court, the ECJ has generally held that a 'tribunal' must have 'the power to consider all the questions of fact and law that are relevant to the case before it',[488]

---

[480] Cf. Ward et al., 'Right to a Fair Trial', paras. 47.54, 47.94ff.
[481] There are exceptions; see, e.g., *Kadi II*, C-584/10P, para. 101; *Liivimaa Lihaveis MTÜ*, C-562/12, para. 72.
[482] *Chalkor*, C-386/10P, para. 51; *Otis*, C-199/11, para. 47.
[483] One may think of the right to free assistance by a lawyer for legal persons (e.g., *DEB*, C-279/09, paras. 46ff); the right of an accused to appear before the court in person (*Melloni*, C-399/11, para. 50) or procedural rights in extradition and expulsion cases (e.g., *Jeremy F.*, C-168/13PPU para. 43; *Abdida*, C-562/13, para. 52).
[484] *Otis*, C-199/11, para. 48.
[485] In more detail, see Ward et al., 'Right to a Fair Trial', paras. 47.52ff.
[486] *Liivimaa Lihaveis MTÜ*, C-562/12, para. 68.
[487] E.g., *Kušionová*, C-34/13, para. 50; the case law is nuanced, however; see further Ward et al., 'Right to a Fair Trial', para. 47.57.
[488] *Otis*, C-199/11, para. 49. The notion of a 'tribunal' is not further explained in the case law. See, however, the case law on the notion of a 'judicial authority' in relation to the European arrest warrant system: *Poltorak*, C-452/16 PPU and *Özçelik*, C-453/16 PPU.

including to review the proportionality of sanctions and penalties.[489] It must be able to exercise this power even if the institution or authority that has taken a certain decision has a (wide) margin of discretion.[490] These general obligations have been specified according to the requirements of specific types of cases, such those where confidential information and state security play a special role, where sanctions are imposed on terrorist suspects,[491] cases on asylum and migration issues[492] and horizontal disputes between private parties.[493]

An important question regarding access to a court in EU law is whether individuals should be able directly to access the ECJ when their interests have been affected by EU regulatory acts.[494] This night, the ECJ has long held, can be exercised only by applicants directly and individually concerned by such regulatory acts, i.e., those especially affected by circumstances that are peculiar to them or that differentiate them from all other persons.[495] Although the ECJ has been criticised for using this restrictive standard, it has confirmed by reference to the CFR that it does not infringe the core of the right to access to a court.[496] Even if very few such direct appeals against legislation are possible, sufficient other remedies are available in the TFEU's system of procedures that can guarantee the rights protected by Article 47, supplemented with remedies provided by national law.[497]

The right to fair trial also encompasses the obligation to decide cases within a reasonable time, which may also be invoked, for example, not only with respect to national proceedings,[498] but also, for example, where the General Court has allegedly taken too long to decide a case. The ECJ has held that, in such circumstances, a claim for compensation may be made to the General Court in respect of the damage allegedly caused[499]

---

[489] *Kušionová*, C-34/13.

[490] *Chalkor*, C-386/10P, para. 59; *Otis*, C-199/11, para. 59.

[491] E.g., *ZZ*, C-300/11, paras. 61ff; *Kadi II*, C-584/10P.

[492] See, e.g., M. Reneman, *EU Asylum Procedures and the Right to An Effective Remedy* (Oxford: Hart, 2014).

[493] *Dekker*, C-177/88; see further Ward et al., 'Right to a Fair Trial', para. 47.72ff.

[494] See further Ward et al., 'Right to a Fair Trial', para. 47.152ff.

[495] *Plaumann*, 25/62.

[496] *Inuit Tapiriit Kanatami*, C-583/11P, para. 75; see also Ward et al., 'Right to a Fair Trial', para. 47.161.

[497] *Ibid.*, paras. 89–104.

[498] E.g., *Puid*, C-4/11, para. 35.

[499] *Gascogne Sack Deutschland*, C-40/12, paras. 80–102; *Guardian Industries*, C-580/12P, paras. 17–19; *Galp Energía España*, C-603/13P, para. 56.

and it is open to the ECJ to find that that procedure has also taken too long.[500]

According to the ECJ, the principle of equality of arms 'implies that each party must be afforded a reasonable opportunity to present his case, including his evidence, under conditions that do not place him at a substantial disadvantage vis-à-vis his opponent'.[501] The aim is to ensure a balance between the parties, including guaranteeing in principle that any document submitted to a court may be examined and challenged by any party to the proceedings.[502] In addition, there may be no unreasonable differences between the parties as regards financial impediments such as court fees or value added tax for lawyers' services.[503]

The right provided by Article 47(2) to be assisted by a lawyer is complemented by the obligation under Article 47(3) to make legal aid available, which, the ECJ has held, can be invoked by both natural and legal persons.[504] It also has considered matters such as the freedom of choice of a lawyer and the principle of legal privilege, which it regards as important, yet which may be subject to restrictions and conditions.[505] The ECJ has adopted the standards and criteria developed by the ECtHR regarding the obligation to provide legal aid.[506] It has held, however, that it is normally up to national courts to decide whether providing legal aid is necessary, and that

> the national court must take into consideration the subject-matter of the litigation; whether the applicant has a reasonable prospect of success; the importance of what is at stake for the applicant in the proceedings; the complexity of the applicable law and procedure; and the applicant's capacity to represent himself effectively. In order to assess the proportionality, the national court may also take account of the amount of the costs of the proceedings (...) and whether or not those costs might represent an insurmountable obstacle to access to the courts.[507]

---

[500] *Galp Energía España*, C-603/13P, para. 57.
[501] *Otis*, C-199/11, para. 71.
[502] *Ibid.*, para. 72; *Unitrading*, C-437/13, paras. 20–1.
[503] *Toma*, C-205/15, para. 48; *Ordre des barreaux francophones et germanophone*, C-543/14, paras. 42ff.
[504] *DEB*, C-279/09, paras. 38–40.
[505] *Akzo Nobel Chemicals*, C-550/07P, paras. 92–7.
[506] *DEB*, C-279/09, paras. 45ff.
[507] *Ibid.*, para. 61.

Generally, restrictive measures may not deprive someone from having effective access to justice.[508]

The principle of equality of arms and the right to be assisted by a lawyer are closely related to the rights of the defence. Article 48 CFR, which is based on Articles 6(2) and 6(3) ECHR,[509] protects the presumption of innocence and the rights of the defence following a criminal charge.[510] While in civil and administrative law cases, Article 47 is mostly applied on its own (or in conjunction with the general principle of defence rights), in cases concerning criminal law matters, Articles 47 and 48 CFR are usually read in conjunction.[511] In its case law the ECJ has detailed the requirements relating to both provisions. It has, for example, developed clear and precise standards for the right of access to documents and information;[512] the right to ascertain the reasons upon which a decision is based;[513] the right of an accused to appear in person at trial and to be heard;[514] and the setting of limitation periods in consumer proceedings.[515] The ECJ has also imposed a number of positive obligations on states to ensure defence rights. In cases on return, extradition or expulsion to which Article 19(2) CFR applies, it has, for example, required that procedures have suspensive effect.[516] It has also held that relevant secondary legislation must be read so as to 'ensure that (...) the delivery of judicial decisions take place in such a way that the rights of the defence enshrined in Article 47 of the Charter are observed'.[517]

---

[508] *Peftiev*, C-314/13, para. 26.
[509] Explanatory Notes to Article 48.
[510] See further H. P. Nehl, 'Article 48. Presumption of Innocence and Right of Defence (Administrative Law)', in Peers et al., 'The EU Charter', 1277–301; D. Sayers, 'Article 48. Presumption of Innocence and Right of Defence (Criminal Law), in Peers et al., 'The EU Charter', 1303–49.
[511] E.g., *Melloni*, C-399/11, para. 49; *Radu*, C-396/11, para. 29. Sometimes Article 48 is read in conjunction with Article 41; e.g., *WebMindLicenses*, C-419/14, para. 83; in other cases, Article 48 is applied on its own; see, e.g., *Eturas*, C-74/14, para. 38.
[512] E.g., *Eturas*, C-74/14, paras. 38ff.
[513] E.g., *ZZ*, C-300/11, para. 53; *Kadi II*, C-584/10P, para. 111; *Unitrading*, C-437/13, paras. 20–1.
[514] *Melloni*, C-399/11, para. 49; *Radu*, C-396/11, para. 39; *A.*, C-112/13, paras. 52–60.
[515] *Kušionová*, C-34/13.
[516] *Abdida*, C-562/13. In cases where Article 19(2) does not play a role, the Court has accepted that states provide for such suspensive effect; see *Jeremy F.*, C-168/13PPU, para. 51.
[517] *A.*, C-112/13, para. 51.

The presumption of innocence of Article 48 may play a particularly prominent role in EU fraud proceedings and in competition law.[518] This provision is generally read in line with the case law of the ECtHR. The ECJ has accepted, for example, that it may be infringed if a judgment by the General Court implies someone is guilty of an offence in spite of a formal acquittal.[519] By contrast, according to the ECJ, the principle is not infringed by typical presumptions and rules for the burden of proof in competition law,[520] nor by statements of fact and provisional opinions given in a preliminary reference by a national court.[521]

Article 49 concerns the principles of legality and the requirement of proportionality of criminal penalties, the latter of which has hardly ever has been invoked directly before the ECJ.[522] Instead it has applied the general principle and referred to its extensive case law on it.[523] The legality principle as provided by Article 49, a modernised version of Article 7 ECHR, is more important,[524] and has proven particularly relevant in cases relating, for example, to competition law, customs cooperation and fisheries policy,[525] and, more recently, in cases concerning criminal offences committed before a member state's accession.[526] The ECJ has held that the principle of legality applies not only in relation to decisions imposing criminal penalties in the strict sense, where it generally closely follows relevant ECtHR jurisprudence,[527] but also to those imposing administrative sanctions.[528] In common with the ECtHR, it has also held that the principle requires that penalties are clearly defined by law in order to provide legal certainty, which is achieved 'where the individual concerned is able, on the basis of the wording of the relevant provision and, if need be, with the help of the interpretative guidance given by the courts, to know which acts or

---

[518] See generally, e.g., *E.ON Energie*, C-89/11P, para. 73.
[519] *Nikolaou*, C-220/13P, para. 35.
[520] E.g., *E.ON Energie*, C-89/11P, paras. 71ff; *FLS Plast*, C-243/12P, paras. 27ff. See more elaborately, e.g., Nehl, n. 510, paras. 48.18ff.
[521] *Ognyanov*, C-614/14, paras. 25–6.
[522] For a rare exception, see *Eni*, T-558/09, para. 165; even here, the Court continued to apply the principle of proportionality rather than Article 49 (3).
[523] See further V. Mitsilegas, 'Article 49. Principles of Legality and Proportionality', in Peers et al., 'The EU Charter', 1351–71, para. 49.25.
[524] See, e.g., *Delvigne*, C-650/13, paras. 53–8.
[525] See further Mitsilegas, 'Principles of Legality and Proportionality', para. 49.15.
[526] *Paoletti*, C-218/15.
[527] *Ibid.*, para. 75.
[528] *Ezz*, T-256/11, para. 71.

omissions will make him criminally liable'.[529] However, although the principle of legal certainty may preclude the retroactive application of a new interpretation of a rule establishing an offence, it cannot be interpreted as prohibiting the gradual clarification of the rules of criminal liability.[530] Nor does the extension of limitation periods for criminal offences, such as VAT fraud, constitute an infringement of Article 49.[531] Finally, given the particular characteristics of the EU legal system, the ECJ has clarified that, although normally national courts are required to interpret domestic law in light of the wording and purpose of directives, this should not result in determining or aggravating the liability in criminal law of those who contravene their provisions.[532]

Finally, Article 50 contains the 'double jeopardy', or *ne bis in idem* principle, corresponding to that found in Article 4 P7 ECHR,[533] which prohibits trial or punishment more than once for the same offence. This article has proven of particular importance in the EU context, not least because not all member states have ratified the ECHR version. In common with the ECtHR, the ECJ has held that the principle applies only in relation to more than one penalty, the criminal character of which is determined by national law, the nature of the offence and/or by its nature and severity.[534] The ECJ usually leaves this assessment to national courts.[535] Since Article 50 refers to 'the same offence' rather than 'the same acts' it is not clear if the ECJ's understanding of the concept of 'idem' as 'identity of the material acts, understood as the existence of a set of concrete circumstances which are inextricably linked together'[536] will be maintained.[537] The Explanatory Notes to Article

[529] See, e.g., *Garenfeld*, C-405/10, para. 48. See also already *Advocaten voor de Wereld*, C-303/05, paras. 49–50.
[530] E.g., *Telefónica*, C-295/12P, para. 147ff.
[531] *Taricco*, C-105/14, para. 57.
[532] *Coronna*, C-7/11, paras. 51–5.
[533] Cf., e.g., J. Tomkin, 'Article 50. Right Not to Be Tried or Punished Twice in Criminal Proceedings for the Same Criminal Offence', in Peers et al., 'The EU Charter', 1373–412; B. van Bockel, *The Ne Bis in Idem Principle in EU Law* (Leiden: Kluwer Law International, 2010).
[534] *Åkerberg Fransson*, C-617/10, para. 35. See also already (without reference to Article 50 CFR): *Bonda*, C-489/10, para. 37.
[535] E.g., *Åkerberg Fransson*, C-617/10, para. 36. This is different, however, in cases concerning penalty decisions taken by the EU institutions in relation to irregularities, for example in relation to quota systems; see, e.g., *Beneo-Orafti*, C-150/10, paras. 70ff.
[536] E.g., *Gasparini*, C-467/04, para. 54.
[537] *Zolothukin v Russia*, HUDOC 10 February 2009 (Grand Chamber), para. 82; Tomkin, n. 533, para. 50.63.

50 further expressly state that the *ne bis in idem* principle applies, not only within the jurisdiction of one State, but also among the jurisdictions of several member states. Particularly given the Schengen arrangements and other forms of collaboration between member states in the context of criminal law, it may be that different national public authorities might exercise enforcement competences in parallel,[538] challenging the ECJ to harmonise the specific requirements of Schengen with those of the CFR.[539]

5.7   Conclusion

The ECJ has come a long way, from the first steps it took in the fundamental rights field in its judgments in *Nold*, *Stauder* and *Internationale Handelsgesellschaft*, to the current application of the CFR in cases about data protection, obligations for Internet service providers and expulsion of asylum seekers. Originally accused of being overly economically oriented and lacking respect for basic entitlements, in several key areas the ECJ can now be regarded as a genuine champion of fundamental rights. Its ability to provide effective protection may still be limited by notions of conferral, subsidiarity, supremacy and uniformity of EU law, respect for national identity and mutual recognition, as well as by its distinctive procedural context, and by the strongly economic rationale of the EU as a whole. However, the dominant economic approach of the early days is now often also complemented by a powerful fundamental rights perspective. Of the four models under consideration in this study both 'separate development' and 'organic convergence' are clearly inappropriate to explain the ECJ's fundamental rights jurisprudence, since as a court of law, it must resolve the cases brought before it authoritatively and definitively. However, both of the other alternatives – 'unification' and 'constitutional pluralism' – apply according to how prescriptive and universalistic the relevant provisions of EU law are. When the ECJ asserts its autonomy in defining the legal obligations of states, and seeks to overrule national constitutional norms, it does so in ways that are generally respectful of fundamental rights. It is equally clear, however, that clashes and conflicts may still occur as a result of diverging national and pan-European views on the level of protection

---

[538] Tomkin, 'Right Not to Be Tried Twice', para. 50.36.
[539] E.g., *Spacic*, C-129/14 PPU, para. 74; *M.*, C-398/12, para. 35; *Kossowski*, C-486/14, para. 31.

certain fundamental rights require, giving rise to complex interactions both between the ECJ and national courts, on the one hand, and between the ECJ and the ECtHR, on the other. Therefore, one of the challenges for the future is for an adequate response to the difficulties arising from these interactions to be provided, especially since it is now unlikely that the EU will accede to the ECHR any time soon.

These difficulties should not be unamenable to resolution, however. This chapter and Chapter 3 have shown that there is already a strongly, though uneven, parallel development of rights, principles and general notions in the ECHR and EU contexts. Although there are significant differences, the ECJ clearly relies on similar principles of interpretation, conditions for justification of restrictions and similar notions of deference and intensity of review. In spite of the many questions that remain open, for example regarding horizontal effect and the difference between principles and rights, the ECJ's approach to necessity and proportionality review, as well as its core rights approach, are commendable though not yet fully clarified and developed. There are, however, ample grounds for confidence that fundamental rights will be soundly protected as the EU continues to develop. There can be little doubt that the ECJ still has valuable lessons to learn from the ECtHR, particularly as far as articulating a more transparent and predictable margin of appreciation doctrine and a proper balancing test are concerned. But the judgments it has delivered since the CFR became binding in 2009 show such refinement that they may even provide exemplars for the ECtHR itself, thereby reversing their more familiar relationship.

6

Summary and Conclusion

6.1 Introduction

The purpose of this chapter is to summarise the key insights from preceding chapters, which have endeavoured to substantiate the core thesis of this study, that the central achievements of the CE and the EU in the fields of human and fundamental rights are the successful institutionalisation of their respective missions in both political and legal spheres; the central trends are their expansion and increasing complexity, multidimensionality and interpenetration; and the central challenges concern how this could, and should, be properly understood, and coherently, legitimately and effectively managed according to four theoretically possible models – unification, separate development, organic convergence and constitutional pluralism. As far as the interface between both organisations is concerned, we also conclude that, while the first of these is inapplicable across the board, and none of the others applies uniformly in all spheres, the latter has particular relevance for the judicial realm, where the most sharply focused problems and dilemmas typically arise.

Our answers to the two 'flip side' questions raised in the Preface, hinted at but not squarely addressed throughout the study, are that the autonomy and separate identity of the CE and EU in the human rights field are likely to be preserved for the foreseeable future and that this is appropriate given their histories and subsequent trajectories. But more coordination, interdependence and convergence – requiring, on the part of all relevant parties, mutual respect and a willingness to engage in dialogue and to negotiate – are desirable in matters of principle and interpretation although, given the respective contexts, other differences in judicial method will remain. However, neither the integration of procedure nor the harmonisation of substantive norms is possible or desirable. In all probability, whatever the results, they will, at best, be unevenly achieved. We begin with the distinction between external and internal activities.

6.2   External Activities

Since there is little prospect of the external activities of the CE and EU becoming more formally integrated or regulated, of the conceptual paradigms distinguished in Chapter 1, separate development, albeit underpinned by some shared but not strongly institutionalised values, is arguably the most applicable here. As indicated in Chapter 1, the CE has both regular and ad hoc contacts with other intergovernmental organisations, including the EU and UN. Under certain conditions, considered in Chapter 3, the ECHR may also bind member states acting outside Europe, for example with respect to the conduct of their armed forces abroad.

By contrast, as indicated in Chapter 4, the activities of the EU beyond the Union, including on the human rights front, are much more extensive and significant. The EU participates regularly in multinational organisations by, for example, issuing statements or sponsoring resolutions in the UN's Human Rights Council. In addition to incorporating political conditionality in its external agreements with third states, it relies on civil and military missions, financial assistance and diplomacy (human rights dialogues, public declarations and private *démarches*) to enhance respect for human rights externally. Addressed to EU institutions and member states, the Council of the EU has adopted a series of non-binding, soft law guidelines on priority issues – including the death penalty, torture and other forms of ill-treatment, freedom of expression and religion, the rights of the child and discrimination against women – designed to provide practical tools for coherent action concerning the promotion of particular human rights beyond the Union's frontiers. The European Parliament (EP) has played a pioneering role in the development of the EU's external human rights policy, and continues to ensure its effectiveness by, for example, publishing annual reports and issuing ad hoc resolutions, holding other EU institutions to account over their inconsistent treatment of third states and exercising its fiscal authority to increase the budget for the EU's democratisation and human rights programmes. For its part, the Commission monitors human rights compliance by third states through a variety of processes.

Rather than impose sanctions, particularly upon strategically significant third states, the EU has demonstrated a clear preference for positive measures intended to incentivise improvements, an approach which may best be described as 'guided convergence'. In the context of the EU's relations with third states the guidance element makes this a hybrid between separate development and organic convergence, and a model that fits the EU's relationship with non-EU members of the European Economic Area particularly well because, in order to gain access to the single market, the latter must incorporate into their national law all relevant EU legislation, including that concerning fundamental rights.

However, the relationship with accession states is probably best described as a species of constitutional pluralism. It is 'constitutional' because, as Chapter 2 argues, the effective institutionalisation of fundamental rights in any legal system inescapably has this characteristic, and 'pluralist' because, in this context, it can and should accommodate the specific legitimate interests of each state applying for membership. The unique 'passive' and 'active' dimensions of accession make it the EU's most effective external policy tool with the highest overall success in delivering tangible improvements in human rights beyond the Union's heartlands. 'Passive' leverage stems from the inherent attraction of membership to applicant states, while the 'active' dimension is a consequence of the EU's accession policy, encompassing negotiation, the Copenhagen criteria, extensive monitoring and financial assistance coupled with a particular emphasis upon the judiciary and fundamental rights. The 'unification' model is not appropriate in this context because the degree of standardisation and harmonisation it suggests is at variance with national sovereignty.

6.3   Internal Activities

In exploring the different possible modes of connection and divergence between the internal human rights activities of the CE and EU, a distinction should be drawn between the extra-legal and legal dimensions. Bearing in mind that, in contemporary liberal democracies public power is always formally exercised within a constitutional and legal framework, for these purposes 'extra-legal' means those administrative, political, economic and other activities and functions pursued through institutions other than legislative or judicial ones, while 'legal' means those that are. In this context the latter concern legislation, adjudicative institutions and procedures, methods of interpretation and substantive human rights law.

Human Rights on the Extra-Legal Dimension

The fact that the CE and EU each pursue human rights activities on the extra-legal dimension through separate institutions with shared foundational principles suggests a hybrid between the separate development and constitutional pluralist models. As more fully documented in Chapter 2, the CE's key extra-legal human rights–related institutions are the Committee of Ministers (CM), the Parliamentary Assembly (PACE), the Secretariat and the European Commissioner for Human Rights. The CM provides executive and formal policy and treaty making functions and supervises execution of the ECtHR's judgments. The chief functions of PACE are to make recommendations, to pass resolutions and to express opinions about, and to monitor state compliance with CE policy. In addition to electing the European Commissioner for Human Rights, the Secretary General and Deputy Secretary General of the CE, PACE, which has no legislative powers, also elects judges to the ECtHR from the lists of three candidates presented by member states. The Secretary General presides over the Secretariat and the CE's bureaucracy and has some monitoring responsibilities with respect to the ECHR. The European Commissioner for Human Rights promotes education in, and awareness of, human rights in member states, including collaborating with national and international human rights institutions and ombudsmen, identifying human rights shortcomings in national law and practice and promoting effective human rights compliance. As part of the office's general monitoring responsibility the Commissioner can also submit written comments to the ECtHR, take part in Chamber and Grand Chamber hearings and receive individual complaints, but cannot adjudicate or present them before any court, or initiate litigation.

As Chapter 4 described, the EU's extra-legal human rights institutions and bodies are the European Council, the Council of the EU (also known as the Council, or Council of Ministers), the Parliament (EP), the European Commission, the European Ombudsman, the EU Agency for Fundamental Rights (FRA) and the European Institute for Gender Equality. Including the head of state or government of each member state, the European Council, as the ultimate decision-making body, sets the EU's broad policy agenda, while the Council (of Ministers) determines policy at a more detailed level and is formally responsible for decision making across almost all areas of EU activity. While the former can be credited with providing the political impetus for the establishment of the EU's fundamental rights policies, the rhetoric of the latter has often been stronger than the action it has taken. Composed of ministers from each member state, and charged with representing national interests at the supranational level, the Council's innate caution tends to derive from the reluctance of national governments to transfer sovereignty to the EU in the fundamental rights and other fields.

The EP, the only directly elected supranational legislature in the world, has been, and continues to be, a leading and arguably the most successful proponent of fundamental rights in the EU. It issues reports and resolutions highlighting areas of concern, raises matters of priority by tabling questions to the Commission and Council and scrutinises the fundamental rights records of other EU institutions and bodies. The European Commission has been closely associated with the EP's efforts in the development of the EU's fundamental rights policy. Mandated to act in the general interest of the EU, and with an overarching obligation to ensure the advancement of EU policies in the light of the treaties, it was the Commission, for example, that first asserted, in 1976, that the Community's political institutions should formally declare their respect for fundamental rights. It has also established numerous expert networks providing independent advice and analysis for EU policy formation in the fundamental rights field. For example, the European Network of Legal Experts in Gender Equality and Non-Discrimination produces, amongst other things, various thematic reports on particular policy issues within its remit. The Commission, Council and EP have all adopted soft law measures, with variable effectiveness, to ensure that fundamental rights are taken into consideration in the EU's legislative process. Since 2010 the Commission has also published an annual report indicating how the EU Charter of Fundamental Rights (CFR) has been taken into account by EU institutions, and by national authorities when implementing EU law.

Set up in 1995 to monitor the administrative practice of EU institutions and bodies, and complementing the introduction of EU citizenship, which requires the provision of an effective mechanism for safeguarding citizens' rights, the Ombudsman reflects the contemporary trend to provide those adversely affected by the exercise of public power with opportunities to complain. Like all such institutions, the Ombudsman's is primarily a reactive investigatory office that lacks the power to develop systematic strategies for effective human rights enforcement. Developing an idea first approved two years earlier, the EU also formally proposed, in June 2005, to expand the remit of its European Centre on Racism and Xenophobia to create the FRA, which came into operation on 1 January 2007. Using the CFR as its main point of reference, attempting to avoid overlap with the CE and networking with national institutions, the FRA is intended to assist member states to safeguard fundamental rights when implementing EU law, and to guide and support EU institutions in all their activities in this respect. To this end, its principal function is collecting, analysing and disseminating objective, reliable and comparable information on fundamental rights in the EU. It has no powers to examine individual complaints, to issue regulations or to carry out normative monitoring for the purposes of Article 7 TEU; nor can it directly advocate particular policies or solutions to human rights problems. Although intended to be non-political, which in this context means not naming and shaming member states, its annual and thematic reports, nevertheless, enable countries with deficient human rights standards to be identified. The European Institute for Gender Equality is another autonomous specialised and decentralised fundamental rights agency, with a more specific remit, which exists alongside the FRA to assist in combatting sex discrimination by collecting, analysing and disseminating objective, comparable and reliable information on gender equality, carrying out surveys and publishing positive examples of non-gender-stereotyped practices.

The fact that the CE and EU have each pursued human rights policy on the extra-legal plane through a variety of separate institutions referenced to different institutional standards suggests the separate development model. However, in spite of their different origins and designs, the CE's and EU's extra-legal human rights institutions have largely the same function – to promote enhanced human rights protection in substantially the same multi-layered political space, and, therefore, inescapably share overlapping spheres of interest. The 'unification' model is, however, also untenable in this context because neither the CE nor the EU has the will or capacity to achieve the kind of top-down integration it suggests. Other considerations ignored, there would be little reason to prefer either of the remaining two models. However, when other relevant issues are considered, 'constitutional pluralism' emerges as the more appropriate because of its particularly appropriate mix of universal standards and pluralistic implementation.

Human Rights Legislation

Of the four conceptual models under consideration, separate development is the most applicable to legislative activity because the CE simply has none at all while the EU has tripartite arrangements. The Commission has an almost-exclusive right to propose legislation, with the Council and EP subsequently acting as co-decision maker in most policy areas. While the legislative powers of the EP have considerably increased from its original toothless, advisory role, the Council remains the EU's principal legislative body with a monopoly in some fields.

A fragmented array of EU legislation, with varying degrees of visibility, has been passed regarding a broad spectrum of fundamental rights, a haphazard approach stemming from the EU's lack of competence to develop a fully fledged fundamental rights policy and its inability to act except where the Treaties provide an adequate legal basis. Apart from one provision ensuring equal pay for men and women, the Founding Treaties originally contained no explicit reference to fundamental rights at all. However, as respect for fundamental rights subsequently became more formally recognised as a founding principle of European integration, the Treaties were gradually reformed to include various provisions to this effect. As European integration deepened, the Community's competence also expanded into areas such as immigration, and further legal bases, from which secondary fundamental rights legislation could be developed, were also accordingly provided. The profile of fundamental rights, therefore, increased in both primary EU law and secondary legislation.

The EU's first piece of fundamental rights legislation, derived from the Founding Treaties, prohibited sex discrimination regarding remuneration in employment. Subsequent legislation broadened the scope of gender equality to other aspects of the labour market, and to other fields such as social security. Secondary legislation later delivered on the competence, granted the Community by the Treaty of Amsterdam, to combat discrimination on grounds other than sex, both within and outside the employment field. Data protection legislation, also originally restricted to matters relevant to the internal market, has also recently been extended to such areas as law enforcement. However, because of the reluctance of member states to delegate social policy competences to the EU – except in the field of occupational health and safety, deemed intrinsically related to the internal market – the Commission has had to interpret relevant treaty provisions widely in order to introduce legislation on such matters as working time.

The CFR has failed to ensure a more coherent body of EU fundamental rights legislation because its provisions do not extend the Union's competences beyond that provided by the Treaties. Nevertheless, it significantly improves legal certainty by codifying, for the first time, all EU fundamental rights in a single written document. Since the Treaty of Lisbon entered into force in 2009, the CFR has also assumed the status of primary EU law, binding member states when implementing EU law and EU institutions themselves. Its substantive content is considered later.

Institutions and Procedures for the Adjudication of Human Rights

The separate development model is also most relevant for the very different institutional and procedural arrangements applicable to the adjudication of human rights complaints under the ECHR and in the EU. As already indicated in Chapters 1 and 2, at its inception it was agreed that the ECHR's main modus operandi should be the 'inter-state process'. But there have only been about two dozen or so such cases in the Convention's entire history, not least because litigation is a hostile act in most circumstances and, therefore, not an ideal vehicle for cultivating European interdependence, the CE's core rationale. As indicated in Chapter 2, by sharp contrast, the rate of individual applications has been rising exponentially since the mid-1990s. For example, between 2000 and 2016, a total of 741,100 were formally received ('allocated to a judicial formation'), an annual average of 43,594.

The Court's increasing case load has presented the Convention system with five main challenges: distinguishing between, and managing, admissible and inadmissible applications; expeditiously addressing those concerning manifest Convention violations; distinguishing between high- and low-priority complaints; responding effectively to those already condemned in the respondent state; and dealing with neither clearly inadmissible nor repetitive applications. Protocols Nos. 11 and 14 streamlined relevant processes. Two more recent ones, Nos. 15 and 16, have also recently been approved though, at the time of writing, neither had yet come into force. Since supervision of the execution of adverse judgments by the ECtHR is the responsibility of the CM, and a matter for negotiation with all member states, the respondent state effectively participates in supervising enforcement against itself. States may find it difficult to correct the systemic source of a violation for various reasons including a lack of clarity in the ECtHR's judgment, political problems, the daunting scale of the reforms required, managing complex legislative procedures, budgetary issues, adverse public opinion, the possible impact of compliance on obligations deriving from other institutions and bureaucratic inertia.

By the end of 2015, Protocol No. 14, the Court's priority policy and the stricter approach to the receipt of complaints by the Registry at last seemed to be reducing the scale of the case overload crisis. However, although it is too early to say whether they constitute merely a temporary blip or the beginning of a new phase, the figures for 2016 also show some reversals in this trend. For example, having dropped from an all-time high of 65,800 in 2013, to 40,600 in 2015, the number of applications allocated to a judicial formation rose to 53,500 by the end of 2016. Of those cases pending by the end of January 2017, 30,500 were repetitive, almost 11,500 were 'priority' and nearly 21,000, constituting the greatest weight on the Court's docket, were neither clearly inadmissible nor repetitive. The alleviation of case overload has, however, been achieved largely as a result of an 'unholy alliance' between states, Strasbourg bureaucrats and NGOs, who for very different reasons, jointly mobilised in the reform debate against any perceived threat to the right of individual petition. Yet, the unfortunate irony is, that in the attempt to defend it, the right of individual complaint has, paradoxically, been undermined, the Court has been confirmed as a 'human rights small claims tribunal', structural violations are now more likely to be institutionalised than resolved and a golden opportunity to improve the protection of human rights across the continent has been missed.

Sending less serious prima facie Convention violations indefinitely to the back of the queue will inevitably result in large numbers of applications not being examined, creating injustice both for those whose complaints cannot be addressed at all and for those for whom judgment is delayed. The state interest is clear – doing as little as possible to satisfy the CM that judgment has been executed. For their part, Strasbourg officials, in common with bureaucrats everywhere, tend to assume that the resolution of administrative challenges lies in micro-managing the existing system rather than in its imaginative re-conceptualisation. And, by prioritising the Convention rights of actual over those of potential victims, the NGOs have endorsed, not only a highly ineffective way of promoting the structural changes that would prevent violations from occurring in the first place, but one that paradoxically institutionalises them by permitting states repeatedly to pay compensation as a modest cost of failing to deal with the source. Since the stark and inescapable fact is that not every meritorious complaint can possibly receive full judicial consideration in Strasbourg, a much wiser strategy would be to concentrate the Court's scarce resources upon judging those that are most serious for the applicant, for the respondent state and for Europe as a whole, and/or that present significant fresh challenges. Indeed, the Court has moved, and been moved, significantly in this direction in recent years. But it continues to be inhibited from fully capitalising on this function because of the demands made by case management and the adjudication of relatively minor repetitive applications that ultimately fail to stem the flow of similar complaints at source.

As Chapters 4 and 5 indicate, the institutional and procedural land-scapes for the judicial protection of fundamental rights are very different in the EU. Since the EU operates on the basis that such rights form an integral part of the general principles of its law, and that respect for them is a condition of the lawfulness of Community/Union acts, in theory, violations of fundamental rights can be litigated before the ECJ: by EU institutions against each other; by member states against each other; by the Commission against member states; by individuals and subnational organisations with legal personality against EU institutions; and by individuals and subnational organisations with legal personality against member states through preliminary references from national courts in on-going litigation. However, in practice, it is rare for any of this to happen. Hence the lack of statistics comparable to those for the Convention system provided elsewhere in this study. At the instigation of the Commission, a member state can be held responsible in infringement proceedings for not complying with fundamental rights provisions such as those contained in relevant directives. By contrast, a member state may invoke fundamental rights to justify its lack of compliance with other EU obligations. Direct appeals, brought by other EU institutions, other member states or natural or legal persons, require the ECJ to direct its attention to the compatibility of EU decisions, and sometimes legislation, with fundamental rights. In dealing with direct appeals the ECJ acts as an administrative law tribunal, taking account of the fact that decisions have been taken by co-equal branches of government with their own distinct-ive sources and types of legitimacy. The principles of conferral and subsidiarity further mean that the ECJ has limited opportunity to develop fundamental rights and cannot, for example, simply read new positive obligations into CFR provisions where there is no such competence for the EU to act. Together these features may contribute to a lack of clarity in how certain fundamental rights are understood in the EU context and how they should be protected at national level by EU institutions. Nor does the ECJ have any jurisdiction in relation to the EU's Common Foreign and Security Policy which may raise human rights issues.

It is very difficult for individuals to complain to the ECJ about a violation of their fundamental rights by EU legislation because this is not available as of right and the threshold requirements are exceptionally high. In principle, natural and legal persons can initiate proceedings for review of the legality of acts of EU institutions only where these are addressed to or are of direct and individual concern to them. The ECJ has interpreted this to mean having been affected as a result of certain attributes peculiar to the specific applicant or by circumstances differentiating him or her from everyone else. Therefore, most cases presented to the ECJ, including those involving fundamental rights, arrive at the court through the preliminary reference route instead. By contrast with the ECtHR, the ECJ does not, therefore, deal with cases that have been fully examined at the national level and closed by judgment. Instead, its opinion and interpretation are sought in ongoing litigation where national courts may still have to establish material facts and assess the reasonableness of an interference. If, having reviewed a provision, including one concerning fundamental rights, the ECJ finds it to be incompatible with EU law, it may be declared null and void. But the ECJ can also leave important questions to national courts. Although neither the direct nor preliminary reference routes require domestic remedies to be exhausted as under the ECHR, each is, nevertheless, an expensive and protracted process. It is hardly surprising, therefore, that the ECJ has heard few human rights complaints from individual applicants, or that judicial review in Luxembourg has led to the annulment of only a handful of EU measures on human rights grounds.

Methods of Interpretation in Human Rights Adjudication

The fact that the methods of interpretation employed by ECtHR and by the ECJ in its human rights adjudication have both distinctive and shared 'constitutional' features suggests another separate development/constitutional-pluralist hybrid. The primary issue the ECtHR has to consider in judging the merits of any admissible application is whether, on the evidence presented, the respondent state has violated the Convention, which generally deprives the ECtHR's judgments of any significant effect beyond the specific facts of any given case. As Chapter 3 more fully demonstrates, this involves interpreting the alleged misconduct in context and determining what the sparse and abstract statements of the relevant rights mean. The ECHR also applies a dozen or so principles of interpretation not found in the text of the Convention itself but identified and developed in the process of litigation over the years. These include primary constitutional principles, such as democracy, effective protection of rights, 'priority to rights' and rule of law/legality; secondary principles, such as proportionality and subsidiarity; and exegetical ones such as the principle of evolutive interpretation. The Convention also operates horizontally between private parties where the ECtHR applies the principle of positive obligations requiring the respondent state to act effectively to protect Convention rights where such relationships may jeopardise them. Because the ECJ inhabits a different juridical space from that of the ECtHR, and has developed its human rights jurisprudence largely in the footsteps of the latter, the ECtHR has had less opportunity or reason to follow the ECJ's juridical method.

By contrast with the ECtHR, the ECJ operates in a much more precisely regulated legal environment, where, depending on context, normative integration and subsidiarity/margin of appreciation are complementary factors, and where judgments are more likely to have *erga omnes* effect than those of the ECtHR. The key interpretive issues the ECJ faces, in the human rights and other fields, are, therefore, significantly more complex, and even principles shared with the ECtHR, such as proportionality, may be approached in different ways. Yet the fact that both courts have very similar foundational-constitutional principles at their disposal, which they apply in a pluralistic fashion (the ECtHR more so than the ECJ), makes the constitutional pluralist paradigm partially applicable here. The central interpretive issues the ECJ has to address with respect to fundamental rights are to determine whether the right in question is part of EU law; if it is, to decide whether or not it has been violated; if it has been, to establish responsibility and to determine whether or not the violation can be justified. The interpretive resources available to the ECJ derive from two main sources: those it has itself developed that have survived the incorporation of the CFR into EU law, and those that have since emerged. Prior to the advent of the CFR, several principles were available to the ECJ as aids to interpretation in adjudication, including in the fundamental rights field. The most fertile, although in some cases underdeveloped, included the EU's core aims and objectives, not least the principle of the supremacy of EU law, the rule of law/legality principle, the principle of proportionality, the margin of appreciation doctrine/doctrine of deference, the doctrine of positive obligations and other more subordinate principles arising from the case law of the ECtHR. However, since the CFR came into effect, the ECJ has increasingly taken it, rather than the ECHR, as its primary point of reference.

The ECJ has defined its main task as contributing to the implementation of EU law, and to the pursuit of the EU's core objectives, including the free movement of goods, services, capital and persons, competition policy and, in the areas of citizenship of the Union, freedom, security and justice. Relevant principles include direct effect, supremacy, harmony and uniformity in the interpretation of internal market and competition law, and, more recently, EU citizenship. By contrast, other principles – for example, subsidiarity, attribution, conferral, mutual respect and recognition, effectiveness and equivalence of national enforcement mechanisms, and respect for national constitutional identity – imply that EU authorities may only exercise those powers and competences expressly accorded them by the Treaties, and also affirm respect for national sovereignty and diversity.

In the EU context the rule of law/legality principle functions as a principle of interpretation in two main ways. The ECJ has held that interferences must be provided by law and has also noted that, in addition to the requirements expressly provided by Article 52(1) CFR, procedural safeguards should ensure effective protection of a given right against the risk of abuse. The CFR's various proportionality requirements assist the ECJ in discharging its interpretive responsibilities. While the ECtHR often resorts to a general balancing approach when rights collide either with each other or with competing public interests, the ECJ typically applies tests of suitability, necessity and often 'least onerous means'. Although the ECJ has not yet developed a fully fledged margin of appreciation doctrine or a 'doctrine of deference', in the context of expulsion or extradition of migrants to states where there might be a risk of persecution, torture, inhuman or degrading treatment, it has, however, left little discretion to member states, requiring strict and full compliance with CFR rights instead. By contrast, if a fundamental right does not appear to have been seriously affected, the case does not concern a particularly important aspect of a fundamental right or it deals with socio-economic principles rather than individual rights, the ECJ is willing to be more deferential. The ECJ has also allowed a wide margin of appreciation where there is little European consensus on certain matters and, where EU institutions have exercised powers in areas requiring complex economic, technical or medical assessments, it has also accorded margins of discretion. While this has usually involved the application of a test of manifest arbitrariness or manifest disproportionality, in some cases (usually concerning sanctions) the ECJ has also added that it must assess, amongst other things, whether the decision had an adequate factual basis and whether the choices were based on objective criteria.

Compared with the ECtHR, the ECJ has had little opportunity to develop a full-fledged doctrine of positive obligations either. Procedural restraints, plus the limitations imposed by the principles of conferral and attribution, leave little opportunity to define obligations and requirements beyond those already provided by EU Treaties and secondary legislation. Indeed, in its CFR case law the ECJ does not expressly refer to positive obligations at all; nor has it relied on any of the factors used by the ECtHR – such as the fair balance, the effective protection of rights or the reasonable knowledge tests – to identify them. While the ECJ has, nevertheless, imposed some procedural obligations on both member states and EU institutions, it is unlikely for reasons already given that it will want to impose any substantive positive obligations other than those already stemming from EU primary or secondary law.

The CFR has compounded the interpretive challenges facing the ECJ in two main ways: determining how it fits with the rest of EU law and the extent to which fundamental rights in the EU may apply to relations between private parties. Article 51(1) CFR requires EU institutions, bodies, offices and agencies not to violate the Charter. The ECJ has also confirmed that the CFR compliance of EU legislation, measures and decisions may be open to review. Article 51(1) CFR also makes clear that member states are bound to comply with Charter rights when implementing Union law. Therefore, according to the ECJ, when a member state transposes a directive into national law, or implements the obligations stemming from a regulation, it must do so in conformity with fundamental rights. However, Article 51(2) CFR stipulates that the Charter does not extend the field of application of Union law beyond the powers of the EU; nor does it establish any new power or task or modify those already arising under, and defined by, the Treaties. The CFR cannot, therefore, be interpreted as providing any new competences to EU institutions actively to protect fundamental rights. Therefore, where the legal issue does not come within the scope of EU law, the ECJ has no jurisdiction, and, consequently, the provisions of the CFR cannot be applied either. Since the ECJ requires a degree of connection beyond merely a close relationship or indirect impact, the mere fact that national and EU legislation govern a particular issue is not sufficient to bring any case arising under the national legislation within the scope of the CFR. But even if legislation, acts or omissions at the national level are not expressly intended to implement EU law, they can still come within the scope of the CFR if they aim to pursue typical EU objectives, or if they relate to fundamental rights in a manner that potentially affects the unity, primacy or effectiveness of EU law. The CFR will, therefore, be applicable when a member state acts under an express mandate contained in EU law, when it implements an issue exhaustively regulated by EU law yet expressly granted a choice, and when a national court is empowered to guarantee the effectiveness of the rights and obligations derived from EU law. Furthermore, in its case law applying fundamental rights as general principles considered previously, the ECJ has held that the acts and omissions of member states may fall within the scope of EU law if they interfere with EU fundamental freedoms, or discriminate directly or indirectly on the basis of nationality.

Article 52 CFR subjects all Charter rights to a generic limitation clause in the following terms: any such restriction must be provided for by law, respect the essence of the rights and freedoms in question and be subject to the principle of proportionality. It must also be necessary and genuinely meet objectives of the general interest recognised by the EU or the need to protect the rights and freedoms of others. Those CFR rights deriving from Community Treaties, or the Treaty on European Union, must also be exercised under the conditions and within the limits defined by those Treaties. According to Article 52(3) CFR and the Explanatory Notes to the Charter, as confirmed by the ECJ, CFR rights that correspond to rights provided by the ECHR must be given the same meaning and scope as relevant Convention rights, although this does not prevent more extensive protection being offered by EU law, a requirement primarily serving to ensure that the general limitation clause of Article 52(2) CFR is not applied to permit restrictions upon non-derogable rights such as the prohibition against torture. The ECJ has traditionally referred to the Strasbourg case law, and continues to do so, when issues arise it has not hitherto considered, but that the ECtHR has, or where there is a risk of divergence between the two systems. Otherwise express references to the Strasbourg case law have increasingly been replaced recently by references to the ECJ's own precedents, and to the CFR, which the ECJ now affirms should be the primary source for fundamental rights in the EU. Article 52(4) CFR states that Charter rights should be interpreted so as to offer a high standard of protection, adequate for EU law and in harmony with common constitutional traditions.

The ECJ has denied that the supremacy of EU law is affected by Article 53 CFR, which states that 'nothing in this Charter shall be interpreted as restricting or adversely affecting human rights and fundamental freedoms as recognised, in their respective fields of application, by Union law' and national constitutions, etc. Consequently, it has held that this provision would only allow national constitutional rights to be applied at the level specifically provided by them if the primacy, unity and effectiveness of EU law were not thereby compromised. The ECJ has also made clear, however, that where there is any doubt, the matter should be referred for a preliminary ruling.

The extent to and the way in which EU fundamental rights affect relations between private parties is determined mainly by relevant EU norms. An employer or trade union may, for example, invoke fundamental rights to justify limiting free movement of workers or services, and private parties may complain that their fundamental EU rights have been violated by other private parties. Horizontal rights issues of this kind may also arise in relation to the implementation of secondary EU law, particularly directives in the non-discrimination, data protection, media and intellectual property law contexts.

Finally, methodologically, the profiles of EU law in the ECHR system, and of the ECHR in the EU system, are very different. Since the EU is not a party to the ECHR, the ECtHR has been presented with very few opportunities to consider the compliance of EU law with the Convention and, when it has, a 'presumption of compatibility' has been applied. By contrast, the ECJ is required to be much more conscious of the ECHR, particularly because respect for fundamental rights as understood by the ECtHR has been a core principle of EU law for decades.

Before finally turning to the substantive human rights jurisprudence of the two systems, it may be useful briefly to summarise the case for constitutional pluralism in this domain. To begin with, and to repeat, the idea of constitutional pluralism has always been about much more than offering a solution to the case management problems experienced by the ECtHR, and the argument has never been that either it, the ECHR or the ECJ should *become* constitutionalised in a pluralist environment. The point is they each *already* have both constitutional and pluralistic features but that this has not yet been as fully recognised, nor have the central implications been as fully understood as they should. What is most required in the transnational legal protection of human rights in Europe, as this model suggests, are institutions facilitating adequate, context-specific protection, which adjudicate only those cases that have systemic significance for the state concerned or for Europe more widely or are sufficiently serious for the applicant to warrant it, which permit variable degrees of national discretion depending upon context, and which produce verdicts and norms which are 'constitutionally reasoned', that is to say, guided more by judicial restraint than activism, and which are tightly referenced to fundamental principles the implications of which are systematically unpacked in judgments even if the resulting norms vary. In other words, the ECtHR and ECJ should strive for the harmonisation of the interpretation of principle, rather than seeking to homogenise or standardise procedure, formal judicial method or norms.

While this is not only a worthy end in itself, it is difficult to see how the crisis of legitimacy and authority from which the ECtHR and the ECJ are increasingly suffering can be resolved without it. And, given the heavy dosage of myth and misrepresentation in the ongoing debate, possibly not even then.

Substantive Human Rights Case Law

It follows from the preceding analysis that the unification model proposes a degree of homogenisation in the substantive human rights case law of the CE and EU that is not possible, not least because there is no institutional or procedural mechanism by which it could be achieved, nor is there ever likely to be. The separate development model is also inappropriate in this context largely because the ECJ has been taking formal notice of the ECHR and the jurisprudence of the ECtHR for decades. Some form of integration or convergence is, therefore, already well under way. The organic convergence model fails to address the risk of inconsistency and incoherence emerging in standards, while also failing sufficiently to appreciate the fact that the ECtHR and the ECJ have long shared common core values and foundational, constitutional and interpretive principles. By contrast, although outcomes are not always the same, the case law of both courts is already underpinned by a framework of common values interpreted by each in similar though not identical ways, generating outcomes that are pluralistic both between states and between the two systems. However, while significant divergences between the Strasbourg and Luxembourg case law have been rare, have generally been corrected and are not the central concern at national level, the key problem concerns the eclectic and unsystematic use of the ECHR and the Strasbourg case law by the ECJ. But, while significant disharmony has so far been avoided, it would be a mistake to take this for granted. Properly understood and applied by all relevant parties, the constitutional pluralist model offers a framework within which the ECtHR, the ECJ and national courts can manage their developing relationship with greater coherence, mutual respect and fruitful dialogue, yet without outcomes being predetermined, thereby achieving an appropriate accommodation between coherence/consistency, on the one hand, and flexibility/diversity, on the other.

In the remainder of this chapter a broad-brush attempt is made to identify the core similarities and differences in the rights jurisprudence of both systems discussed more fully in Chapters 3 and 5, where citations to 'authorities' can also be found. While the principal formal source of the human rights featuring in the case law of the ECtHR and the ECJ's fundamental rights jurisprudence - the CFR and the ECHR - share many substantive features, they also differ in three principal ways. First, the CFR includes rights also contained in the ECHR, but not in precisely the same terms. Second, the ECHR is largely confined to civil and political rights while the CFR also includes a wide range of social, economic, cultural and citizenship rights, similar in kind to those found in the European Social Charter that are not justiciable by the ECtHR. Third, the ECHR provides provision-specific limitation clauses for each right while Article 52 CFR restricts all substantive Charter rights in accordance with a generic limitation clause discussed above in the section on Methods of Interpetation in Human Rights Adjudication.

Since attention will focus upon those rights which are expressly common to both systems, the following rights found in the CFR are not considered any further here because they have no express counterpart in the ECHR, although some of the issues they present may, nevertheless, arise in the Convention provisions cited in brackets: human dignity, Article 1 CFR (Articles 3, 4 and 8 ECHR); the integrity of the person, Article 3 CFR (Articles 3, 4 and 8 ECHR); protection of personal data, Article 8 CFR (Article 8 ECHR); freedom of the arts and sciences, Article 13 CFR (Articles 8 and 10 ECHR); freedom to choose an occupation and right to engage in work, Article 15 CFR (Articles 8, 10 and 11 ECHR); freedom to conduct a business, Article 16 CFR (Articles 8, 10 and 11 ECHR); right to asylum, Article 18 CFR; right to cultural, religious and linguistic diversity, Article 22 CFR; equality between men and women, Article 23 CFR (Article 14 ECHR); rights of the child and the elderly, Article 24 CFR (Articles 8 and 14 ECHR); integration of persons with disabilities, Article 26 CFR (Article 8 and 14 ECHR); the 'solidarity' rights in Articles 27–38 CFR (the right to environmental protection arises under Article 8 ECHR); and none of the citizens' rights in Articles 39–46 CFR, except the rights to vote, to stand for election (Article 3, Protocol No. 1 ECHR) and to freedom of movement (Article 2 of Protocol No. 4 ECHR).

Right to Life

Article 2 ECHR does not provide a right to life as such. Assuming such a right exists, it seeks, instead, to protect it through two distinct obligations. The first sentence of Article 2(1) creates a positive obligation on the part of the state to protect everyone's *right* to life through law (though not to protect his or her *life* through law), while the second sentence of Article 2(1) and Article 2(2) together create a negative state obligation not to deprive anyone of life except through lawful execution (since qualified by Protocol Nos. 6 and 13 ECHR), or by the use of no more force than is absolutely necessary to defend anyone from unlawful violence, in order to effect a lawful arrest or to prevent the escape of a person lawfully detained, or lawfully to quell a riot or insurrection. Subject to wide margins of appreciation, the obligation to protect the right to life by law implies, amongst other things, the provision of appropriate health care to prevent reasonably avoidable deaths; independent and effective legal and administrative processes capable of establishing the cause of unexplained deaths or disappearances and of punishing those culpable (including where state forces are implicated); and adequate protection from foreseeable and reasonably avoidable life-threatening self-harm, harm from third parties and harm from man-made and natural hazards.

This does not, however, include an obligation to permit assisted suicide by mentally competent persons enduring great suffering who, because of their condition, cannot end their lives themselves. The ECtHR has held that there is, at best, a consensus in Europe only that embryos and foetuses are part of the human race with the potential to acquire full legal rights, but no consensus on when, legally, morally and scientifically, human life begins. Member states are, therefore, permitted generous margins of appreciation with respect to abortion. Article 2 CFR states that everyone has the right to life and prohibits the death penalty and execution. Given that the CFR only applies to EU institutions and to member states of the Union as regards EU law, this provision is mainly relevant as an interpretative aid for secondary EU legislation in the fields of asylum and immigration law, health and human reproduction. Thus far it has hardly been referred to at all in the ECJ's case law and has not yet been fully explained in any judgment.

Prohibition of Torture and Inhuman or Degrading Treatment or Punishment

Article 3 ECHR and Article 4 CFR each state, in exactly the same terms, that 'No one shall be subjected to torture or to inhuman or degrading treatment or punishment', a stark prohibition devoid of any express rights or limitations. Therefore, the character and scope of any implied rights or limitations will hinge upon how this provision is interpreted. In spite of the almost-universal consensus to the contrary, it is, however, logically impossible to regard these rights as 'absolute', in the sense of being subject to no exceptions in any circumstance whatever, because where two instances of the same 'absolute' right conflict, one must be an exception to the other, and because, in order to fall within the scope of Article 3 ECHR, the prohibited conduct must cross a seriousness threshold including subjective and/or context-specific factors. Article 3 ECHR and Article 4 CFR should, therefore, be more accurately described as 'formally unqualified' or 'virtually absolute' rights, or 'rights which have a specially protected status'. As with Article 2 ECHR, Article 3 ECHR also generates positive state obligations that include criminalising the proscribed ill-treatment in domestic law, effectively seeking to prevent it, including by third parties and by other states (practicing 'extraordinary rendition' for example) and by refusing to extradite or deport individuals to other states where there are substantial grounds for believing there is a real risk of violation (non-refoulement). The positive obligation includes a duty to conduct independent and effective investigations and to enforce the prohibition appropriately, including by providing adequate remedies.

According to the Strasbourg institutions, degrading treatment or punishment is that which, intentionally or otherwise, humiliates and/or severely debases, and/or shows a lack of respect for dignity and/or which arouses feelings of fear, anguish and/or inferiority capable of breaking moral and/or physical resistance. Inhuman treatment or punishment is the infliction of degrading treatment or punishment, not necessarily intentional, causing either actual bodily injury or intense physical and/or mental suffering above a certain threshold and sustained for considerable periods of time. It is distinguished from torture – deliberate, purposive and prolonged inhuman treatment – primarily by the greater suffering the latter involves. Given that EU institutions are unlikely to have direct physical contact with individuals, and that the implementation of EU law by member states is also unlikely to give rise to such complaints, it is hardly surprising that the ECJ has had few opportunities to reflect upon Article 4 CFR. And, on the few occasions it has, the ECtHR's interpretation of Article 3 ECHR has generally been followed with, occasionally, a slightly different perspective typically limited to very specific facts. However, with the development of the justice and home affairs agenda, incorporating criminal as well as asylum and refugee matters, the international legal principle of non-refoulement may generate further development of relevant EU legal standards, in particular also by use of the separate prohibition of refoulement laid down in Article 19(2) CFR.

Prohibition of Slavery and Forced Labour

Article 4 ECHR and Article 5 CFR prohibit slavery, servitude and forced and compulsory labour. While human trafficking is implicit in Article 4 ECHR, it is expressly included in Article 5 CFR. Article 4 ECHR also lists various kinds of obligatory work or service that do not constitute forced or compulsory labour, including for example, military service and prisoners' employment. Unlike the rights not to be held in slavery or servitude, the rights not to be subject to forced or compulsory labour are derogable under the ECHR. The sparse litigation there has been on Article 4 ECHR has been dominated by mostly unsuccessful attempts by dentists, physicians and lawyers to evade discharging limited public service obligations as part of their professional responsibilities. As with Articles 2 and 3 ECHR states also have positive obligations under Article 4 ECHR to prohibit the behaviour and conditions in question; to act appropriately without assuming an impossible or disproportionate burden where they are, or ought to have been, aware of credible suspicions that a specific person was being, or was at real risk of being, subjected to the prohibited conduct; to conduct effective investigations; and to punish offenders adequately. So far the ECJ has heard very few cases in this field and, where it has, the ECtHR's interpretation of Article 4 ECHR has been followed.

Right to Liberty and Security

Article 6 CFR provides a right to liberty and security of the person in a single clause – 'everyone has the right to liberty and security of the person' – while Article 5 ECHR has no fewer than five clauses, one of which has six further subclauses, twelve elements in total, for the same right. The underlying purpose is to provide an effective, law-governed prohibition against arbitrary/unlawful deprivations of liberty without consent, guided by the core assumption that liberty should be presumed unless one or more of a number of express exceptions, falling broadly into two categories, apply: those relating to the law enforcement process and those concerning specific types of detainee. Two rights apply both to arrest and to detention. Article 5(4) ECHR provides a right to have the legality of arrest and/or detention decided speedily by an independent and impartial court, empowered in adversarial proceedings, to order release if found to be unlawful. Article 5(5) ECHR provides an enforceable right to compensation for breaches of any part of the entire provision. A number of other rights apply only to those under arrest. Article 5(2)

ECHR requires arrestees to be informed 'promptly' (within a matter of hours), in a language they understand, of at least the bare legal reasons for arrest, and of any charge against them, subject to whatever information they may also readily glean from the circumstances. Those arrested on reasonable suspicion of having committed an offence must also be brought 'promptly' – and, where relevant, at reasonable intervals – before an independent and impartial judge or other officer authorised by law to exercise judicial power. They must also be tried within a reasonable time, or released (upon surety if appropriate) pending trial, unless the state can provide 'relevant and sufficient' reasons to justify continued detention. While certain circumstances, including for example the struggle against terrorism, may legitimately prolong the period of pre-trial detention or the period of detention before suspects are brought before a judge, the 'promptness' criterion should not be so flexible as to impair the 'very essence' of the right to liberty. A delay of four days, six hours has been held to be too long. In its interpretation of Article 6 CFR, the ECJ usually refers expressly to the requirements set by the case law on Article 5 ECHR, but has also specified some positive procedural obligations for national courts to follow. In the EU context, Article 6 CFR is of particular importance in the context of migration and asylum, not least because EU directives allow member states to detain third country nationals pending admission, expulsion or return. Similarly, the right to liberty and security is likely to play an increasing role in the Area of Freedom, Security and Justice, which provides a legal basis for criminal justice cooperation including, for example, with respect to the European Arrest Warrant.

Right to Respect for Private and Family Life

Article 8 ECHR, which provides a right to respect for private and family life, home and correspondence rather than rights to these interests themselves, has generated an ever-expanding bundle of intertwined express and implied entitlements, and both positive and negative obligations. It has also increasingly become a residual category, potentially accommodating claims that have failed on virtually every other ground. A useful preliminary, though not a wholly watertight distinction, is between, on the one hand, the right to respect for family life and, on the other, the right to respect for private life, home and correspondence. As far as the scope of the right to respect for family life is concerned, the Strasbourg institutions have recognised, for example, that Convention jurisprudence should reflect the fact that families in contemporary

Europe are complex and fluid, and that de facto reality matters more than formal legal status. 'Respect' for family life also involves positive obligations to provide appropriate legal recognition and procedures, for example, regarding adoption, rights of succession plus custody and rights of access to children following divorce. The 'rights and freedoms of others' and the 'prevention of disorder and crime' limitations under Article 8(2) ECHR are often pleaded by states to defend claims that the right to respect for family life has been violated. The Strasbourg institutions have required, for example, that fair bureaucratic procedures are followed in cases where parents complain about the authorities taking their children into care or about limitations upon rights of access thereafter, while the 'prevention of disorder and crime' exception has caused particular controversy in cases where a recidivist non-national, whose family lawfully resides in a given CE state, contests expulsion or deportation on the grounds that this would breach his/her right to respect for family life. The principle of proportionality and the margin of appreciation play pivotal roles here.

The wide range of privacy-related interests derived by the Strasbourg institutions from Article 8 ECHR has, so far, defied every attempt at comprehensive, rational, consistent and discrete classification. However, one of the most useful distinctions is between, on the one hand, the 'negative freedom' from unwelcome active interference with well-being or integrity, and, on the other, the 'positive freedom' to develop personality, identity and life-style and to exercise autonomy, coupled with the avoidance of unjustified hindrance and supported by appropriate official recognition. Within the first category, a further distinction can be drawn between unwelcome interferences with bodily and non-bodily integrity. But while these are likely to constitute an interference with Article 8(1) ECHR, they may, nevertheless, be capable of being justified if in accordance with law, and necessary in a democratic society in pursuit of one or more of the Article 8(2) exceptions, providing the margin of appreciation and proportionality tests are satisfied. The same is true of the freedom to develop, and to receive appropriate official recognition for, personality, identity, autonomy, sexual relationships, reputation and life style. The relevant case law here is dominated by the quest for a 'fair balance' between the applicant's Article 8(1) ECHR rights and the competing legitimate interests found in Article 8(2), where the principle of proportionality and the margin of appreciation doctrine play variable roles according to the circumstances, including the interest in question and the type of restriction or interference. Article 7 CFR provides a right to respect for private and family life, home and communications in a single clause. In the EU context, the right to respect for family life is relevant primarily to family reunion and expulsions arising from migration and the free movement of persons. Prior to the CFR, Article 8 ECHR was influential in this field. However, although Article 7 CFR has sometimes been used by the ECJ and national courts to ensure secondary EU legislation on family law matters is interpreted consistently with fundamental rights, it has not yet played a very significant role. By contrast, insofar as Articles 7 and 8 CFR specifically protect personal data, it appears that the ECJ is currently taking the lead in developing this right.

Rights to Marry and to Found a Family

Article 12 ECHR provides right(s) to marry and to found a family according to national laws. Providing the Strasbourg legality test has been met, the principles of proportionality, reasonableness and non-arbitrariness are satisfied and any restriction does not impair the very essence of these rights, states have a wide margin of appreciation concerning regulation, regarding, for example, form, capacity, conditions and exclusions. Recognising same-sex marriage remains within the discretion of CE states. Article 9 CFR, which is in substantially the same form as Article 12 ECHR, has not yet played a role of any significance in the case-law of the ECJ.

Freedom of Thought, Conscience and Religion

Article 9 ECHR protects not only freedom *of* but freedom *from* religion, and includes not only individual religion and belief but also that of faith communities. But, in order to benefit from the protection offered by Article 9, a belief system must have a certain level of cogency, seriousness, cohesion and importance and must also respect the ideals and values of a democratic society. Therefore, not all opinions and convictions are covered. The right to believe in the pure, internal sense (*forum internum*) precludes forced conversion, and modification, renunciation or (usually) compelled disclosure of belief. Once the 'seriousness' threshold has been crossed, the state's principal negative obligation is to remain neutral and tolerant, and to refrain from privileging any faith or belief system over any other, or to express views about how it should be practiced, who should lead it, or about its truth or falsity. This includes the educational context where Article 2 of Protocol No. 1 ECHR – the right of parents to ensure their children are taught in conformity with their own religious and philosophical convictions – might also arise.

Positive obligations, exercisable on a non-discriminatory basis, include granting official recognition and/or official registration, and protecting faith groups from harassment and physical attack from third parties. Legitimate restrictions upon the manifestation of religion or belief (*forum externum*) found in Article 9(2) ECHR which are prescribed by law, are then exposed to the democratic necessity test where the principle of proportionality and the margin of appreciation doctrine are of particular importance. Article 10 CFR also protects the right to freedom of thought, conscience and religion. While it is very unlikely that this would ever be directly breached by EU law it may, nevertheless, be relevant to the interpretation of secondary EU legislation, for example, in relation to the expulsion of asylum seekers. Unlike the ECtHR, however, the ECJ defines religion broadly and does not distinguish the *forum internum* from the *forum externum*, public from private, individual from collective or core from peripheral aspects.

Freedom of Expression and Information

Article 10 (1) ECHR provides a right to freedom of expression, which the ECtHR has affirmed is vital for the kind of ideas, views, opinions and outlooks upon which a pluralistic, tolerant, broadminded, progressive and democratic society depends. States have both the negative obligation not to violate Article 10 ECHR and the positive obligation to ensure that the right to freedom of expression is adequately protected between private parties. Access to information has not yet, however, been recognised as a right implied by this provision although it might arise under Article 8 ECHR. Certain forms of expression are excluded from the scope of Article 10 ECHR, particularly those inherently hostile towards core Convention values. The majority of complaints about Article 10 ECHR violations, however, concern liability for alleged defamation where fine balances typically have to be struck between freedom of expression, on the one hand, and the protection of reputations on the other. The legitimate purposes specified by Article 10(2) ECHR are not always easy to distinguish from one another, and the Strasbourg institutions do not always indicate clearly the ground upon which a limitation has been accepted in this context. But blanket bans are difficult to justify, and the ECtHR is typically mostly concerned that any formalities, conditions, restrictions or penalties are proportionate, taking into account content, form, tone, context, who is expressing the views in question and for what purpose, the likely consequences plus the possibility of alternative outlets and the adequacy of procedural safeguards against arbitrary restriction.

However, in cases where an interference with the right to freedom of expression is admitted but justification pleaded, the severity of the penalty will often be the deciding factor. The scope of the right to respect for private life tends to be limited by the right to freedom of expression according to how justified the alleged intrusion is, in terms of, for example, the disclosure of discreditable private conduct inconsistent with a positive public image, or by reference to a genuine public interest in, for instance, the responsible discharge of an important public responsibility. The relationship between freedom of expression and the protection from disclosure of information received in confidence is subject to the proportionality principle and to a wide margin of appreciation, and may also raise issues under Article 8 ECHR. Article 11 CFR protects not only freedom of expression but also freedom of information. In most cases the approaches of the ECtHR and the ECJ tend to coincide. Where, for example, the ECtHR recognises a wide margin of appreciation in relation to restrictions upon commercial expression, the ECJ tends to do likewise. There is some debate, however, about whether the standard of review under EU law is generally lower than that provided by the ECtHR and whether the ECJ's core assumptions are always credible.

Freedom of Assembly and Association

Article 11 ECHR provides rights to freedom of peaceful assembly and of association, the latter of which expressly includes the rights to form and to join trade unions. The positive duty on states to protect the right to peaceful assembly may require finely tuned public order measures, including requirements for prior notification or authorisation, re-routing, dispersal or complete bans, particularly to facilitate the rights of both demonstrators and counter-demonstrators. While the right to freedom of association is one of the hallmarks of a democratic society, Article 11 ECHR does not grant an individual right to be admitted to any particular association; nor does any association have an obligation to admit any particular individual as a member. States also have positive obligations to ensure that legitimate associations receive some form of official recognition (though not necessarily registration), and that the right to freedom of association is observed between private parties. Because of their importance for democracy, states have only a narrow margin of appreciation to restrict, and particularly to ban or dissolve, political associations in pursuit of any of the Article 11(2) ECHR limitations. Where proportionate, the interests of public safety, the prevention of disorder or crime and the protection of the rights and freedoms of others also provide legitimate grounds for banning criminal associations and those seeking to incite racial or other forms of social hatred. Article 11 ECHR also implies the 'negative' freedom not to be compelled to join an association against one's will, a right that has been particularly controversial in the context of compulsory trading associations and 'closed shop' trade unions, which are generally, though not invariably, incompatible with Article 11 ECHR. Although there is a right to strike, it is not unlimited, and while members of the armed forces, police and civil servants have the right to form and join associations including trade unions, and to go on strike, the ECtHR accepts that the relevant margin of appreciation is narrow, the proportionality test more easily accommodates restriction and bans on strikes by certain public servants can be more easily justified than in other contexts. Article 12 CFR provides a right to freedom of assembly and association, which includes the right to form, and to membership of, all kinds of association including political parties and trade unions. The right to collective action may be implicit in Article 12 CFR, but it is, in any case, also expressly provided by Article 28 CFR and the ECJ does not always clearly distinguish between the two provisions.

Right to Education

Article 2 of Protocol No. 1 ECHR provides that no one shall be denied the right to education, and that in discharging educational responsibilities, the state shall respect the right of parents to ensure education and teaching conform with their religious and philosophical beliefs. Although they must refrain from prohibiting private education, states, therefore, have no positive obligation either to provide a publicly provisioned education system or to subsidise private education at any level. And, since the right to education is not absolute, it may be subject to regulation according to a national margin of appreciation in both public and private sectors, providing the effects are foreseeable and reasonably proportionate to a legitimate aim. The positive obligation to respect parents' religious and philosophical convictions is primarily intended to protect against indoctrination. Article 14 CFR protects the right to education in terms similar to those in Article 2 of Protocol No. 1 ECHR. But, since EU competences in the field of education are very limited, there seems little potential for it to be applied except possibly with respect to the interpretation of secondary EU law regarding migration and citizens' rights issues.

Right to Property

There is no right to property as such in the ECHR. Instead, Article 1 of Protocol No. 1 recognises the right of every natural or legal person to the peaceful enjoyment of his or her possessions. Being deprived of possessions is also prohibited, except in the public interest and subject to the conditions provided for by law and by the general principles of international law. The right of a state to enforce such laws as it deems necessary to control the use of property in accordance with the general interest, or to secure the payment of taxes or other contributions or penalties, is also preserved. In common with most other rights in the ECHR, states have both preventive and remedial positive obligations to ensure that the right to peaceful enjoyment of possessions is adequately protected, but generally not from market-related loss of value. The distinctions between 'interference', 'deprivation' and 'control' are not always easy to draw and, even when finding a violation, the ECtHR does not always clearly identify which has occurred. Providing no one ends up bearing an individually excessive burden, states are entitled to balance fairly the right in question against the public or community interest. Subject to the legality test and the principles of proportionality and non-discrimination – which imply, amongst other things, the provision of adequate compensation – states have a generous margin of appreciation in deciding how this should be achieved. Article 17 CFR – modelled on Article 1 of Protocol No. 1 ECHR with a separate clause on intellectual property – has been recognised for decades as a general principle of EU law and a core feature of the EU system. Although the ECJ sometimes refers to the ECtHR's case law, in other contexts it prefers to apply its own jurisprudence. According to the ECJ, the many areas in which the right to property arises generally require that, subject to generous margins of appreciation accorded EU institutions, restrictions should be clear, precise and predictable in their effect, especially where they may have negative consequences. Although Article 17(2) CFR provides a broadly formulated right to intellectual property, it is also not without limits and, subject to generous margins of appreciation accorded EU institutions and national authorities, has to be reconciled with other fundamental rights.

Protection in the Event of Removal, Expulsion or Extradition

While Article 4 of Protocol No. 4 ECHR and Article 19(1) CFR prohibit the collective expulsion of aliens, neither has received much judicial attention so far. However, by contrast, the ECJ has often cited Article 19 (2) CFR, which contains an independent prohibition against returning, extraditing or expelling third-country nationals where there is a serious risk they might be subject to the death penalty, torture or other inhuman or degrading treatment or punishment. Since Article 19(1) CFR is regarded as a codification of the ECtHR's case law on Article 3 ECHR, the ECJ has, therefore, expressly acknowledged that it should be interpreted accordingly. As a consequence of the close correspondence between Article 19(2) CFR and Article 3 ECHR, the ECJ has also recognised a significant overlap with the dignity rights protected by Articles 1, 2 and 4 CFR.

Prohibition of Discrimination

While Article 14 ECHR prohibits discrimination 'in the enjoyment of the rights and freedoms set forth in this Convention on any ground such as sex, race, colour, language, religion, political or other opinion, national or social origin, association with a national minority, property, birth, or other status', there is no express right in the ECHR to equality before the law, although this is, nevertheless, implied by the combined effects of Articles 6 and 14 ECHR. In this context 'discrimination' means the direct or indirect allocation of goods or benefits on an unequal basis without adequate objective justification including by reference to competing rights and interests. Not every difference in treatment, and not every private or social disadvantage will, therefore, be discriminatory. The state has a positive obligation to tackle discrimination, including by affirmative action if necessary, and because of the 'any grounds such as' clause and the indeterminate boundaries of 'other status', the sources of discrimination expressed by Article 14 ECHR are non-exhaustive. However, the pursuit of even legitimate aims resulting in differential treatment must not be disproportionate in their overall effects, alternative means for achieving the same result must have been considered and rejected for good reason, and a fair balance must be struck between the protection of the interests of the community and respect for Convention rights and freedoms. National margins of appreciation may, therefore, vary according to the circumstances, subject matter, background and the position in other CE states. While particularly wide margins are permitted with respect to social and economic policy, by contrast, the margin is narrow, and the justifications for differential treatment must be particularly compelling, with respect to characteristics such as race, sex/gender, sexual orientation, religion, birth, nationality and disability.

Protocol 12 ECHR, which has so far been ratified by, and is enforceable against, twenty CE states, and signed but not yet ratified by a further eighteen, provides much wider protection by prohibiting discrimination in relation to the 'enjoyment of any right set forth by law'. Article 20 CFR provides a right to equality before the law, while Article 21 prohibits discrimination 'on any ground such as sex, race, colour, ethnic or social origin, genetic features, language, religion or belief, political or any other opinion, membership of a national minority, property, birth, disability, age or sexual orientation'. While this is largely a formal affirmation of core goals and key principles of the EU since its inception, these were initially oriented towards the elimination of economic and financial obstacles to European integration. At the same time, however, the ECJ has developed a number of key concepts, such as indirect discrimination, which have meant the case law of the ECJ has had considerable impact upon national non-discrimination law as well as the budding case law of the ECtHR. In litigation arising from national legislation implementing EU law, the ECJ tends to leave it to national courts to decide whether there was a sufficient justification for a difference in treatment. Review by the ECJ varies in intensity according to the circumstances, with much more discretion accorded decision makers in complex policy areas.

Right to Free Elections

In the ECHR context the rights to vote, and to stand for election, have been derived from Article 3 of Protocol No. 1 ECHR, which imposes a positive obligation on states to hold free elections at regular intervals by secret ballot, under conditions that ensure the free expression of the opinion of the people in the choice of legislature. It has been held that, taking national margins of appreciation and any relevant European consensus into account, limitations upon electoral rights must comply with the implied principle of legality, and in particular, must preserve their essence and effectiveness, pursue a legitimate aim in a proportionate manner, protect legitimate expectations and must not be arbitrary or thwart the free expression of the choice of the people. Electoral processes and institutions must also be fair and impartial. Although the principle of universal suffrage lies at the heart of the right to vote, proportionate disqualifications and exclusions, according to age, residence, citizenship, mental incapacity and imprisonment, are not excluded. The rights to stand for election, and if successful to sit in the legislature, are subject to even wider margins of appreciation and to potentially greater formal restriction. Article 39 CFR concerns the rights of EU citizens to vote in elections, and to stand as candidates, for the EP in any member state where they happen to reside. Article 40 provides similar rights for municipal elections, entitlements affirmed for a long time by EU treaties and secondary EU legislation. Until recently, relevant judgments of the ECJ closely followed the ECtHR's case law when signs of a more distinctive approach began to emerge.

Freedom of Movement and of Residence

Article 2 of Protocol No. 4 ECHR provides a right to freedom of movement within a state's territory, subject to familiar restrictions in the public interest, and for the protection of the rights and freedoms of others, which the ECtHR has distinguished, largely according to degree, from exceptions to freedom from arrest and detention. Article 45(1) and (2) CFR concern, respectively, the freedom of movement and of residence of EU citizens, also recognised in Article 20 TFEU, as well as those of third country nationals. Since Article 20(2) TFEU states that freedom of movement has to be exercised 'under the conditions and within the limits defined by the Treaties, and by the measures adopted pursuant thereto', the ECJ has tended to address Article 45 claims under the relevant legislation alone. Nevertheless, it has also invoked Article 45 to confirm that, as one of the fundamental freedoms of the internal market, personal freedom of movement is a fundamental EU right.

Rights to an Effective Remedy and to a Fair Trial

Article 6(1) ECHR provides that, in the determination of civil rights and obligations, or of any criminal charge, everyone is entitled to a fair and public (and by implication an oral) hearing, within a reasonable time, by an independent and impartial tribunal established by law. A 'tribunal established by law' is one rooted in legislation and governed by law, though not necessarily staffed by professional judges, which has the jurisdiction to examine all relevant questions of fact and law, and whose decisions are legally binding and incapable of being overturned by the executive. While 'independence' and 'impartiality' are interwoven concepts, the former refers particularly to the character of courts and tribunals as institutions, and denotes their structural autonomy and the appearance of separation from the parties and other public institutions. 'Impartiality', on the other hand, refers to the integrity of the process of adjudication and to the need to avoid the risk of actual, and/or apparent, judicial bias. The ECtHR accepts as 'criminal' any accusation defined as such by national law. But, in order to prevent states neutralising Article 6 safeguards by re-designating criminal offences as mere administrative infractions, it otherwise determines for itself whether any national legal proceeding amounts to a 'criminal charge', the most influential factor tending to be the severity of the applicable sanction.

What constitutes a 'reasonable time' will depend on all the circumstances of any given case, including the complexity of facts, law and domestic judicial procedure; the conduct of both parties; what is at stake for the applicant; and ensuring that justice is neither unreasonably delayed nor excessively swift. However, although judgment shall also be 'pronounced publicly', though not necessarily in open court, the 'press and public may', according to Article 6(1), 'be excluded from all or part of the trial in the interests of morals, public order or national security in a democratic society, where the interests of juveniles or the protection of the private life of the parties so require, or to the extent strictly necessary in the opinion of the court in special circumstances where publicity would prejudice the interests of justice'. Other rights, not expressly provided by Article 6(1), have also been derived from it, including a general residual right to fairness not exhausted by full compliance with the express terms of Article 6, and the right of effective access to a court where the principle of equality of arms is observed, and to be tried upon evidence obtained in a manner that does not compromise the fairness of the proceedings as a whole. Articles 6(2) and (3) provide a minimum set of defence-related rights only to those charged with a criminal offence, considered in the following section.

Article 13 ECHR provides an autonomous, though subsidiary, right to an effective remedy before a national authority where an arguable case can be made that another Convention provision has been violated, whether or not this is eventually confirmed. Provided the authority in question is sufficiently independent, its decisions have some degree of enforceability and minimum procedural guarantees are observed, national remedies need not be judicial. They must, however, operate effectively in practice as well as in law, and where violations of Articles 2, 3 and 5 have been alleged, thorough and effective investigations capable of establishing culpability and dispensing punishment, to which victims have effective access, should also be conducted. Appropriate relief should be provided and, where necessary, compensation, particularly for delays in the administration of justice in breach of Article 6(1).

Procedural justice and access to remedies have always been key principles of EU law. From a very early stage, the ECJ has recognised that, in both the interests of justice and the effective functioning of the single market, judicial protection should be afforded individuals, companies and administrative bodies whose interests are affected by EU law (the principle of effectiveness), and that this should also be at least equivalent to that normally available in similar cases governed by national law (the principle of equivalence). In three separate, but not numbered paragraphs, Article 47 CFR seeks to achieve this by providing rights to an effective remedy before a tribunal to everyone whose rights and freedoms under EU law have been violated (first paragraph); a fair and public hearing within a reasonable time by an independent and impartial tribunal established by law; a right to be advised, defended and represented (second paragraph); and, where necessary, a right to legal aid for those lacking sufficient resources to ensure effective access to justice (third paragraph).

Unlike Article 6 ECHR, Article 47 CFR is not limited to civil rights and obligations and criminal charges, there is no 'arguable claim' threshold (as for Article 13 ECHR), nor is it restricted to judicial review of decisions taken by EU institutions (as is the right to good administration in Article 41 CFR). On the contrary, Article 47 CFR applies to all cases in which EU and national institutions and bodies take decisions and/or pass legislation. In spite of the fact that the ECJ has made some reference to the ECtHR's case law under Articles 6 and 13 ECHR, it has also expressly stated that, since Article 47 CFR secures in EU law the protection afforded by Article 6(1) ECHR, it is now necessary to refer only to the former rather than the latter. The ECJ has held that, in addition to adequate remedies ensuring effective legal protection in all fields covered by EU law, the principle of effective judicial protection laid down in Article 47 CFR entails the right of access to a court or tribunal empowered to consider all relevant questions of fact and law and to impose proportionate sanctions according to the type of case, such as those involving confidential information, state security, sanctioning terrorist suspects, asylum and migration law. But, as already indicated in the Institutions and Procedures for the Adjudication of Human Rights section, it has long held that, under EU law, individuals should only be able directly to access the ECJ when their interests have been directly and individually affected by EU regulatory acts in a manner peculiar to them, or by reason of circumstances differentiating them from all others. Although the ECJ has been criticised for using this highly restrictive standard, it does not regard it as infringing the very essence of the right of access to a court because, even if few such direct appeals against legislation are possible, TFEU procedures, supplemented by those under national law, provide other remedies that effectively guarantee Article 47 rights. The right to a fair trial also entails the obligation to decide cases within a reasonable time, which as in the ECHR context, depends on the precise circumstances of each case. According to the ECJ, the principle of equality of arms implies that each party must be afforded a reasonable opportunity to present its case, including evidence that supports it, under conditions that do not place him or her at a substantial disadvantage vis-à-vis an opponent. The right to be assisted by a lawyer (second paragraph of Article 47 CFR) is complemented by the obligation on member states under the third paragraph to make legal aid available, where appropriate, to both natural and legal persons, normally a matter for national courts.

Presumption of Innocence and Rights of Defence

The right to be presumed innocent of a criminal offence until proven guilty according to law, intimately linked to the privilege against self-incrimination and a component of the general notion of fairness under Article 6(1) ECHR, is expressly provided by Article 6(2) ECHR. In common law terms this means that the burden of proof lies with the prosecution, while in civil law systems it means that, in its inquiry into the facts, a court should find in favour of the accused where doubts about guilt have not been dispelled. Article 6(3) ECHR also provides a minimum set of rights, essential for the effective preparation and conduct of the defence on terms equal to that of the prosecution (the principle of equality of arms), including a right to be informed promptly, and in detail, in a language that either the accused or his/her lawyer understands, about the nature and grounds for the accusation sufficient to prepare the defence case (Article 6(3)(a)); to adequate time and facilities to prepare a defence, including access to relevant documents, the precise requirements of which will vary according to the particular facts, circumstances, and complexity of the case (Article 6(3)(b)); to defend oneself in person, or with effective legal assistance of one's own choosing, provided freely where sufficient means are lacking and the interests of justice so require (Article 6(3)(c)); to obtain the attendance of, examine and cross-examine witnesses under the same conditions as the prosecution (Article 6(3)(d)); and to a competent interpreter (Article 6(3)(e)).

In cases related to criminal law matters, Articles 47 and 48 CFR are usually read in conjunction. Article 48 CFR provides for the presumption of innocence, which may play a role in EU fraud proceedings and in competition law, and that, in criminal cases, the rights of the defence shall be respected. In applying this provision the ECJ tends to follow relevant case law of the ECtHR and has further specified the requirements following from both provisions, also imposing a number of positive obligations on states. Relevant secondary legislation on jurisdiction and the recognition and enforcement of judgments in civil and commercial matters must also be read so as to ensure that judicial decisions are delivered in such a way that the rights of the defence enshrined in Article 47 CFR are observed. The same is true for secondary legislation in some substantive areas of EU law including asylum and migration.

Principles of Legality and Proportionality of Criminal Offences and Penalties

Article 7(1) ECHR, which prohibits both retrospective criminalisation and the imposition of heavier penalties than those applicable at the time the offence was committed, derives from the rule of law principle. Amongst other things, this requires that crimes and penalties are defined only by law, and that the criminal law must not be extensively construed to an accused's detriment. The ECtHR has held that the prohibition in Article 7(1) ECHR includes, on the one hand, the retrospective extension of the scope of existing offences to acts and omissions not previously covered, but not, on the other hand, to repetitive criminal conduct the mere formal definition of which was changed while the offender was repeatedly committing it, or to the judicial interpretation of an offence that, by resolving doubts about its scope, retrospectively extends its reach, especially where this, accessibly and foreseeably, eliminates an unjust and anomalous exception such as the marital rape defence. Article 7(2) provides: 'This article shall not prejudice the trial and punishment of any person for any act or omission which, at the time when it was committed, was criminal according to the general principles of law recognised by civilised nations.' The rights in Article 7 are non-derogable under Article 15.

Article 49 CFR is in very similar terms. Although the requirement that sanctions should be proportionate has hardly ever been invoked directly before the ECJ, the *lex mitior* principle (that penalties applied retrospectively should be as lenient as those applied contemporaneously) has proven particularly relevant in some cases. The ECJ has also expressly held that it can be relied on not only against decisions imposing criminal penalties in the strict sense, but also against those imposing administrative ones. Generally, it has closely followed the ECtHR's interpretation, including holding that the principle of legal certainty does not prohibit the gradual clarification of the scope of criminal liability. Finally, the ECJ has also held that although national courts are normally required to interpret domestic law according to the terms and purpose of directives in order to achieve the intended result, this should not have the effect of imposing or aggravating any criminal liability not otherwise arising from the directive itself.

Right Not to Be Tried or Punished Twice in Criminal Proceedings for the Same Criminal Offence

Article 4 of Protocol No. 7 ECHR and Article 50 CFR enshrine the *ne bis in idem*, or 'double jeopardy' principle, which provides a right not to be tried or punished more than once in the same state for an offence arising out of the same facts. This does not apply where new facts or a fundamental defect in the previous proceedings subsequently come to light. Both the ECtHR and the ECJ generally approach the principle in the same way although, unlike the ECtHR, the ECJ usually leaves national courts to decide whether or not the issue has a criminal character. Because the double jeopardy principle applies, not only within the jurisdiction of any given EU state, but across several, the ECJ has been compelled to harmonise Schengen requirements and those arising from other forms of collaboration between the member states in the sphere of criminal law.

Appendix A

European Convention on Human Rights

The text of the Convention is presented as amended by the provisions of Protocol No. 14 (CETS no. 194) as from its entry into force on 1 June 2010. The text of the Convention had previously been amended according to the provisions of Protocol No. 3 (ETS no. 45), which entered into force on 21 September 1970, of Protocol No. 5 (ETS no. 55), which entered into force on 20 December 1971, and of Protocol No. 8 (ETS no. 118), which entered into force on 1 January 1990, and comprised also the text of Protocol No. 2 (ETS no. 44), which, in accordance with Article 5 § 3 thereof, had been an integral part of the Convention since its entry into force on 21 September 1970. All provisions which had been amended or added by these Protocols were replaced by Protocol No. 11 (ETS no. 155), as from the date of its entry into force on 1 November 1998. As from that date, Protocol No. 9 (ETS no. 140), which entered into force on 1 October 1994, was repealed and Protocol No. 10 (ETS no. 146) lost its purpose.

Convention for the Protection of Human Rights and Fundamental Freedoms

Rome, 4.XI.1950

THE GOVERNMENTS SIGNATORY HERETO, being members of the Council of Europe,

Considering the Universal Declaration of Human Rights proclaimed by the General Assembly of the United Nations on 10th December 1948;

Considering that this Declaration aims at securing the universal and effective recognition and observance of the Rights therein declared;

Considering that the aim of the Council of Europe is the achievement of greater unity between its members and that one of the methods by which that aim is to be pursued is the maintenance and further realisation of Human Rights and Fundamental Freedoms;

Reaffirming their profound belief in those fundamental freedoms which are
the foundation of justice and peace in the world and are best maintained on
the one hand by an effective political democracy and on the other by a
common understanding and observance of the Human Rights upon which
they depend;

Being resolved, as the governments of European countries which are like-
minded and have a common heritage of political traditions, ideals, freedom
and the rule of law, to take the first steps for the collective enforcement of
certain of the rights stated in the Universal Declaration,

Have agreed as follows:

ARTICLE 1
Obligation to Respect Human Rights

The High Contracting Parties shall secure to everyone within their jurisdiction
the rights and freedoms defined in Section I of this Convention.

SECTION I
RIGHTS AND FREEDOMS

ARTICLE 2
Right to Life

1. Everyone's right to life shall be protected by law. No one shall be deprived
   of his life intentionally save in the execution of a sentence of a court
   following his conviction of a crime for which this penalty is provided
   by law.
2. Deprivation of life shall not be regarded as inflicted in contravention of this
   Article when it results from the use of force which is no more than
   absolutely necessary:
   (a) in defence of any person from unlawful violence;
   (b) in order to effect a lawful arrest or to prevent the escape of a person
       lawfully detained;
   (c) in action lawfully taken for the purpose of quelling a riot or insurrection.

ARTICLE 3
Prohibition of Torture

No one shall be subjected to torture or to inhuman or degrading treatment or
punishment.

ARTICLE 4
Prohibition of Slavery and Forced Labour

1. No one shall be held in slavery or servitude.
2. No one shall be required to perform forced or compulsory labour.
3. For the purpose of this Article the term "forced or compulsory labour" shall not include:
   (a) any work required to be done in the ordinary course of detention imposed according to the provisions of Article 5 of this Convention or during conditional release from such detention;
   (b) any service of a military character or, in case of conscientious objectors in countries where they are recognised, service exacted instead of compulsory military service;
   (c) any service exacted in case of an emergency or calamity threatening the life or well-being of the community;
   (d) any work or service which forms part of normal civic obligations.

ARTICLE 5
Right to Liberty and Security

1. Everyone has the right to liberty and security of person. No one shall be deprived of his liberty save in the following cases and in accordance with a procedure prescribed by law:
   (a) the lawful detention of a person after conviction by a competent court;
   (b) the lawful arrest or detention of a person for noncompliance with the lawful order of a court or in order to secure the fulfilment of any obligation prescribed by law;
   (c) the lawful arrest or detention of a person effected for the purpose of bringing him before the competent legal authority on reasonable suspicion of having committed an offence or when it is reasonably considered necessary to prevent his committing an offence or fleeing after having done so;
   (d) the detention of a minor by lawful order for the purpose of educational supervision or his lawful detention for the purpose of bringing him before the competent legal authority;
   (e) the lawful detention of persons for the prevention of the spreading of infectious diseases, of persons of unsound mind, alcoholics or drug addicts or vagrants;
   (f) the lawful arrest or detention of a person to prevent his effecting an unauthorised entry into the country or of a person against whom action is being taken with a view to deportation or extradition.

2. Everyone who is arrested shall be informed promptly, in a language which he understands, of the reasons for his arrest and of any charge against him.
3. Everyone arrested or detained in accordance with the provisions of paragraph 1(c) of this Article shall be brought promptly before a judge or other officer authorised by law to exercise judicial power and shall be entitled to trial within a reasonable time or to release pending trial. Release may be conditioned by guarantees to appear for trial.
4. Everyone who is deprived of his liberty by arrest or detention shall be entitled to take proceedings by which the lawfulness of his detention shall be decided speedily by a court and his release ordered if the detention is not lawful.
5. Everyone who has been the victim of arrest or detention in contravention of the provisions of this Article shall have an enforceable right to compensation.

ARTICLE 6
Right to a Fair Trial

1. In the determination of his civil rights and obligations or of any criminal charge against him, everyone is entitled to a fair and public hearing within a reasonable time by an independent and impartial tribunal established by law. Judgment shall be pronounced publicly but the press and public may be excluded from all or part of the trial in the interests of morals, public order or national security in a democratic society, where the interests of juveniles or the protection of the private life of the parties so require, or to the extent strictly necessary in the opinion of the court in special circumstances where publicity would prejudice the interests of justice.
2. Everyone charged with a criminal offence shall be presumed innocent until proved guilty according to law.
3. Everyone charged with a criminal offence has the following minimum rights:
   (a) to be informed promptly, in a language which he understands and in detail, of the nature and cause of the accusation against him;
   (b) to have adequate time and facilities for the preparation of his defence;
   (c) to defend himself in person or through legal assistance of his own choosing or, if he has not sufficient means to pay for legal assistance, to be given it free when the interests of justice so require;
   (d) to examine or have examined witnesses against him and to obtain the attendance and examination of witnesses on his behalf under the same conditions as witnesses against him;
   (e) to have the free assistance of an interpreter if he cannot understand or speak the language used in court.

ARTICLE 7
No Punishment without Law

1. No one shall be held guilty of any criminal offence on account of any act or omission which did not constitute a criminal offence under national or international law at the time when it was committed. Nor shall a heavier penalty be imposed than the one that was applicable at the time the criminal offence was committed.
2. This Article shall not prejudice the trial and punishment of any person for any act or omission which, at the time when it was committed, was criminal according to the general principles of law recognised by civilised nations.

ARTICLE 8
Right to Respect for Private and Family Life

1. Everyone has the right to respect for his private and family life, his home and his correspondence.
2. There shall be no interference by a public authority with the exercise of this right except such as is in accordance with the law and is necessary in a democratic society in the interests of national security, public safety or the economic well-being of the country, for the prevention of disorder or crime, for the protection of health or morals, or for the protection of the rights and freedoms of others.

ARTICLE 9
Freedom of Thought, Conscience and Religion

1. Everyone has the right to freedom of thought, conscience and religion; this right includes freedom to change his religion or belief and freedom, either alone or in community with others and in public or private, to manifest his religion or belief, in worship, teaching, practice and observance.
2. Freedom to manifest one's religion or beliefs shall be subject only to such limitations as are prescribed by law and are necessary in a democratic society in the interests of public safety, for the protection of public order, health or morals, or for the protection of the rights and freedoms of others.

ARTICLE 10
Freedom of Expression

1. Everyone has the right to freedom of expression. This right shall include freedom to hold opinions and to receive and impart information and ideas

without interference by public authority and regardless of frontiers. This Article shall not prevent States from requiring the licensing of broadcasting, television or cinema enterprises.

2. The exercise of these freedoms, since it carries with it duties and responsibilities, may be subject to such formalities, conditions, restrictions or penalties as are prescribed by law and are necessary in a democratic society, in the interests of national security, territorial integrity or public safety, for the prevention of disorder or crime, for the protection of health or morals, for the protection of the reputation or rights of others, for preventing the disclosure of information received in confidence, or for maintaining the authority and impartiality of the judiciary.

ARTICLE 11
Freedom of Assembly and Association

1. Everyone has the right to freedom of peaceful assembly and to freedom of association with others, including the right to form and to join trade unions for the protection of his interests.
2. No restrictions shall be placed on the exercise of these rights other than such as are prescribed by law and are necessary in a democratic society in the interests of national security or public safety, for the prevention of disorder or crime, for the protection of health or morals or for the protection of the rights and freedoms of others. This Article shall not prevent the imposition of lawful restrictions on the exercise of these rights by members of the armed forces, of the police or of the administration of the State.

ARTICLE 12
Right to Marry

Men and women of marriageable age have the right to marry and to found a family, according to the national laws governing the exercise of this right.

ARTICLE 13
Right to an Effective Remedy

Everyone whose rights and freedoms as set forth in this Convention are violated shall have an effective remedy before a national authority notwithstanding that the violation has been committed by persons acting in an official capacity.

ARTICLE 14
Prohibition of Discrimination

The enjoyment of the rights and freedoms set forth in this Convention shall be secured without discrimination on any ground such as sex, race, colour, language, religion, political or other opinion, national or social origin, association with a national minority, property, birth or other status.

ARTICLE 15
Derogation in Time of Emergency

1. In time of war or other public emergency threatening the life of the nation any High Contracting Party may take measures derogating from its obligations under this Convention to the extent strictly required by the exigencies of the situation, provided that such measures are not inconsistent with its other obligations under international law.
2. No derogation from Article 2, except in respect of deaths resulting from lawful acts of war, or from Articles 3, 4 (paragraph 1) and 7 shall be made under this provision.
3. Any High Contracting Party availing itself of this right of derogation shall keep the Secretary General of the Council of Europe fully informed of the measures which it has taken and the reasons therefor. It shall also inform the Secretary General of the Council of Europe when such measures have ceased to operate and the provisions of the Convention are again being fully executed.

ARTICLE 16
Restrictions on Political Activity of Aliens

Nothing in Articles 10, 11 and 14 shall be regarded as preventing the High Contracting Parties from imposing restrictions on the political activity of aliens.

ARTICLE 17
Prohibition of Abuse of Rights

Nothing in this Convention may be interpreted as implying for any State, group or person any right to engage in any activity or perform any act aimed at the destruction of any of the rights and freedoms set forth herein or at their limitation to a greater extent than is provided for in the Convention.

ARTICLE 18
Limitation on Use of Restrictions on Rights

The restrictions permitted under this Convention to the said rights and freedoms shall not be applied for any purpose other than those for which they have been prescribed.

SECTION II
EUROPEAN COURT OF HUMAN RIGHTS

ARTICLE 19
Establishment of the Court

To ensure the observance of the engagements undertaken by the High Contracting Parties in the Convention and the Protocols thereto, there shall be set up a European Court of Human Rights, hereinafter referred to as "the Court". It shall function on a permanent basis.

ARTICLE 20
Number of Judges

The Court shall consist of a number of judges equal to that of the High Contracting Parties.

ARTICLE 21
Criteria for Office

1. The judges shall be of high moral character and must either possess the qualifications required for appointment to high judicial office or be jurisconsults of recognised competence.
2. The judges shall sit on the Court in their individual capacity.
3. During their term of office the judges shall not engage in any activity which is incompatible with their independence, impartiality or with the demands of a full-time office; all questions arising from the application of this paragraph shall be decided by the Court.

ARTICLE 22
Election of Judges

The judges shall be elected by the Parliamentary Assembly with respect to each High Contracting Party by a majority of votes cast from a list of three candidates nominated by the High Contracting Party.

ARTICLE 23
Terms of Office and Dismissal

1. The judges shall be elected for a period of nine years. They may not be re-elected.
2. The terms of office of judges shall expire when they reach the age of 70.
3. The judges shall hold office until replaced. They shall, however, continue to deal with such cases as they already have under consideration.
4. No judge may be dismissed from office unless the other judges decide by a majority of two-thirds that that judge has ceased to fulfil the required conditions.

ARTICLE 24
Registry and Rapporteurs

1. The Court shall have a Registry, the functions and organisation of which shall be laid down in the rules of the Court.
2. When sitting in a single-judge formation, the Court shall be assisted by rapporteurs who shall function under the authority of the President of the Court. They shall form part of the Court's Registry.

ARTICLE 25
Plenary Court

The plenary Court shall

(a) elect its President and one or two Vice-Presidents for a period of three years; they may be re-elected;
(b) set up Chambers, constituted for a fixed period of time;
(c) elect the Presidents of the Chambers of the Court; they may be re-elected;
(d) adopt the rules of the Court;
(e) elect the Registrar and one or more Deputy Registrars;
(f) make any request under Article 26, paragraph 2.

ARTICLE 26
Single-Judge Formation, Committees, Chambers and Grand Chamber

1. To consider cases brought before it, the Court shall sit in a single-judge formation, in committees of three judges, in Chambers of seven judges and in a Grand Chamber of seventeen judges. The Court's Chambers shall set up committees for a fixed period of time.

2. At the request of the plenary Court, the Committee of Ministers may, by a unanimous decision and for a fixed period, reduce to five the number of judges of the Chambers.

3. When sitting as a single judge, a judge shall not examine any application against the High Contracting Party in respect of which that judge has been elected.

4. There shall sit as an *ex officio* member of the Chamber and the Grand Chamber the judge elected in respect of the High Contracting Party concerned. If there is none or if that judge is unable to sit, a person chosen by the President of the Court from a list submitted in advance by that Party shall sit in the capacity of judge.

5. The Grand Chamber shall also include the President of the Court, the Vice-Presidents, the Presidents of the Chambers and other judges chosen in accordance with the rules of the Court. When a case is referred to the Grand Chamber under Article 43, no judge from the Chamber which rendered the judgment shall sit in the Grand Chamber, with the exception of the President of the Chamber and the judge who sat in respect of the High Contracting Party concerned.

ARTICLE 27
Competence of Single Judges

1. A single judge may declare inadmissible or strike out of the Court's list of cases an application submitted under Article 34, where such a decision can be taken without further examination.

2. The decision shall be final.

3. If the single judge does not declare an application inadmissible or strike it out, that judge shall forward it to a committee or to a Chamber for further examination.

ARTICLE 28
Competence of Committees

1. In respect of an application submitted under Article 34, a committee may, by a unanimous vote,
    (a) declare it inadmissible or strike it out of its list of cases, where such decision can be taken without further examination; or
    (b) declare it admissible and render at the same time a judgment on the merits, if the underlying question in the case, concerning the interpretation or the application of the Convention or the Protocols thereto, is already the subject of well-established case-law of the Court.

2. Decisions and judgments under paragraph 1 shall be final.
3. If the judge elected in respect of the High Contracting Party concerned is not a member of the committee, the committee may at any stage of the proceedings invite that judge to take the place of one of the members of the committee, having regard to all relevant factors, including whether that Party has contested the application of the procedure under paragraph 1(b).

ARTICLE 29
Decisions by Chambers on Admissibility and Merits

1. If no decision is taken under Article 27 or 28, or no judgment rendered under Article 28, a Chamber shall decide on the admissibility and merits of individual applications submitted under Article 34. The decision on admissibility may be taken separately.
2. A Chamber shall decide on the admissibility and merits of inter-State applications submitted under Article 33. The decision on admissibility shall be taken separately unless the Court, in exceptional cases, decides otherwise.

ARTICLE 30
Relinquishment of Jurisdiction to the Grand Chamber

Where a case pending before a Chamber raises a serious question affecting the interpretation of the Convention or the Protocols thereto, or where the resolution of a question before the Chamber might have a result inconsistent with a judgment previously delivered by the Court, the Chamber may, at any time before it has rendered its judgment, relinquish jurisdiction in favour of the Grand Chamber, unless one of the parties to the case objects.

ARTICLE 31
Powers of the Grand Chamber

The Grand Chamber shall

(a) determine applications submitted either under Article 33 or Article 34 when a Chamber has relinquished jurisdiction under Article 30 or when the case has been referred to it under Article 43;
(b) decide on issues referred to the Court by the Committee of Ministers in accordance with Article 46, paragraph 4; and
(c) consider requests for advisory opinions submitted under Article 47.

ARTICLE 32
Jurisdiction of the Court

1. The jurisdiction of the Court shall extend to all matters concerning the interpretation and application of the Convention and the Protocols thereto which are referred to it as provided in Articles 33, 34, 46 and 47.
2. In the event of dispute as to whether the Court has jurisdiction, the Court shall decide.

ARTICLE 33
Inter-State Cases

Any High Contracting Party may refer to the Court any alleged breach of the provisions of the Convention and the Protocols thereto by another High Contracting Party.

ARTICLE 34
Individual Applications

The Court may receive applications from any person, non-governmental organisation or group of individuals claiming to be the victim of a violation by one of the High Contracting Parties of the rights set forth in the Convention or the Protocols thereto. The High Contracting Parties undertake not to hinder in any way the effective exercise of this right.

ARTICLE 35
Admissibility Criteria

1. The Court may only deal with the matter after all domestic remedies have been exhausted, according to the generally recognised rules of international law, and within a period of six months from the date on which the final decision was taken.
2. The Court shall not deal with any application submitted under Article 34 that
   (a) is anonymous; or
   (b) is substantially the same as a matter that has already been examined by the Court or has already been submitted to another procedure of international investigation or settlement and contains no relevant new information.

3. The Court shall declare inadmissible any individual application submitted under Article 34 if it considers that:
   (a) the application is incompatible with the provisions of the Convention or the Protocols thereto, manifestly ill-founded, or an abuse of the right of individual application; or
   (b) the applicant has not suffered a significant disadvantage, unless respect for human rights as defined in the Convention and the Protocols thereto requires an examination of the application on the merits and provided that no case may be rejected on this ground which has not been duly considered by a domestic tribunal.
4. The Court shall reject any application which it considers inadmissible under this Article. It may do so at any stage of the proceedings.

ARTICLE 36
Third Party Intervention

1. In all cases before a Chamber or the Grand Chamber, a High Contracting Party one of whose nationals is an applicant shall have the right to submit written comments and to take part in hearings.
2. The President of the Court may, in the interest of the proper administration of justice, invite any High Contracting Party which is not a party to the proceedings or any person concerned who is not the applicant to submit written comments or take part in hearings.
3. In all cases before a Chamber or the Grand Chamber, the Council of Europe Commissioner for Human Rights may submit written comments and take part in hearings.

ARTICLE 37
Striking Out Applications

1. The Court may at any stage of the proceedings decide to strike an application out of its list of cases where the circumstances lead to the conclusion that
   (a) the applicant does not intend to pursue his application; or
   (b) the matter has been resolved; or
   (c) for any other reason established by the Court, it is no longer justified to continue the examination of the application.
   However, the Court shall continue the examination of the application if respect for human rights as defined in the Convention and the Protocols thereto so requires.
2. The Court may decide to restore an application to its list of cases if it considers that the circumstances justify such a course.

ARTICLE 38
Examination of the Case

The Court shall examine the case together with the representatives of the parties and, if need be, undertake an investigation, for the effective conduct of which the High Contracting Parties concerned shall furnish all necessary facilities.

ARTICLE 39
Friendly Settlements

1. At any stage of the proceedings, the Court may place itself at the disposal of the parties concerned with a view to securing a friendly settlement of the matter on the basis of respect for human rights as defined in the Convention and the Protocols thereto.
2. Proceedings conducted under paragraph 1 shall be confidential.
3. If a friendly settlement is effected, the Court shall strike the case out of its list by means of a decision which shall be confined to a brief statement of the facts and of the solution reached.
4. This decision shall be transmitted to the Committee of Ministers, which shall supervise the execution of the terms of the friendly settlement as set out in the decision.

ARTICLE 40
Public Hearings and Access to Documents

1. Hearings shall be in public unless the Court in exceptional circumstances decides otherwise.
2. Documents deposited with the Registrar shall be accessible to the public unless the President of the Court decides otherwise.

ARTICLE 41
Just Satisfaction

If the Court finds that there has been a violation of the Convention or the Protocols thereto, and if the internal law of the High Contracting Party concerned allows only partial reparation to be made, the Court shall, if necessary, afford just satisfaction to the injured party.

ARTICLE 42
Judgments of Chambers

Judgments of Chambers shall become final in accordance with the provisions of Article 44, paragraph 2.

ARTICLE 43
Referral to the Grand Chamber

1. Within a period of three months from the date of the judgment of the Chamber, any party to the case may, in exceptional cases, request that the case be referred to the Grand Chamber.
2. A panel of five judges of the Grand Chamber shall accept the request if the case raises a serious question affecting the interpretation or application of the Convention or the Protocols thereto, or a serious issue of general importance.
3. If the panel accepts the request, the Grand Chamber shall decide the case by means of a judgment.

ARTICLE 44
Final Judgments

1. The judgment of the Grand Chamber shall be final.
2. The judgment of a Chamber shall become final
   (a) when the parties declare that they will not request that the case be referred to the Grand Chamber; or
   (b) three months after the date of the judgment, if reference of the case to the Grand Chamber has not been requested; or
   (c) when the panel of the Grand Chamber rejects the request to refer under Article 43.
3. The final judgment shall be published.

ARTICLE 45
Reasons for Judgments and Decisions

1. Reasons shall be given for judgments as well as for decisions declaring applications admissible or inadmissible.
2. If a judgment does not represent, in whole or in part, the unanimous opinion of the judges, any judge shall be entitled to deliver a separate opinion.

ARTICLE 46
Binding Force and Execution of Judgments

1. The High Contracting Parties undertake to abide by the final judgment of the Court in any case to which they are parties.
2. The final judgment of the Court shall be transmitted to the Committee of Ministers, which shall supervise its execution.
3. If the Committee of Ministers considers that the supervision of the execution of a final judgment is hindered by a problem of interpretation of the judgment, it may refer the matter to the Court for a ruling on the question

of interpretation. A referral decision shall require a majority vote of two-thirds of the representatives entitled to sit on the committee.

4. If the Committee of Ministers considers that a High Contracting Party refuses to abide by a final judgment in a case to which it is a party, it may, after serving formal notice on that Party and by decision adopted by a majority vote of two-thirds of the representatives entitled to sit on the committee, refer to the Court the question whether that Party has failed to fulfil its obligation under paragraph1.

5. If the Court finds a violation of paragraph 1, it shall refer the case to the Committee of Ministers for consideration of the measures to be taken. If the Court finds no violation of paragraph1, it shall refer the case to the Committee of Ministers, which shall close its examination of the case.

ARTICLE 47
Advisory Opinions

1. The Court may, at the request of the Committee of Ministers, give advisory opinions on legal questions concerning the interpretation of the Convention and the Protocols thereto.

2. Such opinions shall not deal with any question relating to the content or scope of the rights or freedoms defined in Section I of the Convention and the Protocols thereto, or with any other question which the Court or the Committee of Ministers might have to consider in consequence of any such proceedings as could be instituted in accordance with the Convention.

3. Decisions of the Committee of Ministers to request an advisory opinion of the Court shall require a majority vote of the representatives entitled to sit on the committee.

ARTICLE 48
Advisory Jurisdiction of the Court

The Court shall decide whether a request for an advisory opinion submitted by the Committee of Ministers is within its competence as defined in Article 47.

ARTICLE 49
Reasons for Advisory Opinions

1. Reasons shall be given for advisory opinions of the Court.

2. If the advisory opinion does not represent, in whole or in part, the unanimous opinion of the judges, any judge shall be entitled to deliver a separate opinion.

3. Advisory opinions of the Court shall be communicated to the Committee of Ministers.

ARTICLE 50
Expenditure on the Court

The expenditure on the Court shall be borne by the Council of Europe.

ARTICLE 51
Privileges and Immunities of Judges

The judges shall be entitled, during the exercise of their functions, to the privileges and immunities provided for in Article 40 of the Statute of the Council of Europe and in the agreements made thereunder.

SECTION III
MISCELLANEOUS PROVISIONS

ARTICLE 52
Inquiries by the Secretary General

On receipt of a request from the Secretary General of the Council of Europe any High Contracting Party shall furnish an explanation of the manner in which its internal law ensures the effective implementation of any of the provisions of the Convention.

ARTICLE 53
Safeguard for Existing Human Rights

Nothing in this Convention shall be construed as limiting or derogating from any of the human rights and fundamental freedoms which may be ensured under the laws of any High Contracting Party or under any other agreement to which it is a party.

ARTICLE 54
Powers of the Committee of Ministers

Nothing in this Convention shall prejudice the powers conferred on the Committee of Ministers by the Statute of the Council of Europe.

ARTICLE 55
Exclusion of Other Means of Dispute Settlement

The High Contracting Parties agree that, except by special agreement, they will not avail themselves of treaties, conventions or declarations in force between them for the purpose of submitting, by way of petition, a dispute arising out of the interpretation or application of this Convention to a means of settlement other than those provided for in this Convention.

ARTICLE 56
Territorial Application

1. Any State may at the time of its ratification or at any time thereafter declare by notification addressed to the Secretary General of the Council of Europe that the present Convention shall, subject to paragraph 4 of this Article, extend to all or any of the territories for whose international relations it is responsible.
2. The Convention shall extend to the territory or territories named in the notification as from the thirtieth day after the receipt of this notification by the Secretary General of the Council of Europe.
3. The provisions of this Convention shall be applied in such territories with due regard, however, to local requirements.
4. Any State which has made a declaration in accordance with paragraph 1 of this Article may at any time thereafter declare on behalf of one or more of the territories to which the declaration relates that it accepts the competence of the Court to receive applications from individuals, non-governmental organisations or groups of individuals as provided by Article 34 of the Convention.

ARTICLE 57
Reservations

1. Any State may, when signing this Convention or when depositing its instrument of ratification, make a reservation in respect of any particular provision of the Convention to the extent that any law then in force in its territory is not in conformity with the provision. Reservations of a general character shall not be permitted under this Article.
2. Any reservation made under this Article shall contain a brief statement of the law concerned.

ARTICLE 58
Denunciation

1. A High Contracting Party may denounce the present Convention only after the expiry of five years from the date on which it became a party to it and after six months' notice contained in a notification addressed to the Secretary General of the Council of Europe, who shall inform the other High Contracting Parties.

2. Such a denunciation shall not have the effect of releasing the High Contracting Party concerned from its obligations under this Convention in respect of any act which, being capable of constituting a violation of such obligations, may have been performed by it before the date at which the denunciation became effective.

3. Any High Contracting Party which shall cease to be a member of the Council of Europe shall cease to be a Party to this Convention under the same conditions.

4. The Convention may be denounced in accordance with the provisions of the preceding paragraphs in respect of any territory to which it has been declared to extend under the terms of Article 56.

ARTICLE 59
Signature and Ratification

1. This Convention shall be open to the signature of the members of the Council of Europe. It shall be ratified. Ratifications shall be deposited with the Secretary General of the Council of Europe.

2. The European Union may accede to this Convention.

3. The present Convention shall come into force after the deposit of ten instruments of ratification.

4. As regards any signatory ratifying subsequently, the Convention shall come into force at the date of the deposit of its instrument of ratification.

5. The Secretary General of the Council of Europe shall notify all the members of the Council of Europe of the entry into force of the Convention, the names of the High Contracting Parties who have ratified it, and the deposit of all instruments of ratification which may be effected subsequently.

DONE AT ROME THIS 4TH DAY OF NOVEMBER 1950, in English and French, both texts being equally authentic, in a single copy which shall remain deposited in the archives of the Council of Europe. The Secretary General shall transmit certified copies to each of the signatories.

Protocol to the Convention for the Protection of Human Rights and Fundamental Freedoms

Paris, 20.III.1952

THE GOVERNMENTS SIGNATORY HERETO, being members of the Council of Europe,

Being resolved to take steps to ensure the collective enforcement of certain rights and freedoms other than those already included in Section I of the

Convention for the Protection of Human Rights and Fundamental Freedoms signed at Rome on 4 November 1950 (hereinafter referred to as "the Convention"),
Have agreed as follows:

ARTICLE 1
Protection of Property

Every natural or legal person is entitled to the peaceful enjoyment of his possessions. No one shall be deprived of his possessions except in the public interest and subject to the conditions provided for by law and by the general principles of international law.

The preceding provisions shall not, however, in any way impair the right of a State to enforce such laws as it deems necessary to control the use of property in accordance with the general interest or to secure the payment of taxes or other contributions or penalties.

ARTICLE 2
Right to Education

No person shall be denied the right to education. In the exercise of any functions which it assumes in relation to education and to teaching, the State shall respect the right of parents to ensure such education and teaching in conformity with their own religious and philosophical convictions.

ARTICLE 3
Right to Free Elections

The High Contracting Parties undertake to hold free elections at reasonable intervals by secret ballot, under conditions which will ensure the free expression of the opinion of the people in the choice of the legislature.

ARTICLE 4
Territorial Application

Any High Contracting Party may at the time of signature or ratification or at any time thereafter communicate to the Secretary General of the Council of Europe a declaration stating the extent to which it undertakes that the provisions of the present Protocol shall apply to such of the territories for the international relations of which it is responsible as are named therein.

Any High Contracting Party which has communicated a declaration in virtue of the preceding paragraph may from time to time communicate a further declaration modifying the terms of any former declaration or terminating the application of the provisions of this Protocol in respect of any territory.

A declaration made in accordance with this Article shall be deemed to have been made in accordance with paragraph 1 of Article 56 of the Convention.

ARTICLE 5
Relationship to the Convention

As between the High Contracting Parties the provisions of Articles 1, 2, 3 and 4 of this Protocol shall be regarded as additional Articles to the Convention and all the provisions of the Convention shall apply accordingly.

ARTICLE 6
Signature and Ratification

This Protocol shall be open for signature by the members of the Council of Europe, who are the signatories of the Convention; it shall be ratified at the same time as or after the ratification of the Convention. It shall enter into force after the deposit of ten instruments of ratification. As regards any signatory ratifying subsequently, the Protocol shall enter into force at the date of the deposit of its instrument of ratification.

The instruments of ratification shall be deposited with the Secretary General of the Council of Europe, who will notify all members of the names of those who have ratified.

DONE AT PARIS ON THE 20TH DAY OF MARCH 1952, in English and French, both texts being equally authentic, in a single copy which shall remain deposited in the archives of the Council of Europe. The Secretary General shall transmit certified copies to each of the signatory governments.

Protocol No. 4 to the Convention for the Protection of Human Rights and Fundamental Freedoms Securing Certain Rights and Freedoms Other Than Those Already Included in the Convention and in the First Protocol Thereto

Strasbourg, 16.IX.1963

THE GOVERNMENTS SIGNATORY HERETO, being members of the Council of Europe,

Being resolved to take steps to ensure the collective enforcement of certain rights and freedoms other than those already included in Section I of the

Convention for the Protection of Human Rights and Fundamental Freedoms signed at Rome on 4th November 1950 (hereinafter referred to as the "Convention") and in Articles 1 to 3 of the First Protocol to the Convention, signed at Paris on 20th March 1952,

Have agreed as follows:

ARTICLE 1
Prohibition of Imprisonment for Debt

No one shall be deprived of his liberty merely on the ground of inability to fulfil a contractual obligation.

ARTICLE 2
Freedom of Movement

1. Everyone lawfully within the territory of a State shall, within that territory, have the right to liberty of movement and freedom to choose his residence.
2. Everyone shall be free to leave any country, including his own.
3. No restrictions shall be placed on the exercise of these rights other than such as are in accordance with law and are necessary in a democratic society in the interests of national security or public safety, for the maintenance of ordre public, for the prevention of crime, for the protection of health or morals, or for the protection of the rights and freedoms of others.
4. The rights set forth in paragraph 1 may also be subject, in particular areas, to restrictions imposed in accordance with law and justified by the public interest in a democratic society.

ARTICLE 3
Prohibition of Expulsion of Nationals

1. No one shall be expelled, by means either of an individual or of a collective measure, from the territory of the State of which he is a national.
2. No one shall be deprived of the right to enter the territory of the State of which he is a national.

ARTICLE 4
Prohibition of Collective Expulsion of Aliens

Collective expulsion of aliens is prohibited.

ARTICLE 5
Territorial Application

1. Any High Contracting Party may, at the time of signature or ratification of this Protocol, or at any time thereafter, communicate to the Secretary General of the Council of Europe a declaration stating the extent to which it undertakes that the provisions of this Protocol shall apply to such of the territories for the international relations of which it is responsible as are named therein.
2. Any High Contracting Party which has communicated a declaration in virtue of the preceding paragraph may, from time to time, communicate a further declaration modifying the terms of any former declaration or terminating the application of the provisions of this Protocol in respect of any territory.
3. A declaration made in accordance with this Article shall be deemed to have been made in accordance with paragraph 1 of Article 56 of the Convention.
4. The territory of any State to which this Protocol applies by virtue of ratification or acceptance by that State, and each territory to which this Protocol is applied by virtue of a declaration by that State under this Article, shall be treated as separate territories for the purpose of the references in Articles 2 and 3 to the territory of a State.
5. Any State which has made a declaration in accordance with paragraph 1 or 2 of this Article may at any time thereafter declare on behalf of one or more of the territories to which the declaration relates that it accepts the competence of the Court to receive applications from individuals, non-governmental organisations or groups of individuals as provided in Article 34 of the Convention in respect of all or any of Articles 1 to 4 of this Protocol.

ARTICLE 6
Relationship to the Convention

As between the High Contracting Parties the provisions of Articles 1 to 5 of this Protocol shall be regarded as additional Articles to the Convention, and all the provisions of the Convention shall apply accordingly.

ARTICLE 7
Signature and Ratification

1. This Protocol shall be open for signature by the members of the Council of Europe who are the signatories of the Convention; it shall be ratified at the same time as or after the ratification of the Convention. It shall enter into force after the deposit of five instruments of ratification. As regards any

signatory ratifying subsequently, the Protocol shall enter into force at the date of the deposit of its instrument of ratification.

2. The instruments of ratification shall be deposited with the Secretary General of the Council of Europe, who will notify all members of the names of those who have ratified.

In witness whereof the undersigned, being duly authorised thereto, have signed this Protocol.

DONE AT STRASBOURG, THIS 16TH DAY OF SEPTEMBER 1963, in English and in French, both texts being equally authoritative, in a single copy which shall remain deposited in the archives of the Council of Europe. The Secretary General shall transmit certified copies to each of the signatory states.

Protocol No. 6 to the Convention for the Protection of Human Rights and Fundamental Freedoms concerning the Abolition of the Death Penalty

Strasbourg, 28.IV.1983

THE MEMBER STATES OF THE COUNCIL OF EUROPE, signatory to this Protocol to the Convention for the Protection of Human Rights and Fundamental Freedoms, signed at Rome on 4 November 1950 (hereinafter referred to as "the Convention"),

Considering that the evolution that has occurred in several member States of the Council of Europe expresses a general tendency in favour of abolition of the death penalty;

Have agreed as follows:

ARTICLE 1
Abolition of the Death Penalty

The death penalty shall be abolished. No one shall be condemned to such penalty or executed.

ARTICLE 2
Death Penalty in Time of War

A State may make provision in its law for the death penalty in respect of acts committed in time of war or of imminent threat of war; such penalty shall be applied only in the instances laid down in the law and in accordance with its provisions. The State shall communicate to the Secretary General of the Council of Europe the relevant provisions of that law.

ARTICLE 3
Prohibition of Derogations

No derogation from the provisions of this Protocol shall be made under Article 15 of the Convention.

ARTICLE 4
Prohibition of Reservations

No reservation may be made under Article 57 of the Convention in respect of the provisions of this Protocol.

ARTICLE 5
Territorial Application

1. Any State may at the time of signature or when depositing its instrument of ratification, acceptance or approval, specify the territory or territories to which this Protocol shall apply.
2. Any State may at any later date, by a declaration addressed to the Secretary General of the Council of Europe, extend the application of this Protocol to any other territory specified in the declaration. In respect of such territory the Protocol shall enter into force on the first day of the month following the date of receipt of such declaration by the Secretary General.
3. Any declaration made under the two preceding paragraphs may, in respect of any territory specified in such declaration, be withdrawn by a notification addressed to the Secretary General. The withdrawal shall become effective on the first day of the month following the date of receipt of such notification by the Secretary General.

ARTICLE 6
Relationship to the Convention

As between the States Parties the provisions of Articles 1 to 5 of this Protocol shall be regarded as additional Articles to the Convention and all the provisions of the Convention shall apply accordingly.

ARTICLE 7
Signature and Ratification

The Protocol shall be open for signature by the member States of the Council of Europe, signatories to the Convention. It shall be subject to ratification, acceptance or approval. A member State of the Council of Europe may not ratify, accept or approve this Protocol unless it has, simultaneously or previously, ratified the Convention. Instruments of ratification, acceptance or approval shall be deposited with the Secretary General of the Council of Europe.

ARTICLE 8
Entry into Force

1. This Protocol shall enter into force on the first day of the month following the date on which five member States of the Council of Europe have expressed their consent to be bound by the Protocol in accordance with the provisions of Article 7.
2. In respect of any member State which subsequently expresses its consent to be bound by it, the Protocol shall enter into force on the first day of the month following the date of the deposit of the instrument of ratification, acceptance or approval.

ARTICLE 9
Depositary Functions

The Secretary General of the Council of Europe shall notify the member States of the Council of:

(a) any signature;
(b) the deposit of any instrument of ratification, acceptance or approval;
(c) any date of entry into force of this Protocol in accordance with Articles 5 and 8;
(d) any other act, notification or communication relating to this Protocol.

In witness whereof the undersigned, being duly authorised thereto, have signed this Protocol.

DONE AT STRASBOURG, THIS 28TH DAY OF APRIL 1983, in English and in French, both texts being equally authentic, in a single copy which shall be deposited in the archives of the Council of Europe. The Secretary General of the Council of Europe shall transmit certified copies to each member State of the Council of Europe.

Protocol No. 7 to the Convention for the Protection of Human Rights and Fundamental Freedoms

Strasbourg, 22.XI.1984

THE MEMBER STATES OF THE COUNCIL OF EUROPE, signatory hereto, Being resolved to take further steps to ensure the collective enforcement of certain rights and freedoms by means of the Convention for the Protection of Human Rights and Fundamental Freedoms signed at Rome on 4 November 1950 (hereinafter referred to as "the Convention"),

Have agreed as follows:

ARTICLE 1
Procedural Safeguards Relating to Expulsion of Aliens

1. An alien lawfully resident in the territory of a State shall not be expelled therefrom except in pursuance of a decision reached in accordance with law and shall be allowed:

   (a) to submit reasons against his expulsion,

   (b) to have his case reviewed, and

   (c) to be represented for these purposes before the competent authority or a person or persons designated by that authority.

2. An alien may be expelled before the exercise of his rights under paragraph 1(a), (b) and (c) of this Article, when such expulsion is necessary in the interests of public order or is grounded on reasons of national security.

ARTICLE 2
Right of Appeal in Criminal Matters

1. Everyone convicted of a criminal offence by a tribunal shall have the right to have his conviction or sentence reviewed by a higher tribunal. The exercise of this right, including the grounds on which it may be exercised, shall be governed by law.

2. This right may be subject to exceptions in regard to offences of a minor character, as prescribed by law, or in cases in which the person concerned was tried in the first instance by the highest tribunal or was convicted following an appeal against acquittal.

ARTICLE 3
Compensation for Wrongful Conviction

When a person has by a final decision been convicted of a criminal offence and when subsequently his conviction has been reversed, or he has been pardoned, on the ground that a new or newly discovered fact shows conclusively that there has been a miscarriage of justice, the person who has suffered punishment as a result of such conviction shall be compensated according to the law or the practice of the State concerned, unless it is proved that the nondisclosure of the unknown fact in time is wholly or partly attributable to him.

ARTICLE 4
Right Not to Be Tried or Punished Twice

1. No one shall be liable to be tried or punished again in criminal proceedings under the jurisdiction of the same State for an offence for which he has already been finally acquitted or convicted in accordance with the law and penal procedure of that State.
2. The provisions of the preceding paragraph shall not prevent the reopening of the case in accordance with the law and penal procedure of the State concerned, if there is evidence of new or newly discovered facts, or if there has been a fundamental defect in the previous proceedings, which could affect the outcome of the case.
3. No derogation from this Article shall be made under Article 15 of the Convention.

ARTICLE 5
Equality between Spouses

Spouses shall enjoy equality of rights and responsibilities of a private law character between them, and in their relations with their children, as to marriage, during marriage and in the event of its dissolution. This Article shall not prevent States from taking such measures as are necessary in the interests of the children.

ARTICLE 6
Territorial Application

1. Any State may at the time of signature or when depositing its instrument of ratification, acceptance or approval, specify the territory or territories to which the Protocol shall apply and State the extent to which it undertakes that the provisions of this Protocol shall apply to such territory or territories.
2. Any State may at any later date, by a declaration addressed to the Secretary General of the Council of Europe, extend the application of this Protocol to any other territory specified in the declaration. In respect of such territory the Protocol shall enter into force on the first day of the month following the expiration of a period of two months after the date of receipt by the Secretary General of such declaration.
3. Any declaration made under the two preceding paragraphs may, in respect of any territory specified in such declaration, be withdrawn or modified by a notification addressed to the Secretary General. The withdrawal or modification shall become effective on the first day of the month following the

expiration of a period of two months after the date of receipt of such notification by the Secretary General.

4. A declaration made in accordance with this Article shall be deemed to have been made in accordance with paragraph 1 of Article 56 of the Convention.

5. The territory of any State to which this Protocol applies by virtue of ratification, acceptance or approval by that State, and each territory to which this Protocol is applied by virtue of a declaration by that State under this Article, may be treated as separate territories for the purpose of the reference in Article 1 to the territory of a State.

6. Any State which has made a declaration in accordance with paragraph 1 or 2 of this Article may at any time thereafter declare on behalf of one or more of the territories to which the declaration relates that it accepts the competence of the Court to receive applications from individuals, non-governmental organisations or groups of individuals as provided in Article 34 of the Convention in respect of Articles 1 to 5 of this Protocol.

ARTICLE 7
Relationship to the Convention

As between the States Parties, the provisions of Article 1 to 6 of this Protocol shall be regarded as additional Articles to the Convention, and all the provisions of the Convention shall apply accordingly.

ARTICLE 8
Signature and Ratification

This Protocol shall be open for signature by member States of the Council of Europe which have signed the Convention. It is subject to ratification, acceptance or approval. A member State of the Council of Europe may not ratify, accept or approve this Protocol without previously or simultaneously ratifying the Convention. Instruments of ratification, acceptance or approval shall be deposited with the Secretary General of the Council of Europe.

ARTICLE 9
Entry into Force

1. This Protocol shall enter into force on the first day of the month following the expiration of a period of two months after the date on which seven member States of the Council of Europe have expressed their consent to be bound by the Protocol in accordance with the provisions of Article 8.

2. In respect of any member State which subsequently expresses its consent to be bound by it, the Protocol shall enter into force on the first day of the month following the expiration of a period of two months after the date of the deposit of the instrument of ratification, acceptance or approval.

ARTICLE 10
Depositary Functions

The Secretary General of the Council of Europe shall notify all the member States of the Council of Europe of:

(a) any signature;
(b) the deposit of any instrument of ratification, acceptance or approval;
(c) any date of entry into force of this Protocol in accordance with Articles 6 and 9;
(d) any other act, notification or declaration relating to this Protocol.

In witness whereof the undersigned, being duly authorised thereto, have signed this Protocol.

DONE AT STRASBOURG, THIS 22ND DAY OF NOVEMBER 1984, in English and French, both texts being equally authentic, in a single copy which shall be deposited in the archives of the Council of Europe. The Secretary General of the Council of Europe shall transmit certified copies to each member State of the Council of Europe.

Protocol No. 12 to the Convention for the Protection of Human Rights and Fundamental Freedoms

Rome, 4.XI.2000

THE MEMBER STATES OF THE COUNCIL OF EUROPE, signatory hereto,

Having regard to the fundamental principle according to which all persons are equal before the law and are entitled to the equal protection of the law;

Being resolved to take further steps to promote the equality of all persons through the collective enforcement of a general prohibition of discrimination by means of the Convention for the Protection of Human Rights and Fundamental Freedoms signed at Rome on 4 November 1950 (hereinafter referred to as "the Convention");

Reaffirming that the principle of nondiscrimination does not prevent States Parties from taking measures in order to promote full and effective equality, provided that there is an objective and reasonable justification for those measures,

Have agreed as follows:

ARTICLE 1
General Prohibition of Discrimination

1. The enjoyment of any right set forth by law shall be secured without discrimination on any ground such as sex, race, colour, language, religion, political or other opinion, national or social origin, association with a national minority, property, birth or other status.
2. No one shall be discriminated against by any public authority on any ground such as those mentioned in paragraph 1.

ARTICLE 2
Territorial Application

1. Any State may, at the time of signature or when depositing its instrument of ratification, acceptance or approval, specify the territory or territories to which this Protocol shall apply.
2. Any State may at any later date, by a declaration addressed to the Secretary General of the Council of Europe, extend the application of this Protocol to any other territory specified in the declaration. In respect of such territory the Protocol shall enter into force on the first day of the month following the expiration of a period of three months after the date of receipt by the Secretary General of such declaration.
3. Any declaration made under the two preceding paragraphs may, in respect of any territory specified in such declaration, be withdrawn or modified by a notification addressed to the Secretary General of the Council of Europe. The withdrawal or modification shall become effective on the first day of the month following the expiration of a period of three months after the date of receipt of such notification by the Secretary General.
4. A declaration made in accordance with this Article shall be deemed to have been made in accordance with paragraph 1 of Article 56 of the Convention.
5. Any State which has made a declaration in accordance with paragraph 1 or 2 of this Article may at any time thereafter declare on behalf of one or more of the territories to which the declaration relates that it accepts the competence of the Court to receive applications from individuals, non-governmental organisations or groups of individuals as provided by Article 34 of the Convention in respect of Article 1 of this Protocol.

ARTICLE 3
Relationship to the Convention

As between the States Parties, the provisions of Articles 1 and 2 of this Protocol shall be regarded as additional Articles to the Convention, and all the provisions of the Convention shall apply accordingly.

ARTICLE 4
Signature and Ratification

This Protocol shall be open for signature by member States of the Council of Europe which have signed the Convention. It is subject to ratification, acceptance or approval. A member State of the Council of Europe may not ratify, accept or approve this Protocol without previously or simultaneously ratifying the Convention. Instruments of ratification, acceptance or approval shall be deposited with the Secretary General of the Council of Europe.

ARTICLE 5
Entry into Force

1. This Protocol shall enter into force on the first day of the month following the expiration of a period of three months after the date on which ten member States of the Council of Europe have expressed their consent to be bound by the Protocol in accordance with the provisions of Article 4.
2. In respect of any member State which subsequently expresses its consent to be bound by it, the Protocol shall enter into force on the first day of the month following the expiration of a period of three months after the date of the deposit of the instrument of ratification, acceptance or approval.

ARTICLE 6
Depositary Functions

The Secretary General of the Council of Europe shall notify all the member States of the Council of Europe of:

(a) any signature;
(b) the deposit of any instrument of ratification, acceptance or approval;
(c) any date of entry into force of this Protocol in accordance with Articles 2 and 5;
(d) any other act, notification or communication relating to this Protocol.

In witness whereof the undersigned, being duly authorised thereto, have signed this Protocol.

DONE AT ROME, THIS 4TH DAY OF NOVEMBER 2000, in English and in French, both texts being equally authentic, in a single copy which shall be deposited in the archives of the Council of Europe. The Secretary General of the Council of Europe shall transmit certified copies to each member State of the Council of Europe.

Protocol No. 13 to the Convention for the Protection of Human Rights and Fundamental Freedoms Concerning the Abolition of the Death Penalty in All Circumstances

Vilnius, 3.V.2002

THE MEMBER STATES OF THE COUNCIL OF EUROPE, signatory hereto,

Convinced that everyone's right to life is a basic value in a democratic society and that the abolition of the death penalty is essential for the protection of this right and for the full recognition of the inherent dignity of all human beings;

Wishing to strengthen the protection of the right to life guaranteed by the Convention for the Protection of Human Rights and Fundamental Freedoms signed at Rome on 4 November 1950 (hereinafter referred to as "the Convention");

Noting that Protocol No. 6 to the Convention, concerning the Abolition of the Death Penalty, signed at Strasbourg on 28 April 1983, does not exclude the death penalty in respect of acts committed in time of war or of imminent threat of war;

Being resolved to take the final step in order to abolish the death penalty in all circumstances,

Have agreed as follows:

ARTICLE 1
Abolition of the Death Penalty

The death penalty shall be abolished. No one shall be condemned to such penalty or executed.

ARTICLE 2
Prohibition of Derogations

No derogation from the provisions of this Protocol shall be made under Article 15 of the Convention.

ARTICLE 3
Prohibition of Reservations

No reservation may be made under Article 57 of the Convention in respect of the provisions of this Protocol.

ARTICLE 4
Territorial Application

1. Any State may, at the time of signature or when depositing its instrument of ratification, acceptance or approval, specify the territory or territories to which this Protocol shall apply.
2. Any State may at any later date, by a declaration addressed to the Secretary General of the Council of Europe, extend the application of this Protocol to any other territory specified in the declaration. In respect of such territory the Protocol shall enter into force on the first day of the month following the expiration of a period of three months after the date of receipt by the Secretary General of such declaration.
3. Any declaration made under the two preceding paragraphs may, in respect of any territory specified in such declaration, be withdrawn or modified by a notification addressed to the Secretary General. The withdrawal or modification shall become effective on the first day of the month following the expiration of a period of three months after the date of receipt of such notification by the Secretary General.

ARTICLE 5
Relationship to the Convention

As between the States Parties the provisions of Articles 1 to 4 of this Protocol shall be regarded as additional Articles to the Convention, and all the provisions of the Convention shall apply accordingly.

ARTICLE 6
Signature and Ratification

This Protocol shall be open for signature by member States of the Council of Europe which have signed the Convention. It is subject to ratification, acceptance or approval. A member State of the Council of Europe may not ratify, accept or approve this Protocol without previously or simultaneously ratifying the Convention. Instruments of ratification, acceptance or approval shall be deposited with the Secretary General of the Council of Europe.

ARTICLE 7
Entry into Force

1. This Protocol shall enter into force on the first day of the month following the expiration of a period of three months after the date on which ten member States of the Council of Europe have expressed their consent to be bound by the Protocol in accordance with the provisions of Article 6.
2. In respect of any member State which subsequently expresses its consent to be bound by it, the Protocol shall enter into force on the first day of the month following the expiration of a period of three months after the date of the deposit of the instrument of ratification, acceptance or approval.

ARTICLE 8
Depositary Functions

The Secretary General of the Council of Europe shall notify all the member States of the Council of Europe of:

(a) any signature;
(b) the deposit of any instrument of ratification, acceptance or approval;
(c) any date of entry into force of this Protocol in accordance with Articles 4 and 7;
(d) any other act, notification or communication relating to this Protocol.

In witness whereof the undersigned, being duly authorised thereto, have signed this Protocol.

DONE AT VILNIUS, THIS 3RD DAY OF MAY 2002, in English and in French, both texts being equally authentic, in a single copy which shall be deposited in the archives of the Council of Europe. The Secretary General of the Council of Europe shall transmit certified copies to each member State of the Council of Europe.

Appendix B

Charter of Fundamental Rights of the European Union

(2000/C 364/01)
Nice, 7 December 2000

Preamble

The peoples of Europe, in creating an ever closer union among them, are resolved to share a peaceful future based on common values.

Conscious of its spiritual and moral heritage, the Union is founded on the indivisible, universal values of human dignity, freedom, equality and solidarity; it is based on the principles of democracy and the rule of law. It places the individual at the heart of its activities, by establishing the citizenship of the Union and by creating an area of freedom, security and justice.

The Union contributes to the preservation and to the development of these common values while respecting the diversity of the cultures and traditions of the peoples of Europe as well as the national identities of the Member States and the organisation of their public authorities at national, regional and local levels; it seeks to promote balanced and sustainable development and ensures free movement of persons, goods, services and capital, and the freedom of establishment.

To this end, it is necessary to strengthen the protection of fundamental rights in the light of changes in society, social progress and scientific and technological developments by making those rights more visible in a Charter.

This Charter reaffirms, with due regard for the powers and tasks of the Community and the Union and the principle of subsidiarity, the rights as they result, in particular, from the constitutional traditions and international obligations common to the Member States, the Treaty on European Union, the Community Treaties, the European Convention for the Protection of Human Rights and Fundamental Freedoms, the Social Charters adopted by the Community and by the Council of Europe and the case-law of the Court of Justice of the European Communities and of the European Court of Human Rights.

Enjoyment of these rights entails responsibilities and duties with regard to other persons, to the human community and to future generations.

The Union therefore recognises the rights, freedoms and principles set out hereafter.

CHAPTER I
DIGNITY

ARTICLE 1
Human Dignity

Human dignity is inviolable. It must be respected and protected.

ARTICLE 2
Right to Life

1. Everyone has the right to life.
2. No one shall be condemned to the death penalty, or executed.

ARTICLE 3
Right to the Integrity of the Person

1. Everyone has the right to respect for his or her physical and mental integrity.
2. In the fields of medicine and biology, the following must be respected in particular:
   – the free and informed consent of the person concerned, according to the procedures laid down by law,
   – the prohibition of eugenic practices, in particular those aiming at the selection of persons,
   – the prohibition on making the human body and its parts as such a source of financial gain,
   – the prohibition of the reproductive cloning of human beings.

ARTICLE 4
Prohibition of Torture and Inhuman or Degrading Treatment or Punishment

No one shall be subjected to torture or to inhuman or degrading treatment or punishment.

ARTICLE 5
Prohibition of Slavery and Forced Labour

1. No one shall be held in slavery or servitude.
2. No one shall be required to perform forced or compulsory labour.
3. Trafficking in human beings is prohibited.

CHAPTER II
FREEDOMS

ARTICLE 6
Right to Liberty and Security

Everyone has the right to liberty and security of person.

ARTICLE 7
Respect for Private and Family Life

Everyone has the right to respect for his or her private and family life, home and communications.

ARTICLE 8
Protection of Personal Data

1. Everyone has the right to the protection of personal data concerning him or her.
2. Such data must be processed fairly for specified purposes and on the basis of the consent of the person concerned or some other legitimate basis laid down by law. Everyone has the right of access to data which has been collected concerning him or her, and the right to have it rectified.
3. Compliance with these rules shall be subject to control by an independent authority.

ARTICLE 9
Right to Marry and Right to Found a Family

The right to marry and the right to found a family shall be guaranteed in accordance with the national laws governing the exercise of these rights.

ARTICLE 10
Freedom of Thought, Conscience and Religion

1. Everyone has the right to freedom of thought, conscience and religion. This right includes freedom to change religion or belief and freedom, either alone or in community with others and in public or in private, to manifest religion or belief, in worship, teaching, practice and observance.
2. The right to conscientious objection is recognised, in accordance with the national laws governing the exercise of this right.

ARTICLE 11
Freedom of Expression and Information

1. Everyone has the right to freedom of expression. This right shall include freedom to hold opinions and to receive and impart information and ideas without interference by public authority and regardless of frontiers.
2. The freedom and pluralism of the media shall be respected.

ARTICLE 12
Freedom of Assembly and of Association

1. Everyone has the right to freedom of peaceful assembly and to freedom of association at all levels, in particular in political, trade union and civic matters, which implies the right of everyone to form and to join trade unions for the protection of his or her interests.
2. Political parties at Union level contribute to expressing the political will of the citizens of the Union.

ARTICLE 13
Freedom of the Arts and Sciences

The arts and scientific research shall be free of constraint. Academic freedom shall be respected.

ARTICLE 14
Right to Education

1. Everyone has the right to education and to have access to vocational and continuing training.
2. This right includes the possibility to receive free compulsory education.

3. The freedom to found educational establishments with due respect for democratic principles and the right of parents to ensure the education and teaching of their children in conformity with their religious, philosophical and pedagogical convictions shall be respected, in accordance with the national laws governing the exercise of such freedom and right.

ARTICLE 15
Freedom to Choose an Occupation and Right to Engage in Work

1. Everyone has the right to engage in work and to pursue a freely chosen or accepted occupation.
2. Every citizen of the Union has the freedom to seek employment, to work, to exercise the right of establishment and to provide services in any Member State.
3. Nationals of third countries who are authorised to work in the territories of the Member States are entitled to working conditions equivalent to those of citizens of the Union.

ARTICLE 16
Freedom to Conduct a Business

The freedom to conduct a business in accordance with Community law and national laws and practices is recognised.

ARTICLE 17
Right to Property

1. Everyone has the right to own, use, dispose of and bequeath his or her lawfully acquired possessions. No one may be deprived of his or her possessions, except in the public interest and in the cases and under the conditions provided for by law, subject to fair compensation being paid in good time for their loss. The use of property may be regulated by law in so far as is necessary for the general interest.
2. Intellectual property shall be protected.

ARTICLE 18
Right to Asylum

The right to asylum shall be guaranteed with due respect for the rules of the Geneva Convention of 28 July 1951 and the Protocol of 31 January 1967 relating to the status of refugees and in accordance with the Treaty establishing the European Community.

ARTICLE 19
Protection in the Event of Removal, Expulsion or Extradition

1. Collective expulsions are prohibited.
2. No one may be removed, expelled or extradited to a State where there is a serious risk that he or she would be subjected to the death penalty, torture or other inhuman or degrading treatment or punishment.

CHAPTER III
EQUALITY

ARTICLE 20
Equality before the Law

Everyone is equal before the law.

ARTICLE 21
Non-Discrimination

1. Any discrimination based on any ground such as sex, race, colour, ethnic or social origin, genetic features, language, religion or belief, political or any other opinion, membership of a national minority, property, birth, disability, age or sexual orientation shall be prohibited.
2. Within the scope of application of the Treaty establishing the European Community and of the Treaty on European Union, and without prejudice to the special provisions of those Treaties, any discrimination on grounds of nationality shall be prohibited.

ARTICLE 22
Cultural, Religious and Linguistic Diversity

The Union shall respect cultural, religious and linguistic diversity.

ARTICLE 23
Equality between Men and Women

Equality between men and women must be ensured in all areas, including employment, work and pay.

The principle of equality shall not prevent the maintenance or adoption of measures providing for specific advantages in favour of the under-represented sex.

ARTICLE 24
The Rights of the Child

1. Children shall have the right to such protection and care as is necessary for their well-being. They may express their views freely. Such views shall be taken into consideration on matters which concern them in accordance with their age and maturity.
2. In all actions relating to children, whether taken by public authorities or private institutions, the child's best interests must be a primary consideration.
3. Every child shall have the right to maintain on a regular basis a personal relationship and direct contact with both his or her parents, unless that is contrary to his or her interests.

ARTICLE 25
The Rights of the Elderly

The Union recognises and respects the rights of the elderly to lead a life of dignity and independence and to participate in social and cultural life.

ARTICLE 26
Integration of Persons with Disabilities

The Union recognises and respects the right of persons with disabilities to benefit from measures designed to ensure their independence, social and occupational integration and participation in the life of the community.

CHAPTER IV
SOLIDARITY

ARTICLE 27
Workers' Right to Information and Consultation within the Undertaking

Workers or their representatives must, at the appropriate levels, be guaranteed information and consultation in good time in the cases and under the conditions provided for by Community law and national laws and practices.

ARTICLE 28
Right of Collective Bargaining and Action

Workers and employers, or their respective organisations, have, in accordance with Community law and national laws and practices, the right to negotiate and conclude collective agreements at the appropriate levels and, in cases of conflicts of interest, to take collective action to defend their interests, including strike action.

ARTICLE 29
Right of Access to Placement Services

Everyone has the right of access to a free placement service.

ARTICLE 30
Protection in the Event of Unjustified Dismissal

Every worker has the right to protection against unjustified dismissal, in accordance with Community law and national laws and practices.

ARTICLE 31
Fair and Just Working Conditions

1. Every worker has the right to working conditions which respect his or her health, safety and dignity.
2. Every worker has the right to limitation of maximum working hours, to daily and weekly rest periods and to an annual period of paid leave.

ARTICLE 32
Prohibition of Child Labour and Protection of Young People at Work

The employment of children is prohibited. The minimum age of admission to employment may not be lower than the minimum school-leaving age, without prejudice to such rules as may be more favourable to young people and except for limited derogations.

Young people admitted to work must have working conditions appropriate to their age and be protected against economic exploitation and any work likely to harm their safety, health or physical, mental, moral or social development or to interfere with their education.

ARTICLE 33
Family and Professional Life

1. The family shall enjoy legal, economic and social protection.
2. To reconcile family and professional life, everyone shall have the right to protection from dismissal for a reason connected with maternity and the right to paid maternity leave and to parental leave following the birth or adoption of a child.

ARTICLE 34
Social Security and Social Assistance

1. The Union recognises and respects the entitlement to social security benefits and social services providing protection in cases such as maternity, illness, industrial accidents, dependency or old age, and in the case of loss of employment, in accordance with the rules laid down by Community law and national laws and practices.
2. Everyone residing and moving legally within the European Union is entitled to social security benefits and social advantages in accordance with Community law and national laws and practices.
3. In order to combat social exclusion and poverty, the Union recognises and respects the right to social and housing assistance so as to ensure a decent existence for all those who lack sufficient resources, in accordance with the rules laid down by Community law and national laws and practices.

ARTICLE 35
Health Care

Everyone has the right of access to preventive health care and the right to benefit from medical treatment under the conditions established by national laws and practices. A high level of human health protection shall be ensured in the definition and implementation of all Union policies and activities.

ARTICLE 36
Access to Services of General Economic Interest

The Union recognises and respects access to services of general economic interest as provided for in national laws and practices, in accordance with the Treaty establishing the European Community, in order to promote the social and territorial cohesion of the Union.

ARTICLE 37
Environmental Protection

A high level of environmental protection and the improvement of the quality of the environment must be integrated into the policies of the Union and ensured in accordance with the principle of sustainable development.

ARTICLE 38
Consumer Protection

Union policies shall ensure a high level of consumer protection.

CHAPTER V
CITIZENS' RIGHTS

ARTICLE 39
Right to Vote and to Stand as a Candidate at Elections to the European Parliament

1. Every citizen of the Union has the right to vote and to stand as a candidate at elections to the European Parliament in the Member State in which he or she resides, under the same conditions as nationals of that State.
2. Members of the European Parliament shall be elected by direct universal suffrage in a free and secret ballot.

ARTICLE 40
Right to Vote and to Stand as a Candidate at Municipal Elections

Every citizen of the Union has the right to vote and to stand as a candidate at municipal elections in the Member State in which he or she resides under the same conditions as nationals of that State.

ARTICLE 41
Right to Good Administration

1. Every person has the right to have his or her affairs handled impartially, fairly and within a reasonable time by the institutions and bodies of the Union.
2. This right includes:
   - the right of every person to be heard, before any individual measure which would affect him or her adversely is taken;

CHARTER OF FUNDAMENTAL RIGHTS OF THE EUROPEAN UNION 451

- the right of every person to have access to his or her file, while respecting the legitimate interests of confidentiality and of professional and business secrecy;
- the obligation of the administration to give reasons for its decisions.

3. Every person has the right to have the Community make good any damage caused by its institutions or by its servants in the performance of their duties, in accordance with the general principles common to the laws of the Member States.

4. Every person may write to the institutions of the Union in one of the languages of the Treaties and must have an answer in the same language.

ARTICLE 42
Right of Access to Documents

Any citizen of the Union, and any natural or legal person residing or having its registered office in a Member State, has a right of access to European Parliament, Council and Commission documents.

ARTICLE 43
Ombudsman

Any citizen of the Union and any natural or legal person residing or having its registered office in a Member State has the right to refer to the Ombudsman of the Union cases of maladministration in the activities of the Community institutions or bodies, with the exception of the Court of Justice and the Court of First Instance acting in their judicial role.

ARTICLE 44
Right to Petition

Any citizen of the Union and any natural or legal person residing or having its registered office in a Member State has the right to petition the European Parliament.

ARTICLE 45
Freedom of Movement and of Residence

1. Every citizen of the Union has the right to move and reside freely within the territory of the Member States.

2. Freedom of movement and residence may be granted, in accordance with the Treaty establishing the European Community, to nationals of third countries legally resident in the territory of a Member State.

ARTICLE 46
Diplomatic and Consular Protection

Every citizen of the Union shall, in the territory of a third country in which the Member State of which he or she is a national is not represented, be entitled to protection by the diplomatic or consular authorities of any Member State, on the same conditions as the nationals of that Member State.

CHAPTER VI
JUSTICE

ARTICLE 47
Right to an Effective Remedy and to a Fair Trial

Everyone whose rights and freedoms guaranteed by the law of the Union are violated has the right to an effective remedy before a tribunal in compliance with the conditions laid down in this Article.

Everyone is entitled to a fair and public hearing within a reasonable time by an independent and impartial tribunal previously established by law. Everyone shall have the possibility of being advised, defended and represented.

Legal aid shall be made available to those who lack sufficient resources in so far as such aid is necessary to ensure effective access to justice.

ARTICLE 48
Presumption of Innocence and Right of Defence

1. Everyone who has been charged shall be presumed innocent until proved guilty according to law.
2. Respect for the rights of the defence of anyone who has been charged shall be guaranteed.

ARTICLE 49
Principles of Legality and Proportionality of Criminal Offences and Penalties

1. No one shall be held guilty of any criminal offence on account of any act or omission which did not constitute a criminal offence under national law or

international law at the time when it was committed. Nor shall a heavier penalty be imposed than that which was applicable at the time the criminal offence was committed. If, subsequent to the commission of a criminal offence, the law provides for a lighter penalty, that penalty shall be applicable.

2. This Article shall not prejudice the trial and punishment of any person for any act or omission which, at the time when it was committed, was criminal according to the general principles recognised by the community of nations.

3. The severity of penalties must not be disproportionate to the criminal offence.

ARTICLE 50
Right Not to Be Tried or Punished Twice in Criminal Proceedings for the Same Criminal Offence

No one shall be liable to be tried or punished again in criminal proceedings for an offence for which he or she has already been finally acquitted or convicted within the Union in accordance with the law.

CHAPTER VII
GENERAL PROVISIONS

ARTICLE 51
Scope

1. The provisions of this Charter are addressed to the institutions and bodies of the Union with due regard for the principle of subsidiarity and to the Member States only when they are implementing Union law. They shall therefore respect the rights, observe the principles and promote the application thereof in accordance with their respective powers.

2. This Charter does not establish any new power or task for the Community or the Union, or modify powers and tasks defined by the Treaties.

ARTICLE 52
Scope of Guaranteed Rights

1. Any limitation on the exercise of the rights and freedoms recognised by this Charter must be provided for by law and respect the essence of those rights and freedoms. Subject to the principle of proportionality, limitations may be made only if they are necessary and genuinely meet objectives of general

interest recognised by the Union or the need to protect the rights and freedoms of others.

2. Rights recognised by this Charter which are based on the Community Treaties or the Treaty on European Union shall be exercised under the conditions and within the limits defined by those Treaties.

3. In so far as this Charter contains rights which correspond to rights guaranteed by the Convention for the Protection of Human Rights and Fundamental Freedoms, the meaning and scope of those rights shall be the same as those laid down by the said Convention. This provision shall not prevent Union law providing more extensive protection.

ARTICLE 53
Level of Protection

Nothing in this Charter shall be interpreted as restricting or adversely affecting human rights and fundamental freedoms as recognised, in their respective fields of application, by Union law and international law and by international agreements to which the Union, the Community or all the Member States are party, including the European Convention for the Protection of Human Rights and Fundamental Freedoms, and by the Member States' constitutions.

ARTICLE 54
Prohibition of Abuse of Rights

Nothing in this Charter shall be interpreted as implying any right to engage in any activity or to perform any act aimed at the destruction of any of the rights and freedoms recognised in this Charter or at their limitation to a greater extent than is provided for herein.

BIBLIOGRAPHY

Affholder, S., updated by Lambrecht-Feigl, M., 'The Congress of Local and Regional Authorities: European co-operation close to the citizen' in Kleinsorge, T. (ed.), *Council of Europe (CoE)* (Alphen aan den Rijn: Wolters Kluwer, 2nd edn., 2015), pp. 170–82.

Alfredsson, G., 'A frame an incomplete painting: comparison of the Framework Convention for the Protection of National Minorities with international standards and monitoring procedures', *International Journal on Minority and Group Rights*, 7 (2000), 291–304.

Alston, P., and De Schutter, O. (eds.), *Monitoring Fundamental Rights in the EU: The Contribution of the Fundamental Rights Agency* (Oxford: Hart, 2005).

Alston, P., with Bustelo, M. R., and Heenan, J. (eds.), *The EU and Human Rights* (Oxford University Press, 1999).

Anagnostaras, G., 'Balancing conflicting fundamental rights: the *Sky Österreich* paradigm', *European Law Review*, 39 (2014), 111–24.

Anagnostou, D., 'Introduction – untangling the domestic implementation of the European Court of Human Rights' judgments' in Anagnostou, D. (ed.), *The European Court of Human Rights: Implementing Strasbourg's Judgments on Domestic Policy* (Edinburgh: Edinburgh University Press, 2013), pp. 1–24.

'Politics, courts and society in the national implementation and practice of European Court of Human Rights case law' in Anagnostou, D. (ed.), *The European Court of Human Rights: Implementing Strasbourg's Judgments on Domestic Policy* (Edinburgh: Edinburgh University Press, 2013), pp. 211–31.

Andreadakis, S., 'The European Convention on Human Rights, the EU and the UK: confronting a heresy: a reply to Andrew Williams', *European Journal of International Law*, 24 (2013), 1187–93.

Anon, 'Tribute to Rolv Ryssdal, ground-breaking reformer', *Human Rights Information Bulletin No. 50: The European Convention at 50* (Strasbourg: Council of Europe, 2000).

Arai-Takahashi, Y., *The Margin of Appreciation Doctrine and the Principle of Proportionality in the Jurisprudence of the ECHR* (Antwerp: Intersentia, 2002).

'The margin of appreciation doctrine: a theoretical analysis of Strasbourg's variable geometry' in Føllesdal, A., Peters, B., and Ulfstin, G. (eds.), *Constituting Europe: The European Court of Human Rights in a National, European and Global Context* (Cambridge University Press, 2013), pp. 62–105.

Arnardóttir, O. M., *Equality and Non-Discrimination under the European Convention on Human Rights* (The Hague: Martinus Nijhoff, 2003).

'Discrimination as a magnifying lens: scope and ambit under Article 14 and Protocol No. 12' in Brems, E., and Gerards, J. (eds.), *Shaping Rights in the ECHR; The Role of the European Court of Human Rights in Determining the Scope of Human Rights* (Cambridge Universtiy Press, 2013).

Ashiagbor, D., 'Article 15: Freedom to Choose an Occupation' in Peers, S., Hervey, T., Kenner, J., and Ward, A. (eds.), *The EU Charter of Fundamental Rights: A Commentary* (Oxford: Hart, 2014), pp. 423–35.

'Article 29: Right of Access to Placement Services' in Peers, S., Hervey, T., Kenner, J., and Ward, A. (eds.), *The EU Charter of Fundamental Rights: A Commentary* (Oxford, Hart, 2014), pp. 795–803.

Askola, H., 'Article 5: Prohibition of Slavery and Forced Labour' in Peers, S., Hervey, T., Kenner, J., and Ward, A. (eds.), *The EU Charter of Fundamental Rights: A Commentary* (Oxford: Hart, 2014), pp. 101–19.

Avbelj, M., and Komárek, J., 'Four visions of constitutional pluralism', *European Journal of Legal Studies*, 2 (2008), 325–70.

'Introduction' in Avbelj, M., and Komárek, J. (eds.), *Constitutional Pluralism in the European Union and Beyond* (Oxford: Hart, 2012), pp. 1–15.

Azoulai, L., 'The Court of Justice and the social market economy: the emergence of an ideal and the conditions for its realisation', *Common Market Law Review*, 45 (2008), 1335–55.

Babayev, R., 'Private autonomy at Union level: On Article 16 CFREU and free movement rights', *Common Market Law Review*, 53 (2016), 979–1005.

Badar, M. E., 'Basic principles governing limitations on individual rights and freedoms in human rights instruments', *International Journal of Human Rights*, 7 (2003), 63–92.

Balducci, G., 'The study of the EU promotion of human rights: the importance of international and internal factors', *GARNET Working Paper No. 61/08* (2008).

Barents, R., 'The precedence of EU law from the perspective of constitutional pluralism', *European Constitutional Law Review*, 5 (2009), 421–46.

Basu, S., 'The European Union in the Human Rights Council' in Wouters, J., Bruyninckx, H., Basu, S., and Schunz, S. (eds.), *The European Union and Multilateral Governance* (Basingstoke: Palgrave Macmillan, 2012), 86–102.

Bates, E., *The Evolution of the European Convention on Human Rights: From Its Inception to the Creation of a Permanent Court of Human Rights* (Oxford University Press, 2010).

Bechev, D., and Nicolaïdis, K., 'From policy to polity: can the EU's special relations with its 'neighbourhood' be decentred?', *JCMS: Journal of Common Market Studies*, 48(3) (2010), 475–500.

Beijer, M., 'Active guidance of (procedural) fundamental rights protection by the European Court of Justice', *Review of European Administrative Law*, 8 (2015), 127–50.

The Limits of Fundamental Rights Protection in the EU (Antwerp: Intersentia, 2017).

Bell, J., 'Reflections on continental European supreme courts', *Legal Studies*, 24 (2004), 156–68.

Bell, M., 'Article 20: equality before the law' in Peers, S., Hervey, T., Kenner, J., and Ward, A. (eds.), *The EU Charter of Fundamental Rights: A Commentary* (Oxford: Hart, 2014), pp. 563–78.

'The principle of equal treatment: widening and deepening' in Craig, P., and de Búrca, G. (eds.), *The Evolution of EU Law* (Oxford University Press, 2nd edn., 2011), pp. 611–39.

Bell, M., Schiek, D., and Waddington, L. (eds.), *Cases, Materials and Text on National, Supranational and International Non-Discrimination Law* (Oxford: Hart, 2007).

Bellamy, R., 'The democratic legitimacy of international human rights conventions: political constitutionalism and the European Convention on Human Rights', *European Journal of International Law*, 25 (2014), 1019–42.

'The democratic legitimacy of international human rights conventions: political constitutionalism and the Hirst case' in Føllesdal, A., Schaffer, J., and Ulfstein, G. (eds.), *The Legitimacy of International Human Rights Regimes: Legal, Political and Philosophical Perspectives* (Cambridge University Press, 2014), pp. 243–71.

Benelhocine, C., *The European Social Charter* (Strasbourg: Council of Europe, 2012).

Bernhardt, R., 'The admissibility stage: the pros and cons of a certiorari procedure for individual applications' in Wolfrum, R., and Deutsch, U. (eds.), *The European Court of Human Rights Overwhelmed by Applications: Problems and Possible Solutions – International Workshop, Heidleberg, 17–18 December 2007* (Berlin: Springer, 2007).

Besselink, L. F. M., 'National and constitutional identity before and after Lisbon', *Utrecht Law Review*, 6 (2010), 36–49.

Besson, S., 'The human rights competences in the EU – the state of the question after Lisbon' in Kofler, G. et al. (eds.), *Human Rights and Taxation in Europe and the World* (IBFD, 2011), pp. 37–63.

Bjorge, E., *Domestic Application of the ECHR: Courts as Faithful Trustees* (Oxford University Press, 2015).

Björgvinsson, D., 'The role of the ECtHR in the changing European human rights architecture' in Mjöll Arnardóttir, O., and Buyse, A. (eds.), *Shifting Centres of Gravity in Human Rights Protection: Rethinking relations between the ECHR, EU and national legal orders* (London: Routledge, 2016), pp. 26–45.

Blankenburg, E., 'Mobilization of the German Federal Constitutional Court' in Rogowski and Gawron (eds.), *Constitutional Courts*, pp. 157–72.

Bobek, M., 'The Court of Justice, the national courts and the spirit of cooperation: between *Dichtung und Wahrheit*' in Lazowski, A., and Blockmans, S. (eds.), *Research Handbook on EU Institutional Law* (Cheltenham, UK: Edward Elgar, 2016), 353–78.

Bogg, A., 'Article 31: Fair and Just Working Conditions' in Peers, S., Hervey, T., Kenner, J., and Ward, A. (eds.), *The EU Charter of Fundamental Rights: A Commentary* (Oxford: Hart, 2014), pp. 833–68.

Borreschmidt, N., 'The EU's Human Rights Promotion in China and Myanmar: Trading Rights for Might?', *EU Diplomacy Paper 5/2014* (Department of EU International Relations and Diplomacy Studies, 2014).

Bratza, N., 'Living instrument or dead letter – the future of the European Convention on Human Rights', *European Human Rights Law Review*, (2014), 116–28.

Brems, E., 'The Margin of Appreciation Doctrine in the Case-Law of the European Court of Human Rights', *Zeitschrift für Auslandisches Offentliches Recht und Volkrecht*, 56 (1996), 240–314.

Brkan, M., 'The unstoppable expansion of the EU Fundamental Right to Data Protection: little shop of horrors?', *Maastricht Journal*, 23 (2016), 812–41.

Broberg, M., and Fenger, N., *Preliminary References to the European Court of Justice* (Oxford University Press, 2010).

Bruer, M., 'Establishing common standards and securing the rule of law' in Schmahl, S., and Breuer, M. (eds.), *The Council of Europe: Its Law and Policies* (Oxford University Press, 2017), pp. 639–70.

Brummer, K., 'Enhancing intergovernmentalism: the Council of Europe and human rights', *International Journal of Human Rights*, 14(2) (2010), 280–99.
'Imposing sanctions: the not so "normative power Europe"', *European Foreign Affairs Review*, 14(2) (2009).

Brunnee, J., and Troope, S., *Legitimacy and Legality in International Law* (Cambridge University Press, 2010).

Bünte, M., and Portela, C., 'Myanmar: The beginning of reforms and the end of sanctions', *German Institute of Global and Area Studies Focus*, 3 (2012), 1–7.

Burri, S., 'The European Network of Legal Experts in the Field of Gender Equality', *European Anti-Discrimination Law Review*, 6 (1993), 11–12.

Çali, B., Koch, A., and Bruch, N., 'The legitimacy of human rights courts: a grounded interpretivist analysis of the European Court of Human Rights', *Human Rights Quarterly*, 35 (2013), 955–84.

Callewaert, J., 'The European Convention on Human Rights and European Union Law: a long way to harmony', *European Human Rights Law Review*, (2009), 768–83.

Cameron, I., 'The Court and the member states: procedural aspects' in Føllesdal, A., Peters, B., and Ulfstein, G. (eds.), *Constituting Europe: The European Court of Human Rights in a National, European and Global Context* (Cambridge University Press, 2013), pp. 25–61.

Carrasco, C. M., 'The applicability of human rights instruments to European Union's CSDP operations: framing the challenges', *Cuadernos Europeos de Deusto*, 53 (2005), 53–80.

Carrera, S., and Atger, A. F., 'L'affaire des Roms: A Challenge to the EU's Area of Freedom, Security and Justice', *CEPS Paper 'Liberty and Security in Europe'* (2010).

Carruba, C., and Gabel, M., 'Courts, compliance and the quest for legitimacy in international law', *Theoretical Inquiries in International Law*, 14 (2013), 505–42.

Checkel, J. T., 'International institutions and socialization in Europe: introduction and framework' in Checkel, J. T. (ed.), *International Institutions and Socialization in Europe* (Cambridge University Press, 2007), pp. 3–30.

Chetwynd, H., 'The European Committee for the Prevention of Torture (CPT)' in Kleinsorge, T. (ed.), *Council of Europe (CoE)* (Alphen aan den Rijn: Wolters Kluwer, 2nd edn., 2015), pp. 127–41.

Choudry, S., 'Article 9: Right to Marry and Right to Found a Family' in Peers, S., Hervey, T., Kenner, J., and Ward, A. (eds.), *The EU Charter of Fundamental Rights: A Commentary* (Oxford: Hart, 2014), pp. 269–90.

Christoffersen, J., 'Individual and constitutional justice: can the power balance of adjudication be reversed?' in Christoffersen, J., and Madsen, M. (eds.), *The European Court of Human Rights between Law and Politics* (Oxford: Oxford University Press, 2011), pp. 181–203.

Churchill, R. R., and Khaliq, U., 'The collective complaints system of the European Social Charter: an effective mechanism for ensuring compliance with economic and social rights?', *European Journal of International Law*, 15 (2004), 417–56.

Claes, M., 'The EU, its member states and their citizens' in Leczykiewicz, D., and Weatherill, S. (eds.), *The Involvement of EU Law in Private Law Relationships* (Oxford: Hart, 2013), pp. 29–52.

Closa, C., 'Reinforcing EU monitoring of the rule of law: normative arguments, institutional proposals and the procedural limitations' in Closa, C., and

Kochenov, D. (eds.), *Reinforcing Rule of Law Oversight in the European Union* (Cambridge University Press, 2016), pp. 15–35

Conant, L., 'Compelling criteria? Human rights in the European Union', *Journal of European Public Policy*, 21(5), 713–29.

Coppel, J., and O'Neill, A., 'The European Court of Justice: taking rights seriously?' *Common Market Law Review*, 29 (1992), 669–92.

Costa, J.-P., 'On the legitimacy of the European Court of Human Rights' judgments', *European Constitutional Law Review*, 7 (2011), 173–82.

Costello, C., 'Article 33: Family and Professional Life' in Peers, S., Hervey, T., Kenner, J., and Ward, A. (eds.), *The EU Charter of Fundamental Rights: A Commentary* (Oxford: Hart, 2014), pp. 891–925.

'The Bosphorus Ruling of the European Court of Human Rights: fundamental rights and blurred boundaries in Europe', *Human Rights Law Review*, 6 (2006), 87–130.

Council of Europe, *Highlights 2015* (Strasbourg: Council of Europe, 2016).

Craig, P., 'Article 41: Right to Good Administration' in Peers, S., Hervey, T., Kenner, J., and Ward, A. (eds.), *The EU Charter of Fundamental Rights: A Commentary* (Oxford: Hart, 2014), pp. 1069–98.

'The ECJ and ultra vires action: a conceptual analysis', *Common Market Law Review*, 48 (2011), 395–437.

Craufurd Smith, R., 'Article 22: Cultural, Religious and Linguistic Diversity' in Peers, S., Hervey, T., Kenner, J., and Ward, A. (eds.), *The EU Charter of Fundamental Rights: A Commentary* (Oxford: Hart, 2014), pp. 605–31.

Cruft, R., Matthew Liao, S., and Renzo, M., 'The philosophical foundations of human rights: an overview' in Cruft, R., Matthew Liao, S., and Renzo, M. (eds.), *Philosophical Foundations of Human Rights* (Oxford University Press, 2015), pp. 1–41.

Cullen, H., 'The collective complaints system of the European Social Charter: interpretative methods of the European Committee of Social Rights', *Human Rights Law Review*, 9 (2009), 61–93.

Curtin, D., and Mendes, J., 'Article 42: Right of Access to Documents' in Peers, S., Hervey, T., Kenner, J., and Ward, A. (eds.), *The EU Charter of Fundamental Rights: A Commentary* (Oxford: Hart, 2014), pp. 1099–119.

Curtin, D., and van Ooik, R., 'The sting is always in the tail: the personal scope of application of the EU Charter of Fundamental Rights', *Maastricht Journal*, 8 (2001), 102–14.

Dahlberg, M., 'Should social rights be included in interpretations of the convention by the European Court of Human Rights?' *European Journal of Social Security*, 16 (2014), 252–76.

Dauses, M. A., 'The protection of fundamental rights in the community legal order', *European Law Review*, 10 (1985), 398–419.

Davies, G., 'Legislative control of the European Court of Justice', *Common Market Law Review*, 51(6) (2014), 1579–607.

De Búrca, G., 'After the EU Charter of Fundamental Rights: The Court of Justice as a human rights adjudicator?' *Maastricht Journal*, 20 (2013), 168–84.

'Europe's Raison d'Etre', NYU Public Law and Legal Theory Research Paper No. 13-09, http://ssrn.com/abstract=2224310.

'The drafting of the European Union Charter of Fundamental Rights', *European Law Review*, 26 (2001), 126–38.

'The ECJ and the international legal order: a re-evaluation' in de Búrca, G., and Weiler, J. (eds.), *The Worlds of European Constitutionalism* (Cambridge University Press, 2011), pp. 105–49.

'The evolution of EU human rights law' in Craig, P., and de Búrca, G., *The Evolution of EU Law* (Oxford University Press, 2nd edn., 2011), pp. 465–97.

De Londras, F., 'Dual functionality and the persistent frailty of the European Court of Human Rights', *European Human Rights Law Review*, (2013), 38–46.

De Londras, F., and Dzehtsiarou, K., 'Managing judicial innovation in the European Court of Human Rights', *Human Rights Law Review*, 15 (2015), 523–47.

De Mol, M., '*Kücükdeveci: Mangold* revisited – horizontal effect of a general principle of EU law', *European Constitutional Law Review*, 6 (2010), 293–308.

De Schoutheete, P., 'The European Council' in Peterson, J., and Shackleton, M. (eds.), *The Institutions of the European Union* (Oxford University Press, 3rd edn., 2012), 43–67.

De Schutter, O., and De Jesus Butler, I., 'Binding the EU to international human rights law', *Yearbook of European Law*, 27 (2008), 277–320.

De Vries, S. A., 'The protection of fundamental rights within Europe's internal market after Lisbon – an endeavour for more harmony' in de Vries S. et al. (eds.), *The Protection of Fundamental Rights in the EU after Lisbon* (Oxford: Hart, 2013), pp. 59–94.

De Wet, E., *The International Constitutional Order* (Amsterdam: Vossiuspers UvA, 2005).

De Witte, B., 'Article 53 – Level of Protection' in Peers, S., Hervey, T., Kenner, J., and Ward, A. (eds.), *The EU Charter of Fundamental Rights: A Commentary* (Oxford: Hart, 2014), pp. 1523–38.

'The legal status of the Charter: vital question or non-issue?' *Maastricht Journal of European and Comparative*, 8 (2001), 81–9.

'The past and future role of the European Court of Justice in the protection of human rights' in Alston, P. et al. (eds.), *The EU and Human Rights* (Oxford University Press, 1999), pp. 859–97.

Den Boer, M., and Monar, J., 'Keynote article: 11 September and the challenge of global terrorism to the EU as a security actor', *JCMS: Journal of Common Market Studies*, 40(1), 11–28.

Den Heijer, M., 'Article 18: Right to Asylum' in Peers, S., Hervey, T., Kenner, J., and Ward, A. (eds.), *The EU Charter of Fundamental Rights: A Commentary* (Oxford: Hart, 2014), pp. 519–41.

Denza, E., 'Article 46: Diplomatic and Consular Protection' in Peers, S., Hervey, T., Kenner, J., and Ward, A. (eds.), *The EU Charter of Fundamental Rights: A Commentary* (Oxford: Hart, 2014), pp. 1177–95.

Devroe, W., and Van Cleynenbreughel, P., 'The impact of general principles of EU law on private law relationships' in Hartkamp, A. S. et al. (eds.), *The Influence of EU Law on National Private Law* (Alphen aan den Rijn: Wolters Kluwer, 2014), pp. 187–218.

Diggelmann, O., and Altwicker, T., 'Is there something like a constitution of international law?' *Zeitschrift für Ausländisches Öffentliches Recht und Völkerrecht*, 68 (2008), 623–50.

Dobner, P., and Loughlin, M. (eds.), *The Twilight of Constitutionalism* (Oxford University Press, 2010).

Dörr, O., 'Commissioner for Human Rights' in Schmahl, S., and Breuer, M. (eds.), *The Council of Europe: Its Law and Policies* (Oxford University Press, 2017), pp. 296–313.

O. Dörr, 'European Social Charter' in Schmahl, S., and Breuer, M. (eds.), *The Council of Europe: Its Law and Policies* (Oxford University Press, 2017), pp. 507–41.

Dorssemont, F., 'Article 12(1): Freedom of Assembly and of Association' in Peers, S., Hervey, T., Kenner, J., and Ward, A. (eds.), *The EU Charter of Fundamental Rights: A Commentary* (Oxford: Hart, 2014), pp. 341–77.

'Article 27: Workers' Right to Information and Consultation within the Undertaking' in Peers, S., Hervey, T., Kenner, J., and Ward, A. (eds.), *The EU Charter of Fundamental Rights: A Commentary* (Oxford: Hart, 2014), pp. 749–71.

Dossow, R., 'Cultural Co-operation' in Kleinsorge, T. (ed.), *Council of Europe (CoE)* (Alphen aan den Rijn: Wolters Kluwer, 2nd edn., 2015), pp. 194–201.

Dougan, M., 'The Treaty of Lisbon 2007: winning minds, not hearts', *Common Market Law Review*, 45 (2008), 617–703.

Douglas-Scott, 'The European Union and human rights after the Treaty of Lisbon', *Human Rights Law Review*, 11 (2011), 645–82.

Drzemczewski, A., 'Core monitoring mechanisms and related activities' in Schmahl, S., and Breuer, M. (eds.), *The Council of Europe: Its Law and Policies* (Oxford University Press, 2017), pp. 617–35

'Ensuring compatibility of domestic law with the European Convention on Human Rights prior to ratification: the Hungarian model', *Human Rights Law Journal*, 16 (1995), 241–60.

'The Council of Europe's co-operation and assistance programmes with central and eastern Europe in the human rights field: 1990 to September 1993', *Human Rights Law Journal*, 14 (1993), 229–48.

'The European Human Rights Convention: a new court of human rights in Strasbourg as of November 1, 1998', *Washington and Lee Law Review*, 55 (1998), 697–736.

Dupré, C., 'Article 1: Human Dignity' Peers, S., Hervey, T., Kenner, J., and Ward, A. (eds.), *The EU Charter of Fundamental Rights: A Commentary* (Oxford: Hart, 2014), pp. 3–24.

Dürr, R., 'The Venice Commission' in Kleinsorge, T. (ed.), *Council of Europe (CoE)* (Alphen aan den Rijn: Wolters Kluwer, 2nd edn., 2015), pp. 156–69.

Dzehtsiarou, K., *European Consensus and the Legitimacy of the European Court of Human Rights* (Cambridge University Press, 2015).

Dzehtsiarou, K., and Greene, A., 'Restructuring the European Court of Human Rights: preserving the right of individual petition and promoting constitutionalism', *Public Law*, (2013), pp. 710–19.

Dzehtsiarou, K., and O'Meara, N., 'Advisory jurisdiction and the European Court of Human Rights: a magic bullet for dialogue and docket control?' *Legal Studies*, 34 (2014), 444–68.

Eckes, C., 'Does the European Court of Human Rights provide protection from the European Community? – the case of Bosphorus Airways', *European Public Law*, 13 (2007), 47–67.

Egeberg, M., and Trondal, J., 'Differentiated integration in Europe: the case of EEA country, Norway', *JCMS: Journal of Common Market Studies*, 37(1) (1999), 113–42.

Egli, P., 'Protocol No. 14 to the European Convention for the Protection of Human Rights and Fundamental Freedoms: towards a more effective control mechanism?' *Journal of Transnational Law and Policy*, 17(1) (2007), 1–32.

Eissen, M.-A., 'The principle of proportionality in the case-law of the European Court of Human Rights' in Macdonald, R. J. et al. (eds.), *European System*, pp. 125–46.

Ellis, E., and Watson, P., *EU Anti-Discrimination Law* (Oxford University Press, 2nd edn., 2013).

Eriksen, E. O., *The Unfinished Democratization of Europe* (Oxford University Press, new edn., 2009).

'Why a Charter of Fundamental Human Rights in the EU?' *Ratio Juris*, 16(3) (2003), 352–73.

Evans, M. D., 'Getting to grips with torture', *International and Comparative Law Quarterly*, 51 (2002), 365–83.

Religious Liberty and International Law in Europe (Cambridge University Press, 1997).

Evans, M. D., and Morgan, R., *Preventing Torture: A Study of the European Convention for the Prevention of Torture and Inhuman and Degrading Treatment or Punishment* (Oxford: Clarendon Press, 1998).

Everson, M., and Correia Gonçalves, R., 'Article 16: Freedom to Conduct a Business' in Peers, S., Hervey, T., Kenner, J., and Ward, A. (eds.), *The EU Charter of Fundamental Rights: A Commentary* (Oxford: Hart, 2014), pp. 437–63.

Fabbrini, F., *Fundamental Rights in Europe: Challenges and Transformations in Comparative Perspective* (Oxford University Press, 2014).

Ferraro, F., and Carmona, J., *Fundamental Rights in the European Union: The Role of the Charter after the Lisbon Treaty* (European Union: European Parliament Research Service, 2015).

Fierro, E., *The EU's Approach to Human Rights Conditionality in Practice* (The Hague: Martinus Nijhoff, 2003).

Fischer, H., Lorion, S., and Ulrich, G., *Beyond Activism: The Impact of the Resolutions and Other Activities of the European Parliament in the Field of Human Rights outside the European Union* (Venice: Marsilio, 2007).

Føllesdal, A., 'Much ado about nothing? International judicial review of human rights in well-functioning democracies' in Føllesdal, A., Schaffer, J., and Ulfstein, G. (eds.), *The Legitimacy of International Human Rights Regimes: Legal, Political and Philosophical Perspectives* (Cambridge University Press, 2014), pp. 272–99.

'The legitimacy of international human rights review: the case of the European Court of Human Rights', *Journal of Social Philosophy*, 40 (2009), 595–607.

Føllesdal, A., Peters, B., and Ulfstein, G., 'Conclusions' in Føllesdal, A., Peters, B., and Ulfstein, G. (eds.), *Constituting Europe: The European Court of Human Rights in a National, European and Global Context* (Cambridge University Press, 2013), pp. 389–402.

Føllesdal, A., Schaffer, J., and Ulfstein, G. (eds.), *The Legitimacy of International Human Rights Regimes: Legal, Political and Philosophical Perspectives* (Cambridge University Press, 2014).

Fornasier, M., 'The impact of EU fundamental rights on private relationships: direct or indirect effect?' *European Review of Public Law*, (2015), 29–46.

Fouwels, M., 'The European Union's common foreign and security policy and human rights', *Netherlands Quarterly of Human Rights*, 15(3) (1997), 291–324.

Franck, T., 'Why a quest for legitimacy', *UC Davis Law Review*, 21 (1987), 535–47.

Fraser, J., 'Conclusion: The European Convention on Human Rights as a common European endeavour' in Flogaitis, S., Zwart, Z., and Fraser, J. (eds.), *The European Court of Human Rights and Its Discontents: Turning Criticism into Strength* (Cheltenham, UK: Edward Elgar, 2013), pp. 192–210.

Furtado, C. F., 'Guess who's coming to dinner? Protection for national minorities in the eastern and central Europe under the Council of Europe', *Columbia Human Rights Law Review*, 34 (2002–3), 333–411.

Fuster, G. G., *The Emergence of Personal Data Protection as a Fundamental Right of the EU* (Cham, Switzerland: Springer, 2014).

Galbreath, D., *The Organization for Security and Co-Operation in Europe* (Routledge, 2007).

Garben, S., 'The constitutional (im)balance between "the market" and "the social" in the European Union', *European Constitutional Law Review*, 13 (2017), 23–61.

Gearty, C., 'Democracy and human rights in the European Court of Human Rights: a critical appraisal', *Northern Ireland Legal Quarterly*, 51 (2000), 381–96.

Gerards, J. H., 'Inadmissibility decisions of the European Court of Human Rights: a critique of the lack of reasoning', *Human Rights Law Review*, 14 (2014), 148–58.

'Pluralism: Deference and the Margin of Appreciation Doctrine', *European Law Journal*, 17 (2011), 80–120.

'The discrimination grounds of Article 14 ECHR', *Human Rights Law Review*, 13 (2013), 99–124.

'The prism of fundamental rights', *European Constitutional Law Review*, 8 (2012), 173–202.

'Who decides on fundamental rights issues in Europe?' in Weatherill, S., and de Vries, S. (eds.), *Five Years Legally Binding EU Charter of Fundamental Rights* (Oxford: Hart, 2015), pp. 47–74.

Gerards, J. H., and Terlouw, A., 'Solutions for the European Court of Human Rights: the Amicus Curiae project' in Flogaitis, S., Zwart, Z., and Fraser, J. (eds.), *The European Court of Human Rights and Its Discontents: Turning Criticism into Strength* (Cheltenham, UK: Edward Elgar, 2013), pp. 158–82.

Glas, L., 'Changes in the procedural practice of the European Court of Human Rights: consequences for the convention system and lessons to be drawn', *Human Rights Law Review*, 14 (2014), 671–99.

The Theory, Potential and Practice of Procedural Dialogue in the European Convention on Human Rights System (Cambridge: Intersentia, 2016).

Glendon, M. A., 'Knowing the Universal Declaration of Human Rights', *Notre Dame Law Review*, 73 (1998), 1153–90.

Goldoni, M., 'Constitutional pluralism and the question of the European common good', *European Law Journal*, 18 (2012), 385–406.

Goldston, J., 'Achievements and challenges: insights from the Strasbourg experience for other international courts', *European Human Rights Law Review*, (2009), 603–10.

Gordillo, L., *Interlocking Constitutions: Towards and Interordinal Theory of National, European and UN Law* (Oxford: Hart, 2012).

Gori, G., 'Article 14: Right to Education' in Peers, S., Hervey, T., Kenner, J., and Ward, A. (eds.), *The EU Charter of Fundamental Rights: A Commentary* (Oxford: Hart, 2014), pp. 401–22.

Grabenwarter, C., 'Constitutional standard-setting and strengthening of new democracies' in Schmahl, S., and Breuer, M. (eds.), *The Council of Europe: Its Law and Policies* (Oxford University Press, 2017), pp. 732–46.

Gragl, P., *The Accession of the European Union to the European Convention on Human Rights* (Oxford: Hart, 2013).

Greer, S., 'Being 'realistic' about human rights?' *Northern Ireland Legal Quarterly*, 60 (2009), 145–61.

'Is the prohibition against torture, cruel, inhuman or degrading treatment really "absolute" in international human rights law', *Human Rights Law Review*, 15 (2015), 101–37.

'Protocol 14 and the Future of the European Court of Human Rights', *Public Law*, (2005), 83–106.

'Reforming the European Convention on Human Rights: towards Protocol 14', *Public Law*, (1993), 663–73.

'Should police threats to torture suspects always be severely punished? Reflections on the Gäfgen case', *Human Rights Law Review*, 11 (2011), 67–89.

The European Convention on Human Rights: Achievements, Problems and Prospects (Cambridge University Press, 2006).

The Exceptions to Articles 8 to 11 of the European Convention on Human Rights (Strasbourg: Council of Europe Publishing, Human Rights Files No. 15, 1997).

The Margin of Appreciation: Interpretation and Discretion under the European Convention on Human Rights (Strasbourg: Council of Europe Publishing, Human Rights Files No. 17, 2000).

'Universalism and relativism in the protection of human rights in Europe' in P. Agha (ed.) *Human Rights between Law and Politics* (Oxford: Hart, 2017), pp. 17–36.

Greer, S., and Slowe, R., 'The Conservatives' proposals for a British Bill of Rights: mired in muddle, misconception and misrepresentation?' *European Human Rights Law Review*, (2015), 370–83.

Greer, S., and Wildhaber, L., 'Revisiting the debate about "consitutionalising" the European Court of Human Rights', *Human Rights Law Review*, 12 (2012), 655–87.

Greer, S., and Wildhaber, L., 'Reflections of a former president of the European Court of Human Rights', *European Human Rights Law Review*, (2010), 165–75.

Greer, S., and Wylde, F., 'Has the European Court of Human Rights become a "small claims tribunal" and why, if at all, does it matter?' *European Human Rights Law Review*, (2017), 146–55.

Gribnau, J., 'Legitimacy of the judiciary', *Electronic Journal of Comparative Law*, 6 (2002), www.ejcl.org/64/art64-3.html.

Grief, N., 'Non discrimination under the European Convention on Human Rights: a critique of the United Kingdom government's refusal to sign and ratify Protocol 12', *European Law Review*, 27 (2002), 3–18.

Groenendijk, K., 'Article 40: Right to Vote and Stand as a Candidate at Municipal Elections' in Peers, S., Hervey, T., Kenner, J., and Ward, A. (eds.), *The EU Charter of Fundamental Rights: A Commentary* (Oxford: Hart, 2014), pp. 1057–67.

Groussot, X., 'Constitutional dialogues, pluralism and conflicting identities' in Avbelj, M., and Komárek, J. (eds.), *Constitutional Pluralism in the European Union and Beyond* (Oxford: Hart, 2012), pp. 319–41.

Groussot, X., Arold Lorenz, N. L., and Thor Petursson, G., 'The paradox of human rights protection in Europe: two courts, one goal?' in Mjöll Arnardóttir, O., and Buyse, A. (eds.), *Shifting Centres of Gravity in Human Rights Protection: Rethinking Relations between the ECHR, EU and National Legal Orders* (London: Routledge, 2016), pp. 8–25.

Groussot, X., Lock, T., and Pech, L., 'EU accession to the European Convention on Human Rights: a legal assessment of the Draft Accession Agreement of 14th October 2011', *European Issues* No. 218, 7 November 2011.

Groussot, X., Lock, T., and Petursson, G. T., 'The reach of EU fundamental rights on member state action after Lisbon' in de Vries, S. et al. (eds.), *The Protection of Fundamental Rights in the EU After Lisbon* (Oxford: Hart, 2013), pp. 97–118.

Groussot, X., and Pech, L., 'Fundamental rights protection in the European Union post Lisbon Treaty', *Policy Papers of the Foundation Robert Schuman (European Issue)*, 173 (2010).

Guild, E., 'Article 19: Protection in the Event of Removal' in Peers, S., Hervey, T., Kenner, J., and Ward, A. (eds.), *The EU Charter of Fundamental Rights: A Commentary* (Oxford: Hart, 2014), pp. 543–62.

Guðmundsdóttir, D., 'A renewed emphasis on the charter's distinction between rights and principles: is a doctrine of judicial restraint more appropriate?, *Common Market Law Review*, 52 (2015), 685–720.

Hagemann, S., 'Strength in numbers? An evaluation of the 2004–2009 European Parliament', *European Policy Centre Issue Paper*, 58 (2009).

Halberstam, D., 'Local, global and plural constitutionalism: Europe meets the world' in de Búrca, G., and Weiler, J. (eds.), *The Worlds of European Constitutionalism* (Cambridge University Press, 2011), pp. 150–202.

Harby, C., 'The changing nature of interim measures before the European Court of Human Rights', *European Human Rights Law*, (2010), 73–84.

Harden, I., 'Article 43: European Ombudsman' in Peers, S., Hervey, T., Kenner, J., and Ward, A. (eds.), *The EU Charter of Fundamental Rights: A Commentary* (Oxford: Hart, 2014), pp. 1121–50.

Harmsen, R., 'The European Convention on Human Rights after enlargement', *International Journal of Human Rights*, 5 (2001), 18–43.

Harper, J. L., 'In their own image – The Americans and the question of European unity, 1943–1954' in Bond, M., Smith, J., and Wallace, W. (eds.), *Eminent Europeans* (London; The Greycoat Press, 1996), pp. 62–84.

Harris, D., O'Boyle, M., Bates, E., and Buckley, C., *Harris, O'Boyle and Warbrick: Law of the European Convention on Human Rights* (Oxford University Press, 2009).

  Harris, O'Boyle and Warbrick: Law of the European Convention on Human Rights (Oxford University Press, 3rd edn., 2014).

Harris, D, J., O'Boyle, M., and Warbrick, C., *Law of the European Convention on Human Rights* (London: Butterworths, 1995).

Harris, D., and Darcy, J., *The European Social Charter* (Ardsley: Transnational, 2nd edn., 2000).

Hartkamp, A. S., 'The concept of (direct and indirect) horizontal effect of EU law' in Bernitz, U., Groussot, X., and Schulyok, F. (eds.), *General Principles of EU Law and European Private Law* (Alphen aan den Rijn: Wolters Kluwer, 2013) 189–97.

Heidbreder, E. G., *The Impact of Expansion on EU Institutions: The Eastern Touch on Brussels* (New York: Palgrave Macmillan, 2011).

Helfer, L., 'Redesigning the European Court of Human Rights: embeddedness as a deep structural principle of the European human rights regime', *European Journal of International Law*, 19 (2008), 125–59.

  'The burdens and benefits of Brighton', *European Society of International Law Reflections*, 1 (2012), http://esil-sedi.eu/node/138.

Helfer, L., and Slaughter, A.-M., 'Toward a theory of effective supranational adjudication', *Yale Law Journal*, 107 (1997), 273–392.

Heliskoski, J., 'Fundamental rights versus economic freedoms in the European Union: which paradigm?' in Klabbers, J., and Petman, J. (eds.), *Nordic Cosmopolitism: Essays in International Law for Martti Koskenniemi* (Martinus Nijhoff, 2003), pp. 417–43.

Hennette-Vauchez, S., 'Constitutional v international: when unified reformatory rationales mismatch the plural paths of legitimacy of ECHR law' in Christoffersen, J., and Madsen, M. (eds.), *The European Court of Human Rights between Law and Politics* (Oxford: Oxford University Press, 2011), pp. 144–63.

Heringa, A. W., and Verhey, L. F. M., 'The EU Charter: text and structure', *Maastricht Journal*, 8 (2001), 11–32.

Hervey, T. K., and Kenner, J., *Economic and Social Rights under the EU Charter of Fundamental Rights: A Legal Perspective* (Oxford: Hart, 2006).

Hervey, T. K., and McHale, J., 'Article 35: Health Care' in Peers, S., Hervey, T., Kenner, J., and Ward, A. (eds.), *The EU Charter of Fundamental Rights: A Commentary* (Oxford: Hart, 2014), pp. 951–68.

Hill, D. M., 'Human rights and foreign policy: theoretical foundations' in Hill, D. M. (ed.), *Human Rights and Foreign Policy: Theoretical Foundations* (Basingstoke: Macmillan, 1989), 3–20.

Hillebrecht, C., *Domestic Politics and International Human Rights Tribunals* (Cambridge University Press, 2014).

'The power of human rights tribunals: compliance with the European Court of Human Rights and domestic policy change', *European Journal of International Relations*, 20 (2014), 1100–23.

Hillion, C., 'Enlarging the European Union and deepening its fundamental rights protection', *SIEPS European Policy Analysis*, 11 (2013), pp. 1–16.

Hioureas, C., 'Behind the scenes of Protocol No. 14: politics in reforming the European Court of Human Rights', *Berkeley Journal of International Law*, 24 (2) (2006), 718–57.

Hirsch-Ziembińska, M., 'In Pursuit of Good Administration' (European Conference, Strasbourg, 10 January 2008) DA/ba/Conf (2007).

Hoffmeister, F., 'Cyprus v. Turkey. App.No. 25781/94. At www.echr.coe.int/Eng/Judgments.htm. European Court of Human Rights, Grand Chamber, May 10, 2001', *American Journal of International Law*, 96 (2002), 445–52.

Hofman, H. C. H., and Mihaescu, B. C., 'The relation between the charter's fundamental rights and the unwritten general principles of EU law: good administration as the test case', *European Constitutional Law Review*, 9 (2013), 86–101.

Hogan, G., 'The right to life and the abortion question under the European Convention on Human Rights' in Heffernan, L., with Kingston, J. (eds.), *Human Rights: A European Perspective* (Blackrock: Round Hall Press, 1994), pp. 104–16.

Hovius, B., 'The limitation clauses of the European Convention on Human Rights: a guide for the application of Section 1 of the charter?' *Ottowa Law Review*, 17 (1985), 213–61.

Huber, D., *A Decade Which Made History: The Council of Europe 1989–1999* (Strasbourg: Council of Europe Publishing, 1999).

Hurrell, A., *On Global Order: Power, Values and the Constitution of International Society* (Oxford University Press, 2007).

Hutchinson, M. R., 'The margin of appreciation doctrine in the European Court of Human Rights', *International and Comparative Law Quarterly*, 48 (1999), 638–50.

Ionescu, G., *The New Politics of European Integration* (London: Macmillan, 1972).

Jackson Preece, J., *Minority Rights* (Cambridge: Polity Press, 2005).
   National Minorities and the European Nation-States System (Oxford: Clarendon Press, 1998).
Jacobs, F. G., 'Human rights in the European Union: the role of the Court of Justice', *European Law Review*, 26 (2001), 331–41.
   'The "limitation clauses" of the European Convention on Human Rights' in de Mestral, A., Birks, S., Bothe, M., Cotler, I., Klinck, D., and Morel, A. (eds.), *The Limitation of Human Rights in Comparative Constitutional Law* (Cowansville: Les Éditions Yvon Blais Inc., 1986), pp. 21–40.
Jacqué, J. P., 'The explanations relating to the Charter of Fundamental Rights of the European Union' in Peers, S., Hervey, T., Kenner, J., and Ward, A. (eds.), *The EU Charter of Fundamental Rights: A Commentary* (Oxford: Hart, 2014), pp. 1715–24.
Jaklic, K., *Constitutional Pluralism in the EU* (Oxford University Press, 2014).
Jones, T. H., 'The devaluation of human rights under the European Convention', *Public Law*, (1995), 430–49.
Jowell, J., 'The Venice Commission: disseminating democracy through law', *Public Law*, (2001), 675–83.
Judt, T., *Postwar: A History of Europe since 1945* (London: Pimlico, 2005).
Kamminga, M. T., 'Is the European Convention on Human Rights sufficiently equipped to cope with gross and systematic violations?' *Netherlands Quarterly of Human Rights*, 12 (1994), 153–64.
Keller, H., and Stone Sweet, A. (eds.), *A Europe of Rights: The Impact of the ECHR on National Legal Systems* (Oxford University Press, 2008).
Kenner, J., 'Article 30: Protection in the Event of Unjustified Dismissal' in Peers, S., Hervey, T., Kenner, J., and Ward, A. (eds.), *The EU Charter of Fundamental Rights: A Commentary* (Oxford: Hart, 2014), pp. 805–32.
Kerr, Lord., 'The need for dialogue between national courts and the European Court of Human Rights' in Flogaitis, S., Zwart, T., and Fraser, J. (eds.), *The European Court of Human Rights and Its Discontents: Turning Criticism into Strength* (Edward Elgar, 2013), pp. 104–34.
Khadar, L., and Shaw, J., 'Article 39: Right to Vote and Stand as a Candidate at Elections to the European Parliament' in Peers, S., Hervey, T., Kenner, J., and Ward, A. (eds.), *The EU Charter of Fundamental Rights: A Commentary* (Oxford: Hart, 2014), pp. 1027–56.
Khan-Nisser, S., 'Conditionality, communication and compliance: the effect of monitoring on collective labour rights in candidate countries', *JCMS: Journal of Common Market Studies*, 51(6) (2013), 1040–56.
Kilpatrick, C., 'Article 21: Non-Discrimination' in Peers, S., Hervey, T., Kenner, J., and Ward, A. (eds.), *The EU Charter of Fundamental Rights: A Commentary* (Oxford: Hart, 2014), pp. 579–603.

Kinzelbach, K., 'The EU's human rights dialogues - talking to persuade or silencing the debate?' presented at the Kolleg-Forschergruppe (KFG) Conference: *The Transformative Power of Europe* at Freie Univesität Berlin, 10–11 December 2009).

The EU's Human Rights Dialogue with China: Quiet Diplomacy and Its Limits, vol. VII (Abingdon: Routledge, 2015).

Kitzinger, U. W., *The Politics and Economics of European Integration* (Westport, CT: Greenwood Press, 1963).

Klabbers, J., Peters, A., and Ulfstein, G., *The Constitutionalization of International Law* (Oxford University Press, 2009).

Kleinsorge, T., 'General overview' in Kleinsorge, T. (ed.), *Council of Europe (CoE)* (Alphen aan den Rijn: Wolters Kluwer, 2nd edn., 2015), pp. 71–4.

'The Parliamentary Assembly: Europe's motor and conscience' in Kleinsorge, T. (ed.), *Council of Europe (CoE)* (Alphen aan den Rijn: Wolters Kluwer, 2nd edn., 2015), pp. 75–95.

'The CoE's activities' in Kleinsorge, T. (ed.), *Council of Europe (CoE)* (Alphen aan den Rijn: Wolters Kluwer, 2nd edn., 2015), pp. 105–15.

Klerk, Y. S.,'Supervision of the execution of the judgments of the European Court of Human Rights—the Committee of Ministers' Role under Article 54 of the European Convention on Human Rights', *Netherlands International Law Review*, 45 (1998), 65–86.

Kochenov, D., and Pech, L. 'Monitoring and enforcement of the rule of law in the EU: rhetoric and reality', *European Constitutional Law Review*, 11(3) (2015), 512–40.

Kolb, R., 'The jurisprudence of the European Court of Human Rights on detention and fair trial in criminal matters from 1992 to the end of 1998', *Human Rights Law Journal*, 21 (2000), 348–73.

Kopecky, P., and Ucen, P., 'Return to Europe? Patterns of Euroscepticism among the Czech and Slovak political parties' in Rupnik, J., and Zielonka, J. (eds.), *The Road to the European Union. vol. I. The Czech and Slovak Republics* (Manchester University Press, 2003), 164–79.

Korkeakivi, A., updated by Altenhöner-Dion, C., 'The CoE and the protection of national minorities' in Kleinsorge, T. (ed.), *Council of Europe (CoE)* (Alphen aan den Rijn: Wolters Kluwer, 2nd edn., 2015), pp. 183–93.

Kosta, V, Skoutaris, N., and Tzevelekos, V. (eds.), *The EU Accession to the ECHR* (Oxford: Hart, 2014).

Kranenborg, H., 'Article 8: Protection of Personal Data' in Peers, S., Hervey, T., Kenner, J., and Ward, A. (eds.), *The EU Charter of Fundamental Rights: A Commentary* (Oxford: Hart, 2014), pp. 223–66.

Kratochvíl, J., 'The inflation of the margin of appreciation by the European Court of Human Rights', *Netherlands Quarterly of Human Rights*, 29 (2011) 324–57.

Krieger, H., 'The Conference of International Non-Governmental Organizations of the Council of Europe' in Schmahl, S., and Breuer, M. (eds.), *The Council of Europe: Its Law and Policies* (Oxford University Press, 2017), 314–44.

Krisch, N., *Beyond Constitutionalism: The Pluralist Structure of Postnational Law* (Oxford University Press, 2010).

'The case for pluralism in postnational law' in de Búrca, G., and Weiler, J. (eds.), *The Worlds of European Constitutionalism* (Cambridge University Press, 2011), pp. 203–61.

Krish, N., 'The open architecture of European human rights law', *Modern Law Review*, 71 (2008), 183–216.

Krommendijk, J., 'Principled silence or mere silence on principles?' *European Constitutional Law Review*, 11 (2015), 321–56.

'The use of European Court of Human Rights case law by the Court of Justice after Lisbon: the view of Luxembourg insiders', *Maastricht Journal*, 22 (2015), 812–35.

Kühling, J., 'Fundamental rights' in Von Bogdandy, A., and Bast, J. (eds.), *Principles of European Constitutional Law* (Oxford: Hart/C. H. Beck, 2nd rev. edn., 2010), pp. 479–514.

Kumm, M., 'The jurisprudence of constitutional conflict: constitutional supremacy in Europe before and after the constitutional treaty', *European Law Journal*, 11 (2005), 262–307.

Ladenburger, C., 'European Union institutional report' in Laffranque, J. (ed.), *The Protection of Fundamental Rights Post-Lisbon* (Tartu University Press, 2012), pp. 141–215.

Lambert-Abdelgawad, E., 'The Court as a part of the Council of Europe: the Parliamentary Assembly and the Committee of Ministers' in Føllesdal, A., Peters, B., and Ulfstein, G. (eds.), *Constituting Europe: The European Court of Human Rights in a National, European and Global Context* (Cambridge University Press, 2013), pp. 263–300.

The Execution of Judgments of the European Court of Human Rights (Strasbourg: Council of Europe Publishing, Human Rights Files No. 19, 2002).

Lambrecht, S., 'Chapter 19 – Assessing the existence of criticism of the European Court of Human Rights' in Popelier, P., Lambrecht, S., and Lemmens, K. (eds.), *Criticism of the European Court of Human Rights – Shifting the Convention System: Counter-Dynamics at the National and EU Level* (Cambridge: Intersentia, 2016), pp. 544–6.

Lamont, R., 'Article 24: The Rights of the Child' in Peers, S., Hervey, T., Kenner, J., and Ward, A. (eds.), *The EU Charter of Fundamental Rights: A Commentary* (Oxford: Hart, 2014), pp. 661–91.

Landau, E. C., 'New regime of human rights in the EU', *European Journal of Law Reform*, 10 (2008), 557–76.

Lautenbach, G., *The Concept of the Rule of Law and the European Court of Human Rights* (Oxford University Press, 2013).

Lavender, N., 'The problem of the margin of appreciation', *European Human Rights Law Review*, (1997), 380–90.

Leach, P., 'Access to the European Court of Human Rights – from a legal entitlement to a lottery?' *Human Rights Law Journal*, 27 (2006), 11–25.

'No longer offering fine mantras to a parched child? The European Court's developing approach to remedies' in Føllesdal, A., Peters, B., and Ulfstein, G. (eds.), *Constituting Europe: The European Court of Human Rights in a National, European and Global Context* (Cambridge University Press, 2013), pp. 142–80.

'On the reform of the European Court of Human Rights', *European Human Rights Law Review*, (2009), 725–35.

'The Parliamentary Assembly of the Council of Europe' in Schmahl, S., and Breuer, M. (eds.), *The Council of Europe: Its Law and Policies* (Oxford University Press, 2017), pp. 181–91.

Leach, P., Hardman, H., and Stephenson, S., 'Can the European Court's pilot judgment procedure help resolve systemic human rights violations? Burdov and the failure to implement domestic court decisions in Russia', *Human Rights Law Review*, 10(2) (2010), 346–59.

Leach, P., Hardman, H., Stephenson, S., and Blitz, B. K., *Responding to Systematic Human Rights Violations – An Analysis of 'Pilot Judgments' of the European Court of Human Rights and Their Impact at National Level* (Antwerp: Intersentia, 2010).

Leach, P., Paraskeva, C., and Uzelac, G., 'Human rights fact-finding: the European Court of Human Rights at the crossroads', *Netherlands Quarterly of Human Rights*, 28 (2010), 41–77.

Lebeck, C., 'The European Court of Human Rights on the relation between ECHR and EC-law: the limits of constitutionalisation of public international law', *Zeitschrift für Öffentliches Rectht*, 62 (2007), 195–236.

Leconte, C., 'The EU fundamental rights policy as a source of Euroscepticism', *Human Rights Review*, 15(1) (2014), 83–96.

Leconte, C., and Muir, E., 'Introduction to special issue "Understanding resistance to the EU fundamental rights policy"', *Human Rights Review*, 15(1) (2014), 1–12.

Leczykiewicz, D., 'Horizontal effect of fundamental rights: in search of social justice or private autonomy in EU law?' in Bernitz, U., Groussot, X., and Schulyok, F. (eds.), *General Principles of EU Law and European Private Law* (Alphen aan den Rijn: Wolters Kluwer, 2013), pp. 171–86.

Legg, A., *The Margin of Appreciation in International Human Rights Law: Deference and Proportionality* (Oxford University Press, 2012).

Leijten, A. E. M., *Core Rights and the Protection of Socio-Economic Interests by the European Court of Human Rights* (Meijers Research Institute and Graduate School of the Leiden Law School, Faculty of Law, Leiden University, 2015).

Lemmens, K., 'Chapter 2 – criticising the European Court of Human Rights or misunderstanting the dynamics of human rights protection?' in Popelier, P., Lambrecht, S., and Lemmens, K. (eds.), *Criticism of the European Court of Human Rights – Shifting the Convention System: Counter-Dynamics at the National and EU Level* (Cambridge: Intersentia, 2016), pp. 27–8.

Lemmens, P., 'The relation between the Charter of Fundamental Rights of the European Union and the European Convention on Human Rights – substantive aspects', *Maastricht Journal*, 8 (2001), 49–67.

Lenaerts, K., 'Exploring the limits of the EU Charter of Fundamental Rights', *European Constitutional Law Review*, 6 (2012), 375–403.

Lenaerts, K., and de Smijter, E., 'The charter and the role of the European courts', *Maastricht Journal*, 8 (2001), 90–101.

Letsas, G., 'Two concepts of the margin of appreciation', *Oxford Journal of Legal Studies*, 26 (2006), 705–32.

Lezertua, M., and Forde, A., updated by Sidaropoulos, N., 'The Commissioner for Human Rights' in Kleinsorge, T. (ed.), *Council of Europe (CoE)* (Alphen aan den Rijn: Wolters Kluwer, 2nd edn., 2015), pp. 116–23.

Liisberg, J. B., 'Does the EU Charter of Fundamental Rights threaten the supremacy of community law?' *Common Market Law Review*, 38 (2001), 1171–99.

Lindfeldt, M., 'Article 44: Right to Petition' in Peers, S., Hervey, T., Kenner, J., and Ward, A. (eds.), *The EU Charter of Fundamental Rights: A Commentary* (Oxford: Hart, 2014), pp. 1151–60.

Livingstone, S., 'Article 14 and the prevention of discrimination in the European Convention on Human Rights', *European Human Rights Law Review*, (1997), 25–34.

Lock, T., 'Beyond Bosphorus: The European Court of Human Rights case law on the responsibility of member states of international organisations under the European Convention on Human Rights', *Human Rights Law Review*, 10 (2010), 529–45.

'End of an epic? The draft agreement on the EU's accession to the ECHR', *Yearbook of European Law*, 31 (2012), 162–97.

'The future of EU accession to the ECHR after Opinion 2/13: is it still possible and is it still desirable?' *European Constitutional Law Review*, 11(2) (2015), 239–73.

Loewenstein, K., *Verfassungslehre* (Tübingen: J. C. B. Mohr, 1959).

Loucaides, L. G., 'The judgment of the European Court of Human Rights in the case of Cyprus v. Turkey', *Leiden Journal of International Law*, 15 (2002), 225–36.

Lovecy, J., 'Framing decisions in the Council of Europe: An institutional analysis' in Reinalda, B., and Verbeek, B. (eds.), *Decision Making within International Organizations* (London: Routledge, 2004), 59–73.

Lundestad, G., *"Empire" by Integration: The United States and European Integration, 1945–1997* (Oxford University Press, 1998).

MacMullen, A., 'Intergovernmental functionalism? The Council of Europe in European integration', *Journal of European Integration*, 26 (2004), 405–29.

Madsen, M., 'From Cold War instrument to supreme European court: the European Court of Human Rights at the crossroads of international and national law and politics', *Law and Social Inquiry*, 32 (2007), 137–59.

Maduro, M., 'Contrapuntal law: Europe's constitutional pluralism in Action' in Walker, N. (ed.), *Sovereignty in Transition* (Oxford: Hart, 2003), 502–37.

'Interpreting European law: judicial adjudication in a context of constitutional pluralism', *European Journal of Legal Studies*, 1 (2007) 2, 137–52.

We the Court (Oxford: Hart, 1998).

Mahoney, P., 'An Insider's View of the Reform Debate', paper presented at the *Symposium on the Reform of the European Court of Human Rights, Strasbourg,* 17 November 2003.

'Judicial Activism and Judicial Self-Restraint in the European Court of Human Rights: two sides of the same coin', *Human Rights Law Journal*, 11 (1990), 57–88.

'New Challenges for the European Court of Human Rights Resulting from Expanding Case Load and Membership', *Conference on Human Rights – Dynamic Dimension, London,* 27 April 2002.

'Speculating on the future of the reformed European Court of Human Rights', *Human Rights Law Journal*, 20 (1999), 1–4.

'The relationship between the Strasbourg court and the national courts', *Law Quarterly Review*, 130 (2014), 568–86.

'The European Court of Human Rights and its ever-growing caseload: preserving the mission of the Court while ensuring the viability of the individual petition' in Flogaitis, S., Mahoney, P., et al., 'The doctrine of the margin of appreciation under the European Convention on Human Rights: its legitimacy in theory and application in practice' (Council of Europe internal seminar), *Human Rights Law Journal*, 19 (1998), 1–36.

Mak, C., 'Unchart(er)ed territory – EU fundamental rights and national private law' in Hartkamp, A. S. et al. (eds.), *The Influence of EU Law on National Private Law* (Alphen aan den Rijn: Wolters Kluwer, 2014), pp. 323–53.

Malloy, T. E., *National Minority Rights in Europe* (Oxford University Press, 2005).

Manas, J. E., 'The Council of Europe's democracy ideal and the challenge of ethnonational strife' in Chayes, A., and Chayes, A. H. (eds.), *Preventing Conflict in the Post-Communist World – Mobilizing International and Regional*

Organizations (Washington, DC: Brookings Occasional Papers, Brookings Institution, 1996), pp. 99–144.

Manners, I. A., 'The normative ethics of the European Union', *International Affairs*, 84(1) (2008), 45–60.

Marks, S., 'The European Convention on Human Rights and its "democratic society"', *British Yearbook of International Law*, 66 (1995), 209–38.

Marston, G., 'The United Kingdom's part in the preparation of the European Convention on Human Rights 1950', *International and Comparative Law Quarterly*, 42 (1993), 796–826.

Martínez-Torrón, J., 'The European Court of Human Rights and religion', *Current Legal Issues*, (2001), 185–204.

Martinico, G., and Pollicino, O., *The Interaction between Europe's Legal Systems: Judicial Dialogue and the Creation of Supranational Laws* (Cheltenham, UK: Edward Elgar, 2012).

McBride, J., 'Proportionality and the European Convention on Human Rights' in Ellis, E. (ed.), *The Principle of Proportionality in the Laws of Europe* (Oxford: Hart, 1999), pp. 23–35.

McCormick, J., *Understanding the European Union: A Concise Introduction* (Basingstoke: Palgrave Macmillan, 6th edn., 2014).

McCrea, R., 'Article 10: Freedom of Thought, Conscience and Religion' in Peers, S., Hervey, T., Kenner, J., and Ward, A. (eds.), *The EU Charter of Fundamental Rights: A Commentary* (Oxford: Hart, 2014), pp. 291–309.

McHarg, A., 'Reconciling human rights and the public interest: conceptual problems and doctrinal uncertainty in the jurisprudence of the European Court of Human Rights', *Modern Law Review*, 62 (1999), 671–96.

Mendes, J., 'Good Administration in EU Law and the European Code of Good Administrative Behaviour', *EU Working Papers* 2009/09 (European University Institute, Florence, Department of Law).

Meron, T., and Sloan, J. S., 'Democracy, rule of law and admission to the Council of Europe', *Israel Yearbook on Human Rights*, 26 (1997).

Miara, L., and Prais, V., 'The role of civil society in the execution of judgments of the European Court of Human Rights', *European Human Rights Law Review*, (2012), 528–53.

Michalowski, S., 'Article 3: Right to the Integrity of the Person' in Peers, S., Hervey, T., Kenner, J., and Ward, A. (eds.), *The EU Charter of Fundamental Rights: A Commentary* (Oxford: Hart, 2014), pp. 39–60.

Mitsilegas, V., 'Article 49: Principles of Legality and Proportionality' in Peers, S., Hervey, T., Kenner, J., and Ward, A. (eds.), *The EU Charter of Fundamental Rights: A Commentary* (Oxford: Hart, 2014), pp. 1351–71.

Moravcsik, A., 'The origins of human rights regimes: democratic delegation in postwar Europe', *International Organisation*, 54 (2000), 217–52.

Moreham, N., 'The right to respect for private life in the European Convention on Human Rights: a re-examination', *European Human Rights Law Review*, (2008), 44–79.

Morgan, K., *Labour in Power* (Oxford: Clarendon Press, 1984).

Morgan, R., and Evans, M., *Combating Torture in Europe: The Work and Standards of the European Committee for the Prevention of Torture* (Strasbourg: Council of Europe, 2001).

Morgera, E., and Marín Durán, G., 'Environmental protection' in Peers, S., Hervey, T., Kenner, J., and Ward, A. (eds.), *The EU Charter of Fundamental Rights: A Commentary* (Oxford: Hart, 2014), pp. 983–1003.

Møse, E., 'New rights for the new Court?' in Mahoney, P., Matscher, F., Petzold, H., and Wildhaber, L. (eds.), *Protecting Human Rights: The European Perspective – Studies in Memory of Rolv Ryssdal* (Cologne: Carl Heymans, 2000), pp. 943–56.

Mowbray, A., 'An examination of the work of the Grand Chamber of the European Court of Human Rights', *Public Law*, (2007) 507–28.

'Proposals for reform of the European Court of Human Rights', *Public Law*, (2002), 252–64.

The Development of Positive Obligations under the European Convention on Human Rights by the European Court of Human Rights (Oxford: Hart, 2004).

'The Interlaken Declaration – The beginning of a new era for the European Court of Human Rights', *Human Rights Law Review*, 10 (2010), 519–28.

'The role of the European Court of Human Rights in the promotion of democracy', *Public Law*, (1999), 703–25.

Muir, E., 'The fundamental rights implications of EU legislation: some constitutional challenges', *Common Market Law Review*, 51(1) (2014), 219–45.

'The transformative function of EU equality law', *European Review of Public Law*, (2013), 1231–54.

Müller, J.-W., 'Safeguarding Democracy Inside the EU: Brussels and the Future of Liberal Order', *Transatlantic Academy 2012–2013 Paper Studies No. 3* (2013).

Murdoch, J., 'Tackling ill-treatment in places of detention: the work of the Council of Europe's "Torture Committee"', *European Journal of Criminal Policy and Research*, 12 (2006), 121–42.

'The impact of Europe's "Torture Committee" and the evolution of standard-setting in relation to places of detention', *European Human Rights Law Review*, (2006), 159–79.

Naert, F., 'Accountability for violations of human rights law by EU forces' in Blockmans, S. (ed.), *The European Union and Crisis Management: Policy and Legal Aspects* (The Hague: T. M. C. Asser Press, 2008), 375–93.

Napoli, D., 'The European Union's foreign policy and human rights' in Neuwahl, N. A., and Rosas, A. (eds.), *The European Union and Human Rights* (The Hague: Martinus Nijhoff, 1995), 297–312.

Nehl, H. P., 'Article 48: Presumption of Innocence and Right of Defence (Adminis-
trative Law)' in Peers, S., Hervey, T., Kenner, J., and Ward, A. (eds.), *The EU
Charter of Fundamental Rights: A Commentary* (Oxford: Hart, 2014),
pp. 1277–301.
Nicol, D., 'Original intent and the European Convention on Human Rights', *Public
Law*, (2005), 152–72.
Nolan, A., '"Aggravated violations", Roma housing rights and forced expulsions in
Italy: recent developments under the European Social Charter Collective
Complaints System', *European Human Rights Law Review*, 11 (2011), 343–6.
Novitz, T., 'Are social rights necessarily collective rights? A critical analysis of the
collective complaints protocol to the European Social Charter', *European
Human Rights Law Review*, (2002), 50–66.
 'Remedies for violation of social rights within the Council of Europe: the
significant absence of a court' in Kilpatrick, C., Novitz, T., and Skidmore,
P. (eds.), *The Future of Remedies in Europe* (Oxford: Hart, 2000),
pp. 231–51.
Nowak, M., 'The agency and national institutions for the promotion and protec-
tion of human rights' in Alston, P., and de Schutter, O. (eds.), *Monitoring
Fundamental Rights in the EU: The Contribution of the Fundamental Rights
Agency* (Oxford: Hart, 2005), 91–130.
Nowak, M., and Charbord, A., 'Article 4: Prohibition of Torture and Inhuman or
Degrading Treatment or Punishment' in Peers, S., Hervey, T., Kenner, J.,
and Ward, A. (eds.), *The EU Charter of Fundamental Rights: A Commentary*
(Oxford: Hart, 2014), pp. 61–99.
Nowak, T., 'Of garbage cans and rulings: judgments of the European Court of
Justice in the EU legislative process', *West European Politics*, 33(4) (2010),
753–69.
Nugent, N., *The Government and Politics of the European Union* (Basingstoke, UK:
Palgrave Macmillan, 7th edn., 2010).
Oeter, S., 'Conventions on the Protection of National Minorities' in Schmahl, S.,
and Breuer, M. (eds.), *The Council of Europe: Its Law and Policies* (Oxford
University Press, 2017), pp. 542–71.
O'Brien, C., 'Article 26: Integration of Persons with Disabilities' in Peers, S.,
Hervey, T., Kenner, J., and Ward, A. (eds.), *The EU Charter of Fundamental
Rights: A Commentary* (Oxford: Hart, 2014), pp. 709–48.
O'Cinneide, C., 'Article 25: The Rights of the Elderly' in Peers, S., Hervey, T.,
Kenner, J., and Ward, A. (eds.), *The EU Charter of Fundamental Rights:
A Commentary* (Oxford: Hart, 2014), pp. 693–708.
Odermatt, J., 'A giant step backwards? Opinion 2/13 on the EU's accession to the
European Convention on Human Rights', *New York University Journal of
Law and Politics*, 47 (2015), 783–98.

Ojanen, T., 'Making the essence of fundamental rights real: the Court of Justice of the European Union clarifies the structure of fundamental rights under the charter', *European Constitutional Law Review*, 12 (2016), 318–29.

Olsen, C., updated by Kleinsorge, T., 'Treaty-making in the CoE' in Kleinsorge, T. (ed.), *Council of Europe (CoE)* (Alphen aan den Rijn: Wolters Kluwer, 2nd edn., 2015), pp. 143–55.

Oomen, B., 'A serious case of Strasbourg-bashing? An evaluation of the debates on the legitimacy of human rights in the Netherlands', *International Journal of Human Rights*, 20 (2016), 407–25.

Ost, F., 'The original canons of interpretation of the European Court of Human Rights' in Delmas-Marty, M., and Chodkiewicz, C. (eds.), *The European Convention for the Protection of Human Rights: International Protection Versus National Restrictions* (Dortrecht: Martinus Nijhoff, 1992), pp. 238–318.

Palmer, S., 'The Committee of Ministers' in Schmahl, S., and Breuer, M. (eds.), *The Council of Europe: Its Law and Policies* (Oxford University Press, 2017), pp. 137–65.

Palmer, S., updated by Poirel, C., 'Committee of Ministers' in Kleinsorge, T. (ed.), *Council of Europe (CoE)* (Alphen aan den Rijn: Wolters Kluwer, 2nd edn., 2015), pp. 96–104.

Parry, R., 'History, human rights and multilingual citizenship: conceptualising the European Charter for Regional or Minority Languages', *Northern Ireland Legal Quarterly*, 61 (2010), 329–48.

Paulus, A., 'From implementation to translation: applying the European Court of Human Rights Judgments in the domestic legal orders' in Seibert-Fohr, A., and Villiger, M. (eds.), *Judgments of the European Court of Human Rights – Effects and Implementation* (Baden-Baden: Nomos/Ashgate, 2013), pp. 267–83.

Pedain, A., 'The human rights dimension of the Diane Pretty case', *Cambridge Law Journal*, 62 (2003), 181–206.

Peers, S., and Prechal, S., 'Article 52 – Scope and Interpretation of Rights and Principles' in Peers, S., Hervey, T., Kenner, J., and Ward, A. (eds.), *The EU Charter of Fundamental Rights: A Commentary* (Oxford: Hart, 2014), pp. 1455–521.

Peers, S., Hervey, T., Kenner, J., and Ward, A. (eds.), *The European Union Charter of Fundamental Rights* (Oxford: Hart, 2004).

Pentassuglia, G., 'Monitoring minority rights in Europe: the implementation machinery of the Framework Convention for the Protection of National Minorities – with special reference to the role of the advisory committee', *International Journal on Minority and Group Rights*, 6 (1991), 417–61.

Pescatore, P., 'Fundamental rights and the system of the European communities', *American Journal of Comparative Law*, 18 (1970), 343–51.

Petaux, J., *Democracy and Human Rights for Europe: The Council of Europe's Contribution* (Strasbourg: Council of Europe Publications, 2009).

Peterson, J., and Shackleton, M., *The Institutions of the European Union* (Oxford University Press, 3rd edn., 2012).

Petzold, H., "The convention and the principle of subsidiarity" in Macdonald, R. St. J., Matscher, F., and Petzold, H. (eds.), *The European System for the Protection of Human Rights* (Dortrecht: Martinus Nijhoff, 1993), pp. 41–62.

Phillips, A., 'The 10th anniversary of the Framework Convention for the Protection of National Minorities', *Euopäiasches Journal für Minderheitenfragen*, 3 (2008), 181–9.

Polakiewicz, J., 'The European Union and the Council of Europe – Competition or Coherence in Fundamental Rights Protection in Europe?' *Jean Monnet Conference*, 27–28 May 2008.

Popelier, P., Van de Heyning, C., and Van Nuffel, P. (eds.), *Human Rights Protection in the European Legal Order: The Between the European and the National Courts* (Cambridge: Intersentia, 2011).

Popovic, D., 'Prevailing of judicial activism over self-restraint in the jurisprudence of the European Court of Human Rights', *Creighton Law Review*, 42 (2009), 361–96.

Portela, C., and Orbie, J., 'Sanctions under the EU generalised system of preferences and foreign policy: coherence by accident?' *Contemporary Politics*, 20 (1) (2014), 63–76.

Portela, C., and Vennesson, P., 'Sanctions and embargos in EU-Asia relations' in Christiansen, T., Kirchner, E., and Murray, P. (eds.), *The Palgrave Handbook of EU-Asia Relations* (Basingstoke, UK: Palgrave MacMillan, 2013), 198–210.

Prebensen, S. C., 'Inter-state complaints under treaty provisions – the experience under the European Convention on Human Rights', *Human Rights Law Journal*, 20 (1999), 446–55.

'Evolutive interpretation of the European Convention on Human Rights' in Mahoney, P., Matscher, F., Petzold, H., and Wildhaber, L. (eds.), *Protecting Human Rights: The European Perspective – Studies in Memory of Rolv Ryssdal* (Cologne: Carl Heymans, 2000), pp. 1123–37.

Prechal, S., 'Competence creep and general principles of law', *Review of European Administrative Law*, 3 (2010), 5–22.

Prechal, S., de Vries, S., and van Eijken, H., 'The principle of attributed powers and the "scope of EU law"' in Besselink, L., et al. (eds.), *The Eclipse of the Legality Principle in the European Union* (Kluwer Law International, 2010), pp. 213–47.

Prodi, R., 'A wider Europe: a proximity policy as the key to stability', speech to the Sixth ECSA World Conference in Brussels, 5–6 December 2002 (SPEECH/02/619).

Provost, R., 'Teetering on the edge of legal nihilism: Russia and the evolving European human rights regime', *Human Rights Quarterly*, 37 (2015), 289–40.

Rainey, B., Wicks, E., and Ovey, C., *Jacobs, White and Ovey: The European Convention on Human Rights* (Oxford University Press, 6th edn., 2014).

Reidy, A., Hampson, F., and Boyle, K., 'Gross violations of human rights: invoking the European Convention on Human Rights in the case of Turkey', *Netherlands Quarterly of Human Rights*, 15 (1997), 161–73.

Reneman, M., *EU Asylum Procedures and the Right to an Effective Remedy* (Oxford: Hart, 2014).

Ringelheim, J., 'Minority rights in a time of multiculturlism – the evolving scope of the Framework Convention on the Protection of National Minorities', *Human Rights Law Review*, 10(1) (2010), 99–128.

Robertson, A. H., *The Council of Europe: Its Structure, Functions and Achievements* (London: Stevens & Sons, 2nd edn., 1961).

Roos, C., and Orsini, G., 'How to Reconcile the EU Border Paradox? The Concurrence of Refugee Reception and Deterrence', *Institute for European Studies Policy Brief 4/2015* (Brussels: Vrije Universitei, 2015).

Royer, A., *The Council of Europe* (Strasbourg: Council of Europe Publishing, 2010).

Ruffert, M., 'Secretariat' in Schmahl, S., and Breuer, M. (eds.), *The Council of Europe: Its Law and Policies* (Oxford University Press, 2017), pp. 212–23.

Ryngaert, C., 'Oscillating between embracing and avoiding Bosphorus: the European Court of Human Rights on member state responsibility for acts of international organisations and the case of the EU', *European Law Review*, 39 (2014), 176–92.

Ryssdal, R., 'On the Road to a European Constitutional Court', Winston Churchill Lecture on the Council of Europe, Florence, 21 June 1991, quoted in Alkema, E. A., 'The European Convention as a constitution and its Court as a constitutional court' in Mahoney, P., Matscher, F., Petzold, H., and Wildhaber, L. (eds.), *Protecting Human Rights: The European Perspective – Studies in Memory of Rolv Ryssdall* (Cologne: Carl Heymans, 2000), pp. 41–63.

'Opinion: the coming of age of the European Convention on Human Rights', *European Human Rights Law Review*, (1996), 18–29.

Sadurski, W., 'Partnering with Strasbourg: constitutionalization of the European Court of Human Rights, the accession of central and east european states to the Council of Europe, and the idea of pilot judgments', *Human Rights Law Review*, 9 (2009), 397–453.

Rights before Courts: A Study of Constitutional Courts in Postcommunist States of Central and Eastern Europe (Dordrecht: Springer, 2005).

Safjan, M., and Miklasziewicz, P., 'Horizontal effect of the general principles of EU law in the sphere of private law', *European Review of Public Law*, (2010), 475–86.

Sainati, T., 'Human rights class actions: rethinking the pilot-judgment procedure at the European Court of Human Rights', *Harvard International Law Journal*, 56 (2015), 147–206.

Sardaro, P., 'Jus non dicere for allegations of serious violations of human rights: questionable trends in the recent case law of the Strasbourg Court', *European Human Rights Law Review*, (2003), 601–30.

Sargentini, J., and Dimitrovs, A., 'The European Parliament's role: towards new Copenhagen criteria for existing member states?' *Journal of Common Market Studies*, 54(5), 1085–92.

Sarmiento, D., 'The silent lamb and the deaf wolves' in Avbelj, M., and Komárek, J. (eds.), *Constitutional Pluralism in the European Union and Beyond* (Oxford University Press, 2012) 285–318, pp. 285–317.

'Who's Afraid of the charter? The Court of Justice, national courts and the New Framework of Fundamental Rights Protection in Europe', *Common Market Law Review*, 50 (2013), 1267–304.

Sayers, D., 'Article 13: Freedom of the Arts and Sciences' in Peers, S., Hervey, T., Kenner, J., and Ward, A. (eds.), *The EU Charter of Fundamental Rights: A Commentary* (Oxford: Hart, 2014), pp. 379–400.

'Article 48: Presumption of Innocence and Right of Defence (Criminal Law)' in Peers, S., Hervey, T., Kenner, J., and Ward, A. (eds.), *The EU Charter of Fundamental Rights: A Commentary* (Oxford: Hart, 2014), pp. 1303–49.

Schabas, W., *The European Convention on Human Rights: A Commentary* (Oxford University Press, 2015).

Scheuner, U., 'Fundamental rights in European Community law and in national constitutional law', *Common Market Law Review*, 12 (1975), 171–91.

Schiek, D., 'Article 23: Equality between Women and Men' in Peers, S., Hervey, T., Kenner, J., and Ward, A. (eds.), *The EU Charter of Fundamental Rights: A Commentary* (Oxford: Hart, 2014), pp. 633–60.

'Intersectionality and the notion of disability in EU discrimination law', *Common Market Law Review*, 53 (2016), 35–64.

Schill, S., 'Overcoming absolute primacy: respect for national identity under the Lisbon Treaty', *Common Market Law Review*, 48 (2011), 1417–54.

Schimmelfennig, F., Engbert, S., and Knobel, H., *International Socialization in Europe: European Organizations, Political Conditionality, and Democratic Change* (Basingstoke: Palgrave Macmillan, 2006).

Schmahl, S., 'The Council of Europe within the system of international organizations' in Schmahl, S., and Breuer, M. (eds.), *The Council of Europe: Its Law and Policies* (Oxford University Press, 2017), pp. 874–945.

Schokkenbroek, J., 'The prohibition of discrimination in Article 14 of the Convention and the margin of appreciation', *Human Rights Law Journal*, 19 (1998), 20–3.

Schwellnus, G., 'Social rights: The EU and ILO' in Falkner, G., and Müller, P. (eds.) *EU Policies in a Global Perspective: Shaping or Taking International Regimes?* (London: Routledge, 2014).

Scott-Moncrieff, L., 'Editorial – Language and the law: reclaiming the human rights debate', *European Human Rights Law Review*, (2013), 115–21.

Sedelmeier, U., 'Anchoring democracy from above? The European Union and democratic backsliding in Hungary and Romania after accession', *Journal of Common Market Studies*, 52(1) (2014), 105–21.

Seibert-Fohr, A., and Villiger, M., 'Current challenges in European multilevel human rights protection' in Seibert-Fohr, A., and Villiger, M. (eds.), *Judgments of the European Court of Human Rights – Effects and Implementation* (Baden-Baden: Nomos/Ashgate, 2013), pp. 13–24.

Senden, H. C. K., *Interpretation of Fundamental Rights in a Multilevel Legal System* (Antwerp: Intersentia, 2011).

Senden, L. A. J., 'Soft law and its implications for institutional balance in the EC', *Utrecht Law Review*, 1(2) (2005), 79–99.

Shany, Y., 'Assessing the effectiveness of international courts – a goal-based approach', *American Journal of International Law*, 106 (2012), 225–70.

Shaw, J., and Khadar, L., 'Article 12(2): Freedom of Assembly and Association' in Peers, S., Hervey, T., Kenner, J., and Ward, A. (eds.), *The EU Charter of Fundamental Rights: A Commentary* (Oxford: Hart, 2014), pp. 371–7.

Sicilianos, L. I., 'The involvement of the European Court of Human Rights in the implementation of its judgments: recent developments under Article 46 ECHR', *Netherlands Quarterly of Human Rights*, 32 (2014), 235–62.

Sieburgh, C., 'A method to substantively guide the involvement of EU primary law in private law matters', *European Review of Public Law*, (2013), 1165–88.

'General principles and the charter in private law relationships' in Bernitz, U., Groussot, X., and Schulyok, F. (eds.), *General Principles of EU Law and European Private Law* (Alphen aan den Rijn: Wolters Kluwer, 2013), pp. 233–47.

Siegel, A., 'Beyond Measuring – the Council of Europe's Instruments Contributing to the Progress of Societies', *OECD World Forum on Measuring and Fostering Progress of Societies*, Istanbul, 23–30 June 2007.

Sikkink, K., 'The power of principled ideas: human rights policies in the United States and Western Europe' in Goldstein, J., and Keohane R. O. (eds.), *Ideas and Foreign Policy: Beliefs, Institutions and Political Change* (New York: Cornell University Press, 1993), pp. 139–70.

Simor, J., and Emmerson, B. (eds.), *Human Rights Practice* (London: Sweet & Maxwell, 2000).

Simpson, A. W. B., 'Britain and the European Convention', *Cornell International Law Journal*, 34 (2001), 523–54.

Human Rights and the End of Empire - Britain and the Genesis of the European Convention (Oxford University Press, 2001).

'Hersch Lauterpacht and the genesis of the age of human rights', *Law Quarterly Review*, 120 (2004), 49–80.

Sjursen, H., 'Enlargement in perspective. The EU's quest for identity', *Recon Online Working Paper* 2007/15.

Smith, K. E., 'The conditional offer of membership as an instrument of EU foreign policy: reshaping Europe in the EU's image?' *Marmara Journal of European Studies*, 33 (2000), 1301–59.

'The EU as a diplomatic actor in the field of human rights' in Koops, J., and Macaj, G. (eds.), *The European Union as a Diplomatic Actor* (Basingstoke, UK: Palgrave Macmillan, 2015), 155–77.

'The European Union at the Human Rights Council: speaking with one voice but having little influence', *Journal of European Public Policy*, 17(2) (2010), 224–41.

'The use of political conditionality in the EU's relations with third countries: how effective?' *SPS Working Paper 1997/7* (San Domenico di Fiesole: EUI, 1997), 1–37.

European Union Foreign Policy in a Changing World (London: Polity Press, 3rd edn., 2014).

Smith, M., 'Developing administrative principles in the EU: a foundational model of legitimacy?', *European Law Journal*, 18(2) (2012), 269–88.

Snell, J., 'Fundamental rights review of national measures: nothing new under the charter?' *European Public Law*, 21 (2015), 285–308.

Söderman, J., 'Public Hearing before the Convention on the Draft Charter of Fundamental Rights of the European Union', speech delivered on 2 February 2000 in Brussels.

Spano, R., 'Universality or diversity of human rights? Strasbourg in the age of subsidiarity', *Human Rights Law Review*, 14 (2014), 487–502.

Spaventa, E., 'Article 45: Freedom of Movement and of Residence' in Peers, S., Hervey, T., Kenner, J., and Ward, A. (eds.), *The EU Charter of Fundamental Rights: A Commentary* (Oxford: Hart, 2014), pp. 1161–76.

Stalford, H., 'Article 32: Prohibition of Child Labour and Protection of Young People at Work' in Peers, S., Hervey, T., Kenner, J., and Ward, A. (eds.), *The EU Charter of Fundamental Rights: A Commentary* (Oxford: Hart, 2014), pp. 869–89.

Steyn, Lord., 'Laying the foundations of human rights law in the United Kingdom', *European Human Rights Law Review*, (2005), 349–62.

Stone Sweet, A., 'The European Convention on Human Rights and national constitutional reordering', *Cardozo Law Review*, 33 (2012), 1859–68.

'The European Court of Justice' in Craig, P., and de Búrca, G. (eds.), *The Evolution of EU Law* (Oxford University Press, 2nd edn., 2011), pp. 121–53.

Stubberfield, C., 'Lifting the Organisational Veil: Positive Obligations of the European Union following accession to the European Convention on Human Rights', *Australian International Legal Journal*, 19 (2012), 117–42.

Suchkova, M., 'An analysis of the institutional arrangements within the Council of Europe and within certain member states for securing the enforcement of judgments', *European Human Rights Law Review*, (2011), 448–63.

Sweeney, J. A., 'Margins of appreciation: cultural relativity and the European Court of Human Rights in the post–Cold War era', *International and Comparative Law Quarterly*, 54 (2005), 459–74.

The European Court of Human Rights in the Post-Cold War Era: Universality in Transition (London: Routledge, 2013).

Swimelar, S., 'Approaches to Ethnic Conflict and the Protection of Human Rights in Post-Communist Europe: The Need for Preventive Diplomacy', *Nationalism and Ethnic Politics*, 7 (2001), 98–126.

Szyszczak, E., 'Article 36: Access to Services' in Peers, S., Hervey, T., Kenner, J., and Ward, A. (eds.), *The EU Charter of Fundamental Rights: A Commentary* (Oxford: Hart, 2014), pp. 969–82.

Tamm, D., 'The history of the Court of Justice of the European Union since its origin' in The Court of Justice of the European Union (ed.), *The Court of Justice and the Construction of Europe: Analyses and Perspectives on Sixty Years of Case-law - La Cour de Justice et la Construction de l'Europe: Analyses et Perspectives de Soixante Ans de Jurisprudence* (The Hague: TMC Asser Press, 2013), 9–35.

Thielborger, P., 'Judicial Passivism at the European Court of Human Rights', *Maastricht Journal of European and Comparative Law*, 19 (2012), 341–47.

Thorarensen, B., 'The advisory jurisdiction of the European Court of Human Rights under Protocol No. 16: enhancing domestic implementation or human rights or a symbolic step' in Mjöll Arnardóttir, O., and Buyse, A. (eds.), *Shifting Centres of Gravity in Human Rights Protection: Rethinking Relations between the ECHR, EU and National Legal Orders* (London and New York: Routledge, 2016), pp. 79–100.

Tocci, N., *The EU and Conflict Resolution: Promoting Peace in the Backyard* (London: Routledge, 2007).

Toggenburg, G., 'The EU Charter: moving from a fundamental rights ornament to a European fundamental rights order' in Palmisano, G. (ed.), *Making the Charter of Fundamental Rights a Living Instrument* (Leiden: Brill Nijhoff, 2015), 10–29.

'The role of the new EU Fundamental Rights Agency: debating the "sex of angels" or improving Europe's human rights performance?' *European Law Review*, 3(385) (2008), 385–98.

Tomkin, J., 'Article 50: Right Not to Be Tried or Punished Twice in Criminal Proceedings for the Same Criminal Offence' in Peers, S., Hervey, T.,

Kenner, J., and Ward, A. (eds.), *The EU Charter of Fundamental Rights: A Commentary* (Oxford: Hart, 2014), pp. 1373–412.

Tomkins, A., 'The Committee of Ministers: its roles under the European Convention on Human Rights', *European Human Rights Law Review*, 49 (1995), 49–62.

Torremans, P., 'Article 17(2): Right to Property' in Peers, S., Hervey, T., Kenner, J., and Ward, A. (eds.), *The EU Charter of Fundamental Rights: A Commentary* (Oxford: Hart, 2014), pp. 489–517.

Torres Pérez, A., *Conflicts of Rights in the European Union: A Theory of Supranational Adjudication* (Oxford University Press, 2009).

'*Melloni* in three acts: from dialogue to monologue', *European Constitutional Law Review*, 10 (2014), 308–31.

Trauner, F., 'Asylum policy: the EU 'crises' and the looming policy regime failure', *Journal of European Integration*, 38 (2016), 311–25.

Trechsel, S., 'Human rights and minority rights – two sides of the same coin? A sketch' in Mahoney, P., Matscher, F., Petzold, H., and Wildhaber, L. (eds.), *Protecting Human Rights: The European Perspective – Studies in Memory of Rolv Ryssdal* (Cologne: Carl Heymans, 2000), pp. 1443–53.

Trommer, S., and Chari, R., 'The Council of Europe: interest groups and ideological mission?' *West European Politics*, 29 (2006), 665–86.

Tsagourias, N. (ed.), *Transnational Constitutionalism: International and European Models* (Cambridge University Press, 2007).

Tzevelekos, V., 'When elephants fight it is the grass that suffers: "hegemonic struggle" in Europe and the side-effects for international law' in Dzehtsiarou, K., Konstadinides, T., Lock, T., and O'Meara, N. (eds.), *Human Rights in Europe: The Influence, Overlaps and Contradictions of the EU and the ECHR* (London and New York: Routledge, 2014), pp. 9–34.

Ulfstein, G., 'The European Court of Human Rights and national courts: a constitutional relationship?' in Mjöll Arnardóttir, O., and Buyse, A. (eds.), *Shifting Centres of Gravity in Human Rights Protection: Rethinking Relations between the ECHR, EU and National Legal Orders* (London and New York: Routledge, 2016), pp. 46–58.

Vachudová, M. A., *Europe Undivided: Democracy, Leverage and Integration after Communism* (Oxford University Press, 2005).

Van Bockel, B., *The Ne Bis in Idem Principle in EU Law* (Alphen ann de Rijn Kluwer Law International, 2010).

Van Cleynenbreugel, P., 'Judge-made standards of national procedure in the post-Lisbon constitutional framework', *European Law Review*, 37 (2012), 90–100.

Van de Heyning, C., *Fundamental Rights lost in complexity*, unpublished PhD thesis, Antwerp University, 2011.

'No place like home: discretionary space for the domestic protection of fundamental rights' in Popelier, P., van de Heyning, C., and van Nuffel, P. (eds.),

Human Rights Protection in the European Legal Order: The Interaction between the European and the National Courts (Cambridge: Intersentia, 2011), pp. 65–96.

Van de Heyning, C., and Lawson, R., 'The EU as a party to the European Convention of (sic) Human Rights: EU law and the European Court of Justice case law as inspiration and challenge to the European Court of Human Rights jurisprudence' in Popelier, P., Van de Heyning, C., and Van Nuffel, P. (eds.), *Human Rights Protection in the European Legal Order: The Interaction between the European and the National Courts* (Cambridge: Intersentia, 2011), pp. 35–64.

Van den Berghe, F., 'The EU and issues of human rights protection: same solutions to more acute problems?' *European Law Journal*, 16 (2010), 112–57.

Vested-Hansen, J., 'Article 7: Respect for Private and Family Life (Private Life, Home and Communications)' in Peers, S., Hervey, T., Kenner, J., and Ward, A. (eds.), *The EU Charter of Fundamental Rights: A Commentary* (Oxford: Hart, 2014), pp. 153–82.

Voeten, E., 'Domestic implementation of European Court of Human Rights judgments: legal infrastructure and government effectiveness matter: a reply to Dia Anagnostou and Alina Mungiu-Pippidi', *European Journal of International Law*, 25 (2014), 229–38.

'Public Opinion and the Legitimacy of International Courts', *Theoretical Inquiries in Law*, 14 (2013), 411–36.

'Politics, judicial behaviour and institutional design' in Christoffersen, J., and Madsen, M. (eds.), *The European Court of Human Rights between Law and Politics* (Oxford University Press, 2011), pp. 61–76

Vogiatzis, N., 'The admissibility criterion under Article 35(3)(b) ECHR: a "significant disadvantage" to human rights protection', *International and Comparative Law Quarterly*, 65 (2016), 185–211.

Von Bogdandy, A., 'The European Union as a human rights organization? Human rights and the core of the European Union', *Common Market Law Review*, 37(6) (2000), 1307–38.

Von Bogdandy, A., and Schill, S., 'Overcoming absolute primacy: respect for national identity under the Lisbon Treaty', *Common Market Law Review*, 48 (2011), 1417–54.

et al., 'Reverse *Solange* – protecting the essence of fundamental rights against EU member states', *Common Market Law Review*, 49 (2012), 489–520.

Von Danwitz, T., and Paraschas, K., 'A fresh start for the charter: fundamental questions on the application of the European Charter of Fundamental Rights', *Fordham International Law Review*, 35 (2012), 1396–424.

Vorhaus, J., 'On degradation. part one. Article 3 of the European Convention on Human Rights', *Common Law World Review*, 31 (2002), 374–99.

'On degradation. part two. Degrading Treatment and Punishment', *Common Law World Review*, 32 (2003), 65–92.

Walker, N., 'Reconciling MacCormick: constitutional pluralism and the unity of practical reason' *Ratio Juris*, 24 (2011), 369–85.

'The Idea of Constitutional Pluralism', *Modern Law Review*, 65 (2002), 317–59.

Wallace, S., 'Much ado about nothing? The pilot judgment procedure at the European Court of Human Rights', *European Human Rights Law Review*, (2011), 71–81.

Walter, C., 'Combating terrorism and organized crime' in Schmahl, S., and Breuer, M. (eds.), *The Council of Europe: Its Law and Policies* (Oxford University Press, 2017), pp. 671–95.

Ward, A., 'Article 51: Field of Application' in Peers, S., Hervey, T., Kenner, J., and Ward, A. (eds.), *The EU Charter of Fundamental Rights: A Commentary* (Oxford: Hart, 2014), pp. 1413–54.

et al., 'Article 47: Right to an Effective Remedy and to a Fair Trial' in Peers, S., Hervey, T., Kenner, J., and Ward, A. (eds.), *The EU Charter of Fundamental Rights: A Commentary* (Oxford: Hart, 2014), pp. 1198–275.

Weatherill, S., 'Article 38: Consumer Protection' in Peers, S., Hervey, T., Kenner, J., and Ward, A. (eds.), *The EU Charter of Fundamental Rights: A Commentary* (Oxford: Hart, 2014), pp. 1005–25.

'From economic rights to fundamental rights' in de Vries, S. et al. (eds.), *The Protection of Fundamental Rights in the EU after Lisbon* (Oxford: Hart, 2013), pp. 11–36.

Weiler, J., 'In defence of the status quo: Europe's constitutional Sonderweg' in Weiler, J., and Wind, M. (eds.), *European Constitutionalism beyond the State* (Cambridge University Press, 2003), pp. 7–23.

'Prologue: global and pluralist constitutionalism: some doubts' in de Búrca, G., and Weiler, J. (eds.), *The Worlds of European Constitutionalism* (Cambridge University Press, 2011), pp. 8–18.

Weller, M. (ed.), *The Rights of Minorities: A Commentary on the European Framework Convention for the Protection of National Minorities* (Oxford University Press, 2005).

Weller, M., Vertichel, A., Alen, A., De Witte, B., and Lemmens, P. (eds.), *The Framework Convention for the Protection of National Minorities: A Useful Pan-European Instrument?* (Antwerp: Intersentia, 2008).

White, R., 'Article 34: Social Security and Social Assistance' in Peers, S., Hervey, T., Kenner, J., and Ward, A. (eds.), *The EU Charter of Fundamental Rights: A Commentary* (Oxford: Hart, 2014), pp. 927–49.

White, R., and Boussiakou, I., 'Voices from the European Court of Human Rights', *Netherlands Quarterly of Human Rights*, 27(2) (2009), 167–89.

White, R., and Ovey, C., *Jacobs, White and Ovey: The European Convention on Human Rights* (Oxford University Press, 6th edn., 2014).

Whitehead, L., *The International Dimensions of Democratization: Europe and the Americas* (Oxford University Press, 2nd edn. 2001).

Wicks, E., 'Article 2: Right to Life' in Peers, S., Hervey, T., Kenner, J., and Ward, A. (eds.), *The EU Charter of Fundamental Rights: A Commentary* (Oxford: Hart, 2014), pp. 25–38.

'The United Kingdom government's perceptions of the European Convention on Human Rights at the time of entry', *Public Law*, (2000), 438–55.

Wildhaber, L., 'A constitutional future for the European Court of Human Rights?' *Human Rights Law Journal*, 23 (2002), 161–5.

'The European Convention on Human Rights and International Law', *International and Comparative Law Quarterly*, 56 (2007), 217–32.

'Rethinking the European Court of Human Rights' in Christoffersen, J., and Madsen, M. (eds.) *The European Court of Human Rights between Law and Politics* (Oxford University Press, 2011), pp. 2014–29.

'The role of the European Court of Human Rights: an evaluation', *Mediterranean Journal of Human Rights*, 8 (2004), 9–32.

Williams, A., *EU Human Rights Policies: A Study in Irony* (Oxford University Press, 2004).

The Ethos of Europe: Values, Law and Justice in the EU (Cambridge University Press, 2010).

'The European Convention on Human Rights, the EU and the UK: confronting a heresy', *European Journal of International Law*, 24 (2013), 1157–85.

Wilsher, D., 'Article 6: Right to Liberty and Security' in Peers, S., Hervey, T., Kenner, J., and Ward, A. (eds.), *The EU Charter of Fundamental Rights: A Commentary* (Oxford: Hart, 2014), pp. 121–52.

Wincott, D., 'The Court of Justice and the European policy process' in Richardson, J. (ed.), *European Union, Power and Policy-Making* (London: Routledge, 2001).

Winkler, G., *The Council of Europe: Monitoring Procedures and the Constitutional Autonomy of Member States* (Vienna: Springer, 2006).

Wintemute, R., 'Filling the Article 14 "gap": government ratification and judicial control of Protocol No. 12 ECHR: part 2', *European Human Rights Law Review*, (2004), 484–99.

'"Within the ambit": how big is the "gap" in Article 14 European Convention on Human Rights? part 1', *European Human Rights Law Review*, (2004), 366–82.

Wissink, M., 'Interpretation of private law in conformity with EU directives' in Hartkamp, A. S. et al. (eds.), *The Influence of EU Law on National Private Law* (Deventer: Kluwer, 2014), pp. 119–58.

Wolfrum, R., and Deutsch, U. (eds.), *The European Court of Human Rights Overwhelmed by Applications: Problems and Possible Solutions – International Workshop, Heidleberg, 17–18 December 2007* (Berlin: Springer, 2007).

Wollenschläger, F., 'Article 17(1): Right to Property' in Peers, S., Hervey, T., Kenner, J., and Ward, A. (eds.), *The EU Charter of Fundamental Rights: A Commentary* (Oxford: Hart, 2014), pp. 469–87.

Woods, L., 'Article 11: Freedom of Expression and Information, in Peers, S., Hervey, T., Kenner, J., and Ward, A. (eds.), *The EU Charter of Fundamental Rights: A Commentary* (Oxford: Hart, 2014), pp. 311–39.

Wouters, J., and Hermez, M., '*EU Guidelines on Human Rights as a Foreign Policy Instrument: An Assessment*', Leuven Centre for Global Governance Studies Working Paper No. 170 (Leuven: Leuven Centre for Global Governance Studies, 2016).

Wright, B., 'The Europeanisation of Hungary: institutional adjustment and the effects of European Union integration', *POLIS Journal*, (2013), 271–331.

Youngs, R. (ed.), *Survey of European Democracy Promotion Policies 2000–2006* (Madrid: Fundacíon para las Relaciones Internacionales y el Diálogo Exterior (FRIDE), 2006).

Yourow, H. C., *The Margin of Appreciation Doctrine in the Dynamics of European Human Rights Jurisprudence* (The Hague: Kluwer, 1996).

Zaru, D., and Guerts, C.-M., 'Legal framework for EU participation in global human rights governance' in Wouters, J., Bruyninckx, H., Basu, S., and Schunz, S. (eds.), *The European Union and Multilateral Governance: Assessing EU Participation in United Nations Human Rights and Environmental Fora* (Basingstoke, UK: Palgrave Macmillan, 2012), 49–65.

Zoethout, C. M., 'Margin of appreciation, violation and (in)compatibility: why the European Court of Human Rights might consider using an alternative mode of adjudication', *European Public Law*, 20 (2014), 309–30.

Zwart, T., 'More human rights than Court: why the legitimacy of the European Court of Human Rights is in need of repair and how it can be done' in Flogaitis, S., Zwart, Z., and Fraser, J. (eds.), *The European Court of Human Rights and Its Discontents: Turning Criticism into Strength* (Cheltenham, UK: Edward Elgar, 2013), pp. 71–95.

INDEX